Develo
MANAGEMENT

MANAGING IN ORGANIZATIONS THAT LEARN

𝔹

Developmental Management
General Editor: Ronnie Lessem

Charting the Corporate Mind
Charles Hampden-Turner*

Greening Business
John Davis

Ford on Management
Henry Ford*

Managing Your Self
Jagdish Parikh

Conceptual Toolmaking
Jerry Rhodes

Integrative Management
Pauline Graham

Total Quality Learning
Ronnie Lessem

Executive Leadership
Elliott Jaques and Stephen D. Clement

Transcultural Management
Albert Koopman

The Great European Illusion
Alain Minc

The Rise of NEC
Koji Kobayashi

Organizing Genius
Paul Thorne

European Strategic Alliances
Sabine Urban and Serge Vendemini

Intuition
Jagdish Parikh, Fred Neubauer and Alden G. Lank

Spiral Dynamics
Don Beck and Chris Cowan

Managing in Organizations That Learn
Steven A. Cavaleri and David S. Fearon

* For copyright reasons this edition is not available in the USA

Managing in Organizations That Learn

EDITED BY STEVEN A. CAVALERI
AND DAVID S. FEARON

Copyright © Blackwell Publishers, 1996

First published 1996
2 4 6 8 10 9 7 5 3 1

Blackwell Publishers Inc.
238 Main Street
Cambridge, Massachusetts 02142, USA

Blackwell Publishers Ltd
108 Cowley Road
Oxford OX4 1JF, UK

Library of Congress Cataloging-in-Publication Data

Managing in organizations that learn / edited by Steven Cavaleri and David Fearon.
p.   cm.
Includes index.
ISBN 1-55786-660-0 (pbk.: alk. paper)
1. Organizational learning—Management.   I. Cavaleri, Steven.   II. Fearon, David.
HD58.82.M36   1996
658—dc20
95-49249
CIP

British Library Cataloguing in Publication Data

A CIP catalogue record for this book is available from the British Library.

Typeset in Ehrhardt 10/12 pt
by Best-set Typesetter Ltd., Hong Kong
Printed in the U.S.A.

This book is printed on acid-free paper

To our parents,
Salvatore (Sam) and Hallie Cavaleri
Spencer and Lois Fearon

Contents

Figures

Boxes

About the Editors

Steven A. Cavaleri is Professor of Management at Central Connecticut State University. Dr. Cavaleri is the author of two other books, *Management Systems* and *Omega Corporation*. Dr. Cavaleri holds a Ph.D. from Rensselaer Polytechnic Institute, Troy, NY. In 1992, he was Visiting Scholar in the System Dynamics Group in the Sloan School of Management at MIT, where he conducted research under the supervision of Dr. Peter Senge. He is a Certified Systems Integrator in the Institute of Industrial Engineers, and also consults with several large manufacturing companies.

David Fearon is Professor of Management in the Central Connecticut State University School of Business. His emphasis is the management learning of all employees for total quality. Dr. Fearon earned the 1995 Excellence in Teaching Award from his university and frequently presents his teaching innovations in professional meetings and journals. His Ph.D. is from the University of Connecticut with degrees from Central Michigan University and College.

Contributors

R. Ivan Blanco is an Associate Professor of Management at Barry University, Miami Shores, Florida. He is also the Director of International Business Programs at Barry's Andreas School of Business. Dr Blanco is formerly an executive in the human resources area with the Venezuelan National Airline. He holds a Ph.D. in management from Oklahoma State University.

Kermit Campbell is Chief Executive Officer and President of Herman Miller Inc. Mr Campbell is formerly a Sloan Fellow at MIT's Sloan School of Management and is former chair of the State of Michigan Partnerships in Education Task Force.

Leo Charalambides is Assistant Professor at Eastern Connecticut State University. His writings seek to bridge the areas of information systems, business strategy, and systems thinking. Dr Charalambides holds a B.S. in aeronautical engineering from Rensselaer Polytechnic Institute and a Ph.D. in operations management from the University of South Carolina.

Kathleen DeChant is a member of the faculty of the Department of Management at the University of Connecticut at Stamford. She is an Associate Editor of the *Academy of Management Executive*. Dr DeChant is a former human resources development executive with a financial services company. She holds a doctorate in adult and higher education from Columbia University.

André DelBecq is Professor of Management of the School of Management at the University of Santa Clara. Dr DelBecq is the author of several books and over 80 articles focused on executive decision-making and managing innovation.

David Edgar is Vice-President for Human Resources at Reflexite Corporation. He holds a master's degree in Industrial and Labor Relations from Cornell University.

A. Russell Fanelli is a Professor of Management at Western New England College. He is former Visiting Fellow in Organizational Behavior at Yale University. In addition, Dr Fanelli writes in the areas of communication, leadership, and organizational behavior. He holds a Ph.D. from Rensselaer Polytechnic Institute in Organizational Communication.

William P. Ferris is a Professor of Management at Western New England College. Dr Ferris is past President of the Eastern Academy of Management. He has written extensively in the areas of conflict resolution, team building, and organization development. A former Visiting Fellow at Yale University, Dr Ferris holds a B.S. degree from Dartmouth College and a Ph.D. from Rensselaer Polytechnic Institute.

Laura Freebairn-Smith is the President of Good Work Associates in New Haven, Connecticut, a management consulting firm. She is formerly the Managing Director of the Gesell Institute. Ms Freebairn-Smith is a Visiting Professor of Management at Central Connecticut State University. She is a doctoral candidate at Boston University and holds a master's degree from the Yale School of Management.

Matthew Guyer is Director of Operations at Reflexite Corporation. He holds an MBA degree from Rensselaer Polytechnic Institute.

Stephen Hall is Quality Assurance Manager in the US Household Products Group of Black & Decker Corporation. He is an SME Certified Manufacturing Technologist and an ASQC Certified Quality Engineer. Mr Hall is currently completing a master's degree program in Technology Management.

Craig C. Lundberg is the Blanchard Professor of Human Resource Management in the Cornell University School of Hospitality Management. A leading scholar in the fields of organizational culture and change, Dr Lundberg also acts as consultant to a variety of organizations to surface organizational culture and enhance executive skills. He is immediate past-President of the Eastern Academy of Management. He has published widely in a broad variety of journals and books in the field of management. Dr Lundberg's Ph.D. was earned at Cornell.

Brian Maguire is a founding principal of The Capra Group, a management consulting firm. Before forming the Capra Group, he was Manager in the Manufacturing Consulting Practice of Deloitte & Touche. Mr Maguire is also a former financial manager at Digital Equipment Corporation. He has written several articles on Focused Performance Management, most recently in *Productivity Review*. He holds an M.B.A. degree from Boston University.

Steven I. Meisel is an Associate Professor of Management at LaSalle University, and former Chair of the Management Department at that school. His expertise is in the areas of organizational behavior and managerial skills. Dr

Meisel is active in the Eastern Academy of Management and the Organizational Behavior Teaching Society. He holds a Ph.D. in Group and Organizational Psychology from Temple University.

John M. Montgomery is an organizational consultant and partner, Nuclear Development Associates. He recently retired from his post as senior federal official in the US Nuclear Regulatory Commission. In 1987, he was Executive Assistant to NRC Chairman Lando W. Zech. Dr Montgomery holds a Doctorate in Business Administration from George Washington University where his major studies were in Organization Development, as well as Management Systems and Cybernetics.

William J. O'Brien was Chief Executive Officer of the Hanover Insurance Company for 12 years. Hanover's success has been recorded in a number of books including Peter Senge's *The Fifth Discipline*. He is affiliated with Innovation Associates as a consultant and is on the council of MIT's Organizational Learning Center.

Alexander N. Pattakos is a principal partner in Creative Learning Technologies, a consulting firm that specializes in continuous learning and improvement. He is a pioneer in the field of applying cybernetic bio-acoustic entrainment systems for promoting creativity. Dr Pattakos is formerly the Director of the Graduate Program in Public Affairs at Boise State University. He holds a Ph.D. from Northern Illinois University.

Frederick Reed is currently a computer scientist/cognitive engineer at Analysis and Technology Inc. His work involves the design of human–computer systems. He is also a co-founder of a new company created to develop and market a new form of computing technology based on the principles of autognomics. Mr Reed holds an M.S. in computer science from Rensselaer Polytechnic Institute and is a trained TQM facilitator.

George Roth is Director of Research in the Center for Organizational Learning in the Sloan School of Management at MIT. George has spent over ten years in industry in a variety of marketing and engineering positions at Digital Equipment Corporation. He has also been an account executive at Kodak and General Motors. Dr Roth is an expert in the field of organizational culture and systems thinking. He holds a Ph.D. in management from MIT.

Frank Scalia is President of TriStar Consulting Services, a firm that specializes in management development and training, and is a partner, Nuclear Development Associates. He has held a number of senior human resource executive positions in the manufacturing and insurance industries. He has also been on the faculties of several universities and the Center for Creative Leadership. Dr Scalia earned a Ph.D. in Industrial/Organizational Psychology from Carnegie-Mellon University.

Sharon Seivert is currently President of Great Work, a management consulting firm which is dedicated to driving fear and contention out of organizations. She is formerly CEO of the Central Minnesota Group Health Plan, a consumer-owned, staff-model HMO. She is co-author of *Magic at Work* and *Heroes at Work: Understanding and Transforming Your Relationships, Work, and Self*. She graduated from the University of Minnesota and is a Reiki Master.

John D. Sterman is Professor in the Sloan School of Management at MIT, and Director of the System Dynamics Group. He is co-author of *Modeling for Learning Organizations* by Productivity Press. He is past President of the System Dynamics Society and is a leading researcher in system dynamics.

James A. F. Stoner holds the position of Professor of Management Systems at Fordham University. He is author/co-author of sixteen books including six editions of the noted management textbook, *Management*. Dr Stoner is a leader in the total quality management movement and recently assisted Dr Joseph M. Duran in editing a book on the history of managing for quality. In 1992, Fordham University established the James A. F. Stoner Chair in Quality Leadership in recognition of his work in this field. He holds a Ph.D. in Industrial Management from MIT's Sloan School of Management.

James Thompson is a principal of Gemini Consulting Inc., a world-wide management consulting firm. He was formerly an executive with LeapTec Simulations, a firm that specializes in system dynamics software and consulting. He was Chief Financial Officer of Engineered Coatings Inc., and for over ten years he was Treasurer of Kollmorgen Corporation, where he directed strategic planning.

Cecil Ursprung is President and Chief Executive Officer of Reflexite Corporation, New Britain, Connecticut. Mr Ursprung and the 325 employee-owners of Reflexite Corporation were chosen by *INC.* magazine as "Entrepreneur of the Year" in 1992.

Peter Vaill is Professor of Human Systems at George Washington University's School of Government and Business Administration. He is the author of *Managing as a Performing Art* and *Learning as a Way of Being* both by Jossey-Bass.

Joan Weiner is Professor of Management at Drexel University. She holds a Ph.D. from the Wharton School of Management at the University of Pennsylvania, where she studied under renowned systems theorist Russell L. Ackoff. Dr Weiner is President-elect of the Eastern Academy of Management and a leader in the Organizational Behavior Teaching Society.

Richard E. Wise is President of ValueNet International, a management consulting firm that specializes in expense reduction through innovation. He formerly held the position of Director of Corporate Strategy and Research for the Travelers Companies. He has been a Contributing Editor for *Educational*

Technology magazine. Dr Wise holds a doctorate from Pennsylvania State University.

Nicholas J. Zangari is currently a Vice-President of Mathog and Moniello Insurance, a firm specializing in risk management. Prior to that he was General Manager of the Connecticut office of Hanover Insurance Company. Mr Zangari holds a master's degree from the University of Connecticut and has participated in executive development programs at MIT.

Foreword

At the beginning, there was strategy. It was about allocation of resources, technology, economics, and competitive analysis. The company which could outsmart its competitor won. Transformation science was hardwired, rooted in the sheer intelligence of a few managers.

Then came the world of quality and reengineering. The attention moved to the careful crafting of the firm's key processes, streamlining and aligning them to the goals of the corporation. Process mapping was born, followed by its cohort of team-based change and facilitation techniques. Transformation science remained hardwired, but was placed in the softer context of change management, and moved to the masses.

The world of learning is upon us, undeniably. Learning is not only hard and soft, it is alive. Today, competition is about connecting creatively to the outside world, and accumulating knowledge faster than competitors. Transformation science has moved away from the steely blueprints of mechanical engineering, and adopted the neural networks of biology as its model. As in bio-engineering, the promise of learning in corporate transformation resides in the ability not only to *understand* how learning loops drive behaviors, but also to *influence* the formation of those learning loops to foster performance.

This is what *Managing in Organizations That Learn* is about. In it, you will discover how far learning has traveled from the early pioneering work of Peter Senge at MIT, to a full-fledged body of practical knowledge usable by corporations everywhere. Simply put, this book contains the source of your future competitive advantage.

Francis J. Gouillart
Senior Vice President, Gemini Consulting
Co-author, *Transforming the Organization*

Reviewer's Comments

Readers will want to dip into this diverse and fascinating collection of resources on organizational learning over and over. The lively interviews with leaders in the field, coupled with thoughtful articles by scholars and practitioners, make this a unique compendium for anyone interested in how organizations can become better learners. *Lee Bolman, Marion Bloch Missouri Chair in Leadership, University of Missouri – Kansas City*

Managing in Organizations That Learn is distinguished by its unique combination of contributors – scholars, consultants, and business leaders who are on the leading edge of a learning revolution. Steven Cavaleri and David Fearon are to be commended for the way they have linked the contributions of many writers. The book is much more than the sum of its parts. An especially noteworthy contribution of Cavaleri and Fearon's book is the idea that managers who wish to transform their organizations must begin by transforming themselves first. For those managers who are willing to make this commitment **Managing in Organizations That Learn** will be an excellent guide. *Bill Brandt, Chairman and CEO, American Woodmark Corporation*

I find this book great reading on a topic (how to become "a learning organization") that we constantly struggle with in our organization. It offers many viewpoints. The meshing of academic and practical approaches is a strength and certainly is different than other books on the market. **Managing in Organizations That Learn** provides particularly useful concepts for managers in today's very unstable environments because it introduces, teaches and demonstrates. This is something that practitioners rarely get in literature like this. *Cheryl Harrison, Director, Management Training & Performance Consulting, CIGNA HealthCare*

Managing in Organizations That Learn is a wonderfully thorough guide through modern thinking about how managers create knowledge in organizations. It swoops over and dives into the minds and experiences of hundreds of thoughtful business and academic leaders. This is not an intellectual snack. It is a feast of ideas, of knowledge, of experience. It contains ideas which will excite anyone who is both reflective and is grappling with the creation and maintenance of a learning organization. *Robert Saldich, President, Chief Executive Officer (ret), Raychem Corporation*

I found the book an excellent compendium of thought provoking articles that address all facets of the current management diamond popularly known as "the learning organization". The authors have adroitly compiled in one volume a broad spectrum of views and ideas around this central theme. The examination of the central topic from so many different angles caused me to see interrelationships and get, what for me were, fresh insights into how organizational growth can be fostered. This multidimensional approach to the problem is, in my opinion, the single major contribution of the book. *George Stephan, Chairman of the Board, Kollmorgen Corporation*

Preface

The enterprise of writing a book such as this is one that demands as much human cooperation as inspiration. We wish to thank our many contributors for their diligence and for sharing in our vision for this book. Through the process of writing this book we have become convinced of a compelling need to establish a relationship of reciprocity between managing and organizational learning. Managing as a process of control is doomed to fade into the dusk of history as a new generation of managers steps forward to tap the potential of the learning organization.

Clearly, organizational learning is a potentially powerful, yet often misunderstood phenomena. Enthusiastic managers cannot build organizational learning empires the way that Augustus built Rome. Organizational learning is a uniquely human process that is more amenable to understanding by drawing on the roots of sociology and philosophy, rather than the historical bases of management thinking, namely economics and psychology. Further, much can be gained by examining organizational learning from a cross-cultural perspective. By considering the tribal experiences of Native Americans, the mystical experiences of Europeans, such as Rudolf Steiner, and the Japanese traditions, as expressed by Nonanka, managers may approach some of the universal truths of learning.

We have tried to blend innovative thinking with practicality in this book. For some readers we may not have gone as far as they would like in pushing the envelope of new ideas on organizational learning. Conversely, other readers may find this book to be outside their comfort zone. Overall, we hope that most readers will find this book to be a practical outline for personal and organizational transformation. We do not intend to use the word "transformation" lightly. To us, it implies that organizational learning is a transformative process that requires personal and collective change and yields a recombinant organization that has capacities that extend beyond the limits of many people's imagination. We believe that many managers have learned to live in fear of their own imaginations. If they were to dream too deeply, extreme tension would result from the juxtaposition of what could be with what is. Organizational learning liberates managers to own their dreams . . . in hopes that some of these may become reality.

Acknowledgments

We wish to offer our heartfelt thanks to Rolf Janke for his guidance and support, and to Developmental Management series consulting editor, Ronnie Lessem for his encouragement. Finally, we wish to acknowledge Mary Riso for her fine administrative support.

We wish to thank our loving wives, Linda and Connie, for their patience and support.

We believe the value of this book has been richly enhanced by the interviews with the people whom we consider to be among the leaders in articulating what it means for organizations to learn. Our special thanks go to André DelBecq, Kermit Campbell, Bill O'Brien, John Sterman, Cecil Ursprung, and Peter Vaill.

As we began planning this book we soon realized that much of what we and our contributors wanted to express was more of a vision than a reality. In order to ground this book in common-sense practice and practical wisdom we chose to enlist the cooperation of a number of esteemed practitioner colleagues in reviewing the manuscript. We wish to thank all of them for their helpful remarks and for their encouragement. These reviewers are:

Dennis P. Cunningham, Executive Director, El Hogar del Futuro
Mark Dudzik, Director Human Resources, Connecticut Natural Gas
John L. Fagan C.H.E., Vice-President, Hartford Hospital; President, Connecticut Quality Council
Linda Ferraro, Training Specialist, Loctite Corporation
Sandra Hastings, Director of Staff Development, Connecticut State Department of Labor
Jeffrey Nolan, Consultant, Spectrum Management Group
Robert Rarus, Compliance Officer, US Department of Labor
Michael Raphael Ph.D., Raphael & Associates, Industrial and Organizational Psychologists
Stephen J. Russo, Senior Industrial Engineer, US Surgical Corporation

Steven A. Cavaleri
David S. Fearon

PART I

Managing and Learning

Interview with Kermit Campbell
President and Chief Executive Officer
Herman Miller Inc., Zeeland, Michigan

Interviewer: David Fearon   Date: July 1994

DF: This first question undergirds our book. People would not bother to buy or share our book, if they didn't think that the ideas that they would generate by reading this book could contribute to the lasting success of their organizations. You have achieved superior quality; is that enough? What must Herman Miller now become so as to remain successful in the next five to ten years?

KC: There are two things that are central to the future of Herman Miller. The first is captured in our vision, in our mission statement. Our mission is to liberate the human spirit. This is the basis around which we are building the future of the whole company.

First and foremost, we must liberate the mind, the talents, the skills, the backgrounds, the differences and everything else that we have in our people. We must get all of these things on the table. Actively engaging all of our people will make us the kind of company that we want to be.

We chose "liberation" over being a "command and control" kind of company. That would be a company where we tell people what we want them to think; tell them which parts of their brains to engage; tell them when to do it and when not to do it. The command and control organization would have managers tell people which "box" to play in.

Rather than doing that, our whole focus is on letting people rise to the level of their own competence. We are managing so as to engage everything that they have mastered and have been experiencing in their whole lives.

This is not to say that we don't have a vision as to where the company is going to go; it's not going to be a random walk. Rather, we are setting the parameters, the boundaries of the kind of business that we want to be in.

We are in the business of creating environments. Some of that happens to be hardware, in the form of furniture. We see the future being much beyond that, but still around the work environment. Our people come forth with ideas and with actions that are consistent with the boundaries that we've established. We're going to let them, basically, run as fast and as far as they can run.

The second concern of the company is the whole idea of being, becoming a learning organization. That is how we are going to help ourselves along the way, realizing the potential of the company.

There are many things that we will discuss in the course of this interview, but it all comes down to learning – the learning process.

DF: There is an interesting connection between the mission of liberation and your desire to advance the organization through learning.

KC: I think it's like part of the same universe. Learning is such a personal thing. If you mean it when you say you are going to liberate people, then you're going to allow learning to go on.

It is very instructive to think about what goes on in the early primary years of education. Over the last several decades, we've done a poor job of creating learning environments for our children. We have shackled them, shackled their minds. We've done so many things to keep them from being liberated by destroying their creativity; and yet, we call it "learning." It should have been called "unlearning."

DF: I am part of that educational establishment. I suppose I could claim that we thought we were disciplining minds, not shackling them.

KC: I do think we can learn to recover from what has been foisted upon us during all those decades. Whether in a business, educational, or a religious setting, adults have not lost the gray matter that little toddlers have. We've simply programmed it out. I believe that we can "reprogram" it. That is what we're trying to rediscover in Herman Miller.

DF: When we designed this book to link managing and organizational learning, we wondered if the two processes are antithetical. Over those years of the schooling process, people have learned to be subordinated to higher authorities. This is how we are still positioning management in the workplace. They are the higher powers who do the main thinking for the company, and the workers follow the scripts.

There is nothing wrong with subordination up to a point, but it seems that if the spirit must be liberated, it is being held captive in the superior–subordinate relationship.

KC: It all comes to the leadership.

DF: Spirit has been held captive incrementally over our life spans; more and more subordinating our learning to the learning of others, deferring to the final word of those above us in the organizational structure who learned for us.

KC: I agree with that. The only thing with which I disagree is that I don't necessarily believe that the other, the superior, is learning. You said "deferring to the learning of others." I think it is deferring to the *wishes* and the *dictates* of others. I suspect that the "others" that we are talking about here are anything but learning models. They're too often using, perhaps abusing, this superior position to their own advantage.

The key phrase is "command and control." You know it's the exact opposite of what you must have, the environment you must have for true learning to go on.

DF: How many employees are in the Herman Miller Company right now?

KC: 6,500.

DF: Among the 6,500 there are many who have the responsibility of managing. You are one of them. Command and control is the focus of our conversation right now. Don't many more Herman Miller managers know command and control than those who know how to foster liberation?

KC: Well, it's not "they," it's "we," because we've all come up under that sort of system.

DF: As have I; so, I can't point my finger that far away from myself. What, then, do you do, if your company's future success is to be embedded in this liberation mission? What do you say to those hundreds of Herman Miller managers to reverse old ways and accelerate liberating learning?

KC: First of all, I keep saying it. I think that it's very important that the message be clear and that the message be repeated and I can do this. I'm learning too, of course. I'm on the same learning journey that I'm trying to take this company. And so, as my understanding deepens, and as I come into contact with new thinking, I communicate.

Part of being in, and having, a learning organization is making sure that you have exposure to new thinking all the time. This new thinking can come from inside of us, but most of it comes from the "networks." These are the people, inside the organization and globally, that we allow ourselves to be exposed to. The network is a very important ingredient in constantly letting the organization be exposed to new thinking. My message out into this network has to be clear and it has to be consistent.

The other thing that is very, very important, and I said this from Day One, when I walked in the door of this place, is *teams*. I arrived talking about teams and the formation of teams. Yet, I wasn't smart enough two years ago to talk about "learning teams." I spoke of the way that I wanted people to participate in cross-functional activities and cross-functional teams. Then, I said, "If you don't know what good teams are, watch my team."

We have been building this company through dialogue. My team goes apart for days at a time and just practices dialogue. We're trying to learn the skills of inquiry, so that we're not just telling people what to do. And, we are going beyond listening into probing and understanding what skills are essential for a true inquirer.

This is being done at the top level of management in the company, not just to have it filter down, but as a living example of how we want to be together. By this, we encourage our people to take it through their organizations within Herman Miller.

DF: It must make you and your team feel quite vulnerable.

KC: That's wonderful! We love to be vulnerable.

DF: Now let me hit you with a hard point. That vulnerability, that time away to reflect and so forth, seems like a possible, even easy, thing to do while the business is running well. What if you hit a couple of hard quarters? Would you not all be back at your desks and phones, driving your business hard, the good old-fashioned way?

KC: Well, in fact we started this activity with the top team while in the midst of a very difficult economic period. Two years and four months ago when I walked into this company the situation was rapidly eroding. All the directions were southeast. Yet, rather than just go in and start taking costs out and restructuring and downsizing – we did take some costs out – the main message was that we have to look at how we're doing things, rather than just looking at where we are spending too much money.

We immediately put the main focus on who we are, the kinds of things we're engaged in, and the processes that we're going through to make decisions. In other words, we asked ourselves how to become a "learning company."

Not incidental to, but parallel with that dialogue, we started working on the bottom line issues. The focus remained on the higher ground. I think it quickly helped us to reverse the whole attitude in the company. It changed overnight. There was a defeatist attitude starting to build before then that is no longer evident today.

DF: Was it because everyone initially expected you, the new man coming in from another industry, to "wield the ax"?

KC: Yes, not only that. Even before I arrived there was an air of defeat. Many of the top managers of the company were not certain that the company could be turned around. The industry was sliding and the company was experiencing its first downturn in the history of the company.

DF: Herman Miller has been in business since the early 1900s! This was the first downturn?

KC: Right. They "had it all" from the late sixties, when the office furniture industry really took off. It had been nothing but "go, go." Then, in the late eighties, it all came to an end. These people had never experienced decline. They didn't know what to do and were basically resigned to defeat.

The first thing to do was to turn the morale around, turn the attitude at the senior levels of the company around. Once we did that, and we were able to do it very quickly, we started getting people to concentrate on the right things. The "bottom line" numbers came along after that.

It gives me a great deal of encouragement that, should we go through more periods of downturn, we can keep our minds on the right things. I believe that your mind is basically able to take you over those kinds of recessionary cycles. You simply start doing different things and doing some things in other ways. You don't just follow your business down.

DF: How are you finding the "right things"? Obviously you can't turn to the CEO's manual on your shelf to tell you what the next right things are.

KC: Oh, that's for certain.

DF: It suddenly appears that management books on most shelves are the least likely source for finding the right things to do to keep a company viable.

KC: They will, in fact, tell you exactly the wrong things, as they are all of the old management paradigm.

DF: In the absence of easy solutions, how do you develop the new liberating paradigm for Herman Miller's management?

KC: Well, I think I'm a very good learner and I've had an inquiring mind all my life. My focus throughout has been on personal growth. I try to extend this focus to my organizations. If I were not of a mind to be in a state of constant inquiry, to be focused on my own growth, it would have a fairly negative impact on my ability to do these kinds of things.

This somewhat "cultivates the field"; but, then you still have to plant the seeds. Those seeds come from a lot of people that I exposed my thinking to; some of the best thinkers of our time. George Land has been a mentor and friend of mine for more than a decade. I've learned a lot, which probably isn't enough, and much of that has been influenced by George.

Meg Wheatley is a person who in recent years has started to impact not only me but our company as well.

Peter Vaill is another. I first got to know Peter Vaill through his *Managing as a Performing Art*. I was given that book by a consultant at Dow Corning who knew me quite well. She wrote a long statement in the front of the book which said, "Here's a kindred spirit for you." And so when I read it, it was like I had written it myself! Then, when I finally met Peter, it was just such a wonderful experience.

Speaking of "Peter," I meet with Peter Senge, author of the *Fifth Discipline*, at least twice a year.

Kindred spirits do sort of "flock together as birds of a feather." Jim Autrey is the CEO of Meredith Publishing. He's a poet and has written some really neat poetry books. Jim is another person who is just wonderful to sit down and talk to as a friend and engage in dialogue. He reinforces my thinking. The first time that I met Jim a couple of years ago, we sat in my office together for two hours. It was funny. At the end of that time, we both said the same thing! "We have exactly the same ideas, which is surprising enough; but, not only that, we use exactly the same words to articulate our ideas!" It was the strangest phenomenon – two total strangers thinking the same way and using the same words.

DF: Both you and Jim Autrey bear enormous responsibility for companies, and have for a number of years. One of the nicest phrases in Vaill's *Performing Art* book is that managers are those who "live with responsibility for others."

KC: Right, well you have to live with responsibility. That is why Herman Miller is such a wonderful fit for me. This company was founded by D. J. DePree on these very values. I was talking with some people earlier this morning about how this company has moved through time, from 1923 until where we find ourselves today.

Max DePree tells the "millwright" story in his book, *Leadership is an Art*. Max's father, as a very young owner of the company, learned of the death of a millwright who was in charge of keeping all the machines running in the company. He went to the home of the millwright, whose widow brought out some poetry. D. J. DePree was reading this really beautiful poetry and asked, "Who wrote this?". She said that the millwright wrote it. Mr DePree thought, "We only knew this person in Herman Miller as the person that ran the machinery. But look at who he really was and we didn't know it." That changed his whole life. That little cameo has changed the whole course of the company.

We've never departed from the belief that each of our people have unique and varied gifts to bring to our company. Our liberation mission builds upon this foundation.

That was in the mid-1920s. In about 1950, D. J. DePree was introduced to Dr Carl Frost, who had studied with Joseph Scanlon at MIT. We were the first company in 1950 to incorporate the Scanlon Principles and introduce that Scanlon Plan into the company. Herman Miller has continued through the next 45 years of being as a Scanlon Company. So the whole idea of participative management and employee ownership came here in the late 1940s and early 1950s.

Today, we are in Phase Three as we move into liberation management. It is all consistent with the millwright story. We're building. We're learning. Yet the company, in a sense, has been a learning organization for its entire 70 plus year history. We're just continually unfolding this thing.

DF: A couple years back, however, when financial indicators were "heading south," you could have chosen a harsher course. Many companies have done heavy "deconstruction work." Had Herman Miller downsized, it might have made the figures look pretty good. A shrunken workforce could mean higher levels of productivity. It would look good for you as a decisive leader. Of course, the legacy of the millwright would be gradually lost.

KC: It would have been a real tragedy for Herman Miller had we done that. That was one of the reasons, I think, I was asked by the Board of Directors to come in. They saw within me a set of values that would not allow that deconstructing to happen. But, beyond just the tragedy that would have been for Herman Miller, such tearing down would be a tragedy for any company. It is all wrong. It follows all the wrong instincts. All you have to do is look at the major companies in this country who have been downsizing. Wait for just "n" more months, until they downsize again.

If you get your thoughts right, your positioning right, you understand why downsizing is wrong. The idea is not to lose with layoffs your company's best asset, its experienced people. Rather, the choice is to redeploy your people into ways that add new value to the customer, that really serve the shareholder. If the mind of the leadership is wrong, then you're going to do the wrong things.

DF: Unfortunately employees, even in a company with as much participation as yours, still have to depend on the upper leadership. They can't take matters into their own hands to save a company.

KC: Of course they can't. Not only do they have to depend on top leaders, another way of putting it is that their lives are determined by us! It is not a dependency as much as it's a determinant. If the leadership aims in the wrong direction, then it is going to effect everybody adversely.

DF: Thinking now of Vaill's phrase, "Managing with responsibilities for others," I'm hearing from you ". . . managing with genuine *responsiveness* to others." That again goes back to your willingness to be vulnerable, to be an inquirer, when others may be more assured if you always appear to be certain about the company.

How will you structure the Herman Miller organization over the next several years – departments, units, and relationships – for that responsiveness? How can you, and the managers who work between you and the employees, act as antennae for their creative ideas?

KC: Two years ago, we took out several layers of hierarchy. We eliminated the Executive Committee. I think that the executive committee, certainly in this company, is a complete anachronism in most companies. Such a committee implies that there is a small group of people through which everything must filter for the final decisions. Having an executive committee is the ultimate statement of command and control. I just wiped it off the map. We don't have an executive committee.

We have no Office of the President. There is, instead, a group of 30 people, most of whom report to me as CEO. It is through this new system that we are building what we call a "relational and adaptable organization."

We have developed a company book on this theme called *The Relational and Adaptable Organization: a Conversation with Kermit Campbell*. Christine McClain talked with me with a tape recorder going. She put it together as an in-house document; but it has been widely disseminated outside the company.

The whole idea is that teams, starting at the top, will be self-forming. Each of us in the group of 30 knows our sphere of responsibility. We also know who among our peers will be affected by the immediate action that has to be taken or decision that has to be taken. It is our responsibility to then form teams of people, of our peers and whoever else will be able to make a difference; to pull that team together, make the decision, implement it, and then disband that little team. We don't even call them teams, it just happens.

DF: No kidding!

KC: We don't formalize anything. There are literally hundreds of these going on all the time. Any one of the senior managers may be on a dozen or more of them. Nobody counts, because they're just going and good things are happening.

DF: Now that presumes that there's some kind of agenda, so that they know what to move to and from. How do you manage that agenda without having all the formalistic things that we've used throughout the decades (policy statements, fiats, GANTT charts, etc.)?

KC: I've set the direction of the company. It is my responsibility to set the direction and establish its widest boundaries. Within these parameters, we don't need much more.

DF: It sounds sort of like a popular leadership metaphor that Herman Miller is moving ahead more like a flock of wild geese than a herd of buffaloes. The geese fly in formation, but there is no single goose who is in the lead position for very long. They all seem to know where their flight is going and how to stay together to get there. Whereas, those buffalo blindly follow the head bull, even over a cliff.

KC: Well, occasionally, occasionally I'm there, occasionally I'm the lead goose, but often it's any one of the other 30.

DF: I sense there is a real feeling that your whole group knows what they're after, in regard to the business. But how do you know what your customers are after? Has your company information system changed, so as to keep up with, even ahead of their changing needs?

KC: We're still learning. We don't have the sensing system fully redeveloped yet. We have what we are currently calling a "business operations team." This is a group of about 30 that meets every other month. It's not a decision-making body, because everybody has different jobs to do in their own groups. So we never make decisions in that team. It's there for mutual understanding and focusing the direction of the company. So it is basically a matter of making time for sharing. More and more, we're trying to use it as a type of dialogue, so that we can really gain some of these skills that we're after.

We also have our formal information network with voice mail or electronic mail. We are still evolving these to capture nuances of our overall organizational self-development.

DF: Underneath this general system would be your financial reports, your production schedules and so forth. Those still exist, I assume, for your operating people who need their day-to-day doses of data.

KC: Yes, we have to have budgets. We have to know when we're ahead and behind. But, those operational measures do not occupy the "frontal" part of our brains.

DF: I would like to build on that point. These data sets, under the command and control environment, tended to be hoarded on a "knowledge is power" basis. Upper-level managers coveted their information. Have you, in the cause of liberating Herman Miller people, also liberated company information? Does the working employee know how the company is doing, how you think the company should be doing, and why?

KC: Sure, that preceded my coming here. People were always part of the Scanlon Plan, so they had to know where their bonuses were coming from each quarter and how they were calculated and where they needed to improve. We have a wonderful history of this awareness. But now, we are going even beyond that.

Many company leaders hold financial numbers tightly to their chests, claiming competitive advantage. We're saying that when you do this, it is a competitive disadvantage. If your people don't know where they're going and how they're doing, how can they improve themselves? So, let's not be looking over our shoulders at our competitors. Let's be looking to the light ahead and move toward that. We should not be preoccupied with keeping our information and our ideas close to our chests. Let's use them and share them to get out in front and just keep running.

DF: That's managing in a company that learns, Kermit! Thank you for helping us "see the light" ahead.

KC: It was my pleasure.

I

Managing In and Through the Knowledge Ecology

Steven A. Cavaleri and David S. Fearon

Logic is the beginning of wisdom, not the end.
Spock, *Star Trek IV: The Undiscovered Country*

For many years managers have sought to better understand the mechanisms that govern learning in organizations. More recently, managers have shifted their attention to discerning the practical implications of collective or shared types of learning, as would be found in a "learning organization." We can only speculate as to the reasons why legions of managers have decided that becoming a learning organization is a top priority. We believe that the transformation toward becoming learning organizations that we are witnessing represents nothing less than a sea-change in the way organizations are managed. In our view, these changes are being fueled by the emerging realization that organizational learning yields organizational knowledge, and this special type of knowledge represents a source of power to organizations: market power, technology power, quality power . . . the list goes on.

There are a growing number of signs that managers are developing a deeper appreciation of the importance of organizational knowledge for a company's competitive viability. Business magazines, such as *Fortune*, have touted the importance of intellectual assets and the need to become a learning organization. Some corporations, such as the Canadian Imperial Bank of Commerce, are creating management positions specifically dedicated to supporting organizational learning within their firms. Well-known companies like Polaroid, and emerging companies like Reflexite (featured in this book), are bringing organizational learning techniques and concepts to the shop floor and assessing the learning styles of both individual and teams in manufacturing. Ford, Shell, and Federal Express are working to reshape the way they do business to incorporate both systems thinking and organizational learning into their operations.

From Honda and Canon in Japan, to Swatch and British Telecom in Europe, managers are reconsidering the way they view and use organizational knowledge.

Many companies are beginning to regard organizational knowledge as if it were jet-fuel for propelling innovation, competitiveness, and quality. However, the rush to become learning organizations is being tempered by the growing realization that organizational knowledge is something which takes time to develop and cannot be controlled with precision. Simply, organizations just can't buy, import, or acquire organizational knowledge; rather, they must continually create it from scratch, the old-fashioned way . . . they must learn it! This is what it means to be managing in organizations that truly learn.

It's clear that many organizations are developing structures and processes which are intended to promote organizational learning for the creation of organizational knowledge. Organizational knowledge is a very precious commodity which, like a small amount of refined uranium ore, can be a concentrated source of energy having many possible uses. Much like uranium, the artifacts of organizational intelligence can exist in a number of different states ranging from raw to refined, all having different degrees of usefulness.

Organizational Intelligence

One way to understand the various artifacts of organizational intelligence is to view them as existing on a spectrum of refinement ranging from relatively raw data, to information, then to organizational knowledge, and finally to organizational wisdom. Data are raw facts and numbers which alone are meaningless without a context for interpretation.

Information represents facts which now have a context and are ready for further interpretation. The particular meaning attributed to any set of facts will depend on the potential uses one has for it, as well as one's values. The uncertainty that accompanies the receipt or acquisition of information is that there is no guarantee that it will be interpreted the same way by more than one person. In other words, the extent to which information will create a shared understanding among many people is dubious. Information is independent of the process of knowing. That is, information hasn't yet been internalized by the user, or used as a basis for action. The true test of the value of information is in using it as the basis for effective action.

Once information has been used by a person or group, then it becomes the basis for creating knowledge through the **process of knowing**. In order to have knowledge, one must first experience knowing. One explanation of the process of knowing is offered by scientists Humberto Maturana and Francisco Varela. "Knowing is effective action, that is, operating effectively in the domain of existence of living beings."[1] When people are able to act effectively in a particular circumstance we are inclined to believe it is because of something which they know. If people have knowledge, then they are able to pose a question or raise an expectation that defines those actions which can be effective in a given situation.

The **process of creating knowledge** has been well-described by numerous writers, including Americans Chris Argyris, David Kolb, and Peter Senge, and Europeans Charles Handy, Ronnie Lessem, and Reg Revans. One of the most thought-provoking writers in this area is the Japanese scholar Ikujiro Nonanka. Throughout much of the works of these scholars we are able to find several important themes. First, knowledge often derives from a cyclical process of learning through experience, in other words, an action–learning cycle. Secondly, this action–learning cycle or wheel of learning spins around in a continuous process that includes: (1) theories of how things work, (2) experiences that test the validity of ideas, (3) observing and reflecting behaviors that are used to define meaning found in experiences, and (4) questioning and experimenting with new ideas.

Finally, learning and knowledge creation are subjective processes that depend on how one views self, others, and the way the world works. Another useful explanation of the process of learning through experience that has developed with roots in the biological sciences can be found in the work of biologists Maturana and Varela. By summarizing the process of learning, as these scientists appear to understand it, we may begin to make the important distinction between the various artifacts of organizational intelligence even clearer.

An organic view of learning

Every time people engage in the process of "knowing" they are defining their view of the world to focus on the usefulness of particular actions at certain times. While information may be necessary for the creation of knowledge, it is not sufficient. When people who "know" something take either effective action, or ineffective action, they gain a new level of experience that shapes their future capacity for knowing other things. So the process of knowing is a way of experimenting with information to see if it works for you. Once you discover whether something works, you must then decide whether that discovery is consistent with what you already believe is true.

This comparison takes place through the process known as **reflection**. When people pause to discover the meaning of their experiences in relation to their beliefs we say that they have engaged in the process of **reflecting**. Reflecting is a means of discovering what one really knows (or doesn't know). When people discover that either they know or don't know something, then they have learned through the benefit of their experience.

This completes the cycle of learning that enables people to learn and create knowledge by testing the usefulness of information. In terms of our prior metaphor with uranium, knowledge is highly refined because it has been through the mill of knowing, action, experience, and reflection. Clearly, information plays a very different role in organizations than does organizational knowledge. We have just described a system that reflects the process of creating personal knowledge. The key task of the learning organization is to make personal knowledge available to others throughout an organization so as to enhance each person's ability, and the organization's capacity, to create value for customers.

As a matter of principal, information is most useful in situations which are governed by recurring, standardized, mechanical, and routine situations. Information is most effectively generated by traditional managerial planning and control systems and disseminated by management information systems. On the other hand, organizational knowledge is often critical in ill-defined, human systems characterized by unique sets of circumstances where clear-cut answers are not usually available. For example, new product development processes often draw on accumulated organizational knowledge to decipher customer needs and create products to address these needs. Nonanka has described such processes in detail at several major Japanese companies, such as Honda, Matsushita, Canon, NEC, Sharp, and Kao. According to Nonanka, "The centerpiece of the Japanese approach is the recognition that creating new knowledge is not simply a 'matter' of processing objective information. Rather, it depends on tapping the tacit, and often highly subjective insights, intuitions, and hunches of individual employees and making those insights available for testing and use by the company as a whole."[2]

We define organizational knowledge *as the capacity for effective action, over time, that results from the collective knowing, experience, and reflection of all members of an organization.* It would seem that there are no short-cuts to acquiring such organizational knowledge. In fact, we propose that it is a tremendous asset, like a good reputation, that takes time and patience to build. Ideally, such accumulations of organizational knowledge, over time, will eventually lead to **organizational wisdom**.

Information, knowledge, and wisdom are all enhanced through the infusion of context into the **interpretation process**. The more managers know about a situation the richer the context that they may draw upon in their search to find new meaning amidst the complexity of modern organizations.

We believe that actionable organizational knowledge will be a critical component of competitive advantage for firms in the future. The purpose of this book is to provide a road map of possible stopping points for those manager/explorers who have chosen a path that may lead to being able to assist in the creation of organizational knowledge. Our sense is that this may be a complex, and often illusive, path that turns in ways that run counter to the intuition of many managers and co-workers. We invite you to explore this uncharted wilderness with us as you read this book. As we and our co-authors have ventured this far, our learning about management and effective organizations has been exhilarating. We hope that we have done justice to sentiment in the book that we have created for you.

Actionable knowledge

Effective organizational learning results not just in usable information, but in "actionable knowledge." We regard actionable knowledge as the yeast that helps ferment human interactions into breakthrough innovations. One way to think of actionable knowledge is that it is a form of wisdom which is gained through experience over time.[3] It is the "know-how" that enables people to visualize new ways of creating value in organizations. Typically, collective forms of know-how are the result of organizational learning. Organizational learning is a process of continually redefining the meaning of work experiences. It helps deepen both personal and shared understandings of how things work in an organization (what causes what) and how to create value for customers. For example, in craft organizations such as glass blowing, or the making of musical instruments, the accumulated wisdom of past and current master craftspeople stays alive in the traditions, routines, and values of the organization.

Researchers Scott Cook and Dvora Yanow studied the organizational learning processes of the three major, fine-quality, flutemakers in the United States. All three were located in the greater Boston area; they are: the Wm. S. Haynes Company, Verne Q. Powell Flutes, Inc., and Brannen Brothers–Flutemakers, Inc. As a result of their research they concluded,

> Typically, neither the flutes nor the way they are made have changed when flutemakers have left one of the workshops. Moreover, the organizational know-how entailed in flutemaking at each workshop is, in significant measure, different from that at the others. Although all three know how to make flutes and all follow similar production operations, each makes its own particular flute, one with a unique, unambiguously recognizable style. Thus part of what each workshop knows is unique to it.[4]

Organizational learning often results from a reframing of shared information or accepted common knowledge of how to add value to a product or service. This is in contrast to the "know-why" of comprehending theories or the "know-what" of repeating things that others have done before. All three forms of knowing are important elements for achieving success in organizations. However, the importance of actionable knowledge is of greater importance than ever before due to the simultaneous decline of command and control style structures and the rise of high-speed management.[5]

Today, people in organizations are making more local-level decisions than ever, with less time to make them. Sports teams offer a useful metaphor for the differences in types of organizations. Traditional command and control organizations are like football teams, whereas innovative companies are becoming more like basketball teams. Basketball teams are driven to improvise, while football teams are prone to plan. Yet basketball players are often guided by a strong sense of values and the same legacy of embedded cultural know-how as flutemakers.

For example, a locker-room speech by Indiana University coach Bob Knight gives a sense of the historical continuity present in a team that plays a six month season, and where players stay on the team for a maximum of four years.

> I want to give you an example of what playing here is all about . . . Wetlich coached here for five years and for two years with me at Army. At Texas today, they're playing for the Southwest Conference championship . . . Tommy Miller coached for us here for five years and he had Cornell playing for the Ivy League championship last night. And today, Mike [Krzyzewski], who played for us and coached for us, is playing in the Atlantic Coast Conference championship and to be ranked number one in the country. That all came from here . . . That's what you represent and that's what you're playing for, and that's what you ought to be playing for. Because this is the best way to play basketball – ever.[6]

There are many possible explanations why organizational learning has emerged to become so important to managers. We believe that the changing role of time and speed of change in organizations is a major contributor to this shift. Thirty years ago, managers might typically experience one major shift in technology, product or market in a decade. Today, such changes are commonplace in the space of a year or two. The pace of time, as it relates to human experience in organizations, has accelerated at an unprecedented rate. Learning enables people to recognize patterns over time. Without learning, the changes that managers see from year to year may just appear to be a series of chaotic, discontinuous, events. However, learning can help managers to see the patterns of cause and effect that underlie these changes and enable them to incorporate this understanding to help them know how to create more value in the future than today. So, in essence, organizational learning is important because it enables managers to discern the common threads of causality that shape many of the changes they must face in markets, products, technologies and the like.

Management learning

Unless these understandings of how things change over time can be transferred to a forum where they are generally accepted and understood by others, knowledge will not really be actionable for an organization. We believe that the key to success in creating learning for managers of the future will be to understand how they can help cultivate an environment of actionable knowledge in an organization, where all members can use its fruits to help them understand and act upon changes in their world.

Some management theorists have argued that this meta-world of knowledge can be constructed by well-trained managers as simply as youngsters can build a small-scale house from Lego blocks. Similarly, other consultants and writers have described learning organizations as being inanimate objects which are acted upon and controlled by managers. Our experience tells us that nothing could be farther from the truth. We regard this learning environment as the context that encompasses all work that is done by managers and with which managers must interact in order to cocreate organizational experience. For example, the shared beliefs that govern which management approaches are of the greatest value to an organization are filtered through an organization's memory and culture to influence how managers will act. In essence, this core of organizational knowledge is both a cause and effect of the actions of managers.

Surely there are many other organizational factors, beyond managers, that contribute to the development of organizational knowledge. Perhaps none of these creative influences on organizational knowledge are as important as the work of managers. It is for this reason that the role of the manager, in relation to the shaping of organizational knowledge, is the focus of this book. Given this vantage point, *the purpose of this book is to critically examine how managers may act and think to support the viability of organizational knowledge as a means to creating value for customers.* To better understand how managers have traditionally viewed their relationship to learning in organizations let's take a look back in time.

Going Back in Time

The old saw that "knowledge is power" may have even greater meaning in relation to organizations, since actionable knowledge is the fuel that drives its ability to innovate and compete. Despite this realization, one might argue that managers have long known that knowledge is a source of competitive advantage and that organizations learn. The famous quote by Arie DeGeus, "The ability to learn faster than your competitors may be the only sustainable competitive advantage," may reflect what has been known by many innovative managers, but was incompatible with the prevailing structures and cultures of organizations.[7] If, in fact, knowledge has been regarded as an important source of competitive advantage by managers, then why all the recent interest in organizational learning?

Since the publication of Peter Senge's book *The Fifth Discipline*, in 1990,[8] there has been a subtle, yet important, shift in the way that organizational learning is discussed. Prior to the publication of Senge's book, organizational learning was largely considered to be about objective information acquisition processes. Here, information was regarded as conveying the same meaning to all who would choose to use it. Certainly, scholars such as Chris Argyris called for managers to recognize the importance of modifying their understandings and actions based on feedback; but learning was often taken to be construed as a process of refining one's understanding by adding to one's store of information.

Senge's work has questioned the *modus operandi* of managers at the most fundamental level. It would appear that Senge has thrown a stone at the glasshouse of managers. He implies that information, let alone knowledge, is derived from highly subjective processes based on the beliefs and perceptions of managers. He proposes that all people, including managers, tend to hold beliefs that are both nonsystemic, and incomplete in their outlook.

Upon reflection, some managers may discover that it is their own world view which is inhibiting their own effectiveness. Inevitably, those managers who have regarded management to be an acquired skill, which exists largely external to themselves, may still be trying to reconcile these two opposing views. Similarly, other managers have made the simultaneous realization that it often is their own thinking that limits their performance. However, they are encouraged to know that thinking is something that can be changed, and is within their own control more than it is subject to the demands of others. Senge has offered such managers several means to become masters of their own art and practice of management, namely the tools of systems thinking, personal mastery, mental models, shared vision and team learning. The implications of this shift in outlook from viewing managing as an objective, external activity, to an internal, subjective one are enormous.

This new perspective serves as a basis for creating a learning organization in which processes, such as dialogue, are used to derive new meaning from changing circumstances. This approach to learning in organizations encourages people to engage each other in a mutual process of inquiry that helps them to move closer to some fundamental truth about what makes organizations tick.

In the past, knowledge was viewed as being synonymous with information, and learning meant training and development to most managers. Knowledge was viewed as being objective information that was conveniently packaged and could be distributed easily to individuals and teams through the mechanism of training. The shift of understanding that leads to the realization that much important information can only be accessed through subjective processes involving personal and group inquiry sheds a whole new light on the definition of the term "useful information."

What has changed is the meaning of the processes by which knowledge is created and used in organizations. As Japanese managers have discovered, organizationally useful knowledge is not usually received by individuals, rather it is extracted from the knowledge environment by both individuals and teams. The question of exactly how this organizational knowledge can be extracted from the **knowledge environment** is one this book will address.

Today, many managers are asking the question, "Now that we see how organization learning happens . . . how do we manage it?" Whether organizational learning can be managed at all is a matter of debate. Obviously, we think that managers can play an instrumental role in the process of creating organizational knowledge. It is questionable whether management, as it is often practiced today, will be able to meet the challenge of supporting learning in organizations.

In our view, *the path to reconciling the processes of managing and learning begins with rediscovering work experience, the seed of creating organizational knowledge.*

It is difficult to understand the significance of actions by managers without first knowing what the conventional wisdom for managing is within a given organization. This is to say, although many consider management to be a profession, it is still practiced as an art form in ways, in many roles, that are unique to each organization. The concept of "know-how" applies as much to managing as it does to flutemaking. Management may be considered to be an objective discipline which draws upon a body of external knowledge which is endemic to the profession. Managing may also be seen from a more cultural basis as a set of values and norms within an organization that guides which practices are used and which are ignored.

How people approach managing learning will depend on where they stand in terms of their fundamental view of organizations. If they regard management as a body of external facts, and learning as the process of acquiring such facts, then it is likely that such people will manage learning by providing people with all the information they need. Conversely, people may understand the process of managing as a personal activity that reflects their beliefs as much as it mirrors external facts. They are often likely to see learning as an experience of actively engaging one's environment. If such people desire to manage organizational learning they will be prone to focus upon discovering how shared beliefs and values influence the meaning people attribute to their experiences.

The essence of these two positions is captured by Henry Skolimowski. He has termed these two opposite views as the "yoga of objectivity" and the "yoga of participation." Many managers are trained to be experts in the yoga of objectivity, taking a detached, rational view of situations that discounts the influence of their own subjective views in defining problems.[9] On the other hand, those managers who are steeped in the traditions of the yoga of participation acknowledge that they personally identify with their work and thus see that they are part of a whole system from which they cannot be separated in either mind or spirit. Thus, managers who engage in the yoga of participation often subscribe to a willingness to be personally transformed by the very process in which they are at the center.

Geoffrey Vickers has described how managers operate within a framework of values and judgments known as an "appreciative system" that governs what will be revealed to managers in any situation. Accordingly, those managers who are obsessed with the economic efficiency of operations will have their vision of other important features of their environment obscured by this preoccupation. This may in part explain the fact that permanently failing organizations often behave in ways that suggest that they would rather do what they understand than do what works. By the same token, some organizations are shocked into examining their own appreciative systems by glimpses of their own demise.

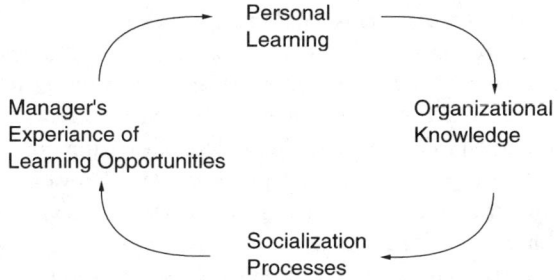

Figure 1.1   Organizational learning as a mirror of culture.

It is highly unlikely that managers will be able to maintain a personal appreciative system that is inconsistent with the larger organization in which they work. In our view, the organizational knowledge or shared know-how that pertains to managing will play an instrumental role in determining how people in that organization will manage, what they will learn, and what they will contribute to the organizational knowledge base. From this perspective, organizational knowledge-creating processes appear to be self-sustaining. If the conventional wisdom in an organization is that managing is a process of applying traditional scientific principles to problem-solving, then this will also govern what is learned by managers. It is clear from this that organizational learning cannot be fully understood without an appreciation of its managerial context (see figure 1.1).

Systems Thinking

If a manager's approach is based on the yoga of objectivity, he or she will be inclined to attempt to directly "manage" learning processes by controlling them. They will try to justify them in terms of measurable data and economic indicators, like a banker would justify an investment in terms of return and payback period. In the nomenclature of systems theory, this approach is an example of "hard systems thinking." There is "soft systems thinking" as well.

Hard systems thinking is a very effective conceptual framework for managing mechanical systems that yield discrete, measurable outputs. On the other hand it is misleading and dangerous when misapplied to organizational learning. Hard systems thinking offers a seductively simple approach for understanding the details of a problem.

In the hard systems approach improvements are seen as stemming from the achievement of four fundamental goals: (1) reduction of uncertainty levels through rationalization, (2) prediction of future states of the system, (3) preparation for these predicted future states, and (4) control of all relevant forms of performance through negative feedback mechanisms, to assure efficiency.

The influence of hard systems thinking is pervasive in most organizations and can be recognized in diverse functions ranging from strategic planning to operations management, and organization design. Its emphasis is upon finding solutions to well-defined problems. For example, when outdoors outfitters L. L. Bean of Maine wanted to better serve their telephone customers they did a hard systems study of the capacity of their telephone system. They discovered that by investing in more lines, more phones, and more customer service operators they were able to shorten waiting times on calls and avoid many lost calls from frustrated callers placed on hold. The problem with such solutions is that if they are regarded by managers as being permanent, then there is relatively little chance for improvement or learning through and beyond this experience. In general, hard systems thinking tends to short-circuit learning by focusing on information, rather than on knowledge, and on creating permanent solutions to problems that replace the human experiences of knowing and reflection with simplified mathematical models of situations.

Soft systems thinking is a more interpretive perspective which is based on the yoga of participation. *It frames organizational learning as a process of continuously redefining people's beliefs and perceptions about how things work.*

British management theorist Peter Checkland has identified a number of assumptions that are characteristic of soft systems thinking: (1) it places emphasis upon learning, rather than goal seeking; (2) it views systems models as being intellectual constructs, rather than as maps of the actual world; (3) it views the world as being problematical, but can be explored using systems models, rather than engineering structures to meet needs; and (4) it talks the language of "issues" and "accommodations," rather than problems and solutions.[10]

"Soft" and "hard" forms of systems thinking are not opposites. As Checkland notes, "the well-defined problem needing a solution is the special case within the general case of issues calling for accommodations" (p. 765). We believe that one of the preconditions for organizational learning is the adoption of a "soft" systems thinking perspective. Again, the perspective we offer is not to replace hard systems thinking with soft systems thinking, but rather to balance the polarity of the managing process and use each approach when it is of greatest value. Managers who singularly espouse only one of these frameworks, at the exclusion of the other, are like carpenters who only know how to use a hammer and to whom all situations appear as nails!

Fostering Organizational Learning

Organizational learning holds the promise of offering flexibility and competitiveness to organizations. It has attracted the interest of managers who are excited by its potential for improving organizational performance. Despite this promise, organizational learning is likely to flourish only under a relatively well-defined set of circumstances. It is argued here that organizational learning may only achieve robust results in organizations whose processes of improvement are founded on "soft" systems thinking.

Organizational learning is not a management technique. It is more accurately described as *the purposeful creation of shared meanings derived from the common experiences of people in organizations*. Learning organizations often operate on the basis of sets of assumptions which run counter to traditional managerial principles used in organizations.

By drawing on the two themes we have just discussed we can see that the process of creating useful knowledge in organizations is not as transparent as one might think. The reasons are three-fold: (1) organizational cultures tend to support the creation of ways of managing that are unique to each organization; (2) the dominant style of managing in an organization tends to reflect the base of organizational knowledge which exists; (3) the way people manage may either alert them to learning opportunities or shield them from learning.

Managers who engage in the yoga of participation and "soft" systems thinking are more likely to learn about their relationship to their surroundings; whereas managers who practice the yoga of objectivity and hard systems thinking are likely to attempt to learn information about the details of their environment. Our point of view is that management approaches which discount the cultural and subjective bases for organizational learning run the risk of creating chaos in the name of learning.

One of the reasons for this potential pitfall is that managers who practice the yoga of objectivity focus their attention on correcting what they perceive as being wrong by exerting control to restore things to their rightful state. This process of correcting errors develops an essentially problem-oriented view of organizational learning. While this may help to understand what has gone wrong, it says nothing about what is right or natural.

Learning is a fundamentally natural process that relies on human experience that unfolds in ways that are unplanned and may not make sense initially. The yoga of objectivity is often confounded by such processes, although they may be essential to the viability of organizations. Let us explore a more natural approach to learning that integrates notions from the fields of anthropology, cognitive science, ecology, and evolutionary biology.

It's Alive!

Traditionally, managers have done just fine by adopting a mechanical view of organizations. That is, they have chosen to regard organizations as operating according to the same working principles of cause and effect as would be found in a machine. The classic example is the clockwork metaphor: a timepiece made up of finely-crafted precision gears all interfacing with perfect synchronicity. These images of "clockwork as organization" have been brilliantly captured on celluloid in Chaplin's vintage film *Modern Times*, and in the 1980s cult classic

Brazil. Undoubtedly, this metaphor is very effective for understanding how to control many stable, repetitive processes that are commonly found in organizations.

On the other hand, such mechanistic models usually infer a role of managers based on physical explanations, rather than in terms of information, energy, or spirit. The penchant for explaining complex behavior in terms of the material aspects of an organization is characteristic of the manager who practices the yoga of objectivity. After all, the logic goes, all reasonable people can see and observe the material aspects of an organization, (profits, product quality, and efficiency), whereas the other dimensions are not reliably measured (learning, culture, and morale). In other words, "if you can't measure it, it doesn't exist."

The difference between materialistic and energy/information approaches is nowhere more evident than in the practices of medicine and healing. Traditionally, allopathic physicians in the West evaluate a person's health by measuring the level of functioning of various organ systems. By contrast, in Eastern cultures there is an emphasis on assessing a person's *qi* or *chi*, their vital life energy force, to know that person's state of health. In Native American cultures, a shaman may try to understand their patients' relationships to their families and communities in order to understand the source of their diseases.

Interestingly, a recent international study of workplace values in 18 countries found that spiritual development was rated more highly than physical development by managers responding in the survey. One of the primary researchers for the study concluded, ". . . this could be a 'wake-up call' for those corporations who believe that they are being very progressive installing gymnasiums and other perks for the physical needs of workers. Could meditation rooms or quiet 'sanctuaries' be the next step for visionary employers?"[11] Indian researcher, Professor S. K. Chakraborty studied senior managers in India between 1983 and 1990, and concluded that senior managers would benefit greatly from the presence of a place to be quiet and at peace: a "mind-stilling room." He notes the potential value of such a room, ". . . mind-stilling room . . . is more fundamental than the provision of clubs and swimming pools. The latter usually lead to a lot of useless exteriorization and to very little genuine relaxation. Usually the consciousness is lowered and vulgarized through such socialization."[12]

Many of the ultra-rational approaches used in the West tend to elevate humans to a position above nature. This perspective devalues the power and wisdom of nature and assumes that people should use their intellect to control natural forces to reach their goals. Since nature is often regarded as being difficult to control and machines are easy to control, it is easy to see how managers could conceive of organizations as machines and themselves as mechanics.

The main difficulty with this perspective is that many critical elements of organizations are fundamentally natural. They don't respond well to control through rational, mechanical means. Employees, customers, and suppliers are all governed by nature, more than they fit the mechanical requirements of any organization. This is not meant to imply that such natural elements of organizations are uncontrollable. Rather, it suggests that organizations benefit when managers use wisdom in blending the natural and the artificial forces in organizations. In the United States, companies such as Digital Equipment Corporation, have experimented with natural work settings. A number of companies in Scandinavia, such as Volvo and SAAB, have devoted considerable attention to creating a more natural work environment for employees.

The learning process is also a highly natural one which does not respond well to efforts at control. Make no mistake, there are always some academics, consultants, and practitioners who will try to control anything that comes their way by seeing everything as nails and pulling out their hammer. One such example is the tendency to take complex ideas and philosophies and reduce them to techniques. Consequently, the learning process becomes focused on objectively learning the new information, rather than seeking to understand how the new philosophy can become integrated into the way they and the organization operate. American managers, for example, have been criticized by people such as the late Edwards Deming for taking the concepts of total quality management (TQM) and using them as turnkey techniques. At the same time Japanese managers have come to regard the same ideas as a guiding philosophy and revere them for their wisdom. The distinctly different yogas of objectivity and participation can be clearly seen in the American and Japanese approaches to TQM. The manager who practices the yoga of participation asks the question for the hundredth time, "What does quality really mean to the way I do my work?" The manager who has mastered the yoga of objectivity asks for the hundredth time, "What can I do to help us win the Baldrige Award?"

Self-Organization

Can learning organizations be managed with utter disregard for natural forces? We think not. Furthermore, such tactics are wholly unnecessary because nature has its own built-in controls that, when understood and appreciated, can be an effective tool in guiding learning processes. These natural forces are called **self-organizing processes**. Our fundamental point here is that nature is even better than humans at controlling itself, over the long run, because it has evolved its own internal governing systems. Scientists and systems theorists often refer to this natural self-organizing process as **autopoiesis**.

The autopoietic perspective proposes that natural systems are autonomous in that they have their own internal controls that lets a system know what conditions seem capable of supporting future growth and survival. In the short run, a system may behave chaotically as a way of defining its own limits and capacities. Managers may find this self-organizing process to be painful, since customers and investors usually prefer stability. However, by intervening prematurely, managers often preclude a system from developing its own internal mechanism of governance that will provide stability over the long run.

Through a process known as **structural coupling**, these systems can become stabilized by evolving internal controls that rely on recurring patterns of interactions that yield long-term stability. For example, populations of animals, such as deer, regulate the size of the herd by the natural process in which deer which are starving from lack of food are less likely to produce new offspring, and those young which are born are less likely to survive under conditions of famine due to the action of natural predators, such as wolves.

The balancing feedback loops present in both markets and nature are programmed to restore stability of a system whenever possible. That is to say, through the process of self-organization systems invent their own patterns of relationships that will solidify over time to encourage the creation of a dynamic balance between the two forces of the natural world – growth and stability.

There is a fundamental relationship between the processes of self-organization, structural coupling, and learning that is essential to the creation of organizational knowledge. Systems that are self-organizing automatically note what actions are effective and what are not. The implication for managers is that when they are able to define their interest in a system in terms of questions or verbalized expectations, then they will have the opportunity to learn. Why? Because a natural system will tell you when you are wrong. The first time you overeat or overindulge in alcoholic beverages, your body usually will send out a very strong message that the actions you took the night before were not effective in supporting the growth and stability of your organism. Just so, a natural self-organizing system will tell managers when customers are dissatisfied. Companies like General Motors, during the 1970s, were often masked from this feedback by strategies and techniques that buffer the effects of customer feedback.

In natural organizations the experience of being in the organization is a learning experience. The natural flow of feedback to the effects of prior decisions create frequent learning opportunities. In the words of Maturana and Varela, "to live is to know (living is effective action in existence as a living being)."[13] What this means is that when organizations are allowed to exist as self-organizing entities, then learning and knowledge come to the surface naturally, because survival depends on it. Furthermore, self-organizing systems highlight the smallest of unnatural imbalances present, whereas in machine-type organizations such imbalances can be ignored for years because the rigid structures that stabilize a firm can mask its inner fragility. However, learning in complex systems is not a simple matter of just making corrections to previous errors. Ground-breaking research by MIT professor John Sterman has found that various impediments can delay or prevent learning feedbacks from functioning and allowing erroneous and harmful behaviors and beliefs to persist.[14]

In sum, our view is that organizational learning is a uniquely natural process, that becomes confounded by the efforts of managers to mechanize or control it. By virtue of its naturalness, organizational learning is more likely to prove to be fruitful when systems are allowed to evolve their own self-referential standards. The reasons for this are simple: "control" and "learn" are antithetical terms.

Managing in Organizations That Learn

Managers can play an instrumental role in generating organizational knowledge, but it is not by controlling the process, but rather by *supporting the work of the forces at play in organizations that naturally support learning*. For example, by helping managers discover their inner mental models and values that influence how they manage. By supporting others in creating a playful atmosphere where people can feel free to experiment with new ideas and be innovative. By creating reward systems that encourage people to engage in thoughtful dialogue with colleagues as to the nature of the problems they face. By serving as role models who are willing to act heroically by publicly surfacing and testing out their own mental models. By leading the formation of a community of learners who are committed to respecting each other's views, and to their own personal development as people and members of a particular organization. There are literally thousands of ways that managers can act in support of organizational learning. This book is intended to offer an overview of a variety of approaches that managers may adopt to promote the creation of knowledge in organizations.

A metaphor that is of value to those managers who are seeking to develop a comprehensive view of natural learning in vitalized environments can be found in the scientific concept of **ecology**. While this word often conjures up images of the physical atmosphere of the Earth, we are using it in a broader sense to describe a field of relations.

The Knowledge Ecology

In the **knowledge ecology**, the relations that we speak of are among ideas and energies. Let's examine the notion of ecology more deeply by discussing the Gaia model of physical ecology.

The Gaia model is a dynamic representation of the interactions among several key parts of the Earth's ecology in which the assumption is made that the ecology is a living system, rather than an inanimate object. The way that one would consider interacting with a living organism is very different from interacting with an inanimate, mechanical one. The "daisy world" ecological model created by scientists James Lovelock and Lynn Margulis is a simple, yet elegant, framework that can help build an understanding of the underlying causal structure that creates the dynamics with which everyone is familiar.[15] The heating and cooling of the Earth during the day/night cycles and the various seasons of the year is an example. According to Lovelock and Margulis, the prerequisites to life are created and maintained by the self-organizing processes of life itself. Simply stated, their model suggests that the flora of the world is composed of three colors: white daisies, black ones, and red earth, or sand. The white daisies reflect light from the sun and help to cool the surface of the Earth. The black daisies soak in sunlight, store heat, and help warm the planet. White daisies prefer warm temperatures and the black ones enjoy cooler weather. Through an autopoietic process, a structural coupling is fashioned in which the different color daisies are continuously engaging in a self-maintaining cyclical web of interactions that help to create a dynamic, yet stable balance in the ecosystem.

If humans sought to intervene to control this system, it is doubtful that they could match the effectiveness of nature in regulating itself. To take the metaphor of daisies one step further, if one wishes to cultivate a patch of daisies there must be a recognition on the part of the gardener that nature will control the growth of the daisies in its own way, and that the most the gardener can do is to assure timely offerings of food, water, and weeding.

If one were to consider ideas in an organization to be the equivalent of the daisies in the Gaia model, what would an ideal knowledge ecology look like? What would the role of the manager/gardener be under such circumstances? One clue to answering this question may come from the work of psychiatrist/ philosopher Gregory Bateson. In his book *Steps to an Ecology of Mind*,[16] Bateson envisions a collection of ideas as a "mind." His ecological perspective on ideas is intended to highlight questions such as, "How do ideas interact? Is there a process of natural selection that governs the fate of some ideas to survive while others perish?" Similarly, one could consider an organization as having a series of shared understandings and memories of past experience which give rise to shared meaning and collective learning. From this perspective, it is arguable that organizations possess some sort of collective intelligence or **organizational mind**. What is the ecology of this organizational mind? What is the relevance of the organizational mind (knowledge/wisdom) to the organizational body (work)? Can the two be understood independent of one another? In the next pages we will describe our vision of living, managing, and learning in the knowledge ecology.

Just as the way we live from day to day determines the quality of the physical ecosystem, the way we manage shapes the knowledge ecology of organizations. Society cannot produce huge quantities of refuse without disturbing the natural balance between the earth and humans. Similarly, one cannot manage à la Genghis Kahn, and then expect to create a "learning organization" that will pay long-term dividends. Just as some people may argue that the balance of the physical ecosystem is both dynamic and delicate, we also believe that the knowedge ecology is this way. To understand this, let's look at the fundamental structures and elements that form the knowledge ecology.

Organizational knowledge ecology exists in the space between task requirements, technology, human experience, and organizational mind. The media of this ecology, like the air we breathe or the sunlight on our skin, is composed of data, information, knowledge, and wisdom.

The core human processes in the knowledge ecology are interpreting, learning, knowing, and being. The media and processes that bring life to the knowledge ecology are all interconnected. Through their work experience people are able to use the tension between work requirements, themselves, and the organizational mind as the basis for creating new meaning. Meaning emerges as data is interpreted, information is learned, knowledge is known, and as people live with wisdom. The relationships among these core elements are depicted in figure 1.2.

In a vital knowledge ecology, situations are consistently seen "in a different light" as new meaning consistently emerges as a result of work experiences. Here, work and learning are viewed as being concurrent: they reinforce each other and flow together. When situations are seen in a different light people discover the newness of the situation by observing and interpreting data and adding those new ideas to the learning cycle.

In a vital learning ecology there is a dynamic tension in meshing task and technological requirements with human experience and the organizational mind. In organizations that are not designed or managed for learning there will be an emphasis on task and technology.

According to British management expert Ronnie Lessem, successful learning environments enable people to be engaged in activities on many personal levels. This approach regards managers holistically in terms of their thoughts, feelings, and actions as they work. Lessem proposes that thinking is most closely related to the creation of management knowledge, feelings pertain to a manager's self, and action relates to managerial skills.[17]

In the nonvital knowledge ecology, work is completed by engaging human experience at the level of action and there will be little interaction with the organizational mind. The organizational mind represents the collective

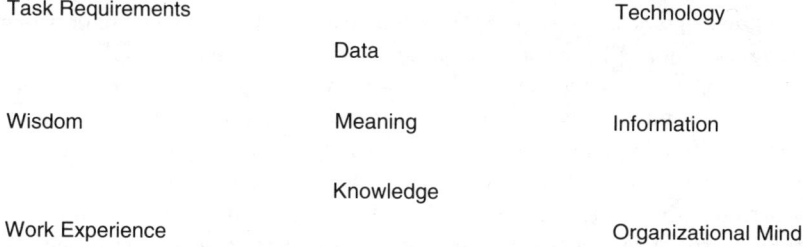

Task Requirements   Technology
                        Data

Wisdom   Meaning   Information

                     Knowledge
Work Experience   Organizational Mind

Figure 1.2   The knowledge ecology.

memory, knowledge, and wisdom of an organization. By interacting with the organizational mind people challenge the prevailing wisdom of how things are done in that organization. This model of organizational knowledge ecology has been designed to further inquiry and to prompt its testing in the reality of the organizational world.

The knowledge ecology is a framework for understanding the underlying forces that affect the processes that lead to the creation of knowledge in organizations. Transforming an organization to one in which people are enabled to engage their work more fully is usually a complex and challenging enterprise. Organization members may find that it is more comfortable to engage work only at the level of action than to include their minds and hearts in their work. On the other hand, work that also offers chances to play and opportunities for creativity can be very attractive to most people. The challenge for most managers is to find the wise balance among these forces where employees can experience work in its fullest, raw form, while still enjoying their work.

Nonanka argues that knowledge is created through a process that flows from direct experience. However, Argyris suggests that managers are often ill-prepared to accept the lessons of their direct experience, so they enact defensive routines to skew their perception of situations to be congruent with their existing beliefs.[18] By diffusing direct experiences in this way they are also diluting potential lessons that may be discovered in a situation. Ultimately, direct knowledge, which has been gained through experience, is the essential ingredient of organizational knowledge. Such action-driven knowledge arises out of the flux between a manager's awareness and activity. In essence, knowledge comes forth from experience and in organizations experience means work. So knowledge and work are intertwined in a delicate dance that easily loses balance in one direction or the other.

If people automatically learn just by doing their jobs, then what is being sought by the many organizations that are hoping to become learning organizations? Our answer is that we believe that both people and organizations learn. However, what they learn depends on the context in which they are learning, and the context is shaped by the way an organization is managed. We believe that most organizations are managed for specific outcomes, not for learning.

One way to conceive of how both action and knowledge may be integrated in the knowledge ecology is through a framework called concurrent learning. *Concurrent learning is a continuous process that seeks to expand people's learning capacities by viewing work and learning as being coterminous activities.* Unlike most work improvement schemes, concurrent learning activities have a dual agenda: to promote innovation in work processes, while helping people to become more aware of their own patterns of thinking. By recognizing the limitations and nonsystemic tendencies inherent in their own patterns of thinking, people now have a source of reference for becoming better systems thinkers. In concurrent learning, systems thinking is the primary tool, systems integration is the framework, and learning and improvement are the goals.[19]

Learning is vital to the long-term health of organizations. For some managers, the validity of this assertion may be difficult to accept. For others it is intuitively obvious and compelling in its attractiveness as a touchstone for their way of managing. We will not try to address or defend the rationale for this "learning imperative." We simply say, based on all that we know and feel, we believe that this statement is true. Moreover, our sense is that most of those managers who share this belief in the importance of learning in organizations will also be struck by the immensity of the challenge to understand the relationship between managing and learning.

While it is arguable that learning is manageable, this book is more concerned with understanding how one's management approach affects the ways in which we learn. The essence of this view is reflected in the following axiom: *The way one manages will affect how an organization learns more than what you do to manage learning.* The way each person manages is reflected in what he or she does most of the time, not just in those special times when the focus is on organizational learning. Our estimate is that 90 percent of the time that managers spend managing does not facilitate learning, but rather is aimed at accomplishing specific outcomes, like increasing output or making sure that a delivery is made on time. However, any time managers manage they are also concurrently shaping the learning ecology, whether they realize it or not. For example, corporate planning processes that direct the efforts of managers exclusively on goal setting, and which reward them for the accuracy with which they achieve these goals, also unintentionally subvert the learning process. They do this by diverting the attention of managers away from what could be learned if they were free to more fully experience the planning process. When a planning cycle culminates by rewarding only the discrete outcomes yielded they are inadvertently contributing to a "dumbing-down" of the organization.

The principles of needing to engage the whole person in the learning process hold true whether we are speaking of the work being that of managing or anything else. In some cultures managers tend to emphasize the mastery of techniques instead of seeking to develop a deeper understanding of an approach. In terms of Lessems's framework, this technique orientation only engages people on the action level and fails to significantly draw upon their thoughts or feelings. Consequently, any learning that arises through the use of these techniques tends to be externalized and superficial. This is not to say that the use of techniques truncates learning. Rather, the point is that *engaging people through the use of techniques alone limits the potential for work to become a learning experience.*

It is easy to be seduced by the simplicity and efficiency of many techniques. It is often more difficult and time-consuming to introduce one's personal thoughts and feelings to the mix. Yet, that is the clarion call for this book. We are proposing that by everyone experiencing work more fully there will be greater opportunity for learning in organizations. When managers make decisions to create systems where technique is valued over learning, in effect, they are shaping the "knowledge ecology" of their organization. When top managers interact with people as economic entities, rather than as whole persons, they have sent a message that they are not ready to engage people fully in their work, and thus they limit learning. When top managers communicate the message, "We are now empowering you to learn," they are practicing the yoga of objectivity if they are providing others with a license to learn, without transforming work to engage people on all three personal levels. Whether you are polluting, sustaining, or supporting this ecology with the way you manage may be critical to the future viability of your organization.

In summary, we have argued that managers whose management style reflects their commitment to organizational learning benefit by working to create, rather than control, the conditions for learning. Systems thinking will enable managers to see that organizational learning is a dynamic process in which balance must be maintained between work and learning. Perhaps, in the knowledge ecology the old Latin phrase will acquire new meaning: *Non schola set vita discimus* ("We don't learn for school but for life").

The Rest of the Book

While notions of living, managing, and learning in a knowledge ecology can be interpreted in a wide variety of ways, this book has been organized around a very simple structure that we hope will enable us to grasp some of the key elements of this ecology.

Part I began with an interview with Kermit Campbell, CEO of Herman Miller Inc. Chapters in Part I examine relationships between managing and learning in organizations. New approaches to managing are considered, as are the ways in which managers can create the essential conditions for learning to blossom. The result of these efforts may produce a dramatic transformation of the very landscape of the organizational learning process that we find in the playing fields of learning.

The chapters in this section examine the changing role of managers in relation to organizational learning. Chapter 2, "The Prism of the New Managerial Mind" by David Fearon and Ivan Blanco considers the implications of how recent patterns of transformation in managerial thinking to encompass all members of the organization will influence learning in organizations. Both this chapter and the one which follows examine the role played by self-development in promoting managerial effectiveness. In "The Learning Manager and the Inner Side of Management," William Ferris and A. Russell Fanelli look at the process of managing from the inside out. By adopting a holistic view of the manager as person they explore the implications of that personal self-discovery for learning in organizations. The process of self-discovery in service to learning has at times been equated with personal pain and awkward situations. However, when organizations are supportive of such efforts to learn by exploration of one's self and one's world there are also ways to view the landscape of the workplace as a literal playing field for learning. Kathleen DeChant's chapter "The Playing Fields of Learning" seeks to map out the terrain of the learning organization and locate the potential places where work and play intersect to support learning.

Part II begins with an interview with noted organization theorist André DelBecq. This section considers the experience of managers who want to serve as the catalyst for creating the conditions of learning. The inner work of managers is viewed as the starting point from which all else follows. The result of this inner work is both an emerging sense of creativity and a quest to lead others into the realm of the knowledge ecology.

Chapter 5, "Creating the Conditions for Learning," by Richard Wise, takes the view of the manager who believes in the value of learning in organizations and wants to know what circumstances must prevail to support the emergence of broad-scale organizational learning. In many organizations the cornerstone for organizational learning will be laid on the foundation of creativity and innovation. In chapter 6, Alex Pattakos examines the dynamic relationship between personal creativity, innovation and organizational learning. Organizational learning is a powerful, yet subtle process. It is a process that bridges the personal and shared experiences of organization members. One emerging view suggests that leadership is the most critical function in organizations that can maintain and strengthen this bridge. Stephen Meisel and David Fearon consider the role of the learning leader in building a learning organization in their chapter, "Leading Learning."

Part III is headed by an interview with John Sterman, Director of MIT's well-known System Dynamics Group. This part of the book considers teams and information in designing and supporting the knowledge ecology. Both operator and management teams are essential to the formation of the emerging knowledge ecology. In chapter 8, "From Individual and Team Learning to Systems Learning," George Roth analyzes a comprehensive effort to develop systems thinking and organizational learning capacities of people in a major US automobile company. The support of top management is always critical to the success of such projects. However, top management teams are often incapable of fully knowing the requirements of organizational learning programs unless they have functioned as a learning group themselves. In "Transforming The Top Management Team Into a Learning Group," Laura Freebairn-Smith discusses the major challenges that face top management teams that are seeking to become self-renewing learning systems. As various teams and groups in organizations begin to learn together they will have a desire to communicate more frequently than ever. The demands this will place on the information systems of an organization are unprecedented. The way information-related functions are conceived and implemented by managers places an important role in organizational learning. In "Information pathways to organizational knowledge," Steven Cavaleri, Leo Charalambides, Brian Maguire, and Stephen Hall take a broad view of the informational needs of the learning organization.

Part IV begins with an interview with innovative management thinker and educator, Peter Vaill. He discusses his view of the future organizations that will operate as total learning systems. This part adopts a systemic perspective that emphasizes the role of relationships, values, and integration of parts to the whole. The idea of the integrative manager who manages for learning is the focus of "Relational Management" by Nicholas Zangari and Steven Cavaleri. Often the transition to becoming a learning organization is fraught with uncertainty and anxiety related to issues of identity, values, and autonomy. The persons who choose to step forward to confront such issues on the path toward becoming a learning organization might be described as heroic leaders. Their journey through the culture of an organization is described in "Learning From The Core: The Heroic Leader and the Conscious Organization" by Sharon Seivert, Alex Pattakos, Fred Reed, and Steven Cavaleri. On the path toward becoming a learning organization many of the beliefs that have been accepted as part of traditional cultures are challenged and begin to crumble under the light of scrutiny. People are often left to wonder if there are other ways of thinking about organizations that may be more natural in their ability to support learning. One possible framework that is considered for this purpose is the field of autognomics, which is the focus of "The Implications of Autonomy for Learning in Organizations" by Fred Reed and Sharon Seivert. Even the most innovative of learning managers must eventually come to terms with the prevailing structures, practices, and routines of the organizations where they work.

Part V starts with an interview with Cecil Ursprung, CEO of Reflexite Corporation, *INC.* magazine's company of the year in 1993, along with two Reflexite colleagues, David Edgar and Matthew Guyer. This part of the book examines a number of core management functions as they relate to the knowledge ecology. Planning, structure culture, and organizations of the future are all considered from this perspective. A case vignette of Reflexite Corp looks in greater detail at the inner workings of a knowledge ecology.

The transformation toward becoming an effective learning organization usually requires that managers reconsider the way they use standard managerial tools such as planning and culture-building. In "Integrating Learning and Organizations," John Montgomery and Frank Scalia draw on decades of personal experience as executives managing in the public and private sectors to look afresh at the pragmatic challenges of managing for performance. In "Strategic Planning as a Tool for Building Learning Capacity," James Thompson and Joan Weiner explore a new view of planning as a vital cog in the learning process. During the decade of the 1980s many managers became aware of the strategic importance of organization culture. In "Managing in a Culture That Values Learning," Craig Lundberg re-examines the role of culture as a tool for helping to create learning organizations. As people in well-known organizations begin to creatively manage for learning it is becoming increasingly clear that managing in the learning organizations of the future may look very different than it does today. In the final chapter, James A. F. Stoner explores the future of the relationship between managing and learning in organizations. Can these two seemingly opposing forces co-exist in organizations that increasingly value learning? Stoner will offer a provocative view of these prospects. Finally, the epilogue to this book is in the form of an interview with Bill O'Brien. Bill is the former CEO of the Hanover Insurance Company and a pioneer in the creation of an organization that both learns and performs.

Notes

1 Humberto Maturana and Francisco Varela, *The Tree of Knowledge* (Boston: Shambala, 1987), p. 29.
2 Ikujiro Nonanka, "The knowledge-creating company", *Harvard Business Review*, Nov./Dec., 1991, pp. 312–20, quote p. 313.
3 Chris Argyris, *Knowledge for Action* (San Francisco: Jossey-Bass, 1993).
4 Scott Cook and Dvora Yanow, "Culture and Organizational Learning", *Journal of Management Inquiry*, 1993, vol. 2, no. 4, December, pp. 373–90.
5 D. Cushman and S. King, *High Speed Management* (Albany, NY: SUNY Press, 1992).
6 J. Feinstein, *A Season On The Brink: A Year with Bobby Knight and the Indiana Hoosiers* (New York: Simon & Schuster, 1987).
7 Arie DeGeus, "Planning as learning", *Harvard Business Review*, March/April 1988, pp. 70–74.
8 Peter M. Senge, *The Fifth Discipline: The Art and Practice of the Learning Organization* (New York: Doubleday, 1990).
9 Henry Skolimowski, "The methodology of participation and its consequences", Unpublished manuscript, Institute for Social Research, University of Michigan.
10 Peter Checkland, "From optimizing to learning: A development of systems thinking for the 1990s", *Journal of the Operational Research Society*, 1985, vol. 36, pp. 757–67.
11 *Genesis Neural Network News*, 1st quarter, 1995 (A. Pattakos, ed.), Delaware, Ohio, Bio-Innergy Systems Inc., quote p. 1.
12 S. K. Chakraborty, *Management by Values* (Oxford: Oxford University Press, 1991), p. 18.
13 Maturama and Varela, *The Tree of Knowledge*, p. 174.
14 John Sterman, "Learning in and about complex systems", *System Dynamics Review*, 1994, vol. 10, no. 2–3, pp. 291–330.
15 James E. Lovelock, *Gaia: A New Look at Life on Earth* (Oxford: Oxford University Press, 1979).
16 Gregory Bateman, *Steps to an Ecology of Mind* (New York: Ballantine Books, 1972).

17 Ronnie Lessem, *Total Quality Learning* (Oxford: Blackwell, 1991).
18 Argyris, *Knowledge for Action*, p. 25.
19 Steven Cavaleri and David Fearon, "Systems integration through concurrent learning", *Industrial Management*, July/August 1994, pp. 27–30.

2

The Prism of the New Managerial Mind

David S. Fearon and R. Ivan Blanco

Dana Gilbert, machine operator in the Grand Bay Manufacturing Company's recently modernized plant, looked over the latest run of components stacked near the lot of 355 SEs that the third shift had made. He noticed how much alike the two parts looked. "They had better be damned sure they don't mistake a 355 for a 992 when these go to final assembly," he mused, "or, it will take the customer days to figure out why their fuel system is acting up." His thoughts then turned to the Stanley tape rule that he had been using last night in remodeling his kitchen. It was fluorescent green, making it much harder to lose in the debris on his floor. "Hey, why not add a bright color band to these components?" he thought. At break, Dana went over to the final assembly area and tried out his brainstorm with June Cowperthwaite, an assembler whom he had known for years. He knew she would not laugh at him. June ascertained that there had been times when the components had been mixed up when hand-filling rush orders. The two agreed to talk up the idea to their supervisors, Jim Rich and Kevin Trefrey.

Dana and June are two of the 420 managers of the 420 person Grand Bay Plant. Let us qualify that. Two *undisclosed* managers. Convention would have it that this manufacturing business is managed by the Chief Executive Officer, Langley Richards, and his 37 "top reports," down to the two supervisors about to hear from "their" employees about the color-banding idea. Dana and June just work there. The purpose of this chapter is to ask the reader to look far beyond the conventional Langley Richards management system to discover how organizations are really managing to learn.

Dana's innovative idea, if it survives the hierarchy to which it must now be addressed, could improve Grand Bay's quality and add to the "bottom line." It arose in Dana's **managerial mind** and made sense in June's **managerial mind**. They were both thinking about the company, at the moment they gazed at the two nearly identical components which Dana held out for June's comparison. In the sense which we would like to convey in this chapter, they were thinking, with responsibility *as* the Grand Bay Company. In that moment when they also contemplated how to make their own work go more smoothly, they were learning for Grand Bay. Every one of those 420 employees think, talk about their thoughts, and test their insights in action. Everyone, therefore, manages Grand Bay and its organizational learning, as work goes on each day.

Imagine the overall gains in organizational learning and effectiveness if we were to recognize, and cultivate our companies to use the managerial minds of all employees. A barrier to this happening, however, is the traditional, external-ized status of management itself. It stands above work – the very source of Dana's insight – separating employees into managers and nonmanagers. Manag-ers are those held responsible for the performance of the company. They control and coordinate its work. Nonmanagers just do their jobs. Perhaps the most difficult, but essential, thing we ask readers to do is let go of the bureaucratic principal undergirding the exclusivity and mystique of managers for decades: to command and control the work of others. This chapter proposes transforming management from a status to a state of mind. We believe this will greatly amplify and intensify learning at individual, team, and organizational levels. This would return responsibility for the enterprise to all working members of the organiza-tion. Koopman points out: "Before industrialization, man produced goods be-cause of his drive to deliver good work productively, and because of his innate desire to be creative. The quality of the product was superior – made by his own hands and exchanged for other goods and services. The purpose of work and the worker's purpose were inseparable."

Industrialization gradually took that away as, he explains. ". . . The purpose of work was separated from the worker's purpose."[1] We observe that it was given over to managers. Times call for it to be returned and shared, for now all must constantly learn if the organization is to survive. What work has to teach about organizational effectiveness goes largely unheeded by those who are supposed to manage. Conversely, lessons these managers are learning for the organization are often kept above the shop and office floor, so as to not distract workers with "complexities."

With every one of its 420 members managing Grand Bay, those who used to be *the* managers would still have much to do among their associates. Their new work would be to bring out and help to focus the managerial brainpower of their technical associates on doing those things which create the greatest value for all to whom Grand Bay matters – its customers, owners, and employees.

Supervisors Jim Rich and Kevin Trefrey would welcome Dana and June's natural inquiry about the look-alike parts as still another chance for them to do their managerial work. While the change they shepherd through may seem infinitesimal, when viewed from high above a shop floor the size of two football fields, there could be many hundreds of such work-inspired events going on among people all over Grand Bay. That is how we believe organizations can transcend current performance, doing so by the "experiential management" of all its members.

Organizational learning is the purposeful creation of shared meanings de-rived from the common experiences of people in organizations. **Experiential management**, as we define it, is a special kind of meaning that people make of the *organizational* nature of their work, as they also think about its technical nature: management made in the managerial mind. The color-coding solution is Dana Gilbert's "management" for Grand Bay at that moment.

Such a departure from the usual definitions of management comes from the "soft systems" perspective which Cavaleri and Fearon have highlighted in the first chapter of this book. Among its principles are that all events are subject to various interpretations and that there are no problems "out there" waiting to be solved. Rather, problems become enacted through people's conditioning and perceptions. A "soft systems" view is that an organization is the mental creation of its members, all its members, not just its executives, we would add. "An organization can be seen as having an existence which is in the collective mind of its members," says Cavaleri. "Here, the collective perceptions of the members of an organization, are the *system*, for them." We build on this point by speculating that the organization also exists, lives, and dies, in the individual mind of each member; hence the term the "managerial mind."

As Cavaleri explains, "Ideally, organizational learning is seen as resulting in greater awareness among employees of the subtle workings within the organization that help shape performance."[2] The microbasis of our argument is that employees are also the prime source of knowledge about these workings. Ideas of this nature come to them out of a transcendent sense of responsibility which is engaged in work. Experiential management was beginning to happen, once again, for Grand Bay, when Dana Gilbert's managerial mind went to work on the problem of mistaking the two similar parts, an issue which began as a technical problem, but grew in its organizational implications as he considered the dilemma of end-user customers whose engines fail by virtue of the mistaken identity of the parts. Once the idea left his head, in conversation it began on one of the countless organizational learning cycles of the living Grand Bay organization.

It must be noted, before we go on, that Grand Bay is a fictional company, created for this exposition of a new management system. It is a composite of many of today's transitional organizations that we know as management educators and consultants. Couching our ideas in the Grand Bay parable allows us to get into the heads of some of its members to "see" their work from the vantage points of their managerial minds. Indeed, we go so far as to "see" and describe the managerial minds therein.

Work – The Medium for What Organizations Teach and Learn

Work – human efforts to responsively create something of value – is the magnanimous, but hidden teacher of organizations. From the moment that the first task is begun in a cycle of work to the moment its product is put to use by the customers who determine its value, work "tells" its performers how well the organization is doing from moment to moment. Work also foretells how to innovate and improve, by releasing mental images of desired future states. Yet work teaches best those who are of an **attentive mind**.

The color coding idea found this mind in Dana Gilbert, who pooled his thinking with June and others. Six months later, brightly colored components flowed through the system, each one burnishing Dana's pride in managing that innovation for Grand Bay. This was somewhat of an accidental gain. The company is stuck somewhere between a more democratic structure, by default, because of the laying off of many managers, and still being managed from the traditional, command control perspective. In this case, Rich and Trefrey were eager to try out some of their recent TQM facilitation training, and their boss needed a "win" too. The idea lived. Many ideas in the minds of workers, perhaps most, are never expressed or fall out of cycle. Company suggestion programs do tend to preserve a higher rate of ideas, but in the United States yields of implemented ideas are negligible, when compared to businesses in Japan.[3]

Work is common ground for all members of an organization; yet traditional notions of management's role and the principles of organization presumes that knowledge and decision-making ability is concentrated in top management. Ironically, much of what work has to teach is lost to those who are, by assignment, supposed to lead and manage.

Organizations worldwide now face an era of astounding changes in requirements for staying alive. Yet, most try to change while holding on to standardized hierarchical models for organizing and managing, models that worked in the past but have little relevance to what customers and investors value today.

Langley Richards, Grand Bay's new CEO, knows this all too well. His in-basket receives new stacks of brochures and flyers every day inviting him and his managers to read, view, attend, listen to, books, magazines, conferences, video and audio tapes – all telling him that managers should lead the quality revolution from the top. That it is up to him and his VPs to keep this 87-year-old rust belt company alive. "Hell," Richards said to the air-brushed visage on the cover of the glossy brochure atop his basket. "You spend a week in this chair with those interest payments on my predecessor's capital expenditure binge biting you in the butt, then see if you have anything worth teaching me for $2,200 at that fancy hotel!" Langley has his doubts.

An organization gambles with its future when only its small cadre of managers try to do all this survival learning for the rest. What is needed is rapid organizational adaptiveness which, while it may be steered from the top, has to be managed from the bottom where work happens.

The flow of lessons from work is greatly enhanced and commingled with the view of the top, when there are efforts to cultivate the managerial minds of all employees. Our message to Langley Richards and other appointed managers is, "Lead this kind of learning, by orchestrating work-embedded managerial thinking and your fellow employees will figure out how to save and earn the pain of those interest payments away."

Improving the Quality of Experiential Management

Undertaking to bring out and use the managerial minds of all releases what Peter Drucker has defined as the life-force of organization – their managerial thinking. He says in an *Atlantic Monthly* cover story that, ". . . because the knowledge society perforce has to be a society of organizations, its central and distinctive organ is management [whose major function is] to bring people – each possessing different knowledge – together for joint performance."[4] Considering this role, Drucker adds that "managers need both the knowledge of work and discipline and understanding of the organization itself – its purposes, its values, its environment and markets, its core competencies." This sets forth the stakes and broad criteria for improving the quality of management in organizations. Yet, it stops at opening the boundary between manager and nonmanager. We say, take the next step. Every worker needs to have these understandings and core competencies, and *can* learn, regardless of the appearance of complexity. According to Drucker, "The essence of management is to make knowledge productive."[5] Who should be excluded from doing this for their organization?

A book written in 1977 was titled *The Managerial Mind*.[6] It assumed a mentality uniquely associated with being in charge, with getting things done through others. A reader in those days may have aspired to having a managerial mind, or become resigned to not having one, thereby following those who do. Some have it, some don't. Those who do, climb the ladder. That may have been so in the preceding era. The book's authors reflected the prevailing view that management learning is for and by the few in charge, those with a "policy orientation" which bridges the gap between management science on the one hand and the limitations of theory in practice on the other. Managing was the work of superiors. Today, it would significantly improve the quality of management to remove its exclusivity and acknowledge the managerial mind of each employee. Its existence, development, and daily use is the natural outgrowth of lifetimes of learning to be members and customers of organizations. Granted, Dana Gilbert, a loyal machinists' union member with a technical high school education, might balk at our labeling his good organizational sense as "managerial." Yet, to do so would lower a wall in his commitment to Grand Bay, releasing into its (fixed) thought systems a great deal more of his creative energies and ideas.

That day, Dana's experiential management for the color-coding ignited with the think-ing of June Cowperthwaite, whose own commitment to the company was great enough that she would not let it fade, after her brief conversation with Dana. She gathered some facts about mismatched components over several months' time. Dana was right, the two he made and several from line "D" looked much alike to those who sorted them into bins and those who grabbed them off the carts when hand-filling rush orders. June saw the chance one day to hold a spontaneous "seminar" on the situation, when two engineers and area manager Brud Crosby stood nearby. Two days later, Dana and she had rigged several components with color tapes. June pulled up the charts she had made on the computer, then asked the three to try sorting and picking the components as fast as they could. Then, she put in the colorized components. Eureka! The engineers rushed off with orders from Brud.

Work "tells" the mind when something extraordinary arises in otherwise normal task cycles. The range and strength of our reactions depends, in part, upon our personal sense of freedom to do what seems best, under the circumstances. Those who consider themselves highly limited in authority – lacking the official power to make substantive changes – would tend to do little and say less. This results in weak, or poor quality experienced management of the situation. Others say and do more to manage the situation. It depends somewhat upon the design of the system and the relationships in which work is performed. Mostly, it is a matter of spirit. We notice, *we care*, therefore we act. The moment after Dana made the connection between his product and the colorful Stanley tool, he might have thought, "Forget it, this would be just one more time when the engineers would accuse us operators of meddling in their business." But he loves being part of this company, and relished the quality of the management that he helped provide.

Each minute change in the content of work or its process, subtly, powerfully, and eventually transforms the entire organization. This is similar to the way El Niño winds, a force of enormous global power, are sustained by thousands of "little" winds. Katy Sawyer explains in a *San Francisco Examiner* article:

> The climate-boggling condition known as El Niño is born of a "dance" between the Pacific Ocean and the tropical wind, scientists now understand. In much the same way that a human conversation can change mood without each partner's knowing exactly who was responsible, small perturbations in the water temperature and wind speed amplify each other until together, they can change the world.[7]

The managerial thoughts of those Grand Bay people amplify each other over time to transform their organization. While we look at what managers do for causes of organizational change, we overlook where most of the managing that matters is really going on and how each moment of good or poor management recreates Grand Bay.

New Paradigm Context

This realization did not come to us in a flash of insight. It has been surfacing in our study of modern genres of management – total quality management, systems thinking and dynamics, and the learning organization. We note the certainty of those who are interpreting these genres that attaining ever-higher levels of quality is the *sine qua non* of just being in business, let alone being one of the best companies. Thus, competitive ideas of management itself need to take into account:

- the supremacy of customer value;
- the necessity of unbounded cross-functionality;
- the passion for continuous improvement;
- the centrality of team working in all performance arenas;
- the treatment of the organization as a total system.

Managing was once about maintaining orderly activity in settled routines, and still is in many struggling organizations. The pursuit of world-class quality standards has reversed this axiom. The new purpose of management and leading is to keep things perpetually unsettled. The emerging role of the manager is to foster broad-based, constant experimentation within key processes and systems. It is now an open question as to what must be done to provide superior value to customers, investors, and employees. So, the manager, once the "maintainer" of status quo, is now its "disturber." This shift from maintaining to continually innovating organizations brings management, as professional knowledge and practice, to the same threshold as the organizations which subscribe to it. Often postmortems on failed organizations concluded that they were managed to fall apart that way. What is needed is management that creates a superior unity of purpose between employees and customers, to which all managers are subordinates.

Paradoxically, even models derived from new concepts associating management with quality, systems, and organizational learning retain the deeply etched assumption that work cannot be well managed unless there are managers separated from the workers to *do* the important managing.

There is a growing global movement toward self-management which is shifting responsibility from the separated manager to the team. One of its pioneers, Fred Emery, writes, "After 40 years of experimentation and innovation I think we now know how to achieve the productive participation of the workforce at the enterprise level." Advocating change by participative design, Emery strikes the chord that resonates throughout this chapter and book, "The simple truth is that organizations harnessing the mental power of all their employees outperform organizations that have brilliant leadership yet fail to harness the mental powers of all their workers."[8]

To this end, we offer new constructs which we call **experiential management**, introduced at the opening of this chapter, **all-member management**, and the **prismatic managerial mind**.

All-Member Management

A more fruitful direction for meeting the new competitive imperative is for *all* members of the company to require each other to freely exercise their managerial minds for the organization. In this way, management is no longer just an organizational status, but a shared state of mind. We call this **all-member management**. Like the "all-terrain" vehicle that can go along in rough and suddenly changing terrain, all-member management, figuratively and collectively, anticipates and self-organizes systems through attending to the lessons of work, so as to "hold" the organization on its most competitive track. CEO Langley Richards would not have to make all-member management happen at Grand Bay, as still another intrusive change initiative driven down from the top. It would be better for him to allow it to emerge from people's natural sense of responsibility.

Over ten years ago, management educator Peter Vaill warned:

> American behavioral science has been – we have been – saying the wrong thing. For decades we have tried to say the wrong things better and better, for within our disciplinary matrix we have had trouble saying anything else. As long as we continue to say the wrong thing – no matter how well we say it, no matter how "reliably" and "validly," no matter how elegantly and mesmerically – it *still* will be the wrong thing.
>
> . . . The "wrong thing" American behavioral science has been saying to practitioners is what I call "facts-and-methods." We have busily collected facts and invented methods, and then told manager-leaders that if they want to be effective they have to absorb our facts and learn our methods.
>
> The best among us are living proof that we have been saying the wrong thing, for the best among us have understood in our own ways, dim and acute, florid and dry, spare and prolix, what enterprise is really about: the enterprise is really about what it means *to be in the world with responsibility*.[9]

Responding to Vaill's last point, "living in the organization with responsibility" is the core of all-member management. Consider responsibility not as something given by managers to workers, but as a state of being, as the life-force of the organization.

By definition, responsibility involves personal ability to act without superior authority, to be trusted, depended upon, accountable. Effective work happens when we allow each other to act *responsibly* according to agreed-upon processes and promised outcomes. Such work designs and arrangements are carried in our heads, despite the plenitude of manuals and software that seem to be the repositories of work and organizational designs. These insights from work are learned, refined, and expressed *responsively* among people upon whom the successful conduct and results of work depend. They are expressed in words and actions as natural forms of actionable knowledge that we have introduced as organizational meanings which arise in work as **experiential management**.

To be responsible is to be the source or cause of something. Employees are sources of something greater than well-executed tasks. They have, and sometimes express, intimate knowledge of the organization's vital signs. Each knows and imagines the current and future state of the organization from their unique standpoints. Each of us, pipe-fitter, accountant, clerk, or college professor, is a potentially bountiful source of reflection and direction for the entire organization. Harness it.

Ironically, Langley Richards and his VP for Operations, Brian Severn, hired an outside consulting firm several months ago who went immediately to rank and file employees to discover how to fix an order-filling process plagued by redundancies. Learning from employees through interviews and observations, the outside firm translated the solutions for management and charged them a pretty penny for "their" re-engineering design.

The New Prism of the Managerial Mind

If only Richards and Severn could have seen what those consultants were open to seeing – the active managerial minds of all those employees involved in the order fill process. What is needed is a conceptual tool that does this for one and all. The backward "pull" of the conventional images of management is so great that the central idea of the employee as a source of powerful organizational meanings could fade. Thus, we have crafted what we hope is a vivid symbol of the managerial mind. It involves picturing the managerial mind as if it were a brightly shining, crystalline, tetrahedral prism (see figure 2.1).

The prism rests in a mental webbing of many specialized "minds" constituting the unique intelligence of each member of the organization. There would also be the "family mind," the "spiritual mind," the "career mind," and others, each developed over a lifetime to concentrate memory of what matters most to the person for continuing well-being. In this regard, the managerial mind knows, mainly from life experience, how to work well, and what works well, in all sorts of organizations.

There is no such prismatic mind, of course. We propose it as a soft system thinking tool. Jerry Rhodes suggests in his book, *Conceptual Toolmaking*, that we learn to use mental processes as if they were tools in our minds. He says that "the

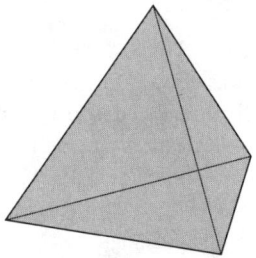

Figure 2.1   The prismatic managerial mind.

whole idea of the conceptual tool is to represent the complexity in simple form. Thus, it can be grasped, accessed, and remembered very fast indeed."[10] Our variation on this advice is to view the "mind" as a tool used in the *mental* process of managing.

This special mind is shaped and acts like a translucent prism, as it refracts and reflects light into mental images about work as it goes on in its process and organizational settings. Thus, the **prismatic managerial mind** generates meanings which enlighten individual and organizational performance. While this mind retains lessons from the past, it is oriented to current and coming events in the life of the organization, drawn to do so by the immediacies and urgencies of work.

It directs our thoughtful attention to extraordinary occurrences in the flow of work, continually assessing if novel situations will enhance or retard well-being. It responsibly has us ask ourselves, in these unsettling moments:

1 Am I (are we) doing the right thing now?
2 Am I (are we) doing it in the best way?
3 To whom does this matter?

Answers to oneself about these questions constitute for us, at the same time, answers to:

1 What tasks must now be done;
2 How;
3 With whom; and
4 Why.

We may then test our new managerial realizations with others whose work also impinges the situation in question. These dialogues enrich the shared meanings which are the managerial products of and for organizational learning.

> *Laura Jackson, Purchasing Agent, ponders an e-mail message from Engineering asking her to get some preliminary price quotes on special brightly colored paints that will adhere to treated metal. A quick phone call to that department brings to her mind just the paint they need, something she once ordered when she was in a Navy safety task force.*

The symbol of the prism was chosen to stand for the mind, because its facets are physically and dynamically integrated into a handsome, useful whole. Living with responsibility for the organization can be interpreted to happen in four, well-integrated facets, as well:

1 Keen awareness of **work** as it is happening;
2 **Process,** or a concerned sense of how it should be going on;
3 The social **context** of those we answer to, to whom the work matters, and who matter

to us. The fact that these people, and the work we are doing for and with them, matter to *us* engages:

4 Our self.

It is our self who aligns and energizes the other three aspects into responsible managerial thinking. To illustrate, we revisit the first moments of Dana Gilbert's success with the color coding notion.

> *Nearly halfway through a fairly routine shift, he had a moment between lights flashing on poles calling for attention to his team's automated parts assembler, to notice the close similarity between the two types of components. The work facet of his mind flashed an inquiry to his process sense which revealed to him the total process in which the part he was making was done. "Nothing out of the ordinary here, but what might this mean to the folks downstream?" – an instantaneous connection to the context facet wherein he could see implications for errors leading to problems for customers, and therefore for Grand Bay. Now here is where the fourth aspect, his self, made the difference in his subsequent actions. To put it bluntly, it told him whether he "gave a damn." While there may be some inherent gain for the company, did it matter to him, Dana Gilbert? Upon realizing that it did matter to him – call it his pride – a flow of creative ideas was released creating the notion of the color coding by connecting to his do-it-yourself memories. He was then personally motivated and self-led to go over and talk with June Cowperthwaite during his break, instead of drinking a coffee and finishing the sports page.*

As we proceed, it must be acknowledged that it is beyond our current capacity to give a scientific explanation of what that managerial mind might be like. We fashion this conceptual tool largely from intuition. It seems more like the "right thing" to teach about management, in light of what Vaill has said about the "wrong things" we too have been teaching. Here, then, is more about how we imagine the managerial mind looks and works.

Each of the four aspects of responsibility are translated into a facet of the prism which integrates them into the managerial mind as shown in figure 2.2.

Facet 1 – **work** – brings information to mind as it is anticipated, experienced, and reflected back upon. Work is the activator of the managerial mind. It is the

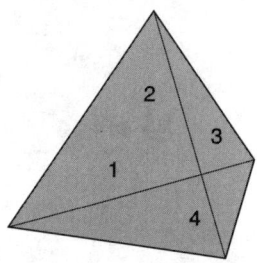

Figure 2.2   Facets of the managerial mind.

organization's purposeful behavior, so when we attend to work, we are watching, hearing, feeling the organization *live*. Tasks of work "talk" to the mind, noting as they flow past what is being accomplished or what is not. They "say" what is happening with or without hitches, surprises, and other perturbations. The concreteness of work gives it its fact base. Yet, the mind associates much with work beyond the concrete to bring out important abstractions and distractions. The more fascinating the work, the more compelling its "mind talk."

Work continually replants our attention to the next point of action, and the next, as the work of typing this sentence draws attention to the space about to be filled with the next sentence. "There is always the chance," says work, "that what comes next will flop or propel performance to a higher plane." Work is timed in events, seconds, minutes, hours, even days. Events can mark endings and beginnings, descending problems and transcending opportunities. All but the most mechanized work holds out such enticing possibilities. Dana Gilbert, encouraged by this and other recent successful uses of his organizational savvy, is looking forward with the anticipation of a trout fisher. The next cast just might land the granddaddy of breakthrough ideas.

Just as at the moment a piano key is struck, as the player's eyes read that note on the sheet music, they are also glancing down the score to prepare fingering for the key strikes, the **work facet** of our managerial mind mentally harmonizes current and anticipated tasks. There will be "clinkers" in work as there are in the music, along with rifts of improvisation. The information that enters through work is refracted to the process facet in plus or minus signals to be checked against how things are supposed to be going.

Impulses of dissonance or harmony question or confirm the rightness of the process we have "in mind" at that moment. This generates what Deming, the quality management philosopher, called "task knowledge," in which there is understanding of the technology and rules of operation.

Earlier that same day, June Cowperthwaite had been pulled off her normal position in the line to help hand pack still another rush order. "What the heck is going on here," she

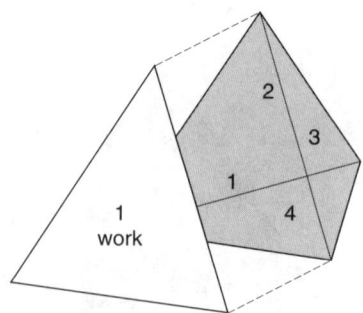

Figure 2.3 The work facet.

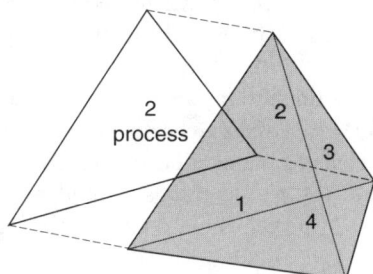

Figure 2.4   The process facet.

had mused. "We went through automation in order to cut these special order packing frenzies to a minimum. Not only are they losing me from the 'regular' work, but we are all making mistakes here for which I know we will catch it from management."

To learn what is on Jane's or anyone's managerial mind, just encourage them to talk about work. We tend to strongly identify ourselves, our competence, and our memberships by what we do for work.

Facet 2 – **process** – mentally arrays tasks of work along conceptual lines and among parameters known or anticipated for each type of familiar work. Processes operate in systems and give life to them. Here in the managerial mind, systems thinking figuratively happens.

Work's plus and minus flashes of thought from facet 1 are reflected off the mental models and maps that have been etched in this facet by real and educative experience. This facet of the prismatic managerial mind ascribes value to incoming plus and minus work information, instantly registering the relative health of the process, and thus the systems it serves.

Intuition tells us there is always a "better way" to do or replace this work. June could tell that these rush order side processes were harming not only her regular system, but signaled breakdowns "somewhere back there where the orders were being taken and customers were being promised what the plant could not normally deliver." This restiveness made her receptive to Dana's idea later that day to at least reduce the errors in picking the wrong components.

In the language of total quality management, Michael Stahl explains that "a process is a grouping of activities that take an input, add value to it, and provide an output to an internal or external customer."[11] There are virtually thousands of discrete processes running the collective work of all 420 members managing Grand Bay.

Of particular importance to a company like Grand Bay are the core business processes, those which cut across the entire organization and are most vital to delivering profitably valued goods and services to customers. Dana and June almost accidentally initiated a change that made a difference to customers receiving and relying upon those finished products. The more they are helped to become aware of these core processes, the more likely they are to place higher value on signals from work that the health of these processes are again at stake.

The **process facet** continually reconstitutes our awareness of the systemic nature of work. The TQM tool of flow-charting or process mapping, when done by a team whose work covers a major process, usually reveals suprisingly complex knowledge of "the way we do things around here for our customers." Consideration of the "we" who get things done illuminates and is reflected upon the **context facet**.

Facet 3 – **context** – brings to mind, in each moment of noticing, holistic images of the total organization in action. Further, they flash images of the organization in its future. This shows us the "big picture" which is the context of our work – the technology, related organizational units, the company, and beyond to our industry and many environments. It is our unique glimpse of the present and future, the way the company is, ought to be, or might be, if things get better or worse. This is *not* the exclusive viewpoint of the top executives, who we tend to think do the strategic thinking for the organization.

Work and process reflections reveal a wide spectrum of recollections and visions that some would call the "big picture," but we call this facet "context," because responsibilities are struck and carried out in *webs of dynamic human relationships*. Our awareness of these provides an internal sense of organizational structure. It may look far different than the traditional charting of divisions, departments, and managerships. This facet shows us, in the moment of reflection, who to see and who to avoid, and who to please, to change the work system.

Dana has played a part in Grand Bay for 19 years, following his father and grand-father to yield decades of Gilbert family experience in this enterprise. His co-worker, Bob Capra, was one of the last hired before last year's freeze. Each explores his managerial notions within very different context facets. Dana is showing Bob the ropes.

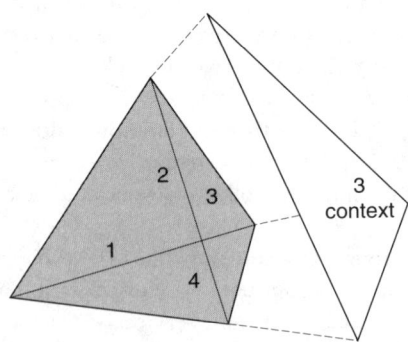

Figure 2.5   The context facet.

Bob, on the other hand, is applying his knowledge of his previous place of employment, a distributor of Grand Bay products to their current situation. He was the one who told Dana several days before how often he processed returns from unhappy manufacturing customers, only to discover they had used the wrong parts.

Management has been traditionally related to the marshaling and conserving of resources. It is here, in the social context, that thoughts instantly turn to others with the power to provide resources as needed. Will what is happening jeopardize the flow of resources back to the unit from the greater organization? Can improvements be made that increase the flow? All resources flow into human systems in terms of relationships that people doing the work have with people providing the resources – the internal and external customers and investors.

This social context facet "knows" or "learns" about relationships that impinge upon successful work. These relationships extend through process and into systems, and beyond to the ever-widening networks of people who comprise the whole organization and its customer and supplier environments. Relationships occurring closest to the moment where work is being "managed" must be sustained by strong social bonds, if the changes which come to mind are to be acted upon. The plus or minus signals reflected from the process facet bring up images of us connecting or disconnecting from others. This is according to our sense of the value the outcomes of work has in sustaining these primary relationships and those beyond.

Dana and June had wondered if their color-coding idea would "survive" the hierarchy. This meant they realized their interdependency in developing and implementing such a change and wondered if management would care for their suggestion. Fortunately, Dana knew several of the brass from "way back" when they worked with his dad or with him before they were promoted. He talked about the idea with three friends in the plant administration by staying after his shift ended and dropping into offices. June found a very receptive ear the next day from her supervisor, Kevin Trefrey, who reported to one of Dana's three contacts.

The context facet of the managerial mind is the locus of *caring* to make accommodations with others to form and sustain social bonds. It brings to mind a trajectory of those persons to whom a better managed work situation will matter. This calls upon us to decide if we are running a gauntlet or a receiving line. Total quality management categorizes these stakeholders as internal and external customers, coproducers, suppliers, and investors. In a flash, the managerial mind can "picture" these people and their look of satisfaction or dissatisfaction. "Is it going to be worth it?" we instantly ponder. If not, we once again quell our managerial mind.

Facet 4 – self – answers this context question, "is it worth it to me?" When affirmative, this facet opens to our innermost being, and releases our spirit. This infuses the managerial mind with brilliant, creative energy. When the answer is

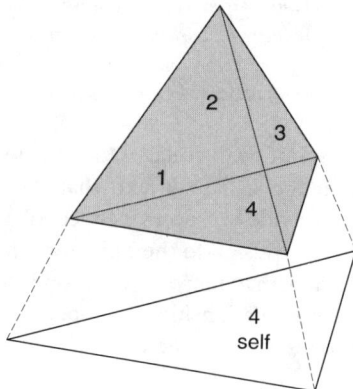

Figure 2.6   The self facet.

negative, this facet starts closing, leaving the other three "in the dark." Kevin Trefrey made it worth it to June to press forward with the color-coding idea, for it would be worth it to him.

The self facet is a window to our genius – the creative totality of our intellectual and spiritual powers. It is the base of the prism, seating the managerial mind in our greater being and grounding the signals reflected and refracted from the other three facets. It flashes inspirations on the other three facets: a time-saving work step, a new twist that makes a process serve two aims, a master-stroke idea about including the down-line customer differently than usual.

It is so often said and written that the top leader has the "vision" and tells the rest about it, a notion which may help justify their compensation packages, but is hardly useful for revitalizing companies. Instead, consider our proposal that each of us does the "vision thing" naturally, some more brilliantly than would ever be noticed unless we talk to each other. For it is in the stories we tell about the future that the transcendent messages can be found.

We all have depths of genius, barely tapped in a lifetime. Some of us believe this about ourselves and each other more than others. It shows in our work and teamwork. When we care, our inner brilliance shines into the managerial mind in flashes of insight. These show us how to save money and time, revitalize waning products, spin off services into whole new lines of business, bring an alienated co-worker back to the fold. The best ideas come to those high in self-belief.

This fourth facet brings intellectual force to the moment of considering what work is telling us. It allows to "see" in our minds the interaction of task, process, and context, to understand what is going on as a whole, and assess the value of expected outcomes to securing the future for our organization, and therefore, ourselves.

Revealing the Idea Spectrum

According to the *American Heritage Dictionary*, a prism is a homogeneous, transparent solid . . . It is used to produce or analyze a continuous light spectrum. So do the four facets of the managerial mind combine to simultaneously create and analyze momentary spectrums of managerial knowledge that appear and disappear like rainbows. The "light" that comes to the managerial mind is information, mainly flowing from work, where our attention is occupied.

Viewed three-dimensionally, a prism admits light at its surfaces, but takes it deep into its core where all aspects converge and seem to go on forever. Let us assume that the outer faces of the managerial mind admit information as would a prism light, generated from what comes to mind from moment to moment. Just beneath that surface are recent memories of experiential managements that succeeded, failed, or are still forming. Information is translated into rough knowledge of the situation, but the fuller spectrum of possibilities is not yet revealed.

If the power of the fourth facet – the self – where our genius is activated is released, in other words, if we recognize in this rough pattern that what is happening does matter to us, then the thought is pulled deeper toward that infinite core of possibilities resting in our imaginations.

"Way in there" where edges of the facets intersect, can be seen what we call **future memories**. These instantly reveal better, same, or worse conditions "if" things were to change rather than to stay the same. The scenarios are more vivid when we suspend our rationality to see what our imaginations have to offer. As Mark Twain said, "You can't depend upon your judgment when your imagination is out of focus."

There is dynamic mental interplay within this prism, revealing a spectrum of managerial thinking from fact-based reality to faith-based *ideal*. Revelations, coming as we work, arch across gaps in what is (or at least is perceived to be what is) to what ought to be. In the stream of work events, we can concurrently "see" the company that is (or at least the company as we think it is) and the company of the future. This energizes native restlessness to "go at it" another way, try something new, revise a policy, bend a rule.

The main work of Sloan Colby, Grand Bay's Director of Marketing, is to learn what their manufacturing customers need and see to it that they get it from Grand Bay, not from its competitors gunning for their long-standing place as market leader. He had not heard about the color coding change until this morning, when he was congratulated by a purchasing agent, Laura Jackson's boss, who rarely had a good word to say, particularly after the price increases brought on by the massive plant automation. This new information penetrated his mind as he was driving back to the plant, and was about to be forgotten, while he scanned the radio dial for easy listening music. Then, the fourth

facet opened, and he was suddenly envisioning an entire line of visually coded parts.
"Wow!" Colby is energetically pursuing this new prospect company-wide and with their
prime customers, with CEO Langley Richards running interference.

If All Members Manage, What of Managers?

Information that is attracted to the managerial mind comes also from sources
beyond work: books, articles, news stories, conversation. Yet it seems that the
richest information flows in from directly experienced work where we can learn
directly from the consequences of our actions. What is "new" is more
impactfully noticed, plotted, and compared in the spectrum of knowledge reflecting one's past and future organizational histories. Uncertainty opens inquiry; we begin again to learn for the organization. Rarely can we acquire or
create experienced management alone. We talk to others, and through these
dialogues, construct new meanings about what is and should be going on. It is
this mutual reconstruction or reorganization of work experience that directs the
course of subsequent work. All this managing is going on with scarcely a
manager around to make it happen. It would be more powerful if there were
formally designated managers around to appreciate it.

Regardless of position or level, all members create ideas, which manage the
members themselves, their groups, and simultaneously, the system which the
organization has now become. Each idea contains, faintly or vividly, the essence
of what a change means to the vitality of the organization. A goal of our **All-
Members Manage** model is that each will develop the desire and capacity to
see the organization that comes to mind as we perform its work.

Stahl defines management as the "creation and continuous improvement of
organizational systems that when used by organizational members lead to increased value for the customers of its products and services."[12] Rather than
being just users of these manager-created systems, we would extend Stahl's
definition to all workers. *Management is the co-creation and continuous improvement of organizational systems which are kept in mind by all who responsibly use
them.*

Among us, in any organization, there would still be persons acting among,
rather than over, others as managers. Yet, their main contributions would be to
support the rest of us in expressing our managerial learning and thinking into
the organizational behavior of our enterprise, our businesses, our schools, our
governments. Traditionally managers get things done through others, and
workers are "their" instruments of goal attainment. Generally, these managers
may not "see" the integrative prism described in this chapter, and only see the
work, process, and context as isolated planes. The typical job description may
further impede their vision. Managerial positions traditionally delimit the
boundaries that isolate business functions from each other, as in Vice President
for Finance and Administration or Director of Materials Management.

Managing, as proposed in this chapter, would still include formal managerships associated with functions, key processes, or product areas. These managerships are accountable for the quality of all managerial thinking as measured by signs of healthy, self-renewing processes with continuously improving products. However, if management also involves experiential knowledge of the work of the organization, an inner state of mind in all its people, the quality of this thinking is vital to the organization. Thus, experiential management must be cultivated, shared, and allowed to be "heard" where it will cause the most beneficial changes.

It would be the new role of the Manager of Engineering, for example, to cocreate conditions with colleagues, so that their product designs reflect sensitive understanding of critical contingencies for every other part of the organization. Do they find others receptive to creative ideas? Are they often "blind sided"? Has communications technology been brought to their workstations? Do they have easy and ample access to persons across all lines, including suppliers and customers? People will freely make those many accommodations mentioned earlier in this chapter with far less concern for turf or for stepping on bosses' egos.

> *Before Dana had stopped the last spilling yards of the metal stripping that had jumped its cogs, he saw shift manager Jackson Lopez coming his way doing double time. "I have already called Materials Management, Dana, and they have the new roll halfway up the floor. Ask Jerry to set it up. We need to hustle over to Greg Lansing's office. He has Pittsburgh on the phone. They want to know how that shipment was behaving. After you fill them in, tell me who we need to 'educate' and how I can help." In the old days, Dana mused, seeing a supervisor charge down the line meant heads would roll. Now, it means help is on the way.*

Where once managers were linked to each other to serve as the organization's primary learning/deciding system, the "unbounded" organizations are discovering ways to link all minds. It is the work of the new manager to develop and sustain these pathways, to foster collaboration for the customer's sake. Just as a clear glass prism has optical qualities that reflect light, so the prism-like managerial minds carry enlightening ideas among people, through their daily conversations. This makes collective thinking and action more possible and competitively potent.

> *Essentially, a middle manager like Production Coordinator Jackson Lopez, using his computer to train his thoughts, visualizes the flow of inquiries and answers that come up and through his assigned area. It is his purpose that all employees will know new realities and potentialities in time to innovate.*

Senge's definition of the new leader managers as designers, stewards, and teachers who are responsible for learning[13] complements our vision of Lopez helping Gilbert and Cowperthwaite. He is so close to the action, or in it, that he rapidly spots and frees "optical" impairments, which lets them go ahead and manage change.

There is a continuum of atmospheres ranging from where, ideally, all forms of organizational learning shine forth, shading to the opposite where most are kept in the dark to accentuate the power of those doing the keeping. Fear does the darkening. One of Deming's 14 principles, "Drive out Fear," is our charge to all new managers.

> *Jackson Lopez was aware of the negative impact he could have had, were he to have "lost his cool" at the tenth prolonged machine stoppage on his watch. Yet he knew that invectives left residuals in the atmosphere long after the machines were fixed. Truth was, essentially, his only tool. That all parties to this problem with supplies would have quick access to factual information and people who could translate it into lasting improvement was his contribution, the seventh of the day, and it was only 9:40 a.m.*

The prism-conscious new manager works to ensure that healthy information systems are extant to link all processes and their organizational context. One powerful way to bring this system fully "on-line" with all members is to develop a common language unique to their enterprise and setting. While it is obvious why functional specialists communicate with their rather exclusive technical terms, everyone knows that they can make the translations to help others understand them, if it matters. It does, when the learning atmosphere is at stake. For what is learned is what the organization next becomes, for better or worse.

The Organization that We Keep in Mind

It is in the **context** facet that Grand Bay exists in Dana's mind, June's and Langley's too. Yet, do each see the same Grand Bay? Surely not, and they are not likely to, unless their talk reveals to each other what they think Grand Bay is. Are we proposing that June, an hourly worker whose pay is still measured in pieces of parts that pass through her hands, has a partial image of Grand Bay, while her CEO sees it all? To the contrary, we believe she sees it all too and manages accordingly.

This is supported in Ronnie Lessem's *Total Quality Learning* by his theory of the holographic managerial mind. Lessem affirms that the "ultimate organizational form" is the **holographic** mental field of the creative manager, where "learning and managing, operations and finance, knowledge and skill, and intuition become both discrete and separate phenomena and holographic reflections of each other." According to Lessem's imagery, holograms are a special type of optical storage system, "where the part is in the whole; and the whole is in each part."[14] Each member is a part of an organization, yet *the whole of the organization is reflected in the person.* This calls into question the organizational competence or "savvy" of all members, not just those who carry designations as executives, managers, and supervisors.

Our faith in the Dana Gilberts of this world leads us to assert that each employees' managerial mind recreates and imprints pictures of the total organization in each work situation. It is what the organization means to them, totally, at a given moment. *The new manager's work, that we are proposing, is to care for the quality of those mental pictures.* Doing so is to foster unbounded dialogue, see that all employees are richly supplied with information from and about the company, and help people fill in the murky spots and fill out their visions of the organization one, five, ten years hence.

There are 420 persons working *as* the Grand Bay Manufacturing Company. Thus, there are 420 versions of the company in their minds; and many more of Grand Bay, when we count customers, suppliers, and other stakeholders in the extended organization. While "managing" work situations, each of us learns, indirectly, what significant others think our organization looks like. These holograms can be shared and modified as members talk with each other, until there is some certainty that they all know the same company pretty well.

Before the 1970s, organizations slowly evolved over decades, assuring most members plenty of time to fix in mind a general, enduring imagery of the organization. Today, and in the future, there is little time for gradually orchestrating changes of the official organization in people's minds, at least by traditional means (i.e. company newsletters, cascading training, employee reorientation). New media, much of which are not yet invented, are needed, if those 420 minds are to be linked and changed so that the organization learns in time.

Prospects for a Paradigm Shift

The prismatic managerial mind may be a more likely locus of organizational creation and control to achieve this agility. But, what chance does it have of being embraced as an alternative to dominant separate manager–nonmanager models? As Kevin Lewis of Chevron Petroleum Technology Company wrote recently,

> . . . organizations say that people are their most important resource because it is politically correct to do so. After years of downsizing, rightsizing, or de-recruiting, these words ring hollow for many employees. The irony of the situation is that organizations find themselves in the position of having to rely on employees whose development has not been a priority to do the work that will restore the organization to profitability or improve its competitiveness.[15]

Prospects for a paradigm shift toward all members managing would not seem good on the surface. If, however, managers discover in time that they alone cannot restore their organizations, even with the help of outside consultants and in accordance with the advice of management gurus, then the timing of our proposal may be right after all. Let us assess the prospects for Grand Bay.

The Grand Bay Company has been an organization much like those cited by Lewis. Its people "suddenly" find their company competing, at home and abroad. Where once they were the US market leaders, today they can barely detect where they stand among global competitors and customers. Several top management groups tried, over the past seven years, many of the "sizings" referred to in Lewis's statement. The company's once blue chip stock price dropped precipitously. It is just now inching back to pay stockholders dividends slightly higher than a bank certificate of deposit.

Having let go many of its younger newcomers, Grand Bay is now populated with a mainly baby-boom-aged workforce. Instead of looking forward to easing off into prepaid retirement, these seasoned veterans find they must now go "back to zero." Due to a recent infusion of high-tech systems, most workers, even the managers, have to start over mastering the new skills that will keep them employed. Paid retirement is no longer inevitable to their Grand Bay careers. Worry is spreading like a bad flu.

These changes are driven by customers who now shop the world, and whose requirements for quality and expectations of value soar with each Grand Bay sales success. They are also driven by investors who can move their stake to another company on the other side of the world, with a click of the "mouse" of their PC's investment software.

Dana Gilbert is one of the remaining 420 employees who mentally creates one of the 420 "versions" of this company, whenever he thinks about his work. Operating a state of the art, computer-assisted final assembly system of six linked machines, Dana's "mental picture" of his company is in constant flux; yet he has a strong sense of his lineage with past workers. His father and grandfather worked for Grand Bay, and he would like his son and daughter to do so, when they finish college. He recalls feeling great pride at the recent Centennial celebration, when he walked past a montage of old pictures of his predecessors.

In his managerial mind, Dana muses, "We made those old gizmos as fast as they could invent them in those days, and we're making their latest versions today." He ruminated, "Faster, for damn sure. Better? I'm not so sure about that anymore. They are still working with smoke and mirrors up there in corporate."

Some events, like the Centennial, are suddenly extraordinary, so perturbing that there is a shift and the holographic picture of Grand Bay becomes substantially different. The new CEO, Langley Richards', speech at the ceremony was still full of references to a future of rapid product diversification and distribution. Yet Dana pondered over the short cuts and corner cutting he knew they were taking to beat "ridiculously" tight product-to-market cycle times. "I would hate to be flying in a plane that has one of our 359-Series D parts on the engine, if we keep making them on the cheap." Even as Dana paused in this moment of dissonance over the relative quality of his products – the contrasts of the inflated rhetoric of the speeches, family pride in the well-regarded Grand Bay label, and doubts about the future – he was mentally recreating "his" Grand Bay Manufacturing Company.

This meant to Dana more machine set ups, seven-day, 24-hour-day schedules, and more capital expansion. "Or does it?" he mused, "The boss was throwing some financial terms at us like 'economic value added.' When I asked Greg, standing next to me, what the Hell that means, he said 'stockholders and top execs get more . . . you fill in the rest.'"

Dana sensed that, again, the rules of the game were changing. A year ago they shut down five manual assembly lines, to be replaced by the work his new team of operators now does with one, integrated, computerized system. He was grateful to be picked to make the changeover, although he felt that they should have kept his and one other semi-automated line going to take up the slack when all that fancy technology broke down.

After 16 years with the company and 11 months with this new automated system, is the Grand Bay that Dana has in mind more like the "real" organization than the one held by the new CEO, Langley Richards? Has Dana's managerial learning and thinking improved over time? Perhaps so, in both instances, if we assume that the flows of events have deeply etched the basic Grand Bay Manufacturing **organizational character** in the minds of all its stakeholders. It would be so in the way that one is first a stranger, then an acquaintance, then a friend, perhaps becoming a loved one.

Dana Gilbert and his teammates were trained in the manufacturing and business support processes that govern their machines. They have come to "know" them as second nature. Still looking for consistently higher rates of output of high quality and low costs, these processes are constantly, somewhat methodically, revised. They are also constantly, somewhat chaotically, modified, as jerry-rigging and other quick fixes sneak in. Were their manufacturing subsystem to fail to develop to its specified standards, it might even be radically redesigned. Dana and his co-workers would know how, if their responsibility to do so were to be acknowledged by specialists eager to get their hands on another "re-engineering" problem. The diffusion of organizational learning at Grand Bay crosses functional lines and floors of the plant as situations arise in the work of one that leads to the work of another.

After payday, Dana makes a beeline to the payroll office to complain about a shortage in his check. That overtime amount had to be wrong. Five minutes into an initially heated conversation with Ellen Cote, a payroll clerk, the two have brought the whole company out in their minds. It becomes clear in each of their minds that mistakes were made by an "out-sourcing" payroll service that seemed to be beyond the reach of union grievances. Dana and Ellen's discourse, like the myriad of work conversations going on all over the plant, is leading to new, broader realizations about the changing nature of Grand Bay.

"Outsourcing payroll? What else are we not doing any more?" quipped Dana. Both had things to "fix" about their processes, when Dana went back to the shop floor and Ellen to her computer.

CEO Langley Richard's inner managerial work brings forth ideas for and about Grand Bay that are different from, but not necessarily more important than, what Dana is composing to keep those machines purring and Ellen to debug the EDI system to the payroll supplier.

The general management of this company is realized in the thousands of daily accommodations and adjustments people like Dana and Ellen make across "lines," desks, counters, phone and fax lines. These accommodations and adjustments are like the living brain cells of an organization, dying when accommodations cannot be created or sustained, flourishing when they do.

Our prism-like managerial mind focuses and intensifies the images that come to people as they work, converse, and otherwise experience the organization. These images continually alter each employee's view of how and why the organization goes about its business. Since everyone else is doing somewhat the same, it is the collective thinking and rethinking of organizational members that drive actions from within. Ideas flow from individual thinking, through talk, to the collective thinking of groups, and ultimately the entire membership. Insofar as this thinking is harmonized, management is more integrated than fractionated. The organization is *enabled* rather than disabled. Sometimes it is not, as in the case of Grand Bay's "failed" TQM campaign.

Two years ago, Dana glanced at the TQM poster in the lunch room. He had heard something about "ISO 9000 or something" certification that the plant was going after. The person whose name he attached to that mountain of paperwork and those interminable meetings had left in a shakeup in the front office. "He must have stepped on many toes," Dana mused. Johnson was the "quality guy." Dana put two and two together. "I guess that fad is finally over too."

Dana may have been "wrong" in this assessment, but it is his thought to hold. Each time he hears about quality, he pulls in his neck and looks for the wiping rag. He is listening to his "inner manager" rather than the explanation of company officials. An employee's inner mental manager acts as the main processor of work, process, system, and organizational information, shaping it into actionable ideas about how to "keep on going." It creates, holds, hides, and divulges, releasing or withholding energies that make change happen. Some of this managerial "know-how" is derived, in part, from aspects of formal education; even a management education.

To think critically about work as it happens is to think managerially. Those who have learned to appreciate how they learn to understand things of a complex social nature are closest to knowing how to build this "mind" into an important personal and organizational asset. Formal education aside, it is work and participation in an organization that freely shapes and develops the managerial mind.

It takes an open mind and willingness to learn from and with others to broaden and deepen the managerial mind. World-class organizations have widened and customized the media available to all employees to communicate.

Moreover, to have the outgrowth of this openness is distinctive **managerial resourcefulness**. Such organizations create a force of employee innovators who largely direct themselves at solving problems that were once thought insoluble.

> *Grand Bay's third shift operators in Dana's machine complex were constantly "bugging" the first shift crews with the many changes they seemed to be getting away with while the professionals were home asleep. Dana wondered what it would be like to just go ahead and fix the things they knew how to fix, as those night owls do. But he would have the trades union and management on his neck. He mused about the freedom of that third shift, then shuddered at the idea of those graveyard hours.*

Like Dana, each Grand Bay employee decides daily how important it is to exercise and execute thoughts of organizational and performance improvement. When Dana connects the value of having these insights to gains of mind that come with expressing them into uncertain situations, there is a greater likelihood that he will offer more. In other words, he comes to appreciate what he can do beyond the tasks and processes of his system of integrated assembly machines.

In today's turbulent environments, extraordinary situations arise frequently, overlapping and often compounding each other in real time. There is little opportunity to take matters "upstairs" and work out new orders, and even less time to rehearse the performance altering decisions made in coursing streams of work.

> *In just five minutes, Dana's six-person first shift team had five "breakdown" lights on at four opposite ends of the 100 × 100 foot manufacturing cell; an engineer arrived with a group of Asian engineers touring the plant and expecting an impromptu lesson "from the operator's point of view"; an e-mail bulletin popped up on screen alerting all employees to attend end-of-shift information sessions on "new realities in the cost of health benefits"; and, it was revealed that three of those lit lights were caused by the sixth bad batch of semifinished materials from a sole vendor's not just-in-time shipment. The next coffee break seemed days away.*

Integrating the leading, managing, working, and, most importantly, the feeling of these changes into everyone's role bodes well as a vital evolutionary step brought on by the state of perpetual disturbance in organizations. More than ever, people are working and managing "without a net." All strive, through learning, to keep their own balance while helping co-workers keep theirs. This is, ideally, accomplished by quickly sensing tremors in the lines of **work**; checking disorders against **process** orders to detect and assess gaps; then, creating situation-arresting accommodations, often crossing organizational lines to bring focus to the problem. In other words, they are viewing and changing work through the **prisms** of their managerial minds.

Management Learning

John Burgoyne has defined management itself as "learning on behalf of organizations."[16] This chapter's conceptual tool takes this definition to heart and carries it perhaps beyond Burgoyne's definition, and his audience of "only" managers, to *all* employees. Thus, management education is needed by all who learn on behalf on the organization.

Responsible employees, sensitized to the managerial value they can extract from their work, would be receptive to training and information once restricted to managers. Yet, there is a gap to be closed. Books, articles, tapes, workshops and conferences about all dimensions of managing and leading organizations address the Langley Richards of the world, not the Dana Gilberts.

These resources were produced with conventional managers (only) in mind. There is heavy, lingering influence of the **command and control** presumption, where the informed few decide for the uninformed many. Many of these works are written esoterically, that is for an elite cadre of "superiors" in whose language "subordinates" are not prepared to learn.

At Grand Bay, Dana, Ellen and several hundred other members of that company are producing countless managerial decisions a day that are subtly shaping Grand Bay's destiny. What "the manager" should know, what "the manager" should do, "what the manager should ask and learn," can be read by employees like Dana Gilbert as what "I" should do in my own way.

There are tools emerging from experience with, and of, the most innovative companies that are more likely to fit the "hand" of whoever takes them up to better understand change situations. The quality field offers for use in cross-disciplinary teams such tools as: statistical process control, Pareto analysis, flow charting, fishbone analysis and process re-engineering and quality function deployment.

Tools for developing the learning organization are just emerging and are comprehensively reported in the *Fifth Discipline Field Book*.[17] Among these are: storytelling for systems thinking, creating ladders of inference, creating scenarios, team dialoguing, composing an organization's "learning news media," and the powerful "learning labs and flight simulators."

Creativity and innovative-thinking-enhancing tools are increasingly plentiful, particularly for stimulating and accelerating the rate of new product development. An employee can now learn to manage with brainstorming, mind-mapping, deep relaxation exercises, and "free-falling from 35,000 mental feet up."[18]

Most of these new resources can be accessed through multiple channels of books, software, networks, articles, films, and conferences. Ideas can then be traced down paths of the research to source organizations that learned them. At many nodes of this network are innumerable resource organizations, based in universities or free-standing, which make their presence known to heads of firms through advertising.

The all-members manage model is also consistent with the employee involvement movement, perhaps taking it a step beyond. Edward Lawler of the Center for Effective Organizations at the University of Southern California, provides landmark research on conditions in high-involvement organizations and the emerging shape of employee involvement practices. These are work settings where employees have "considerable amounts of information, power, knowledge, and rewards," writes Lawler, citing structural changes to support high involvement through self-managing work teams, job enrichment programs, skill-based pay systems, and gainsharing.[19]

All these tools and their underlying theories can be adapted to use in raising and focusing the "connotative powers" of all members to accelerate the learning and performance of their organization.

Conclusion

Dana Gilbert looked across the classroom at the several other shop floor workers, two engineers, a supervisor and, could it be possible, the CEO! "Richards here as a student?" It was the opening minutes of a four week, in-plant Kaizen (continuous improvement) course. There was the CEO, dressed casually, notebook open.

"Well, I'll be damned," Dana muttered, "There is hope for this old place yet."

There is hope for Grand Bay and for all our organizations. It rests in ending the traditional detachment of management from work. Employees are learning from work and managing for the company in ways even they do not fully realize. The new prism metaphor of the managerial mind is offered to help them and those who manage in the lingering tradition to discover what they have in common – the need to secure their company's future when nothing about how to do that is certain. Accepting this as a fundamentally new reality, they can concentrate on improving the quality of each other's management learning, regardless of status and roles.

Learning is the continual reconstruction of experience into meaningful wholes, management for complex organizational situations, for example. Experiential management is made up of meanings that each of us, alone, and in concert, make of what is and should be going on as we do the work of our organization.

All through this chapter, we have talked about Dana Gilbert. Yet, not much will change at Grand Bay, even after the Kaizen workshop with Langley Richards, unless Dana *himself* discovers he has such a fine managerial mind and likes the difference.

"Say, Jim," says Dana, eight months after the day he ended the mistaken parts identity problem, "You are my supervisor, and I respect that, but you make me feel like a back-seat driver. I have a great feel for this place and our business. Don't ask how I got it or know it, but believe it, because I do. You do too. But, why not try going a whole day without calling our shift 'my men,' and saying 'I' have decided we do this or that. Bill, Alonzo, Steve, and I deserve the 'we' in your conversations with top brass. The new IMS link to that terminal over there shows us that productivity in our area goes up 2–4 percent every quarter. Jim, we all managed that!"

And they did.

Notes

1 A. Koopman, *Transcultural Management* (Oxford: Blackwell, 1991), p. 42.
2 Steven Cavaleri, "'Soft' systems thinking: a pre-condition for organizational learning", *Human Systems Management*, 1994, vol. 13, no. 4, pp. 259–67.
3 See Total Employee Involvement Institute research, Norwalk, CT.
4 Peter Drucker, "The age of social transformation", *The Atlantic Monthly*, November, 1994, p. 56.
5 Ibid., p. 58.
6 C. Summer, J. O'Connell and N. Peery, *The Managerial Mind* (Homewood, IL: Richard D. Irwin, 1977), p. 4.
7 Katy Sawyer, "El Niño: wind, ocean dance changes world weather", *The San Francisco Examiner*, reprinted in the *Maine Sunday Telegram*, Jan. 15, 1995, p. 3C.
8 Fred Emery, "Participative design: effective, flexible and successful, now!", *Journal of Quality and Participation*, 1995, vol. 18, no. 1, Jan./Feb., pp. 6–9.
9 Peter Vaill, "Process wisdom for a new age", in J. Adams (ed.), *Transforming Work* (Alexandria, VA.: Miles River Press, 1984), p. 21.
10 Jerry Rhodes, *Conceptual Toolmaking: Expert Systems of the Mind* (Oxford: Blackwell, 1994), p. 36.
11 Michael Stahl, *Management: Total Quality in a Global Environment* (Cambridge, MA.: Blackwell, 1995), p. 224.
12 Ibid., p. 415.
13 Peter Senge, *The Fifth Discipline: The Art & Practice of the Learning Organization.* (New York: Doubleday, 1990), pp. 298–300.
14 Ronnie Lessem, *Total Quality Learning: Building a Learning Organization* (Oxford: Blackwell, 1991), p. 256.
15 Kevin Lewis, "Executive commentary", *Academy of Management Executive*, 1994, vol. VIII, no. 4, November, pp. 28–30.
16 John Burgoyne, "Managing by learning", *Management Learning*, 1994, vol. 25, issue 1, pp. 35–56.
17 P. Senge, A. Kleiner, P. Roberts, R. Ross and B. Smith, *The Fifth Discipline Fieldbook: Strategies and Tools for Building a Learning Organization* (New York: Doubleday, 1994).

18 A. Pattakos and L. Garrett, '"Managing" creativity for continuous learning,' in *Creative Decision Making* (Boise, 10: Creative Learning Technologies, 1992).

19 E. Lawler, S. Morhman and G. Ledford, *Employee Involvement and Total Quality Management: Practices and Results in Fortune 1000 Companies* (San Francisco: Jossey-Bass, 1992), p. 2.

3

The Learning Manager and the Inner Side of Management

William P. Ferris and A. Russell Fanelli

Much has been written about how to lead and how to manage. For years researchers have sought to learn the best ways to elicit optimal performance from subordinates, associates, peers, and even superiors. This book is an attempt to elaborate on leadership and management strategies that might serve to improve organization function by establishing learning organizations: organizations that are able to manage their own development, improvement and growth as well as that of their members. In other words, the leaders and managers of such organizations must build systems that will stimulate learning and growth within organizational members so that the organization can remain vibrant in its own development. In this connection, few things are more important to that learning and growth than what is going on within the inner selves of those leaders and managers.

This chapter will explore a side to the organizational member with management responsibilities that is not often discussed in management books and articles: the **inner side of management**. It is our assumption that the learning organization must be managed by "learning managers," people who are always open to new ideas and who have a personal investment in the growth and development of their employees and their organization. Their goal is to learn how to optimize the personal growth of themselves and their employees because they realize such growth will optimize their organization's development. And for people to become true learning managers, they must be able to access their inner selves; before they can help others grow, they must be in touch with their own personal growth. Studying how to treat one's subordinates, associates, peers, and superiors, how to act toward and with them, while important, is not nearly enough. We have to know how to treat ourselves. Of course, staying physically fit, eating properly, and getting enough sleep are critically important. But equally important, yet too often overlooked, is managing one's inner self, one's mental, spiritual, and intuitive faculties for optimal growth, development, and achievement. It is this side of ourselves that is going to be ultimately responsible for developing the special insight and vision and creativity that will make our part of our particular organization unique and extraordinary as well as optimally functional.

Managing one's inner self to gain such "optimality" requires no less than consideration of a whole new way of regarding oneself and interacting with one's environment, from job to family to off-hour pursuits. It is a commitment to enhancing the quality of one's life in every respect because it is not possible to be as good a manager as one can be, to be a learning manager, and not be functioning in an optimal manner physically, mentally, and spiritually.

The process of accessing the inner side of management can be assisted by reference to the literature, now gaining more and more currency, that deals with such topics as spirituality, soul, intuition, deep reflection, and the development of vision. When consideration of these topics is applied to management, it leads to the concept of the development of the holistic manager, the manager as a whole spiritual and psychological human being, not just an organizational cog (see such other books in this series as Ronnie Lessem's *Developmental Management* and Jagdish Parikh's *Managing Your Self*).[1] This chapter will reference such literature in describing how the practice of optimal management is incomplete without consideration and employment of inner management.

Since a large part of managing so that organizations learn involves problem-solving, let us begin by considering a very common theory of problem-solving that adopts a learning style approach. Most helpful in the context of the developmental approach of organizational learning is the Kolb model of experiential learning.[2] According to this model, the process of learning is grounded in how we experience the environment and how we conceptualize our place in relationship to our environment. It requires the resolution of conflicts between opposing ways of adapting to the environment. The first of these conflicts is between what Kolb calls **concrete experience** and **abstract conceptualization**; the second is between **active experimentation** and **reflective observation**. In other words, do you learn better by visualizing examples of something or by reading about principles and theories; secondly, do you learn better by trying something directly or by watching others and considering your observations carefully? In sum, learning can be accomplished both by action and reflection, and people are usually good at one or the other, but not both. Most managers are best at action but they fail to fully reach their learning potential if they do not carefully consider becoming more skilled in the modes that are connected to reflection. For example, an action-oriented manager must always be doing something or risk being "beaten to the punch." Frequently, we are advised to move forward, and "don't look back or the competition will be gaining." Reflection is seen as something for "ivory tower" types who "are not living in the real world."

Kolb divides learning styles into four types: **accommodators, assimilators, divergers**, and **convergers**. In Kolb's terms, most business persons are especially strong in the more action-oriented style of the accommodator. We have found, however, that organizations that do not attend to the functions that are the strengths of the accommodator's opposite, the assimilator, do poorly as learning organizations because they lack the conceptual and theoretical background necessary for thoughtful growth. They may not be short on enthusiasm but they are frequently short on patience and planning. A famous example of this was Coca Cola's decision to rush into the marketplace with "New Coke," supplanting its old tried and true coke formula only to discover that New Coke would meet serious resistance. The facts of this situation suggest that the performance of this product could be improved if greater attention was devoted to planning and market research.

Like assimilators, divergers are also oriented toward reflection, but rather than being planners and modelers, they tend to have a great many creative ideas and to take a genuine interest in the differences and divergences among personalities. They are good at brainstorming ideas but not normally interested in following their ideas to a logical and complete conclusion. Business tends

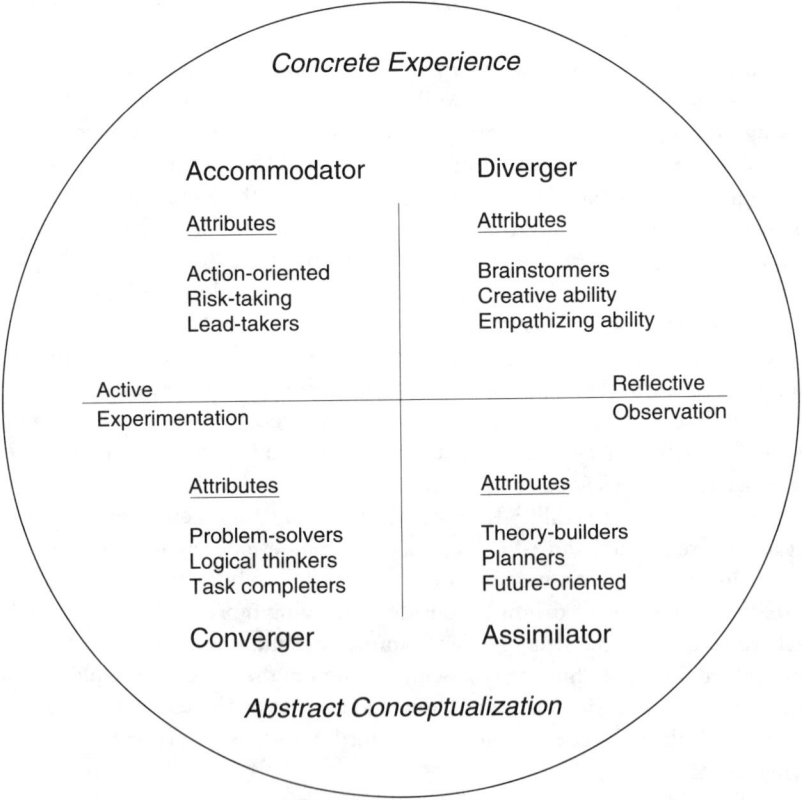

Figure 3.1   David Kolb's four learning styles, their attributes, and their relationships to types of cognitive activity. Source: Based on Kolb, *Experiential Learning*, 1984.

to value their opposites, the convergers, who think logically and systematically and whose strength is in the action-orientation of complete follow-through. Yet, if we are interested in developing a learning organization, we must take another look at the value of reflection in stimulating creativity and new perspectives.

Only by mastering the elements of inner management can we return reflection to its rightful place in the management problem-solving process. In order to accomplish the integration of action and reflection, several things are essential. First, we must become skilled at accessing our inner selves if we are to be open to such reflective qualities as inspiration, intuition, and spiritual understanding. The necessary psychological foundation for such an approach requires an integrated adult ego state and a secure sense of self-esteem. We cannot be open to learning and inspiration if we are anxious about how we are coming across to others and unable to make ourselves properly vulnerable to the constant possibilities of new learning. Second, the many barriers to inner managing must be overcome. Examples of barriers abound. Unbreakable paradigms of "how we've always done it around here" deter the creativity of paradigm shifting and developmental managing. Promotion of fear prevents risk-taking and discourages initiative. Perhaps worst of all, structural policy barriers – rigid chain of command, overuse of prescribed protocols, denigrating raise and compensation systems, to name a few – act to stimulate organizational ignorance: the learning of counterproductive behaviors rather than optimization of performance. Third, actual techniques and practices that one can utilize to become more fit to manage from the inside must be learned. These include the use of environmental feedback from family and play as well as work, the development of personal psychic vision and energy, and the painstaking learning of how to explore and expand one's spiritual mind-set through such practices as fulfilling one's spirituality, valuing art, and practicing meditation and even breath control. We will deal with each of these necessities in turn, and conclude with some discussion of the human resource ramifications of such an approach for the learning organization.

Inner Management and its Prerequisites

At its most exhilarating, inner management involves being at a level of human perception only rarely experienced, a level of timeless concentration and focus that seems to transcend everyday life. At its most mundane, it simply involves the reflective discipline of careful planning with a view to maximizing available resources. In this chapter, we will focus on the more exhilarating level, which is also normally the least accessible for most managers. We will begin by describing this level in more detail, and then go on to discuss the psychological foundation needed to undertake the important task of accessing it.

Who has not experienced the elation of climbing to the top of a small mountain, or winning an important athletic contest, or being so engrossed in a book or movie or computer program as to lose track of the passage of time? Athletes call it being "in the zone" or "unconscious," social scientists say **in flow**, and Buddhist teachers describe "becoming one with the Universe." It is those times when you have felt most exhilarated to be human, most infused with the excitement of being alive. Unbelievably to some, many people have reported their most exhilarating moments have occurred when they were at their job. Mihaly Csikszentmihalyi, researcher on the flow phenomenon and author of *Flow: The Psychology of Optimal Experience*, describes workers in flow as having lost track of time, "being so involved in an activity that nothing else seems to matter."[3] The phenomenon is characterized by an intense concentration, an absorbing sense of challenge, and ultimately, a deep feeling of satisfaction. People in such professions as surgeon, professional athlete, artist, and teacher have reported these peak experiences as common to their work; in fact, people in a great variety of other jobs have also reported the phenomenon. Invariably, the moments occur when people are doing their very best work. In his books on the "inner game" of tennis, Tim Gallwey reports that even beginners can achieve the sense of being in the zone through mastery of inner tennis: letting go of judgment and self-criticism and allowing the body to take over one's strokes.[4] When beginner and expert alike achieve the inner game, they are operating at peak proficiency. So, while confidence in self is required to tap inner resources, uncommon competence is not. But for us, the question becomes, how could a learning manager achieve such peak experiences on a regular basis as part of the normal work day? And how could an organization teach its members to operate "in flow," thus optimizing its own performance? First, the psychological conditions for such a possibility have to be present.

Some key ideas from current theories of motivation and behavior that have been tested across cultures are relevant here. Victor Vroom, in his **expectancy theory**, suggests that one must feel competent before even deciding whether or not to attempt something.[5] This would be especially important if the thing to be attempted were new and involved some risk. Albert Bandura originated the concept of **self-efficacy** to describe the sense that you have when you feel you can accomplish the thing contemplated.[6] This proceeds from a foundation of self-esteem. You feel good about yourself (self-esteem) and that allows you to feel that you have the competence, or can develop it, to accomplish whatever you decide needs to be done. Finally, Abraham Maslow developed a theory of motivation and growth that suggests that people naturally seek growth and, ultimately, **peak experiences**.[7] Given what we know from these theories and the thousands of studies that have corroborated them, we can only conclude that a sense of competence, self-efficacy, and desire for growth and peak experience are psychological prerequisites for learning managers who wish to manage from the inside, as much as for the employees whose inner selves they wish to access.

Generally found correlated with these psychological prerequisites is a sense of **learned optimism** – you are generally optimistic about yourself and about life; you see the glass half full rather than half empty; you have a "can do" attitude and a confidence that things will turn out for the best, not all by themselves, but with a little application.[8] Although there is some research to indicate that positive self-esteem is either developed early in life, or is difficult to develop later, nevertheless, it can be learned.[9] Educational foundations and government agencies across the United States are spending millions in an attempt to develop it in school children.[10] Returning to our tennis example, when a coach with a high degree of self-esteem is able to access the inner self of a beginner by encouraging belief in that person's natural abilities, and then reinforcing the success that can be generated, the beginner will begin to develop learned optimism and achieve a sense of "flow." Similarly, managers who value their own managerial abilities can access flow for themselves and their employees on the job as long as they can facilitate awareness of self-esteem.

Closely tied to the need for a strong sense of self-esteem is the development of what has been called **ego energy** in the individual.[11] Ego energy is defined as "the chronic desire to define oneself through behavior in a way that demonstrates to others that one is valuable and unique."[12] Thus, it is driven by a sense of pride in one's individuality, one's uniqueness as not just any human being,

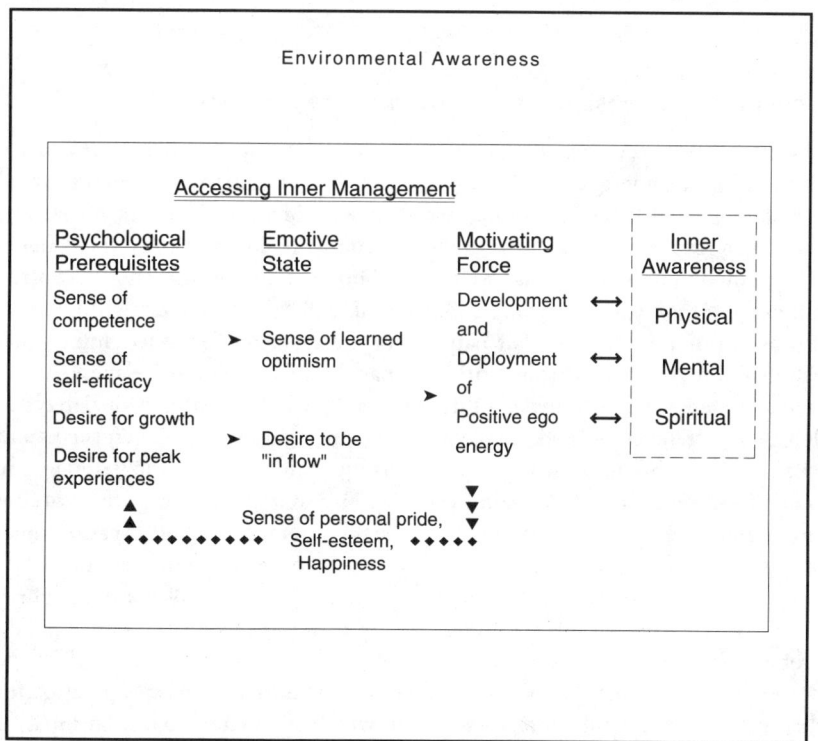

Figure 3.2   Accessing inner management.

but as a human being who shares characteristics with many other humans, yet who is also different in some important way. How does this relate to inner managing? It is up to managers to make use of the positive natural pride in genuine accomplishment that all of us want to feel in connection with our contribution at work. For managers to do that, they must be in touch with their own ego energy as well as that of those they want to influence.

Ego energy can be either positive or negative. It is positive when it is directed toward developmental and organizational goals. It is negative when it is deployed for the advancement of the individual's interests at the expense of other organizational members or the organization itself. For example, it is negative when it is directed against the organization in activities that can range from playing practical jokes on other employees, to deliberate sabotage or theft, to pursuit of a hidden agenda, to simple obstructive or counterproductive behavior. The danger is that positive ego energy may be replaced by apathy at the work site and allowed to surface in creative behaviors only off the job. The organizational leader and learning manager must become invested in creating opportunities for the development of pride and self-esteem, thus directing the ego energy of all in a positive way. When this occurs, a circular process ensues in which the positive ego energy that is generated reinforces the psychological prerequisites that are required to develop the positive ego energy in the first place.

Developing a sense of environmental awareness

Another of the prerequisites for managing from the inner self is to try to see things with beginners' eyes. By this we mean that learning managers must take a fresh look at what they are doing from the point of view of the naive observer, cultivate a responsive awareness of the environment, and recognize the dangers of ingrained mindless habits as well as the boredom and indifference that often comes from a job where learning no longer takes place. Excitement, enthusiasm, and even fun are not just what happens at the weekends or other times when employees may be away from work, but part of a working environment where people are challenged to make a difference and are rewarded appropriately for doing so. Organizations and people who are continually aware of themselves and what they are doing, with a mind to learning new ways of doing things, are young in the excitement that comes from seeing something new in the working environment. Routine and boredom are signs of employee and organizational old age. It is the responsibility of the learning manager to counteract organizational senility by encouraging, promoting, and rewarding observation, reflection, and creative problem-solving. In fact, we believe that learning and problem-solving are the manager's most important jobs and always ought to be perceived of as opportunities. Everything in the manager's life is preparation for this role of learner and problem-solver in which action and reflection must be united. Certainly managers can and do manage without accessing their inner side, but if they remain closed to themselves and to inner management, they will not be learning managers and they will become deterrents to a learning organization rather than its essential building blocks. Much that we discuss later in this chapter is meant to assist managers in becoming better at inner management so that they can become genuinely effective as learners and problem-solvers in a true learning organization.

Ben and Jerry's ice cream company is one in which employees are treated like valued customers and respond by "taking more responsibility for their jobs."[13] At Ben and Jerry's, people take precedence over profits and the end result is that the company can't make the product fast enough to keep pace with demand. Managers model learning themselves; they are aware that their behavior is visible to others in the organization and that they are examples more by what they do than by what they say. Managers model learning by paying close attention to what is happening in the organization and with the work group. They focus their interest and energy on the jobs people are doing and the context in which that work takes place, and they listen to what their people have to say. One production line worker made this comment: "We actually can talk to Ben and Jerry, and they tell us what's going on. We do a lot of listening at these meetings. They're very informative and help us know what's happening."

Although this injunction to keep a watchful eye on the workings in the environment may seem obvious, in practice few managers are aware of what employees think, do, and say on the job. Our own experience conducting climate surveys in large and small businesses indicates that many managers are blind to important employee attitudes and behaviors. This blindness is especially prevalent at the top of the organization, but can be found throughout most companies. Additionally, when employees are anxious, worried, and insecure, they become expert at hiding what they think while seeming to be open and straightforward with management. The consequences are disastrous for learning in the organization.

We spent over a year trying to improve the quality of the products sold by one company in the northeast United States. The CEO and his executive group were ignorant of the abuses taking place on the shop floor while the supervisors responsible for making the product seemed indifferent, themselves, to the sloppy work habits of their crews. As long as orders continued coming in, the old ways seemed satisfactory. However, changes in the marketplace resulted in a continued increase in returns from various customers no longer content with the products being sold to them.

When supervisors were made aware of the problem and told it was necessary to improve their products, at first they were hostile. Weekly group meetings were necessary to bring people together to discuss common interests and problems. Slowly, supervisors became aware of their responsibility to their customers and other people in the organization. A pride in producing first-rate goods began to surface and they started to challenge one another to begin paying attention to difficulties they had been content to ignore in the past. They started to make suggestions and take risks which were supported by the executive group. For the first time in years a sense of excitement could be felt at group meetings. Supervisors had been given a wake-up call. They responded by paying attention themselves and encouraged their people to do the same, not so much telling workers what to do as simply being more available on the shop floor. There they systematically began to learn how to increase quality and output, and subsequently to recommend to the plant manager ways to improve the manufacturing process.

In terms of Kolb's model, our manufacturing group had been relying heavily on concrete experience gained from many years of producing the same goods. Now these products were increasingly being returned because the standards in the industry had become more stringent. It had become necessary to do some problem-solving to find out what had gone wrong, to develop new models to improve production, and to experiment with some of the suggestions made by the work group to improve product quality. Reflection needed to be integrated with action; the reward for supervisors and workers alike would be the sense of achievement and satisfaction that comes from reaching the highest quality standards in one's work, and the sense of being "in flow" or "in the zone" that can go with that. People were able to alter the work process in a way that produced a noticeable difference and gave them pride as well as building their self-esteem. Supervisors who had become complacent on the job and had lost any excitement they once had for going to work, actually welcomed this challenge. People who had been simply putting in time and doing as little as possible to be productive were now engaged. The opportunity to find better ways to do business and to change the production process brought excitement to meetings which had become little more than gripe sessions. For the first time in years supervisors looked forward to coming to work.

For the learning manager the lessons here are clear. First, the manager needs to see clearly what has to be done and communicate this vision to the team. Second, managers need the determination to pursue goals vigorously even when hardship and obstacles are encountered. Third, managers need an extraordinary amount of patience. Just as people have a long history of learning ineffective ways of dealing with problems, organizations also have these counterproductive histories. The learning manager understands that quick fixes seldom resolve long-standing learning dysfunction and disability. Many good starts made by employees have been later undone by managers who were unwilling to be patient and have faith in almost all workers' needs to grow as valued individuals. And fourth, managers need to value the new perspectives and suggestions brought by employees who sometimes have little experience or little in common with the supervisors or little apparent connection to the traditional way of doing business. In order to reflect this value and to encourage such thinking and inspiration, risk-taking must be fostered rather than stifled or punished.

We have seen that what learning managers do better than others is to focus their attention on the work people are doing in the organization and the context in which that work takes place. Employees know if their boss is paying attention by simply looking to see if the manager is out at the sharp end where work is being done, or back in the office protected by a secretary, or in countless meetings where problems are talked about but rarely solved. Seldom are the people who are actually doing the work of the organization invited to these meetings. Instead, managers who are once, twice, or three times removed from producing goods or providing services carry clipboards to meetings where action without reflection originates, action that seldom makes a difference in how work actually gets done.

Learning managers know that they must patiently work to get out to the sharp end of the company again, where business is being done. They know that the most valuable meetings they attend are the impromptu meetings with their people on the firing line who are doing the business of the corporation. This behavior represents the kind of pulse-taking and paying attention that matters to employees and separates serious managers from those who hold the title without actually making a difference in how people work or what they produce. It can only be accomplished by managers who are in tune with the working environment and especially with the people who are such a critical part of that environment. And it must be accomplished by managers who are self-assured and in touch with themselves, and who do not feel their authority challenged by the better ideas of nonmanaging line personnel. Only then will a relationship founded on mutual interests and concerns develop.

Thus, learning managers get to know employees through their work and the problems they encounter in producing products and services. In our lives most of us have experienced the genuine satisfaction of having someone take an interest in our work. We can remember the excitement in our voice and the feeling of self-worth we experienced as we talked about what we were doing on the job. The best managers understand the need employees have to tell someone what they are doing and what they think it means, not only to themselves, but to the work of the group.

Paying attention and developing awareness seem so obvious and so simple. Actually, they are neither. Managers' lives are filled with hurry, worry, and distress. To understand what has been lost from the past we need only take a few moments to view small children at play and observe the total attention they give to what they are doing. It is this single-mindedness as well as the ability to ignore distractions that we seek to recapture as we focus on the work at hand. In the experience of working with employees, managers have the potential to discover something new if they are open, interested, and without fear. Thus, their job is to help people truly experience the work they are doing, its importance and value. From the point of view of inner management, managers cannot do this until they are aware of themselves physically, mentally, and spiritually.

Physical, mental, and spiritual awareness

Deepak Chopra, MD, in his book *Ageless Body, Timeless Mind*, discusses the need for **physical awareness** in detail.[14] He presents medical evidence to show that people who are in the closest touch with their bodies can affect and effect healing from the deadliest diseases. They can assure longer lives for themselves and gain a greater state of alertness. The well-known Type A personality so common in business, the person who is always doing three things at once and is always in a hurry, in reality is less productive than the one who is able to be truly engaged in one task at a time and be alert to all possibilities that may present themselves to such a heightened awareness. And, of course, the Type A person also lives a shorter and more unhealthy life. Living in harmonious interaction with one's body, especially including regular meditation, has been shown to bring physically dysfunctional behaviors (like high blood pressure and heart-beat) under better control, to decrease such debilitating feelings as hopelessness, and to extend one's life span. Chopra demonstrates how every cell in one's body contains intelligence; to the degree that you are not in contact with all cells, you limit your own intelligence. He discusses many studies and real-life examples of people who did poorly or even lost their lives in situations that were not hopeless simply because, not in touch with their full body, they became apathetic or totally discouraged. Managers who fall prey to loss of awareness of self or loss of interest in personal happiness and self-mastery, risk apathy, burnout, and even early death, not only for themselves but also for those for whom they have some responsibility.

Being **mentally aware** of oneself requires attention to self-mastery. All growth psychology as well as much of the world's spiritual tradition emphasizes the primacy of fulfilling one's potential. Yet loss of awareness can emerge in this context, too. Part of self-mastery includes knowing which of your limits are real and which are artificial.[15] As Jagdish Parikh says in his earlier referenced book about how to become a master manager, you have a choice: you can remain a seed your whole life, or you can choose to flourish and grow. You can adopt and pursue an inner vision from your increased state of whole body alertness, gaining ideas and creative energy from your environment and your reading, or you can live within the visions of others.

Warren Bennis and Bert Nanus in *Leaders: Strategies for Taking Charge* have much to say about **vision**.[16] They interviewed 90 leaders including 60 CEOs, half of whom were from Fortune 200 companies, and 30 other leaders from various nonprofit organizations and the US government, to learn what they had in common. All focused extraordinary attention on vision, and the authors write extensively on where these leaders found the inspiration for their visions. Most visions came from reading, especially history and philosophy, but also from reading about the state of the art in all fields, not just their own. Ideas for vision were, in fact, most likely to come from another field. Starting points for the vision were often reflection on the ideal – what things at the home company would be like if they were going perfectly. In their reflections, these leaders saw problems as opportunities. Finally, many ideas that can play a part in formulating a vision can come from reading future-oriented material that makes predictions about what life will be like in future decades, and even from reading good science-fiction.[17]

For mid- and lower-level managers, the concept of vision might shift to visualization of how things within their departments or work-sites would be going if they were going ideally. It is not dissimilar, though a bit more complicated, than the process by which an athlete visualizes perfect tennis serves or basketball free throws just prior to execution. You as manager would open your mind to all its possibilities, thus adopting the "revisioning" posture of Parikh's master manager. This requires letting go of your ego and its potential to allow expression to the bad side of pride, the side that can get you in trouble because it is associated with a fear of how you are perceived. By remaining open to your own intuition, that power beyond sensing and reason that gives you ideas and inspiration, you allow a vision to take shape in your mind.[18] More and more of the world's attention is turning toward understanding the nature and necessity of valuing intuition.[19] If you are going to have a vision of how the department, the team, or the organization should change, or even proceed, your creative and inspirational powers will be barren without an active involvement of intuition. But to be ready for that, you need to be free of anxiousness and fear of judgment by others. Only then will you be approaching a state of mental readiness and thus be prepared to seek spiritual awareness.

Related to mental awareness but also different in many ways is **spiritual awareness**. Your spirituality involves your emotions, your search for personal happiness, your sense of who you are, and your perception of your relation to your values and perhaps to a greater power or being. The importance for managers of dealing with their emotions in a positive manner has been widely written about in the management literature. Certainly, the more a manager can present positive emotions such as empathy, enthusiasm, pride in the work of others, satisfaction, and genuine liking or unconditional positive regard for others, the more subordinates and associates will be environmentally encouraged to perform at optimal levels. However, managers' negative emotions such as frustration, anger, discouragement, disapproval, and disliking will discourage workers. Yet pretending to be positive without genuinely feeling that way will usually be seen through; such lack of truth to self robs a manager of credibility. But are we expected to be paragons of positive emotions? No, because that would not be human. Instead, we need to cultivate our ability to experience positive emotions for our own personal benefit as well as for the benefit of our work as managers. And we must come to an acceptance of our negative emotions and the need to learn to deal with them in a way that does not debilitate our inner selves. In short, we must attend assiduously to our spiritual selves.

Many authors have written on spirituality. Two notable ones are Thomas Moore, a former Catholic monk, in *Care of the Soul* and Jack Kornfield, a Western Buddhist who became a clinical psychologist, in *A Path with Heart*.[20] Of course, the work of Buddhist masters such as Thich Nhat Hanh, some of whose ideas will be taken up later in this chapter, has long been noteworthy. And the Bible, Torah, and Koran, for centuries the world's most authoritative religious texts, can provide the deepest spiritual inspiration. Here we will focus especially on some of the ideas of Moore and Kornfield.

By soul, Moore does not mean one's spirit that seeks immortality but rather "a quality, or a dimension of experiencing life and ourselves. It has to do with depth, relatedness, value, heart, and personal substance."[21] "Care" means what a nurse does, including attention, devotion, healing, managing, and nurturing. His point is that we ignore our soul's care to our detriment as holistic beings. Worse, we deny who we are. Rather, we should be working with "what is, rather than what you wish were there."[22] Throughout the book he relates mythology, the range of human emotions, virtues, vices, senses, and psyche to the individual soul.

For Kornfield, the spiritual path that must be followed for a person to be whole is the "path with heart," a way of being that requires integration of mind, body, and emotions. The purpose of choosing it is "to discover peace and connectedness in ourselves and to stop the war in us and around us."[23] For example, we must avoid compartmentalization of our lives into such artificial divisions as work and nonwork, office and home. Instead, we must demand from our professional life the same focus, concentration, and empathy that we employ in our personal lives. These two lives are not separated but are united in us. This requires a state of mindfulness that seeks an awareness of all things at every moment. Such demons as anger, fear, grasping, boredom, judgment, restlessness, and doubt attempt to distract us, but by becoming aware of them we can master them and replace them with the qualities of spiritual maturity. Without enumerating all of these qualities and explaining them in detail, suffice it to say that they include the following: nonidealism (the capacity to love and to withhold blame or judgment, as well as not to demand a perfection that can never be attained); kindness (the ability to turn anger into forgiveness); patience; immediacy (ability to live in the present moment); open-mindedness; flexibility; and relatedness (understanding one's relatedness to all other persons and things).

For most managers, even attempting to put some of these ideas into practice would represent major change. Just the concepts of withholding blame and not demanding an unattainable perfection take years to master. Yet spirituality cannot be ignored in one's professional life any more than it can be ignored in one's personal life. And managing from the inside clearly means managing from the heart. Later in this chapter, we examine some specific techniques that can help managers grow from the inside.

Common Organizational Barriers to Inner Managing

Although focus on the inner side of managing is just beginning to gain interest, there are other reasons why inner managing has not been much studied in business. Significant barriers are raised against it in the very essence of business as it is commonly practiced. For example, the nature of competition is such that most businesses must attend to short time frames in all that they do. Competition to satisfy customers in the shortest possible time, quarterly reports to satisfy shareholders every 90 days, the high cost of money, and constantly changing government regulatory requirements are four of the most common factors that seem to militate against the management of enterprise using techniques of inner management. Yet, it is our contention that far too much is lost from not using such techniques in this environment. In other words, we risk rushing headlong into the same mistakes, inadequacies, and deficiencies over and over again if we don't stop to take advantage of the potential of our entire being, not just our capacity to act quickly. The following section will detail some of the barriers to inner managing and their costs, as well as suggest some ways of mitigating them as barriers.

If it is important for learning managers to access their inner selves in order to be effective as managers, it is almost as important for them to be able to do so in an environment of free and open communication with the workforce. Employees must be as open to the ideas, feelings, and good intentions of their managers as managers are to be open to them. If there are unspoken hostilities, feelings of distrust, or other unexpressed elements of poor morale present, accessing inner management will be difficult at best. Becoming a learning manager and inspiring employee growth in such an environment will be almost impossible.

Overcoming lack of feedback

Lack of **feedback** in the learning process is among the most critical problems for the manager and a nearly insurmountable barrier to effective inter- and intrapersonal communication. Here, we stress not only the importance of effective feedback in the day-to-day operations of the business, but also the necessity for systematic feedback systems within the organization. In other words, both managers and their employees need to learn how they are doing from charts, graphs, records, journals, production numbers, customer response cards and surveys, and a variety of non-supervisor-dependent sources. Feedback cannot be relegated solely to verbal interaction with workers. It is the role of the learning manager to assist in setting up these systems and to monitor them as well.

As mentioned earlier, true learning managers get out on the floor where the work is being done and pay attention to people and their problems, taking notes as appropriate. They use their notes to take actions that show employees that they care about them and what they are doing; the most effective managers ask what they can do to help and then follow through. They also make sure employees are rewarded appropriately for learning and contributing on the job. Helping employees to understand how their work contributes to the overall goals of the organization as well as to the employees' personal goals is probably one of their most important functions. It almost goes without saying that they actively work to keep open the lines of communication within the group while developing a team of people who see their interests as being satisfied by the contributions of the group as a whole. Finally, and perhaps most often overlooked, they establish an audit system that allows them to know what employees think about the manager's work.

Feedback and meaningful work are a powerful combination for the learning manager who understands that the typical employee takes little interest in the job and gets no feedback from management about the products or services produced. Most employees live in a feedback vacuum. The way out for the learning manager is to keep the lines of communication open and feedback flowing freely between employees and management. As Ken Blanchard has frequently repeated, "Feedback is the breakfast of champions."[24] Managers would do well to type this statement on a card and place it in some prominent place on their desk as a frequent reminder of their responsibilities in regard to regular, specific, and meaningful feedback.

Feedback instruments should allow employees to communicate their thoughts about the climate of the organization anonymously. When we work with managers in organizations, they often question us about the necessity of making some forms of feedback anonymous. We are convinced that employees often hide their true thoughts and feelings from their managers and appear to be satisfied with their jobs when they are not. Years of being hurt have conditioned many of them to shy away from stating their thoughts honestly and openly. They have learned that it is safer to say what they think the manager wants to hear instead of what they really think. Some employees believe that management may use the employees' honesty against them when it comes to the time for raises and promotions. This honesty is thought to be too high a price to pay for responding to questions about work when the answers might not make any difference in the way employees are managed or how they are treated.

In *Theory Z*, William Ouchi makes a case for anonymous feedback when he says, "A manager who has worked hard at being more cooperative and participative, who has intellectually embraced a new approach, is hardly a reliable first judge of personal progress."[25] He recommends that a brief feedback instrument be sent out to subordinates for their candid reactions to the manager. We recommend that the learning manager establish a focus group to construct a brief feedback instrument. The manager can add items and questions to those supplied by employees working without managerial personnel present. When employees respond, the manager can be reasonably certain that the feedback represents not only what the manager thinks important, but also what employees truly want the manager to hear.

Many learning organizations have systematically constructed "360 degree" feedback systems that allow organizational members to receive feedback from all stakeholders who have any connection whatsoever to their work. Such organizations include Alcoa, British Petroleum, Burlington Northern Railroad, General Electric, General Motors, Hewlett-Packard, Herman Miller, 3M, UPS, and Whirlpool, to name a few. Hoechst Celanese Corporation's experience is typical. Managers receive feedback from superiors, peers, and subordinates, all of which go into a "Leadership Feedback" developmental plan for the manager. Training programs' curricula are taken from results in the aggregate.[26] In fact, for feedback to be complete, customers, vendors, shareholders, and site community members should also be involved.

In addition to feedback from all other sources, we agree with Al Huang and Jerry Lynch in *Thinking Body, Dancing Mind* when they recommend that learners give feedback to themselves in the form of positive affirmations.[27] This recommendation is echoed by Chopra, who reiterates that the feedback we give ourselves is of critical importance in the self-learning that must precede managerial interventions at work. Our recommendation to managers that they practice being patient with their employees applies to the self as well. Overcoming limitations, doubts, false starts, and mistakes as the manager seeks to involve employees in the accomplishment of high goals is a challenge of the highest order and one not easily accomplished. The greater the achievement sought, the more patience needed by the manager both with self and others.

Overcoming the lure of carrot and stick managing

Another barrier for the learning manager to overcome is pervasive belief in the **carrot and stick** approach to motivation. This is the outworn Theory X approach of enticing the donkey with a reward carrot just out of its reach (or even just within it) and alternatively hitting it with a stick to coerce it to do what you want out of fear of pain. Too many managers see this apparently work a few times and conclude it is the only way to achieve results. However, growth psychology has long since discredited this approach. And it is absolutely inconsistent with inner management because it relies on fear. Fear and its relatives – anxiety, jealousy, envy, and other forms of negative ego energy – have no place in tapping the inner resources of managers. We believe strongly that it is not the business of the learning manager to manipulate employees into doing what Frederick Herzberg calls "idiot work" by blandishments or threats. Herzberg thinks of "idiot work" as any mindless, repetitive task better done by a machine.[28] Managers know instantly what Herzberg is talking about and often respond with indignation or resentment arising from a feeling of guilt coming from the knowledge that the manager has tried to convince others to do work the manager knows is demeaning, degrading, or both. In *Walden Two*, B. F. Skinner tried to overcome this problem by formulating a plan where everyone has to share the unpleasant jobs in the community.[29] While Skinner's utopian view on this subject is unlikely to gain much commitment in the business community, managers do need to show themselves ready to make the same sacrifices as the employees in the group. As always, the manager is the model who must do much more than just "talk the talk." To be effective managers must demonstrate by timely action that they are in fact who they say they are.

Of course, learning managers are responsible for more than simple willingness to do the distasteful jobs of the organization; they have the even more significant task of making work meaningful. We realize that this assignment will make great demands on the creative abilities of managers and their teams. What is at stake strikes at the very heart of employee motivation; that is, helping people take pride and satisfaction in the work they do and the product or service they produce. All true motivation and work is generated by the need people have to be associated with an enterprise that makes demands on the best they can give. Giving work meaning for self or others without access to inner management is virtually impossible.

Overcoming lack of trust

Still another barrier to inner managing and learning is **inappropriate competition** within the work group and organization. Learning managers realize the importance of reducing or eliminating dysfunctional competition within the group, fostering a caring environment, and building relationships based on trust.

A classic example of how managers create distrust using inappropriate competition occurred a few years ago on one of our consulting assignments. After we advised on the importance of feedback systems, the CEO agreed to a series of measures that would provide feedback to round the clock work crews on how well they were doing. As consultants, we wished to gather the data so that the five plants involved could compete against each other, thus appealing to a sense of plant pride for good results. The CEO, however, insisted that crews' posted results be compared against each other within plants so that he could discover who the weakest supervisors were. Despite our protests, he persisted. A great deal of negative ego energy was unleashed. Some crews refused to do required maintenance on their machines in order to get better crew results at the expense of machines breaking down on another crew's shift. Others selected "gravy" orders for production, "sticking" later crews with shorter and more time-intensive jobs. Some even sabotaged incoming crews' materials and machines outright in an attempt to keep from looking bad themselves by comparison to later crews. The supervisor whom the CEO previously considered his best one, came in last in the sweepstakes because he had the self-esteem to ignore how he might be perceived on production measures in order to help other crews whose supervisors were less experienced with their problems. In short, through use of a classic Theory X tactic, this CEO did more to ruin trust, while at the same time introducing serious doubts into his own perceptions of supervisors, than if he had personally gone around to tell his employees that he didn't trust them.

In other consulting contexts, we have experimented with various forms of group games illustrating the value of cooperation over dysfunctional competition. We have discovered that managers and employees have frequently learned not to trust one another but rather to behave in a "what's in it for me?" fashion which undermines attempts to build solid communication and feedback networks. Ideals of cooperation, trust, and sharing, which managers and employees prize in words, are often ignored in actions. The results of these games have always illustrated fierce competition and joy in this opportunity to compete. It is as if managers and employees prefer to compete, even if they must lose, rather than win at the cost of having to cooperate. This insight indicates the extent of the challenge for the learning manager interested in reducing the barriers to learning and sharing in the organization.

At least part of the answer to the manager's problem of reducing competition within the work group is to develop the work group into a team with a shared purpose and common goals. The sense of satisfaction derived from working in a closely knit, high functioning team is often even greater than the satisfaction of a personal victory over another. Teams require individuals to channel competitive instincts into victories over self for the good of something greater than self. All over the world models from the world of sports abound which demonstrate the ability of people to commit themselves to the team. The quadrennial World Cup Football (soccer, in the US) tournament attests to the great interest and importance people place in the work of the team.

In his phenomenally popular book *The Seven Habits of Highly Effective People*, Stephen Covey encourages the manager to think "win/win."[30] In other words, the secret of resolving any situation is to arrange or derive benefits for all involved and major loss for none. This is a principle underlined in our contention that employee goals must be served concomitantly with organizational goals for positive ego energy to become prevalent within the learning organization. In his next book, *Principle-Centered Leadership*, Covey builds on many of the ideas mentioned in *Seven Habits*.[31] He provides a lengthy treatment of the work of W. Edwards Deming and mentions Deming's scathing indictment of American competitiveness, scarcity mentality, and lack of common purpose. Deming wisely counsels managers to promote an abundance mentality within the organization and even beyond. An abundance mentality understands that there is enough for everyone in a collaborative environment that prizes sharing over hoarding. For a start, we think it is enough for learning managers to examine their own motives, demonstrate an interest in others, and work to build an effective team at home and on the job.

In addition to assuming an abundance mentality, learning managers are particularly careful to maintain the highest expectations for all of their people and an enthusiasm for them and their work. They are not blind to faults and weaknesses, but they understand that most people will live up to the expectations managers have for them. High expectations promote a learning environment in which the climate is friendly and encouraging, the feedback is frequent, the amount of information given to learners to help them with the task is abundant, and the outcomes give employees a chance to stretch their skills and abilities. All the evidence now available to us indicates that employees are an incredible resource of talents only waiting for the chance to be developed under the right encouragement and guidance. High expectations are a potent intellectual force against the barriers to establishing an effective learning organization.

Lou Holtz, the football coach at Notre Dame University, rightly points out that the three questions employees ask most often of managers are, "Can I trust you? Do you care about me? and Are you committed?" The first two questions get right to the heart of the issue which the learning manager must resolve. When employees experience trust and caring they become less fearful and more willing to say what they think about the work they are doing. They become more willing to contribute to the work group and more able to develop satisfaction and pride in their work. Mistakes and false starts are not seen as embarrassing events, but as necessary steps in the learning process. Employees are granted what the noted psychologist Carl Rogers has called "freedom to learn."[32] This freedom can only take place in an atmosphere of trust.

In this connection, we must mention Rogers' noted concept of **unconditional positive regard**, which he defines as "an outgoing positive feeling [about a person] without reservations, without evaluations." It says that no matter how you or others might judge a person, you will find something positive in your regard for him or her. According to Rogers, true listening which engenders trust and comes from unconditional positive regard, takes place when managers are able to establish relationships in which they accept employees for what they are as human beings and recognize the great value resident in being a person. This is a lesson learned well at Ben and Jerry's. The active listener/ learning manager does not attempt to force change, but allows for change to happen uniquely with each employee. No employee will feel his or her idea is stupid or irrelevant when unconditional positive regard is present. Being truly listened to is indeed a growth experience and one that can only take place in an atmosphere of trust.

Overcoming the organizational paradox of the double bind

A barrier that is more subtle than some of the others is that of the **double bind**. Double binds are debilitating organizational communication patterns in which members are paralyzed or rendered dysfunctional by two or more messages with conflicting meanings that are sent simultaneously to the member/receiver(s) on different communication channels. For example, if a manager tells an employee that he or she is always available for help but does so in a tone of voice that suggests the employee will be considered less intelligent to ask for that help, the employee can become paralyzed. Employees who ask for the proffered help feel they risk looking stupid and endangering their raises or even their continued employment if they do so too often. Sometimes, it won't be the negative tone of voice of the manager but rather the way the manager has set up barriers to communication by arranging an office to reflect a position of power or giving orders about access to a secretary or other gate-keeper. Another example might be the invitation of some managers to employees to be creative or innovative in the face of a myriad of policies that require rigidly prescribed behavior.

Managers should be on the lookout for paradoxes of this type within their organizations as well as in their own behavior. Employees who find themselves faced with such double binds really have only three choices: become paralyzed, leave the field (situation), or stick doggedly to one of the messages paying no heed whatsoever to the other. All of these choices are bad ones for the organization. True learning organizations and learning managers work assiduously to keep from double binding employees. Nevertheless, double binds can come up despite the best intentions, since having many managers in an organization inevitably creates low coordination of communication and policy. The best antidote is therefore to keep communication and trust as high as possible. **Metacommunication**, or communication about communication, is the key to prevention, much as it is critical to any operational phase of an organization that wishes to learn from itself.

Techniques and Practices to Become Fit for Managing from the Inside

This entire chapter has attempted to stress that the best management comes from an integration of action and reflection and that the learning manager is on duty whether at work or play, at home or at the office. Outmoded thinking stresses segmentation and compartmentalization of employees' lives. Contemporary managers are challenged to employ the whole person, not some fragmented part. The whole person uses adaptive skills and energies to manage life and living with family, friends, and community. A learning manager can make use of a whole life to become a better manager, not just what can be learned from management texts and on-the-job training.

How active listening contributes to awareness

Earlier we stressed the importance to managing from the inside of awareness and alertness to what is going on at all given moments. Any cue missed in the environment hurts one's ability to make sense of the world as well as to create any new sense of order or harmony from it. The importance of listening has been stressed in many places, yet it deserves primary attention in any section on techniques and practices to become fit for managing from the inside. We include the following quotation from Carl Rogers' recent book, *A Way of Being*, because it says so clearly what learning managers need to understand if they are to genuinely encourage openness, trust, and learning in the organization:

> . . . what I really dislike in myself is not being able to hear the other person because I am so sure in advance of what he is about to say that I don't listen. It is only afterward that I realize that I have heard what I have already decided he is saying; I have failed really to listen. Or even worse are those times when I catch myself trying to twist his message to make it say what I want him to say, and then only hearing that. This can be a very subtle thing, and it is surprising how skillful I can be in doing it. Just by twisting his words a small amount, by distorting his meaning just a little, I can make it appear that he is not only saying the thing I want to hear, but that he is the person I want him to be. Only when I realize through his protest or through my own gradual recognition that I am subtly manipulating him, do I become disgusted with myself. I know too, from being on the receiving end of this, how frustrating it is to be received for what you are not, to be heard as saying something which you have not said. This creates anger and bafflement and disillusion.[33]

Rogers' suggestions about **active listening** are enormously important for the learning manager. Perhaps most significant is the sense of humility he suggests must accompany any genuine attempt to understand others, to empathize with one's organizational associates.

We recommend that the learning manager practice five key skills to better understand employees and engender trust in the organization. Each of these skills requires the manager to focus on what the employee is saying in the present moment and to concentrate fully on the communication taking place. First, if there is any confusion about what the employee is saying, managers should try to restate their understanding of the comment. The following reply is one way to begin: "If I am hearing you correctly, you think that we should . . ." Second, the manager might invite the employee to continue talking if it appears that such prompting is needed. Comments such as, "I'd like to hear more about that idea," or open-ended questions that invite further contributions, instead of looking for answers the manager already possesses, are appropriate. Third, managers should always remember to touch base with the emotional response of employees to any communication event. Questions such as, "How do you feel about this change in schedule?" give employees the chance to level with the manager about their feelings. Fourth, the manager can make inferences that let the employee see that the manager is thinking ahead to the possible implications of the employee communication. Fifth, the manager should always be aware of the nonverbal content of the conversation. Employees are marvelous sensing instruments when it comes to nonverbal communication.

If the manager is not interested, is angry, or distracted, the employee will immediately pick up these nonverbal signals intuitively.

Without a focus on the present moment and the ability to be mindful of what is happening in the environment, the manager's work becomes a series of frustrations which are reflected in dysfunctional communications throughout the day. Given these conditions, it is easy and natural for employees to see themselves as part of the problem, not the solution. Good work does not come from angry, impatient, self-centered managers. Nor, as we have pointed out, can these behaviors be hidden successfully. The nonverbal communication of the manager continually gives the signals employees come to trust and rely on. For one last example, we include the most common nonverbal sign employees see: the eye dart of the manager to a watch or clock signaling impatience and time pressure. The wise employee stops talking immediately, for to continue is usually a waste of time. It should be clear to learning managers that they must get their own house in order before they can be expected to be a useful influence at work.

The significant contribution of film and drama to inner management

What about when the learning manager is not at work? As might be guessed, we feel that there is no time when the learning manager cannot be employed in inner management. Three of the many times when a great deal can be learned about management are when you are going to the movies, going to a play, or reading a novel or other literary work. We will provide examples of each.

A vast number of movies can teach us a great deal about management. MBA courses using film and literature are just now starting to become current in graduate business programs in the United States. Of course, any films with generals, presidents or sea captains as protagonists bring up important issues to a manager. Some examples include the following: charismatic leadership and the advisability of imposing one's will on followers in *Moby Dick*; pitfalls to avoid in first taking charge in *The Caine Mutiny*; getting the most out of your followers in *Stand and Deliver*; exploitation of your followers and issues of diversity in *Glory*; idiosyncratic behavior as leader in *Patton*; inadvisability of making discipline public in *Henry V*; miscommunication and failure to listen to the inner self in *The Remains of the Day*; and the unadulterated joy and "flow" of doing work that one loves in *Babette's Feast*, among countless others. To watch these films or to read the books on which they are based without thinking of one's role as a learning manager in a learning organization is a great mistake.[34]

In a similar way, drama brings up important issues for reflection. *Antigone*, the classic Greek play by Sophocles, is commonly used in academic workshops in the United States for large organizations to discuss the nature of "constructive loyalty" and development of the wisdom to know how the obsessive pride embodied in negative ego energy can blind one to knowing when to violate one's own rules. *Saint Joan* and *Major Barbara* by G. B. Shaw are two other plays that bring up significant issues for learning managers. American playwright Arthur Miller has written a number of plays that provide important insights into the nature of how and how not to manage in business situations. In *Death of a Salesman*, issues of dealing with burnout and with bankrupt dreams emerge. In *All My Sons*, Joe Keller, a factory owner building airplane engines during World War II, forgets his responsibility to the truth under the pressure of time and profits. He ships out engines with defects to save his reputation and business. Several of the engines fail, killing American servicemen. When Keller's son Larry, also a pilot, finds out about his father's crime, he commits suicide by crashing his plane. Keller finally comes to realize that unethical business conduct – in this case, making money for one's family at the expense of unknown fliers – is not any more morally acceptable when one thinks it is only to benefit one's family. The learning manager experiences the emotional impact of this tragedy and is able to relate it to his or her own consideration of family, personal pride, and career in relationship to the potential harm of unknown others in making business decisions.

The humanities can bring to life better than any management text what the learning manager needs to know to lead the organization effectively. While we have stressed the art of film and drama as helpful to the learning manager, a great many novels and short stories are also helpful. In fact, all human art forms contribute to the manager's ability to manage from the inside.

Additionally, much can be learned by the manager who carefully studies the history of great leaders, especially the lives of Jesus, the Buddha, Socrates, or other great religious leaders and philosophers. These leaders have at least three things in common: an unswerving devotion to the truth, a concern for others at the expense of their own safety and well-being, and a focus on every moment as of the highest importance. Clearly, anything we can learn or relearn about how to put these goals into practice in any aspect of life will be extremely helpful to us in our managerial roles in a learning organization.

Alerting the senses, meditation, and breath control

Mindfulness is a state of the highest significance for the manager who wishes to access inner management. It is derived from the Buddhist notion of becoming what you are doing by concentrating all your senses only on what you are doing. Thich Nhat Hanh describes it as "the miracle by which we master and restore ourselves."[35] He quotes Zen Master Thuong Chieu, who wrote, "If the practitioner knows his own mind clearly, he will obtain results with little effort. But if he does not know anything of his own mind, all of his efforts will be wasted."[36]

What exactly is this mindfulness? It is focusing completely on what you are doing. For example, when you are driving, it is being alert with all of your senses to every aspect of the act of driving, not thinking about arriving. It is stopping at yellow lights and taking the time to consider exactly what you are doing instead of seeing the yellow lights as a signal to accelerate. It is tasting, smelling, and thinking about your food instead of seeing a meal as a necessary but time-consuming interruption. It is the height of awareness and the antithesis of mind-wandering. It is living in the present moment, not in the past or future. It is the opposite of Type A behavior. And it must be practiced hourly if one is to become proficient at it. Incidentally, none of this excludes the need to plan for the future or to meet emergencies, two managerial necessities. It only suggests that behaving with total alertness allows one to be open to all the possibilities of a situation whereas trying to do three things at once, which many managers mistakenly consider a necessity, too often results in doing three things poorly.

A wide variety of books reference mindfulness and the need to include meditation as a way to develop proficiency. Meditation is a highly valued activity in the East that is very little understood by Western managers. However, many Western authors as well as medical doctors have come to understand its value in helping people learn to concentrate, providing deeper rest than sleep, and even adding years to one's life. This chapter cannot provide methodology on how to meditate, but we must emphasize the value of meditation in relieving stress and focusing energy before important events of the day begin. Additionally, we would be remiss if we did not stress the importance of breathing in connection with meditation and even mindfulness itself. As Nhat Hanh says, "Breath is the bridge which connects life to consciousness, which unites your body to your thoughts. Whenever your mind becomes scattered, use your breath as the means to take hold of your mind again."[37] He suggests the best way to combat stress is to breathe in while saying, "I breathe in and I am calm," and breathe out while saying, "I breathe out and I smile." In fact, for him, as well as for many Buddhist masters, proper breathing is more important than eating.

To connect our discussion more directly to a set of practical strategies, it may be useful to cite the work of Chopra once again. He proposes ten keys to active mastery of the inner life and takes a few pages to explain them. They are of sufficient interest to list them below:[38]

1 Listen to your body's wisdom, which expresses itself through signals of comfort and discomfort.
2 Live in the present, for it is the only moment you have.
3 Take time to be silent, to meditate, and to quiet the internal dialogue.
4 Relinquish the need for external approval.
5 When you find you are reacting with anger or opposition to any person or circumstance, realize that you are only struggling with yourself.
6 Know that "the world out there" reflects your reality "in here."
7 Shed the burden of judgment – you will feel much lighter.

8 Don't contaminate your body with toxins, either through food, drink, or toxic emotions.

9 Replace fear-motivated behavior with love-motivated behavior.

10 Understand that the physical world is just a mirror of a deeper intelligence.

Clearly, it is not possible for most managers to be completely successful in practicing these keys. However, they do constitute valuable strategies in pursuing the goal of holistic managing as well as achieving inner peace.

Developing the inner side of organizational members

If developing the inner side of oneself is critical to an effective learning manager, quite obviously, developing the inner side of one's employees and fellow organizational members must be equally as important. Clearly, it is incumbent upon such managers to assure the self-esteem and self-worth of their employees, to encourage the deployment of positive ego energy within the organization, to facilitate the conditions for reflection as well as action, to stimulate creativity, intuition, effective visualization, and attention to the moment, and to generally assure the best chance for a sense of flow to pervade the workplace. This will require managers to do such things as persuade people of their competence and ability to develop in areas in which they are not currently competent. It will require setting aside time, perhaps in off-site retreats but not solely on special occasions, for the purpose of reflection and deference to the inner self. It will necessitate the elimination of blaming and its replacement by genuine problem-solving in shared responsibility teams. And it will require reward of employee developmental activities such as growth experiences and education. In short, managers who are committed to their own inner growth lose credibility if they are not equally committed to that of their peers and those who report to them.

Human Resource Ramifications of Managing From the Inside

Earlier in this chapter, we mentioned several general barriers to this approach such as lack of feedback, belief in carrot-and-stick motivation, lack of trust, and organizational double-binding patterns. It is probably not possible to adopt a learning approach without also giving serious thought to modification and change of several familiar institutional human resource strategies and policies. In the current chapter, we can only suggest some of the areas requiring attention. Nevertheless, they are areas that have long gone only weakly challenged, and that now must undergo a severe challenge as part of the thought process necessary to design a learning organization with learning managers.

Significance of a healthy work environment

We believe it is the learning manager's responsibility to pay close attention to the working environment of employees and help them make that place one of healthful living and attractiveness. Sterility and even ugliness are all too common in the workplace. We think it is self-defeating to ask employees to give their best when they are surrounded by gray, antiseptic, unpleasant environments. Clean, bright colors reflect life and living where creative thinking and concern for quality can best be called forth. Managers should be aware of the irony involved in asking employees to pay attention to details of quality when in paying attention they will clearly see the low regard management has for them as evidenced by the ugliness of the surroundings. Managers should take every chance they get to involve employees in designing working environments which promote creative, healthful living. Cleaning up the workplace and making it genuinely livable and workable is a clear signal to employees that management is ready to get serious about business. It is difficult to expect either managers or employees to be spiritually and psychologically committed to an organization that does not seem to value its own environment.

Implications for jobs

Jobs as we have known them are undergoing vast changes as organizations become more oriented to learning. They are no longer the static set of functions and responsibilities that they used to be. With the advent of the self-managing team, as well as the dynamic nature of advancing technology and the changing home and family needs of the workforce, jobs no longer remain the same for 90 days at a time. Now that we are discussing the need to tap the positive ego energy of all employees and to honor the interdisciplinary nature of managerial and, indeed, employee vision in a corporate world where one's survival depends on change, restricting employees to the confines of the usual ten-function job description seems ludicrous. Additionally, employees in the learning organization are expected to develop in many directions and to assist in a variety of ways in achieving the goal of improved quality of product as well as employee life. They can hardly be restricted to an obsolete job description.

Obsolescence of the performance appraisal system

The annual performance appraisal in which you spend an hour or so with your boss discussing, or even battling over, a series of subjective ratings, whose "validity" you must acknowledge by your signature, has long been as obsolete as the job description it no longer matches. Now, if learning managers are interested in developing their employees "for excellence" on shared responsibility teams and encouraging them to be partners in the development of the organization itself, this performance system is in the way.[39] In its place, in keeping with the new focus on two-way or 360-degree feedback which we have discussed, will be a system of managers and employees regularly seeking input from each other on a project-by-project basis. Feedback of this sort requires all those providing it to be specific and objective; it decries the possibility of reducing a year's activity to a set of eight or ten numbers or ratings. It focuses far more strongly on the developmental aspect than the evaluative, in keeping with the philosophy of a learning organization. The old notion of the importance of appraisal is not totally dead. Managers are still responsible for guiding and assessing their employees. However, now employees along with other stakeholders are responsible for returning the favor. And all will fail unless they provide detail, objectivity and timeliness, and feel free to speak their mind instead of avoiding the truth or responding to hidden agendas.

Pay secrecy policies as an obstacle

Despite the prevalence in many organizations of pay secrecy policies requiring employees not to divulge their salaries or raises, these policies fly directly in the face of the concept of a learning organization. They are also an impediment to the learning manager who is, after all, attempting to develop an environment of trust and reinforcement for the deployment of positive ego energy. Secrecy says, we don't trust you with this information. Or, alternatively, it says, if you find this out, you will see that we have made many mistakes and may be in the process of one now. It also says, by corollary, that although there may be good reasons for why the compensation system here seems distorted and unfair, we don't think you are smart enough to understand them and we don't think we are smart or articulate enough to explain them to you. In any case, you may be too emotional to handle the knowledge.

We think that there is no place for such implied communication in a learning organization. It devalues the employee and it devalues the manager. Instead, employees need to know why they are being paid the way they are so that they can utilize this information to be better at what they do. If they find certain achievements and qualities rewarded at their organization, then they need to learn how to duplicate these achievements and qualities for the betterment of themselves as well as their organization. After all, how people are paid is perhaps the most telling of feedback systems, especially after worker supply and job demand factors are accounted for. Such an important feedback system must be available to all, just as it is in union and government environments.

The United States legal system is leading the way in questioning the need for secrecy in a great many aspects of organizational life, but we don't think it will be long before many other countries' legal systems follow that lead with regard to what can be made available to the public, including organizational members. For those who live in a democracy and work in a truly participative and empowered environment, knowledge of pay is too great a part of learning what is valued not to be shared throughout the organization. For these reasons, and since it is relatively hard to police anyway, we think pay secrecy as a policy will slowly erode and disappear over the next several years. Learning managers must take advantage of this trend for their own sake and that of their organizations.

Selection and promotion policies that can help

Selection and promotion are probably two of the most important human resource functions in an organization. Most managers feel that if they could just hire the right people for the right positions in the first place, most of their problems would be solved. All employees in an organization carefully observe the qualifications and belief systems of new hires and promotees for clues about the values and corporate strategy of the upper management members who have made the hiring decisions. In a learning organization, employees, themselves, would be involved in the search and placement process for both new hires and promotions. Workers have an important stake in their new colleagues since all are likely to be working together on teams and focus groups sharing similar goals. Certainly, managers make the decisions, but in an organization that values feedback and participation, all must be involved to some degree. Also, managers will have an opportunity to reinforce what is valued in discussions to prepare for the hiring process. Such philosophical discussions help to solidify understanding of the organizational culture among all those involved. A significant benefit is that this policy will pay dividends as employees who have a share of the decision will be more likely to help their new colleagues develop, and to be vested in their success, since they were involved in the hiring decision. In addition, promotion policies can demonstrate to employees the rewards that are possible with successful development. Of course, it is clearly not always appropriate to promote rather than to hire from outside, but it should usually be done when possible. The message of passing over inside candidates to hire from outside can be very discouraging unless it is carefully handled.

Discipline as self-discipline

If discipline is to be used by the learning manager in the service of promoting employee growth in a learning organization, it cannot be something done to people who don't "shape up" or "toe the line." In an environment of open communication, it must become self-discipline. Employees must all feel a stake in the importance of their shared mission. They must either articulate their own rules for dealing with counterproductive behaviors or, at a minumum, help to enforce existing rules and policies in which they feel ownership. In a learning organization, managers continue to hold employees accountable for their promises and basic behavior agreements but employees are more motivated to maintain discipline because they realize its place in learning and developing. They are quicker to take responsibility for their work and behavior when their ideas and feedback are valued. "Acting out" is a form of negative ego energy and usually occurs in an attempt to become noticed, except for those cases of people with severe psychological or personal problems. With the advent of employee assistance programs (EAPs) and the cooperation demonstrated in teams, these problems are being handled more responsibly than ever. In a learning organization, it is rare to give up on an employee. The assumption that all employees can learn and grow, just as the organization can, is critical to the foundation upon which such an organization must rest.

Conclusion

Peter Senge, proponent of the "learning organization," traces the management application of the concept of the interrelationships among small changes people make in organizations and how the smallest changes affect the entire system.[40] According to Senge, "small changes can produce big results – but the areas of the highest leverage are often the least obvious."[41] Although he does not specifically address the subject of inner management in the same way we have, he does dwell on the notions of personal mastery and the importance of building shared visions. He emphasizes the principle that learning employees can change, and that the total of their changes can add up to a greater whole for the organization. We have suggested that the search has to begin within, in the vast, largely untapped potential of human beings to transcend their environment through peak experiences, flow, mindfulness, even control of their involuntary bodily functions. A wide variety of writers have attested to this untapped physical, mental, and spiritual potential. In an organizational era of self-managed teams and increased cooperation, the value of developmental vision in an organization is too great to overlook.

In this chapter, we have presented an overview of the required psychological elements to managing from the inside as well as the characteristics of such management. We have discussed some of the barriers to such an approach and how they might be overcome. We have also described a number of techniques and practices – some originating from the East and some from the West – that must become part of the resources of learning managers who realize they must progress in this direction. Throughout, we have stressed the need to integrate action and reflection. And we have introduced the vast human resource ramifications of the entire approach, including the necessity and direction for change that is essential to learning organizations. If managers are to expect and encourage learning, they must have the support of their organization. But beyond that support, they must look inside as well as outside for the vision and energy to fulfill the mission of maximizing the development of human potential for their organizations.

Notes

1 Ronnie Lessem, *Developmental Management: Principles of Holistic Business* (Oxford: Blackwell, 1990), and Jagdish Parikh, *Managing Your Self: Management by Detached Involvement* (Oxford: Blackwell, 1991).

2 David Kolb, *Experiential Learning: Experiences as the Source of Learning and Development* (Englewood Clifts, NJ: Prentice-Hall, 1984).

3 Mihaly Csikszentmihalyi, *Flow: The Psychology of Optimal Experience* (New York: Harper & Row, 1991), p. 4.

4 Tim Gallwey, *The Inner Game of Tennis* (New York: Random House, 1974) and *Inner Tennis: Playing the Game* (New York: Random House, 1976).

5 Victor Vroom, *Work and Motivation* (Melbourne, FL: R. E. Krieger, 1982, originally published 1964).

6 Albert Bandura, *Social Foundations of Thought and Action: A Social Cognitive Theory* (Englewood Clifts, NJ: Prentice-Hall, 1986).

7 Abraham Maslow, *Motivation and Personality* (New York: Harper & Bros., 1954, 1970), and *Religions, Values, and Peak-Experiences* (New York: Viking, 1970).

8 See M. Seligman, *Learned Optimism* (New York: A. A. Knopf, 1991).

9 Ibid.

10 In the United States, tens of millions of government dollars have been spent on raising self-esteem in public-school children.

11 See R. Kilmann et al., *Managing Ego Energy* (San Francisco: Jossey-Bass, 1994).

12 W. Ferris, "Mobilizing ego energy", in Kilmann et al., p. 202.

13 J. Laabs, "Ben and Jerry's caring capitalism", *Hartwick College Classic Leadership Cases* (Hartwick College: Oneonta, NY, 1993), p. 35.

14 Deepak Chopra, *Ageless Body, Timeless Mind: The Quantum Alternative to Growing Old* (Glendale, CA: Harmony Books, 1993).

15 See M. Seligman, *What You Can Change and What You Can't* (New York: A. A. Knopf, 1994).

16 Warren Bennis and Bert Nanus, *Leaders: The Strategies for Taking Charge* (New York: Harper & Row, 1985).

17 See, for example, Alvin Toffler, *Powershift: Knowledge, Wealth, and Violence at the Edge of the 21st Century* (New York: Bantam, 1990).

18 Jagdish Parikh, Friedrich Neubauer and Alden G. Lank, *Intuition: The New Frontier of Management* (Oxford: Blackwell, 1994).

19 See also W. A. Agor (ed.), *Intuition in Organizations: Leading and Managing Productively* (Beverly Hills, CA: Sage, 1989).

20 Thomas Moore, *Care of the Soul: A Guide for Cultivating Depth and Sacredness in Everyday Life* (New York: Harper Collins, 1992), and Jack Kornfield, *A Path with Heart: A Guide through the Perils and Promises of Spiritual Life* (New York: Bantam Books, 1993).

21 Moore, p. 5.

22 Ibid., p. 9.

23 Kornfield, p. 29.

24 K. Blanchard and S. Johnson, *The One Minute Manager* (Berkeley, CA: Berkeley Books, 1983), p. 67.

25 William Ouchi, *Theory Z: How American Business Can Meet the Japanese Challenge* (New York: Avon, 1993), pp. 95–6.

26 See M. E. McGill and J. W. Slocum, Jr., *The Smarter Organization: How to Build a Business that Learns and Adapts to Marketplace Needs* (New York: Wiley, 1994), pp. 225–6.

27 Al Huang and Jerry Lynch, *Thinking Body, Dancing Mind: Tao Sports for Extraordinary Performance in Athletics, Business, and Life* (New York: Bantam Books, 1992).

28 Frederick Herzberg, *Motivation to Work.*

29 B. F. Skinner, *Walden Two* (New York: Macmillan, 1976).

30 Stephen Covey, *The Seven Habits of Highly Effective People* (New York: Simon and Schuster, 1989).

31 Stephen Covey, *Principle-Centered Leadership* (New York: Simon and Schuster, 1992).

32 Carl Rogers, *Freedom to Learn* (Columbus, OH: Charles E. Merrill, Macmillan, 1969).

33 Carl Rogers, *A Way of Being* (Boston: Houghton Mifflin, 1980), p. 13.

34 For a powerful novel (made into a less than inspiring film) that can teach an immense amount about how to manage effectively, see Richard Adams, *Watership Down* (New York: Avon Books, 1975). For an account of the use of fiction in teaching MBA and undergraduate management courses, see William Ferris, "A Humanistic Approach to Leadership Skill-Building," in J. Bigelow (ed.), *Managerial Skills* (Beverly Hills, CA: Sage, 1991), pp. 54–70.

35 Thich Nhat Hanh, *The Miracle of Mindfulness* (Boston: Beacon Press, 1987), p. 14. See also T. Hanh, *Peace is Every Step* (Boston: Beacon Press, 1991).

36 Hanh, *Miracle of Mindfulness*, p. 37.

37 Ibid., p. 15.

38 Chopra, *Ageless Body, Timeless Mind*, pp. 258–260.

39 D. Bradford and A. Cohen, *Managing for Excellence* (New York: Wiley, 1984).

40 Peter Senge, *The Fifth Discipline: The Art and Practice of the Learning Organization* (New York: Doubleday, 1990), as well as P. M. Senge et al., *The Fifth Discipline Handbook: Strategies and Tools for Building a Learning Organization* (New York: Doubleday, 1994).

41 Senge, *Fifth Discipline*, p. 63.

4

The Playing Fields of Learning
Kathleen DeChant

Introduction

Webster gives 14 definitions for the word, "play." Inherent in most of these definitions is the idea of taking active part in something: whether it be a game, a performance, or some other activity. In the same dictionary, the word "field" is identified as "an area where practical work is done . . ." and "an area of observation." It's interesting to link and reflect on these definitions in combination. They imply that a playing field might be construed as an engagement in a relatively pragmatic experience which can be observed, or perhaps even reflected upon. For children, this might translate into "playing house" or "playing cops and robbers," where play tries to imitate life, and imagination is a substitute for experience.

For adults, playing fields will, of course, be different. Previously acquired knowledge, as well as experimental behavior, is applied to real life or simulated but realistic scenarios. For most adults employed by business organizations, playing fields can range from classroom settings in training programs to challenging job assignments. What is learned will vary with the nature of the playing field, the experience itself, and the learning abilities of the players. Learning outcomes will tend to be task-centered and solution-oriented.

Understanding such "playing fields" is like piecing together a puzzle: there are a number of parts that must fit together before a total picture emerges. The individual, the learning process, and the context in which learning takes place constitute the key pieces. This chapter will explore the puzzle by looking at:

- the "players," that is, people who work in organizations, and the kinds of playing, that is, learning skills, necessary for successful performance and personal development;
- the "games" or methods, to see how they can be constructed or approached to maximize the potential for learning;
- the "fields" of learning, or the organizational environment in which learning is expected to take place to determine what impedes or facilitates learning.

Playing Skills . . . Or, What Makes People Effective at Learning?

In today's firms, the pace of change and the heat of competition calls for workers who are effective at "learning on the run," who are capable of shifting mindsets and acting innovatively, and who can engage others in collaborative learning so that both they and their organizations learn. The first step in building continuous learning skill is to know what is meant by learning at the individual and group levels.

Behavioral and cognitive theorists differ in their definitions of learning while social theorists offer a third view. For behavioralists, the learning is in the action; for cognitive theorists, the learning is in the thinking; and for social theorists, it is a combination of both. What is the definitive position today? In truth, there is no one universally accepted definition for learning.[1] Several years ago a study conducted by Saljo[2] asked a number of people what they meant by learning. Their answers revealed five different conceptions of varying complexity:

1 An **increase in knowledge** which portrays learning more in terms of an outcome than a process. Knowledge for knowledge's sake.
2 **Memorizing**. The transfer of units from an expert source into the learner's head.
3 The **acquisition of knowledge which has practical utility** and is applicable to current problems.
4 The **abstraction of meaning**. Viewing what is learned beyond the context of the situation as potentially applicable to other situations.
5 An **interpretive process**, aimed at understanding meaning. A process in which the learner views what is learned in relation to his/her values and experience and the outside world.

Apart from viewing the responses as a variety of definitions, we can also say they represent points along a continuum of learning from lesser to greater complexity, requiring lower to higher level skills.[3] This, in turn, suggests that there is a broader concept that needs to be considered when discussing learning and that is **the ability to learn how to learn** and to **differentiate among situations with respect to the type of learning skills required**. Learning, then, is the acquisition of content and the development of a repertoire of approaches to new learning. Adults who are skilled at learning have, as a result of engaging in various learning experiences throughout their lives, been able to develop competence in learning how to learn. Furthermore, the more skilled learners hold a concept of themselves as learners and seek to increase their learning competence as they move through new experiences.

Learning how to learn

Why are some people more competent at learning than others, particularly learning from experience? Several years ago a study by the Center for Creative

Leadership in Greensboro, North Carolina, discovered that when managers were exposed to the same types of job assignments, high performing managers reported they learned more than those whose performance was average. What factors accounted for the difference? Can the findings of this study be extended to others? If so, how? There are many theories around what is involved in developing learning skill. Limited space prevents me from reviewing the extent or nature of these theories. Instead, I will focus on what is for me the key competency, that is, the ability to give direction to and take responsibility for our learning activities and behavior.[4] This ability is generally described as **knowing how to learn**. Through the exercise of what Langer calls "mindfulness,"[5] we become aware of ourselves as learners in every situation and subsequently come to exercise greater control over our learning strategies. Practicing such mindfulness increases the probability that learning will happen.

Because new job assignments are, for most people, the source of new knowledge or skill, they present a perfect opportunity to practice mindfulness. The goal of mindfulness in learning from job assignments is to increase one's learning by exercising greater intent, control, and deliberation in approaching the task. This is possible to do if one considers (a) the key inputs to the assignment, (b) the learning needs of oneself and others involved in the assignment, (c) optimal strategies to meet these learning needs, and (d) sources of feedback on one's performance as a means of identifying additional learning needs and resources.[6] The strategic framework for learning mindfulness presents an approach for tackling new job assignments which addresses these four dimensions.

Learning inputs	Learning needs	Learning methods	Feedback
Situational history	My learning needs	Formal learning strategies	Sources of feedback
Vision of assignment at completion	Others' learning needs	Informal learning strategies	Methods of obtaining feedback
Personal history of applicable strengths			Implications of feedback for additional learning
Organization context			

The first column, **learning inputs**, focuses on the factors surrounding the assignment that will determine what needs to be learned and who will be involved in the learning process. The learner needs to ask the following questions to get at the context for the assignment or situational history, the ultimate vision of the assignment's outcome or end results, the learner's personal history of applicable strengths, and the organizational context in which the assignment is embedded.

1 What is the significance of this project to the organization? What implications does this have for what needs to be learned and who needs to be involved in my learning?
2 Has anyone done anything similar to this assignment before? What can be learned from that person's experience?
3 What is my vision of this assignment? How do others see it?
4 What have I done before that I can apply to this assignment?
5 What skills, abilities, and knowledge do I have that are relevant to this assignment?
6 What organizational beliefs, values, or assumptions will be affected by this assignment? What resistance might challenges to these provoke?

Based on responses to these questions, the learner is ready to outline the **learning needs** of him/herself and others. "Others" refers to anyone in the organization whose input, approval, cooperation or compliance will be needed to complete the assignment. The learner should consider him/herself as a facilitator of the "education" of these people. Knowledge of the assignment and what it entails will be important for gaining support in whatever form necessary.

Once learning needs have been uncovered, tactics, or **learning methods**, for addressing these needs must be identified and planned. These tactics might include formal learning events such as attending a training program or, more likely, a series of informal learning situations that might include conversations with key people, meetings, visits to field operations offices, reading documents, and so forth.

Finally, as the learner progresses through an assignment, it is critical to obtain **feedback** on initiatives taken. Such feedback is a good source of information about learning needs that remain to be met.

The experience of an engineer I will call Ray is a good example of how mindfulness in a job assignment can make a difference. Ray was charged with introducing a new technology for detecting the presence of high voltage in telephone lines. At the outset of this task, he took the time to use the Strategic Framework for Learning Mindfulness to plot his course. With respect to situational history, he learned that an earlier technology that was used several years ago had proved unreliable. Consequently, most of the linemen were skeptical of all technology for this purpose. In addition, the organization was generally resistant to change, particularly those which were not mandated by corporate engineering. He decided, as a result, that he needed to find a champion in engineering and a few of the newer linesmen who would be willing to support the new technology. He would "educate" them on the nature and benefits of the new technology.

In terms of his strengths, Ray counted on the fact that he had been successful introducing new ideas in the past. Regarding his learning needs, he had to become thoroughly familiar with the device and how it worked under the most adverse conditions. He also needed to compare it to the earlier, less reliable, technology as well to determine its advantages.

With respect to others' learning needs, Ray believed both managers and linesmen needed to understand the new technology. In particular, management needed to know the costs and benefits associated with it. To meet these learning needs (his and others), Ray attended a demonstration of the technology, tested it out at difficult locations, discussed the procedures for working around high voltage with several company representatives, and developed a report for management on the details of his findings, stressing the merits of his recommendation. He was open to feedback throughout his project, modifying his strategy accordingly. After the technology was successfully introduced in a pilot region, he monitored it against accident reports to support wider usage.

As demonstrated by this example, the benefits of mindfulness in learning are many. Candy points out that

. . . stepping back from a task, stepping outside ourselves, enables us to consider how it can best be accomplished and to examine and shape our thoughts, feelings, and actions . . . it (enables) us to examine, imagine, choose, design, and manage the experiences we have, to shape our own evolution through many transformations in one lifetime.[7]

Collective learning

In today's learning organizations, teams are integral to both individual learning and organizational learning processes. As Senge indicates, "Team learning is vital because teams, not individuals, are the fundamental learning unit in modern organizations. This is where the rubber meets the road; unless teams learn, the organization cannot learn."[8] The use of task forces, committees, problem-solving teams, self-managed work teams, and high performing teams has become a standard practice in most firms.

In discussing team learning, we need to recognize that it is different from individual learning because it is a shared experience with shared outcomes. The learning is collective in nature. As such, what it takes for groups to learn is different in many ways from what it takes for individuals to learn.

However, just as learning mindfulness increases the likelihood for individuals that learning will be enhanced and increased, this applies also to teams. When a team, for example, frames itself as a learning group, its experiences and effectiveness are changed qualitatively.[9] A goal of "learning" is more open-ended than a goal of "getting the task accomplished." It encourages generative thinking on the part of the team. Individual members who are released from the single-minded focus of task accomplishment feel more freedom to engage in associative thinking. They also find it easier to alter their own mindsets if they feel they are trying to learn as a route to achieving goals.

Mezirow and Senge both insist that the ability to engage in transformative or generative learning depends on the ability to identify and suspend assumptions in order to subject these assumptions to rational evaluation.[10] This is easier said than done. However, by framing work as a learning process, group members find it easier to dissociate themselves from particular visions of the ultimate team product or task accomplishment.[11] In most instances, the act of creating a learning mindfulness in the service of achieving a task promotes dialogue among members and produces collectively constructed knowledge – the heart of team learning.

Learning mindfulness can be achieved by first paying attention to the learning processes of the team (see figure 4.1). These processes consist of **collective thinking and acting** which are usually inextricable linked together. Teams "think" using two cognitive or mental processes called **framing** and **reframing**. Framing is the initial perception of an issue, situation, person, or object based on past understanding and present input. An example of framing in a team's learning process is its perception of its purpose when it is first assigned a task or project. When this perception is changed as a result of group discussion or analysis, the learning process of reframing has occurred. In this example, reframing involves challenging the team's initial mandate or hammering out consensus among members as to the nature of the mandate.[12]

Collective thinking processes are usually paired with action. In fact, action frequently "reshapes what we are doing while we are doing it."[13] In team learning, two forms of action stand out: **experimenting** and **boundary crossing**.

Experimenting can be systematic and scientific or it can occur as a result of trial and error. A team can set up an experiment with a set of planned conditions, observe the results, and learn from what happens. Or it can experiment serendipitously, running ideas up the organizational flagpole to see what happens. The team can do this as a collectivity or a few members can experiment on its behalf.

Boundaries are the intangible lines that separate person from person, group from group, and group from organization. Team members cross boundaries when they ask for help, collaborate with someone inside or outside the group to accomplish a task, or actively seek or listen to another's opinion. Boundary crossing involves bringing into the team the ideas, insights, information, or data from the outside to facilitate its learning and thus its movement toward its goal.

The final component in the team learning process links thinking and action. It is called **integrating perspectives**. This is a synthesis process in which divergent views and new input merge through group member dialogue resulting in collectively held understandings. Reframing generally occurs as a result of integrating perspectives. Thus, when a marketing team examines input from customers and salespeople, then, as a result of collective discussion, revises its views of what a new product launch should look like, it has integrated perspectives and reframed.

INTEGRATING PERSPECTIVES

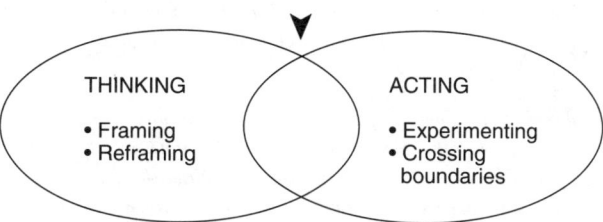

Figure 4.1   Team learning processes.

Teams can become conscious of their learning processes by reflecting on questions which pertain to the team learning processes.

1 Do we challenge our assumptions? With what results? (Framing/Reframing)
2 What can we do to make sure we get and use input from people inside and outside our group? (Boundary crossing)
3 What can be done to create an atmosphere where team members feel free to experiment with new behaviors and ideas? (Experimenting)
4 How can we work at developing a better integration of our diverse views and knowledge in the service of our mission? (Integrating perspectives)

In newly formed teams or those that are dysfunctional, these learning processes are not used very much. Individuals may be learning, but as a whole, the group is not learning. The processes are inhibited by barriers posed by individual differences, by varied levels of commitment to the team's not yet understood or agreed upon mission, and by diverse professional or organizational backgrounds of group members. The individual viewpoints of most members are largely unknown because sharing does not go much beyond giving superficial or safe information. Members are hesitant to test out their ideas, and personal viewpoints are generally withheld by some members. A team at this stage is a **fragmented learning group**.

The Production Systems Team in the MIS Department of the Brewster Company (pseudonym), a large paper manufacturing company, illustrates what I mean by a fragmented learning group. The following are excerpts from interviews with team members. Here are their responses to the question, how does your team work?[14]

> *Nick: It's still piecemeal; there's no one major project that . . . everyone in the group is working on. . . . there's a group of us – subgroups if you will – that are working on certain projects, but the team itself is not working on one massive project. It's a team, I guess, because we're working on related projects, but I don't know if it's truly a team. . . . I think we're still trying to find a definition ourselves.*

John: (We) never really acted as a team so (we) never really took on any endeavor as a team. Everybody was working on their own and the only team work we really did was when everybody would come back and report what they're working on. . . . It was this person doing his own thing, come back and say how things are going for them. But as far as trying to tackle anything as one unit, one team, they never really attempted that.

Roland: It definitely isn't one of the most cohesive teams, and the reason I feel that we are not as cohesive as the other teams, the mix of backgrounds we had on that team was really diverse as far as the technologies worked with, the backgrounds we came from . . . so I think we are more diverse than most of the other teams and I think that contributes to a lack of cohesion.

Walt: We started out kind of fumbling around saying, "well, we've got to do something different" from just wondering what's going on and then we decided to meet every day at 9 a.m. so we could at least say "if we're supposed to be communicating and talking to each other about what's going on and looking at what needs to be done, what resources are available, priorities are to do that, we better just discipline ourselves to start communicating."

These perspectives from four of the five members of the Production Systems Team illustrate the single issue that became the bane of its existence, that is, the inclination of people to think and act as individuals rather than as members of a team.

When a group moves past this stage, members offer individual views but frequently defend them as the team seeks to find the one best perspective rather than hammer out shared meaning through integration and shaping of members' multiple views. Teams at this stage of learning are usually more effective at operating within existing paradigms; they are not generally open to breaking new ground or challenging strongly held organizational assumptions. A team at this stage is a **pooled learning group**. Teams operate at a pooled learning level where they are capable of problem-solving and decision-making, but not necessarily innovation.

When teams reach the stage where the learning processes are used frequently and well, they become **synergistic learning groups**. For example, teams at this level actively experiment with new ideas and behaviors, adding to both member and group capability. Members are committed to their roles as team players, pulling together their ideas, skills, and resources to create, innovate, and challenge. The team actively constructs new knowledge, often altering or discarding individual members' long-standing assumptions and beliefs in order to accomplish the team's mission.

A team's level of learning is related to its maturity but is also framed by its task. Many relatively experienced groups can function well at the pooled learning level. High-performing teams or teams charged with accomplishing an innovative or groundbreaking task, however, generally must operate at the synergistic level in order to be effective.

The Games: Effective Strategies for Creating Learning Experiences

What I hear, I cannot remember.
What I see, I do remember.
What I do, I understand.
Chinese Proverb

Researcher Annie Pyle interviewed 100 senior executives about the practice of running large organizations and management development practices that assure quality performance: ". . . all spoke of learning and experience . . . in the context of other issues."[15] They found it difficult to speak of learning when it was separated from experience. Their learning was in the "doing" of daily work. We turn, now, to the second piece of the learning puzzle, the "games" or methods by which people learn at work.

Learning in today's organizations can be described in terms of the human resources development matrix illustrated. Along one axis initiatives range from those which are structured or formal to those that are incidental or informal. The other axis refers to the initiator of the learning – from self-directed to organizationally directed.

FORMAL		
	• Degree programs	• Teleconferences
	• Outside conferences	• Training programs
	• Professional organizations	• Offsite conferences
		• Learning laboratories
	• Self-initiated and self-planned experiences in job assignments	• Self-managed teams
		• Action learning
	• Coaching/mentoring exchanges	• Performance discussions using self-ratings
INFORMAL	• Networking	
	SELF-DIRECTED	*ORGANIZATIONALLY*
		DIRECTED

The most effective approaches to human resource development fit the environment of today's organizations where time is at a premium and where learning must be problem-centered and immediately applicable. At the same time, such approaches meet the needs of individuals as adult learners; that is, they enable them to:

• learn continually and informally as they adjust to changes in their roles and organizational situations;

- actively participate in the learning process;
- learn in light of varying individual characteristics;
- capitalize upon past experiences as a resource in learning.

Which are the learning methods that fit the criteria outlined above? Any methods where learning is centered around the acquisition of information or **knowledge that** as well as the skills to apply it, or **knowledge how** will do the job. They include classroom simulations, outdoor adventure learning, and action learning.

Simulations

Before an individual can be an airline pilot, an air traffic controller, or a reactor operator, that individual learns the set of complex skills required for the job in a simulated environment where mistakes won't result in lost lives or widespread property destruction. This makes perfect sense, doesn't it? Developing skills on the job in these professions is really not a feasible option. While the jobs of managers and other key people in organizations such as engineers, designers, planners, and analysts may not have as dramatic an impact, their mistakes can involve both legal and financial risk. While knowledge that can be imparted in classroom settings, knowledge how can really only come from hands-on time at the controls.

In such cases, a simulation is an appropriate strategy to use to develop the skills people need. Simulations can be designed to parallel the work environment. A simulation is "a structured learning experience addressing a learner's entire range of on-the-job performance or a subset of that range including the most critical performance."[16] A simulation goes beyond the normal classroom experiential exercise. Such exercises generally focus on a set of concepts taught at an earlier time. Simulations require learners to bring past experience to bear as well as new concepts recently learned in a situation or setting that parallels what the participant will encounter on the job.

In some instances, the simulations go beyond building skills that will be used daily. They can be designed to pose "what if" scenarios to provoke new thinking and instill proactivity in the learners. Simulated environments often operate over several time periods called "rounds," where job proficiency is developed over time through the acquisition and application of complex decision-making and problem-solving skills in increasingly difficult situations. An example of such a simulation is one that focuses on product development, in which product managers learn to increase the firm's number of new products while at the same time reducing product development/introduction cycle times and managing the existing portfolio.

The latest addition to the micro world of simulations is what is known as a flight simulator, which involves the use of computers. The MIT Sloan School has produced several ready-to-use simulators including the well-known People

Express Management Flight Simulator which is available on Macintosh and MS Windows. You start this simulation by taking over an airline company with just three planes and gross revenues of $32 million a year. You face decisions in the areas of human resources, aircraft acquisition, marketing, pricing, and service scope. Depending on the quality of your decision-making, you can either fly the airline into the clouds of prosperity or bring it crashing into the ground of bankruptcy. Continual feedback provided via the computer allows you to observe and reflect on the impact of your decisions.

Strategy flight simulators allow management teams to test-fly strategic options without actually crashing the business. Such a simulator was a choice of Deutsche Aerospace AG of Germany, a heavy industry where trial-and-error learning on the job is a high risk activity that can be extremely costly. Actual and "what if?" scenarios are built into the computer model to challenge existing views and promote out-of-box thinking. At Royal Dutch Shell, simulators incorporating systems thinking have been used since the early 1980s. Recent business applications have included the rapid evaluation of a wide variety of options to improve the efficiency of the logistic operation of a Singapore refinery, the quantification of strategic options for one of its European operations, and modeling a new recruitment system.

Action learning

Action learning is growing in popularity as a method for creating a playing field for learning. In my estimation the recent success of action learning can be attributed to several facts:

1 It involves actually taking action on real organizational issues, not just recommending action or analyzing someone else's problems. The organization receives an immediate benefit and, in effect, learns, too.
2 Participants learn with and through each other, promoting individual and group development.
3 The learning is in the performing. Participants have a vested interest in getting results and are recognized accordingly.
4 The skills developed are reapplicable because they have been developed in the context of the participants' organization.

In brief, action learning is a process in which a small group of people, usually five, work together in what is known as a set on real problems which have no preset solutions. The diagnosis is based on real-life contacts with real people, not merely on statistics or a written account drafted by a third party, as in business cases or most classroom simulations. Each action learning set has a project adviser whose role is to help enrich the experience by highlighting all the learning opportunities for the individuals and their teams. The advisers guide the teams through active reflection on their actions. Reflection of this kind helps team members confront their own experiences and theories, altering them as needed. Such reflection is necessary if the learning is to transcend the action learning situation and become transferable to future situations.

An interesting example of the kinds of individual, team, and organizational learning that can emerge from a playing field created by taking an action learning approach is the Grace Cocoa experience. Currently, Grace Cocoa, a subsidiary of W. R. Grace, Inc., is the world's largest industrial supplier of chocolate ingredients, such as cocoa powder. It processes 12 percent of all the cocoa beans in the world. With 16 locations in nine countries, it is an international company with around $700 million in annual sales. Grace Cocoa was created from two different companies owned by W. R. Grace for over 25 years and some smaller acquisition made around the time of the merger. A reorganization into three large business divisions was only the first step in shaping the new company. Each organization had a different culture; there was little cross-functional contact. A survey of top managers revealed some very specific needs at the individual, group, and company levels:[17]

- teamwork to facilitate cross-functional/divisional group efforts;
- trust development to enhance fair and predictable behavior;
- leadership skill development to work cross-functionally, cross-culturally, and globally;
- communication techniques to ensure that relevant information reached employees, enabling them to do their job;
- conflict management in cross-cultural settings;
- innovation and continuous improvement to ensure future competitiveness;
- global employee development career paths.

An action learning program was created which ran for four weeks in five to six day sessions over the course of six months. The first participants to be selected were managers at relatively high levels whose jobs required them to interact on a global basis. They were assembled into cross-functional, cross-cultural, and cross-organizational teams of five people each. Issues were identified in four areas: quality, customer needs, new product development, and logistics; each team was assigned a single area.

On an individual level, participants have acquired a renewed commitment to self-development and continuous learning. At the team level, they have learned to work effectively in groups, specifically with respect to the importance of clarifying goals, putting together operating norms, identifying roles and responsibilities, sharing leadership, and exchanging information to increase team and organizational learning. At the organizational level, the New Products Team produced over 100 new ideas and generated the first consolidated worldwide product guide. The Customer Needs team created a new global strategic process to enhance customer satisfaction. The Logistics team has generated annual savings of $1.5 million. The Quality team has put together a seven-phase program to address quality issues.

Individuals learned, teams learned, and so did Grace Cocoa. This second result is a major benefit of action learning programs, that is, the organization learns as well as the program participants. I will refer to this aspect later.

Outdoor adventure learning

Just before I sat down to write this section of the chapter, I stumbled across a reprise of an article that was originally featured in *Harvard Business Review* in 1977.[18] The article describes retrospectively the experience of one of the men on a raft trip designed to foster teamwork among the four participants (the fifth rafter was the expert). While the point of the article then and now is to illustrate the unconscious efforts of men to work together to hold onto their power and, as a result, undermine women in leadership positions, it raised a different issue for me.

In reading about the adventure, it seemed to me that the bulk of the group's time was focused on the task of maneuvering the rapids, handling the chores required to maintain the physical integrity of its members, and mediating various interpersonal conflicts as they arose. The author only began to gain insight into his experience after he'd returned from the white water trip. No time was set aside for reflection about the team and what was happening to it during the trip. I'd like to discuss this in light of the perspective given by Mike Broussine of the Bristol Business School in relation to its approach to creating playing fields of learning around outdoor experiences (see p. 110).

Reflecting on the *HBR* classic article and Broussine's approach to outdoor education, it's relatively easy to conclude that any educator worth his or her salt should set up and debrief an exercise properly to maximize its learning potential. I think, however, that the lessons to be learned from these two examples go a bit further. In my estimation, the most critical dimension of all outdoor adventure training as well as the other learning examples described in this chapter is the opportunity they give for **reflection in and on action**.

Most of what people do at work lies at the interface of theory and practice, where the individual brings knowledge and skills to a situation and is often forced to think and learn when there is a disjunction between past experience and the current situation. In these instances, new knowledge, skills, or attitudes may be created, although they may go unrecognized as such. It is up to the facilitators of learning experiences, that is, the creators of the learning fields, to help people to individually and collectively crystallize that new knowledge and articulate it so that they recognize the breadth and depth of what they have learned.[19] The type of facilitation can often determine the type of learning that follows an experience. Good facilitators and educators encourage learners to reflect upon their experiences and to appreciate the richness and the completeness of their learning.

A final example drawn from an action reflection learning program conducted by the Management Institute of Sweden illustrates and confirms this criterion for effective playing fields. The management team of a Scandinavian company

Outdoor Adventures as Development
by Michael Broussine
Bristol Business School, University of the West of England

The senior manager sulked as the rest of the top management team got on with building the bridge over the stream with the scaffolding and wooden beams. Noel had just suggested a way out of the difficulty the team was facing, but Peter, the CEO, silenced him. "Quiet, Noel! We've got our plan and we've just got to get on with it. There isn't time!"

The team failed miserably; the bridge would not safely take the weight of one person, let alone six. These people looked despondent as they trooped indoors along with their facilitator. After ten minutes of high tension, the team began to talk about what they did well and what they did badly in the exercise. Noel said, "I just want to say that I felt really fed up, Peter, when you told me to shut up. I could see we weren't going to do it. And what's more, you're always doing that to me in our meetings. I've had enough of it, frankly."

Peter looked hurt. The others were quiet. The atmosphere got even more tense until finally Peter asked, "Did I? I didn't realize . . ." The incident, and the subsequent debrief turned out to be a highly significant metaphor for this team's ineffectiveness which has been used by team members, including Peter, ever since.

At the Bristol Business School we have developed an approach which makes a distinction between outdoor management development and "outdoor training" or "adventure training." Certainly OMD shares various respectable antecedents with outdoor or adventure education. Their roots go back to scouting, military officer selection in the Second World War, and youth adventure training schemes such as the Duke of Edinburgh's Award. While acknowledging the progenitors which are common to both outdoor training and OMD, we argue that the branch we are concerned with has evolved to an extent that it would be a mistake to regard them as synonymous, as some training organizations do. To do so perpetuates the myth and misconception which surrounds OMD. The example of the experience of the top management team above illustrates well the need to keep the physical component of OMD in perspective. The key processes, namely, those processes which enabled learning and change for the team, were not so much the physical exercise, but rather the interpersonal and group dynamic which it catalyzed, together with the crucial subsequent debrief.

This is not to say that the physical challenges were not significant to the learning. An independent evaluation of such programs revealed that "outdoor courses were a most powerful learning experience for participants

Continued on p. 111

... very many comments testify to the reality of the experience to management, and to participants' experience of managing within the (agency). There is strong evidence that managers were able to identify their own and others' strengths and weaknesses, using this as a positive learning experience for behavior change on return to their places of work."

The physical nature of the task – whether it be building a bridge, going on a scavenger hunt, climbing a hill, or even white water rafting – appeals to the playful side of adults when learning from experience. Indeed, participants in OMD report that learning and change occurs which is more potent and enduring than may be imagined being achieved through more didactic methods of management training.

had come to the Institute to participate in a development program to improve their effectiveness as a team and to work at the obstacles that were preventing them from performing innovatively.

The managers were separated into pairs, given questions to use to interview each other, and told to proceed across a snow-covered field along a lantern-illuminated pathway to a frozen lake in the forest. They trudged the mile or so down to the lake and found a blazing campfire along the shore set up near a cave in the hillside. Snow had begun to fall and the temperature was dropping. As they approached the lake, members of the team hurried to the warmth and comfort of the blaze. They also discovered some food in a basket nearby. Pretty soon they were ensconced around the fire, comfortable and full, chatting about the results of their interviews, the picturesque setting, and things in general.

One of the managers interrupted his conversation to point out the figure of an old man crossing the frozen expanse of the lake. He was headed toward the small group. The man, bent over with age, had a disheveled, rather unkempt appearance. As he approached the group, it was obvious that he was dirty and smelly as well. He looked somewhat like a hermit who had been living in the woods. He made his way up to the fire and began to warm himself. Several managers edged away. Soon, he bent down and opened the old canvas bag he had been carrying and pulled out a string of sausages to cook over the fire. He offered the group some of the meat, but everyone politely refused.

After he had eaten a few sausages, he began asking group members questions. He asked them who they were and what they were doing at the lake. One manager explained that they were members of the management team of a local company who had come to participate in a training program. The old man proceeded to ask more questions which were, surprisingly, penetrating and thoughtful. Several members of the management team had, by now, moved away and were engaged in their own conversations, ignoring both the old man and what he had to say. Undaunted, the man persisted with the few people whose attention he still held. His questions became more pointed and provocative. Intrigued, a few of the managers responded and soon a lively dialogue ensued with even more managers joining in.

Abruptly, the old man got up and walked away – back across the lake. He left the managers who talked with him with a sense of amazement at the insights they had gained from this brief, unanticipated, but intense encounter. Within a short time, the fire began to die out, and the chief executive officer announced it was time to go back to the training facility. The group rose and began the trek back.

When the management team reached the conference room, they were surprised to see the old man sitting in a corner of the room. The program facilitators instructed the team to sit down. As they did so, the old man stood up. No longer was he bent over with age; he appeared younger now. He removed his tattered hat and coat to reveal a clean shirt and jeans. He pulled off a wig and scruffy beard and used a nearby towel to wipe his face and hands. The facilitators introduced the old man as Michael, one of the program's trainers.

Michael began his talk by upbraiding the team, reminding them of their lack of openness to sources of new ideas, suggesting that their fixed mindsets prevented them from seeing the breadth and depth of learning in new experiences. The management team, duly chastised, agreed. "How will you," Michael challenged, "act innovatively as a management team when you aren't open to new experiences, no matter what form they take?"

This story not only points to the effectiveness of action learning, but to the absolute value of reflection to collective and individual learning.

Shaping the Playing Fields: Evolving a Learning Culture

The ordeal and ecstasy of learning

I have chosen as a subheading for this section the title of Plato's remarkable metaphor about education.[20] In it he describes one of the prisoners of an underground cave who had never been exposed to anything more substantial than shadows. The prisoner is freed from his chains and brought out into the fresh air and sunlight. He is initially delighted but soon shrinks from the painful brightness and strangeness of the never-before-experienced surroundings and attempts to return to the cave. Before he retreats, he realizes that the world outside the cave is one that is right and real for human beings. He resists returning to the cave and the world of illusion it fostered, but recognizes that he has an inescapable duty to go back and help others see their illusions.

In this parable Plato illustrates the process of learning as one individual's remarkable encounter with a truth that exists above and beyond any one person. It is a process, however, that is a harrowing experience both for the individual and the other people in the cave at the moment they are introduced to this truth. The ecstasy comes from the discovery of the truth; the ordeal is in the process of accepting and sharing it.

This haunting metaphor of individual and collective learning is, I think, one that can also be employed to characterize an organization's journey toward the creation of a climate that fosters effective playing/learning fields. The rewards of learning are many and quite desirable; however, the path to learning is often difficult, particularly because it demands that both individual and organization change. And, it's no secret that both find change easy to resist.

Brundage and Macheracher found that "environments that reinforce the self-concepts of adults, that are supportive of change, and that value the status of learners will produce the greatest amount of learning."[21] More recently, such environments have become known as learning organizations or, as Peter Senge states, places "where people continually expand their capacity to create results they truly desire, where new and expansive patterns of thinking are nurtured, where collective aspiration is set free, and where people are continually learning how to learn together."[22] In short, a learning climate is one where learning is both individual and communal and where there are virtually no limits imposed on learning. If organizations want to minimize the "ordeal" and optimize the "ecstasy" of learning at both the individual and collective levels, they need to ensure that the following become norms of their culture.

Management supports learning endeavors   People who participate in programs designed for learning are encouraged, recognized, and utilized, not penalized for the time spent away from the job. At a recent program I facilitated on team leadership, several participants wore bleepers. Their work was punctuated periodically with the sound of the beeper signals followed by quick exits from the classroom to the nearest telephone. Needless to say the impact on these individuals and the teams of which they were members was negative.

What is learned is integrated into the operation of the organization Learners are able to take what they learn and apply it. Comments such as, "This is great stuff but it won't work because my manager won't buy it" will not be heard. The organization will, for example, value the individual or team that spends hours and hours developing a solution to a problem in a training program by accepting the solution and facilitating its implementation.

Learners are not constrained by real or artificial boundaries in their pursuit of knowledge   When the end goal is to learn, people are not prevented from doing so by hierarchical, procedural, or political constraints. One example that comes to mind is that of a chemist in a major cosmetics company who was having difficulty solving a problem with a new cold cream formula. After several weeks of fruitless efforts, she discovered that another chemist in a competing product line had encountered and successfully resolved a similar problem. "Why don't you give him a call," I asked, "and find out how he addressed the issue?" "I can't," she replied. "It's confidential information. His product line competes against ours within the company." Who is the real loser here?

Learners view others not only as resources but as collaborators in their learning   Considering that organizations are living systems where a change in one component affects one or more of the others, in most instances the learning of one individual has implications for the learning of others, even the entire organization. The term **community of learning** is a good one to describe this phenomenon. If we begin to see organizations as communities of learning, we would realize that our learning belongs not just to us but to others in the organization. The idea that you and I are learners in the context of our team and our organization produces an attitudinal change as well as a conceptual shift. Not only do I see you differently, I also alter my behavior in working with you. I take responsibility as architect of my own learning and as a support to yours.

In a community of learning, open inquiry and dialogue are practiced on the playing fields of learning. People feel free to challenge assumptions, take risks, and experiment with new behavior in the name of learning but do so in a way that produces generative results. In one of the companies used as a foundation for our research on team learning,[23] a manager who was part of what was referred to as a synergy team remarked, "We started out with a ground rule of being brutally frank (in the interest of openness and learning). What we discovered was we focused on being brutal. We revisited that ground rule . . . (and changed it) to becoming respectfully frank." The climate of the team changed to one that valued candor and challenge, but not at the risk of alienating some members and silencing others.

The L-Factor: Panacea or Cure?

Learning, or what I call the "L-Factor," in adult and organization development, is not a new phenomenon; it's been going on since the dawn of the universe, so to speak. Is the recent attention being given to it merely a fad? Are the expressions "learning team" or "learning organization" on the way to becoming overused buzzwords? Or, is "learning awareness" truly an ageless, enduring concept, a shift in the way we ought to view what organizations and the people in them do, the DNA of individual and organizational growth?

We turn to world-renowned anthropologist Margaret Mead for some insights into this question of learning awareness as an integral feature of effective individuals and organizations with the implication that its presence belies the existence of effective playing/learning fields in organizations. She describes how we need to think about learning in terms of a "vivid truth of the new age," that is, "no one will live all his life in the world into which he was born, and no one will die in the world in which he worked in his maturity."[24] She explains what she means by noting that contemporary life changes at frequent intervals, and that those intervals are even shorter for individuals who work at the cutting edge of science, technology, or business. What was taken for granted or successfully practiced at one point in time must be "unlearned or transformed to fit the new state of knowledge or practice." Learning must take place not only at special times and in special places, but through the activities of daily life: "from the technician who must handle a new machine to the factory supervisor who must introduce its use, the union representative who must interpret it to the men, the foreman who must keep the men working, the salesman who must service a new device or find markets for it . . .".[25] In other words, learning must be the underlying motivation for all that we do.

The L-Factor – or as Mead describes it – the vivid truth of the new age, is not something that is optional. It is absolutely imperative! The consequences of ignoring it are grave. On an organizational level, one has only to look around at the companies once called "excellent" that have gone out of existence or are struggling to survive to realize the cost of learning mindlessness. Or one might note the consequences of blocking learning for the sake of perpetuating some established paradigm or reaching some predetermined outcome.

The benefits of learning as a strategic imperative are many. Two examples come to mind. One is when learning is part of the organizational philosophy; the other when it underlies team operations. In the first instance, the company is IKEA North America, where the president, Goran Carstedt, views himself as a teacher and his company as a community of learners.[26] IKEA was founded nearly two dozen years ago by Ingvar Kamprad in Sweden with the mission of providing well-designed furniture to the many rather than the few. His feeling was that ordinary people deserved to have their lives made more comfortable at prices they could afford.

This philosophy has inspired a strategy and a set of management practices that sound very much like the definition of a learning culture as described by Brundage and Macheracher earlier in this chapter. Learning is central to the company's development. Its organizational structure is decentralized and promotes freedom with responsibility. The learning mode across the organization is one of a curious attitude with a lot of experiments that grow out of an open, trustworthy dialogue with customers and employees with systematic follow-up. Barriers to learning and employee development are constantly worked against. There are few titles, no notable perks for managers such as parking spaces or special dining rooms. The headquarters of IKEA N.A. is located next to one of its stores in Pennsylvania; everyone eats in the company cafeteria in order to observe and interact with customers and each other. Managers are required to work in the warehouse or store once a year as part of Anti-Bureaucratic Week. They load furniture, unpack boxes, help customers, all in the interest of learning.

When describing his organization's learning attitude, Carstedt said that the company strategy is blue and yellow (the colors of the Swedish flag) mixed with stars and stripes (US flag) and maple leaves (Canadian flag). In other words, the idea is not to follow unquestioningly orders issued from the parent company in Sweden, but to make managers, employees, and customers partners in learning how to reach the goal of creating a better life for all.

The second example is one of learning teams at Boeing used to build the new 777 passenger jet. Because of the teamwork displayed within and across teams, the plane flew its first successful test flight with fewer than half the number of design glitches of other new product launches.[27] To build the jet, the company created a hierarchy of teams involving 10,000 employees and 500 suppliers. There were 200 cross-functional teams headed up by a management team of five or six top managers from various disciplines with the bottom-line accountability for producing the plane on time and within budget. In the middle were 25 to 30 two-person teams of leaders from engineering and operations with the responsibility of overseeing the 200 plus work teams.

A wonderful example of the impact of team learning happened when two Boeing teams discovered a problem. One team had designed the passengers' oxygen system to fit in the same spot another team had slotted for something called a gasper – a nozzle that shoots fresh air toward the passenger. A third team known as the integration team came in not to mediate a dispute, but to work with the two teams so that together they arrived at the optimal solution for the plane – a special clamp that held both systems together. This collective learning prevented the problem from ending up as it would have in the past; the conflict would not have been discovered until the plane was being manufactured.

Conclusion

Yes, the L-Factor is here to stay because it is central to being human. Individuals learn, groups learn, organizations learn, and even societies learn. To fail at learning means that human preparedness to face the myriad of challenges posed by everyday existence goes underdeveloped. However, contemporary "playing fields" are more challenging to create and operate than ever before. In the past, human learning has been relatively successful at adapting to environmental changes and challenges as they presented themselves. **Maintenance learning** was generally the hoped for outcome. Such learning produced relatively fixed outlooks, methods, or rules for handling known and recurring situations. It enhanced our ability to solve problems that were givens. It helped us to sustain an established way of life. While an indispensable part of functioning, maintenance learning as a standard process is no longer enough.[28]

For long-term survival, particularly in these current turbulent times, **innovative learning** must become the norm. This type of learning is critical to change, renewal, restructuring, and problem reformulation. The primary features of innovative learning according to Botkin, Elmandjra, and Malitza are anticipation and participation. Anticipation "implies an orientation that prepares for possible contingencies and considers long-range future options."[29] Participation requires inclusion in the learning process by all those affected by the potential outcome of the learning. Learning opportunities are systemically viewed, without boundaries and barriers posed by organizational structures and culture. Communication is open and active. The "playing field" is less contrived and controlled.

If learning as a strategic initiative and as an individual and group competency is to permanently take hold, if our current infatuation with the L-Factor is to endure, we need to make sure we create the playing/learning fields that will develop, in individuals, groups, and organizations, the ability to learn innovatively and continuously – to make the L-Factor as central to work as it is to life.

Notes

1 See P. C. Candy, "How people learn to learn", in R. M. Smith et al. (eds) *Learning to Learn Across the Life Span* (San Francisco: Jossey-Bass, 1990), pp. 30–63.

2 R. Saljo, "Learning about learning", *Higher Education*, 1979, vol. 8, pp. 443–451.

3 Candy, "How people learn to learn".

4 Ibid.

5 E. Langer, *Mindfulness* (New York: Addison-Wesley, 1989).

6 See K. Dechant, "Making the most of job assignments: an exercise in planning for learning", *Journal of Management Education*, 1993, vol. 18, no. 2, pp. 198–211.

7 Candy, "How people learn to learn", p. 87.

8 P. Senge, *The Fifth Discipline: The Art and Practice of the Learning Organization* (New York: Doubleday, 1990), p. 10.

9 See E. Kasl, K. Dechant and V. Marsick, "Living the learning: internalizing our model of group learning," in D. Boud, R. Cohen and D. Walker (eds), *Using Experience for Learning* (Buckingham, England: Open University Press, 1993), pp. 143–56.

10 J. Mezirow, *Transformative Dimensions of Adult Learning* (San Francisco: Jossey-Bass, 1991). Also Senge, "The Fifth Discipline".

11 Kasl et al., "Living the learning".

12 See K. Dechant and V. J. Marsick, *Team Learning Survey* (King of Prussia, PA: Organization Design and Development, Inc., 1993).

13 D. Kolb, *Experiential Learning* (Englewood Cliffs, NJ: Prentice-Hall, 1984), p. 26.

14 E. Kasl, V. Marsick and K. Dechant, "Teams as learners: A research-based model of team learning, styles, processes, and conditions", Unpublished manuscript, pp. 10–11.

15 A. Pyle, "Past, present and possibility: An integrative appreciation of learning from experience", *Management Learning*, 1994, vol. 25, issue 1, p. 159.

16 P. Hybert, "Simulations for corporate training", in *Pursuing Performance*, a quarterly publication of Svenson & Wallace, Inc., Naperville, Illinois, Summer 1994, p. 19.

17 P. Mata and C. Dennis, "Working the global network: the Grace Cocoa Experience", Presentation given at European Foundation for Management Development Annual Conference at MiL Campus in Klippan, Sweden, on June 9, 1994.

18 R. Schrank, "Two women, three men on a raft", *Harvard Business Review*, May–June 1994, pp. 68–80.

19 See P. Jarvis, *Adult Learning in the Social Context* (London: Croom-Helm, 1987).

20 Plato, "The ordeal and ecstasy of learning", in R. Gross (ed.), *Invitation to Lifelong Learning* (Chicago: Follet Publishing Company, 1982), pp. 28–34.

21 D. Brundage and D. Macheracher, *Adult Learning Principles and their Application to Program Planning* (Ontario: Ministry of Education, 1980), p. 26.

22 Senge, "The Fifth Discipline", p. 3.

23 Dechant and Marsick, *Team Learning Survey*, p. 12.

24 M. Mead, "No one can 'complete an education'", in R. Gross (ed.), *Invitation to Lifelong Learning* (Chicago: Follet Publishing Company, 1982), p. 83.

25 Ibid., p. 84.

26 G. Carstedt, "Learning in action: the IKEA experience", Presentation given at European Foundation for Management Development Annual Conference at MiL Campus in Klippan, Sweden, on June 9, 1994.

27 B. Dumaine, "The trouble with teams", *Fortune*, 5 September, 1994, pp. 86–92.

28 W. Bennis and B. Nanus, *Leaders: The Strategies for Taking Charge* (New York: Harper and Row, 1985).

29 J. Botkin, M. Elmandjra and M. Malitza, "Bridging the 'human gap'," in R. Gross (ed.), *Invitation to Lifelong Learning* (Chicago: Follet Publishing Company, 1982), p. 257.

PART II

Learning Through Working

PART II

Learning Through Working

Interview with André DelBecq

Professor, University of Santa Clara School of Management

A Silicon Valley Perspective on the New Learning Organization

Interviewer: David Fearon   Date: June 1994

On a windy day in Windsor, Ontario, Canada I had an opportunity to interview André L. DelBecq regarding his perspectives on the new learning organization. There was some symbolic appropriateness in visiting with André in Windsor across from Detroit. He grew up near the greater Detroit/Windsor auto complex in Toledo, Ohio. His father was in the machine tool business, a technology underpinning the automotive industry. From where we sat we could view the auto plants just across the river in Michigan and up river in Windsor that were symbolic of mid-century American economic power. André's early scholarship was deeply imbedded in these traditional midwestern organizations. However, over the last 15 years after moving to the Leavey School of Business at Santa Clara University in Silicon Valley, his scholarship has charted the organizational, and leadership challenges associated with the turn of the century industries of electronics and bioscience. Now a senior scholar and Dean of Fellows for the Academy of Management, it was an opportunity to ask how he perceives the new learning organizations from his position in the heart of an international complex which has symbolized the information age.

DF: Perhaps we could begin by asking what you see are the causes for the movement towards learning organizations in our contemporary society.

AD: We can all recite a litany of reasons for changes in organizations: increased competitiveness, a move towards cognitive work, the presence of highly educated specialists, global business pressures, etc. However, I think the issue that is the keystone that brings down the old organizational order and provides the central rationale for the new organizational order is the impact of the speed of information transfer . . . the fact that immediately, worldwide, everyone has access to the latest information, best practices, and design elements for solution building. This implies a need for an entirely different type of organization structure.

Recently I attended a conference at the University of Southern California dealing with the most recent research on an organizational issue. The conference ended at noon and I caught a commuter plane back to Northern California from Los Angeles. I had to make a telephone call that afternoon to a colleague at the the École Supérieur de Commerce de Rouen, in Normandy, France. My French colleague said, "This afternoon in my graduate class we discussed the conference that you attended in L.A. and I have a couple of questions for you." I wasn't even back in town before the information was disseminated from the conference at the University of Southern California to INSEAD and from INSEAD to the École de Commerce in Normandy. The key points of the Conference in L.A. had already been discussed, and were being refined by European educators!

This speed of information transfer forces organizations to make much greater use of the intellectual capabilities of each employee, particularly technical and scientific cadres. Because of the rapidity of information exchange, it is necessary to empower these employees to move quickly. You no longer have the luxury to wait until everyone in the organization understands and agrees upon everything. Rather, to enter a competitive window, it is necessary to create subsidiarity, allowing small business units within large organizations to move with great speed. So it's access to information which requires speed in implementation that is really driving the new organizational designs. As Andy Grove, CEO at Intel says, "There will only be two organizations in the future: the quick and the dead."

DF: Do you see this fundamentally changing the way that organizations are managed? How does this build a need to release that intellectual capability to deal with such rapid change? Does this change the nature of management itself?

AD: Yes, absolutely! What this implies is that the most powerful current currency for technology advancement is "local knowledge" in the sociological sense. Employees who are intimately involved with a particular subknowledge base in terms of both technological perspective and closeness to customers, and who also understand the strategic forces of a differentiated market segment and feel empowered to act on their information and insight, are now the new decentralized locus of action.

This is not to say that this decentralized expertise creates action that is unduly precipitous. Decentralized organizational players must also engage in as much search as possible with other organizational and market boundary spanners and obtain as many heuristics, both factual and analytical, as well as intuitive and judgmental, as possible. Before acting, they need to cross-check their information with alternative perspectives. Thus as decentralized business segments construct their particular response, they are enriched by massive amounts of shared information. **But to do this well and to do this quickly, maintaining an action orientation of decision speed, requires a very different kind of organizational learning.**

DF: The manager as the "intervener" in the workplace process might then inadvertently be the manager as the "interruptor." In the past employees felt bound to get permission or to check with someone in a superior position. So interrupted, employees were less able to focus energy on their own searches and to decide what new kinds of information was required.

AD: If as an organizational player, I am very much involved in decentralized strategic action, and I feel empowered to respond to a particular challenge within my sphere of "local knowledge," and if I am working 70 hours a week gathering information and problem-solving with respect to a subsidiary business challenge, I can hardly expect the rest of the organization members to be paying equal attention to my focus. This implies that in the new "speed to design to market organization" we have to accept both suboptimization and decentralization where employees are empowered in their particular area of knowledge and responsibility to continue to move quickly while at the same time constantly searching for contributing information and briefing the rest of the organization on their activities.

DF: The tissue is starting to separate, is it not?

AD: Indeed, this decentralization involves special challenges for aggregating efforts strategically. If we have parts of the organization highly focused on different concerns, there has to be an organizational intelligence center concerned with the aggregation of information based on both the exchange between the boundaries of these groups, and also investigating developments associated with the entire portfolio of organizational entities. In this sense, the new "Headquarters" function is much more like an office of central intelligence. It's in this intelligence center that concern with "big picture" overview and broad environmental or market developments is analyzed.

So we have created a situation where we have very specialized units with in-depth local knowledge dealing with highly focused, suboptimal efforts; and we also have an office of central intelligence concerned with overall directional strategy identifying broad issues and gaps. Obviously there has to be an exchange of information between these two parts of the organization's structure. Thus, we have not done away with strategic management, but are combining decentralized strategy with overall "portfolio" strategy. But the managerial function at "Headquarters" is more focused on the overall strategic concerns, and is no longer micromanaging or overcontrolling a subunit's empowered effort.

Within the subunit we have highly competent individuals who are very confident in their technical competencies and strategy relative to their market segment. At Headquarters (office of central intelligence), we have people who are very competent in large macro intelligence gathering, overall industry trends, and broad market changes. We have to build an interface between these two forms of cognitive specialization. This interface is not accomplished by having some "superordinate" individual who knows more than anyone else over controlling. It is accomplished by building an interactive dialectic which assures the exchange of information between these two arenas of organizational intelligence.

DF: Exactly! That to me is the pivot for this book. The theme of the book is that new designs seem to be emerging in our imaginations about this "new" organization. There has been a great deal said and written recently about performance and its importance to stakeholders. In what ways does your view of an organization deal with designing and transforming an organization to optimize learning as it relates to performance?

AD: I think that performance, in the sense of quality, efficiency, cost control, and bench mark speed is a *sine qua non* of contemporary adequacy. So yes, you will have to be concerned about quality. Yes, you will have to be concerned about moving down the cost curve. Yes, you will have to be concerned about meeting customers' quality expectations. But, short-run excellent performance in and of itself will not lead to survivability.

Survivability will also depend on the ability of the organization to anticipate future developments and innovate more rapidly than its competitors. This means that the organizational system that you must create is one which is extraordinarily porous relative to the gathering of information in anticipation of the future. Innovative organizations will be searching for information regarding new technologies, developments in science and research, changes in market structures and customer expectations, comparative organizational bench marks, etc. A systematic capability to gather information must be in place to improve the ability of the organization to make strategic choices.

The exchange of such information (presuming at the moment that we can create the capacity to gather and manage it) involves an enormous amount of total organizational learning in very short periods of time. So we are confronted with a paradox. We have to be open to much more learning, but we have to process it and make decisions more quickly. This calls upon us to design an organization that is simultaneously both extremely open and at the same time able to process information and make timely decisions and implement timely action. This is at the core of the new challenges in organization design. Without decentralization and subsidiarity the decision system is overwhelmed.

DF: As I am listening about these requirements for learning – the amount of energy and information that needs to be brought in, worked up, and integrated into strategic action – I have a sense of hopelessness. How are we going to manage organizations to such a level of extraordinary capacity?

AD: Well, the interesting thing is that there are organizations in extraordinarily turbulent environments who are doing this at the present time very well: electronic firms, computer firms, bioscience firms as well as many other firms in highly competitive areas. High performing companies are already very successful implementing everything about which we have talked. And if you meet the people who are doing the tasks, they are normal people like you and me.

DF: They aren't gods?

AD: They aren't gods. They aren't heroic. But they are advantaged because they work in a set of organizational arrangements and within an organizational culture that makes it possible for them to respond to these challenges. It is not that the organizational requirements and design to accommodate these new challenges are mysterious. We can document organizations in which this is done by competent, but not "exceptional" individuals. The right organizational design does not require extraordinary, heroic individuals.

DF: That's good news. The ability of individuals to accomplish this assimilation of information and act upon it, consciously or unconsciously, implies that they have placed a value on learning that is intrinsic to the company. Do you think it is more conscious than unconscious? Do you see learning and the knowledge that they generate within their businesses as reflecting organizational designs that are different?

AD: The first attribute of these firms with respect to information processing is that they spend an enormous amount of time scouting. "Scouting" in the sense that they send people outside the firm to gather information. They send their core work groups to science centers to gather information about emerging science and technology. They send their core people to other organizations to find out what types of internal arrangements they have made to be a quality provider. They send their core people to spend time with the customers so that they can internalize new needs in the marketplace. These organizations are very proactive in seeking information "over the horizon" in anticipation of future developments. As a footnote, they combine existential scouting (being in other places and interacting with other people) with electronic information searches, since many interactive clues are missed in liaison knowledge.

As Leland Kaiser, the futurist, has said, "The future is just an unfurnished room." However, when organizations conduct scouting, they are able to discover the type of fixtures, systems, technologies and customer needs, etc. that are likely to be placed in that future space which they then can cocreate.

High-performing firms expect their core workforce to help anticipate and furnish the future. They expect the core workforce, itself, to put together their combination of insights with their own competencies to create new forms of products and services. The entire organization, each employee, is engaged in creating the future as opposed to responding to it five years later when their competitors already have a head start.

DF: It seems to me that you would have to structure organizations in a different way if you are to carry on the tasks you just described: creating the scouting roles, processing the information, and acting on the information. Are you carrying in your head some kind of vision of the "new organization?" What would it look like? And would that vision have something to do with being able to optimize learning?

AD: We have already discussed one big feature. First, it will be important to decentralize strategy. No single organizational entity or set of organizational players can scout everything. No one can pay attention to clues with respect to all aspects of the business, all market segments, all customer groups, all technological imperatives. So the world of scouting and the sharing of strategic information is decentralized.

Second, scouting is future oriented. Everyone feels that part of their work obligation is to create the future, not simply deliver the present. This implies that exploratory studies and feasibility modeling are a normal part of the workload. The precondition here is for "slack" to be present. If everyone is so busy doing today's work and does not have time to design tomorrow, when tomorrow arrives it is a surprise for which the organization is not prepared.

Third, this implies an organization willing to experiment. The organization must mandate and fund experimentation and learning before new designs or services become a competitive requirement. A great deal of organizational learning must occur well before the organization is actually in the market with a new product or service.

Fourth, this implies careful attention to evaluation of all key workers in terms of their contribution to future learning, not just present work. It is ruthless in the sense that no one can be excused from participating in creating the future. It is forgiving in the sense that since you are dealing with future variables, it must encompass experimentation and inevitable failures. Because you are anticipating the future in time and learning, you can tolerate mistakes while conducting experimental tests as part of learning. However, at the point at which you promise performance to the customer, your integrity is on the line. You must deliver what you promise.

I can't overemphasize the fact that all core players in the organization are responsible for being strategic and future oriented, not simply doing present tasks. This means we are finally hiring the whole person. Whether you are talking about someone in facilities management, inventory management, information systems, manufacturing, in every unit of the organization there is an obligation to be future and strategic in perspective.

DF: One of our traditional understandings of organizational structure is the "manager over subordinates" system. You said the new organization would be decentralized; but how much of that manager/subordinate pattern do you envision in the future? We have seen the flattening and broadening of the span of control. What's coming after this that will allow the fluidity that you have just described?

AD: I like Ray Miles's phrases when he describes the role of the new manager. He indicates that the role of management is to "govern civilized discourse and manage markets." Managing discourse is used in this sense to mean receiving, sorting out, and confronting disparate information gracefully, doing your best to see that useful ideas from the variety of interface sources are incorporated in problem-solving. "Markets" is used to imply that within the context of this discourse, entrepreneurship is encouraged and multiple experiments, sometimes in contradiction with each other, are tested, allowing the most successful to survive in the market. This is different than managers as controller of all specifics as in the past.

DF: Absolutely!

AD: We really don't know how to describe the new managerial role in its wholeness. Obviously these behaviors require a different profile for the manager. The former was an individual with great technical knowledge, very concerned about careful analysis, and with an orientation towards power and control. The new manager is someone who is interested in and comfortable with heuristics, able to operate on the basis of both data and intuition, able to empower others to take risks, and willing to learn experimentally by doing, not overanalyzing. The new manager must be comfortable with an indefinite fuzzy boundary between the various parts of the organization and components of overall strategy.

The new role requires not only a new set of skills, but probably individuals with a different set of aptitudes than those possessed by individuals who formerly rose to upper management in the bureaucratic organization.

DF: I thought of this next question, parenthetically, because I am always interested in management education, as I know you are. Will this new manager profile make a difference in management education? How we organize the material, the kinds of folks we attract to teach our students, the ways we facilitate learning so that individuals can grow into new roles? Are we there or close to being there and am I simply not giving our academics fair credit?

AD: I think we are going to see new types of role specialization as opposed to one "managerial" type. For example, we will see individuals who are very good at invention and creativity, who are often inner-directed, independent, politically less sensitive, irreverent towards authority, and disinterested in political systems. These individuals will work within the suboptimal core technology units as project leaders. On the other hand, the individuals managing at the interface have to be more socially sensitive, and much more interested in participating in political processes and influence. The notion that an individual can simultaneously or even sequentially play all roles is going to disappear.

Individuals will have a chance to grow their career horizontally, rather than grow a career vertically. Task specialists, entrepreneurs/intrapreneurs will move from project to project, being increasingly compensated for new competencies, and gain sharing in contributions created by their project. Other individuals interested in boundary spanning and social and political influences will operate between projects and missions, and between mission groups and the central intelligence headquarters unit. For this form of differentiated leadership to work, we are going to have to change the notion that there should be an enormous difference in status between people occupying liaison/coordinator activities, and people engaged in entrepreneur, task specialization activities. We are going to have to surrender the notion that either role is superior, but rather understand that they are different forms of contribution. For example, you would want to have a skeptical, very analytical senior scientist in your laboratory; but that's not the profile of the optimistic entrepreneur trying to implement innovation. In turn, the boundary spanning manager has still a different profile. We are going to see a collapsing of the differential salary structures associated with leadership differentiation, and an increase in salary differentiation based on competencies within each of the varied roles. Robert J. House and I have just completed a study of technology CEOs which documents the differentiated profile between types of high tech leadership.

DF: Carrying it back to the way we organize courses of study and executive management programs, it seems to me we management educators have remained involved in the vertical while many new organizations are rapidly working their way towards the horizontal. So we have a challenge on our hands to change schooling, I would think.

AD: Yes, very much so. I think what will happen is that people will continue to enlarge their competencies relative to their own particular set of talents. For example, if you have a very good project manager, over the course of career history, he or she will manage more complex projects, and manage projects in a variety of different organizations. This manager will manage projects first at the sub-business unit level, then at the company level, and then at the industry level. However, his or her career path doesn't go from project management to boundary spanning manager. We don't really know what the new career paths will look like. It certainly will not be the vertical lock-step career paths of the past. There will emerge a variety of horizontal career phases with increasing complexity, challenge and risk which will be appropriately compensated.

DF: So, if we notice these new career patterns, we can begin to think of how we can be there to respond with a variety of teaching interventions and information. My concern is that we don't have to continue to design our courses (and write our books) around the roles that we have focused on in the past. Instead, we would do so more around "impact areas" or "missions" as you are calling them.

AD: The whole concept of the new organization is that each of us, relative to the roles that we would choose to play, will have to be constantly learning. At the same time none of us is capable of learning everything that is needed for organizational success and we will be increasingly interdependent.

So now we have to start coupling this array of talent, insight, and perspective. The coupling will be more like jazz, where there is a lot of constant improvising and fluid movements by players in and out of prominent focus, as opposed to a carefully constructed classical score.

DF: My study of managing for quality over the last eight years has shown me that we have organizations like the Juran Institute that can teach us how to design an organization or redesign an organization so that quality is a consideration in every step of every process. Can we, likewise, design so that learning can be managed in the strategic way that you have described earlier in your comments?

AD: Yes, there are some design features that increase the probability of effective learning. We have talked about organizations that increase external scouting with particular attention towards changes that are going to occur over the horizon. We have talked about slack. Unless you have time and resources to invent the future, you won't try to do so because you are too busy delivering the present. Another aspect of design that we haven't talked about is learning to manage each sequential stage of the developmental process. We will have to design the appropriate parameters for each phase of the cycle from conceptualization to feasibility study to pilot to implementation. Each of these phases require different resources, different organizational arrangements, and different channels of communication. There have to be roles in the organization that focus on each stage as well as roles that facilitate the transfer between stages. I have written about managing phases of innovation elsewhere.

Finally, since we are demanding such high performance, we will have to give people a chance to lie fallow to retool and relearn between intensive missions. We can do that in a number of ways. We can create opportunities inside the organization for individuals to take time to think, to increase their knowledge, and to refresh themselves after completing a complex mission. Or we can share rewards at the end of a mission with sufficient generosity so that individuals can develop their own strategies for relearning, perhaps outside the organization at universities or in other complementary organizational settings.

DF: Buy themselves a sabbatical?

AD: Yes. What you cannot do is to burn people out in very intensive time-driven missions without any strategies for renewal. So another major design aspect of the learning organization is to build in renewal strategies that are either self-managed or organizationally managed and facilitated.

DF: As we say in the preface to this book, we don't need another tome that bashes conventional managers. They have been pretty well beaten up in the popular media. Managers have gotten the message that business can't be done in the same way. If you could contrast some of the differences between how one manages through control, and how one manages so that learning occurs, what would your reflections be?

AD: We talk a great deal in the literature about "open systems learning"; but we really haven't institutionalized such learning. Open organizations would have managers with systematic strategies and processes for scanning the environment, linking with customers, interfacing between business units, and intelligence gathering between generations of organizational cadres. It is important to pay particular attention to youth in the sense of individuals who are new to organizations and new to project or mission since these are precisely the people who were not co-opted in the past solutions. You would be open to a great deal of experimentation where people can learn through experience, and would not require theoretical or analytical proof prior to permission to experiment.

This implies a managerial style that is truly open to readjustments in strategy from all these sources of learning. This is a world of fluidity and tentativeness. This is not the old organization with one best way, etc. This is an organizational context in which learning is occurring up to the point at which you make a commitment to a customer with respect to the product or service that you can deliver with integrity. At that point, you have to be able to deliver without exaggeration and with surprising sensitivity to service needs, and of course open to customer feedback both in design and enactment.

DF: I see a basic contrast in structures and management in the organization you are describing: the previous organization emphasized control, it was about closing down, closing gaps, identifying "the" decision. It was about "finishing off" problems (competitors for that matter) as opposed to keeping the organization open and attentive.

My mental image of what you are telling me is that the new structure supports simultaneous finishings and reopenings; that there is always a better way ahead which makes it acceptable and desirable to reopen to "case" of any matter that had been previously settled. It implies a constant reopening to keep the learning flowing.

AD: One of the interesting consequences is that we create a world of temporary systems, temporary assignments, and temporary teams. Further, each mission group has a shortened life cycle with the ability to do a hand-off which allows others to step in and continue to make changes. By these hand-offs to new teams you create a capacity in the organization that is greater than the capacity of any single individual or any single team. This ability to have continuous innovation through new groups tackling problems from new perspectives is one of the new forms of "organizational surplus." It stands in contrast to the old system of the same group growing stale in the same position.

DF: So in the new organization there is not a single manager reaching up and pulling a switch and saying, "This is all that needs to be said and all that needs to be done." This metaphorical switch is there in reach of all who can, on their own initiative, bring closure to an issue or a project. All participants can also choose to switch "back on," when learning has brought fresh insights into view.

AD: Look at the implications of these "mission driven" approaches for career paths. We demand greater speed for team goal accomplishment. We expect each team to finish its work in a specified period of time and then to do a hand-off. In like manner, we have shorter life cycles for leadership positions; whether president or vice-president or project director in a firm, or President of the United States. All senior managers have a mandate and program for their term in office, just as each high performing team has an explicit or implicit mandate. We are increasingly aware that no set of talents is good at everything or has equal contribution to make to different phases of problem-solving.

By this fluidity of movement in and out of mission prominence, we allow the evolution of projects, programs, and organizational agendas to be moved forward to a different stage of problem-solving by a new generation of talent. However, this also implies that people who have expended great energy and taken great risks to deal with prior challenges in an intensive time-driven effort have to have honor as they do a hand-off. They have to be treated with dignity when their mission is completed and they have to have time to rebuild their energy and knowledge base and rediscover new missions. They cannot be treated as "has beens." We have not developed adequate models in human resource management for handling this kind of fluidity, although firms like Apple and Intel which have institutionalized mini-sabbaticals are frontier organizations experimenting with these new challenges.

DF: In our domestic culture we actually abhor "has beens." You know that we do not like to see Mickey Mantle at 65 years of age. Instead we would prefer to remember Mickey when he was perfect. We have a long way to go, culturally, in understanding and allowing this kind of rejuvenation; not just the person's rejuvenation, but the rejuvenation of our image of the person as someone ready and able to go on to something else.

AD: That is where shifting the emphasis to 'mission," not position, changes the whole concept. The concept is that I can accept a mission in Denver to revitalize a certain program; and at the end of the mission, I can go back to headquarters in California and spend the time enlarging my repertoire of skills. When the next mission arises in Florida, I bring to that not only the experiences of Denver, but the learning that has taken place in between the two missions. Each one of these missions has its own integrity and its own dignity. Dignity is no longer associated with remaining in a position in California. This kind of movement from mission to mission with an opportunity to enhance skills between missions can be very self-actualizing.

DF: I could look forward to that kind of life-style!

AD: There are even opportunities to better integrate family concerns with work concerns. If you have teenagers who like skiing, you can accept a mission in Colorado during the ski season. If you have an elder in need of specialized care for a period of time you can refuse a mission. There are little ways in which personal and organizational needs can be melded.

DF: By being able to volunteer and negotiate missions, your energies will be "pumped"! You would be able to take on challenges enthusiastically.

On the phone we talked a bit regarding theories of organization behavior that are extant at the moment in which we examine these new organization forms. What are some of the gaps in theories of organization behavior that we will have to develop that we should be aware of?

AD: I think the configuration is pretty well understood: It will be flatter, more decentralized, will emphasize spontaneous horizontal communication, will be environmentally more porous and open, will empower faster and more responsive decision-making, and will encompass task-specific missions. I think this general framework of the new organization is agreed upon. In order to operate within that framework, however, we discover huge gaps in our knowledge.

For example, we are still struggling with managing decision-making where there is never enough information. We still are limited in our skills at creating teams that are flexible and allow people to move comfortably through a series of fluid assignments. We don't provide the kind of training and skills necessary to be effective team members. We are confused about team-based reward structures, and still tend to put responsibility on the individual as opposed to creating shared responsibility among team players. At an organizational level, we don't help people think through their career as a portfolio of evolving competencies. Individuals are struggling to manage career strategies on their own. In short, we are still much better at understanding behavior necessary to manage stable systems than we are at understanding behavior requirements for very fluid systems.

DF: Yes, that is descriptively true, and developing knowledge on dealing with temporary systems will be an important key.

AD: There are additional problems at the industry and societal level. We haven't developed the portability of benefits so that people can move between organizations and rationalize their career at the industry level. We don't know how to cope with the challenges of labor mobility that these systems create. In short, we have the rough outlines of the organizational configuration associated with new designs, but the internal skill sets and the external support systems are still inadequate and primitive. We keep regressing to former notions of hierarchically focused equity based on stable organizations and vertical career patterning within a single firm as opposed to the new temporary systems and movement between firms.

DF: Exactly, exactly. We have a huge amount of work to do then, don't we?

AD: Yes, it is as if we have an artist's sketch of the outside parameters of the building, but all the internal systems to make life inside that building survivable are only weakly understood, and the external infrastructure at the societal level is still missing.

DF: Do you have any examples of some literature that is emerging that would help us in that regard? There are lots of ideas out there that seem to be on the borders of this new challenge, that are maybe knocking on the door to be let in.

AD: Perhaps we can learn something from the literature that is exploring multiple cultures in international studies. If we were to treat organizational subunits as differentiated cultures (scientific, technical, engineering, customer, manufacturing) and instead of predetermining what the structure and behavior should be, simply allow each subculture to evolve by asking the diagnostic questions: "What is working? What is impeding us?" I think we would facilitate rapid evolution. Our difficulty is that we still try to impose a former bureaucratic culture and set of norms on all organizational entities, believing that constancy across organizational units is desirable. I think we have to let go of constancy and allow for much more organizational differentiation evolution.

Having said that theory is lagging, it is important to note we already have a certain number of individuals in high-performing organizations whose instincts and intuitions based on what they have learned by doing can be tapped and codified. This in-depth knowledge from learning has just barely penetrated our theoretical literature which I think lags by about half a decade much of what is happening in the field. It is for this reason that managers are more inclined to read *Fortune* and *Business Week* than they are to read the *Academy of Management Journal* or the *Administrative Science Quarterly*. It is not that they don't value the careful reasoning that is part of our tradition in academia; rather it is that our theory is largely addressing problems of a simpler level of complexity than the world in which they live. So they turn to biographical reflections from skillful practitioners, and case stories describing new developments in companies written by journalists, since our academic modeling hasn't caught up.

DF: There is an appetite for that literature among practitioners, and they seem to be able to decode which lessons are useful for their own uses. I don't know that we have learned from practitioners how and what they learn by reading the thoughts of other practitioners. Maybe one of our approaches could be to learn more from those who are learning from each other rather than going in and doing our usual research surveys, etc.

AD: I think organization behavior (OB) has tended to continue to focus at the micro level; that is, it has tended to focus on the individual and the stable internal work team. In fact, the big changes are occurring at the interface of organizational aggregation and in temporary teams. In this sense, scholars of business strategy are often perceived as more relevant than scholars of organization behavior because the strategists are addressing problems at the macro level where many of the challenges are occurring.

DF: We want to be sure that this book is not just about learning at the individual and group levels. We are opening inquiry about learning in all zones of an organization, including interorganizational activities. This draws us into communication with very different scholarly groups. One of the co-authors has been doing a lot of work as a business culture anthropologist attempting to make translations between practice and theory. Developing this book as a team of authors is much like operating as one of the new organizations we have been describing. We have to learn very rapidly, be highly integrative and disintegrative, abandon notions of management that no longer work, and be open to new learning. We management educators do not want the epithet, "We learned too little, too late."

AD: Academics are suffering greatly by being a protected monopoly. Many universities possess a relative geographic monopoly. Universities are also government subsidized in many instances. This has allowed the university researcher the dysfunctional luxury of being more inclined to focus on his or her individual interests as opposed to focusing research on the needs of the marketplace. Further, to be responsive to the needs of any society in a period of transition implies that we have to use modalities of analysis that are tentative. We must admit that we are doing pilot research with soft methods as opposed to using modalities of analysis that are more refined and associated with more advanced learning. In our field we seem to have an enormous cleavage between a few people who are willing to be very much involved in the emergent realities of these new organizational forms, and a larger set of scholars who are more involved in the exchange of ideation surrounding more traditional intellectual models. As a result, academics are being moved out of the center of dialogue with institutional leaders by virtue of the fact that they aren't spending their time focused on the survival concerns of administrators in these new very fluid organizations.

DF: I can't agree with you more. I think this is an interesting segue way to the notion of service. When we talk about the academic community being internally focused and not having a sufficient sense of service to our outside customers, we are touching a critical aspect of our book. In the book we are going to devote a portion of the manuscript to the examination of the nature of service itself. It seems that the discovery of the "pull" of service expectations has had a huge impact on which organizations survive. Reflecting on how an organization that learns could also improve its service is a critical issue for this effort.

AD: "Service pull" is *the* most visible change reflected in my discussions with players in the technology firms in Silicon Valley. Half a decade ago technology firms were all "technology push." At the present time, they have shifted to a form of "market pull." They have reoriented themselves toward solving customer problems. This is not just a cultural or attitudinal shift. It also implies organizational rearrangements. Again, much of this reflects the impact of the information age. The customers know much more about alternative products and services available in the market, and if they don't know they simply get on Internet and find out. They can talk to providers/users anywhere in the world describing their need and exploring who might do the best job of responding to their need. So customers are no longer beholden to single supplier sources, and this change requires that organizations be structured in order to be far more responsive to differentiated customer needs.

DF: The organization cannot be captured by salespeople.

AD: In fact at the present time organizations have to *anticipate* the needs of customers, not just meet today's customer needs. They have to create a flexible architecture in product and service design that allows them to modify their product or service as new aspects of technology evolve and new client needs emerge. This requires anticipation three to five years into the future even while they are building today's product. This is an extraordinary change in the world of technology which only a short time ago said, "Here it is. It's our best. Take it or leave it."

DF: It seems to me that this would have a forceful effect on the value of learning in an organization; because, in the old system you learned, then you produced, then you sold, then you learned, then you produced, then you sold. Now you are saying that in order for that anticipation of the future to be incorporated, you are constantly learning and integrating future anticipations into the design of the present product.

In this sense, you have even changed the character of service itself. Service used to mean actions you took after the sale, or actions undertaken to deal with defects. Furthermore, you would even charge customers or require them to purchase a service contract to deal with these actions. One could suspect that we used to be comfortable designing flawed products, just to make service bucks. Now you are saying that serving requires the ability to visualize the product in the hands of the customer, not just in the present tense but several years out and to design the product to meet not only present needs but in anticipation of future needs.

AD: That is correct. Successful firms are creating architectures that allow tremendously differentiated products to be provided for different sets of customers building on a flexible based technology.

As a metaphor think of two American success stories in vehicle manufacturing: pick-up trucks and Harley Davidson motorcycles. You never see two pick-up trucks on the road that are exactly the same. Every purchaser adds something different . . . tool kit, rifle rack, an additional fuel tank, bicycle rack, etc. In this sense the stripped model of the pick-up truck is a base upon which each individual can start meeting personal needs. Likewise you seldom see a Harley Davidson as a stock model. After purchase each Harley quickly becomes a separate personal expression as the standard model is modified, personalized, stylized individually. These examples are nice metaphors for the future. Whether it is a medical service or an electronic product, people want to be able to build on the foundation design, twisting it to meet their personal needs, requirement, and preferences. Those organizations that understand that variety and flexibility are critical will create platforms that will accommodate this kind of customer differentiation. Organizations that help customers personalize the product or service are going to be the ones that are most successful.

DF: Absolutely! Knowing what those personal demands are and having this knowledge translated into capacity for design variation and execution is what an organization learns and can take to the bank.

I would like to change our discussion toward the issue of organizational culture. What is culture going to mean in the new organization?

AD: In the old organization we largely associated culture building with the skills of and prerogative of office associated with the transformational leader. We normally thought that establishing culture was primarily a responsibility of top management, particularly CEOs. There is a big problem with this conception in the new decentralized organization. It remains true that senior leaders today have a heavy role in overall organizational directing and culture. However, each business subunit will itself have to have the capacity to develop cultural norms, not incompatible with the larger organization but emphasizing aspects that are unique to its subsidiary functioning.

I expect to see parallels to what is emerging in the European Economic Community. How can you simultaneously be more European and at the same time be more French or Spanish? The parallel is this: How can you at the same time be more Hewlett Packard, but at the same time have a culture that is particular to the Medical Instruments Division?

What we are learning is that there remains a need for an overarching culture, but one that allows for a good deal of subunit diversity. Culture building in Silicon Valley is as much a concern of a design team, a customer service team, or an engineering systems team as it is the concern of a single CEO like Andy Grove or T. J. Rogers. Inside the bowels of the organization, although there is an overarching context, much of the culture that touches the individual is right down in the operating unit.

Now, America ought to be very good at doing this. The current remembrance of the Normandy invasion should remind us that much of the success was not because of a perfect master plan developed by Dwight Eisenhower. We were successful because when the master plan began to tear apart due to unanticipated circumstances, individual combat units felt free to take the initiative, decide what to do, and operate independently. In that sense, one of the strengths of the American military is creating a culture so that at the combat unit level there is freedom to exercise tremendous initiative.

This is a nice metaphor for culture in the new organizations. It is not enough to have culture at the corporate level, you have to have empowerment and a culture that provides freedom and allows for differentiation at the unit and team level.

DF: In a learning organization where lessons can be shared and cultural transfer can be more horizontal, the old notion that management sets down all aspects of culture, and sanctions any deviation, no longer seems to apply. By contrast, in the older organization there was actually recrimination if there was cultural deviation.

My sense of what you just shared is that while there may be an overarching culture, there are also units within the new organization that have their own unique culture and that what they have learned following their particular culture can also be shared with other parts of the organization.

AD: People need community, an identity with a country as well as with a region. We see this in the increasing emphasis on being Norman in Normandy, not simply French; while at the same time being a new European. We have a lot to learn about melding particularized cultures and values with overarching organizational cultures' values. So culture, like every other tool of management, at one and the same time is very macro and very subsidiary. We do not yet understand how to be comfortable with this paradox.

DF: Hopefully this book will be bought and read by a number of men and women who we are calling innovative managers and who understand that they are in a sea of change. They will be passionate about surviving personally and professionally. How would you answer those who will say to you: "Well, this is all fine for those hot shots in companies in Silicon Valley. But you know, I work for Acme Screw and Bolt; it is going to be a long while before I can start managing so that my organization is flexible and can learn as you are describing." What do you say to those people about some of these ideas that seem to be a bit off in the future from their present experience? Is there some place that they can start? Some steps that they can begin to take in this direction?

AD: Well, the first precondition for the new workforce is that you have to be educated and have well-developed skills regardless of the organizational level. You have to be a more skilled worker in a manufacturing cell in the mid-1990s than you had to be on a manufacturing assembly line in the mid-1970s. Likewise, up the skill ladder. It doesn't matter at what level you're operating, all positions require a greater investment in human resources. (The average company in Silicon Valley, by the way, is spending about $18,000 per employee at the lowest skill levels for training and development.) So the first thing to say is that both you and the organization have to make a much greater investment in your competencies than was true in the past. This increase in education will increase with acceptance of the concept and ability to move geographically in less "other directed" environments.

The second precondition is that organizations have to hire whole people. You are no longer hiring an individual to perform specified restricted tasks. You're hiring the total person as a true partner in your business and mission. Each employee has to understand the big picture, customer needs, and the latest technologies associated with serving these needs. No member of the organization can be isolated from the strategy of the company, its evolving technologies, or from customer contact. This results in a context where some of what used to be thought as "managerial viewpoints and prerogatives" now become partner prerogatives of all employees. This means that all employees have the right to some flexibility in managing their time, the right to invest in themselves and develop new competencies, the right to be away from the company interacting with customers, the right to search for solutions outside the company. As a consequence every employee, in fact, will participate in creating the new organization through innovating, and these innovations will change the nature of a company's strategy. So no one will really be in a position of saying, "my company is old fashioned and this doesn't apply." Instead, each of us must say, "My career requires that I respond to these new challenges and help co-create my new company."

DF: Initially at least, each individual has to test his or her own values in this regard. Each individual has to make sure that we are looking at each other as complete persons, not simply as a pair of hands or someone fulfilling a limited task. We have to see the wholeness of our co-workers and we also have to examine our own personal wholeness. There is a lot of wrestling right now with rethinking how each of us conceives the world of work. While we are talking and writing, there are people out there caught between two eras.

AD: One of the difficulties that complicates this period of transition is the tremendous employee displacement, white collar managerial workers, not simply blue collar machine operators. If Silicon Valley is a test bed for the future, you will see that labor mobility must be rationalized at the level of the Silicon Valley industry cluster, not inside a single firm. The average person in Silicon Valley, over the course of ten years, works for four different companies. They sign on with Apple until a mission is complete, then move to Intel until a mission is completed, then sign on at another company until a mission is completed there, etc. So you can ask: "Are they Apple employees? Are they loyal?" The answer is: "They are loyal to the mission while they are at Apple; they are loyal to Intel while they are at Intel completing its mission, but in many ways they are employees of Silicon Valley, that is, not employees of a single firm." How do we link prior notions of a career that enhances the culture of a single firm?

We are just beginning to conceive of labor forces at the industry cluster level, and we are not clear on how to manage this labor mobility. However, this kind of labor mobility is not simply a function of Silicon Valley, but exists in other major industry clusters – in the Great Lakes machine tool cluster, for example. We have always thought of managing the labor force, investing in their training, and so on as a "company" matter. This change to the industry level of resource exchange raises some interesting questions for us as a society. It seems an anomaly that we are trying to push health care, for example, as a company responsibility while at the same time we have a mobile labor force in which attachment to companies is relatively shorter. So at both the societal and organizational levels, we are seeing an emergent reality that we don't yet know how to manage.

DF: It reminds me of the Guild period. In the old days the Guild collected the money and took care of pensions and so forth. Members basically moved around in the region performing their craft, but the Guild was there as an overarching organizational form. We may be returning to that period.

AD: Yes, we may see the emergence of new craft groupings of professionals in our society. And these professional groups may become the contravailing power that protect the scientists, engineers, and professional workers in the way that labor unions protected blue collar workers in the past.

This leads to a painful aspect of the unsettled period that diminishes the present excitement. There is the possibility for enormous mischief during periods of paradigm shifts in organizational arrangements. For example, we had carefully constructed rubrics associated with avoidance of discrimination and fair employment practices that worked in bureaucratic structures. Now we are creating highly empowered self-designing teams where we argue the "chemistry has to be right" for the team to function. One could easily mutate this into "women wouldn't fit into our team."

We provided a certain amount of family economic stability by laws associated with unfair firing practices. Now are utilize downsizing and mission termination as means of adjusting employability with no obligation to displaced workers, and weakened safety nets. In short, until organizational and societal practices evolve appropriate norms, protecting the players in the new organization, both workers and professionals, there is great possibility for greed and exploitation as we make the transition to new organizational arrangements. We have not developed the social conventions that prohibit inhumane treatment in the new organizational forms in a manner parallel to the arrangements that were in place for more stable bureaucracies.

DF: My hunch on this is that those with greedy behaviors will act as lethal viruses, unleashing problems within the business without any particular anti-dote in place to cope with them. Business infected with these viruses cannot survive. I am hoping, therefore, the more ethical businesses are going to be the survivor in the competitive marketplace because they are conscious of the destructiveness associated with these negative possibilities. They will work out ways to self-organize and protect their employees and the employees will work out mechanisms for self-protection without necessarily regressing to older forms of government and legal intervention as the prop.

AD: Well, if we evolve shared norms as opposed to resorting to lawyers and artificial codification of rules and regulations that would be a desirable outcome. But this implies that such concerns for employee protection and well-being have to be a legitimate part of the dialogue between the new workforce and management. At the present time management is much more focused on and skilled with respect to issues such as high performance, high efficiency, quality control, and reduction of costs than they are in issues such as skill rebuilding, protection between missions, and portability of benefits. Unless management begins to focus on the needs of their competent workforce in the way that they are focusing on the needs of the competent organization, we will be headed for severe difficulties. Conversations about personal development, adequate slack, opportunities for retraining, equity sharing, etc. are not getting equal time in the literature about new organizations. In the long run I am optimistic. In the short run, I think we are going to see a good deal of dysfunctional behavior.

DF: Well, this is the last point. We have been experiencing exciting response to the idea of this book, *Managing in Organizations That Learn*. I would like to believe this is because it is timely to write a book about management focusing on a new way of managing compatible with the new organization. Have we come upon something important here?

AD: In periods of great stability, organization is an independent variable. You enter the organization and its structure defines your culture, your career path, etc. By contrast, in periods of rapid change, organizations are a dependent variable. Structural arrangements are simply temporary systems which have to be readjusted in order to meet the demands of customer and technology.

We are now moving into a world where we live in true open systems – globally open, market open, technology open, and informationally open. This will result in organizational arrangements which are much more ephemeral. Those organizations that will succeed are those organizations that create capacity to learn quickly. They will be organizations which empower change and are action biased dependent on quick learning. So it is appropriate to have a book centered on *learning*, which is probably the predominant contemporary organization challenge.

5

Creating the Conditions for Learning
Richard E. Wise

Introduction

Philosopher and literary critic Allen Tate once described the "one or two educated men" he had met during his lifetime.[1] The first was a man the 68-year-old Tate remembered from his childhood, a farmer and lawyer born in Kentucky about 1840. The man attended a small, secular college in the South, then served in the Confederate army. After the War, he "read" the law in the office of an older lawyer, while teaching mathematics at his alma mater and writing books on conic sections and integral calculus. "I could not then have understood that he saw no difference between his vocation and his avocation, or that he did not know which was which," Tate writes.

From early spring to early fall, the farmer-lawyer suspended his law practice to devote time to his farm. During those seasons, when not in the fields, he could often be found under a tree in the far corner of the yard, reading Mommsen's *History of Rome*, or Lord Clarendon's *History of the Rebellion*. At other times, he repaired to the abandoned ice-house behind the house, where he conducted chemical experiments in his laboratory

> for what purpose and to what conclusion I do not know; and I doubt that he knew: he was only increasing his knowledge. . . . (He) was not a professional scholar. He knew a little about many things . . . mathematics, science, the ancient classics, agronomy, the law; yet all of the little that he knew was alive in his daily life and was constantly brought to bear upon the human condition as he could know it in his place and time.[2]

Tate's second figure *was* a classical scholar. Herbert Cushing Tolman was born in Massachusetts, educated in the classics at Yale, studied at the great German universities, and returned to the United States to teach at Vanderbilt University. "In bearing and temper, he was remarkably like his non-academic counterpart in Kentucky." He was also a specialist: besides Latin and Greek, he had mastered Sanskrit, Ancient Persian, and Babylonian cuneiform.

Writes Tate:

> This man, a great scholar on the Renaissance model, no more than the Kentucky farmer-lawyer, knew the difference between vocation and avocation, between labor and leisure. These men were both in the strict sense amateurs, for what each did in his own way was done in the love of excellence. The competitive "advancement of knowledge" – produce or perish – the ostensible purpose of our university scholar, was incidental to the love of excellence.[3]

Such love of excellence and lack of distinction between work and the rest of life is not limited to those who toil in intellectual fields. Existential phenomenologist Martin Heidegger tells of a cabinetmaker's apprentice:

> His learning is not mere practice, to gain facility in the use of tools. Nor does he merely gather knowledge about the customary forms of the things he is to build. If he is to become a true cabinetmaker, he makes himself answer and respond above all to the different kinds of wood and to the shapes slumbering within wood . . . to wood as it enters into man's dwelling with all the hidden riches of its nature. In fact, this relatedness to wood is what maintains the whole craft. Without that relatedness, the craft will never be anything but empty busywork, any occupation with it will be determined exclusively by business concerns.[4]

These are but three individuals, and we have all known a handful of people like them. Whether "educated people" in some sense or not, they are above all good learners. What might it be like to have an entire organization populated with learners like these?

Imagine a workforce so inspired by the mission, vision, values, potential, and possibilities of the firm that people see no difference between vocation and avocation, between labor and leisure. Imagine employees so captivated by what they do that they do it mostly to increase their knowledge, and then willingly share that knowledge with others. Imagine colleagues so attuned to the cadence of the enterprise, and with a collective experience base and world view so broad and so diverse, that virtually every field of intellectual and commercial pursuit is alive in their daily lives, and brought to bear upon situations as they understand them in their place and time. Imagine workers so intrinsically motivated that, whether generalists or specialists, they do what they do for the love of excellence: a learning organization, in a classic sense.

That would be wonderful, one might respond, but it would be quite impossible. Productivity would suffer and, besides, the love of excellence, or the love of anything for that matter, it notoriously inept at getting one ahead in the world. Or is it?

It is a Friday morning in 1995, at nine o'clock sharp. More than a hundred employees of Symmetrix Inc., in Lexington, Massachusetts, assemble in the company's amphitheater for a meeting that will last three hours or more.

Clients, prospects, job candidates are all invited to attend, on one condition: all must participate in the vigorous discussion that will follow.

As the weekly meeting gets under way, it becomes clear that this is no exercise in corporate groupthink. In fact, it's just the opposite. An associate might offer a brief presentation on a new technology, or a partner might lay out some thorny issues confronting a new client. But whatever the topic, people are quick to challenge their colleagues' reasoning and assumptions, or their own. At one Friday meeting, the chief executive officer, inspired by an associate's dilemma, jumped up to argue against his own conclusions on an earlier case.

> "What we want to do is avoid the myopia of groupthink," says Symmetrix' president. "Our Friday forums allow us to see reality through multiple eyes. This helps us generate collective knowledge; it assures that as a firm we keep on learning." The right atmosphere, he says, is the key. People have to feel free to speak and try on unconventional ideas. "Once you have that base condition set, people with diverse skills and expertise will share opinions with each other."[5]

This is what a learning organization looks like. It's not surprising that Symmetrix, a management consulting firm, places a great deal of value on continuous learning in the organization. Intellectual capital is its stock-in-trade, and management realizes that the only way to compete today is to make your own intellectual capital obsolete before someone else does.

What is surprising is that so many other managements have taken so long to reach that same conclusion. The conclusion itself is nearly inescapable: in an era of aggressive competition, global markets, rapidly changing technologies, thinner margins, reduced cycle times, increasing expenses, limited capital, flattened organizations, demanding customers, impatient shareholders, querulous regulators, and a proliferation of products and services, no firm can survive if its people wait for a few managers at the top to tell them what to do each day. The firm will be left in the dust of more agile competitors. This is true regardless of the core business. The need for transformation is clear.

This chapter provides an overview of the learning process in people and organizations, then outlines some of the changes that are needed to transform the traditional organization into one that values and sustains continuous learning across the enterprise. The chapter revolves around three premises.

The first premise is that learning is a natural process at which most people, as individuals, are naturally quite adept. The capacity for substantive learning – acquiring new knowledge, divining its dimensions and implications, rendering the appropriate behavioral response, and modifying or confirming the learning in light of the feedback the behavior generates – already exists in most people. And they carry their tendency and capacity to learn, as well as a lifetime of background, education, experience, and insight, with them when they leave the house to go to work.

The second premise is that many of the organizational configurations and management systems and processes we have instituted over time to reduce risk and control uncertainty have had the unintended effect of stifling people's natural tendencies toward learning, either by not valuing it or by overtly punishing it. These aspects of the traditional organization that get in the way of learning must be modified or removed in order to make progress.

The third premise is that creating the conditions for learning in organizations now will require fundamentally new and different approaches to managing valuable intellectual capital. The issue is ultimately one of value creation: How do we manage people in a way that creates extraordinary value for customers, shareholders, the organization, and the people themselves?

Learning: A Natural Act

People are naturally good learners. Learning is an activity in which most of us have been actively and continuously engaged from the earliest moments of life, and little can stop us in our perpetual, if usually unconscious, quest for new things to learn.

Learning is a complex set of events that involves attention and sense-making, not just stimuli and responses. Withdrawing one's hand from a hot stove is not learned behavior, but the tendency to avoid hot stoves in the future is. Not all learning is intentional, not everything learned is taught, and not all learning outcomes are desirable. People can learn math, for example, and generalize what they know to problems never encountered before. They can also learn to hate math, and avoid situations where they may have to use it.

Figure 5.1 illustrates some key events in the learning process. It has a lot to say to business leaders, for two reasons. First, some of what is known about how people learn bears directly on how managers must lead in a learning organization. Secondly, the learning process in individuals is in many respects a metaphor for the learning process in organizations. So it seems worthwhile to examine the model briefly here. Later on, elements of the model will be related to some action steps for creating and fostering a learning organization.

The model has four main elements: **preconditions for learning**; the **cognitive processes and trial behaviors** that constitute learning; **consequences**, that is, confirmation or contradiction of the efficacy of the learning; and **feedback** to the memory banks.

Readiness, attention, and **motivation** are three preconditions of learning. All learners come to all learning situations with a certain amount of readiness to profit from the experience. They have to have the prerequisite knowledge, background, and experience, or social skills, or attitudes and dispositions to learn. If they don't, then that readiness has to be developed, or the energy spent trying to learn will be largely wasted.

In addition, people think with what they know. If a learner's knowledge,

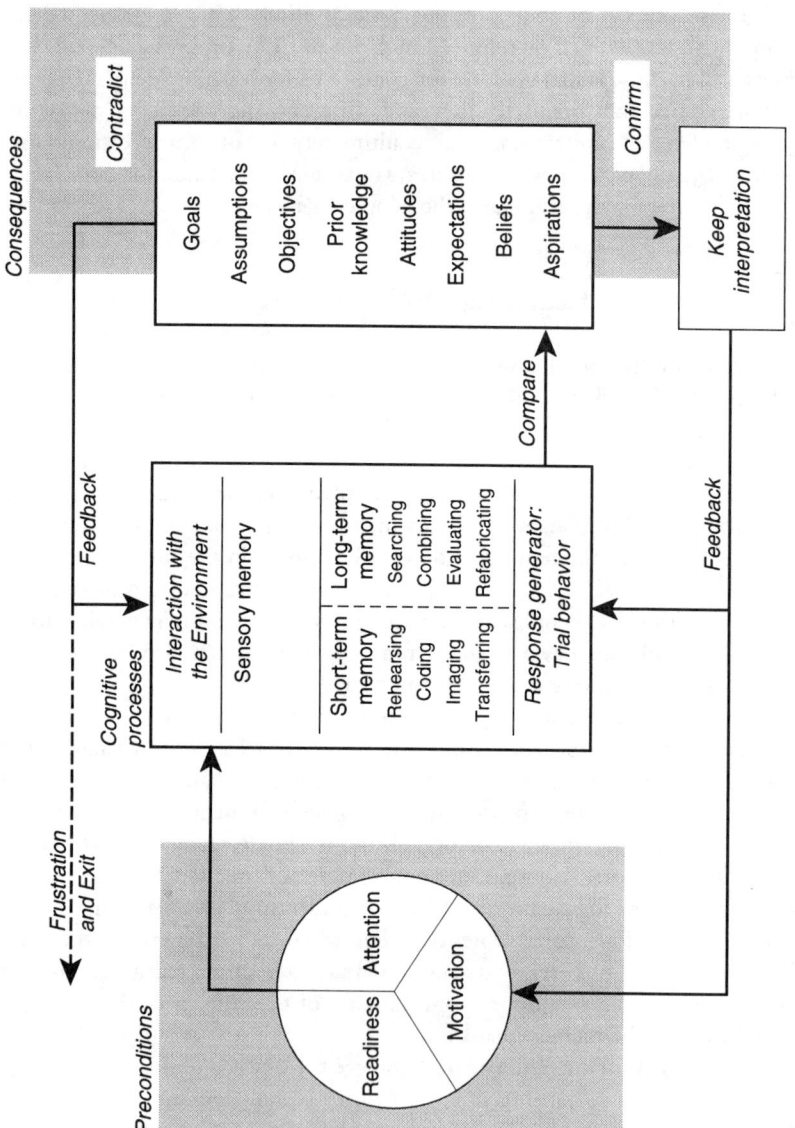

Figure 5.1 A model of the learning process.

of feedback; achievement and affiliation needs; level of aspiration; perceived locus of control; attribution of success, and many other "personological" variables influence one's motivation to learn. However, they don't all influence learning in the same way: a variety of subtle and often complex "aptitude treatment interactions" appear to mediate motivation and achievement.

What is known about motivation and learning holds three clear messages for managers in organizations that aspire to become "learning organizations."

The first message is that the performance appraisal and reward systems you probably use now may actually hinder people's motivation to learn. The reason is that the essence of productive learning is making mistakes. People learn from mistakes and have to make mistakes to learn thoroughly. Good learners make a lot of mistakes. They take roads that lead to nowhere. They follow ideas and trains of thought that yield no benefit. They spend time and have nothing to show for it. They take risks and lose. All the while, they learn.

Most performance appraisal systems are designed to punish this kind of behavior. How would your appraisal system rate a worker who appears to daydream and waste time, tinkers incessantly and seemingly aimlessly, makes mistakes, draws diagrams and throws them away, spends a good part of the day fiddling or talking to people, and comes up with ideas that don't work? Probably not very kindly . . . even if the employee's name were Edison.

In addition, learning is notoriously resistant to extrinsic rewards, especially financial ones (unlike other work-related behaviors). You can't buy insight, and curiosity is not for sale. As employees, people expect and probably deserve periodic increases in pay. But to link such extrinsic rewards to *learning* productivity only reduces intellectual risk-taking and makes learning less intrinsically satisfying.

The second message is that reward and punishment are absolute, but success and failure are relative. The goal in any organization is "success" in some terms. But success and failure are relative, and depend on what *the individual* is trying to achieve (level of aspiration). For example, reaching a goal one has personally set for oneself is generally considered to be successful. But getting within "goal region" (e.g. nominated but not elected) can also bring feelings of success, as can making progress in the right direction on a project or an assignment. Just selecting a socially appropriate goal can be a successful experience (which is why everybody who carries a folded copy of the *Wall Street Journal* carries it with the title folded outward!).

The third message is that **framing** and **process feedback** are everything. Managers of good learners frame problems and issues in ways that engage them in activities that give rise to learning: defining, questioning, observing, classifying, discriminating, generalizing, verifying, applying, hypothesis testing, and so forth. Good learners seldom need to be told what problems to solve or how to solve them, but it can be useful for the manager to let them know what elements the solution set should contain. This helps avoid a "guess what the manager is thinking" dilemma.

Managers also need to monitor and provide frequent feedback on how the learning process is going. Feedback is everything. Good learners don't need to be told whether they have gotten the right answer or come to the right conclusion – in fact, doing so can build resentment among them – but they do need frequent process feedback, often in the form of questions, to gauge how learning process is going.

Not everyone processes feedback the same way, however. Employees with relatively high achievement needs are more likely to benefit from task-oriented feedback (like "What a good job you're doing"), while those with relatively high affiliation needs are more likely to benefit from relationship-oriented feedback ("What a good group you are").

Elaborating what is known about the "human information processing system" is beyond the scope of this chapter. But several points are germane because they provide useful insights for participants and managers in any learning organization. First, though, we should develop a common (if superficial) understanding of how information is processed and how learning happens.

The processes of cognition – attention, sensation, encoding, imaging, searching, storage, rehearsal, retrieval, combination, evaluation, refabrication, transfer, and so on – represent continuous attempts to make sense of, and bring order to, an information-rich but chaotic environment.

The information a person has to work with at any moment comes from three sources: (1) the present circumstance, which includes some focal stimulus; (2) previous memory, which holds representations of past experiences and functional skills; and (3) the feedback received as a consequence of action, which feedback comes partly from the reaction of one's social and nonsocial environment and partly from one's own sensations. Information takes time to be processed and, during processing, appears to pass through several stages, each with its own characteristics and limitations.

If any learning is to take place at all, information must first be registered perceptually: seen, heard, felt, or somehow registered in consciousness, or sensory memory. The two major characteristics of this memory are high capacity and rapid decay. **Sensory memory** will record for a few moments a nearly exact replica of the event in the environment. But if the information is not converted to a more durable form within seconds, it is lost.

Sensory memory appears capable of registering vast amounts of information, but events that are the focus of attention are registered with greatest clarity. The focus of attention can be determined either peripherally (the brightest, the loudest, the most salient characteristic) or centrally (that which we expect to perceive or want to focus on). It is during these brief moments that pattern recognition and encoding for later processing begin.

There is no real agreement on how encoding is accomplished or what form it takes. Some hypothesize that it is largely a matter of converting experience into words. Others suggest it is image-like, retaining many of the characteristics of the original sensory experience. Still others assume an abstract representation that is neither verbal nor pictorial. In any case, encoded information is more durable than preprocessed information, and can be passed from sensory memory to **short-term memory**.

Short-term memory is what we are aware of at any given moment. It is highly active, but of limited capacity. Evidence suggests we can hold in short-term memory only about seven (plus or minus two) items of information at a time. An item of information may be very simple or highly complex, which is why the chess master can appear to remember so much more than the novice. The novice remembers individual moves while the master remembers clusters and patterns, each of which involve many moves.

To keep information alive in short-term memory, we must engage in rehearsal. Rehearsal retains information beyond the time when it would be naturally lost or displaced, and allows further encoding for transfer to **long-term memory**. Without rehearsal, information is lost or displaced in about 20 seconds.

Information processed into long-term memory can pass from consciousness and still be remembered. Whatever form the representation takes, it is highly durable. It has been argued that information that achieves long-term storage is never forgotten. Whether it can always be retrieved is another matter.

Many different kinds of information are represented in long-term memory, as the distinctions among episodic, semantic, and procedural memory make clear. **Episodic memory** is the ability to recall factual details of one's history. Facts of this sort have spatial and temporal marking, and are recalled less for their substance and more in terms of the context of their occurrence.

Semantic memory has to do with one's knowledge of the world: the facts and concepts a person knows, without necessarily knowing how or when they were acquired. Semantic memory is one's repository for the meanings of the world. **Procedural memory** is the memory of "knowing how" as opposed to "knowing that." It is the repository for what one can do with facts, concepts, and episodes, as opposed to what those entities are.

When we are asked to recall an experience or to explain what we remember of an event, we draw on all three types of long-term memory. And the response is not a mere regurgitation of the original experience. Performance in such circumstances is partly constructive. Fragments of the original experience may be remembered, but the gaps are filled in with constructions based on our general knowledge of the world.

Remembering a few things allows us to induce or deduce what other things are likely to have happened. Thus, performance in any situation is a function of how the current situation is sensed, what recollections one has of previous similar circumstances, and one's ability to construct alternatives for behaving that are sensible in light of these two informational inputs.

One kind of inductive process, **concept learning**, is essentially a classification device. The process of concept formation affords some economy for memory and behavior because instances of the same category can be treated identically and need not be distinguished. In most theories of semantic memory, concepts, not individual instances, are the basic content elements.

The mind also works deductively. That is, we can use our knowledge of the world for making decisions about what must logically be the case given the circumstances. If all As are Bs and all Bs are Cs, then it is logically (deductively) true that all As are Cs. Although certain nonlogical operations appear from time to time, the use of reasoning and deduction is one way we have of predicting our own or others' behavior from fragmentary memories of previous events.

Problem-solving and **decision-making** are two other high-level cognitive processes of which we as learners are capable. A person is confronted with a problem when (1) there is a personally meaningful goal to be achieved, and (2) the individual's repertoire of behavior does not include any readily available response that will allow achievement of the goal.

The production of appropriate response alternatives is what problem-solving is all about. Problem-solving appears to have two distinct stages, analysis and synthesis. In the analysis step, the learner attempts to identify relevant attributes, dimensions, and patterns of the problem, and searches for rules or principles that might be used to solve it. In the synthesis step, the learner generates alternative solutions, in an attempt to find a unique one that fully but parsimoniously solves the problem.

Decision-making then involves selecting and implementing the alternative considered best for the situation and, once feedback confirms the rightness of the judgment, the solution set is coded and stored for later use in similar situations.

The "rightness of the judgment," however, may still be debatable. My own work with insurance underwriters indicates that human judges can attend to only three to five informational "cues" at a time; that different judges value these cues in different ways; and that people usually are not able to say with accuracy which cues they value most in taking judgments and making decisions.[8]

Similar information-processing mechanisms are at work in learning organizations. For groups of learners, there are continuous attempts to make sense of an information-rich but chaotic environment. Often in such groups there is active disagreement as to the nature of the problem or issue at hand and the relevance of available information.

Group attention needs to be focused to facilitate information processing, and information usually needs to be represented in a variety of forms, such as charts, diagrams, timelines, written descriptions, and so on. The creative processes of option-generation, analysis, hypothesis testing, synthesis, judgment-taking, and decision-making ensue, as the group attempts to agree on high-quality outcomes. And feedback on the efficacy of the outcome modifies the group's experience base and further bolsters the group's competence.

In an attempt to organize and structure what is known about how people (and, metaphorically, organizations) learn, several hierarchies of learning have been proposed over the years. These schemes attempt to order the events of learning from extremely simple cognitive tasks to highly complex ones.

The hierarchy proposed by Gagne,[9] for example, is both developmental and situational: It describes learning through maturation as well as the cognitive preconditions for learning any highly complex task or skill. Gagne's model was, at first, logically rather than empirically derived but, as the basis for thousands of dissertations and research studies, it has supported empirical research quite well.

Other researchers led by Professor M. David Merrill of the University of Utah took a slightly different approach, in order to show the interaction of what is learned and how learning is used. That approach is shown in figure 5.2.

The horizontal axis shows four types of learnable information: **facts, procedures, concepts,** and **higher-order principles** or rules. Notice how these correspond to the episodic, procedural, and semantic memory systems. The vertical axis shows two types of performance, and two performance conditions for each type. Information can be remembered, and that learning can be demonstrated by either verbatim recall or equivalent restatement. Or information can be used in either previously encountered or novel situations. Three of the cells are logically empty: The only thing you can do with a fact is remember it verbatim (e.g., "Columbus discovered America in 1492").

One early use of this approach was to document the correspondence between what was taught and what was tested in Navy training programs. All students

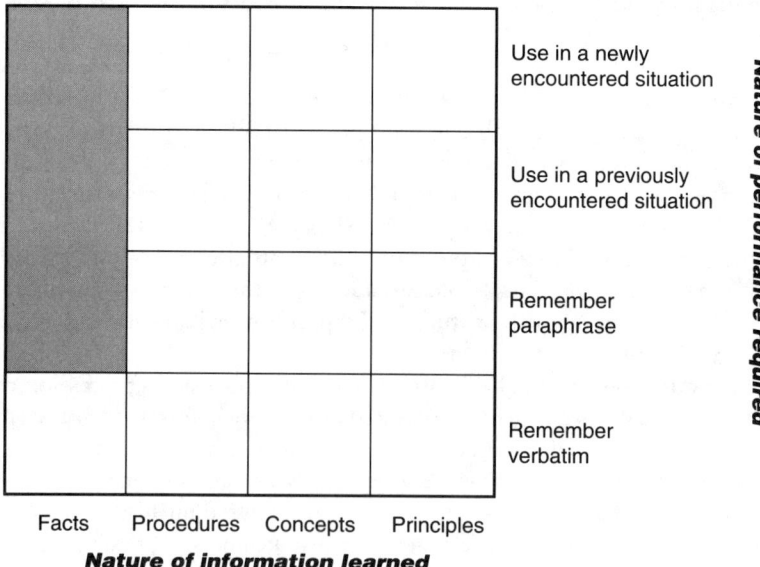

Figure 5.2   Task-content combination matrix.

have had the frustrating experience of being taught relatively low-level informa-tion ("Columbus . . . 1492"), and later being tested at a much higher level (e.g., "What was the impact of Columbus on early 16th century scientific explora-tion?"). Or the equally frustrating opposite experience: The instruction teaches the impact of Columbus, the test asks for the names of his three ships. This approach offered a way to diagnose the problem when student test performance was low; the instruction, the test, and the student could be examined in turn, systematically.[10]

If we overlay the traditional organizational hierarchy on this model, as in figure 5.3, we can gain some insights about the nature of many people's work today and the changes that will have to come about *en route* to becoming a learning organization.

We can see, for example, that most workers' jobs involve little more than remembering facts, procedures, and lower-level concepts, and using them in previously encountered situations. The workers are capable of much more, but they are seldom asked for much more.

In the traditional organization, management typically reserves for itself the right to apply the principles of the business to newly encountered situations. Some time later, policies, procedures, and rules will be carefully written so that any new approaches are institutionalized, thus relieving workers of the burden of having to think for themselves.

In the learning organization, everyone will be franchised to learn and to produce at even the highest levels of intellectual performance. Limitations may

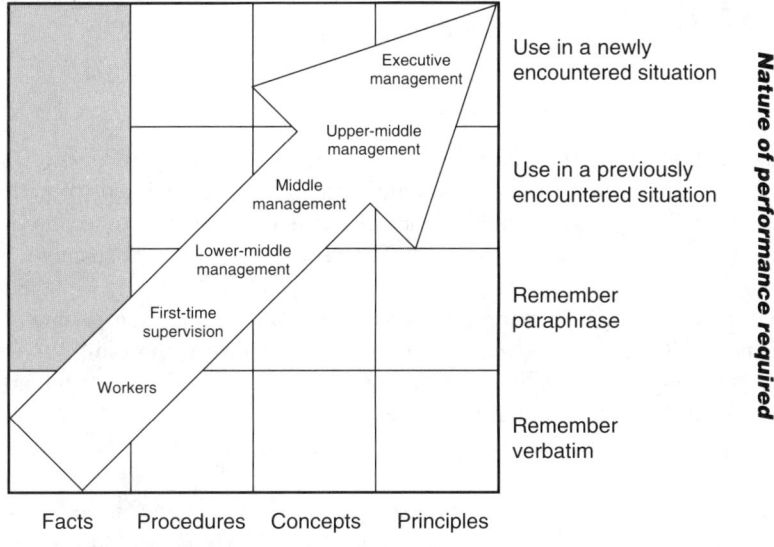

Figure 5.3 Task-content combination matrix and layers of the traditional hierarchy.

come from individuals' abilities, but not from organizational boundaries and layers of charts.

Barriers to Learning at Work

Over the years, companies have embraced a variety of organizational forms and management systems to enhance communication, reduce risk, and control uncertainly. But these configurations and control systems have had an unintended effect: They have stifled people's natural tendencies toward learning, either by not valuing it or by overtly punishing it. The ironic result is that many firms now face greater uncertainty and higher risk than ever before: the risk that competitors will make their intellectual capital obsolete before they do.

Three major categories of institutional impediments to learning deserve mention here:

1 The design of the organization, specifically, the traditional hierarchical bureaucracy as a way of organizing people;
2 The design of the "job" as a way of organizing tasks;
3 Various human resources planning, control, and development systems and processes, including performance appraisal and salary administration systems; and "management development" approaches.

Not included in this discussion are such factors as physical barriers, office and building layout, that make communication and interaction difficult. Also not included are the "institutional imperatives" of the firm – the culture.

Structure of the organization

Whatever its merits may have been in terms of Taylor-like efficiency, the hierarchy has become an expensive and cumbersome impediment to getting work done. The cost is measured financially and in terms of cycle times, product and service quality, communication effectiveness, customer satisfaction, and employee loyalty.

Until very recently, hierarchies offered a certain stability, security, and convenience. They allowed managers to compartmentalize responsibility (while often diffusing accountability), specialize work, and provide career opportunities. Unfortunately, hierarchies developed too many layers. For example, in one insurance company in the late 1980s, there were 11 layers of management, just in the personnel department!

The number of layers in an organization can lead to financial, operational, and cultural problems. The financial problem is that an organization with more than about four layers is just too expensive to maintain. This can be appreciated by considering that the lowest person in the hierarchy must generate enough revenue to pay for all or part of everyone above him or her. Or, in the personnel department's case, someone or some group has to produce enough sales to pay for all of their own management plus all of the personnel department.

The operational problems have to do with both responsiveness and communication effectiveness. With highly compartmentalized responsibilities, it's easy to lay off a problem as "not my job." In fact, it may not be anyone's job, in which case, the problem remains unsolved. If the problem is a customer's, it may not be addressed at all, until a competitor decides to solve it.

Culturally, the problem with hierarchies is not that they are too high, it's that their chief message is to inform people that most of the business is none of their business. Yet in a global, technology-oriented, information-intensive, service economy, every member of an organization will need to have a holistic view of the enterprise as well as a stake in its success.

Peter Drucker has noted that organizations, once built like pyramids, are now more like tents.[11] Indeed they are. And what's left of the hierarchy when you strip away the layers, titles, perks, rules, working hours, job descriptions, manuals, procedures, meetings, memo wars, intrigue, voice mail, petty demagoguery, turf battles, political maneuvering, appraisal forms, self-aggrandizement, excuses for nonperformance, suits-and-ties, cultural symbols, and everything else that too often connotes "the firm"?

What's left is the heart and soul of commerce: the competencies and desire of committed people to put their own resources at risk in order to create value as defined by somebody else – a customer – who is willing and able to pay for it. That is, and always has been, the essence of enterprise.

Inside Drucker's "tent," assets, business acumen, capabilities, and desire are what count. There are no other renewable sources of competitive advantage. Knowledge is inventory, to be turned as rapidly as possible. And people become disposed to learning as never before. Why? Because three important preconditions for learning are at last fully in place: readiness, motivation, and attention. Looking for new things to learn becomes a way of life.

Going forward, the most successful learning organizations will probably be characterized by a dearth of layers. There will continue to be corporate responsibilities and reporting relationships, of course. But they are likely to be transitory, and project- or opportunity-oriented. Spans of control (to the extent that the concept continues to have operational relevance) will be very broad, structurally reinforcing the fact that the manager no longer serves as taskmaster, overseer, chief decision-maker, goal setter, and quality checker. Those powers will remain with the people themselves.

Jobs and the structure of work

The job as a way of packaging work is a relatively recent invention, a product of the industrial revolution. Before there were jobs *per se*, people worked just as hard and provided for themselves and their families by performing shifting clusters of tasks, in a variety of locations, according to schedules set by the seasons and weather. The jobs that emerged in the factories of the early nineteenth century were considered dangerous and inhuman, an unnatural way to work.[12]

Fortune magazine reported in September 1994 that, "Now the world is changing again. The conditions that created jobs 200 years ago – mass production and the large organization – are disappearing." And with the disappearance of the conditions that created jobs, we are losing the need to package work that way.

Organizations are now being transformed from a structure built out of jobs to a "field of work needing to be done."[13] Jobs as they exist today are artificial units superimposed on this field. Together, they are supposed to cover all the work that needs to be done. But in a period of rapid change, jobs become "rigid solutions to an elastic problem." You can rewrite a person's job description occasionally, but not every week.

Jobs – those position-described, performance-objective-defined, Hay-point-rated, organizationally slotted packages of things to do in eight-hour bites – impede organizational learning in two ways. First, they distract the employee from the real focus of the enterprise, which is competing for delighted customers.

Second, they often inadvertently reward the wrong behavior. Instead of being rewarded for getting results, the job holder is more often rewarded for "doing his (or her) job," regardless of the outcome. Over time, employees may consistently opt for those courses of action that pose the lowest personal risk, not the highest organizational rewards. At such a point, learning and renewal become exceedingly difficult.

The "de-jobbing" of the workplace at this time provides an opportunity, for those who would recognize and seize it. The opportunity now is to redirect workers' focus toward the real mission of the enterprise, and find ways to realign their self-interests so that they are more congruent with those of the organization.

Human resources planning and development systems

A variety of human resources planning and development approaches have had the unintended effect of stifling learning in the organization. The performance appraisal and salary administration systems used in many large firms are prime examples.

Management by objectives is one commonly used approach. Performance objectives and measurements for the coming year are mutually agreed to at the beginning of the appraisal period. Interim feedback is provided periodically (usually quarterly). At the end of the appraisal period, performance on each objective is rated and, by some mechanism, a summary rating is obtained. The summary rating provides input into the salary administration system to determine the employee's annual raise.

Management by objectives has deservedly received a lot of praise over the years. Certainly, having objectives is better than not having them, and specifying expected results early on gives focus and discipline to the effort. But incorporating MBO into the employee appraisal system has several compelling drawbacks.

First, the summary ratings almost always present some threat to self-esteem. As a result, they encourage self-protective behavior, "CYA" activities, and excessive documentation; and discourage openness, information sharing, risk-taking, and mistake-making.

Second, the appraisal system is individually focused and top-down. Despite efforts to create involvement and buy-in ("mutually-agreed objectives"), most employees in firms that use this approach know that what will happen is what the boss wants to happen. And, although organizational learning is a uniquely team-oriented phenomenon, there are few mechanisms for measuring and rewarding team performance and individuals' contributions thereto.

Third, a year is too long. In most industries, key players have little idea what they will be doing a year from now, other than "whatever it takes" to keep the enterprise moving ahead.

For many workers, the world of work thus becomes little more than an extension of primary and secondary schooling, where an authority figure makes assessments and assigns grades; where, as one manager once told me, "an ounce of image is worth a pound of performance"; and where there is a clear if curious distinction between learning and getting grades.

This approach to performance appraisal usually works in tandem with a salary administration "grid." The grid crosses performance rating (on, say a 1 to 5 scale) with salary level relative to salary midpoint for the job grade. Cell entries represent annual percentage pay increases, with a "key cell" (average performer at 95 percent to 105 percent of midpoint) prescribing an inflation-level salary increase. Workers whose performance is high and whose pay is relatively low receive the largest pay raises; those whose performance is low and whose pay is relatively high may receive little or no increase.

While this approach has a certain logic and may be useful for planning the salary budget in large organizations, it does little to foster a climate in which organizational learning can flourish. There are at least three reasons for this.

First, as with the formal performance appraisal, a year is too long to wait. Employees make contributions throughout the year, and should receive various financial and nonfinancial rewards as results are achieved.

Second, the existence of the reward table lets the employee decide at the outset how hard he or she wants to work. For example, if it is widely known that only 10 percent of employees will be rated 1, an employee can decide early on whether the marginal reward is worth the incremental effort. I remember one employee who calculated that, on his salary, "the marginal benefit of busting my hump for a year is a dollar a day."

Third, this approach to salary administration disconnects the company's interest from the employee's interest. If the company is wildly successful, the employee will get 4 percent; if it nearly founders, the employee may get 3 percent. There has to be a closer correspondence between the company's financial success and the employee's financial rewards.

Going forward, it is likely that these approaches will fall by the wayside. They are administratively cumbersome, and add little value to the enterprise. Their effects on performance, motivation, and commitment are inimical. They are rigid solutions to elastic problems. In their place will likely emerge appraisal and reward systems that are more team-based, self-administered, performance-contingent, and time-bounded.

Implications for leadership development

Leadership development is a critical activity in the learning organization. This is distinguished from the more traditional "management development" or "supervisory skills training," wherein people are taught about managing (Maslow, Theory X, etc.). The challenge is to train managers to assume a new role: the role of **inquiry manager**. This is similar to the role of the "inquiry teacher" described by Postman and Weingartner.[14]

In the learning organization, the manager of the enterprise is also the manager of the medium. A major challenge for managers thus becomes how to preserve and extend the behaviors of good learners into team and, ultimately, larger organization settings.

The beliefs, feelings, and assumptions of managers are the air of the workplace, and they determine the quality of life within it. The attitudes of the "inquiry manager" are reflected in his or her behavior. Among the small but growing number of such people, you will observe that:

1 They rarely tell people what work to do.
2 The basic mode of discourse with employees is questioning, and the inquiry manager emphatically does not use questioning to exercise power or seduce the employee into guessing what the manager is thinking.
3 The inquiry manager refuses to accept a simple statement as an answer to a question.
4 The inquiry manager encourages employee–employee interaction as opposed to manager–employee interaction, and generally avoids being the judge of the quality of ideas expressed.
5 The inquiry manager rarely summarizes, to avoid closure.
6 The organization and its processes develop from and reflect the abilities of people, and not necessarily some "logical" structure.
7 The inquiry manager frames problems and issues for employees, to engage them in mathemagenic activities – activities that "give birth to learning" – defining, question-

ing, observing, classifying, discriminating, generalizing, verifying, applying, hypothesis testing, and so on.

Above all, the inquiry manager has to get rid of, not just try to mask, any sense of innate position superiority, or that "I got mine," or even that "I deserve my position and its perks." Unless and until managers believe that, given the chance, almost everybody can think as well as they can, solve problems as well as they can and, given the chance, possibly run the organization as well as they can, the transition to a learning organization will be well nigh impossible.

These behaviors and attitudes amount to a definition of a different role for the manager – the inductive manager, the inquiry leader. The traditional boss, like the traditional job and the traditional hierarchy, is defunct.

Keeping the Target in View

I conclude with an image offered earlier in the chapter:

Imagine a workforce so inspired by the mission, vision, values, potential, and possibilities for the firm that people see no difference between vocation and avocation, between labor and leisure.

Imagine employees so captivated by what they do that they do it mostly to increase their knowledge, and then willingly share that knowledge with others.

Imagine colleagues so attuned to the cadence of the enterprise, and with a collective experience base and world view so broad and so diverse, that virtually every field of intellectual and commercial pursuit is alive in their daily lives, and brought to bear upon situations as they understand them in their place and time.

Imagine workers so intrinsically motivated that, whether generalists or specialists, they do what they do for the love of excellence.

This is the target we need to keep in view. A learning organization, in a classic sense.

Notes

1 Allen Tate, "Several thousand books", *The Sewanee Review*, July–September, 1967, vol 78, no. 3.
2 Ibid.
3 Ibid.
4 Martin Heidegger, "What is called thinking?" (*Was heisst Denken?*), trans. by F. D. Wieck and J. G. Gray (New York: Harper & Row, 1968).
5 M. C. Driscoll, "Never stop learning", *CFO*, February 1995.
6 See R. M. W. Travers, *Essentials for Learning* (New York: Macmillan, 1972).

7 Ibid.
8 W. G. Stillwell, D. A. Seaver and W. Edwards, "A comparison of weight approximation techniques in multiattribute utility decision making", *Organizational Behavior and Human Performance*, vol. 28, no. 1, August 1981.
9 R. M. Gagne, *Conditions of Learning* (New York: Holt, Rinehart and Winston, 1985).
10 M. D. Merrill, R. E. Richards, R. V. Schmidt and N. D. Wood, *The Instructional Strategy Diagnostic Profile Training Manual* (San Diego, CA: Courseware, Inc., 1977).
11 T. G. Harris, "The post-capitalist executive: an interview with Peter F. Drucker", *Harvard Business Review*, vol. 71, no. 3, May–June 1993.
12 W. Bridges, "The end of the job," *Fortune*, September 19, 1994, p. 79.
13 Ibid.
14 N. Postman and C. Weingartner, *Teaching as a Subversive Activity* (New York: Dell, 1969).

6

Closing the Loop: The Dynamics of Creative Learning*
Alexander N. Pattakos

Introduction

The call for creativity and innovation in contemporary organizational life can be heard loudly and clearly from all corners of both the academic and practitioner communities. Indeed, it would be fair to say that creativity is becoming a cornerstone of the quest for continuous quality improvement, including total quality management (TQM), as well as the growing interest in "re-engineering" and related organizational transformation efforts. Parenthetically, it is important to note that this has not always been the case; indeed, the emphasis on statistical process *control* typically runs counter to intuitive decision-making and right-brain thinking processes. In order to sharpen their competitive edge, however, more and more organizations are finding reasons to search for practical ways to unleash their creative potential. While the motives for these efforts may not always be clear or consistent, and the expected return on investment from such initiatives may not be precisely or rigorously specified in advance, it is apparent that doing business in the "same old way" is being challenged more frequently by even the most conservative-minded leaders and managers.

This chapter is about what Dr Edward De Bono, the originator of the concept of lateral thinking, has referred to as **serious creativity**. According to De Bono, "Almost every major business advertises itself as 'the creative corporation.' There is a huge amount of lip service given to the central importance of creativity, but . . . this lip service is not accompanied by any serious effort to use creativity."[1] Indeed, to the extent that creativity is "used" by organizations in any systematic way, it is often assigned a role that is removed operationally from the *core* business, such as in research and development. Creativity, under this

* The author would like to acknowledge the contributions of his business colleague, Linda A. Garrett, Vice President, *Creative Learning Technologies, Inc.*, who assisted in the development of many of the ideas and concepts introduced in this chapter.

scenario, is viewed more as an adjunct function to the organization as a whole rather than as a staple of organizational vitality, both in terms of capacity and performance. In situations where the creative function is more widely acknowledged and promoted, it frequently is presented simply as a part of the organization's repertoire of problem-solving tools and techniques or, worse yet, as one of the latest management "flavors of the month" that requires only temporary lip service and tolerance from the rank-and-file since eventually it will be replaced by some "new paradigm."

This chapter addresses the myriad of challenges, including the frustrations, associated with creativity enhancement in organizations. In order to do so, it examines creativity and the creative process in a particular context, that is, a context of organizational learning. Linking creativity and learning in this way, as will be explored in detail later, establishes a new mental model for building organizational capacity and provides a conceptual backdrop for introducing the notion of **creative learning** as a distinct (and desirable) characteristic of learning organizations. Moreover, because the author believes that one cannot have organizational renewal or transformation without personal renewal or transformation, this chapter naturally seeks to confront issues and questions pertaining to "human potential" on both individual and collective levels. From a slightly different view, Larry Wilson, a principal in Wilson Learning Systems and co-author with Ken Blanchard of *The One-Minute Salesperson*, has observed that, "You can change without growing but you can't grow without changing." By definition, we will see in this chapter that, in order to accommodate the creative tension that drives personal and organizational improvement, creative learning is directed towards the latter kind of change process. Furthermore, it is important to underscore here that growth, as used in this chapter, does not refer simply to size; rather, it is an evolutionary and multidimensional concept with an emphasis on human system development.

Defining Serious Creativity

Creativity, it should be noted, is a messy and confusing subject; it conjures up different meanings depending upon the context in which it is used. According to De Bono, at its simplest level, the notion of creativity "means bringing into being something that was not there before."[2] In contrast, Dr Frederic Flach, a noted pychiatrist and expert in stress management, has underscored that "the creative act does not create something out of nothing. It rearranges, combines, synthesizes already existing facts, ideas, and frames of reference."[3] Flach, however, also views creativity in a "serious" vein, much like his colleague De Bono. Creative behavior to both of these respected authorities is goal-oriented, that is, it is a response to a situation, broadly defined, that calls for a novel but adaptive solution.

The understanding that creativity, by definition, *is* serious business in an increasingly complex and competitive environment has surfaced as a staple of contemporary leadership and management. It has been observed, for instance, that the barriers of inertia and attitude, which stop creativity from even starting, are embedded in rigid and often hostile organizational cultures. Infusing creativity and innovation in these organizations requires a "new paradigm" in leadership, as well as a value set that supports and actually provides incentives for continuous learning and risk-taking.[4] In their management best seller, *In Search of Excellence*, Thomas J. Peters and Robert H. Waterman, Jr. describe one of the characteristics of excellent firms as a "simultaneous loose–tight" structure. These firms had at the same time some very clear tight objectives ("fostering a climate where there is a dedication to the central values of the company"), with individual freedom to operate in creative ways to achieve those objectives ("tolerance for all employees who accept those values").[5] It is significant to note that Peters and Waterman placed heavy emphasis – they even used the term "faith" to capture the essence of this guiding principle – on a common set of operating values that were focused explicitly on quality, innovativeness, informality, customer service, and people.

Fostering creativity at work, to be sure, still rests firmly on individual initiative. Indeed, Robert Fritz, a composer, artist, writer, and entrepreneur, is careful to distinguish between creativity and "creating." According to Fritz, "It is possible for *creativity* to exist without having the creative process. It is also possible to have the *creative process* without having creativity."[6] What this suggests is that creative capacity requires both the ability and willingness to act. If a person, no matter how "creative" he or she may be reputed to be, does not engage in the act of creating, creativity and the creative process are analogous to the tree falling in the forest when no one is around to witness or hear the event. Moreover, because of its intimate connection to human potential, creativity has been called "a lifestyle, a personality trait, a way of perceiving the world, a way of living and a way of growing."[7] Put differently, creativity represents the essence of our individuality. In effect, suffice it to say for now that, as we allow our creative potential to become manifest, the process of "creating" serves to define the boundaries of our unique identity as human beings.

The roots of creativity have intrigued both researchers and practitioners across a wide range of disciplines for many years. In this regard, theoretical perspectives and classificational schemes for explaining creative phenomena have appeared in all kinds of media, with varying degrees of acceptance. Typically, creativity has been classified according to its primary focus, that is, person, process, or product, and has been approached theoretically from one or more of the following perspectives: psychoanalytic, behavioralistic, or self-actualization.[8] The published literatures on these subjects are extensive, although their practical application to the organization and management experience is only just beginning to develop. In this chapter, only those elements that seem to meet this latter need will be covered.

Perhaps the most common references to creativity associate it with right-brain thinking. This approach is grounded in **brain dominance** theory, exemplified most notably by the work of Ned Herrmann, who has led the way to measure and profile the "creative brain," based upon what has been described as a holistic view of brain functioning.[9] Indeed, the plethora of literature describing the functions of the two sides of the human brain, and, in particular, the popular bias to associate creative thinking with the "right" hemisphere, has prompted De Bono to put out a cry against what he calls "hemispheric racism." Certainly, strategies to compensate for rigid, linear approaches to thinking, problem-solving, and decision-making by triggering the "right-brain" experience have contributed significantly (both quantitatively and qualitatively) to creativity enhancement in organizational life. By the same token, it would be naive, indeed, to invest in anything other than a truly holistic approach to human systems development – one that engaged the total person, individually and collectively, in mind, body, and spirit. As discussed later in this chapter, it is precisely this kind of strategy that comprises the *sine qua non* of creative learning.

The whole-brain approach to creativity, which essentially is physiological in its fundamental orientation, has helped to intensify and broaden the continuing dialogue(s) over the nature of "mind," and, especially, the structure of consciousness. The arguments that attempt to map a science or philosophy of mind cover a broad spectrum of views. Professor John R. Searle, for instance, postulates that "mental phenomena are caused by neurophysiological processes in the brain and are themselves features of the brain."[10] To Searle, what is going on in the brain is neurophysiological processes and consciousness and nothing more – no rule following, no mental information-processing or mental models, no language of thought, and no universal grammar. Other researchers exploring the new cognitive neuroscience underscore the central importance of the linguistic domain on human consciousness. Professors Humberto R. Maturana (Chile) and Francisco J. Varela (France), in their search for the biological roots of human understanding, conclude that:

> We humans, as humans, exist in the network of structural couplings that we continually weave through the permanent linguistic trophallaxis of our behavior. Language was never invented by anyone only to take in an outside world. Therefore, it cannot be used as a tool to reveal that world. Rather, it is by languaging that the act of knowing, in the behavioral coordination which is language, brings forth a world. We work out our lives in a mutual linguistic coupling, not because language permits us to reveal ourselves but because we are committed in language in a continuous becoming that we bring forth with others. We find ourselves in this co-ontogenic coupling, not as a preexisting reference nor in reference to an origin, but as an ongoing transformation in the becoming of the linguistic world that we build with other human beings.[11]

Constructing "mind" out of the brain has opened up new avenues for developing models that intend to explain visual perception and cognition, memory, and related functions of the intellect.[12] Moreover, explicit attention is being paid to the neurophysiological bases of creative and intuitive thinking.[13]

Are minds, as suggested by MIT Professor Marvin Minsky, ". . . simply what brains do?" Or, are there models of mind and consciousness that transcend the boundaries of orthodox materialism? Professor Erich Harth, for instance, takes us out of the old Newtonian world of machine models of the brain and into the almost mystical realm of contemporary physics. In his view, both consciousness and creativity arise from specific structures – the relays within the sensory pathways linking the sense organs and the cerebral cortex – that send information back and forth. This information, moreover, when it reaches the cortex, is filtered and personalized through improvisation, much like the way children talk to themselves as they practice their language ability. Human consciousness and the creativity that it exhibits, according to Harth, are embedded in a messy, largely intuitive "hall of mirrors" within the biology of the brain.[14]

Another perspective that stands in stark contrast to the neurophysiological models that traditionally have attracted the scientific community in large numbers is represented by the work of physicist Nick Herbert, who draws upon the key features of quantum theory to explain human consciousness. Founding his argument on the attributes of quantum systems, that is, randomness, "thinglessness," and interconnectedness, he posits that mind is a fundamental process in its own right, much like light or electricity, and that it interacts with matter at an equally elemental, that is, subatomic, level.[15] Human consciousness, according to this view, is associated only with quantum systems. In this connection:

> A quantum system may be distinguished from its classical cousins by the number of possible courses of action that are in fact open to that system. If there is only one possible outcome, as, for instance, in a deterministic computer program, then the system is a classical Newtonian one. If, however, there is more than one possible outcome, the system is quantum.[16]

Inner mental states, including what we perceive to be expressions of creativity, are held to be manifestations of a quantum reality rather than simply the results of certain, albeit complex, biological interactions or the software programming that controls the brain's computerlike "hardware."

In his encyclopedic study of the "roots of consciousness," which draws upon multiple frames of reference – historical traditions, folklore, and scientific research and theories – Jeffrey Mishlove, a leading figure in the field of parapsychology and an expert in the practical applicaton of intuition at work, presents further evidence to support the distinctively quantum character of the human mind.[17] Moreover, he explores a wide variety of phenomena long relegated to the realm of the "supernatural" and offers a multidimensional view of reality that expands the meaning of consciousness well beyond the outer limits of neurophysiological explanations and models. Levels of consciousness, it seems, include not only phenomena that reside beneath our threshold of awareness, commonly referred to as the **subconscious mind** but also phenomena that transcend conscious awareness, that is, the so-called **nonlocal** mind (or **superconsciousness**). In the lexicon of quantum theory, this state or principle of nonlocality has also been referred to as universal or collective consciousness.[18]

Creativity, it should be noted, has been defined explicitly in terms of consciousness levels. Arthur Koestler, in this regard, viewed creativity as the balancing between the conscious and the unconscious minds and therefore observed that the creative person is "multi-level headed" as opposed to level headed.[19] This perspective is consistent with one advanced by neurobiologist, William H. Calvin, whose research into the structure of consciousness, which is as philosophical as it is scientific, places creativity at the "margins" of conscious thought. According to Calvin,

> Consciousness involves our operating on the margins, against the enormous background of automatic things. It's something like civilization, where we can drive a car without understanding a carburetor, use a radio without being able to build one, improvise jazz without being able to tune a piano, create electronic music without understanding the innards of the black boxes. *Consciousness doesn't always involve creativity and choice, but they're close relatives, much more so than mere awareness.*[20] [emphasis added]

The creative act, therefore, can be perceived effectively as the process of balancing, if you will, multiple dimensions of "knowing" or understanding across a spectrum of consciousness planes. These planes operate simultaneously, if not in parallel fashion, below (i.e., the subconscious) as well as above (i.e., the superconscious) the threshold of human awareness. On a metaphysical plane, individuals, who are capable of plugging into the so-called superconscious or nonlocal mind, are said by some observers to have attained a "higher creativity."[21]

It has also been proposed that all acts of perception are acts of creativity. Professor Calvin, in this regard, suggests that "We create the world that we see. We surely modify it with experience, but it's an invented world. How we emotionally react to something may, in turn, affect how we see it in the future. Literally."[22] To paraphrase the Greek philosopher, Heraclitus, "you never walk through the same river twice." One could reasonably take this proposition one step further and say that you cannot even walk through the same river *once*, since it is changing constantly (or, at least, our "perception" of the experience is undergoing continuous change). In the language of quantum theory, consciousness, by definition, requires that the frame of reference of the observer be taken into account.[23] The saying, "Where you stand is where you sit," takes on added import as a metaphor for the new physics. In this context, our ability to cast both a wider and a finer net around our "reality" is fundamental to our capacity to be creative. Indeed, events that deviate from Newtonian laws – the paradigm guiding most organizations and management systems today – may occur in our everyday world without being observed simply because we are not looking. The following parable, attributed to Sir Arthur Eddington, a distinguished astrophysicist, raises this possibility:

> In a seaside village, a fisherman with a rather scientific bent proposed as a law of the sea that all fish are longer than one inch. But he failed to realize that the nets used in the village were all of a one-inch mesh. Are we filtering physical reality? Can we catch consciousness with the nets we are using?[24]

Another, perhaps more straightforward, conception of creativity defines it in terms of associations or connections between disparate phenomena. Simply put, creativity can be defined as the art of making connections. Neil McAleer, a journalist, referred inspiringly to creativity as "a passionate, exciting and challenging effort to make just the right connection amid the buffeting chaos of everyday life."[25] Moreover, the ability to make the "right" connection, as discussed in the next section, requires a combination of openness, flexibility, and related personal attributes that are easy to specify and prescribe but more difficult to practice for most individuals. While the author would like very much to develop (or unleash) the "Robin Williams" and "Jonathan Winters" personality dimension of the clients with whom he works as one of his creativity enhancement goals, psychological barriers, such as emotional armoring, obstacles imposed by organizational culture, and so forth, make this something that is much easier said than done.

Serious creativity, moreover, requires both passion and action. In light of our earlier discussion about the relationship of consciousness to creativity, it also draws heavily upon the human mind's ability to create images. Creative imagery or visualization is often loosely equated with imagination. Albert Einstein, in what now has become one of his most famous quotations, said that "imagination is more important than knowledge." Alex Osborn, the originator of the process of "brainstorming," also underscored the importance of imagination to creativity. However, creativity, he wrote in *Applied Imagination*, is "imagination combined with intent and effort."[26] Clearly, to Osborn, only what we are calling serious creativity could be applied effectively to the kind of problem-solving and decision-making challenges facing most modern, complex organizations.

Creativity, as defined here, can be applied both conceptually and practically to even those processes, products, services, and so on, that seem to be no more than *replication* efforts. It could even be argued à la Heraclitus that there is no such thing as "replication." This issue notwithstanding, empirical research reported from Japan looks at creativity from a similar perspective. Unlike in the United States, small, incremental "improvements" or modifications to replicated events in Japanese industries comprise significant outputs of the creative function.[27] The central value attached to *original* (is there really such a thing anyway?) breakthrough ideas as manifestations of "creativity" in organizations seems to be primarily an American (or, at least, Western) phenomenon.

Determinants of Creative Behavior

It is not surprising that research has shown that the natural level of personal creativity, irrespective of how it is operationalized and measured, decreases over time dramatically after about five years of age. Various acculturation factors, such as schooling, family, religion, employment, government, are usually identified as the reasons for this decline in behavior (not necessarily in "capacity" or potential). On the positive side, there is also evidence suggesting the possibility of a reversal of this downward trend at mid-life. The extent to which this reversal occurs is largely a personal matter, especially related to an increased awareness of human potential. The choices made by adults to discover the "meaning of (their) life" have received considerable attention in the popular press and personal development/self-help literatures. Indeed, as the first wave of "baby-boomers" reaches the half-century mark, it can only be expected that matters associated with the adult metamorphosis will become even more important to society-at-large. The implications of this transformation in the United States will be profound – influencing public policies, working environments, societal institutions and relationships of all kinds, and individuals (their sense of being, self-worth, and so on).

Mark Gerzon, writing in his recent book, *Coming Into Our Own*, likens the adult metamorphosis to a series of "quests" – for wholeness, for deep healing, for love, for a calling, for meaning, for interdependence, for integrity, and for the sacred or spiritual. To Gerzon, adults at mid-life need not experience a "crisis"; rather, he envisions the second half of life as a new beginning, as the point from which the quests noted above can become truly manifest. He underscores that, "Particularly as longevity increases, our capacity to grow throughout adulthood becomes absolutely critical – not only to our personal happiness but to human survival."[28] Because creativity has been conceptualized in this chapter as being linked fundamentally to human potential and individuality, efforts to reverse the downward trend identified here should not be considered lightly. On the contrary, unleashing the creative spirit in all of humanity seems to be a threshold requirement for survival, not just a strategy for self-actualization or peak performance.

What, then, are the observed, as well as the hypothesized, correlates of creativity? In other words, what characteristics or attributes seem to determine or influence (i.e., both facilitators and obstacles) levels of personal creativity? Put differently, what factors distinguish creative people from those who appear to be less creative? Moreover, what are the "ideal" elements of a working (or living) environment that support and even may provide a catalyst for unleashing the creative potential of individuals?

It has been observed that "creativity is expressed more in one's attitude than in a set of mental strategies or techniques of thought."[29] Moreover, the same authors contend that the "creative attitude" can be expressed in one phrase: **a willingness to take risks**. One's fear of failure, therefore, is proposed as the ultimate attitude test for creativity. The "courage to create," as Rollo May eloquently described it in his classic work by the same name,[30] exists within each of us. Unfortunately, it is often very difficult for people to find the courage to go through the fears that prohibit their creativity from surfacing. This seems to be especially the case in certain environments, such as the workplace, where the traditional management paradigm breeds fear and works against the principles of total quality, productivity, and innovation. Building upon W. Edwards Deming's call for managers to "drive out fear" in order to achieve high levels of quality, consultants Kathleen D. Ryan and Daniel K. Oestreich have articulated strategies to overcome "creative paralysis" and build a high trust work environment.[31]

The significance of attitude in relation to creativity should be underscored for several additional reasons. It has been established, for instance, that a positive outlook is tied closely to creative behavior. To quote Henry Ford, "If you think you can, or you think you can't, you're right." Not only does negativity work against the creative process, it has been found to lead to increased stress and, concomitantly, to physical illness and disease. The ability and willingness to maintain a positive attitude during times of duress are therefore not only attributes of creative people but also of wellness. One only needs to read about the horrifying experiences in the Nazi death camps described by Viktor E. Frankl[32] to gain an appreciation for the strength of positive thinking as a tool for personal survival. Moreover, Professors Charles C. Manz and Chris P. Neck have found that the establishment by workers of "constructive thought patterns," in terms of their beliefs and assumptions, internal dialogues (i.e., self-talk), and mental images, improves both personal and organizational performance. They conclude that, "Management of thought in organizations is perhaps the ultimate frontier to be explored in the pursuit of employee and organizational effectiveness. There is probably a great deal of truth to the idea that the managers at their best only influence the way employees manage themselves."[33]

Another attitudinal dimension related to creativity is sense of humor. Interestingly, Dr Edward De Bono considers humor to be ". . . by far the most significant behavior of the human brain."[34] As a correlate of creativity, humor also helps to reduce (and manage) stress, which clearly is a major consideration in managing complex organizations in the current era. Stress management has also been linked directly to creativity, both as a facilitator when it is present and as an obstacle when it is not. Resilience to stress, moreover, has been identified as a key element in health and wellness in general, as well as a determinant of job performance. Conversely, psychiatrist Frederic Flach has declared, based on his professional experience as an expert in stress management, that "creativity is an essential part of resilience."[35] In this connection, Dr Flach notes that the creative process adheres to the laws of disruption and integration – both potential stress inducers – and provides courses of action for dealing with both of them.

Other correlates of creativity that have been gleaned from research and practice include: an awareness of thinking style(s); an awareness of, and sensitivity to, the various blocks to creativity that exist within one's environment; a reliance on and trust of one's intuition; a preference for flexibility; an openness to challenge and perhaps reframe one's assumptions (i.e., mental models); a sense of purpose (compare to the "coming into our own" quest described earlier); a value set that is supportive of creative action; diversity of experiences and opportunities; and high self-esteem. These qualities or attributes, when considered together with those discussed previously, provide a composite profile that obviously is ideal and difficult to attain (both for individuals and organizations). Indeed, it has been proposed that a truly creative person is one who has attained the idealized, "self-actualized" state first introduced by Abraham H. Maslow in the early 1950s. Individuals at this level of human development are said to:

1 perceive reality more accurately and objectively; tolerate and even like ambiguity; are not threatened by the unknown.
2 accept themselves, others, and human nature.
3 be spontaneous, natural, genuine.
4 be problem-centered (not self-centered) non-egotistical; have a philosophy of life and probably a mission in life.
5 need some privacy and solitude more than others do; are able to concentrate intensely.
6 be independent, self-sufficient and autonomous; have less need for praise or popularity.
7 have capacity to appreciate again and again simple and commonplace experiences; have zest in living, ability to handle stress, high humor.
8 have (and are aware of) their rich, alive, fulfilling "peak experiences" – moments of intense enjoyment.
9 have deep feelings of brotherhood with all mankind; are benevolent, altruistic.
10 form strong friendship ties with relatively few people; are capable of greater love.
11 be democratic, unprejudiced in the deepest possible sense.
12 be strongly ethical and moral in individual (not necessarily conventional) ways; enjoy work in achieving a goal as much as the goal itself; are patient, for the most part.
13 have a more thoughtful, philosophical sense of humor that is constructive, not destructive.
14 be creative, original, inventive with a fresh, naive, simple and direct way of looking at life; tend to do most things creatively – but not necessarily possess great talent.
15 be capable of detachment from their culture; can objectively compare cultures; can take or leave conventions.[36]

In order to acquire all of these attributes, eventually the steep challenge of maneuvering one's way up to the top of Maslow's hierarchy of needs will have to be faced. Creativity, in this sense, is not merely *related* to human potential on an intimate level. Indeed, the creative spirit plays a much more basic (and profound) role in the evolutionary path of human beings. Creativity, as an expression of individual self, comprises the very seed(s) from which human potential becomes manifest. In this connection, there are some who believe that the capacity for creative action is synonymous with healthy living, and that its absence (that is, the absence of creative capacity) is the direct result of faulty development of the concept of self.[37] Jagdish Parikh, moreover, examines in great detail the concept of self and proposes that "managing your self" is a staple of human systems development and contemporary business management. He offers a model of personal growth in which human beings, who are like "seeds" with a tremendous amount of dormant potential, have critical choices to make:

> . . . either feel the "comfort" or "security" of remaining a "seed" all your life or take a more dynamic courageous attitude, and fertilize and nurture the seed. Then you will enable the "seed" to break through its "barriers," and blossom through various evolutionary stages into a fully grown plant or tree, with all the richness of its flowers or fruits. . . . This involves gaining access to and experiencing higher levels of consciousness and going beyond ego, thereby opening up alternative, but hitherto dormant, channels of knowing. This is what "managing your self" is about.[38]

Advocating a process of "detached involvement," Parikh demonstrates how organizations can maximize their return on investment in human potential through self-management. The ultimate impact of this approach, indeed, is on the organization, leading to its progressive transformation. It is significant to note that he places creativity at the core (i.e., heart and soul) of organizations which not only are experiencing peak performance but also are "centered," "aligned," "attuned," and "alive."[39]

On a personal level, the goal of detached involvement clearly suggests the need to attain a heightened level of awareness about one's "self." In effect, this is exactly what the process of "meditation" is all about – heightened awareness. Parikh underscores the importance of meditation as a tool for self-management and it is slowly becoming a part of academic training in business administration and related fields.[40] The results from an international survey of workplace values conducted between late 1992 and early 1994, moreover, underscore the importance of intrapersonal needs of workers, including the need for spiritual development, and suggest that "meditation rooms or quiet sanctuaries" may be the next step for visionary employers.[41] In his careful analysis of the results of courses on values training for senior managers at the Indian Institute of Management at Calcutta, conducted between 1983 and 1990, Professor S. K. Chakraborty found the "construction of a sound-proof *mind-stilling* room" to be an institutional innovation that, in his opinion, was essential for enhancing organizational performance and vitality. More explicitly, he urged:

... all senior or top management to provide for a *mind-stilling* room, which is a more fundamental need than the provision of clubs and swimming pools. The latter usually lead to a lot of useless exteriorization and to very little genuine relaxation. Usually the consciousness is lowered and vulgarized through such socialization. The *mind-stilling* room should provide management with an alternative facility to sit in during working hours and calm down ruffled tempers, restore nervous equilibrium, allow the mind to render authentic feedback, and even to pray if so inclined.[42]

A recent article in *Fortune* revealed the importance for leaders to "heed the voice within" and described the need for a new management skill – reflection – in the fast-moving new economy. Citing the experiences of mainstream corporations such as AT&T, PepsiCo, and Aetna, various forms of "introspection" training are now being integrated into management development programs. This kind of training is linked directly and explicitly to another mission-critical skill for both individuals and organizations – an aptitude for continuous learning. Moreover, the benefits of meditation are introduced, and illustrations of how it is used in practice are provided. In this regard, it is highlighted that the CEO of Silicon Graphics has been meditating daily for a decade in order to sharpen his own intuition. The article concludes with a discussion of the goals of successful introspection, whether it is accomplished through meditation or by some other means: (1) increased objectivity; (2) passion for continuous learning; (3) increased self-confidence; (4) heightened sense of personal responsibility; (5) increased tolerance for ambiguity and paradox; (6) increased propensity for action; (7) a balance in life; (8) increased access to creativity and intuition; and (9) egolessness, a state of mind that comfortably transcends selfish concerns.[43]

It is interesting to note that the efforts described above to foster increased introspection or reflection in the workplace can also be viewed as creativity enhancement initiatives. This is the case even in those situations where increased creativity is not the articulated goal or part of the conscious intent. Increasing creativity at work, however, by opening up options for visualization and imagery experiences, as well as through relaxation of conscious attention (such as in the case of the mind-stilling room), has proven to be very effective.[44] One of the most *avant garde* approaches to enhancing creativity in the work environment involves the use of emerging sound technologies that are designed both to relax and energize mind, body, and spirit. Donatos Pizza, a midwestern pizza chain, recently installed a new system called the NEST® (Naturally Enhanced Sound Transmission) in its corporate headquarters as a tool for employee capacity-building and wellness. The author is presently conducting an evaluation of the effects of this technology on a number of work-related factors, including creative thinking and stress levels. The preliminary results are promising in these and other areas, and suggest that the notion of mind-stilling rooms or sanctuaries deserves increased attention by leaders and managers in all types of organizations.

Collective Creativity: Seeing the Forest and the Trees

Although the goal of enhancing personal creativity is inherently valuable to organizational vitality and performance, it is not sufficient by itself to develop the kind of organizational capacity envisioned in this chapter (or this entire book, for that matter). At this point, our attention therefore turns to a higher, that is, *collective*, level, that is, groups, teams, organizations. In short, how do we take advantage of "creative communities"? Creative **synergy** between individuals is obviously a desirable commodity in light of all of the previous material covered in this chapter. How does it occur, and what do we need to do (or can we do) for this synergy to occur? Within organizations of different types, what factors seem to inhibit this kind of collective consciousness or energy from manifesting itself? Are certain organizational forms more (or less) appropriate for creative synergy than others?

It should be noted that, even within traditional hierarchies, expectations are increasing that individual contributors (i.e., nonmanagerial employees) will demonstrate their creative potential to further organizational success. On an operational level, what happens when different organizational entities (or subentities within an organization) hold incongruent value perspectives or exhibit contradictory behaviors about the creative process? What if there is not a common, shared vision about the creative function for the organization? Must there be one? Can creativity be mandated from above? How can we reconcile the *source* of creativity at a personal level with the requirements imposed by collective action?

Collective creativity suggests more than creative collaboration in groups. Brainstorming is an illustration of the latter. As the father of "brainstorming," Alex Osborn, has said, by definition and practical design, it is "nothing more than a creative conference for the sole purpose of producing a checklist of ideas – ideas which can serve as leads to problem-solution – ideas which can subsequently be evaluated and further processed."[45] Collective creativity, moreover, is not simply the use of "groupware" or electronic meeting systems (EMS) technologies in state-of-the-art facilities. On the contrary, tapping into the creative potential of groups, teams, organizations, and so forth, is much more than a tabulation and aggregation of individual inputs. The process of making connections and gaining creative insights, while similar to that used on a personal level, necessitates higher levels of trust and risk-taking when applied to more than a single entity.

Dr Brian O'Leary, a former NASA scientist-astronaut, transferred his interest in exploring "outer space" to "inner space" and subsequently experienced a remarkable personal transformation. Concerned about collective consciousness and behavior as well as about understanding our world and our place in it, he has concluded that:

> . . . the key to our *collective synergism* is to forgive the past, feel the perfection of the moment, suspend judgment, open our hearts, let go, and take our free fall into ourselves and the universe. No one knows what the future will hold, but it is clear that we are in the midst of an exciting revolution in thought, feeling, and intuition . . . there is a higher power guiding us from within and without.[46]

Besides the metaphysical and new science leanings reflected in this statement, which are not that far away from some of the perspectives shared about creativity (e.g., Willis Harman's "higher creativity"), learning organizations (e.g., Peter Senge's reference to "metanoia") or the emerging "new paradigm" in business (e.g., Margaret Wheatley's "learnings about organization from an orderly universe"),[47] O'Leary identifies an interesting set of challenges and opportunities for collective action.

Significantly, there is a group communication process that addresses many of O'Leary's operational concerns about facilitating or encouraging collective synergism. **Dialogue** is such a collaborative process and it has received considerable attention as a way to transform communication, with the ultimate goal of transforming business and other organizational "systems."[48] Doug Ross has introduced the following "working understandings" of how dialogue works (or, at least, should work) in groups: (1) identify and suspend assumptions (e.g., mental models); (2) establish collegial regard (i.e., engage with each other as equals); (3) provide for a spirit of generative inquiry (i.e., be open to and invite new ideas); (4) encourage active listening (e.g., use of "talking stick"); and ensure that the "context" of the group is maintained through some means of facilitation (e.g., a facilitator who has no responsibility other than to monitor the dialogue).[49] To be sure, engaging in true dialogue is easier said than done. Further discussion about this process can be found elsewhere in this volume.

Collective creativity and innovation are also becoming significant issues on an interorganizational level. The emergence of corporate networks, strategic alliances, and similar interorganizational arrangements has increased dramatically the targets of opportunity, as well as the challenges, for collective decisions. Dialogue and other forms of communication are also crossing functional and jurisdictional boundaries at an accelerating rate as electronic forums, such as the Internet, provide new points of contact between organizational members. Robert K. Mueller, for example, has observed that, as we move to more open organizational system structures, "Networking provides tremendous power to get ideas accepted or new actions underway and can empower an organization to alter its course or accept change."[50] It remains to be seen how well dialogic communication and other ways to achieve collective synergy work at the interface between organizational entities. Because we now live in the "Age of the Network," it behooves us to examine closely this issue. As Jessica Lipnack and Jeffrey Stamps, two experts in the field of network management, recently concluded, "Networks bridge the self and the group, the daily and the eternal, the mundane and the sacred, and carry us into the 21st Century."[51]

The more that we are able to see both organizations and interorganizational networks as **learning systems,** the more we will be able to increase the likelihood of achieving collective synergy. Creativity at this level is essential for ensuring the "health" of systems that not only are undergoing rapid change but also are seeking continuous improvements in performance. As the pressures to engage in whole systems thinking continue to increase, whether everyone is conscious of them or not, the demands and expectations for creativity in organizations will escalate as well. Seeing both the forest *and* the trees will become an increasingly valuable core competency for workers, individually and collectively. How well entities of different types are able to see the connections between what may at first appear to be entirely unrelated elements, concepts, ideas, and so forth, is a staple of systems thinking, a precondition for organizational and interorganizational learning, and a virtual map in the "management" survival kit required to navigate what Peter Vaill has referred to as the "permanent white water"[52] associated with doing business in the current era.

Creativity: What Does *Learning* Have to Do With It?

Throughout this chapter, there has been an implication that creativity and learning are *interdependent* processes occupying two sides of the same coin. In this regard, it has been well established, both theoretically and practically, that creativity is a "learnable" skill irrespective of the level of creativity that one may reputably possess at any given point in time. This is precisely why specialized organizational entities, such as the Creative Education Foundation (CEF), have been created, and why a wide assortment of creativity "trainers" and consultants can be found across the corporate landscape seeking opportunities to build the capacity of organizational members (and, ideally, the entities of which they are a part) to be more creative.

In an address at the Massachusetts Institute of Technology in 1955, Alex Osborn, who was instrumental in the CEF's evolution, submitted that "creativity is an art, an applied art, a workable art, a teachable art, a learnable art, an art in which all of us can make ourselves more and more proficient, if we will." In a similar vein, but from a distinctly organizational perspective, we do not want simply to create "learning organizations"; instead, our mission should be to develop *creative* learning organizations. Indeed, it can be said that all organizations, to some degree, are learning organizations. It has been observed, moreover, that "all organizations engage in some form of collective learning as part of their development."[53] The question of interest here, however, has to do with the kind of learning that actually occurs – that is, the extent to which "learning" explicitly draws upon (and builds) the *creative* potential that exists within the organization. In their book, *Quantum Learning*, Bobbi DePorter and Mike Hernacki pay considerable attention to the linkage between creative thinking and learning.[54] In this regard, it is clear that the idea of "paradigm shifting," which comprises a major concern for understanding and dealing with organizational dynamics, is tied intimately, perhaps even symbiotically, to the creative process. Learning to "change ladders" will not (and does not) happen without creative effort. By "closing the loop" between creativity and learning, organizations will become not just learning systems but "living" true expressions of open, dynamic, and holistic *human* systems.

Figure 6.1, in this regard, shows how creativity may be tied to the learning organization concept, as well as identifying where many of the key elements discussed in this chapter fit into an overall scheme focused on personal and organizational transformation. The concurrent goals of cultivating "resilient" individuals, building "empowered" teams, and creating "learning" organizations, all within a context of creativity, provide a solid foundation for unleashing human potential for the highest good of all involved. It will not be sufficient or

Figure 6.1   Creative learning loop.

prudent simply to "mandate" creativity in modern, complex organizations. Nor is it going to be enough to expect these organizations to accelerate learning in order to do more of the same, even if then they will be able to perform more effectively or efficiently. The dynamics of **creative learning**, on the other hand, present a new and composite paradigm, one that promises to reframe the purpose of both of these key dimensions, as well as integrate them into a whole that, indeed, is greater than the sum of its parts. Unleashing the creative spirit in this way will enable people and organizations not only to probe but also to extend the "boundaries of rationality" that Herbert Simon[55] once said limit human performance.

Notes

1 Edward De Bono, *Serious Creativity: Using the Power of Lateral Thinking to Create New Ideas* (New York: HarperCollins, 1992), p. viii.

2 Ibid., p. 3.

3 Frederic Flach, *Resilience: Discovering a New Strength at Times of Stress* (New York: Ballantine, 1988), p. 156.

4 See R. D. Gamache and R. L. Kuhn, *The Creativity Infusion: How Managers Can Start and Sustain Creativity and Innovation* (New York: Harper & Row, 1989). See also H. P. Sims and P. Lorenzi, *The New Leadership Paradigm: Social Learning and Cognition in Organizations* (Newbury Park, CA: Sage, 1992).

5 Thomas J. Peters and Robert H. Waterman, *In Search of Excellence* (New York: Warner Books, 1982), pp. 318–25.

6 Robert Fritz, *Creating* (New York: Fawcett Columbine, 1991), p. 6.

7 G. A. Davis, *Creativity is Forever* (Dubuque, Iowa: Kendall/Hunt Publishing, 1986), p. 2.

8 Ibid., pp. 21–30.

9 Ned Herrmann, *The Creative Brain* (Lake Lure, NC: Ned Herrmann Group, 1995).

10 John R. Searle, *The Rediscovery of the Mind* (Cambridge, MA: MIT Press, 1994), p. 1.

11 Humberto R. Maturana and Francisco J. Varela, *The Tree of Knowledge* (Boston: MA Shambhala, 1992), pp. 234–5.

12 See, for example, S. M. Kosslyn and O. Koenig, *Wet Mind: The New Cognitive Neuroscience* (New York: Free Press, 1992) and M. S. Gazzaniga, *Nature's Mind: The Biological Roots of Thinking, Emotions, Sexuality, Language, and Intelligence* (New York: Basic Books, 1992).

13 Erich Harth, *The Creative Loop: How the Brain Makes a Mind* (Reading, MA: Addison-Wesley, 1993) and C. Hampden-Turner, *Maps of the Mind* (New York: Macmillan, 1981).

14 Harth, *The Creative Loop*.

15 Nick Herbert, *Elemental Mind: Human Consciousness and the New Physics* (New York: Dutton, 1993).

16 Ibid., p. 187.

17 Jeffrey Mishlove, *The Roots of Consciousness: The Classic Encyclopedia of Consciousness Studies* (Tulsa, OK: Council Oak Books, 1993).

18 Ibid., pp. 316–18, 329.
19 Arthur Koestler, *The Act of Creation* (New York: Macmillan, 1964).
20 William H. Calvin, *The Cerebral Symphony: Seashore Reflections on the Structure of Consciousness* (New York: Bantam, 1990), 77–78.
21 See W. Harman and H. Rheingold, *Higher Creativity: Liberating the Unconscious for Breakthrough Insights* (Los Angeles: Jeremy P. Tarcher, 1984).
22 Calvin, *The Cerebral Symphony*, p. 229.
23 See N. Friedman, *Bridging Science and Spirit: Common Elements in David Bohm's Physics, the Perennial Philosophy and Seth* (St. Louis: Living Lake Books, 1994).
24 Ibid., p. 27.
25 Neil McAleer, "The roots of inspiration", in Jane Henry (ed.) *Creative Management* (London: Sage, 1991), p. 12.
26 Alex F. Osborn, *Applied Imagination* (New York: Charles Scribners, 1953).
27 See M. Basadur, "Managing creativity: a Japanese model", *Academy of Management Executive*, 1992, vol. 6, no. 2, pp. 29–41.
28 Mark Gerzon, *Coming Into Our Own: Understanding the Adult Metamorphosis* (New York: Delacorte Press, 1992), p. 288.
29 R. Schank and P. Childers, *The Creative Attitude: Learning to Ask and Answer the Right Questions* (New York: Macmillan, 1988), pp. 56–7.
30 R. May, *The Courage to Create* (New York: Bantam Books, 1975).
31 Kathleen D. Ryan and Daniel K. Oestreich, *Driving Fear Out of the Workplace: How to Overcome the Invisible Barriers to Quality, Productivity, and Innovation* (San Francisco: Jossey-Bass, 1991).
32 V. E. Frankl, *Man's Search for Meaning* (New York, Norton, 1975).
33 Charles C. Manz and Chris P. Neck, "Inner leadership: creating productive thought patterns", *Academy of Management Executive*, 1991, vol. 5, no. 3, pp. 87–95.
34 De Bono, *Serious Creativity*, p. 8.
35 Frederic Flach, *Resilience: Discovering a New Strength at Times of Stress* (New York: Ballantine Books, 1988), p. 156.
36 Davis, *Creativity is Forever*, pp. 4–5.
37 See D. W. Winnicott, *Playing and Reality* (Harmondsworth, Middlesex: Penguin Education, 1980).
38 Jagdish Parikh, *Managing Your Self: Management by Detached Involvement* (Cambridge, MA: Blackwell, 1994), p. 29.
39 Ibid., pp. 150–1.
40 See M. Ray and R. Myers, *Creativity in Business* (New York: Doubleday, 1986).
41 D. G. White, *International Workplace Values Survey, 1994* (San Francisco: The Compass Group and Sterling & Stone, Inc., 1994).
42 S. K. Chakraborty, *Management by Values* (Delhi: Oxford University Press, 1991), p. 118.
43 S. Sherman, "Leaders learn to heed the voice within," *Fortune*, August 22, 1994, pp. 92–100.
44 See W. C. Miller, *The Creative Edge: Fostering Innovation Where You Work* (Reading, MA: Addison-Wesley, 1987) and T. Rickards, *Creativity at Work* (Brookfield, VT: Gower Publishing, 1988).
45 Osborn, *Applied Imagination*, pp. 151–2.
46 Brian, O'Leary, *Exploring Inner and Outer Space: A Scientist's Perspective on Personal and Planetary Transformation* (Berkeley, CA: North Atlantic Books, 1989), p. 176.

47 See W. Harman, *Higher Creativity* (New York: Jeremey-Trucker, 1984), P. Senge, *The Fifth Discipline* (New York: Doubleday, 1990), and M. Wheatley, *Leadership and the New Science* (San Francisco: Barrett-Kochler, 1992).

48 See S. Deetz, *Transforming Communication, Transforming Business: Building Responsive and Responsible Workplaces* (Cresskill, NJ: Hampton Press, 1995).

49 Doug Ross, "Dialogue as collaborative process: an organizational perspective", *Vision/Action*, Summer 1994, pp. 3–7.

50 Robert K. Mueller, "Corporate networking: how to tap unconventional wisdom," in J. Henry (ed.), *Creative Management* (London: Sage, 1991), p. 157.

51 Jessica Lipnack and Jeffrey Stamps, *The Age of the Network: Organizing Principles for the 21st Century* (Essex Junction, VT: Oliver Wight, 1994), p. 232.

52 Peter Vaill, *Managing as a Performing Art* (San Francisco: Jossey-Bass, 1989).

53 E. C. Nevis, A. J. DiBella and J. M. Gould, "Understanding organizations as learning systems," *Sloan Management Review*, Winter 1995, p. 74.

54 Bobbi DePorter and Mike Hernacki, *Quantum Learning: Unleashing the Genius in You* (New York: Dell Publishing, 1992), pp. 291–325.

55 H. Simon, *Administrative Behavior: A Study of Decision-Making Process* (New York: Macmillan, 1961).

7

Leading Learning

Steven I. Meisel and David S. Fearon

Effective leadership is the new bottom-line of organizations and this is defined by how well organizations learn. At one time, management was defined by the mastery of the tools and technology of the job along with a knowledge and ability to apply power within the political reality of the corporate system. If power and technical skill are not enough in today's organizations, then what does the manager now need to know?

In a 1994 article, Kevin Barge[1] makes an interesting observation on the nature of leadership. Barge noticed that in the hit movie, *Jurassic Park*, two types of dinosaurs ruled the jungle island. The first was the huge Tyrannosaurus Rex. T Rex trampled through the forest trying to kill everything in sight. But time and again the characters in the film escaped death by hiding or in other ways taking advantage of the monster's poor vision and tiny brain.

In spite of the size and reputation of T Rex, the truly frightening dinosaurs were the velociraptors. These fast-moving hunters worked in packs, learned from each encounter with the humans, and communicated what they learned to each other. The "raptors" overcame the electronic defenses, overwhelmed the heavy weapons of the guards, and provided most of the real movie mayhem. In a prophetic statement shortly before becoming a raptor meal, the movie's big-game hunter observed that, "They think about what they are doing . . . that's why they are so dangerous." The few humans who survive in the story do so, not because they are tougher than the raptors, but because they ultimately outwit them.

Barge's observation is thought-provoking. Sheer size and ferocity are not nearly as effective as strength and speed paired with the ability to learn. In the Jurassic world of the movie or the modern jungle of the competitive corporation, we lead and win by being smarter than the competition.

In the long run, organizations and individuals both work smarter by learning from experience. How this learning takes place, and the role of the individual in creating organizational learning, is the subject of this chapter.

Combining Managing, Leading, Learning

The traditional concept of management is that of command and control. At its best, management is a set of skills applied within a set of rules. Managing maintains the resources of the organization by meeting the demands of the current reality. It is more a process of adaptation than innovation. However, an organization that fails to look ahead to emerging realities soon finds itself in trouble. Newer views of management recognize this problem and have added the role of the leader to the work of management.

Leaders are expected to articulate the vision of the organization, to set a direction, and to inspire people to move in that direction. Although leadership is seen as vital to the growth of the organization, there are no reliable guidelines for leading. All of us have different images of a leader, but there is no single attribute that clearly states the nature of the activity. We have trouble defining leadership yet we know it when we see it and do it.

This chapter suggests that learning is a core aspect of leading. Leaders are those who consciously learn from experience and share their learning with their organization. Although it is true that not everyone who learns will be a leader, everyone who leads must be a learner.

Leaders are often seen as biased toward a personal path of action over reflection. Learners, on the other hand, are seen as biased towards a personal path of reflection over action. In reality, managers are not faced with this "either-or" decision. Managing is an act of balancing the polarities of action and reflection to choose and hold a course of action for the organization. Managing, as we envision it, is generating and organizing knowledge that holds everyone on this course. In a constantly changing environment of scarce resources, organizations do not have the luxury of many managers providing and directing multiple courses of action and other designated learners (i.e. staff specialists) passively reflecting on events as they unfold. Managing, leading, and learning need not be separated, for all can be done by each member of the organization.

The act of creating learning in an organization is an act of leadership. It assumes: (1) finding a gap in the information needed by the organization; (2) accepting the risk to experiment on various new courses of action; (3) organizing a search for the acquisition or creation of new information; and (4) converting this information into workable knowledge.

In our rendition of leadership, **leading is a function of learning**. In a way, leadership is the "fuel" that ignites and sustains the "burn" of learning, until management knowledge is gained. This chapter proposes a continuous process of action and reflection that energizes what we call the **Managing/Leading Learning Cycle**.

The Active Nature of Learning

Learning has been characterized as the changing of behavior to create actions that correspond better to the goals of the learner.[2] In other words, more effective, more competent behavior.

Learning can take place in a variety of ways but individuals typically learn concurrently in three different modes: cognitive (thought); affective (feeling); and behavior (action). These are not mutually exclusive and, in fact, we need all three to make sense of our experiences. Profound learning takes place when we are concurrently learning in all three ways and thoughtfully integrating each dimension.

The process of learning is an interesting puzzle. Learning is a nonusable activity that creates knowledge as a usable resource. Acquired or created knowledge has to be managed into actual organizational functioning in order to be of use to the organization. It moves by dissemination and diffusion into the thoughts and actions of pertinent organizational performers, eventually to be integrated into daily functioning as a value-added resource which informs and guides work.

For individuals, learning most often takes place in a continuous fashion. David Kolb[3] describes this "learning cycle" as a process of: (1) **doing** – in which one gains experience; (2) **reflecting** – considering what that experience feels like and means; (3) **thinking** – in which we analyze and put the experience into some usable category; and (4) **deciding** – making some choices based on what we have learned (see figure 7.1).

The difficult and interesting nature of this cycle is that it is continuous. Once we make choices we create new experiences and begin "redoing." Learning is not really a product. It is known by its knowledgeable performance outcomes. Learning generates a behavior irrevocably different than any that preceded it. Acts of learning are propelled by a "one-way valve" effect. Something once learned cannot be reversed. What is learned may not be consciously used, but always informs our actions. Once children learn that there is no Santa, their world view is forever changed.

The Management/Leading Learning Cycle

Learning means moving from old known ideas to the unknown. Raw information is assimilated to become the "new known." This transformation is driven by the awareness on the part of the individual learner that a knowledge gap exists. The learning process moves us from (1) awareness of the decay of old ideas; entering (2) a state of naive learning (the state of open-mindedness); then, (3) a restored sense of utility, having created improved knowledge. We release the "old known" to explore the unknown by inventing and testing the "newly

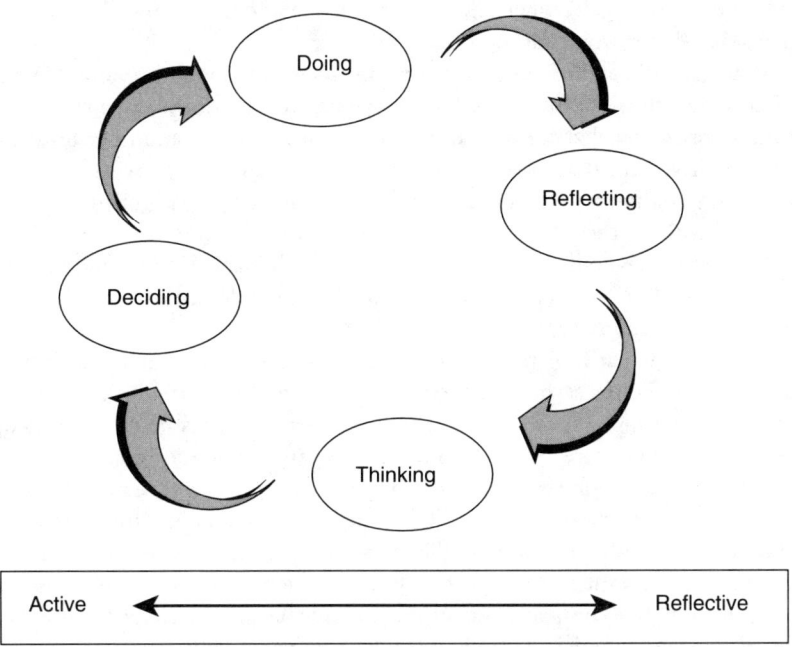

Figure 7.1   Kolb learning cycle.

known." Constant renewing of knowledge is the engine that drives revolutions of the learning cycle determining organizational and individual performance. This is represented in figure 7.2.

The **managing phase** of the M/LL Cycle works initially to hold onto the "old known" for repeated use. It is released by an insight and act of leadership into learning where the "new known" is created. The work of management is

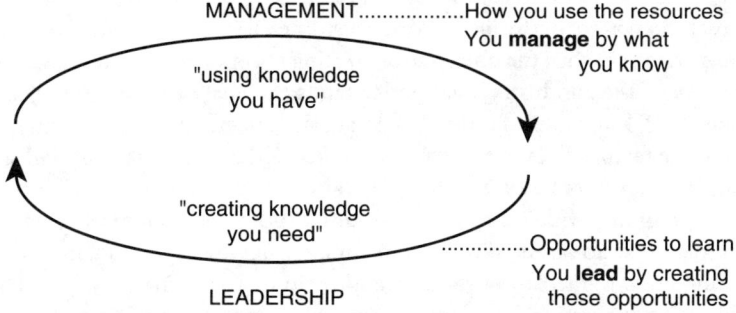

Figure 7.2   The managing/leading cycle.

completed in the cycle, when the new known is made the "known"; that is, the knowledge the organization now goes by.

Juran calls the end of any improvement process "holding the gain."[4] We try to freeze the knowledge produced in managing, so that we can make regular use of the information that we hold in mind. When an organization performs in a stable environment that allows for the slow turn of customer/investor requirements, this holding period can be quite lengthy. However, in a globally competitive marketplace, the demands of customers, investors, and technology break fast and are never-ending. Unfortunately, any "gain" achieved is soon followed by an inevitably rapid decay of knowledge. An example of this is found in the American auto industry.

After World War II, cars had pretty much the same utilitarian look. Customers demanded better styling. United States auto makers learned that style was the most important aspect of product differentiation. This certain knowledge prevailed as gains were realized. However, as Japanese imports began to offer style with better engineering, the Big Three (GM, Ford, and Chrysler) countered only with ever more styling. Their practice wisdom of building cars almost led them to corporate extinction. The half-life of information in today's turbulent work environment runs ever faster. Knowledge is a constantly moving target. Automobile companies no longer wait for the next "car year" to bring out new or improved models. Introductions happen constantly.

What an organization knows represents the prime renewable asset of the firm. Management is charged to increase and preserve these assets, to be the steward of organizational learning resources. Ways in which the organization manages to move from known to unknown to known are through such information-gathering and generating techniques as: gap analysis, quality measurement, financial and management audits, customer requirements, and environmental scanning. The SWOT Method of the strategic planners (Strengths, Weaknesses, Opportunities, and Threats) represents a continuous learning process leading to changes in products and services, operations, and sometimes even the basic mission of the organization. The work of managing heavily involves the operation, use, and extension of information systems.

The need for continuous learning has been recognized by many, if not all, of the great corporate performers. Motorola, Inc. has launched top-to-bottom training programs with the objective of creating a workforce that is on top of the technology of their industry, that understands the goals and procedures of the company and, most importantly, will create and encourage independent thinking from the factory floor to the executive offices. Many organizations talk about training and development but Motorola is also "walking the walk." The current training program (widely known as Motorola U) already commits each individual to at least 40 hours of planned learning programs a year. Plans currently in motion are designed to push the training up to 160 hours per year. This is roughly the time equivalent of four college courses and is projected to cost the company as much as $600 million a year.[5]

Why would one of the world's most successful companies feel the need to put even more of their resources into learning programs which go far beyond simple training? The answer is found in the fact that the leaders of the company believe that in the business wars of the coming decade, the most crucial elements of competitiveness will be responsiveness, adaptability, and creativity. For the individual as well as the organization, these are the outcomes of cycles of well-managed learning leadership.

The Interactive Nature of Leadership

Leadership emerges in virtually every group activity. Leading never looks exactly the same from one situation to another; because, leadership, like water, conforms to the shape of the container that holds it. The usual view of an organization is that of a pyramid with the leader at the top. But imagine this pyramid laid on its side and we can see another common view of leadership. We are leading at its forward point by aiming the organization's attention at better ways to penetrate the marketplace. Leading also occurs at the wide end of this wedge as we interact to propel the organization forward while steering with corporate strategy and vision.

The high profile, mediagenic corporate style of Lee Iacocca or Frank Perdue can be contrasted with the strategic brilliance of Microsoft's Bill Gates or the "hippie executive" model personified by Ben and Jerry of ice cream fame. All these personality types are not only a function of individuals but also of the organizational environment in which they work. Behaviors that result in effective leadership at General Motors will almost surely not work in a small software firm. The search for specific traits that a person can use to "be a leader" has never been successful. However, there are a few ideas about leading that cut across industrial and cultural lines and seem important in every type of organization.

Pauline Graham makes the point that the functions of management cannot be separated from the obligation to lead. In her words, "the leader who is not a manager turns out to be flawed and so does the manager who is not a leader." Leadership brings both power and responsibility and the first task of leadership as well as the special contribution of leadership is "ability to organize all the forces there are in an enterprise and make them serve a common purpose."[6]

Few would argue with Graham that this is a key leadership quality, but we still want to know how to get this done. The task that provides direction for leadership in all types of organizational settings is to find ways for people to learn about their work and from their work.

Organizational and individual learning are necessities in the "right-sized" organizations of the 1990s. Companies can no longer have a small cadre of an organization's members doing all the major organizational learning and thinking. Everyone has to be released from work *per se* to also do the learning work of the organization. The manager's job transcends doing the learning for the company to making sure everyone in the company learns. The reason for this is that there is simply too much to be learned in today's globalized situations for the task to be the responsibility of any one person or group.

Every worker should be viewed as an interactive agent who, upon engaging in a task or exploring a particular problem, should be presented with opportunities for active exploration, investigation, and understanding of that particular process. We are all knowledge workers. Once something has been acted on, the leader's particular task is to provide a way for the individual, the team, and the entire organization to transfer and apply that experience to enhance the entire organization's knowledge.

The **leading phase** of the M/LL Cycle, then, is about connecting with action rather than demanding action or framing a vision. Leading the charge or being the driving force when needed are still important behaviors in meeting the demands of the organization. However, in our model, the critical task in everyday effective functioning is leading the learning.

Management as Organizational Knowledge in Action

Typically, managing is seen as effective utilization of current resources (human, capital, and information) to "do things right." Within the M/LL Cycle, management is a special, pervasive form of organizational knowledge alive in action. Management conveys (usually through managers) how these resources are meant to be distributed and used in performing the work organization most necessary to sustain an organization in its competitive environment.

This chapter proposes a different view of managing, more in tune with a learning organization. In this view, management is that aspect of workable organizational knowledge that is about how the organization gets things done, in order to produce what is promised to the customer. Management ideas are conveyed in words and action by all members of the organization. Like all tacit forms of "knowledge-in-use", it is revealed through organizational performance. The Japanese idea that the most important aspect of car building is "fit and finish" was proven right, not by their stated beliefs, but by sales in a global market.

Conventionally, the management is the group of persons who are "in control" of the organization. However, our meaning of management vests knowledge of the organization where it more naturally lies – in the minds of all its performers. If the organization wants everyone to be responsible for the quality of the work, then everyone needs to see how everything fits together. The workforce needs to understand the business and its competitive environment. In other words, everyone must think managerially.

A recent example of this is the decision of the Harris Corporation, a $3.4

billion electronics conglomerate, to use the Zodiac Game as a tool to help every one of their 8,500 employees worldwide to begin "thinking like a manager." The game is a hands-on simulation that allows players to move cash through and around the organization in quarterly business cycles. No one actually wins or loses, but they get feedback on effective use of resources. Even the least sophisticated employees report an increased appreciation of the connection between satisfying customers and sustaining the economic life of the company. This board game was designed for the company to help profit-making responsibility flow even to the lowest rungs of the company. According to Harris's training manager, "Empowerment is not typically taken this far, but we decided that it's better having 8,500 people looking out for the welfare of the company than just a few."[7]

In traditional roles, managers are set up as gatekeepers of separated units of the organization. They are the ones to go through to reach those clustered within their functional or locational boundaries. Further, these gate-keeping managers are supposed to be intellectually and emotionally detached from work and workers, so as to be more objective. This system of management, most closely associated with bureaucratic organizational designs, fixes most of the responsibility for organizational change with managers, rather than their employees. In fact, a most common notion of the manager is one who gets the organization's work done through others.

The Total Quality Management movement has revealed the detachment of managers from nonmangers to be a main flaw in the still prevailing paradigm of commanding-controlling management. When managers hold their attentions above the workers the company loses access to a primary source of change information, that is, the hands-on knowledge of customers, suppliers, and the "works" of production and support systems.

In a learning environment, those designated as managers have particular responsibility to help employees become aware of their own leading, managing, and learning responsibilities and opportunities. Learning can be seen as part of the work of each. Co-learners are any others throughout the organization whose attention to learning in a given work situation is also needed to improve or innovate performance.

By its usual connotations managing means conserving, preserving, and accounting for holdings, as in the management of financial assets. All management notions of worth include ideas for preserving and developing the organization. This is called **stewardship** and simply means protecting vital organizational assets. To this act of stewardship, we add the necessity of making certain that workers at every level know what is needed to understand and do the work of the company. When these knowledge assets are shared effectively, people carry on in their jobs and carry out their tasks with confidence.

The stewardship view of managing produces a prime paradox. For learning to take place, the manager must be both the protector of organizational stability and the one who initiates risk in the system. Leading begins with a troubling of the mind, in questioning the unquestionable rightness of any point of management, even while it seems that the organization is succeeding. Holding on to strongly held management beliefs about the "right ways to do things" usually keeps change from happening. Failure to adapt to changes in the business environment will quickly erode performance. This is why leadership matters. It is the antidote to overmanaging a situation by holding too long to the established way.

Feeling good about the way things are going makes it difficult to let go of successful methods and become commited to their replacement. The organization has worked hard for its many competitive competencies. It is hard to give any up, yet this must be done when the resource mix supporting performance is constantly changing.

When the leaders of Microsoft spend as much time thinking about competitors and company failures as they do about their current successes, we can be sure they are preparing for the future by learning in the present. Microsoft executives advance their ideas through the corporation, not through presentations but by defending their product or performance under a barrage of questions often lead by CEO Bill Gates. This is the Socratic method applied to business planning. Only by knowing as much as possible about the product and competitors can fast decisions be made. But Microsoft dominates its industry and Gates has been compared to Henry Ford in the impact he has had on world business. How can they change with so much success driving them forward? Gates has recently suggested[8] that the Microsoft workforce has gotten too old to create breakthrough change. This is an amazing notion when we consider that the average age of Microsoft's employees is 31. Gates' solution is to try to have as many as 80 percent of his co-workers be less than five years out of college. This may or may not be feasible or even desirable, and it may be more symbolic than operational. But, literal or virtual, it does send a strong message throughout the corporation that new ideas must push old knowledge aside.

A major management problem is how to face conceptual waste and toxicity; how to get rid of dysfunctional, outdated knowledge. This is particularly difficult because some organizational knowledge becomes culturally embedded as organizational routines, policies, and techniques. Even the company mission and overarching policies can block renewal, and could be wholly reconceptualized. (Xerox is now "The Document Company" and giant steel manufacturer Unites States Steel became "USX" as it re-engineered itself into a diversified manufacturing, service, and distribution company.)

How can managing renew organizational knowledge without people knowing exactly what is useful or valid? The now traditional hierarchical organization, where those who managed (conservators of organizational knowledge) are largely separate from those whose work they control, has kept management away from the power of grassroots, work-embedded, leading. While they may allow some of the more modest forms of employee involvement in policy-level decision-making, the distance is kept with the onus of sanctions for "stepping out of line." This does not go far enough for rapid organizational learning or performance renewal.

Managing so that organizations learn calls for expedited internal communications through which co-workers can make inquires, share possibilities, and re-form ways of performing. The "manager" in this situation only slightly resembles the conventional supervisor. Co-workers do not work *for* the manager, they work *with* the manager for the customers. Conversely, this manager concentrates on learning performance of the unit among co-workers.

While the traditional supervisor rests easiest when things are running smoothly, this is when the learning manager is most alert. It means the sounds of approval may be drowning out the first, disquieting "crackles" of inevitably changing customer requirements.

Requirements for producing a better product or service, however, rarely indicate just a single unit change. Most renewal comes with changes in cycles that run across units and processes. Thus, the traditional, "go through me" manager risks being a bottleneck. Better for this model of organizational leading and learning is the "go with me" manager who brings anyone seeking performance improvement to wherever they need to go to learn in their area of concern. Further, this manager goes with them into any other part of the organization and its environment where they help instigate and run through the Managing/ Leading Learning Cycle.

Leading Learning

The **learning phase** of the cycle is the time of the free-falling search into the unknown. Acting as a learning-leader, the role of the "go with" manager is to foster creative and timely renewals of all performances for customers; to assure continuous improvement or well-timed innovation. This means suspending the authority of one's expertise and joining others in a risky, yet potentially rewarding, **state of doubt**.

Leading has traditionally been defined as a process of influencing the behavior of others in a direction desired by the person who is attempting to lead. This is done by "telling or selling" a vision of the direction and directing adoption of a prescribed solution for its fulfillment. Great leaders are said to be those who set inspiring visions, cut paths to them, and direct the "footwork" to getting there.[9] People follow this leader by virtue of his or her reassuring certainty that they are on the right course.

Paradoxically, it is basic to rapid and pervasive performance renewal to lead from certainty to uncertainty. Learning leaders are those individuals who enable the organization to question successful processes and point the way to needed change. Learning is that phase, cycling concurrently with leading, when honesty about uncertainty is needed the most. People follow the lead in healthy doubt, hopeful, but not assured that a better way will be found. One is being a **learning leader** when exercising these skills and abilities:

1 **Hearing the "crackle" of change, and fostering conditions that also amplify the "hearing" of co-workers.** A customer service representative notices repeated client comments about the use of the product. Her challenge is to get others in the company to hear the same thing. She collects data from her clients and those of other reps, looks for patterns, and brings the emerging information to the attention of her co-workers. In doing so, she begins to lead the organization in learning.

2 **Formulating and stating the unsettling question, and supporting and listening to the questioning of co-workers.** The customer service rep could be discouraged if no one else reports the same problem. She needs to find out why others are not complaining. Is there only an isolated problem or are the other reps not asking the right questions?

3 **Creating images and expressing how things ought to be to meet changed requirements and inviting and considering expressions of co-workers.** The rep goes to her team leader with observations and questions. He "goes with" her to other reps and the production people to share the information. The customer service team agrees to look at the data and survey other clients. This may turn out to be a transformational point for the company or it may be a blind alley. Either way, learning is under way.

4 **Trying out new behaviors, until the right combination emerges; joining co-workers in their experiments as well.** If the survey leads to the knowledge that change in production, and changes to better satisfy the customer, are needed, then learning has occurred.

5 **Sharing the benefits, as well as the costs, of change with co-workers.** The rep who initiated the learning does not take full credit for the improvement. She recognizes that change is a collaborative effort made possible only when others are open to learning. Taking personal credit for a team effort closes down future opportunities for organizational learning.

In summary, learning in an organizational context is how we go about acquiring and creating knowledge in interaction with those who can help us form reliable meanings (co-workers, customers, suppliers, experts). Acquiring knowledge is the search for new needed knowledge which can be integrated into basic operations.

Nonanka[10] reports a good illustration of an individual leading organizational learning. When the Toshiba Company set out to make their electronic bread maker, they perfected the programmed mixing, cooking, and timing but the special texture of home-made bread eluded them. Countless hours in their R&D labs did not help. Finally, a young engineer offered to apprentice herself to a master baker in a Tokyo restaurant. In her stay of several months, she learned that bread texture is most affected by the amount and method of kneading the dough.

Her information eventually became knowledge as she personally learned how to make the bread properly. She returned with this to the Toshiba labs and they began to search for ways to make one person's knowledge available to the entire organization. Information on baking technique was not enough to create the product. What was necessary was the building of knowledge, the distribution of that knowledge to the engineers and designers and, through them, to a successful product development. Individual experience became company expertise but this would not have been possible without the initial questioning about the texture of the bread. Technology created a clever product that was probably close enough to be successful but the process of turning individual learning into organizational knowledge created better bread and new profits.

How do we get from better bread to a better climate for organizational change? The Toshiba example illustrates a process by which knowledge is formed by transforming information to create value and meaning in a specific context. Learning happens concurrently with all forms and levels of work, functional, technical, and managerial. Organizational learning is really testing the current "management theory" of performance to see if it creates value.

Leading engages and sustains actions that enhance learning. Without it, learning is not likely to happen. An act of leadership begins when one musters the courage to hear the "crackle" of changing requirements (initiating questions). It goes on to create a managed change process (initiating investigation). This invents a situation – an awareness of a gap in performance and performance knowledge that identifies the need for learning. Leading is, in many ways, a function of being willing and able to create a structure for mutual learning.

When co-workers trust the learning structure, they accept the learning leader in themselves and others. Those who have a track record in this regard make others confident that the structure and the learning outcomes will be helpful and facilitative and not get individuals or the organization into trouble. Instead, they will bring them out of the troubling situation to a new state of management. The last stage of the learning process is changing minds, as learners exchange old ideas for new, installing them in on-going performance as management innovations.

Leading learning should not be left to the learning specialist (consultant, in-house "re-engineers," CEO), but rather must be integral to the work of everyone in the organization. A salient observation of the nature of organizations is that what firms do better than markets to create organizational change is the sharing and transfer of the knowledge of individuals and groups within an organization. Kogut and Zander[11] pointed out that if knowledge is held only at the individual level, then firms could change simply by employee turnover. Toshiba would have needed only to fire the engineer and hire a baker. We know only too well that this does not work. It is not enough to know how to bake bread. The multiple roles of product development, manufacture, and distribution demand an organizational knowledge beyond that of any one skill or individual.

Organizational Education

Organizational learning is both a cause and an effect of organizational change. It takes different forms throughout the organization, happening in seemingly random patterns that show up in all sorts of observable performances. When these patterns follow intentional organizational designs, they are educational. While some theorists assume that organizational learning must be continuous, as in the spirit of Kaizen that drives the Juran and Deming-inspired quality movement, organizational learning is also discontinuous. The former assumes a steady state of change, where the latter acknowledges a turbulent environment serving up countless surprises. Mastering these more chaotic moments allows for opportunistic learning often remembered in stories, myths, and company legends.

One such legend was born when a CEO decided to make his employees fully informed about the business. The Springfield Remanufacturing Company (SRC) was a money-losing division of International Harvester bought out by a group of its own managers with a lot of courage and even more debt. Company CEO Jack Stack explains,

> What SRC remanufactures are engines and engine components. We take worn-out engines from cars, bulldozers, eighteen wheelers, and we rebuild them, saving the parts that are in good shape, fixing the ones that are damaged, replacing the ones beyond repair. But, in some ways, engines are incidental to what we do. Our real business is education. We teach people about business.[12]

The people being taught are the employees of this now thriving firm. All employees were taught the fundamentals of business (production scheduling, inspection and warehousing, personnel issues, etc.) and were encouraged to use the financial information system as a way to understand the performance of the company. As co-learners, the employees began to understand the realities and demands of the entire business as opposed to the problems of just their own jobs. They bought into the goals of the firm literally as well as figuratively (as of 1994, employee-owned shares in SRC averaged $30,000).

The lesson to be learned from Springfield Remanufacturing is that an informed workforce is not necessarily the first thing any plant manager might wish for, but Stack believes that "when you appeal to the highest level of thinking, you get the highest level of performance." A system of continuous learning that grew out of organizational chaos, yet is anticipated in organizational design, allowed this firm to survive and flourish.

Organizational survival depends on both planned and unplanned learning. Because of this, there needs to be a design to marshal and capture valuable lessons. We see this as a need for an educational design incorporated into the overall organizational architecture. This keeps the matter of learning and renewal in focus within the main streams of organizational management. Such learning focuses the organization and creates a flexible framework based on the following precepts:

1 Schedule work with time for reflection, alone and with teams and work groups.
2 Design an information system that conveys knowledge learned and needed to be learned to all employees.
3 Lower barriers between and among functional units and locales.
4 Develop more diagnostic tools to build an understanding of the learning styles and needs of all employees.
5 Gather data that leads to keen awareness of the conditions that promote or suppress learning.

Organizational education aimed at performance enhancement is more than training or management development. While it encompasses these traditional human resource development functions, we envision it as a deeply embedded system of facilitated work-inspired learning. It brings about the absorption of new ideas that renew all kinds of working knowledge, always including the special knowledge that we call "management."

The learning leader continually builds the capacity of co-workers through observing processes, mentoring, motivating, and appraising. The analogy often used is the manager as coach. However, some observers of leading and managing have suggested that a clearer image is that of the "team captain" – fully involved in the game with responsibilities for action but also charged with the task of focusing the will of the team to the task at hand.

A learning leader visualizes and takes the path of mindful being – leading out to the unknown, inviting along the way those co-workers willing to join. Habits of organizational behavior are difficult to change and the replacement of old habits is actually more a process of unsettling the organizational way of doing things. "If it ain't broke, don't fix it" is a saying that is more comforting than correct. Thus, organizational education must be sensitive to real fears and reservations as a precondition to learning.

Both individual and organization must risk becoming, momentarily, what Peter Vaill calls the "reflective beginner"; letting go of expert, highly formalized knowledge to learn anew.[13] In a similar way, Hammer and Champy's[14] concept of "process re-engineering" calls for radical removal of all assumptions of what the process is supposed to do and why. This is clearly disturbing to all involved. It is not easy to decide that everything you know may be useless and then act to test that assumption. Organizational education supports the timely genesis of ideas which transform work and organization.

Energizing Learning

Without learning leadership, people will be inclined to hold on to what they think brought about performance success, even if those attributes have ceased being useful. Instead, the changing situation calls for innovation – the introduction of something new into the stream of thought from which performance flows.

Leadership senses and articulates newness but when it "oversells" novelty it threatens management with apparently unusable or nonimplementable information. This runs counter to the impulse of stewardship. When newness is "undersold," there is not enough power to lift attention to new possibilities. It is in the dynamic interplay of these opposing forces for stability and change that learning is energized.

The polarity of stewardship and innovation is a natural tension of organizational life. This creates the energy of contrast that fuels the learning process. To break the hold of "conservative" management dictum, there must be sufficient force and change-driven energy to overcome the tender grip of the known.

Changing the form or mix of material and financial resources presents less of a problem than the changing of information that people hold in mind. The very substance of the organization, at any moment in time, is who its people collectively think they are as members of the firm (e.g., "We are General Electric"; "We are the IRS"). Traditionally, what each person does defines what he or she means to the organization ("I am a GE pipe fitter"; "I am an IRS agent"), at any moment in time.

Learning changes the identity of each employee; sometimes subtly, sometimes radically, but always at the cost of certainty. While people, as employees, can be directed to move around to other parts of the organization, they are not "moved" to change their minds unless they learn why.

Organizational Metacognition

Learning differs from training in that there is a conscious reflection on our experience. Not just, "what did we learn?" but, "what does it mean, how can it be used, and how does the experience fit with our prior understanding of what we know?" This is known as **metacognition**. Simply put, this is experienced as constantly thinking about one's own problem-solving processes. Organizational learning is based in the metacognition of people who know themselves as members of the organization.

An example of metacognition driving organizational change can be found in the response to the recent earthquake in Kobe, Japan. In the aftermath of the disaster, the Professional Engineering Societies of Japan immediately began to assess the errors in their assumptions of earthquake engineering. Structural engineers, architects, and seismologists were brought to Kobe to study the effects of the quake in an immediate way. Interestingly, they invited experts from around the world to join them on the site of the disaster. News reports pointed out that, prior to this event, Japanese engineers had disparaged the knowledge of United States and other experts in the field. Faced with overwhelming evidence of the gaps in their own knowledge, the engineering societies tasked all their members with rethinking both the technical aspects of their work as well as the cultural barriers that made it impossible to work in a collaborative way with colleagues from around the world. An early understanding made possible by this opening of professional minds was the realization that buildings built to withstand smaller tremors were thus rendered more vulnerable to quakes of greater force.

The cognitive bias of Japanese engineers was brought to the surface by the experience of the Kobe earthquake. Similar, but less dramatic, examples exist in virtually every organization. Management consists of knowledge and skills along with a particular set of cognitive processes that constitute a "way of knowing" reality. This includes specific ways of asking questions and using cognitive tools or knowledge to build fact nets, develop arguments, and reach conclusions.[15] The earthquake engineers were faced with the realization that their ways of knowing were flawed. To their credit, they began immediately to change not only what they knew but how they would go about learning from that point forward.

Learning is more than the acquisition of technical skills and bodies of knowledge. Thinking skills and cognitive orientations that encourage self-awareness and reflective behavior are necessary for reframing, analyzing problems, and creating knowledge. As professional knowledge and technical skills become increasingly ephemeral in nature, managerial thinking needs to be added to the list of managerial process skills.[16]

Professionals learn their field in an explicit manner. Courses in finance, economic forecasting, or management information systems are generally aimed at building competence in content and technical areas. Professional thinking, on the other hand, is taught implicitly by reading and discussing the work of experts. At the graduate level, professionals teach by modeling the thinking skills of their disciplines. Examples include medical diagnostic thinking taught during rounds, legal thinking developed through case discussions, and scientific thinking taught through graduate student participation in faculty research projects.

Management education also models thinking through case study, role playing, and classroom exercises. Unfortunately, while our training for processes and technology has become more explicit, our training for thinking has not kept pace.

Metacognition is the awareness and control over cognitive processes. Control involves setting goals and subgoals, planning the next cognitive move, monitoring and evaluating the effectiveness of cognitive strategies, and revising them. Examples of strategies are reasoning, transformation, and synthesis. Research has found that those who monitor and control their cognitive processing during tasks perform better than those who do not.[17] Metacognitive sophistication, particularly cognitive mobility – the ability to move from one mental process to another using both hemispheres of the brain in an efficient, integrated manner – should be considered a major goal for management education. However, direct instruction in metacognitive strategies for effective thinking and learning rarely takes place.

In management, there are three groups of metacognitive strategies: **framing**, **creative problem-solving**, and **critical thinking**.

Framing strategies provide understanding of the diversity of perspectives that can be taken with respect to any given issue. The levels of analysis include both the organization as a whole and discrete problems.

Creative problem-solving strategies encompass the use of synthesis, intuition, use of metaphors, brainstorming, imaging and visioning. Creative thinking also includes Kim and Senge's notion of "generative learning."[18] In this concept, thinking has a multiplier effect. Simply, as we expand our consideration of a problem in a creative way, questions and answers to new areas are revealed. In solving a scheduling problem, for example, new insights may occur into distribution, marketing, or management of human resources.

Critical thinking strategies are the traditional, rational directed activities that include: induction, deduction, assumption surfacing, evaluation of alternatives, the Delphi technique, scenario analysis, formal planning, and procedural rationality.

Managers need to be skilled in a variety of modes. In his description of how strategists solve problems, Ohmae[19] is clear that the best solution comes only from a combination of rational analysis, based on the real nature of things, *and* nonlinear brain power (imagination) to reintegrate data into a new pattern. Theorists working in both management and education agree that the problems of the future require both analytical and intuitive skills. Intuition (the "gut feeling") and rationality are not antithetical, but closely related through knowledge, judgment, and experience. They are equal and necessary partners in problem-solving.

An investigation of the types of thinking employed by all levels of managers reported in the *Journal of Management Studies* in 1993 found that all of the managers found to have flexible decision styles utilizing the four modes of sensing, intuiting, thinking, and feeling were top executives (CEOs, COOs, and CFOs). The author concluded that, to be effective, managers need to utilize a combination of analytical and interactive styles.[20] It is not surprising, however, that managers are rarely aware of their reasoning processes as they occur. We seldom design training programs or college courses with the specific objective to develop the capability in managers to create and think in alternative frames of reference as well as to use different modes of thought. We would argue that *all* employees are going to need this capability enhanced to manage in organizations that learn.

The Nature of Management Education

Management education has been characterized as being overly concerned with the development of functional learning at the expense of integrative (or cross-functional) understanding of business. The organization of most business schools into discrete departments representing the major subdisciplines approximates the chimney-like functional departmentalization of most organizations. This presents difficulty in the generation and integration of innovative ideas. Students are trained to respond to behavioral problems from an organizational behavior perspective and to crack scheduling problems from an operations perspective, and are encouraged to "think like accountants" when learning audit procedures. This aspect of the B School culture has raised reasonable concerns that management education is overly "tools-oriented" at the expense of critical thinking. Many business school graduates seem unable to recognize common themes in business situations, have low tolerance for ambiguity, and far too often have only one way to think through a problem.

Programmed learning for planned problems is an acceptable format in a world where there is little risk and certainty prevails. Unfortunately, this is seldom the case in the current business environment. Flexibility and adaptability to constant change are the key predictors of organizational viability. The individual who can contribute and thrive in this environment is one who is not locked into the rigid thinking which characterizes intellectual departmentalization.

People who are working to learn their job in the operational sense are often surprised by the blinkers they have put on when asked to rethink the basic assumptions about the work and the purpose it serves in the organization. The effort seems to be directed entirely to individual learning and deflects attention from organizational learning.

In addressing this problem, Daniel Kim[21] makes the distinction between operational learning: the steps needed to complete a particular task or "know-how"; and conceptual learning: the acquisition of "know-why," thinking about why things are done, challenging the nature of prevailing assumptions, reframing problems in radically different ways. Management, as the outcome of the M/LL Cycle, is best when it informs both the how and why.

Developing metacognitive skills

A first step in developing metacognitive skills is to create awareness of: (1) the kinds of thinking we employ: self-knowledge; (2) the kinds of thinking best used by managers in different situations: managerial applications; (3) the kinds of thinking required to learn and use the knowledge and skills we teach; thinking flexibly; and (4) the understanding that learning is a continuous cycle that demands the integrated functions of both managing and leading.

In 1995 the Intel Corporation discovered that their new computer processor chip caused mathematical errors in rare situations of complex calculation. This posed little problem for the average user and, taking a pragmatic view, Intel decided it was not necessary to offer to replace a faulty chip. Customers (and the marketplace) responded with outrage, sales fell off, and their competitors jumped to take advantage of the situation.

To summarize at this point, this chapter presents our interpretation of the action-reflection dynamics and interplay of management, leadership, and learning. Learning is the activity that links managing and leading. Individuals and teams lead, follow, and learn according to the demands of the firm at any given moment. But within each worker lies the responsibility and the power to create breakthrough ideas that renew the organization. The power to create, convey, and complete these ideas comes through a continuous interplay of mental processes and organizational actions of our Managing/Leading Learning Cycle.

Interpreting the Managing/Leading Learning Cycle

Three basic ideas of management are proposed here:

1 **Managing is knowing what you know about effective organizational performance.** We manage data and processes, and use current knowledge to meet organizational goals.
2 **Leadership is about courageously acquiring knowledge.** Leading is about becoming aware of needing to know something, suggesting or providing the structure for getting things done. It is having a track record that lets people feel confident that the considered structure and the outcomes will work and not lead individuals or the organization into trouble.
3 **Learning is a search.** We look for new needed knowledge which can be integrated into the organization to become a seamless part of the organizational functioning. We try to take the unknown and the innovations and make them commonplace.

In its simplest form (characterized in figure 7.2), the work of learning is a continuous cycle of use of resources and acquisition of new information resources. A more detailed version of the M/LL Cycle (figure 7.3) will be introduced and discussed in the remainder of this chapter.

Management and leadership happen simultaneously. Managers are not working on one or the other but on many aspects of both at once. Different problems and issues demand different actions. Managers must be continuously both adapters and innovators. Every day has many different tasks with no discernible "management track" or "leadership track."

Leading learning requires each person to have the courage to jump between the known and unknown to release the learning energy of the organization. We work through the known/unknown dilemma by suspending assumptions and being willing to say, "I don't know." In a learning organization "I don't know" is seen as a positive developmental step in the M/LL Cycle.

People in the managing/leading cycle are identified as leading or managing depending on which problem is being worked on and where in the cycle the

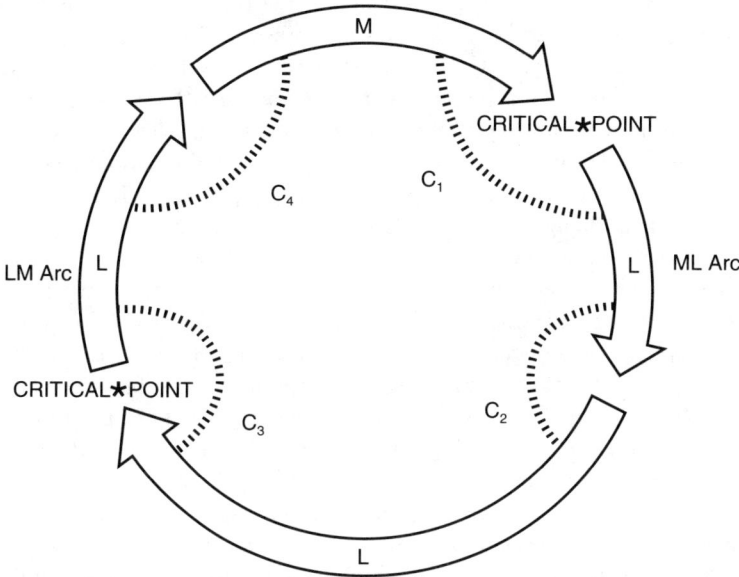

Figure 7.3 The managing/leading learning cycle – Key C the connectors, C_1 use of experimental design, C_2 commitment to learning as leadership, C_3 transforming information into useful knowledge, C_4 accept and install new ideas.

problem happens to be. Is it a problem of managing current knowledge or of needing (and leading the search for) new knowledge? Consequently, people have to be both leader and manager.

A cycle is a time interval in which a characteristic, periodically repeated event (or sequence of events) occurs. Its end is marked by complete execution of this sequence. The total quality view of managing has elevated organizational awareness of this sequencing as a value-adding process. The mapping of production or product life cycles has become a common tool for continuous improvement.

Each individual who contributes to a given process, regardless of position or role, is responsible for managing and leading from the learning generated in cycles of that work. There are also group (team, department, etc.) cycles, intergroup, and even interfunctional cycles of organizational work. These tend to either confound or complement individual improvements and innovations, depending upon the awareness of all performers of their interdependencies and how well they cooperate.

Organizations cycle through countless daily performances, some operating along somewhat concrete lines held in mind as their "management" – the known way to get things done. Other processes operate more naturally, beneath the conscious level. These happen in self-organizing patterns by which organizational systems operate in informal ways to achieve formal goals.

Sometimes the cycles may be slow and difficult to discern. These are the long, lazy arcs of managing and leading that characterize the stable environment and the mature organization. But, the more common experience is the "permanent white water"[22] of a turbulent environment or a highly customized organization. These are characterized by a short managing arc (the life span of usable knowledge) and a longer but faster leading arc (the need for learning to be as close to real-time as possible).

If a manager's experiences in cycles of organizational work tend to mainly reward preserving organizational knowledge in the managing (M) arc, they may rise to positions of influence, but not have sufficient strength in leading (L) when releasing old ways of managing become necessary. This results in an overmanaged organization which holds back change, denies the need for installation of new knowledge, and is so busy churning information that significant learning cannot be accomplished. This is a disabled environment where the search for ever more data becomes its own obstacle to change. Information becomes the enemy. Learning leaders really earn their pay in the organization when they make decisions in conditions of ambiguity with the available information and time as another bottom line.

Managing/Leading Learning Cycles that fall short of completion are disturbing to individuals and the organization. There are, however, counteracting forces that deny or dismiss the disturbances of decaying cycles. They seem to emanate from those persons believing they have much to lose if the processes in which they play a part are redirected from what they know and do well. All of us have been, and will be again, one of those "recalcitrant" persons, needing the reassurance that change is not the enemy of good management.

Anything ventured in a given M/LL Cycle is really just a theory – an assumption that what is going on will "work" for those who perform the work and receive its product. It is sometimes difficult to accept, however, that this outcome should be the beginning of the next cycle of the same process: "Shall we go on managing in this way in the next round?" Proof of a successful outcome is found in courageously measuring performance at the cycle's end and facing the inevitable gaps. There is always the chance that what seems certain to work in managing and leading will, in fact, fail. Knowledge of this should "wake up" the need for leading more learning in organizations.

The learning leader does not split the roles of manager and leader. Instead, both roles exist in seamless and ongoing creative tension. Learning links the roles and creates organizational energy in place of the potential role conflict. To operationalize this, managers need to act in ways in which management is not at cross-purposes with learning leadership. Some ways to achieve this are:

• Recognize the critical points on the Managing/Leading Learning Cycle (see figure 7.3).

- Understand that organizational learning also encompasses meeting the customer's requirements.
- Be continuously sensitive to the "web." That is, design practices and systems to do an internal organizational scan as well as the more obviously accepted environmental scan.
- Develop skills to translate the knowledge in ways the organization can understand and use the learning.

Using the M/LL Cycle

Think of the Managing/Leading Learning Cycle rotating within larger cycles of individual or group work (e.g., a bank teller handling a customer's transaction, a sports team running a planned "play," a salesperson planning and executing a sales presentation, an interiors production team completing their assembly on an automobile and sending it down the line). We perform at the top of the work cycle according to what we *know* to be the right way to proceed. This corresponds to the managing (**M**) of the M/LL Cycle.

1 We begin with "Managing," because this is the most commonly understood and practiced organizational behavior. Managing behavior is often derived from the logic of how what is planned leads to what has been promised. The resources of the firm are set to work in support of the plan. Very quickly, however, the plans begin to fall apart under the weight of a complex environment of human and technological change.

2 These "unplanned for" surprises push the mind out from management to consider alternatives and into the managing-leading (**ML**) arc of the cycle. Here, managing is becoming leading through the process of letting go of fixed ideas of how things are supposed to be done. This is brought on by awareness of the need for new knowledge for organizational competency, and is characterized by a realization that what you have in mind does not work any more. This reflects the short life span of useful knowledge in a turbulent business environment.

3 As the work proceeds, leading learning is necessary in response to understanding that the organization needs new knowledge. A task force might be put together or existing process action teams (PATs) or employee involvement groups might take on the task of identifying areas of study. In project team organizations, the knowledge gap may have been identified by the team before anyone else in the organization has noticed the threat to performance. No matter how the learning process begins, real readiness for change and learning is enabled when persons who feel responsible for the outcomes of work confront their doubts and "let go" of their certainty that what, how, and why they are currently doing things remain unchallenged. In this sense, learning leaders embrace Vaill's concept of the "reflective beginner" as a

valued and expected behavior. They go back to "square one" and question even the most successful operating assumptions to draw out creative alternatives.

4 As these reflective activities of learning (L) move through the ML arc to become an active process of search and acquisition of knowledge, the work of learning leaders changes. In this phase, audits and various types of experimental designs are used to gather data. Focus groups of both internal and external customers can provide both answers and further questions to be pursued.

   Nonlinear learning techniques are often utilized in this phase. Brainstorming, environmental scanning, reframing the problems, and "imaging" new products or processes are used to encourage and nurture lateral thinking. The emphasis is on pulling out of every available resource the radical ideas and innovations that characterize "break-through" learning. Time and resources specifically committed to these creative problem-solving activities are often known as "skunk works" – a catch-all description of structured efforts to think without constraints and with a maximum of team communication.

   Throughout this process, leading is characterized by the concurrent facilitation of learning. The role of the leader is to help individuals and the organization search for new ideas while also fully engaged as a learner.

5 Learning and leading arrive back toward the top of the cycle at the leading managing arc (LM). Leading learning becomes managing through the process of translating information into organizational knowledge. This new knowledge is characterized by managerial utility and fit with the organizational culture and tasks.

   In this part of the cycle, the power of leading is demonstrated by getting new ideas accepted so they become part of the managed resources of the organization. In addition, old knowledge that has lost currency is thrown out at this stage. This process of installation and deletion is very difficult for both individuals and organizations. It recalls the textbook definitions of leadership as a process of influence within the organization. Learning leaders collaborate to generate the influence to make this happen.

   Experimental design for the testing of new knowledge is also a task for the learning leader in this stage of the M/LL Cycle. Learning the utility of new ideas is generally a function of trial and error. However, much of our experience is that a new process or product is developed and put in place without a clear understanding of how to judge the success or failure of the innovation. Even a company as market savvy as Coca Cola, Inc. could probably still produce warehouses full of "New Coke" as canned testimony to the consequences of putting an idea into play without adequate experimental design to test consumer response.

   The concept of experimental design is fully but simply articulated by the Deming cycle of quality improvement.[23] In this model, the process of experimentation leading to improvement is a purposeful action of managerial process. The steps in the cycle are: "plan" – set objectives for work; "do" – implement the plan; "check" – evaluate the performance of the product or process based on critical measures; and "act" – make improvements based on the experience. The Deming cycle is a restating of the basic scientific method used by researchers in every field but rarely identified as a critical aspect of leadership. Yet, without a clear commitment to this learning process, breakthrough performance will be only the result of chance.

6   This final phase, where new knowledge is instilled and installed as management, is very much the test of top-level commitment to the learning process. A process action team that finds no hearing for its findings and no way to implement changes will soon accept reality and lose interest in the task. The learning leader must also be politically adept. Even in the most supportive organizational culture, influence is a scarce resource and leading learning demands attention to the process of discovery as well as an understanding of how to get things done in the organization.

Critical points

There are two critical points in the M/LL Cycle that the learning leader needs to stay aware of in order to maintain effectiveness:

1   *Between the managing arc and the managing-learning arc.* This is the place in the cycle that begins the awareness that what is known to the organization is no longer sufficient for organizational competency. This provokes an assertion of leadership in the managing/leading continuum. If leadership misses this "wake-up call" the organization continues to manage with current knowledge until that resource is depleted. This leaves the organization unable to respond to environmental change and on its way to extinction . . . a brontosaurus looking for an ice age!
2   *Between the leading arc and the leading-managing arc.* After the learning search occurs and information is discovered that is potentially meaningful to the task and the people, the work of influence and installation begins.

When we are leading learning in the M/LL Cycle, we must consider both translation and implementation so learning can move from individual or group knowledge to organizational knowledge. At the same time, "old knowns" must be discarded not only to make room for new knowledge but also to create unimpeded paths for new ways of doing things. Leading learning will have little meaning to the organization if a new set of "knowns" cannot be integrated into the organizational culture and processes.

Failure to acquire and use the influence necessary to effect this integration will leave the organization rich in ideas but devoid of meaningful action. Just as awareness of a knowledge gap is key to the start of the leading process, ability to implement learning is the key to creating knowledge ready to be a managed resource for the organization.

The connectors

The arcs of the M/LL Cycle are linked by four, sometimes invisible but always critical, connectors (see figure 7.3):

C_1 Use of the experimental design to check and correct "old knowledge." ("We have a lot of knowledge but is it all still useful?")

C_2 Commitment to learning as a function of leadership. ("Accepting that there is a lot we do not know.")

C_3 Translation of information into useful knowledge. ("We know a lot, but what part of this matters most to the organization?")

C_4 Getting new ideas (the "new known") accepted and installed. Along with this is the conscious deletion of the "old known." ("We now have in mind how we need to manage, but we still have to work it into the next cycle of practice.")

If any of these four considerations fail to connect or hold, the M/LL Cycle breaks down. Work goes on unrenewed.

A run-through of the M/LL Cycle

A way of understanding this model is through the sequence of actions of the individuals leading the learning. It all begins in a day's work.

1 **Performers "step off" into action according to what they know.** In the terms of our model, "they manage to perform with current knowledge."

2 **As events unfold, in or out of the expected sequence, performers realize there are extraordinary occurrences.** These raise the issue that the knowledge being used is not the knowledge they need.

3 **It is at this critical point, in the friction of disturbance, that leadership is sparked, if allowed.** It forms as a shared realization that a better way is needed or possible. We say "if allowed" because there are many barriers to both leading and learning in organizations.

4 **Leadership releases energy for the search for new management information. Learning is engaged by the search.** The search continues until compelling answers are found or invented to become new knowledge. We again qualify this step with "if allowed," for the people may chose to hold on to the familiar. At this critical point in the cycle, "management" can seem impervious in its highly comfortable zone of certainty.

5 **Leading impels learning at this point, or renewal fails.** It means letting go of certainty, trusting that a period of relative chaos will stir the fires of creativity. Leading releases learning, which is a natural response to becoming separated from the firm ground of the known, to leap to a new reality.

6 **Finally, "answers" are shaped into knowledge for managing the next cycles.** These are formed and recognized, on their surface, as policies, procedures, rules, and informally as rules of thumb, shorthand, and "the way to get it done now."

The M/LL Cycle runs through rarely balanced phases of managing, leading, and learning. In a given situation, the "size" (or power) of one or more phases may be greater or less. Consequently, learning ranges from "just tinkering" to profound breakthrough, depending on how much the management is changed and re-formed.

The cycle is completed only to be re-entered as new information reaches its limits of usefulness. Leading the learning process is a continuous task that often seems at odds with traditional organizational activities.

Barriers to Leading Learning

Releasing learning and learners is a critical part of the cycle. Some who are managing may be innovative in learning but never become learning leaders. Too often they misread the organization and never seem to find the fit between knowledge and learning. Others only want to play with new ideas and never study the customer–organizational realities to understand the variables of implementation of new knowledge. Finally, some excellent learners fail to share acquired information with implementers who can put the ideas to work.

It would be a mistake to believe that individuals or organizations are inherently committed to learning. In fact, learning is often messy, challenges experience and closely held assumptions, and occasionally runs counter to the common sense of the organization. When we act as learning leaders, we are not always appreciated. It is sometimes difficult to work with a manager who uses a *carte blanche* empowering style. There are no rules to follow and questions regarding process or implementation may be answered with, "Go find out." Unfortunately, many people believe that they are "finding out" by asking the manager.

The greatest barrier to learning in the organization is often our inability to "unlearn," to leave the comfort of work-tested ideas of the way things are supposed to be done. If the people of an organization are accustomed to authoritarian leadership and following orders, the leader has to first change their attitudes, train them in the new ways, and convince them, by example, that the new method is of as much benefit to them as it is to the business.[24]

This is especially difficult when managers and organizations neglect to reward learning efforts on an individual level and, instead, focus almost exclusively on performance. In this case, readiness to learn must precede effective use of the M/LL Cycle. The structural changes to create teams and quality systems in an organization are not sufficient to nurture learning. Changes in procedures and reporting relationships need a complementary change in organizational culture. In a system where individuals have learned that it may be risky to question or show their lack of understanding, it is unlikely that the organizational learning can take place.

Swieringa and Wierdsma[25] describe four common strategies used to avoid the pain of learning in organizations. The first is "collective blindness" in which the group acts as if the problem simply does not exist. The Audi company refused to consider the possibility that their car was defective. Instead, they blamed drivers for confusing the gas and brake pedals: a position they held until the market for their product was seriously eroded.

"Collective avoidance" occurs when the team avoids learning by shaping views, opinions, and conclusions to conform only to those the organization wishes to recognize. Swiss watch designers and researchers fully agreed that nonmechanical, digital timepieces could not work to the standards of their industry. A view that the Casio company successfully dispelled in a very short time.

"Collective reluctance" is the third major barrier to learning. This is charac- terized by an insecurity which drives individuals and teams to produce only what they believe the formal hierarchy wants. In recent months, the General Electric Corporation has endured negative publicity and substantial fines for the unethical and illegal actions of some executives from its Kidder Peabody invest- ment bank subsidiary. CEO Jack Welch, considered to be one of the smartest of corporate leaders, was unable to explain how so much could have gone so wrong without being noticed by anyone in his normally astute organization. One answer ventured by an anonymous middle-manager is that no one wanted to tell the boss how bad the situation had become. When an organizational group knows what is undesirable in a situation (and is in a position to change it), but allows the situation to continue, "collective reluctance" is present.

A situation opposite to GE's can occur when a group recognizes the problem and is willing to deal with it but lacks the technical or political knowledge to do so. This is a function of "collective ignorance," a barrier to learning only overcome through increased communication. The organization needs to move information on both content and process issues from the source to the work unit in order to support and enable change. This type of problem is often addressed through technical training, and staff development programs as well as access to outside consultants and information-generating techniques such as communica- tion audits and employee involvement groups.

These and other barriers to learning can be overcome if interest in creating a learning environment is embraced at the highest levels and embodied in all activities of the firm. The greatest predictors of an effective learning environ- ment are visible as acts of leading learning by example throughout the organization.

Implementation

Implementing the Managing/Leading Learning Cycle means releasing the learners in all of us who perform the work of the organization, consciously viewing ourselves as being in parallel communities of learners and co-workers. The learning community in the workplace is voluntary. No one can be effectively ordered to join others in learning, while it may still be possible to do so in work. This also means commitment of time and other resources to the learning objective are differentiated from work objectives.

Changes in organizational culture are necessary as the manager begins to understand that the concurrent learning community is: (a) valuable, (b) needs to exist in all organizations, and (c) needs to make learning happen as part of the functional organization, not as an add-on or occasional event. This includes acting in ways in which managing – acting as conservator for organizational knowledge – is not at cross-purposes with learning, the searching out of knowledge to replace the old. Even more importantly, managers/leaders need to embrace the notion that they are not the sole source of learning, The work of "management" is expanded to include the mandate to create shared learning opportunities and responsibilities throughout the workforce.

Learning leaders also need the technical "know-how" to recognize the critical points in the M/LL Cycle, to develop skills in environmental scanning processes both internal and external to the organization.

Finally, managers need to understand that learning is a function of meeting the customers' requirements and that the constant demand of leadership is to translate information gained in order to create usable knowledge for the organization.

Swieringa and Wierdsma[26] describe this as a change to a "collective process in which old hands learn together with newcomers, and higher echelons with the more lowly." This creates a learning process both for those who have "thought it out" and for those who must "carry it out," everyone learning together as a natural, everyday work experience.

Changing Basic Organizational Processes

In order for learning to move to the foreground as an organizational objective, the basic processes of organizational life need to change. Organizational practices, policies and procedures tend to be artifacts of the "M" side of the M/LL Cycle; but there is no inherent reason why these cannot reflect the demands of the L side as well. Some examples of how these changes can occur include:

1 **Accounting** – moving from "counting" to using "accounting" to suggest new ways of managing the resources of the organization (i.e., activity-based costing).
2 **Performance evaluation** – change from an evaluative focus on performance to evaluating learning competence. This means accepting mistakes and temporary failures. "Temporary" because the learning response is to correct the problem followed by questions intended to find out why the error occurred. A discussion of alternative

paths is followed by the question, "What did you learn from this?" The mistake becomes temporary and not likely to be repeated.

3 **Financial analysis** – should be more than net present value. A structural change should support the idea that the primary reason for financial information is to enable users to make better operational decisions.

4 The process of running a meeting needs to change to be learning-focused. Agenda setting and protocol need to move away from the generation of predictable results and achievement of consensus. An experimental design that questions assumptions of both success and failures and leaves room for disagreement should be integral to the meeting.

Divisions of companies as different as DuPont and Kodak, as well as smaller manufacturers like Springfield Remanufacturing have begun educating employees to understand the financial implications of their decisions.

In a learning organization, a supervisor can use a financial report to make a cost-benefit analysis of the cost of expedited repair versus lost production If financial statements are the critical piece of understanding the health of the organization, the information should be as widely held as possible.

All the above are management functions that can be transformed into one seamless activity that includes managing and leading. In 1994, the National Academy of Sciences studied various techniques designed to enhance performance in the organization. Performance was found to be a function of learning, not of innate ability, and the researchers found that cooperative learning and team training were the most effective methods for creating improved performance.[27]

To this end, the M/LL Cycle is based on the belief that learning is a core part of leading and creates an irrevocable change of behavior resulting in organizational competence. Working tests the "managing" of any process. Leading brings attention to the results of that test, and learning replenishes the resources of the organization. When all three events are balanced and synchronous, performance is enhanced.

This concept goes against conventional wisdom that roles of management and leadership are separate, as are those of manager and "nonmanager," leader and follower. These distinctions may be convenient for distributing power and information to those who are supposed to manage and lead, but they mask the deeper probability that accelerated performance improvements come when performers are fully engaged in learning.

This model proposes the integration of roles of manager, leader, and learner within streams of organizational and individual actions. Organizational effectiveness flows from the full engagement of the workforce in all three behaviors. Every organization is driven by performance standards. We propose to add an explicit "bottom line" for learning. As we respond to the need to learn, we manage and lead in degrees that enhance both the organization and ourselves.

Notes

1 J. K. Barge, "Putting leadership back to work", *Management Communication Quarterly*, 1994, vol. 8, no. 1, pp. 95–109.
2 B. Kogut and B. Zander, "Knowledge of the firm, combinative capabilities, and the replication of technology", *Organizational Science*, 1992, vol. 3, no. 3, pp. 383–97.
3 David Kolb, "Management and the learning process", *California Management Review*, Spring, 1976, vol. 18, no. 3.
4 See the Juran Trilogy, J. M. Juran, *Managerial Breakthrough* (New York: McGraw-Hill, 1995).
5 K. Kelly, "Motorola: training for the millennium", *Business Week*, March 28, 1994, pp. 159–62.
6 Pauline Graham, *Integrative Management: Creating Unity from Diversity* (Cambridge, MA: Blackwell, 1991), p. 122.
7 *Philadelphia Inquirer*, January 14, 1995.
8 J. A. Byrne, "The horizontal corporation", *Business Week*, Dec 20, 1993, pp. 76–81.
9 C. Argyris, "Teaching smart people how to learn", *Harvard Business Review*, May–June 1991, pp. 99–109.
10 See I. Nonanka, "The knowledge-creating company", *Harvard Business Review*, November–December 1991, pp. 312–20.
11 B. Kogut and U. Zander, "Knowledge of the firm, combinative capabilities, and the replication of technology," *Organizational Science*, 1992, vol. 3, no. 3, pp. 383–97.
12 J. Stack, *The Great Game of Business* (New York: Doubleday, 1992).
13 From Peter Vaill's keynote address to the Eastern Academy of Management 1994 Conference, Albany, N.Y. May, 1994.
14 M. Hammer and J. Champy, *Reengineering the Corporation: A Manifesto for Business Revolution* (New York: HarperCollins, 1993).
15 See R. Lessem, *Total Quality Learning* (Oxford: Blackwell, 1991).
16 See J. Swieringa and A. Wierdsma, *Becoming a Learning Organization: Beyond the Learning Curve* (New York, NY: Addison-Wesley, 1992).
17 See E. Kruger and S. Meisel, "Creating metacognitive thinking in the classroom", *Proceedings, Eastern Academy of Management*, May, 1994, pp. 247–50.
18 Daniel H. Kim, "The link between individual and organizational learning", *Sloan Management Review*, Fall, 1993, pp. 37–50.
19 K. Ohmae, *The Mind of the Strategist* (New York: McGraw-Hill, 1982).
20 P. C. Nutt, "Flexible decision styles and the choices of top executives," *Journal of Management Studies*, 1993, vol. 30, no. 5, pp. 695–721.
21 Kim, "The link between individual and organizational learning", p. 39.
22 Peter Vaill, *Managing as a Performing Art* (San Francisco: Jossey-Bass, 1989).
23 See W. E. Deming, *Out of Crisis* (Cambridge, MA: MIT Press, 1986).
24 See C. Argyris, "Good communications that block learning", *Harvard Business Review*, July–August 1994, p. 151.
25 Swieringa and Wierdsma, *Becoming a Learning Organization*, p. 125.
26 Ibid., p. 19.
27 R. A. Bjork et al., *Learning, Remembering, Believing: Enhancing Human Performance* (Washington, D.C.: National Academy Press, 1994).

PART III

Linking Teams With Systems Learning

Interview with John D. Sterman

Professor of Management Science
Director, System Dynamics Group
Massachusetts Institute of Technology

Interviewer: Steve Cavaleri   Date: June 1994

SC: What is your specific interest in organizational learning?

JS: Change in all areas of human existence is accelerating, in many cases out-stripping our ability to understand and manage it. Worse, many of the problems caused by the accelerating changes in technology, in population, in the environ-ment – and in the complexity of these problems – arise as a result of our own actions. Our ability to learn, both individually and organizationally, needs to accelerate as well, lest the consequences of the changes we are making over-whelm us. My particular expertise is in the role of modeling and the use of simulation, particularly system dynamics simulation, to help people improve their mental models. We need to develop what I call "actionable knowledge," that is, knowledge that enables people to take new and different actions. The learning we need is not merely an increase in our intellectual knowledge, but an expansion of our capabilities to act in ways consistent with our true aspirations.

The basic difficulty that people face as individuals and groups is that the normal process by which we learn about everyday activity is trial and error. But for the type of systems in which we now find ourselves, such as business, the trials, the different policies that we try out, don't produce feedback rapidly enough for us to learn. The knowledge of results, the feedback we need to evaluate the effectiveness of our policies and thus decide whether we should continue or try something different simply doesn't exist. A basic principle of systems thinking is that cause and effect are distant in time and space. In business and organizational life, in your life as a family member or member of a community, almost all of the important consequences of your actions are delayed and have consequences far removed from your local situation. We simply never get information about many of the most important consequences of our acts. Worse, frequently the short-term and local effects of an action are opposite to the long-term and distant effects. If you rely on the locally available information, on the short-term results of your decisions, you'll be making decisions that, despite your best intentions, destroy the system.

SC: Can you give us an example?

JS: A classic example that everybody is familiar with is the "tragedy of the commons." Consider any fishing grounds. The sensible, economically necessary course of action for the individual captains is to fish as aggressively as they can, to install the latest technology in their boats, so they can maximize their catch. The local feedback they get from, say, putting in a new sonar system, is that they can find the fish better and increase their catch. So while the local feedback and incentives for each captain encourages them to take ever more fish, the delayed and distant consequences of course are a more rapid decline in fish stocks. Since the fish are commons, it is worthwhile for all the boats to do the same. People reason "If I don't get them someone else will." The result is often that fish stocks decline to the point of commercial extinction, putting all the boats into dry dock and forcing everybody into the unemployment lines. Reliance on local, short-term feedback and local, short-term incentives leads to long-term ruin for an entire community. Just this has now happened to the George's Bank fishery, wiping out the fishing industry in New England and maritime Canada.

The main challenge facing managers seeking to improve the quality of learning is to bring the delayed and distant side-effects of our actions into the here and now. The whole notion of side-effects, of course, reveals how deeply embedded the short-term and local perspective is in our thinking. There's really no such thing as "main" effects and "side" effects. There's just effects: You make a decision, and it has effects – it alters the real world. We consider some of these effects to be main effects – the effects we intended, the ones we can anticipate or account for in our mental model. The effects that are not anticipated in our mental model, the ones that surprise us, that run counter to our goals, we call side-effects, as if they were somehow secondary or of lesser importance, but of course they're not. They're just the things that we weren't thinking about, the feedbacks that weren't accounted for in the framework of our mental model. So the challenge is to improve our mental models by expanding their temporal and spatial boundaries. To do that we usually will need some type of simulation, some type of virtual world, because in the real world of social action there is simply no way that we can experience the distant and delayed consequences of our actions within the time frame we have to make decisions. So modeling and simulation are necessary ingredients for successful individual and organizational learning.

By the way, this doesn't mean that modeling and simulation are sufficient. There are multiple impediments to learning. Besides the problems I just mentioned, learning is often thwarted by the poor interpersonal communication skills and defensive routines we use to relate to one another. Another major problem is the poor quality of our inquiry skills – our ability to think scientifically, to test our theories. For example, research in judgment and decision-making shows clearly that people suffer from literally dozens of cognitive errors and biases. We fail to consider sufficient alternatives when contemplating a decision or imagining explanations for a phenomenon. We tend to seek evidence consistent with our prior beliefs instead of subjecting our beliefs to test. These failures of scientific reasoning can prevent learning even if one has developed a perfect model.

One of the big developments in the past few years in the field of system dynamics has been a broader use of methods to deal with these impediments and an explicit recognition of the role of these other methods in the process of modeling, so that the barriers to learning that can thwart the improvement of our mental models are addressed. There's a history of models that captured some of the problematic issues very well, but which didn't have any impact on the organization because these other issues relating to the inquiry skills or group process of the client team weren't properly addressed. This has changed. Increasingly, modeling is seen more as a total intervention rather than as a technical tool. After all, people are modeling all the time, building mental models, revising mental models. Formal modeling helps make those mental models more explicit so that others in your organization can understand better the basis for your actions and beliefs, and thus provide the foundation for a dialogue about testing those assumptions and revising them in light of feedback from both the real world and the virtual world of the formal models.

SC: John, what do you mean by "modeling"? There are different types of models; especially in industrial engineering and the hard sciences, there's all kinds of modeling. What kind of modeling are you speaking of specifically?

JS: There are lots of different kinds of models and there should be because there are lots of different purposes. Models must be built for a purpose. You need to have a focus, a problem that you're trying to address before you can decide what kind of model you need. All models are wrong. They are all simplifications, abstractions, distortions of reality. It must be so: Even if a perfect model existed, you could no more use it than you could use a map of the United States whose scale was 1 mile = 1 mile. Thus the first stage of modeling is to become clear about what it is you really care about. What problem are you trying to address? What decisions do you have to make? And given that purpose, what needs to be included in the model, and what can be left out? Only by choosing wisely what to leave out can you develop a model that can prove useful. Of course, the need to tailor the model to the purpose is true for mental models as well, though we usually don't think too carefully about our mental models.

So, there are many modeling techniques, each with its own assumptions, uses and limitations. The particular kind of modeling I'm interested in is system dynamics, that is, modeling the feedback structures that give rise to problematic behavior in organizations (or other systems, including systems in ecology, physiology, physics, chemistry – anywhere there are dynamics). By feedback structures, I mean the physical and institutional "plumbing," if you will, of an organization, plumbing that is tied together by the decision rules or policies of the people throughout the organization. These structures form networks of feedback loops, self-reinforcing and self-correcting processes from which the evolution of the system over time emerges. This is what we call the problem of "dynamic complexity," as opposed to "combinatorial complexity."

Let's take project management as an example. Let's say you're designing a new product or managing a large-scale construction or software development project. There's a combinatorial complexity issue: For example, in developing a new aircraft you might have several million different parts that all have to be designed to function without interfering with one another and that can be assembled in a sensible and efficient sequence. Managing the coordination of so many elements is a problem of combinatorial complexity. There's a number of modeling tools to help, such as PERT, Gantt charts, critical path methods, CAD/CAM tools and so on. But there's a dimension of project management that doesn't relate to how many different parts there are, how many lines of code there are in your software, but depend on dynamic complexity. Suppose for example the customer changes the specifications after the project has begun. Such changes occur often in large projects because the customers needs change, the available technology changes, and so on. As you respond to the change you might find that now you're running behind schedule. So you might add resources, for example, hire more programmers. In the long run, adding programmers should boost the rate of coding and speed the completion of the project. But, what may happen is that the project could fall further behind. Why? As you add programmers you're diluting the experience base of your team, you're increasing the coordination and training burden for the members of the team, you're going to have more meetings, you're going to have longer meetings. With less experienced people you're going to lower the productivity of the experienced folks on your team as they help with training and answering the questions of the inexperienced people. You're going to see a higher error rate coming from the inexperienced people. Productivity may actually drop, forcing people to work longer hours. Longer hours might then increase fatigue and burn-out and lead to a still higher error rate and still lower productivity in a vicious cycle. If this goes on long enough, if the experienced people are frustrated by not being able to get their work done, by being tired, by having to train all these inexperienced people, by having to go to more meetings, by having to redo work that they already thought they'd done, then some of them might quit. If they do, then you've got to hire still more inexperienced people, closing the reinforcing feedback and leading to still lower productivity. These are problems of dynamic complexity. They arise from the multiple feedback loops that are created by the decision processes of each individual on a team. While these decision rules are usually locally sensible, the result, as they interact with the decisions of others, is to worsen the situation. system dynamics modeling is designed to help us understand that dynamic complexity.

SC: So are you saying that the members of this team, let's say the programmers, would themselves model their own team, or is it more likely that somebody from the outside would be brought in to model the team, or is it some combination of the two?

JS: You could do it different ways, depending on the purpose. However, what we've found over the years is that the people who build the model develop deep insight into what's going on in the system, while the consumers of a report or presentation of model results do not. Insight leading to actionable knowledge develops from the process of modeling, from the process of collecting the information, eliciting the mental models of the actors in the system, formulating hypotheses about how the system is structured, testing them out through simulation, comparing against the data, identifying gaps, going back for more information, revising the model, and looping back again. Modeling is an iterative process. The product, the model, isn't that important *per se*. It's what has gone on in the modeler's head, the changes in the modeler's mental model, that really count. If, after going through that deep learning process, the modeler then turns around and tries to transmit to the client or managers what they've learned, usually there's a disconnect. The results are not transferred. The more profound the transformation in mental models, the more severe this dilemma becomes. Most likely you are asked to build a model because there's a serious difficulty in the organization. The model is more likely than not to show that current structure and current policies are the source of those difficulties. If you simply try to transmit that message to the very people who are responsible for those structures and policies, they will surely be rejected. "Your model is too simple," they will say, or "your model is too complex, we can't understand the assumptions." Or they will say both at once, and reject the recommendations. The modeling process has the greatest potential to transform an organization precisely when the results of the model are most threatening and most likely to be rejected. Our approach is that the clients, that is, the people's whose behavior you need to change in order for effective action to take place, must become the modelers. They must participate in the conception, design, and evaluation of the model in some meaningful fashion, so that it's *their* mental model that's evolving throughout the learning process.

SC: How would you respond to the manager of a team that says; "If you want my team to build a model, then they're going to have to learn about modeling and that's going to take a lot of their time. Is the process of learning to model really cost-effective?"

JS: Modeling should only be used for important problems. It should be used for the issues that are most central, most fundamental – not for those that are merely urgent. If the stakes are high then it is worthwhile to put in the effort. That is the only responsible choice. At the same time, the costs of modeling have dropped significantly over the past decade, and the ability of ordinary managers to use models effectively without special training has increased dramatically. Thirty years ago you had to be comfortable with computers, you had to be willing to learn traditional programming languages. Only a small fraction of the population, typically people with engineering or computer science backgrounds, were willing or able to do it. The result was you had an expert consultancy methodology where the modelers were technical experts who were asked to develop the model and bring back the results. Today, hardware and software are so easy to use that the technical barriers to modeling have fallen dramatically. Any manager can be working with the modeling tools that are now available within the first afternoon. But, and this is a big "but," ease of use doesn't mean that it's easy to build a good model. It's still hard to build a good model. What you're saying when you say "it's hard to build a good model" is precisely that it is hard to develop a deep understanding of a problematic situation. Gaining insight into the source of persistent problems is subtle, it's fundamentally a creative process and will never be routinized. What today's tools mean, however, is that nearly all of your time can be devoted to what's important – the learning process – with very little time wasted on the mechanics of software, simulation languages, and so on.

The progress has not only been in technology, but also in the development of useful protocols for modeling, that is the processes by which people work with the tools. We've now developed a set of tools ranging from tools for eliciting and recording the mental models of participants, for structuring feedback hypotheses as diagrams even without computers, to "management flight simulators" that enable literally anyone from grade school kids to CEOs to engage in the modeling process. So the technical barriers and the process barriers continue to fall. It still takes time to develop a deep understanding of how a system operates. There are still people out there who are so deeply caught in the trap of "fire fighting" that they have no time for reflection. The long-term consequences of their previous actions have fed back to create crises that force them into still more ill-considered, short-term responses. The cost of taking time from fire fighting may appear to be high, but the costs of not doing it can be even higher. We often find that managers, in all good faith, based on their current mental models, take actions to restore the health of the organization that in fact are undermining its continued viability.

Q: I think what you're suggesting is that by modeling in this way there's an attempt to go to the underlying belief system of managers rather than intervene on the level of behavior, as most other management approaches do. How does your system dynamics modeling-based approach differ from other management approaches? Can you give an example of this?

JS: There's an ongoing debate as to whether what you want to do is change the behavior first and have people's attitudes follow, or whether you change the beliefs first and hope that the appropriate behavior will follow. Like most sterile debates over such dichotomies (Chickens first or eggs? Nature or nurture? Believing what we see or seeing what we believe?) there is a powerful feedback between the two, not an either/or choice. Knowledge and action must develop in tandem, and the better we do on the one, the easier is the other. I do think it's helpful to have people demonstrating and providing examples of different behaviors that might be more appropriate, but I don't think that this alone produces sustained change unless people also have the means to understand the basis for different actions.

Let me give you an example from the early days of system dynamics. A project was done at an electronics firm to help them understand why their business was so volatile, so cyclical, over time. At certain times they had long backlogs, delivery delays were stretching out, they were operating around the clock, but a few quarters later they would find order books shrinking, experience excess capacity and would be forced to lay off their workers. A model was developed that explained why that was happening, what the role of the firm's own production scheduling policies were in exacerbating the instability. The modelers designed better policies which were actually put into place. The new decision rules for production were very simple, so simple they could be easily calculated from information about inventories, work in process, backlogs, and so on. The new policy worked – production volatility declined, product availability increased, and market share stabilized. However, the mental models of the managers hadn't really changed. The decisions these rules suggested didn't fit with their mental models. So they began to say things like "It's been quite a while since this rule was put into place. The market is changing, the economy is changing, but our decision rule hasn't changed in response." So they began to tweak it, overriding the recommendation of the rule and substituting the judgment coming from their mental models. Pretty soon the rule wasn't being used at all, they instead reverted to their mental models. Since their mental models hadn't changed, of course the instability returned. So here the behavior had changed, but the understanding of why it needed to change hadn't. Even though the system had improved, people reverted to their old mental models, causing the previous problems to resurface.

SC: Would you say that to sustain behavior, ultimately there's a need for managers to explore their mental models, whether it's in the form of modeling or just discussing their basic beliefs about how things happen?

JS: Right, I agree. People do need to be constantly surfacing their mental models, challenging them, testing them. Better decision rules, better structures, better designs will flow from the constant interplay of changes in the mental models, experimentation in both the virtual world and the real world, re-evaluation of the mental models, and new experiments. It is a continuous feedback process. Reflection without action is sterile; action without reflection is dangerous.

SC: Do you see systems thinking, in terms of verbal discussions and so forth, being an entree to modeling or can people go directly into modeling without knowledge of the formal theory of system dynamics or systems thinking?

JS: Some people advocate the use of conceptual modeling tools alone. By conceptual modeling tools I mean things like system archetypes, causal loop diagrams, hexagon diagrams or other ways of mapping how you see the system operating. There's no question that mapping your mental models, creating diagrams or using archetypes, can be very powerful. Most of the time it is useful to begin a modeling process with a flexible process starting with elicitation of people's mental models, a process that lays bare the purposes, values, and assumptions people hold so that disagreements can be acknowledged and discussed. Even if people can't agree on certain issues, they should at least agree on the purpose, boundary, and time horizon of any model that might be developed as a way to help resolve the disagreements about substantive issues.

The underlying question, though, is different. You are really asking, "Is it sufficient to have a conceptual model building process alone?" There are a number of practitioners and consultants who believe that if you expose the assumptions of the mental model, then use qualitative modeling tools such as system archetypes or causal loop diagrams to produce a diagram that represents the team's consensus model of how the business operates, that this is sufficient to produce productive and meaningful learning. I don't think this happens very often. There are two fundamental constraints on our ability to understand the complexity of the systems in which we are embedded, but the conceptual modeling tools only help with one of them. First, our mental models don't tend to incorporate much feedback, we don't have a good appreciation of time delays, we don't have a good appreciation of accumulations, of stocks and flows, of nonlinearities. The research clearly shows these to be very difficult concepts for most people. Our mental models tend to be "dynamically deficient" – there's a lot of dynamic complexity in the systems we're called upon to manage and it's hard for us to see. That's where conceptual model-building tools have great power. The conceptual tools not only elicit people's knowledge and record it for everyone to see, but they help improve that understanding because they encourage people to think about issues such as "Where are the feedback loops? Where are the time delays? What are the long-term side-effects of our decisions?"

The conceptual mapping tools are essential in improving our mental maps of how a system is structured. But having a good mental map is only part of the story. Let's say we have a perfect cognitive map. It would be so complex and so have many feedback processes that it would be completely impossible, and I mean that literally, for people to look at that map and understand what its dynamics would be, to understand what the effects of a new policy would be. To use your cognitive map to make inferences about the future dynamics of the system you have to simulate mentally the interactions of all the different elements. Jay Forrester frequently likens this problem to solving in your head a hundredth-order nonlinear differential equation system, but, frankly, that's an underestimate, because a hundredth-order system would actually be quite a considerable simplification from the real-life systems people have to deal with. Evolution did not equip us with the capability to simulate intuitively the type of complex, dynamic systems we have created for ourselves. The result is an interesting dilemma. The better job you do with the conceptual modeling tools – the better your mental map of how a system works, the less able you are to use that map to make reliable inferences about the consequences of new policies or new structures you may want to put into place. The solution is to test the models, to test your hypotheses about the consequences of new policies. In most of the social systems we are concerned with, experiments in the real world are prohibitively costly, unethical, or simply impossible. Simulation then becomes the only means to determine the consequences of policies you might want to try.

SC: The practical reality is that managers have to manage on-line and yet they gain great insight by jumping into the virtual reality of modeling and simulation, so it seems as though there's an important decision to be made about how often you're going to jump in and out of the actual systems and the virtual system and how deeply you will delve into either system. How do managers know the right balance of the two?

JS: Modeling doesn't exist in a vacuum. In a well-designed learning process there's a continuous cycling between the virtual world of the models and the real world of the organization. In the virtual world you test out theories, you practice and develop your skills, your try experiments that couldn't be done in the real world. You might try extreme conditions that you can't or don't want to induce in the organization – such tests are often more instructive than continuing the status quo. Then, drawing on your improved understanding you then design and conduct experiments in the real world. The results of these interventions give further insight to improve your mental model and to help revise your formal models, leading to a still deeper round of testing in the next iterations. So just as airline pilots constantly go back to the simulator to refresh their skills, managers need to be moving continuously between the practice field of the virtual world and the real world of the organization.

SC: Can you provide an example where this type of program based on creating a virtual world has been effective?

JS: Sure, there are a lot of organizations now using modeling in this fashion to create and continue the learning process. The Du Pont Corporation, for example, has developed an interactive management flight simulator to help improve maintenance productivity in its chemicals plants. Actually it's a board game, there's no computer involved. The learning laboratory consists of a several-day workshop with the participants ranging from lowest grade hourly mechanics to plant managers and senior vice presidents. At the beginning they do some exercises – such as skits – to "open up" and build trust in the group. These exercises help people become willing to talk about the things that really matter in the maintenance dilemma as opposed to "safe" topics like new database technology to track equipment histories – the technological solutions that people are always happy to talk about. For example, everybody knows preventive maintenance is more effective than reactive maintenance, after all, "a stitch in time saves nine." Often maintenance managers asks plant managers to let them do more preventive maintenance work. However, in these plants there is enormous pressure to keep the plants running and to reduce down-time, so they'll often be turned down because preventive maintenance means taking functioning equipment off-line to perform inspections (some inspections can be performed while the equipment is operating, but some can't). The plant managers say "I need that machine, you can't take it down for preventive work, because so much of our other equipment is already down – if you were doing your job right in the first place we wouldn't be in this situation." Well, that starts to get into the things that really matter.

One purpose of the workshop and game is to help people surface those attitudes and practices and talk about them. Most important, it creates a virtual world in which people can experience what it might be like to pursue a proactive maintenance culture, which in many cases they may have never experienced in their entire careers. They discover the fundamental long-term/short-term trade-off (you can save money now by cutting preventive maintenance, but then breakdowns increase and costs rise later). They discover the vicious cycle that pulls a plant into a trap of low equipment reliability, high maintenance costs, inadequate resources for preventive maintenance, still more breakdowns, lower revenues, still lower maintenance resources. They also can learn how to escape from the trap, what the time constants are, what the challenges are. It is essential to note that there is an underlying computer model, a system dynamics model, that forms the basis for the game. By basing the game on the model, the developers ensured that the dynamics people experience in the game are realistic. Typically people have to play the game more than once before it can begin to change practices in the plant. It's something that they will go back to from time to time. Several thousand people have now experienced this over the past few years and we have data from a variety of plants showing a steep learning curve with equipment reliability going up sharply in most plants that have been through the program, while in comparable plants that haven't used the game, but tried traditional approaches to maintenance, the learning curve is much shallower and costs have continued to rise.

It's an interesting example because the game isn't arbitrary but grew out of and reflects the relationships and parameters of a carefully constructed and carefully validated system dynamics model. The game is the vehicle for creating a learning environment that allows a much larger group, a more diverse group of people, to experience the learning process that the model building team from Du Pont went through themselves, but without requiring everybody to become a system dynamics modeler. It's been a very successful intervention.

Notes

For further information, see:

J. S. Carroll, J. D. Sterman and A. A. Marcus, "Playing the maintenance game: how mental models drive organizational decisions", in R. R. Stern and J. J. Halpern (eds), *Nonrational Elements of Organization Decision Making* (Ithaca, NY: ILR Press, forthcoming).

J. D. W. Morecroft and J. D. Sterman (eds), *Modeling for Learning Organizations* (Portland, OR: Productivity Press, 1994).

J. D. Sterman, E. Banaghan and E. Gorman, "Learning to stitch in time: building a proactive maintenance culture at E.I. Du Pont de Nemours and Co." Case study available from John Sterman, MIT Sloan School of Management, Cambridge, MA 02142.

J. D. Sterman, "Learning In and About Complex Systems," *System Dynamics Review*, vol. 10, no. 2–3.

8

From Individual and Team Learning to Systems Learning*

George Roth

Introduction

This chapter explores systems learning issues that relate to the process of managing. It begins with a case from the work of the MIT Center for Organizational Learning with the Lincoln Continental program team at Ford Motor Company. The Lincoln Continental program team case is described as a way of providing an empirical foundation for the conceptual ideas which serve as the basis for the discussion of team and systems learning.

The Ford Lincoln Continental Case Study

Learning program established

Automobile magazine called the 1995 Lincoln Continental "a thoroughly happy, all-around excellent machine," and said that Ford "should take the organizational magic created by the Continental team and bottle it."[1] But learning can't be bottled. The Lincoln Continental program team at Ford didn't use magic, but it didn't take a business-as-usual approach to developing the car either. The team decided to build the Lincoln Continental using organizational learning concepts proposed by Peter Senge in *The Fifth Discipline*. Ford had been working with ideas conceptually for a number of years, and the Lincoln Continental

* I am indebted to particular colleagues at the MIT Center for Organizational Learning – Fred Kofman, Bill Isaacs, Dan Kim Ed Scheiw, and Peter Senge – for conversations from which many of the ideas presented in this paper developed. I am also thankful for the editorial assistance of Ginny O'Brien and Kenlin Wilder.

program was an opportunity to apply and test learning and these concepts in the process of developing a vehicle. The managers of the Lincoln Continental program management team had worked on numerous other vehicles and they were determined to avoid some of the problems they had encountered in the past. The team's goals were dual: to manage the Lincoln Continental program in a way that would accomplish objectives, while respecting and engaging the engineers who designed and developed the vehicle; and to launch a disruption-free process that would not result in last-minute changes when production started.

Senge proposes that organizations can gain competitive advantage from individual and collective learning. He recommends a continual cycling back and forth between study and practice in order to improve collective learning capabilities. His approach synthesizes the "core disciplines" of using systems thinking, understanding mental models, developing personal mastery, building shared vision, and team learning. The Lincoln program management team agreed to work with MIT researchers, who would help the team learn these new tools and techniques while the researchers studied how their application impacted business results.

The entire program team included over 200 full-time engineers, who not only worked together, but who also worked with other engineers across the Ford organization. A "core" program management team led the effort and all the other development teams reported to it.

Core Team Learning

The core program management team held meetings two days a month for eight months to develop a shared vision of the automobile design and to apply organizational learning concepts. The managers emphasized their shared view that engineers, not just managers, needed to develop personal initiatives, both in learning together and in trying out new car development ideas. This core team, which consisted of cross-functional managers, learned new techniques for observing, assessing, and reflecting on their management approaches. The meetings provided an opportunity for them to learn tools and techniques associated with organizational learning as they engaged one another as colleagues in an ongoing process of inquiry and personal reflection.

As part of the core team's work, managers gathered data throughout the program by interviewing engineers. When problems arose, rather than the more typical management mode of telling engineers what to do, managers asked the engineers to share their thoughts and make suggestions. These techniques provided managers with a new perspective on how their own attitudes, behaviors, and thinking influenced the engineers they managed. They learned that mistrust between managers and engineers had previously affected critical aspects of the product development process.

Learning labs

Workshops, called learning labs, were created as practice fields where managers could learn new techniques for reflecting on their own thinking and reasoning processes, for inquiring into how others thought, and for communicating more clearly and carefully.[2] **Systems thinking** – seeing individual jobs as part of a complex independent network of tasks and responsibilities – was emphasized. Through the use of a specially designed computer program, which simulated the consequences of their decisions, teams were able to see the projected effects of decisions they might make over the years that it normally takes to develop a new vehicle. The core team subsequently taught the engineers the techniques it learned. Engineers on the development teams went through the learning labs between September 1992 and August 1993.

In the learning labs, managers shared their insights about the consequences of the ways in which they managed the engineers, and in addition to the labs, managers created a number of other interventions that promoted open discussion and interaction with engineers. Throughout these exchanges, the managers discovered how their past responses to engineers had created a punitive atmosphere, leading people to hide problems.

Old problems addressed

One particularly critical problem in past vehicle development was that parts for various prototype models were commonly late. Engineers didn't report problems until the last minute, so problems often only surfaced as deadlines to build prototypes approached and physical parts had to be ready. One area where delays were most noticeable was in the change request (CR) system that engineers worked with: CRs are documents that engineers submit to indicate concerns or to request changes on car components. As core team managers examined the attitudes and behaviors of the engineers, they discovered that the engineers were accustomed to being criticized if they identified problems without knowing how to solve them. Therefore, although managers wanted engineers to provide timely information regarding changes, engineers hesitated to do so for fear of criticism and other reprisals. Engineers' skills were evaluated by the number of CRs outstanding and the time it took to find solutions to those CRs. Because of the way engineers were treated, managers reasoned, they tended to delay the identification of problems until they knew the solutions.

Figure 8.1[3] is a simplified version of a causal loop diagram produced by the core program team. The key problem is the central issue, "parts behind schedule." At the left are a series of forces (many involving exponential growth) that contribute to increasing numbers of part changes and late decisions. At the right are many of the "fixes" that the conventional system uses to "solve" the parts behind schedule problem, and the unintended consequences of those fixes (staffing shortfalls, the taking up of supplier time to help engineering) that actually make the problem worse.

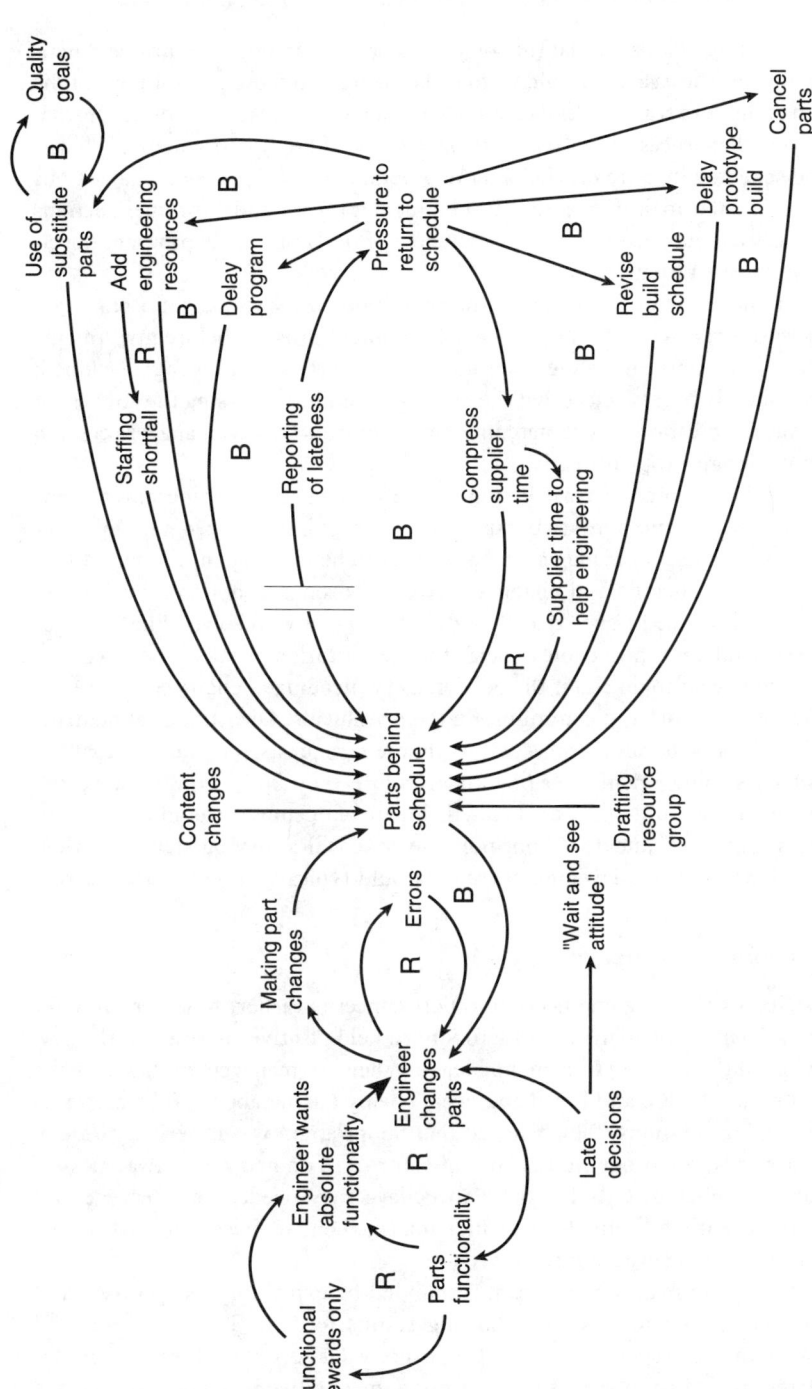

Figure 8.1 The core team's view of "parts behind schedule."

R = reinforcing loop
B = balancing loop
|| = time delay

The core team learned that the sooner it identified and communicated potential problems, the easier it would be to make changes to those parts. In one of the meetings the core team developed a system map using causal loop diagrams that displayed the process involved with late parts. The systems map of "parts behind schedule" (figure 8.1) helped the program team think about what actions they could take to improve the development process and how their actions systemically influenced not only the lateness of parts but other program development considerations.

Team members were able to see the significant cost savings that occur when changes to parts are made early in the development process, before investments are made in tooling, and while other interrelated parts are still being developed. It subsequently became clear that the leverage point in addressing the lateness of parts was the creation of a climate in which engineers trusted managers enough to report design problems early.

As the importance of trust became more evident, establishing an environment of openness and honesty became an explicit goal for the program management team. Managers made conscious efforts to be more open, requested that people report concerns and changes early, and promised not to punish those engineers who raised issues that they didn't know how to solve. The management team did not want people to delay the identification problems because they didn't know what to do about them. Managers encouraged engineers to use the CR system to report and communicate their problems. Over time, as the managers' behaviors became consistent with their requests, engineers began to submit CRs more openly, writing them before they knew how to solve the problems they identified. The increased climate of openness brought issues and problems out more quickly. At one point, over 500 CRs were outstanding, when other programs at the development stage would typically have less than 200.

New problems emerge

The success in getting engineers to report concerns earlier, however, brought other problems. Not all managers across Ford held positive views about the new behaviors of the Lincoln Continental team. When top management first saw the high number of CRs, and heard engineers openly talking about problems without providing solutions, they believed that the program was in serious trouble. In their words, the program was "out of control." Top managers' awareness of the large number of CRs led them to believe they needed to intervene and become more directly involved. Senior management requested formal review meetings and greater accountability.

The program management team responded by explaining its approach and the reasons for its actions, and showing results to date. They also included engineers in the response process. Engineers went to review meetings to describe their work, the progress with the program, and their excitement about the learning approach. Instead of managers simply reporting project progress according to milestone measures, engineers also presented what they were learning to senior management. Having engineers presenting learning at program review meetings was extremely uncharacteristic, and although senior management responded positively in the meetings, they were still concerned that the program was "out of control." Additionally, in order to pay for other initiatives in managing the program, the Lincoln Continental program management team made requests to top management asking for money beyond the amount originally budgeted. These funding requests, made at different points in time in the program, were needed to support an initial off-site meeting with all the engineers, to colocate engineers, to pay for an additional prototype, and to support subsequent funding of the MIT group. Colocation had not been part of the initial program plan, but extra funds to colocate the engineers from various other functions were provided. Costs for a three-day off-site meeting on organizational learning and cycle-time reduction for 150 engineers were approved. Funds were approved for building an extra prototype, which could be continually updated with the newest physical version of available parts. The expenditures for work with the MIT Center for Organizational Learning, originally funded by a corporate department, later came directly out of the program budget.

Throughout the course of the Lincoln Continental program, the core team had engineers and team leaders make presentations to senior managers, not only to report on the progress of the hardware, but also on their reactions to how the learning orientations were affecting them. Team managers continued to promote this new learning approach, but top management were mostly interested in technical considerations about the car and its development process. At one of these review meetings, after presenting car progress and learning approaches, a top executive responded that the organizational learning initiatives were fine, but "don't let these things get in the way of your job."

The core program management team, from their perspective, began to feel that its learning efforts were not being respected or valued by senior management, that only results counted. So team leaders stopped talking about the process and instead emphasized results: they prepared detailed statistical and graphical reports of project metrics to comply with top management's demands. The program management team believed the results would demonstrate the value of the learning process. Team leaders felt the results they achieved weren't possible without the learning approach they used.

The "Ford 2000" Plan

In the spring of 1994, Ford publicly announced its Ford 2000 Plan. Under this initiative, Ford plans to become a stronger global competitor.[4] The company is reorganizing "its worldwide sales, manufacturing and engineering operations to better take advantage of global markets and break down internal barriers."[5] Ford

2000 contains implications for vehicle development and program team functioning that emphasizes a more technical foundation and approach. Under the
initiative, managers are chosen for their technical understanding and engineering backgrounds in vehicle development.

The Lincoln Continental program team set new company records for product development metrics such as availability and quality of parts in all prototype builds. The pattern of CRs in the program was high at the beginning of tne
program but decreasing as the vehicle approached its manufacturing launch
date; this was in marked contrast to a typical pattern of low CR numbers at the
beginning of a program increasing to high numbers as launch approaches. In the
past, as engineers got closer to production, they scrambled to meet tight deadlines and then reported concerns and problems that could no longer remain
hidden. The strategy of the program managers to flush out problems early in the
development process, when they were less costly to fix, appeared to have
worked. The Lincoln Continental program "was able to save $50 to $65 million
that we would have spent correcting late designs or rebuilding production
tools."[6] The building of production vehicles began one week earlier than
scheduled: Parts were already in inventory and fit and finish issues had been
resolved.

The Ford 2000 efforts to become a stronger global competitor brought a new
emphasis on product development approach along with reductions in managerial ranks and grade reductions for many positions. As *Automobile* reported, "in
spite of this success, several of the key managers on the Continental team are
leaving the company. Although no one's talking, it seems that they were not
rewarded for their good works with promotions and bigger jobs, and absent
those offers have chosen early retirement."[7] Program managers and the program
team were early adopters of a new learning-oriented approach for managing.
This scenario of not appearing to be recognized for their innovations raises an
age-old issue of what happens to early adopters when they come up against the
larger system that they are a part of. The timing and changes associated with
Ford 2000 affected many managers through the project development operation.
Personnel decisions were made before the Lincoln Continental was completed.
Top management had made the decision to improve the company's ability to
integrate new technologies into its vehicles and wanted people with extensive
engineering experience to manage future programs. Team leaders, however,
believed that the openness they permitted by allowing engineering teams to
experiment with new approaches was not perceived in the most positive way by
top management. The Lincoln Continental core team ultimately realized that
their fate was in part determined as a repercussion of having failed to effectively
communicate the value of the learning efforts to top management.

Learning is a continual process and organizational learning at Ford continues
to evolve. A group of "Leaders for Learning" continues to promote and test
organizational learning concepts across the organization. "Ford's highest-level
executives have taken an interest in the Continental team and wants to know
what made it work so well."[8]

The process of building skills and capabilities for learning and system thinking has been under way at Ford since 1988. These efforts were gradual and were what developed the understanding that led to learning efforts on the Lincoln Continental program. Learning concepts have spread beyond any single program to several other initiatives in different divisions. With the numerous and broad-based projects under way, as for example the Electronic Fuel Handling division's initiative involving over 400 people in 20 teams,[9] it is likely that organizational learning at Ford will continue for some time to come.

From Individual and Team Learning to Systems Learning

Learning in organizations requires new capabilities and approaches in management. Individuals learn through direct experience, but team learning is a more complex process. And the transition from team learning to **systems learning** is even more complicated, requiring new skills and insights into how individuals learn about larger systems as well as how those larger systems learn from the individuals and teams working within them. The learning dynamics which emerge among these various levels of organizations stand out in bold relief in the Lincoln case study. The Lincoln case provides an empirical foundation for the discussion of team and systems learning.

The work with the Lincoln Continental Program team formally started in October of 1991 as one of the first projects undertaken by the Center for Organizational Learning (COL) at MIT. The COL is a consortium of major companies established by Peter Senge and his fellow MIT researchers. The purpose of the center is to develop knowledge for building learning organizations through testing theories of learning. The center's action research approach brings researchers and practitioners together to study organizational learning processes while they actively work together to help teams develop and improve their learning processes. The Lincoln Continental case examines key issues at three different levels: individual learning of managers; learning in and across teams; and an investigation of how the Ford organizational system influences, and is influenced by, the team learning process.

Team learning and associated organizational changes take place within a larger organizational context. At various points in time, the differences between how a team learns to operate more effectively, and how the larger system continues to operate, create conflict. As the Lincoln team members learned, they both affected and were affected by the larger Ford organization, and the process was not without conflict.

The paradoxical influence of individuals

Individual-level learning includes awareness, motivation, action, and feedback. In team-level learning, these concepts become problematic. In a real world where multiple incidents occur continuously, "reality" is infinitely complex. Individuals learn through recognizing certain phenomena and how those phenomena correspond to individual expectations.[10] In collective settings, such as teams, team members continue to interpret individually even though events or actions are commonly observed. Team members are attuned to and notice different observable facts in the same event. Team norms influence what people can say.

In human systems, such as business organizations, collective properties are perceived and acted on by individuals, who paradoxically both influence and are influenced by the larger system.

In complex systems, awareness is extremely important. Complex systems have delays in feedback and separation in time and space between actions and consequences. With multiple events occurring in a complex system, different individuals are aware of different events. Even when the same events are observed by different individuals, these events are often perceived, interpreted and described in different ways. Awareness includes not only what people notice, but what is perceived and how it is interpreted.

A challenge in team and systems learning is to bring out the different interpretations of the same events and create an awareness of different observable facts. How people interpret a shared situation, and what they are attuned to, becomes increasingly problematic in large organizations, where sheer size and complexity make it increasingly unlikely that people will have a common experience from which they can develop common understandings. What people notice and how they interpret it relates to their individual expectations, motivations, actions, and feedback. Developing a common understanding in teams and organizations of what is important, what it means, and how different individuals impact one another is part of the process of learning. In the Lincoln case, the cross-functional nature of the program's core management team helped it to uncover systemic problems and helped it to develop deeper understanding of the nature and interrelationship of those problems, but the team never developed a common understanding with senior management. The senior managers were not fully aware of the learning process; they perceived and interpreted the results one way, while the core program management team interpreted results in a different manner.

Teams in organizations

More and more frequently organizations use teams to deal with the accelerating pace of external change as well as to handle the increasing complexity and interdependency that is needed for completing internal tasks.[11] Team issues include how members deal with one another and how team members interact with nonteam members. The frameworks that have been utilized for teams have predominantly drawn on group research where the emphasis is on internal interactions among group members, rather than on how the group functions in its larger environment.[12] Group performance, however, correlates with both internal group processes as well as the ability of the group to manage its boundaries.[13] The importance of a team's role, behaviors, and strategies toward the environment in affecting performance has been confirmed.[14] Every team has boundaries and boundary activities. Team members actively acquire information or resources from others inside and outside the group. These activities also relate to how team members persuade others to support the team. The ability of a team to manage its boundaries, and thus its external environment, has been positively correlated with the results teams produce. Unfortunately, the Lincoln Continental core team had difficulty in enlisting top management in understanding the value of the learning processes it used.

Research shows that activities which span organization boundaries are important to team performance,[15] and have implications for team and organizational learning. Teams create conditions that influence the flow of information as well as the team's relationship with its larger environment, both in terms of how the team learns from the organization and how the organization learns from the team. The dependence on organizational conditions that teams encounter is an important consideration in making a conceptual and pragmatic transition from team to organizational learning. Teams have a critical function in promoting learning in larger systems. Learning issues in a team also reflect what are likely to be issues in the larger organization. As a team begins to operate differently, it can set a tone, provide an example, and establish capabilities for collective learning.

However, learning at an organizational level adds increasing complexity and scope to learning efforts. Learning across teams within organizations appears to be more problematic than learning within teams.[16] As units within larger organizations, teams have been shown to be able to produce outstanding results. The Lincoln team results were remarkable in terms of cost and time savings. There is, however, little evidence that what a team learns can be transferred and replicated within the larger organization.[17] Although the Lincoln Continental program succeeded in achieving goals, top Ford management did not attempt to replicate the program development team; instead, the Ford 2000 Plan emphasized that new car development teams be composed of managers who were technically trained. Promotions would be based on technical skills, expertise, and knowledge rather than new learning techniques. The failure of the larger system to learn from the team is most clearly evidenced by the extent to which efforts of the team are rejected.[18] Leaders and members of innovative teams are often ostracized, and the concepts and approaches the team utilizes to achieve results are rarely adopted more widely. Top Ford management had difficulty attributing success to the teams learning efforts.

The strategies used by the Lincoln Continental core team were not unilaterally accepted by other managers. Teams following traditional practices often appear to succeed more frequently than innovative teams, yet traditional practices are more likely to result in only incremental improvements. In order to produce extraordinary results, innovative teams operate in ways which are contrary to organizational norms. The innovative team accomplishes results using methods that are counter to prevailing practice, knowledge, and wisdom. The team's actions may threaten what people hold to be true. If results are achieved based on new ways of thinking, and new capacities for action, then the thinking and capacities of other people and teams might be rendered obsolete. Thus, innovative teams threaten the knowledge base in their organizations. At Ford, program review meetings are used as a mechanism to report details and progress. In these meetings visual aids like charts and graphs help to create an image of being in control through the display of factual knowledge. The Lincoln Continental team tried unsuccessfully to communicate its program accomplishments and learning at a personal level. However, without the ability to report on organizational learning with visual aids, statistics, and numerical details, the credibility of their learning efforts were suspect and questioned.

Organizational learning: the system learns

At an organizational level, a learning organization is "an organization that is continually expanding its capacity to create its future."[19] Creating a future means getting what is desired, and having the capability to consistently achieve intentions. In teams, as with organizations, the definition of learning is not as straightforward as it is with individuals. Teams and organizations are made up of multiple people with different perspectives and various desires. The multifaceted nature of what is desired by the people involved makes it difficult to determine whose intentions are, or are not, being achieved.

Creating a desired future requires a common understanding of what that future is and how people will create it. There are no "ideal" learning organizations, or corporate statements, that specify what aligns a particular group to a future they want. A learning organization is not one where academics or top managers define something that others desire, but one where individuals throughout the organization take part in shaping the definition.

A common dilemma is that people in positions of authority, including experts in theories of learning organizations, specify what a learning organization is and isn't.[20] But a learning organization, by definition, never is or isn't something: It's a process of collectively deciding what an organization wants to become, and then developing a process to work toward that "becoming."

Any set of particular characteristics for a learning organization is determined by the culture of the organization when it starts. The work of the COL is based on the premise that a learning organization needs to develop the capability to define and then to create its own future.[21] That future is based on the commitment of individual members living out personal visions as part of the organization. Part of the research efforts focus on developing and studying tools and methods for people to use in thinking and acting in ways that allow them to articulate and create their desired future.

The conventional wisdom in managerial practice is that results speak for themselves. If a team produces extraordinary results, the wisdom holds that other people's desires to improve performance will lead to the innovative teams' methods being widely adopted. However, there is a delay in time between implementing a process which uses innovative methods and achieving results. During that time, people can form negative assessments of the innovative team that are often not reexamined in light of positive results. As teams begin to operate in new ways, they distance themselves, psychologically and physically, from the influences of the organization. As team leaders and members adopt new ways of working together they challenge conventional practices. Others within the organization are likely to resist the approaches being taken. The team becomes insular, managing its boundaries, protecting and nurturing its new approaches, until it can produce the desired results. The combination of operating in ways which seem contrary to conventional practice, and being protective, are often interpreted negatively by other people in the system. Once they form generalizations, they seek evidence to confirm their assessments.

The Lincoln Continental program team went through these phases. In order to develop a climate which fostered openness and trust, teams behaved in ways that were uncharacteristic at Ford. The requests and responses from the team's managers to top management raised concerns that the program managers were not as focused on the car as top management believed they needed to be. Senior managers were concerned about the high number of CRs being reported in the program; they were concerned the Lincoln program was "out of control." The program management team worked to assuage top management's fears by providing detailed reports on program metrics. When these statistics on quality measures and availability of parts provided evidence that the program was successful, senior managers attributed that success to their own actions in bringing the program "under control."

The Lincoln Continental Program illustrates the conditions in organizations where managers efforts to manage and inhibit learning. The program team managers created an environment where people were more open, took risks, learned, and were given more autonomy. However, the team managers were unable to engage their bosses and create a similar environment with them. Managing upward required different conditions and capabilities than managing subordinates. The core team managers saw these conditions as a dilemma. The learning environment created for the Lincoln Continental working teams was not characteristic of the larger organization. The conditions which provided both Lincoln Continental program managers and team members latitude for new ways of thinking and acting left them feeling uneasy in interacting with the larger system. One aspect of the gap which existed between the program management team and the Ford organization had to do with differences between managing and learning. The philosophies, thinking, and consequently actions that underlie management are different from those that support learning.

Learning versus managing

Overcoming traditional behaviors, attitudes, norms, and assumptions for management is a challenge to developing organizational learning. The environment created by managerial practices affects the ability of people to learn together and collectively become more effective. Many common managerial practices, and managers' assumptions about what it means to manage, can counter learning. Because managers have a highly influential role at team and organizational levels, it is particularly relevant to ask whether there are fundamental incompatibilities between prevailing concepts for management and requirements for learning.

The word "manage" derives from the Latin *manus,* meaning hand. The derivation of "manage" arises from the concept of handling or training. One who manages takes direct responsibility for the performance of others. Webster's Dictionary definitions of "manage" include: getting a person to do what one wishes, especially by skill, tact, and flattery; and making others docile or submissive. These definitions provide some evidence for why managerial behaviors may be counter to behaviors that support learning.

The authority system and hierarchy implicit in notions of managing people are antithetical to the conditions necessary for learning. When people move from being managers to becoming learners they take a different stance toward the world. In a learning organization, the manager moves from the stance of trying to control outcomes to that of the learner, who inquires into what contributed to the outcomes. This is a shift from knowing to learning. The difficulty in making this shift is that people have to discount their existing knowledge so that they can learn something new. It took the Lincoln program management team eight months to "unlearn" their management style, and as one of the managers said, they had ". . . to learn how to quit being bosses."

Preparing for learning requires recognition of ignorance. In many cases it also means admitting mistakes. Learning may require recognizing that the knowledge base from which a manager achieved his or her career success may no longer be valid. Shifting to a learner perspective requires people to write off significant chunks of the intellectual capital they have accumulated in attaining their present position and status. Learning requires examining and taking responsibility for the very basic ways in which individuals think and act in the world. If individuals can't separate who they are from how they think and act, learning can raise questions about who they are.

Consider the example of a manager who has become successful by telling people what to do. He has risen to his high rank by living in this pattern. The people who work for him have accepted this, and they too are successful, in part because they are obedient. But problems arise for the manager when the company starts hiring new people who aren't that obedient and who want to be empowered. The manager feels he needs to disempower them or he will be in trouble. What the manager really needs to do is examine his belief that people need to be obedient. However, once the manager begins to ask these questions, what happens to his certainty about how to manage?

Learning starts with inquiring about what isn't known. But when managers say they don't know, they put themselves at risk. When managers take knowing stances, they are less likely to be open to different possibilities, to seeing problems from different perspectives. The greatest learning challenge for managers is to admit that they don't know, and although an open admission may put them at personal risk and may cause some chaos, new possibilities will arise out of the confusion. When managers start the process of examining themselves and asking difficult questions, they become less interested in looking good, and more concerned with how they can be effective. What are the norms of management, and how might creating conditions for learning be counter to them?

One of the Lincoln program managers admitted the risks involved with new learning and acknowledged that if he had been younger and really worried about getting promoted he might not have been able to change his mindset regarding managing and might not have been able to say, "Hey, I need a hand." The manager also reported that the change taking place was really happening within him. The transition from managers to learners has a personal component. This type of transition requires people to question their automatic thinking, the basis of their knowledge, and their deeply held beliefs and assumptions. Once individuals go through transformative change, they often become proponents of change in others. When managers create conditions where change and learning can take place, they become catalysts for systems learning in their organizations. The Lincoln Continental program team managers learned they did not need to have an answer every time engineers came to them with a problem. They learned that if they responded, "I don't know, what do you think?" they created new possibilities for engineers to propose ideas they might not have mentioned otherwise.

On an individual level, making a mistake or experiencing a breakdown between one's intentions and the results of actions can jolt a person into an awareness of new possibilities. But in complex systems, it is more difficult for people to discover the gaps between what they expect and what actually happens.[22] Learning is a way to accomplish goals, not only by closing the gap between intentions and results, but by creating conditions where gaps are consciously identified, examined, and become a source for collective action.

The concept of managers controlling subordinates is reinforced by institutional-level theories of organizations as bureaucratic, formalized structures that use mechanistic operational methods.[23] The predominant type of work during the industrial age, when managerial practices were developed, was action-centered. People could be observed and evaluated based on what they did. Traditional work and management practices in American companies today are still biased in this way. The bias for action, where "doing" is most highly valued, creates limitations for reflection, and thus for learning. Reflection, thinking, and planning aren't as highly valued, in part because these are activities that can't be

		Knowledgeable about cause?	
		No	Yes
Expectations achieved?	**No**	Uninformed failure	Informed failure
	Yes	Uninformed success	Informed success

Figure 8.2   Matrix of alternative project outcomes.

observed. Both managers and employees are evaluated and rewarded based on what they do, not on how carefully they think through what they do. The challenge to collective learning in this action-centered orientation is illustrated through the matrix of alternative project outcomes shown in figure 8.2. A project which an organization undertakes can be characterized by both its success or failure – whether or not it meets its expectations – and by how knowledgeable people are about what caused that success or failure.

As projects are carried out in organizations, it might be best to examine them not only for their success or failure, but for the processes and thinking that supported the outcomes. This approach to evaluating projects adds a learning element. In a learning organization, not only would managers be assessed on their abilities to produce successful outcomes, but an equally important criteria for their evaluation would be whether or not they could articulate and examine the processes that led to success. More important, if a project does not achieve its expectations and is a failure, having ways of knowing the reasons for failure is crucial. It can be more important to the longer-term success of an organization – which depends upon developing an ability to collectively learn – to have an informed failure than an uninformed success. To some degree, the Lincoln Continental program is presently an uninformed success for Ford. There is no process to broadly share the learning and rationale behind the approach, and consequently the program's successful results can be attributed to many factors which don't include learning. Developing ways of being informed about why some actions succeed or fail is particularly important to learning in complex systems.

Systems concepts and learning

John Sterman recently reviewed learning in complex systems in a *Systems Dynamics Review* article. He proposed that the dynamic complexity of systems, inadequate and ambiguous feedback, systematic "misperceptions of feedback," nonlinearities, inability to mentally simulate our cognitive maps, poor inquiry skills, and poor reasoning skills are barriers to learning.[24] These limitations to learn are found in organizations. Individuals are limited in their abilities to conceptualize dynamic complexity and both flawed cognitive maps and judgmental errors are magnified in organizations. Protection of entrenched interests, defensive routines, and information that is limited, ambiguous, and misperceived make it even harder for people to learn from their actions. To successfully overcome barriers to learning in complex systems, certain issues must be addressed and effective methods "must" include the following: tools to elicit participant knowledge, to articulate and reframe problems, and to create maps of the feedback structure of a problem; simulation tools and management flight simulators to assess the dynamics of those maps and to test new policies; and methods to improve scientific reasoning skills, strengthen group process, and overcome defensive routines for individuals and teams.[25]

Sterman's review clarifies what individuals need for learning in systems. Not only are there complex and difficult considerations for how individuals conceptualize roles in organizations, but there are also considerations for how others in the organization assess those individuals or teams that learn and change. For example, if individuals or teams develop systemic perspectives about themselves and their organization, they are likely to be more effective in the actions they take. Thus, the more they think about their organizations as complex entities, the more they will attempt to explain their reasoning and the more they will be open to understanding alternative viewpoints and perceptions. The more people recognize that others hold different mental models, acknowledge delays in feedback, and accept multifaceted perspectives, the more learning is likely to take place. The greater the ability to understand why people react to behaviors, the greater the ability to notice how the larger organization responds to individual learners.

The tools, methods, theories, and philosophies that teams adopt to facilitate learning and enhance effectiveness are influential in altering individual and collective behaviors. Those altered behaviors can be seen by others within the organization as significant variations from what is typical, expected, and accepted. People who have not been exposed to the tools, methods, theories and philosophies of learning, often interpret the new behaviors from a traditional perspective. The new behaviors are often significantly different from existing approaches, yet the interpretation of those actions by people in the organization is based on traditional expectations and mindsets. Thus, as was the case with the Lincoln Continental teams, learners may be viewed as "out of control."

The history of interventions in organizational development offers considerations for organizational learning initiatives. There is a history of teams achieving results within an organization, but a failure of results being extended more widely.[26] Innovative teams can produce extraordinary results; however, not only do they often fail to spread learning, the teams themselves are often later eliminated by the larger organization. The eventual outcome is demoralized team members, who once were highly motivated. Contrary to the rational expectation that processes which lead to superior business results are quickly adapted and broadly implemented, these learning and change efforts can thus be suppressed within the larger organization.

Communicating the learning process

Another explanation for the failure of organizations to learn from teams is based on how a team informs the larger organization about its learning and behaviors. Early in the Lincoln Continental program, when the core team was not able to convince top management about its learning approach, the team decided to let the results speak for themselves. The core team kept its conversations with senior managers focused on the results achieved, and stopped talking about the process. As they set internal product development records, core team managers thought that the results would speak most loudly. However, by giving up talking about their approach and reasoning, it is likely that the core team managers sent mixed signals to top management.

For larger systems to learn they need to receive clear messages about a team's learning. The Lincoln Continental program's goals were achieved, and the teams' behaviors demonstrated that they learned. However, there is little evidence that the learning extended to the larger system. Because the Lincoln Continental teams felt rebuked when they described their learning processes, they decided to wait until they had produced results to tell others about the merits and effectiveness of their approach. The Lincoln Continental managers and team members were also reluctant to emphasize the personal change they were experiencing in the learning process. They were concerned that what they said might carry an implicit message: since they had changed, others must also change. Yet, by not talking about the depth of personal change they experienced a key element of the learning process was lost. In retrospect, they realized that it should not be a great surprise that the larger system rejected the behaviors and discounted the results that the team produced.

As the core program team became engaged in the learning process, team members' values and norms changed, and changed in such a way that they failed to consider or deal with the gap between themselves and the rest of the organization. A barrier between the teams and the larger system emerged which served, in part, to protect teams' innovative learning efforts. The barrier also appeared to limit the ability of the Lincoln Continental teams to learn about the larger system, particularly about how its efforts were perceived. The behavior of team managers in supporting the empowered decision-making of engineers, in requesting additional support, and in producing a large number of CRs, raised concerns for top management. Before top management understood the reasoning behind the Lincoln Continental team's behavior, they may have established assessments about the program and its managers.

It is likely that top management was concerned that the program would not achieve expectations. In a large, complex development program there are multiple sources of information, formal and informal, about how the vehicle is progressing and how the program team is performing. Top managers, like everyone else, were likely held captive by their own conceptual processes, which tends to filter the information they notice. This prompted them to accept only ideas which were consistent with their assessment. Perceptual filters affect what information people pay attention to and how that information is interpreted. Thus, top managers might have called the program "out of control" because the behaviors they observed and paid attention to were inconsistent with theories they held about how a program should be managed. Furthermore, when top management intervened, driving the program team to report in a manner more consistent with their expectations – both in terms of outward behaviors and metrics emphasized – it was plausible for top management to consider its interventions successful.

A dilemma, endemic to traditional management practice, occurred at the beginning of the Lincoln Continental program and probably contributed to this situation. The COL research staff asked the program team managers how they planned to involve top management. The team's response seemed reasonable: They did not see the need to involve the top management until there were results – why bother top management without data to back up their requests or assertions? Team leaders weren't initially certain of the results they would produce or what implications they would uncover that might require top management support.

In corporate cultures where being in control and appearing knowledgeable are expected managerial characteristics, people make themselves vulnerable when they admit uncertainty about their ability to accomplish goals. However, as stated earlier, admission of ignorance, or "not knowing," is an essential step in a learning process. Admitting ignorance creates an opening for collecting new information or trying new methods.

Once the team withheld information until it had results, it was hesitant to engage higher levels of management. Once there was enough data to show measurable results, team managers were more inclined to convince management they were right, rather than share their learning process and the questions that were raised. Convincing top management of a particular point of view is a substantively different task than engaging them in learning. The openness and inquiry through which the program teams and program team managers learned was different from the approach that program team managers took in interacting with top management.

In hindsight, a premise that managers had counted on throughout their careers – that results speak for themselves – may have had counter-intuitive consequences. That is, the effects were almost the opposite of the manager's expectations. Throughout their careers, managers were convinced that producing results was what mattered most. When they finally achieved results, they relied on those results to win over skeptical top managers. Yet, rather than receiving the rewards they expected, the managers were not promoted. Without a sustainable communication process through which the program team managers could engage top managers, there was limited learning in the larger system.

Language as a tool

The importance of awareness, motivation, action, and feedback in learning in complex systems was mentioned earlier in this chapter. The significance of these concepts is particularly relevant to communication and the language used in communicating. Language is a tool for making collective sense. In order for people in organizations to have productive conversations they need to have common ways of talking about and understanding common events. The limitations of language include not only dealing with multiple meanings, but also consideration for what concepts can be expressed. The ability to inquire begins with developing common language through which understanding can occur. Once common language exists, it can be used for inquiry into, and discussion about, problems.

A very particular kind of language, however, is needed to represent and inquire into problems that are complex and multifaceted. How to represent complex systems in such a way that people can talk about them is a challenge for organizations. Using a systemic structure is one way of explaining systems.[27] What happens in a system can be described, at one level, as an event. Repeated observation of a system provides data on a second level, as patterns of events. Patterns of events are described in ways which are different from the events themselves. For example, statistics on defects in a production process describe a pattern with only limited information on why the product was produced.

Systems thinking approaches have created ways to describe systems not just in terms of the elements that make it up, but in terms of the relationship among those elements. Causal loop diagrams and system archetypes provide a language at another level for characterizing interrelationships and interdependencies of a system's elements.[28] The Lincoln team used causal loop diagrams to help them understand why delays in parts were occurring (see figure 8.1). Causal loop diagrams and stock and flow diagrams are techniques for mapping important conceptual relationships such as decision-making variables and material and information flows within systems. Using these tools creates awareness of relationships among the system's components and helps to promote collective inquiry. The system diagrams and archetypes describe factors and posit theories that explain patterns of events based on the causal and systemic structure that created them. They provide a new lens and language for people to use.

Reflection, feedback, and theory

Learning doesn't occur without feedback, and feedback doesn't make sense without taking time to reflect on the information the feedback provides. A problem in most large companies is that the people who are often promoting change are so busy that they never have the time to study and reflect on what they are doing. The predominant value and orientation in American companies is toward action. The Lincoln team set aside specific time for reflection. For example they met from seven to nine on Wednesday mornings to think about and discuss the program. Greater reflection in corporate America is needed so that more learning can take place.

Learning also cannot occur without theory. The link between theory and learning is critical. Theory, which is the reasoning behind actions and decision-making, needs to be articulated to guide collective actions. For a group of people to act in a coherent fashion, they need to operate from the same set of guiding principles. In organizations, however, the theories that are expected to guide collective action are often tacit. Chris Argyris points out a greater problem: theories that are actually put in use are often different from those espoused, and that difference has a tendency to become undiscussable in the workplace.[29] This undiscussability limits possibilities for learning. Learning on a collective or systems level can take place only when theories that actually guide behaviors are articulated. The Lincoln Continental core team members espoused the theory that engineers could be open and honest without fear of punishment. And, for the most part, the espoused theory and the theory-in-use were the same. Occasionally managers would slip back into an old way of operating and engineers would get reprimanded. However, because the team was putting effort into learning, and because the theory was explicit, when people did lapse into old ways, they were quick to recognize the discrepancy between their behaviors and the espoused theory, and they were able to make amends and change their actions. Making theories explicit allows people to be informed and guided. People can test the theories by behaving in accordance with them and reflecting on results. Once theories are articulated, they create a possibility for conversations about why people do or don't behave in accordance with them.

Theories, whether articulated or not, influence expectations. The Lincoln Continental core program team members described the theory behind their reasoning in decision-making. They talked about what they observed, the interpretation they made from those observations, how they drew further inferences, and how they made generalizations that brought them to their decisions. Going from observable information, to developing some interpretation about that information, and incorporating that information as part of a generalization, is a fundamental process of the human mind.[30] The challenge for managers is to make theories explicit so they can be considered and tested.

Conclusions

Business organizations tend to operate in ways that are not conducive to individual or collective learning; thus, companies limit their abilities and competencies. To operate more effectively and competitively, organizations need to promote learning and support the development of processes that build shared meaning and understanding. The learning process in individuals provides a framework for thinking about learning in teams and systems. On an individual level, managers need to experience greater freedom to ask questions and to let go of the stance of "knowing." As managers learn to suspend their assumptions and stay open to new ideas, the potential for new possibilities and for new shared meaning to flow through their teams and the system increases. As managers learn better methods of communicating with teams, and teams learn how to share their knowledge, the systems within which they work will develop greater abilities to learn. There are no guarantees or pat formulas – each organization will need to find its own way down the path of learning. The organizational culture will influence how individuals and teams work and learn together, and how individuals and teams learn and communicate will determine the evolution of learning within the organization. However, one thing is certain, the more that individuals and teams within the system are open to raising questions, rather than providing answers, the more potential the system has to learn.

Notes

1 R. Ceppos, "Lincoln Continental: opportunity rang the doorbell, and this time they invited it in", *Automobile*, March 1995, pp. 82–85.
2 Daniel Kim and Peter Senge, "Putting systems thinking into practice," *Systems Dynamics Review*, Summer-Fall 1994.
3 Adapted from Daniel H. Kim, "A framework and methodology for linking individual and organizational learning applications in TQM and product development", MIT Ph.D. dissertation, 1993, pp. 282–96.
4 J. Flint, "One world, one Ford," *Forbes*, 20 June 1994, pp. 40–41.
5 "Borderless management: companies strive to become truly stateless", *Business Week*, 23 May 1994, pp. 24–26.
6 C. M. Solomon, "HR facilitates the learning organization concept", *Personnel Journal*, Nov. 1994, p. 60.
7 Ceppos, "Lincoln Continental", p. 85.
8 Ibid.
9 Solomon, "HR facilitates the learning organization concept," pp. 56–66.
10 H. R. Maturana and F. J. Varela, *The Tree of Knowledge, The Biological Roots of Human Understanding* (Boston: Shambhala, 1992).
11 K. B. Clark and T. Fujimoto, "Overlapping problem-solving in product development", Working Paper 87-048, Harvard University Graduate School of Business Administration, Cambridge, MA, 1987.
12 For review of groups literature see D. Gladstein, "Groups in context: a model of task group effectiveness", *Administrative Sciences Quarterly*, 1984, vol. 29, pp. 499–517.
13 D. G. Ancona, "Outward Bound: strategies for team survival in the organization", *Academy of Management Journal*, 1990, vol. 33, no. 2, pp. 334–65.
14 D. G. Ancona and D. F. Caldwell, "Bridging the boundary: external process and performance in organizational teams", Working paper 3305-91, 1991 Sloan School of Management.
15 Ibid.
16 B. A. Stein and R. M. Kanter, "Building the parallel organization: creating mecha-

nism for permanent quality of work life", *The Journal of Applied Behavioral Science*, 1980, vol. 16, no. 3, pp. 371–88 and W. B. Chew, D. Leonard-Barton and R. E. Bohn, "Beating Murphy's law", *Sloan Management Review*, Spring, 1991, pp. 5–16.

17 M. Beer, R. A. Eisenstat and B. Spector, "Why change programs don't produce change", *Harvard Business Review*, November–December 1990, pp. 158–66.

18 For failures in organizational development and learning in organizations see P. Mervis and D. Berg (eds) *Failures in Organizational Development and Change* (New York: Wiley, 1977), A. Pettigrew, *The Awakening Giant: Continuity and Change in Imperial Chemical Industries* (New York: Blackwell, 1985) and R. S. Kaufman, "Why operations improvement programs fail: four managerial contradictions", *Sloan Management Review*, Fall 1992, pp. 83–93.

19 P. Senge, *The Fifth Discipline, The Art and Practice of the Learning Organization* (New York: Doubleday, 1990), p. 14.

20 A. DiBella, "The learning organization: a concept of being or becoming?" Working paper presented at Eastern Academy of Management, Albany, NY, May 1994.

21 "MIT Center for Organizational Learning, 1995", Paper available from Center for Organizational Learning, MIT Sloan School of Management, Cambridge, MA.

22 J. D. Sterman, "Learning in and about complex systems", *Systems Dynamics Review*, 1994, vol. 10.

23 D. S. Pugh, D. J. Hickson and C. R. Hinings, "An empirical taxonomy of work organizations", *Administrative Science Quarterly*, 1969, vol. 14, pp. 115–26.

24 Sterman, "Learning in and about complex systems", pp. 2–3.

25 Ibid.

26 R. E. Walton, *Innovating to Compete: Lessons for Diffusing and Managing Change in the Workplace* (San Francisco: Jossey Bass, 1987).

27 Senge, *The Fifth Discipline*, p. 52.

28 Ibid.

29 C. Argyris, *Overcoming Organizational Defenses* (New York: Prentice-Hall, 1990).

30 Maturana and Varela, *The Tree of Knowledge*.

9

Transforming the Top
Management Team into
a Learning Group
Laura Freebairn-Smith

*Learning, then, is not something that requires time out from being engaged in
productive activity; learning is the heart of productive activity – it is the new
form of labour.*

Ronnie Lessem
Total Quality Learning

Today's Top Management Team

An organization's top management team is critical for its long-term health.
This chapter looks at how the management team can increase and sustain its
ability to learn, as well as encourage ongoing learning throughout the organization. Today, the primary function of the top management team is to learn, to
encourage learning, and to share its learning in a meaningful way. Top management teams can and must break out of the perceptual confines created by their
position and power to enhance the entire company's ability to learn and be more
successful on a variety of scales – profitability, employee turnover, customer
satisfaction.

In most organizations, there is at least one top management team. When
there is more than one top management team, the number of teams
generally reflects the number of levels within the organization. For example,
there could be a middle management team and a top management team. In
smaller organizations there is usually only one top management team. Whether
the company is large or small, relatively flat or hierarchical, there is an inner
circle, the top leadership in the organization, making key decisions about the
company.

The top management team includes people selected by the Chief Executive

Officer (CEO), and its membership is a reflection of what the CEO considers critical for the company. It is not uncommon to find the standard functions represented on the team – finance, marketing, and production. Additionally, in many companies these days, the human resources are included as well. The composition of other top management teams may include leaders of its various divisions or subsidiaries. The membership of such teams is usually determined by the structure of the company and the CEO's view of what information is important for leadership and decision-making. Company structure drives team membership and vice versa. This can be a problem in learning organizations because structure confines vision and information, as will be shown later.

This group, the top management team, is critical for the life and health of the company and to some degree for the life and health of its vendors, its employees, and its customers. Top management makes strategic decisions on an incremental daily basis and at times in a more dramatic, large-scale way such as during acquisitions or mergers. The top management team bases its decisions on information which it acquires from various sources and in various ways. For example, one CEO of a large division said, "I like to go have a cigarette on the loading dock; that's where I find out what is really happening in the company."

Current information sources for many top management teams include financial reports, customer surveys, employee letters, staff meetings, networking with other CEOs, and industry publications. This information comes to the top management team through a variety of filters. Examples of filters are: the manager's definition of the problem and therefore what information is relevant; the limited scope of the questions on the employee survey; the company's implicit norms about openly sharing concerns; and, in all cases, the top managers' "personal information" filters such as personal experience, professional training, ethnicity, and world view.

This chapter emphasizes the problem of acquiring and utilizing information with a self-learning top team. It looks at the various attributes of top management teams and how each attribute affects the team's ability to learn and sustain learning throughout the organization. The following attributes will be examined:

- Vision;
- Group membership;
- Boundaries and shared meaning;
- Information and its interpretation;
- Insulation from the environment;
- Learning to learn: ego versus openness – the catch-22 of top management.

The chapter ends with some specific exercises for improving the top management team's ability to learn and share its learning with the organization. And finally, the chapter poses some questions for future consideration.

Being at the Top is Different (Creating Vision, Utilizing Power)

Top management teams are different from other teams primarily because of their leadership role, which gives them access to and control over resources, and thus gives them power. They have a relative advantage in terms of expertise, knowledge of the business, and experience in the business and/or industry.

The top management team's responsibilities include clarifying the company's vision, setting strategic direction, determining policy, and modeling behaviors that shape the company's internal culture. Because of these responsibilities and high visibility, the top management team must become a self-learning system if its goal is to have the entire company become a learning system. The top management team is the guiding light or north star for the organization. How it behaves dictates the organization's culture, values, and priorities.

Nonmanagement staff are highly attuned to the nuances of top management's values. In one company, the senior executives publicly stated that they supported a company-wide diversity effort. They showed up at one or two meetings for the first five minutes and put out a few memos on the subject. With little more activity from top management, the staff quickly realized diversity was not a priority and change was not going to happen. Attendance at diversity meetings fell dramatically.

This example dramatizes the top management team's role as the north star, the guiding light for the entire organization. Think of how many times you have heard staff say, "The boss wears jeans so I do." Or "The boss never goes home before 9:00 so I guess family is supposed to come second to work here." The top management team should not underestimate its power, through both symbolic acts and the deployment of resources, to create behavior patterns in the organization.

If the top management team models self-learning, other members of the organization will follow suit if they are provided with the necessary support and skills. One of the first steps on this path is creation of a **shared vision** for the future. The vision needs to address both internal and external goals. A strong vision aims for an achievable, yet challenging, future. In doing so, it becomes the barometer for progress and for people to choose to work at the company.

The vision should include the desired internal culture. Articulating how it will *feel* to work in the company and the interpersonal values that will hold sway are important parts of creating a long-term vision. In addition, the vision should not be a static sentence or two posted around the office. It needs to be revisited regularly, talked about, mulled over, and changed as needed.

Learning is driven by a constant process of change – a process of taking in new information and adjusting frameworks to utilize the new information. The vision of a learning company needs to be part of an ongoing dialogue within the company. Maintaining and encouraging this dialogue is top management's primary job. However, because of the power differential between top management and other staff that exists due to the hierarchy within most organizations, it is difficult to maintain dialogue. Many staff members fear reprisals for saying something "unpopular." And, as will be discussed later, top management often learns how to "not hear" input or negate input that is counter to their world view. Thus there are some fundamental forces in hierarchical organizations that must be addressed in order for purposeful learning to happen.

Who is at Our Table? (Group Membership and Norms)

There are two aspects to top management team membership which affect its ability to learn: (1) the design and culture of the team as a whole and (2) the individual characteristics of the team members. This section will focus mainly on the first aspect since much has been written about the impact of individual characteristics on team functioning,[1] although the two are linked.

Overall team design and culture

Membership　Historically, a review of industry practice suggests that the composition of the top management team has changed to some degree in more innovative companies, particularly those that want to become learning organizations. Not only has the gender and racial make-up of some teams changed, but so has the professional expertise of the top management team. It has expanded to include human resources, lawyers, environmentalists, and other areas that were of little of no concern to companies many years ago.

For example, 20 or 30 years ago, the issue of organizational culture or organizational development was rarely considered important. A common response of managers to organizational development initiatives had been, "Let's not waste time doing that touchy-feely stuff," "Human resources' purpose is to issue paychecks and make sure my pension is up to date." However, organizational development is now seen as an integral part of the company's success and so a human resources representative is part of the upper management team. In the future, we may consider the sanitation department to be critical enough to merit a seat at the top management team table.

In the past, the top management group has been a relatively small group of people. Recently, in some organizations, the top management team is growing as the need for information expands. Management needs more people who are capable of bridging the elusive boundary between the organization and the environment, armed with as much information about the organization as possible. This calls for an increased size of the top management team as well as a heightened emphasis on all functions that bridge that boundary, such as the clerk behind the car rental counter. Boundary spanners are key sources of information, the cornerstone of a learning system.

Top management team membership is a potential problem for a team that seeks to learn more effectively. One of the most important factors in becoming a learning system is information (access to it, ability to see it objectively, ability to analyze it, and to see its larger patterns). If the top management team is composed of people who represent the current structure of the company, their views will drive the content of the team's work. For example, a large insurance company may be divided into lines of business – auto, health, life. Each line of business is headed by a vice-president who sits on the top management team. The company is highly decentralized and so each line of business has its own marketing, finance, and other staff departments. As a result, the top management team gets information based on a mental model of various lines of business. The problem in this example is not seeing a holistic view of the customer. For example, one customer might need all of the various insurance products, but packaging and selling the lines of business as an integrated unit that meets all of the customer's insurance needs becomes difficult with the current organizational structure.

The concern here is that the original *content* of an organization's work dictates the membership of the top team. The result is that team members perpetuate the organizational structure that keeps them on the team (see figure 9.1) even if the content of the organization's work has changed and calls for a new structure – truly an empire builder's delight. Jack Welch's work at GE is an example of a CEO restructuring the company and the top management team to fit new work *content*. In a nutshell, work content drives organizational structure, which drives top management team membership. Then top management team membership dictates company structure which is often at odds with new work content.

This dynamic is particularly problematic for a learning organization. Past successes or behaviors block new and often critical information from entering top management's dialogue. This can ultimately result in organizational failure.

In addition to the overall structure and products or markets of the organization dictating membership on the top management team, there are other roots of team membership, other reasons why a person is included in the inner circle. These reasons also affect how the group learns. Many times the CEO's professional training will bias his or her selection of top management members. If the CEO came up through finance, he or she might continually pick people who have a finance background. The end result is that a certain "language" begins to dominate the group, for example, the language of finance, or the language of marketing. Expanding the "language" skills of all the team's members can enhance its ability to learn and be innovative.

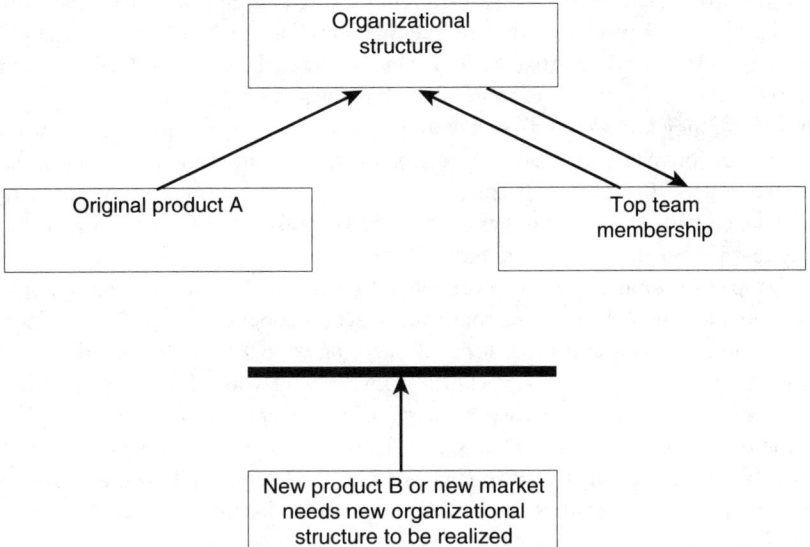

Figure 9.1   Organizational structure and top management team membership.

Shared vision   As mentioned earlier, another key attribute of the overall team culture is the team's shared vision or alignment about future direction. Peter Senge mentions that the Bosom Celtics basketball team:

> . . . demonstrate(s) a phenomenon we have come to call "alignment," when a group of people function as a whole. In most teams, the energies of individual members work at cross purposes . . . (W)hen a team becomes more aligned, a commonality of direction emerges, and individuals' energies harmonize . . . There is a commonality of purpose, a shared vision, and understanding of how to complement one another's efforts.[2]

The need for a shared vision on any team is well-documented. But for the top management team, because of the ongoing nature of their work and its impact on every aspect of the company, a shared long-term vision is more critical than for ad hoc teams. At the end of the chapter, there are exercises to work on your group's and your organization's vision.

Culture   All teams have a certain culture or norms which dictate what is acceptable or unacceptable behavior. These norms impact how relatively open or closed the group is to input or information, how well it deals with conflict, and how able it is to learn. For example, some teams have a culture of joking. The norm is to communicate through jokes or subtle put-downs. Other groups have "no-conflict" norms. When tension arises the group disbands or talks around the issue. Each group has its own culture and articulating this culture is a first step towards learning. Typically, different cultures develop ways of responding to organizational pressures that may either limit or enhance the potential for learning. Organizations that have a tendency to close themselves off from sources of uncertainty, in response to such pressures tend to stick to doing what they think they know (stasis), or try to discover new ways of operating by using old models of reality and creating a new world view in their own image (self-referencing). Cultures that are more open may alternate between times of being overloaded with information that doesn't always make sense (confusion), or they may learn from these experiences.

A top management team is more likely to continue learning if it has an open and questioning culture, one that encourages dialogue, not just discussion. Discussion is a back and forth form of parrying or jockeying for position. The ultimate goal is to figure out who is right or who wins. Dialogue is a deep exploration of meaning and the ultimate goal is to reach a shared understanding of the organization's issues. Dialogue requires an individual openness to feedback. In a later section, *Learning How to Learn so Others Can Learn*, the issue of individual ego and openness to new information is discussed in detail.

Size   The size of the team can range from three to thirty. A group of more than 30 becomes a mob. Each size has its own benefits in regards to learning. Much has been written on the effects of group size so comments here are limited. Team size falls into three generic categories – small (3–5), medium (6–15), and large (16–30).

A small team (3–5 members) can more quickly develop shared meaning about information and can be more cohesive sooner. Its downside is limited information. With fewer people, there is less information. For a small company or one in a very stable environment, a small top management team can often learn well enough to keep the company healthy.

A medium-sized (6–15 members) management team offers the benefits of the small team with increased information flow. However, as with all groups, the larger size increases the complexity of the group relationships and issues. The larger size also means that the group must spend more time developing a shared understanding about their work.

A large team (16–30) has the benefit of having the most information and highest potential for diversity of individual characteristics. However, groups of

	Internalizing	Inquiry
Open	Confusion	Learning
Closed	Stasis	Self-referencing

Figure 9.2   Cultural styles of dealing with organizational pressures.

this size tend to be unwieldy and information is not easily shared in a consistent way. Group dynamics are difficult to manage in this size group.

Led or leaderless   A small number of companies are trying out leaderless top management teams. If the team is focused on learning, leaderless teams have the added benefit of removing hierarchy within the team. This can at times allow for greater communication and sharing since the power dynamic is shifted. However, leaderless teams run the risk of not being able to coherently use information to move towards a clear vision. Also, in leaderless teams, there is often a *de facto* or emergent leader due to the person's tenure, skills, or another attribute which gives her or him power. It is rare to find a truly leaderless team.[3]

Individual characteristics of team members

The team's ability to learn and succeed is greatly affected by the individual characteristics of the team members. Individual characteristics include:

- Age;
- Race;
- Ethnicity;
- Marital and parental status;
- Sexual orientation;
- Professional background;
- Individual learning styles;[4]
- Ability to have dialogue or discussion;[5]
- Self-development/maturity;
- Openness/ego.

The degree of difference or similarity among group members along these various characteristics has been widely discussed. Some theorists[6] believe that similarity is more helpful to group functioning while others believe that difference is more productive. Similarity is often believed to lead to quicker decision-making while difference is believed to lead to more creative solutions.[7] Neither belief holds up consistently in research. There are too many variables at play. However, Dyer's[8] four attributes of successful teams, plus other attributes from observed teams provide strong indicators of health and productivity:

Conflict is resolved openly and in a timely manner.
People are respected and their expertise is utilized appropriately.
There is an atmosphere of trust and support.
Goals are clear, understood, and challenging but not daunting.
The team has fun.
People understand and accept their role.
People know when and how to both lead and be led.
Process and task are attended to equally.[9]

These characteristics apply to both top management and other organizational teams. There is one individual member attribute that is particularly critical for a learning team – the ability to manage one's ego. This is discussed in detail in the section on *Learning to Learn so Others Can Learn Too*.

Top management team checklist

A quick analysis of your top management group's key characteristics can help you determine whether it is on the path to becoming a learning system and whether it is supporting innovation of learning throughout the company. Rate your top management team on the following items:

Characteristic	Always true	True most of the time	Occasionally true	Rarely true	Never true
	5	4	3	2	1
(a) At least 60% of the team have different professional training or experience.					
(b) At least 40% of the team is female.					
(c) We spend less than 30% of our time on crisis resolution.					
(d) Our team members know each other's children's names.					
(e) We discuss our team's purpose at regular intervals.					
(f) Each team member is responsible for staying in touch with at least one external source of information.					
(g) Each team member has a particular skill that is recognized and utilized by the entire team.					
(h) We argue regularly and conflict is resolved and dealt with openly.					
(i) We have fun.					
(j) We recently invited a nonteam member to speak to the group.					

Continued on p. 255

Characteristic	Always true	True most of the time	Occasionally true	Rarely true	Never true
	5	4	3	2	1
(k) I have undertaken some form of self-development or self-analysis in the last three years.					
(l) The leader of our team knows how to use the copier.					
(m) We meet at least once every two weeks.					
(n) A staff member in our organization has made a meaningful change to an internal system within the last month.					
(o) We know how the replacement for our team leader will be picked if s/he leaves.					
TOTALS					

Scoring: Total your scores under each column.
Add the score under each column together for a total score.

15–25:   Your team is not yet functioning as a learning system and might be experiencing problems functioning (even as a team at all). There are probably power struggles going on that are not discussed. Be sure that the team is taking enough time to work on its own process issues (its ability to work together as a team). You might consider some strong intervention measures such as retreats, team building exercises, and outside consultation assistance.

26–50:   Your team has the basic attributes of a learning, healthy team. You might consider having the entire team complete the checklist, and then focus on those items that were ranked the lowest by the most people on your team. You can develop your own exercises to enhance the weaker characteristics or you could seek outside help.

51–75:   Your team is quite healthy and is probably learning on a continuous basis. The key is to maintain that health by balancing process and task work. Do not take the team's health or learning ability for granted; continue to work on the team

Continued on p. 256

members' individual learning abilities (openness, curiosity, information processing) as well as the team's sense of purpose.

© 1994, Good Work Associates; Please do not reproduce without permission; 203/773–3516.

The following case[10] illustrates several points about top teams in learning organizations. Through events in a public sector organization, we see how an organization can utilize small events to increase its ability to learn. We also see the powerful role of the leader or CEO of an organization, as well as the need to redefine who is a "member" of an organization. And finally, we examine how creating a shared view of reality, or shared meaning, is a critical piece of any learning organization.

Bikes and bureaucracy bump heads with the learning organization

One day in December, Loring was riding his bicycle down a steep hill in San Francisco. (Are there any nonsteep hills in San Francisco?) An old and dear friend of Loring's had recently died, and Loring was distracted by thoughts of their college years together. As he turned a corner, Loring's front tire got caught in a large hole in the street. The bike flipped over, throwing Loring violently to the ground and breaking the ball of his arm where it meets the shoulder socket. While Loring was lying on the ground waiting for the ambulance, a man from the San Francisco water authority came up to Loring and said, "You should sue the City; that hole has been there for months." The man then disappeared.

The ambulance arrived quickly and took Loring to the hospital. While he was waiting in the emergency room, another man appeared, a nice man who asked Loring a lot of questions. He said he was a claim adjuster for the City of San Francisco.

Loring was in a cast for months, taking pain-killers to deal with the broken arm. After his arm began to heal, Loring decided to sue the City. This decision began a long process which, after three years, was still not resolved. In the third year of the case, Loring attended an arbitration hearing with his lawyer, a lawyer for the City, and lawyers for each of the two construction companies, Company A and Company B. The two construction companies were represented because it was unclear which of them was potentially responsible for not repairing or at least not marking the hole.

As the story unfolded on the stand, it became clear that in June of the year of the accident, the City of San Francisco decided to put out its

Continued on p. 257

road repair contract to bid because it was unhappy with the performance of its current provider, Company A. Company A and Company B both competed for the contract. Company B was selected in July; however, it took five months to sign the contract and Company A's contract had lapsed in June. When the new contract was finally signed in November, no work had been done on any City roads during that time. In addition, new work had been piling up; Company B inherited a significant backlog of road repair work. The result was that holes were not filled and roads were left in poor condition, and Loring rode his bicycle into one of the holes.

Other interesting things began to come out at the hearing. Who was the man from the water company, the one on the day of the accident who said to Loring, "You should sue"? Somehow the water company had no activity records to trace this man down. In addition, for some reason prior to the hearing, the City could not identify the claims adjuster who had appeared in the emergency room.

At the hearing, the adjuster was presented as a surprise witness. When asked how he could have gotten to the emergency room so fast, he admitted that the City had received a call from the water company. How did the water company know about the accident if the man on the scene was not a water company employee? This question was not answered.

As a result of Loring's accident, the system (the City Public Works Department, the courts, and others) began to address the question of "Who is responsible for this accident?" The question was addressed in the context of the legal system as exemplified by the arbitration hearing. This is a classic example of a nonsystemic, nonlearning approach to solving a systemic issue. If the question is resolved in court, very little – if any – organizational learning will occur because the players in the courtroom are not concerned with or are unable to translate the results into system-wide learning.

The question of "Who is responsible?" *is* valid in the legal context; the current purpose of our legal system is to determine responsibility for actions against people, property, and socially determined values. The problem in the case of the potholes is that nonsystemic thinking (e.g., a court-based decision) rarely results in long-term change. We see that court-based solutions often **overcompensate** for a problem or provide a **short-term fix**.[11] Learning top management teams need to avoid both these types of corrective actions.

What do bicycles and potholes have to do with top management teams and learning? Let's look at Loring's accident from the perspective of the Mayor of San Francisco who decides that resolution of this seemingly small problem is an opportunity to resolve larger system issues. The mayor decides that she wants the top management team for this issue to both *be* and *create* a learning organization.

Why the mayor? In this case, the mayor is the leader or CEO of the City of San Francisco. Her role and purpose is to make the City a high-functioning system for all its constituents, not just employees or taxpayers. The mayor asks a series of questions:

What "organization" is this team working in?
What is that organization's "purpose story"?
What is the purpose of this team in particular?
Who should be on this team given the purpose of this organization?
How will the team learn what it needs to learn and pass that learning on to other people within the organization?

The Walls Around Us (Shared Meaning and Systems)

One of the key questions for any top management team is "Where does the organization begin and end?" Defining the **boundaries** of the organization, and therefore who is in and who is out, affects the team's ability to learn: too broad a definition and the team will be hamstrung by excessive input, too narrow a definition and key constituents and critical information can be overlooked.

From a systemic viewpoint, the case of the potholes affects all of San Francisco's citizens, both taxpayers and nontaxpayers. The issue also affects vendors to the City, the court system, the purchasing office for the City, and other groups. This simple event highlights the connection between all aspects of the City and its residents. This is not a linear problem; it is not a subset of the system; it is an issue affecting the entire system with a broad definition of "the system."

Given the breadth of systemic issues and the need for system-wide learning, the mayor puts together a team which includes representatives from various agencies, Loring, the arbitrator, and the construction companies. She takes a broad definition of her organization (City government) and defines the team as part of the government of the City of San Francisco. This is a wider definition of the government than is used in daily practice; the Mayor has broken out of a mental model that says the City government boundaries only include a small group of people, namely employees. This broad team will bring information that a narrower team could not bring to the table; a team of City employees only would see the world and the problem from a distinct and narrow perspective.

At this level, leaders are continually helping people see the big picture: how different parts of the organization interact, how different situations parallel one another because of common underlying structures, how local actions have longer-term and broader impacts than local actors often realize, and why certain operating policies are needed for the system as a whole.[12]

The top management team needs to develop shared meaning about the problem and the available information. The group needs to understand what happened, how it happened, and why it happened. Shared meaning arises out of this type of analysis and dialogue. If the Public Works Department sees the problem as due to the Purchasing Department's rules, and Loring sees the problem as the Public Works Department's fault, it will be hard to reach a solution that allows the system and its participants to learn.

In addition to thinking about the pothole problem from a systemic viewpoint, the Mayor challenges the team to think about the City's purpose story. "By focusing on the purpose story – the larger explanation of why the organization exists and where it is trying to head – leaders add an additional dimension of meaning."[13]

The team's purpose could have been narrowly defined as "ensure that such accidents do not happen again" or "keep the roads well maintained." These two purpose stories are examples of "event" thinking (the one accident) and "patterns of behavior" thinking (keeping the roads maintained). These two types of thinking look at and respond to the isolated event (the accident) or a series of similar events which have created a pattern (a series of suits or complaints about the roadways). These types of thinking have value and can assist a company if it is part of a broader type of thinking that results in learning, namely thinking about systemic structures, the organization's purpose story, and creating shared meaning.

Our hypothetical top management team, in order to be a learning system and to create a learning organization, needs to take a different approach. They need to look at the system level issues and the purpose story of the organization, the City of San Francisco. On a systems level, we see that the extremely long delay between information and action in the City bureaucracy leaves gaps in service which create unhappy (and sometimes wounded) residents. While waiting for the system to respond in a more long-term way, the system makes quick fixes such as paying court settlements or possibly patching the road with makeshift materials.

A system's view also shows us why public sector groups have large bureaucracies with extensive paperwork. Because they are spending public monies, taxpayer dollars, on publicly shared goods, it is essential to avoid the possibility of graft as much as possible. The only way government has solved this problem is to create onerous procedures with extensive records. This results in long bidding procedures and slow responses to problems.

The purpose story for our top management team is to make the City of San Francisco the most desirable and safe place within which to learn, live, play, and grow old. Potholes on steep hills definitely do not fit in the picture created by this purpose story. The systems learning shows us that the deeper issues are public accountability for expenditures. The challenge for the team is to determine how to speed up contract bidding and allocation, without negatively impacting the public's ability to determine whether funds are appropriately used and graft is avoided.

How Do You Spell "Bicycle"?

As stated earlier, one of the key problems for a learning organization is the transmittal, reception, and utilization of information. Information is currently presented to us primarily through two mediums – the written word and the spoken word. It is important to have a shared understanding of how the words are used and formed, and what they symbolize. "Perhaps most subtly, language programs the subconscious. The effects of language are especially subtle because language appears not so much to affect the content of the subconscious but the way the subconscious organizes and structures the content it holds."[14]

The written and spoken word, whether on paper or via computer, are one person's personal construction of reality, that person's way of naming the world. The recipient of the information also has her or his own constructs around language. Let's look at an example. Imagine that you are the CEO of a large company. Your human resources director comes to a top management meeting with the results of a recent employee survey. One of her findings is that employees, particularly women, feel that they are excluded from informal networking opportunities. You ask the human resources director to say more. She says that the women who responded to the survey (40% of the women in the company, and women are 52% of the companys workforce) noted that most informal networking events were scheduled in the evening, a time which conflicted with their family obligations and thus blocked them from access to these important tools for advancement.

You, as the CEO, hear this information third-hand – employee to survey, survey to human resources director, human resources director to you. In addition you are a man with a wife who stays home to take care of the house and family. You worked your way up the ladder by attending hundreds of evening and weekend events. Your initial reaction to the human resources director is that the survey does not represent a majority of women and there is no way to change these networking opportunities since many of these events are built around client needs. Yet you also know women are leaving the company because there is no way to advance to the top and maintain their families.

You decide to talk to some female employees directly and to some customers as well. After a few interviews, you realize that their complaints are valid and that the women are experiencing this conflict more acutely but no less often than men in similar positions. Solutions appear as a result of your discussions: make the events even later in the evening so women can go home and then come back; make certain weeks of the year off limits for evening events. And much to your surprise, even the clients would like to do more during the work day than in the evening because, also much to your surprise, many of the clients are now women and young men with families.

By acquiring information in new ways (first-hand or through new media), a manager's mental models about the organization can change. For this CEO, it was critical to talk to female employees and customers directly. This allowed him to see that both the company itself and the external environment had changed since he had risen in the organization.

Your personal experience and world-view impact how you see the world and how you interpret data. One of the keys to becoming a learning organization and learning management team is to break out of your own mental models (or constructions) to see data in new ways. The more direct the communication and the more detailed the dialogue, the greater the learning. For management, this is a constant struggle. Information transmittal is difficult to manage if there are too many layers of interpretation, too many layers of management levels, too little time for interpretation, and a limited ability to see different models. The issue of insulation is discussed later but first, here is one more example of how people construct their world and language to fit their world-view.

I was speaking at a large convention in a four-star hotel in New York City last year. Before beginning my talk, I asked one of the hotel stewards where I could find a restroom. He pointed me down the hall to the left. I quickly found a door marked "Women" but as I was opening it, I noticed another door marked "Women" barely 20 feet away on the left. Neither door was marked wrong; they were both for women and the men's room was on the right. Why two bathrooms for women so close together? Women immediately know the answer to this question – women use the bathroom more often and it takes them longer to use it. What's most important here is not the answer but the fact that one of the architects of the hotel was a woman. She approached design from a women's perspective.

Our experience is reflected in everything we do. In order to change what we do, we have to expand our experience. How we ask questions, what we report, and how we filter information matters greatly especially for top management teams that are making critical strategic decisions.[15]

Insulation is for Houses, Not Management Teams

There are three **learning screens** important to the top management team. A learning screen is any system that filters data before the data is used. Some screens are helpful, others detrimental to organizational health (which is the point of all organizational learning from a capitalist perspective; Socialists or Marxists might see organizational learning as a way to improve social conditions but that's a topic for a different chapter).

The three primary learning screens relevant to the top management team are:

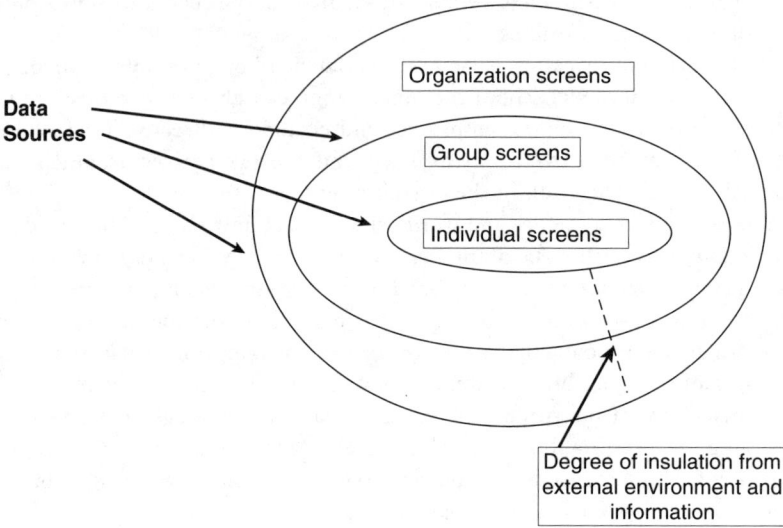

Figure 9.3   Organizational levels of insulation from data.

1 The individual team member's world view/data interpretation methodology. Examples of measures of this are Myers-Briggs and Lessem's work. The Myers-Briggs Type Indicator (MBTI) helps managers understand their personal way of receiving and interpreting information. Through the use of a simple but elegant diagnostic tool, it places people along four spectrums (e.g., introvert to extrovert, sensate to perceiver). Ronnie Lessem's work in *Total Quality Learning* discusses seven learning styles, such as the reactive learner or energized learner. Managers tend to have a dominant style but also have a range. Knowing one's style can help managers seek out other kinds of learners and information that they may not see because of their preferred learning style.

2 The top management team's culture. Does the team have a culture which precludes certain information, certain ways of learning? The team's culture will adversely or positively affect the overall learning.

3 Insulation: the organization's openness to the external environment and top management's openness to the internal environment.

The group's degree of insulation from the external environment affects its ability to learn, as does its insulation from internal environment (see figure 9.3). Learning "will require seeing the company as a system in which the parts are not only internally connected, but also connected to the external environment, and clarifying how the whole system can work better."[16]

Learning to Learn So Others Can Learn Too

How will the team learn what it needs to learn and pass that learning on to other people within the organization? Today, the primary function of the top management team is to learn, to encourage learning, and to share its learning in a meaningful way. It may have to step out of the way once the information or learning is shared so that staff can translate the information into action and draw their own learning from it. "In essence, the leader's task is designing the learning processes whereby people throughout the organization can deal productively with the critical issues they face, and develop their mastery in the learning disciplines."[17]

Learning requires several steps: access to information, comprehension of the information, ability to absorb the information, and ability to utilize and change the information within a feedback loop.[18] Not only does the top management team need these abilities but it must also create them within the organization.

True learning is **interactive**: it allows the learner and the teacher to interact and affect each other's mental models and ways of operating. An example from computer software highlights the difference between interactive learning and passive learning. Many software programs claim to be interactive. They give the user a variety of options at various points in the program. The user can usually choose from a range of options – A, B, or C. This is not interactive in the deepest sense.

Interactive software allows the user to **change** A, B, or C. More importantly, truly interactive software or any learning system allows the user to **add** D, E, and F, and the system learns from the user's mistakes and preferences. For example, a highly interactive word processing system would learn that the typist likes indented paragraphs and would change the default settings after a certain number of uses of this paragraph style by the typist.

The top management team must become like the interactive software, analyzing its own activity, its environment, and the activity of those who use it (employees, customers, and vendors) in a constant cycle of learning. Several tools are critical for this:

1 The team is open to outside information; its boundaries are semipermeable.
2 The team gets at least some of its information first-hand; not all information comes from third-level sources.
3 The team is willing to analyze its own functioning; it is willing to look at its own group process.
4 The individual team members are willing to take the emotional risks of self-analysis, self-development, and deep dialogue.
5 The team regularly challenges its mental models; it uses framebreaking exercises to stay open to other possible models.[19]
6 The team translates its learning into meaningful interactive guides for staff learning.

We have already discussed the first three items on the above list in prior sections. The fourth item means that the top management team member must be able to get his or her ego out of the way so that information can get in. This is one of the catch-22s of a top management team. Individual ego is what has brought the managers to the table. Their egos have produced success for the team members – it has gotten each of them into the inner circle. As a result, most top management team members are convinced that their world-view is accurate. If one's world view is accurate and has produced successful behavior, why bother to examine or question it through dialogue and self-analysis? "Cultivating understanding in isolation can lead to reliance on self-defeating, quickly obsolescent, local truth, and ignoring the contexts of others usually runs the danger of narrow-mindedness and a false sense of security."[20]

Chris Argyris, in an article for *Harvard Business Review*,[21] notes that professionals avoid learning because it is hard to hear criticism or information that refutes one's mental models. He develops the concept of **defensive reasoning** which keeps smart managers from learning. Defensive reasoning is the result of a set of values which work to avoid embarrassment or threat. An example is the value "to remain in unilateral control." Control allows the manager to avoid embarrassment but it also blocks out information.

The following case in the private sector highlights how difficult it is to be a learning top management team, and highlights one of the key barriers to successful top management learning – ego – which we've discussed. This case also shows us two remaining aspects of becoming a learning system: overcoming history's legacy and levels of insulation.

The athletic salesmen

Twenty years ago, a group of men, all white, started a sports magazine[22] in their garage. Over the years that magazine grew and became the premier media vehicle in its sport. The company grew too, adding more men, all of whom were athletes in the sport and most of whom were salesmen, since the company's existence depended on the ability of its staff to sell ad pages. The staff had a good time working at the magazine; there was camaraderie, many games, lots of conventions, drinking, and fun. What better than to earn a living while playing a sport you love?

As the company grew, it expanded into other sports, eventually adding three more sports to the team of magazines. The company continued to be successful with its highly cohesive internal culture which exactly mirrored the culture of their target market: upper class, white, and male. The fast track in the company was through sales since this was still viewed as the most important activity for the life of the magazines. Being in sales demanded that you be proficient in the sport, travel extensively, and be one of the boys.

The company continued to grow, and by the mid-1980s a larger publishing firm made a buy-out offer. The owners accepted and the sports magazines became a subsidiary of a much larger publishing empire. The publishing empire was happy to have the small subsidiary especially since it contributed 30 percent of the empire's profits. With this kind of performance and growth, the empire kept out of the way, only occasionally sending down corporate directives.

Continued on p. 265

> But something began to happen at Sports, Inc. The staff grew to 450 people within five years. More women joined the staff. And the outside world discovered a concept called "diversity," which was creating dramatic paradigm shifts in the more progressive corporations as well as other facets of society.
>
> Sports, Inc.'s top executives, a group of five white men in their fifties, all salesmen by training, with wives at home taking care of the kids, were unaware of this paradigm shift. With only five senior executives, all with the same world view, not much new information penetrated the inner circle. The little that did was from men like them in the company who were moving up the ladder. Any information counter to their world view that did get through the wall around the senior executives was always discounted. The messenger was unfit in some way. But little information flowed in or out of the senior executive group; the formal channels of communication were underdeveloped, and they trusted the staff so little that most information was kept secret.

The next challenge for the top team is to create interactive learning for the entire organization by translating team learning into meaningful interactive guides for all employees. It does this by:

- Tolerating ambiguity ("I don't know," "I'm not sure yet");
- Encouraging risk-taking[23];
- Modeling learning both individually and as a team;
- Challenging staff's mental models;
- Making the system open and reactive to staff input so that the system learns as staff learn.

An example highlights the last characteristic. In its early years up until the late 1980s, the Yale School of Organization and Management was a learning system. This was shown in many ways, but particularly in the inclusion of students on various committees including the curriculum committee and the admissions committee, both powerful decision-making bodies for the school. Students were not included in just a token way; they were given equal votes with the staff and professors who served on those committees. And in the case of the Admissions Committee, students constituted 67 percent of the committee (8 out of the 12 members). The students' presence ensured that the school was constantly learning about what worked and didn't work in terms of entrance criteria. For example, the students on the committee might note that a stronger math background ensured more success in the school, and would bring this out in the selection criteria. Or conversely, the students might note that too many of their classmates had investment banking backgrounds and would thus select new students to better round out the student body experience.

Giving students or clients or staff a true voice in sharing information and changing the company is difficult because of the vulnerability that is required. As we've noted earlier, egos and fear often stand in the way of this type of learning. "The caring relationship, then, is intrinsic to both quality and to learning. The interweaving of thought, feeling, and action becomes a precondition for both total learning and quality management."[24]

Developing a Learning Practice for Your Top Management Team

Cases and abstract analysis are helpful in imagining what your top management team as a learning system might look like and what it might contribute to your company's bottom line. However, moving from old models of the team to a new model of a learning system takes concrete action. As in all learning, the concrete steps are part of a loop: theory, test, reflection, question.[25] The team is simultaneously learning in two loops – one about themselves as a learning team, the other about the focus of the company's work as a learning process.

Various authors talk about a set of skills or ways of thinking that enhance learning. According to Senge,[26] there are five learning disciplines for the learning organization as a whole: systems thinking, personal mastery, mental models, building shared vision, and team learning. Lessem looks at seven phases: imagine, foresee, conceptualize, grasp, explore, respond, react. Debono uses his "six thinking hats"[27] to enhance creativity and learning: white for neutral and objective, red for emotional, black for negative, yellow for positive, green for new ideas, and blue for control and organizing the thinking. There are many other books with techniques for enhancing team functioning. Below are four sample exercises for your top management team to enhance its ability to learn.

System patterns

Ask each team member to draw a picture of the company. The picture cannot be an organizational chart nor can it be a written document. For example, some people draw a picture of a circus, others might draw a picture of a field of landmines. Ask each person to share their picture and why they chose that metaphor. What are the details in the picture? For example, who is the ringleader in the circus? Who do the horses represent?

After sharing each individual picture, ask the entire team to develop a shared view of what it is like to work in the organization. Discuss the pros and cons of this metaphor. What would the team like to change about this system? What aspects of the system block the team from learning or the organization from learning?

You can do the same exercise with a narrower focus on the team. Ask people to draw a picture of what it is like to be a member of the top management team, and repeat the exercise using this narrower focus.

Clarifying personal vision

Ask the members of the top management team to individually respond in writing to the question, "If you woke up tomorrow and your personal vision was realized, how would your life, this company, and the world be different?"

Ask each top management team member to develop a personal "mission" statement based on the above answer. Ask each member to make two lists: what currently blocks me from achieving my vision; what currently supports me in achieving my vision.

Have a group discussion about the blocks and supports. What role does the organization play? Where does learning fit in each person's vision?

Getting new "data"

Ask each team member to interview one customer about the company's product or service. Have three or four standard questions that are asked, but then challenge the team member to create four more meaningful questions which will enhance the team's learning.

Share each team member's data with the entire group. Make a list of "surprises" (things that the team didn't know) and "confirmations" (things the team assumed and that were confirmed by the interviews).

Discuss how the surprises can make the company more successful.

Discuss how it felt to collect the data, to be talking to customers.

Creativity and framebending[28]

Ask each team member to take out a piece of paper and pen. Give each team member an empty paper cup. Tell them they have 60 seconds to write down as many uses for the paper cup as they can think of. Anything goes. They should avoid self-censoring as much as possible.

After 60 seconds, go around the room asking for one item from each person's list. Write down the items on newsprint or a blackboard as people call them out. Ask people not to repeat ones that are already on the list at the front of the room. Keep going around the room until all ideas are on the list. Read the list. Ask for any additions.

Discuss how this exercise applies to the creativity of the team. Was it useful to start on an individual basis? Is it always useful to start that way? Why or why not? How would the exercise have been different if the group had brainstormed together? How can the group apply this technique to its own learning?

Conclusion and Questions for the Future

In conclusion, the top management team's ability and willingness to continually learn will ensure the success of the organization in the years to come. To do so, it must break out of the confines created by its status in the hierarchy and gain access to information in new ways. This is not easy.

As in all learning, there are questions that remain. Three to consider as you develop your top management team's learning ability are:

1 Do we need to stop using the word "manager" in order to shift our paradigms? Does the historical concept of manager interfere with the ability to learn by creating ego-attachment to the power and control that are historically attached to the concept of manager?
2 Does amount of available time matter? Does this type of learning require a certain amount of time for reflection and, if so, what happens in times of crisis?
3 How will a workforce of people from various cultures and international workforces impact an organization's ability to learn?

Notes

1 See Jonathan Gillete and Marion McCollom (eds), *Groups In Context* (Reading, MA: Addison-Wesley, 1990), David Berg and Kenwyn Smith, *Paradoxes of Group Life* (San Francisco, CA: Jossey-Bass, 1990), and Richard Hackman, *Groups That Work (And Those That Don't)* (San Francisco, CA: Jossey-Bass, 1990).
2 Peter Senge, *The Fifth Discipline* (New York: Doubleday, 1990), p. 234.
3 Laura Freebairn-Smith and Jonathan Moss, *Teams At The Top: Literature Search* (Boston, MA: Boston University Executive Development Roundtable, 1992).
4 Ronnie Lessem, *Total Quality Learning* (Cambridge, MA: Blackwell, 1991).
5 Senge, *The Fifth Discipline*, pp. 237–40.
6 Freebairn-Smith and Moss, *Teams At The Top*.
7 Ibid.
8 William G. Dyer, *Team Building: Issues and Alternatives* (Reading, MA: Addison-Wesley Publishing, 1987).
9 Task refers to the actual work or product of the organization and activities related to doing that work. Process refers to how the group works together, group culture, and the psychological aspects of organizational life. Many organizations neglect process, and focus too much on task. Process should be an ongoing maintenance activity for the health of the organization. Doing process work sporadically is akin to doing your bookkeeping whenever you feel like it. Note that list is adapted from Dyer, *Team Building*.
10 Parts of this case are true and parts are fictitious.
11 Senge, *The Fifth Discipline*.

12 Ibid., p. 353.

13 Ibid., p. 354.

14 Ibid., p. 366.

15 Further reading on this topic can be found in Dorothy E. Smith, *The Everyday World As Problematic* (Boston, MA: Northeastern University Press, 1987), Arlie Russell Hochschild, *The Managed Heart* (Berkeley, CA: University of California Press, 1983), and Michel Foucault's extensive work on this subject.

16 Senge, *The Fifth Discipline*, p. 343 (quote from Ray Stata of Analog Devices).

17 Ibid., p. 345.

18 Also see Nonanka's work on this subject, e.g., I. Nonanka and H. Takeuchi, *The Knowledge-Creating Company* (New York: Oxford University Press, 1995) and I. Nonanka, "The knowledge-creating company", *Harvard Business Review*, Nov.–Dec. 1991, pp. 312–20.

19 Edward De Bono, *Six Thinking Hats* (Boston, MA: Little Brown, 1985).

20 Lessem, *Total Quality Learning*, p. 22.

21 Chris Argyris, "Teaching smart people to learn", *Harvard Business Review*, May–June 1991, pp. 99–109.

22 Names and details have been altered to protect anonymity.

23 See Gifford Pinchot, *Intrapreneuring* (New York: Harper and Row, 1985).

24 Lessem, *Total Quality Learning*, p. 14.

25 Ibid., p. 27.

26 Senge, *The Fifth Discipline*, pp. 375–6.

27 De Bono, *Six Thinking Hats*.

28 I first encountered this exercise in a course taught by Dennis Perkins, Ph.D. at the Yale School of Organization and Management.

10

Information Pathways to Organizational Knowledge

Steven A. Cavaleri, Leo Charalambides,
Brian C. Maguire, and Stephen Hall

*Wisdom I take to be the knowledge of the larger interactive system –
that system which, if disturbed, is likely to generate exponential curves of
change.*

Gregory Bateson, *Steps to an Ecology of Mind.*

Introduction

The purpose of this chapter is to examine the question: How can information be stored and used more effectively to promote learning and create knowledge in organizations? The chapter is organized into several distinct sections: (1) new ideas, (2) tools, and (3) experience. The first section considers the strategic relationship between information, learning, and competitiveness in organizations. The next part of the chapter examines several approaches to using information in organizations, namely system dynamics, coordination science, and focused performance management (FPM). Finally, the concluding section recounts an experience in using information to promote learning at Black & Decker Corporation.

People who are regarded by others as being intelligent are usually known for being able to learn quickly and respond effectively to different types of circumstances. Similarly, organizations may perform, over time, in ways that suggest to observers that there is a collective intelligence that may be guiding the actions of that organization. Organizational intelligence may be defined as the capacity to link learning and knowledge, with effective action in the face of uncertainty. More specifically, intelligent organizations are those that are able to: (1) recognize patterns amidst changing circumstances, (2) develop and use conceptual tools that help them to understand how things work, and (3) become conscious of the relative effectiveness of their actions in supporting the achievement of their larger purpose.

As many entrepreneurs know, businesses that have floundered at one point are often the most stable in the long run, because they have discovered their weaknesses and limitations before they became fatal. Conversely, organizations that have long track records of success often are at the greatest risk for failure. There are four main reasons why such organizations are at risk, and they all are rooted in organizational knowledge and intelligence. First, such organizations simply "don't know what they don't know." Second, they don't have a way discovering what they don't know.

> People in organizations usually get rewarded for displaying what they know, rather than by revealing what they don't know. One organization that has taken steps to counteract this pattern is the Canadian Imperial Bank of Commerce. Their first move to help employees learn was to eliminate training. Here, employees are given the responsibility for improving their level of competency to raise their work performance. Various learning resources, such as software and books, are provided to these employees by the bank, and special rooms are dedicated to learning. The success of this new approach is being measured in terms of the numbers of new ideas created and put into effect, numbers of new products introduced, and changes in income resulting from new revenue sources.[1]

Third, the "Billings Principle": "It ain't what you don't know that hurts you; it's what you *do* know that ain't so." Finally, failing organizations often meet their demise because, as Albert Einstein stated, "Problems cannot be solved by the same level of thinking that created them."

Clearly, organizational vitality can be enhanced when the members of an organization have access to a means for discovering their own collective biases and blind spots. When employees are able to collaborate in their use of conceptual tools, such as systems thinking and TQM, they learn more deeply about themselves and their work environment. As companies that have used TQM have found, feedback pertaining to the consistency of operating processes helps to improve quality, as well as promote learning about that system of relationships that effect quality. Feedback plays an instrumental role in both control processes and in learning. Our view is that most organizations are limited in their ability to learn as a result of the presence of restrictions in understanding and using feedback. We believe that there are three main causes for such restrictions that we call **feedback bottlenecks**. They are: (1) a lack of systemic thinking in organizations, (2) the absence of a commonly understood language that all organization members share, and (3) limited capacity for coordinating work interdependencies by using information. Feedback is information that is capable of mirroring an organization's performances. However, much like the curved mirrors often seen at amusement parks, the meaning of feedback can be distorted by the incomplete and nonsystemic mindsets of managers. When managers are able to understand how feedback links the various causes and effects of organizational performance they can begin to see their own role in this system with greater clarity. Such clarity helps them to learn by providing a common framework for discovering how the system really works.

The language of feedback can be found in fields such as cybernetics and system dynamics, that explain the behavior of complex systems in terms of recurring, circular patterns of information and action.[2] Feedback also can enable managers to gain greater objectivity while learning. The presence of feedback enables managers to contrast their personal experience with data from other sources, which are usually outside their direct experience. The ability to jump back and forth between one's personal experience of a system and the data-driven features of it can provide rich opportunities for learning. Douglas Hofstadter notes, "It is an inherent property of intelligence that it can jump out of the task which it is performing, and survey what it has done; it is always looking for and finding, patterns."[3]

This theme is also woven through the work of systems theorist C. West Churchman. Churchman's work on the design of inquiring systems suggests that in the process of designing a system teams must learn about the essence of what will enable such a system to work effectively. During that process of clarifying which information is most useful for completing this design it is likely that the designers will bump into their own biases and nonsystemic notions about how things work. This can be a great learning opportunity for groups as a result of the heightened objectivity that results when people compare their findings. Simply, when there are many points of view about the nature of something, such as how to increase quality, and these observers can both observe themselves and others in discussion, then there is great potential for learning and the system becomes a mirror of what the designers know and believe. This point is cogently made by Churchman:

> Designers wish to create computers to "solve problems," "observe patterns," and so on. But whatever ability the computer attains in any of these directions becomes objectively valid only because the designers observe that the computers are functioning in a certain manner. To understand what the computer is doing objectively, it is essential to know what the designer is doing. The "fact" that computers "solve problems" is as much a description of the behavior of the designer as it is a description of the output of the computer program.[4]

What the group of designers does is bound to what they know as a group and how they perceive what they have done. As these designers work to improve the quality of the computer their understanding of the meaning of the feedback they receive will shape what they do in the future.

New Ideas

Learning and information technology

Nowadays, to be successful in the global business arena, a company must consistently provide more value to its stakeholders than its competitors. To the company's customer stakeholders, superior value means (a) (in an ideal sense, fully) customized products and/or services, (b) coupled with flexible and responsive prices, and (c) delivered in a collaborative (i.e., enabling, empowering) manner and on a long-term basis.

To properly address these functionality and affordability needs, the company should develop a sustainable relationship with each specific customer. The fundamental purpose of that relationship is learning – as an end in itself as well as a means to that end. As an end, learning is maintaining or improving the contribution that the product/service makes (in connection with the customer's use of it) to the attainment of the customer's purposes. As a means, learning is maintaining or improving the company's understanding of how the customer's purposes drive his or her functionality and affordability needs.

The delivery of this kind of outstanding organizational performance is not the result of random behavior. Rather, it is the outcome of appropriate learning processes as the organization's employees go about doing their daily work. Information technology (IT) can provide the communication platform or channel to help bring about "appropriate learning processes."

Learning entails improvement in the results of **inquiry**. Inquiry is the acquisition of information, the processing of knowledge and the achievement of understanding by people concerning a subject (domain of inquiry) of interest to them. Understanding is a prerequisite to further inquiry or action.

An organization is a purposeful, collaborative (as well as competitive), structured, practical, and distributed inquiry system. It is distributed to the extent that it "exists" in the minds of the organization's members (ideally *all* its employees, i.e., managers and workers) and, occasionally, even in the minds of the organization's stakeholders (i.e., employees, suppliers, allies, customers, etc). The organization inquires so that it can take action intended to bring about results consistent with its purposes. These purposes, in turn, are driven by the needs of the various organizational stakeholders. Consequently, the ultimate judges of the "improvement in the results of inquiry" are the affected stakeholders.

Modern IT sports impressive capabilities in terms of speed, capacity, convenience, and electronic transportability of knowledge among people and their "external memories" (i.e., databases). Thus, for example, the announcement of an upcoming conference on information technology presents the following scenario of the so-called "International Office of the Future".

International Office of the future

As the participants arrive at their local conference room, the walls near the conference table light up with live video images from similar meeting sites held at other locations around the world in reasonable proximity to the meeting participants. Participants feel as if they are all present in the same room. Following introductions, the group leader, assisted by a "cultural broker," presents an agenda that includes phases of electronically supported problem framing, creative brainstorming, information organization, consensus formation, and generation of action plans.

Group members are invited to present their opinions and participate in the discussions verbally as well as through use of a wide variety of technology interfaces including personal notepads, wireless digital assistants, and conventional laptop computers enhanced with electronic pens and voice recognition as well as keyboards. Electronic "agents" directed by group members seek out relevant information that may bear on the topic at hand and help cluster participant comments.

As the meeting draws to a close, some participants record on diskette information that they want to personally retain. Other participants send meeting information directly to their office computers to continue their work and seek additional input. In addition, public information is stored in a team memory to be accessed and used by other stakeholders and in future meetings.

Participants leave the meeting with a sense of accomplishment, commitment, and personal satisfaction in the meeting process and product. One might imagine that the participants in such a technologically mediated meeting are developing a complex new product, such as an automobile or a piece of software, or negotiating a specific, sophisticated service, such as a bank loan, for a specific institutional customer. More importantly, this meeting can be only a small part of an electronic platform to "appropriate learning processes" among these individuals.

This kind of futuristic IT does not come cheap. Actually, the cost of maintaining the technology itself and training the users far exceeds that of the initial investment. Like many other capital expenditures, the company about to invest in it is bound to ask the question: is it all worth it? In other words, as a result of the use of this IT by the employees, will the organization develop a more sustainable relationship with its customers? Will there be any relevant learning and will it be significant enough to stimulate sales and/or reduce costs in a sustainable manner? These are the questions that we will try to examine in this section.

Organizational learning

A past mistake is the difference between the means that an authorized employee actually chose and the means the employee should have chosen so that the ends that he or she is responsible for would have been realized. (A similar definition applies to future or likely mistakes.) Learning is the long-term reduction in the frequency and extent of mistakes associated with a particular domain. The organization's overall purpose (its mission) should determine the ends (goals/objectives) that the employee is responsible for.

Organizational learning (OL) is improvement in the results of organizational inquiry and action through the reduction of mistakes. In an alternative sense, OL is the improvement in the competencies of the organization. Competencies include the information, knowledge, and associated methods that are relevant to the domain of inquiry and remain with the learner(s) after the experiences of the mistakes have been understood.

OL is experientially coproduced by the individual and his or her learning environment. For example, the mission is not "given" to the organization unilaterally. Rather, the organization "negotiates" it with its stakeholders. In a similar fashion the employee (or rather the organizational role that she or he plays) "negotiates" the respective goal/objective with the organizational mission. For example, the well-known management by objectives (MBO) process is an attempt to formalize these negotiation tactics.

However, even when particular goals appear to be "intuitively obvious" to all the relevant parties (e.g., quality), the technical challenge remains of identifying what are the relevant means and what should they be so that the ends are realized. In the simple environment and hierarchical organization of the past this was relatively easy. The boss could easily explain it to the employee. However, in the complex environment of the present there is no individual who possesses all the relevant information and knowledge to explain it. To a large extent, it must be learned from (and through) the collective experience of the learning community.

Thus, organizational learners (individuals or organizations) are also teachers. They learn from and teach their relevant stakeholders by interacting with them in appropriate ways, for example, through a dialogue. Interacting learners/teachers who share a common cause comprise a learning community. Usually, a particular learner belongs in multiple learning communities. Such a community is situation-specific and is composed of the focal employee and the stakeholders of his or her work, that is, subordinates, colleagues, and superiors. These individuals may be customers of the employee's work outputs and/or suppliers of necessary inputs. Furthermore, they may be in the same or different line of work, within or across the boundaries of the organization in question. Indeed, some of these boundaries may transcend national cultures, as in employees in the HQ of a Japanese company having to formally interact with research branches in the United States or Europe.

OL is **distributed and distributive learning**. That is, in the final analysis, learning for the benefit of the organization takes place in the minds of its members and stakeholders. These individuals are very diverse in terms of purpose, preferred inquiry mode, knowledge type, and so forth. Therefore, there are many different forms of organizational learning. Furthermore, processes and information systems that claim to facilitate OL should also address the personal inquiry needs of the "carriers of the organizational competencies." Otherwise, the intended learners will neither promote nor nurture OL to the extent and in the form that the organization needs.

OL is particularly relevant to the survival and prosperity of organizations in inquiry and innovation-intensive industries such as accounting, consulting, law, education, engineering, and technology. In these instances, organizational inquiry is continuously trying to keep up with the functionality and affordability needs of the customers and the corresponding offers that the company makes to them in terms of products/services. In other words, inquiry is open-ended and a priori ill-defined.

Organizational learning and communication

Organizational knowledge can be social or individual. If individual, it may be conscious or nonconscious. If social, it may be scientific or collective. The difference between the two is that the former is not embedded in the behavior of the organization (it is objective), while the latter is.

Appropriate interaction among the learners/teachers of a learning community suggests the need for efficient and effective communication. However, due to the rapid change in and complexity of organizational knowledge, participants find learning-oriented communication to be a very challenging and novel undertaking. A number of contextual factors make it even worse. To deal with this challenge there should be some degree and form of intellectual discipline in the learner's inquiry as well as in the ways the outputs of that inquiry become the inputs to the inquiries of other members of the community. That is, for the sake of the organization's success, there should be some structure in the collective and practical search for meaning. The most appropriate way to introduce and maintain this discipline is within a framework for dealing with organizational issues in a strategic manner ("strategic" is here defined to include much more than the simple allocation of economic resources). This framework aspires to address the most fundamental questions that one would ask of an organization, that is, what is it for, and whom is it for?

According to this framework all members of a learning community carry in their minds a "picture" of how they believe things were and/or are. This is a descriptive model of the problem. They are also likely to carry a mental model of how things "should" be if the goal in question (as they understand it) is to be achieved in the future. This is a prescriptive model of the problem. To deal with a problem, the focal employee must examine the repercussions of possible actions using a model with descriptive as well as prescriptive parts.

From the perspective of the organization this is a local model. Financial managers, operations analysts, and advertising executives all deal with local models. A global model would be one that explicitly addresses organization-wide goals and objectives. Senior executives are said to deal with these strategic models.

It is unlikely that the local model of one learning community member will agree with that of another. Clearly, before the action, there is no way of knowing which model is correct. However, after the action and using the requirements of the global model as a standard of comparison, one local model is likely to have been closer to the perfect hindsight solution than most of the others. The records of some individuals in terms of correct models may be better than others. That is, they may be better learners. Consequently, it behooves focal employees to compare their local model with that of others as they think about which means to employ.

Organizational language and systemic inquiry

In the process of dealing with problems, a learning community creates and shares meaning. It does so through the subjective creation, interpretation, critique and recreation of its own system of symbols (i.e., language). Sharing local models with others who have similar backgrounds in terms of knowledge domain (e.g., among financial analysts) is relatively easy. Sharing local models with others who have different domain backgrounds, however (e.g., an advertising plan with engineers and lawyers), is an altogether different story. As was stated above, due to competitive imperatives, members of an organization should now belong to multiple learning communities. Therefore, an organizational language should exist to link the various learning communities. At present, there is no organization language (other than the precise "language of accounting" that is limited to specific aspects of an organizational problem) to facilitate the efficient expression and effective comprehension of so-called communicative models of the mental models of the organization.

An organizational language should be a learning system (not a set) of symbols. A system of symbols conveys meaning which individual symbols – taken separately – cannot convey. This collective meaning is embedded in and derived from the communicative model that the learners use to share their own mental models. Clearly, it should be logically consistent and relevant to the organizational situation at hand (even if it is a novel one) as perceived by (ideally) all the learners – no matter how diverse the knowledge tradition of their particular organizational roles may be.

A learning symbol system contains passive as well as active symbols. The language itself "learns" along with helping the users learn. It is a language about and for learning (learning on the part of and for the benefit of the organization and its stakeholders, i.e., meta-learning). In other words, organizational learning languages must explicitly support systemic (not systematic) inquiry and action within and across learning communities.

Systemic inquiry (or thinking) is the intentional, holistic, consistent and interdependent incorporation of as many relevant perspectives (points of view), knowledge types, and methodological approaches to the work of a purposeful learning community as possible. One of these perspectives, possibly the dominant one in organizational inquiry, is that of the organizational strategist. Put another way, systemic inquiry directly confronts the forces that tend to limit learning in organizations[5]. It is constant, negotiated yet productive interplay between analysis and synthesis, between the parts and the whole, between the inside and the outside, between content and context, between the scientist and the humanist, between the philosopher and the practitioner, and so on.

Organizational language and information technology

The ultimate purpose of all information systems in an organization-as-an-inquiry-system is **learning support**. This is the facilitation of the purposeful creation, sustainable development and, above all, innovative use of a systemic organizational language by the members of the learning communities that the organization participates in. This facilitation may take place "on line" as well as "off line" (i.e., electronically and nonelectronically).

Learning support is the ultimate purpose simply because it does not "put the cart before the horse" as most existing systems do. It does not address the questions: "Now that we have the information, what do we do about it, how do we synthesize it?" or "To which organizational task, problem, issue, concern shall we (can we) offer this information?" Rather, it addresses the questions: "Who are the interested parties? What are the organizational purpose(s) that they may negotiate? What are the inquiry methods that can be (may be) used by the parties to ascertain the needs that are driven by these purposes? What knowledge should these methods generate and consequently what are the information needs that these inquiry methods will (may) have?" Assisted by learning support systems, members of an organizational learning community are able to create individual/personal communicative models as well as a conversational communicative model for the inquiry at hand. Through these models they can visualize the intellectual capital of the firm as a purposeful system of work relationships, information flows, and knowledge exchanges.

A communicative model is a repository of electronic, action-oriented representations of the interdependent issues that the learners face as part of their work requirements. These representations are machine extensions of the human memories of the learners as well as the collective memory of the learning community, in terms of content, and more importantly, process. This feature is a critical requirement for long-term organizational learning despite employee turnover and internal reassignment as well as disruptively intermittent (i.e., chaotic) work patterns.

Boland and Tenkasi[5] use the term "hermeneutic support systems" instead of learning support systems. They identify the following design principles:

1 Communicative model ownership by a particular actor;
2 Hyper-textual exploration of a model's structure;
3 Ease of exchange and critique of models by various actors;
4 Model indeterminacy or "openness";
5 Simultaneous reductionism and expansionism; and
6 Mixed communication media.

From the ensuing discussion one will be able to conclude that existing information technologies and tools already address most of these requirements. Clearly, the challenge will be in the synthesis of the various capabilities. For example, with respect to the last design principle, a communicative model should include a wide variety of visual and auditory symbols (textual, schematic, etc), analogies and metaphors as well as the capability to create new "Esperanto" types of symbols. In this way, learners will be able to "capture" and use the subtlety and scope of all forms of knowledge (social/individual, explicit/implicit).

The primary function of a conversational communicative model is to provide the technological and methodological means to establish boundaries, organize, structure and, in general, manage over the long term the "learning inquiry debates" that take place within an organizational learning community. A key outcome of these debates are the "lessons learned" and the "good practices verified/validated."

Often these learning debates revolve around experiments (real or simulated) with phenomena that are external to the learners. Consequently, some of these electronic representations should take the form of quantitative models of causal relations suitable for analysis. For example, securities firms are currently creating systems of so-called "uncommitted models" (the fourth design principle). These modeling platforms are uncommitted in the sense that their basic structure is always subject to revision based upon (a) simulated results, (b) actual results, and (c) insight gathered from other members of the relevant learning community. However, whether the situations are real or hypothetical, the important thing is to make sure that these simulation models help the individuals deal with the problem at hand as well as learn from this experience.

Above all, this technological platform should make it easy for the users to reflect, explore, argue about, and improve upon the relationships among the symbols – be they similarities or differences. Eventually these learning interactions will lead the organizational stakeholders to pursue consciously the most fundamental question of the organization's existence. This question amounts to the negotiation of the organizational purposes as well as the interpretations of these purposes by all the interested parties. The fifth design principle will apply to these negotiations.

Learning support systems

Some current technological factors will facilitate the learning support function of organizational information systems, while others will be obstacles. The most prominent enabling factors are the two major technical developments which account for most of the tremendous improvement in the functionality of information technologies.

1   The technological convergence of computer and communication technologies. Soon there will be no bits and pieces. Technologically, this unification is being made possible by digital technology (in computers and TV as well as all forms of telecommunications) with very high bandwidths in terms of processing (microprocessor speed), storage (low cost, extremely high capacity hard drives and optical media), as well as transmission (fiber-optic cable coupled with high speed modems and eventually ISDN).

2   The dominant metaphor of the computer as a calculator is being replaced by the metaphor of the computer as only one part of the so-called information appliance (a kind of polyfunctional, multi-modal, super video-telephone). Through friendly graphical user interfaces (e.g., icons, pull-down menus, windows, etc.) and hypertextual linkages among and within compound document bases, an individual will use a particular version of this appliance to communicate with a wide variety of entities in his or her environment (human and other) by means of multiple digitized media, such as text, data, graphics, audio, and video. Furthermore, in the not too distant future, this interface will be intelligent. That is, users will be able to delegate simple tasks for the information appliance to execute in a manner that best fits their particular inquiry needs (work style, job context, etc.)

Component technologies   The Internet is the most dramatic manifestation of these two developments. For example, it is now possible to use multimedia technology to capture and convey the abstract richness of one's model of an issue to a degree not possible or widely available only a few years ago. Thus, the way the model of a problem or project is physically represented can take the form of a "compound document" (the sixth design principle). This document may be composed of a simple diagram, accompanying text, a photograph, a spreadsheet containing associated cost-benefit computations, an audio and/or video clip and so called "hot links" to an executable computer program for demonstration purposes. Thus the elements of one document can be linked with other elements (in the same or different document) through the wizardry of hypertext technology, a form of ad-hoc, design-as-you-go, nonlinear, relational database technology (the second design principle). For example, an engineer can distribute drawings with superimposed annotations by reviewers without losing control of the originals (the first design principle). Because of another emerging technology called object-oriented programming, in the future programming the "hot" or "live" linking of the data in a compound document with the relevant database(s) will become more efficient. Furthermore, because of what is becoming the dominant enterprise IT architecture, that is, client-server technology, it will not matter where these databases are located. They might be inside the corporation, distributed among the various corporate locations, or outside the corporation, accessible through dedicated interorganizational systems (for example, Electronic Data Interchange or EDI) or the Internet.

Interestingly, the most rapidly growing part of the Internet is the World Wide Web (WWW). This is nothing else but a huge collection of (potentially) compound documents that are linked in an open-ended way through hypertext technology (the fourth design principle). That is, people can reach a document they are not aware of by following links from previous documents in the search. In the not too distant future users will be able to assign the relatively structured parts of their search to an "intelligent agent" while they concentrate on the relatively unstructured parts. This agent is simply a powerful searching program with its own form of artificial intelligence and learning behavior.

Client-server technology and advanced digital telecommunications have a lot to do with the freedom that users will be enjoying accessing the compound documents they are interested in from anywhere in the world. This access may be in the context of a live video conference on the information appliance. Thus, even located far apart from one another, participants in this virtual office will be able to jointly edit a particular electronic, multimedia model through so-called "document conferencing software." Also called whiteboard software, existing packages let two or more users view and annotate the same screen over a phone, local area network, or remote locations.

Put together, all these component technologies make possible a class of information system platforms the primary function of which can be (although, in general, it is not yet) to support the communication of complex ideas and concepts among diverse users. These platforms are called "groupware." Currently groupware is being used primarily to eliminate waste in existing document management processes. The best known and most widely used groupware is Lotus Notes. This product essentially combines, directly or indirectly, most of the capabilities listed above with two others: multiple views of the same compound document and automatic replicated updates of local document bases. When users make a change to their copy of a document, that is physically located in their own computer, the change is promptly propagated to all the other copies of the same document no matter where they may reside on the Notes-managed network system and in a manner that is transparent to all the users involved. In other words, a user does not "send a message" to others. Rather, she or he updates the appropriate parts of the electronic repository. Intended recipients are then reminded of updates to the repository that they have not read. Each person can then choose to examine these updates in the sequence and manner that matters to the inquiry needs of the learning community or the individual in question.

Obstacles to learning support systems The most significant obstacles to the creation of learning support systems are not technological. Rather, they are the prevailing mindsets and capabilities of its present and potential users as well as beneficiaries. Thus, most organizations still perceive (as they have since the early days of organizational computing) the primary function of information technology to be the mechanical processing of raw data into low-level, objective information. Transforming this information into high-level, subjective (i.e., problem-related) information and knowledge is still a very low priority of current information systems.

Because most current information systems have been designed from this mechanical perspective, major technical difficulties will be encountered in modifying them so as to serve the needs of the new strategic learning support systems. This tradition is also a major obstacle to the development of the appropriate capabilities of the individuals who should be demanding and using these new types of information systems as well as those that should be designing them. To make matters worse, as an object of research, this topic is receiving almost no attention from the scholarly community. Finally, the development of the new information systems will be further delayed by a host of motivational factors (e.g., more reflective, more substantive thinking is not welcomed equally by all), and cognitive factors the causes and implications of which we know very little of. For example, the mental model for the individual's "organizational self" of how things should be may conflict with the mental model of the individual's "personal self" of how things should be. Worse, the individual may not even realize the existence or implications of this conflict. One of the reasons for this is that both models reside in the same domain, that is, the individual's mind.

Information technologies and models

In this section we provide a brief overview of the various information technologies and tools that may apply to the sharing of each of the four types of communicative models: local vs. global and organizationally descriptive vs. organizationally prescriptive. In general, the number of choices diminishes as one moves from relatively well-defined to relatively ill-defined issues and problems, from relatively local to relatively global models, and from descriptive to organizationally prescriptive models. Obviously, a learning support system must provide access to all types of communicative models efficiently and effectively.

Sharing local and descriptive models   Most systems in this category provide technologically mediated methodological support to the cognitive mapping process. This is a process of creating and sharing relatively well-structured, descriptive mental models (e.g., cause and effect diagrams) of relatively ill-structured situations. Examples include SODA and Decision Conferencing. In general these structuring techniques require the assistance of a trained facilitator. The lack of an internal, experienced facilitator is a major impediment to the use of this technology.

Simpler, less intrusive, more descriptive and general purpose, groupware-based systems are argumentation support systems. Using a rhetorical method individuals learn to structure and record in a network fashion the content and context of the key elements of a conversation. These systems are billed as "organizational intelligence systems" because of such capabilities as instant meeting minutes and meeting memory. The latter implies that it is possible for someone to track the history of a decision: what exactly was decided, why and what was known at the time the decision was made.

In general, the field is in its infancy. The few commercially available systems (such as QuestMap from Corporate Memory Systems) have not yet seen much use outside of relatively well-bounded, project-oriented domains such as software development. Also, it is not yet clear to what extent the communicative model created is a "live" (conversational) one. Therefore, at this time any claim of explicit contribution to organizational learning would be premature. However, because of their rhetorical origin and tolerance for tacit knowledge, in the future systems such as these will become core elements of learning communication support systems.

Closely related to the previous category is the use of system dynamics.[6] These are computer simulation models (or "microworlds") of part(s) of a mental model, suitably filtered and organized. Participants can use such models for experimentation, cooperation, and learning. In this case learning takes place indirectly. That is, the individual does not receive feedback about a mistaken action from the real world domain. Rather, the source of this feedback is a mathematical model of this domain. One can presumably verify the representational validity of this type of model through direct observation and comparison.

Sharing global and descriptive models Under the general heading of computer systems analysis and design one can find an extremely rich and mature collection of technologically supported problem formulation methodologies. These tools are used in major, mechanical data processing systems projects that are critical to the organization's mission, for example, basic accounting functions, process control, and so forth. The methodologies themselves have little to offer to learning support systems. However, the way in which the user interface of these methodologies has been technologically implemented does have something to offer. Furthermore, "live" hypertextual linkages to the compound documents that are the outputs of these methodologies may be highly desirable for business process reengineering and total quality management types of organizational debates.

"Enterprise models" are attempts to built networks of mathematically interconnected data models of the critical parts of an organization (and even its stakeholders). Because they make heavy use of object-oriented programming, these models are much richer in terms of their representational validity than conventional simulation models. That is, the modeler can use an object to capture and encapsulate the key operational as well as financial characteristics of the organizational entity being modeled. Consequently, a computer simulation is possible that is much more informative to the modeler and revealing to the audience. Since they help capture the explicit and social aspects of organizational knowledge, links to models such as these will be a key feature of future argumentation support systems.

Sharing local and prescriptive models   According to the traditional view Group Decision Support Systems (GDSS) and Executive Information/Support Systems (EIS/ESS) are employed to help discover the "right" analytical model of the objectively defined problem at hand. The latter is a relatively mechanistic interpretation of the physical (or resource) aspects of the organization and its technologic/physical as well as economic relationships with its stakeholders. To some extent, groupware technology was developed to address the requirements of these types of systems.

Strictly speaking the use of the adjective "prescriptive" is not justified in this category. This is because there is no "conscious" (formal, explicit) discussion/debate going on concerning all of the organization's purposes (ultimate, i.e., vision/mission and intermediate, i.e., goals/objectives) and how these purposes should drive the specific action(s) being contemplated in connection with a specific organizationally local problem.

The closest that current practice comes to this ideal is the "inquiry center concept," that is, whatever organizational prescriptiveness there is, is mostly manifested in a strategically implicit manner. In general, it goes beyond the idea of "distributed cognition" because it explicitly recognizes that the parties to the discussion (learning community members) are not only the organization's employees but also the organization's stakeholders – starting of course with the customers and then going on to suppliers. In other words, this concept recognizes the need for well-defined paths between the domains of the learning community members and the physical domain that hosts them. At the present time these paths are ad hoc and experimental. Groupware applications are being employed but primarily for coordination and simple communication. Examples include weapons systems development at Lockheed Missile and Space, the Knowledge Xchange system of Andersen Consulting, and the elaborate employee goal-setting system at Cypress Semiconductor. However, collaborative exploration of meaning (e.g., a quasi formalized vocabulary for use in the electronic annotations) has yet to take place.

Sharing global and prescriptive models   Because of its explicit "strategicness," this category constitutes the essence of an organizational learning support system. From the limited perspective of "scientific knowledge" one might argue that "enterprise models" can be pushed into this role. That is, the enterprise model of the focal organization can somehow be modeled to interact with those of key stakeholders (customers, suppliers, etc.) as well as relevant competitors in one sort of super global model. Using game theory one might explore alternative scenarios concerning the behavior of the focal organization, the stakeholders, and competitors.

With parallel computing and real time data capture and processing such a mega-model may indeed one day be possible (at least in industries, such as the airline industry where relevant data is generally available). However, no matter how exhaustive, this effort will be incomplete in a macro sense (industry-wide) and more importantly in a micro sense (intra-company). Thus, an endeavor such as this might help the senior executives learn strategic content. To learn strategic process, however, it must be enriched by a strategic argumentation framework. The situation will be far more challenging for lower level employees because their understanding of the strategic positioning of their company is limited to begin with.

What is needed, therefore, is a facility to support strategic learning in a background/transparent mode, as part of one's everyday routine. Making the organization-wide creation of an organization language a reality should start with electronic communication (E-Mail, Fax, EDI), data storage and retrieval techniques, and meetings (synchronous as well as asynchronous). These should be explicitly tied to new product development and/or similar projects which are key to a company's survival, for example be the development of the learning support infrastructure itself.

Programmers at 3M have started this effort by maintaining a "design log" in which they attempt to capture the content as well as process associated with the various decisions that they have to make from the perspective of the designers themselves as well as their customers (corporate users). Formalizing such a log, extending its scope, and driving it by all the relevant members of the organization and its stakeholders would be useful in developing a learning support infrastructure.

Learning support systems and managerial action

The learning language and the "learning support systems," rather than information and the corresponding "information processing systems," constitute the real "glue" of the organizations of the future. What can practicing managers do to make this vision a reality? The immediate answer is, by themselves, not much. However, working with the other members of their learning community they can do a lot.

1 Recognize/accept/practice the logic above and get colleagues in the learning community to do the same. Make the development of this language a key aspect of all the process improvement work of this community.
2 Become a proficient user of the new integrated groupware technologies on a local, group, corporate, and world basis. Understand technical capabilities, limitations and future directions. Explore the various kinds of interpersonal competencies that are required for effective facilitation of electronic group meetings.
3 Learn about existing inquiry methods and techniques of representing mental models even if these happen not to be within the customary knowledge domain of the learning community in question. Start experimenting with these methods and techniques within the context of the available groupware technologies. That is, the learners themselves should create applications that enable the community (as well as other communities associated with it) to carry out its work as well as reflect upon its learning

performance – in terms of knowledge content mastered and social inquiry process improved.

4 As existing data-driven ("legacy") information systems are upgraded and migrated to client-server (network) architectures, insist that proper linkages ("hooks") between them and the new "language support systems" be included. This should take place even though the "owner" of an operational system may object because it adds to the cost of such a system.

5 Above all, embark upon the personal, intellectually challenging, lifetime study of the philosophical underpinnings and practical ramifications of "systemic inquiry."

Summary of communicative models

In a learning organization the primary purpose of the management information systems (MIS) function is to provide the "IT logistical platform" upon which sister disciplines (e.g., marketing, operations, finance, etc.) will build a continuously evolving "master" information architecture (organizational language) for systemic collaboration. This form of hermeneutic collaboration is the creation, revision and intermittent transfer of one party's communicative model (verbal, schematic, mathematical, etc.) of a focal problem to the problems of the other parties that are relevant to organizational action *within the constraints "imposed" by the global (i.e., strategic) communicative model.*

This language will enable the creation of a dynamic, hypermedia "organizational lessons learned" compound document base. As a minimum, these lessons will pertain to "What did we learn about this subject that matters to our company's future prosperity (as well as our own)?" as well as "What did we learn about the ways we should go about learning on these subjects?"

This document base will be dynamic because, while it would primarily apply to well-structured situations, it would enable organizational conversations or debates into the strategically relevant but unknown. Thus, learning support systems will not be separate from existing, operational systems in the organization. Rather, they will be fully integrated with them and, from the user's point of view, enclose them.

Tools

System dynamics

System dynamics is a problem-solving approach developed by Jay Forrester, professor emeritus at MIT, during the late 1950s. It uses computer simulations of systemic relationships to explain changes in performance over time. In the system dynamics perspective, organizations are viewed as being composed of numerous linked stocks and flows. Stocks are those collections of organizational resources, such as inventories, profits, employees, or knowledge that accumulate. Stocks are filled and drained by various inflows and outflows. For example, stocks of finished goods are drained by customer orders and they are filled by

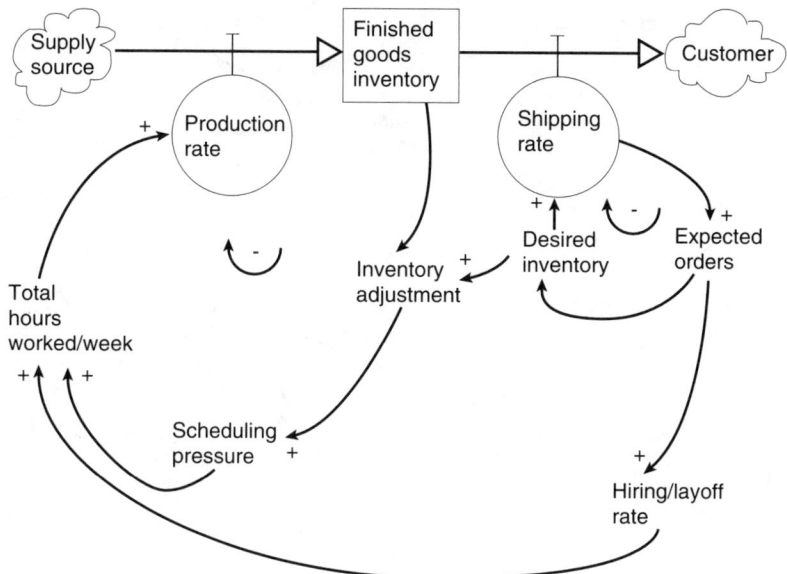

Figure 10.1 Integrated stock and flow system.

production of new goods. In this view, these stocks are linked by feedback loops that control the rates of filling and draining and ultimately the level of these stocks over time (figure 10.1).

Computer simulations of a particular stock and flow system in an organization are based on system dynamics models. A modeling process that is commonly used is one in which the employees who work in the areas of concern work along with a modeling expert to diagram how they believe that system works. During the modeling process it is most likely that the prevailing assumptions of managers and the shared knowledge of a team will be revealed. System dynamics theorists, such as John Morecroft, Peter Senge, and John Sterman, have noted the importance of this step in the modeling process for organizational learning. The mere act of trying to generate a conceptual model causes team members to draw on their own personal understandings of how the various relationships present in a system cause it to perform a certain way. For example, a team might hypothesize by lowering prices for the company's product demand will skyrocket, therefore planned plant capacity should be adjusted to handle the expected orders. The decision to adjust plant capacity will be affected by time delays in the processes of capacity acquisition and implementing plans. Figure 10.2 illustrates how this set of relationships might be represented in the form of a causal loop model. In doing so, it helps team members to understand how this system acts to influence performance over time. It also serves as a vehicle for surfacing both individual and shared assumptions about how the systemic structure of the organization effects performance. John Morecroft has

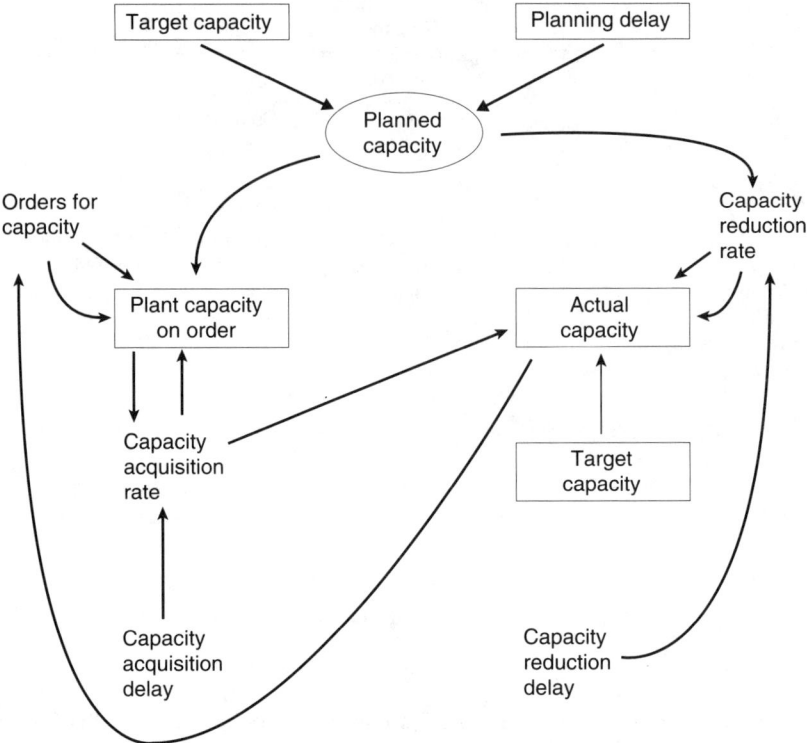

Figure 10.2 Causal diagram for plant capacity changes.

proposed that such system dynamics models can have three different purposes. They can be: (1) used as maps that capture and activate knowledge, (2) seen as frameworks that filter and organize knowledge, and (3) used as virtual worlds for experimentation, cooperation, and learning. Once the model is completed, it becomes the basis for creating a computer simulation. Once the simulation is built and run, it enables the team of managers to test the validity of their notions about how the feedback loop systems influence performance. This becomes the basis for further discussion and learning. Researchers such as Peter Senge have devoted attention to examining the role of dialogue and conversation in modeling and learning.

The essence of this approach is that the understanding of feedback mechanisms in organizations can fuel learning. The tools of system dynamics, such as systems thinking, modeling, dialogue, simulation, and the creation of computer-simulated virtual worlds can assist managers in knowing how to take effective action in complex, dynamic systems. The language of systems dynamics can also serve as the basis of a common language for discussing causal relations within an organization.

One system dynamics methodology that has specific relevance to information systems is Ernst Diehl's strategy support model. According to Diehl, system dynamics and information systems when used together have a synergy that can enable managers to develop deeper insights into the drivers of performance and facilitate group decision-making. Diehl notes, "While models are useful for exploring tacit assumptions and for making mental models explicit, they lack advanced data manipulation and retrieval capabilities of information systems. Executive information systems, on the other hand, provide efficient ways to access data, but they fall short in helping the decision-maker reexamine their thinking or reframe the problem in a new way."[7] Diehl has developed a software package known as "S**4" (Strategy Support Simulation System) for this purpose. S**4 offers flexible report generating capabilities, dynamic data analysis, and dynamic "what if" analysis. The claimed benefits of using this system are: (1) questions become focused around core variables and leverage points, (2) attention shifts towards seeing longer trends in dynamics over time, (3) appreciation of the importance of interconnectivity increases, and (4) strategic assumptions are made explicit and get tested. Overall, system dynamics is an approach that can enable managers to see how information, in the form of feedback, can produce changes in an organization's performance over time. Through the process of developing and using models, managers are able to learn together about their own shared belief systems. System dynamics offers a unique perspective that enables managers to incorporate the role of feedback and information into an organization's learning framework.

Coordination science

Coordination science attempts to understand the interdependencies among work activities in organizations. In the coordination process there is an effort made to identify different kinds of dependencies and determine the types of coordination processes that can be used to manage them. A key building block of managing coordination is the use of computers to assist people in working together more effectively. There is a particular emphasis here on the development and use of various groupware technologies. These computer-assisted cooperative work tools are designed on the basis of concepts from a number of fields such as linguistics, artificial intelligence, philosophy, organization theory, and decision theory.

A core assumption of coordination science is that information technology is growing to be so powerful and affordable that the costs of coordination in organization are declining dramatically. Thomas Malone and Kevin Crowston have proposed that coordination science is evolving through a process that will soon revolutionize the way organizations will be managed and learn. The effects of coordination science are predicted to include:

- **First order effects**: Substituting information technology for some human forms of coordination;

- **Second order effects**: Increasing the overall amount of coordination in organizations;
- **Third order effects**: Encouraging a shift toward the use of "coordination intensive" structures in organizations.[8]

The need for coordination technologies, such as information/learning systems, appears to be greater than ever as organizations move to create flatter, more laterally directed structures. Many decisions which are usually made at the top and filtered down are now being made at local levels by teams. According to Malone, "To make effective team decisions, more people have to know more things, and so more communicating needs to occur. It's the communicating that the technology mix can help with. It makes it cheaper and easier."[9] As access to information technologies becomes greater, the number of people who can be informed of decisions rises and this enables the creation of a richer base of organization knowledge. At MIT a number of coordination technologies have been developed to assist both learning and decision-making processes in organizations. One, which serves as a knowledge repository, is called "Answer Garden." While many organizations are just getting comfortable with e-mail and various groupware technologies, it's clear that organizations of the future will be looking to such technologies as ways to promote learning by enhancing organizational memory and facilitating communication among organization members. Another way of promoting learning in organizations is through an approach known as Focused Performance Management.

Focused performance management

Focused performance is a flexible framework and process to focus, manage, and learn from experience in organizations. It creates a reinforcing cycle that uses high-access information to connect performance to stakeholder value. This is accomplished by using high-speed, high-access information about performance to drive the process of making cross-functional trade-offs. That is, managers of local areas of a business are not capable of distinguishing the relative value of their department's contributions to stakeholders as compared with other groups in the organization. By engaging organization members, on a cross-functional basis, in the process of assessing how their unit helps create value for other units they are in a position to learn deeply about the systemic interactions in the business. In the focused performance approach information management systems are combined with systems thinking and total quality to create a pathway for learning in organizations.[10] Historically, information systems have been designed around command and control-oriented management principles. As has been explained earlier in this book, many of these principles run counter to the spirit of learning in organizations. Focused performance seeks to create an information structure that produces greater balance in the bases for action in a company. Typically, companies limit their own capacity for creating value and learning by relying too heavily on financial measures.

Too often reliance on financial performance indicators produce nonsystemic efforts which are largely directed at controlling costs. How many companies are willing to trade off maximizing productivity or controlling costs over customer service or organizational learning? The problem is that critical performance becomes divorced from outcomes by virtue of the availability and concreteness of measures.

In the focused performance system information requirements are defined in terms of quality and adding value to stakeholders. By defining information requirements in this way it enables managers to connect their actions and decisions with the learning capacities of the people in the organization. The need to refocus information requirements toward building human capacities are often ignored in many organizations. Companies often invest sizeable amounts of money in funding to enhance the capacities of their employees without first refocusing the measures and incentives that drive performance.

The focused performance management approach (FPM) is based on nine basic principles that translate into five "enablers" for assisting managers in improving performance in organizations.[9] The nine principles are:

1 Emphasis is on balancing the interests of constituent groups.
2 Top management *owns* performance, responsibility is not delegated.
3 Connect measures of process value based on how constituents would measure performance.
4 Performance gaps drive cross-functional scope of effort.
5 Agile processes come together based on what matters.
6 High-speed, high-access visual information reduces time needed to learn and discover what matters most.
7 Democratic involvement, fully informed citizenry.
8 Align the enablers of performance and get out of the way.
9 Individuals are responsible for their own learning. People must understand the total system to participate fully in decisions.

The five enablers of FPM are:

1 Develop a sound vision and strategy to delight constituents.
2 Define what matters and its drivers.
3 Align employee motivation with objectives.
4 Enable people to act.
5 Ensure freedom to act.

Ultimately, the goal of a focused performance system is to direct all human systems away from local and random influences and toward the cross-functional and strategic value-driven concerns of constituents (figure 10.3) The focused performance path all begins with the foundation of defining context. This is where the tools of systems thinking, organizational learning, and TQM all are critical. In this system performance-driven information provides both direct and indirect feedback to organization members that can serve as the basis for defining the context increasingly clearly.

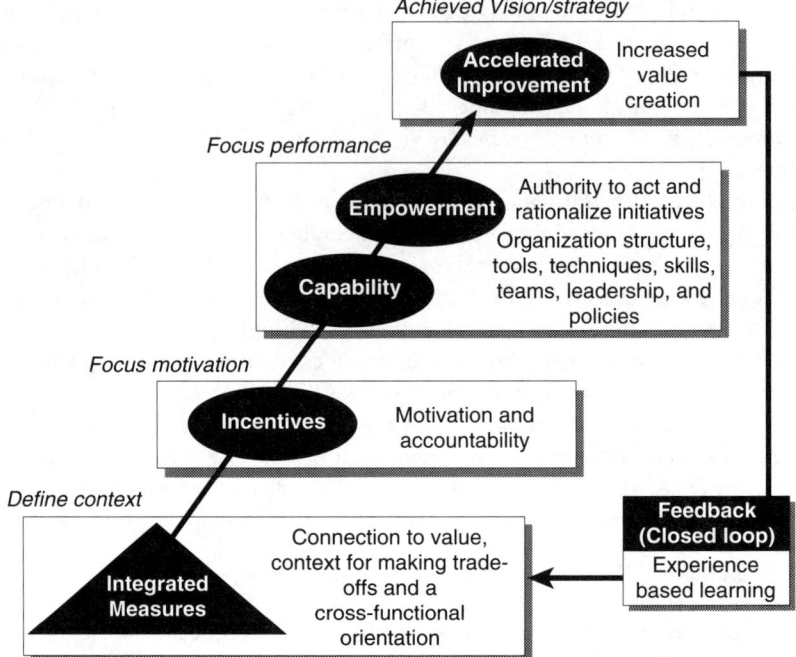

Figure 10.3   The focused performance path. Note: All rights reserved 1996, Brian Maguire and the Capra Group.

Focused performance in action   FPM has been used with positive results in various manufacturing companies. At one medium-sized process manufacturer this system produced notable results. With virtually no incremental increases in staffing or capital investment the following results were achieved:

- On-time delivery was improved from 60 percent to 95 percent.
- Order fulfillment lead time was cut by 25 percent.
- Inventory stocking levels were cut by 50 percent.
- Sales volume increased 8 percent in a no-growth market.
- Shareholder value rose by 70 percent.

In creating an FPM system managers will gain greater clarity in understanding an organization's value-drivers by continually seeking to discover answers to the following questions:

- How can employees learn by measuring "what matters"?
- How can performance measures be created which are integrative and help people to connections among the various systems in an organization?
- How can performance feedback be used to help people better understand how to enhance stakeholder value?

Experiencing Quality and Learning

No matter what the problem or the approach, no discussion of organizational learning and quality can exclude the word "change." One definition from the *Random House College Dictionary* defines change as "to transform or convert." Since the 1970s, American industries have been attempting to transform themselves to meet the challenge of global competition. Change is one of the most important words in organizations today, yet it often is one of the most difficult to accept. Often change is accommodated by adopting new technologies. Change typically causes discomfort for organization members because it requires that people take risks in situations where risky behavior may be perceived as having dire consequences.

In response to the global quality challenge, an alphabet soup of quality improvement techniques has arisen, as well as a barrage of consultants to teach them. Quality improvement tools ranging from Demand Flow Technology (DFT) and Statistical Process Control (SPC) to Kaizen and Quality Function Deployment (QFD) have been adopted, with varying degrees of success. There are many quality "success stories" that are held as examples of the value of these tools and techniques. Organizations such as Florida Power & Light, Motorola, Ford, Chrysler, and General Motors have become widely known. To many observers it is apparent that those who use these tools fall into the trap of thinking that such tools will be a cure-all for many problems when, in fact, they are more likely to serve as useful sources of information that collectively form a larger plan designed to resolve systemic issues and transform the way in which we manage those systems. Yet, clearly, such fundamental systemic issues and transformations can't be adequately addressed without the broad-scale meaningful involvement of a workforce that is learning both individually and collectively.

The theme of this section focuses on the fact that information management is critical to both the decisions we make on a day-to-day basis, and to supporting individual and organizational learning. Therefore, the way we gather, process, disseminate, and manage information is critical to supporting quality and learning. Successful information management requires that managers have the ability to transform their beliefs to suit both current and future needs, in order that they, and their companies, stay competitive. If they do not, they generate the risk of creating beliefs which provide a false sense of security that everything is all right around them, when in fact it may not be. This section will demonstrate how the concepts of systems thinking and information management relate to these goals of quality and learning, and how they apply to organizations, and to Black & Decker specifically.

Black & Decker US Household Products Group (USHPG) has been located in Connecticut since 1986, and is responsible for houseware products wranging from toaster ovens and coffeemakers, including the Dustbuster® vacuum and the Snakelight™ flashlight. The quality assurance function at Black & Decker maintains responsibilities which include overseeing quality engineering activities for new product development; working with various functions in developing and defining internal work systems; auditing new and returned products where the feedback information is paramount for developing and refining those work systems to ensure that a quality product is delivered to the consumer.

When products are returned from a consumer because they are defective, or the wrong color, the wrong size, or a host of other reasons, consumers are given a new one or a refund. The cost of the replacement or refund must be accounted for financially and is charged against an account called "warranty returns" for that particular product. Each product has its own account. In its simplest terms these accounts represent the additional monies that Black & Decker pays out for not doing things right the first time.

Black & Decker produces and sells literally thousands of products worldwide year after year. Products are also returned from consumers worldwide year after year. The quantity and cost of each product returned is recorded, tabulated, tracked, and analyzed. But why all the attention to this seemingly minute detail of return rates? The best way to explain this is to consider this company as if it belonged to the employees. If this were "our company" and we sold 10,000 units of a product at $15 each we would have a total finite income of $150,000. That seems like a lot of money at first, but with this money we must meet all the costs and expenses associated with producing those 10,000 products such as: rent, salaries of employees, electricity, water, telephone, supplies of components and raw materials, and so forth. We also need to invest a portion of our revenue into our future for growth, such as buying new equipment and hiring more employees. If we had a 10 percent return rate, this would translate to $15,000 which would have to be refunded to consumers when they returned our product and would now leave this much less to pay and invest in everything else. One of the objectives as an owner is to minimize the warranty returns which have a direct, negative affect on consumer satisfaction levels.

To compound this problem, at least in the case of Black & Decker, products are not produced, sold, and returned all in the same day. If this was the case there would be direct feedback in which any problems from consumers would be identified and corrected immediately. For Black & Decker it is estimated that the time between when a product is produced and when it is returned by a consumer averages roughly between 18 and 24 months. This is an incredibly long time to go without any formal feedback regarding the quality and durability of the product. If the return rate continued unchanged during that period of time, a significant amount of defective products could be produced, making the total dollars paid out potentially very large. It is imperative that functions such as manufacturing and engineering receive timely, reliable feedback of the nonconformities of products from the quality assurance group in order to effect timely actions.

Since around 1989 Black & Decker USHPG has experienced an increase in warranty return charges. This increase, although not damning to the business financially, was none-the-less viewed as an area to target and reduce its negative effects to the bottom line. Current Vice-President of Quality & Engineering Services, Dennis Harrison, was hired, among other things, to address the situation. After careful review, planning, and orchestration Harrison, and his staff helped the organization realize a greater than 30 percent reduction in warranty charges in two years (see figure 10.4). This was due largely to two major avenues of focus: first, a concise approach to understanding and controlling the level of quality that the company was currently producing; and second, a deliberate attempt to define, in writing, procedures detailing how they currently were managing the business. Documented procedures were lacking in many areas, making it very difficult to manage programs with any consistency. These procedures were a necessity in order that the company could be consistent in our day-to-day activities and thus able to manage from one program to another with consistency. By defining these procedures they also had the added benefit of a vehicle by which to formally change them and disseminate the changes to the organization.

Prior to considering a systems thinking approach to performance improvement and organizational learning Black & Decker believed one of their main responsibilities was to ensure that reports were distributed to the business on a timely basis. They now have a greater grasp on the expanded role and responsibilities of this area. Their concerns now include the type of infor-

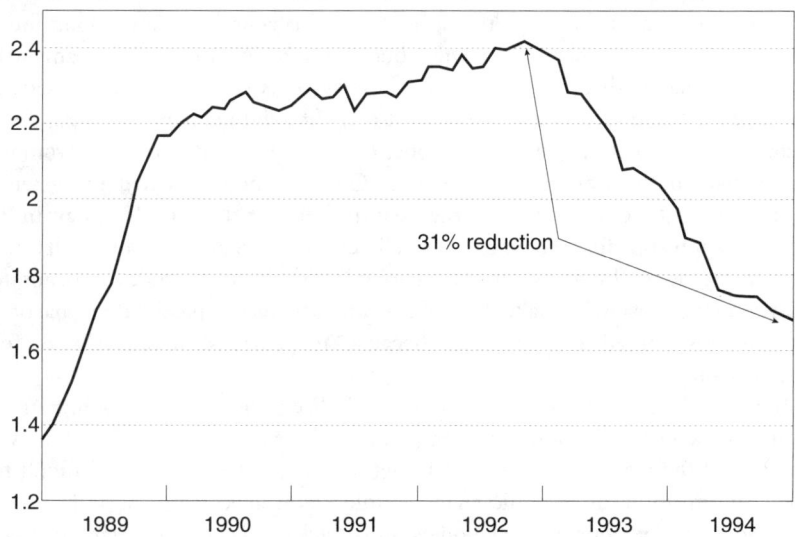

31% reduction

Figure 10.4   Black & Decker USHPG warranty return charges. Note: Data represents trending only. Not reflective of actual return results.

mation required, the systems which must be created to obtain this information, and determining the way in which this information will be managed is paramount in order for a company to move forward and be competitive. One natural area for the company to begin experimenting with improvement of performance was with the theories of organizational learning and systems thinking. They believed these concepts and tools relate directly to the warranty return charges program since it was an area where a lot of attention was already being paid.

Since the quality assurance department is the critical focal point where information is gathered, processed, and disseminated, it was believed that any positive changes made in this process would benefit both the consumer as well as Black & Decker. The first step to improve the process was to understand Peter Senge's five disciplines of the learning organization.[11] The first discipline, "systems thinking," suggests that in order to understand the system, it is necessary to contemplate the whole, not just the individual parts. If you are physically part of the system it is even harder to see the whole system. In the case of the warranty return system, the best way to understand the whole was to develop a causal loop diagram. By doing this it was possible to visualize the determinants of the systems behavior which had not been considered before. This process alone enabled an understanding of the information management process to develop by recognizing how these factors fit into the whole warranty return process. The analysis of the causal loop diagram identified a number of critical feedback loops. The understanding of the relationship between information and performance developed through the diagramming process.

One theory that has developed regarding causal loops is that the existing systemic structures, the loops themselves, drive certain behavior among individuals and team members. From these behaviors the individuals and teams will move in a specific direction. People in these systems truly try to be proactive, and continue their efforts until things get bad enough to generate change. This change comes about only when someone, or something, intervenes to promote the change to the underlying structure. One key point learned in systems thinking is that we must give up the assumption that there is always an individual responsible for problems. Instead, everyone shares responsibility for problems generated by a system. This sounds simple, yet in today's corporate environment, those who make it on the inside fast track typically don't participate in this shared responsibility because it provides no advantages for advancement.

Because "mental models," Senge's third discipline, are deeply ingrained assumptions, generalizations, or even pictures or images that influence how we understand the world and how we take action,[12] it can be extremely difficult to effect any meaningful systemic changes unless you look deeply at and understand your own personal mental models. For Black & Decker, the desire to effect meaningful changes to the warranty return process overrode their own personal mental models. By outwardly challenging their own mental models, by decreeing that nothing was sacred relating to the warranty return process which the quality assurance function had direct control over, this forced them to reconsider their traditional ways of doing things.

As Black & Decker move forward to improve the warranty return program, the employment of Senge's other disciplines: "personal mastery," "building shared visions," and "team learning," have been somewhat tested on a limited basis. This is not because they apply less importance to these, but merely that they have not had as much opportunity to address these disciplines in the short time since they have started this program. Another effort to use these ideas is dealing with the task of defining Black & Decker's acceptance standards process. These standards represent agreed-upon samples for primarily aesthetic imperfections by various functions within the organization such as marketing, industrial design, manufacturing, engineering, and quality.

Since beginning this effort to systemically improve quality Black & Decker have changed their perspective in analyzing results to understand that decisions carry both long- and short-term consequences and the two are typically diametrically opposed. Often, people are aware of the long-term negative consequences of the short-term fix, yet they proceed with the short-term decision anyway. The leverage here, in regard to the warranty return program, has centered on ensuring any fixes identified are well-thought-out and that all people involved are educated in the consequences of the fixes. If long-term consequences are negative, then all parties involved must understand that decisions must be made to ensure a harmonious understanding of the consequences by as many people as practically can be allowed. Furthermore, the traditional constant focus on short-term fixes lessens the ability to effectively implement fundamental long-term policies. Typically, those people who are directly involved only see the short-term, positive results, but are blind to the long-term problems which become inevitable. For the warranty return program Black & Decker have sought leverage in educating all parties involved that although short-term fixes may be necessary, the fundamental solution is the main focal point.

Notes

1 T. Stewart, "Your company's most valuable asset: intellectual capital" *Fortune*, October 3, 1994, pp. 68–74.

2 G. Richardson, *Feedback Thought in Social Science and Systems Theory* (Philadelphia: University of Pennsylvania Press, 1991).

3 D. Hofstadter, *Godel, Escher, Bach: An Eternal Golden Braid* (New York: Vintage Books, 1979).

4 C. W. Churchman, *The Design of Inquiring Systems* (New York: Basic Books, 1971), p. 150.

5 R. Boland and R. Tenkasi, "Designing information technology to support distributed cognition", *Organization Science*, August 1994, vol. 5, no. 3, pp. 456–75.

6 J. Morecroft, "Design of a learning environment: the oil producers microworld", *Proceedings of the International System Dynamics Conference* (Utrecht, The Netherlands, 1992), pp. 465–74.

7 E. Diehl, "The model as a lens: combining modeling and data support systems to aid in executive decision-making", *Proceedings of the International System Dynamics Conference*, 1992, pp. 137–140.

8 T. Malone and K. Crowston, "The interdisciplinary study of coordination," *ACM Computing Surveys*.

9 J. Dix, "Changing the way business works", *Network World, Collaboration*, January 10, 1994, pp. 34–36, quote from p. 35.

10 Focused Performance Management is the creation of the Capra Group, New Britain, CT 06051.

11 P. Senge, *The Fifth Discipline* (New York: Doubleday, 1990).

12 Ibid., p. 8.

PART IV

Learning Communities: Balancing Managing and Learning

Interview with Peter B. Vaill

Professor of Human Systems and Director, Doctoral Program, George Washington University

Interviewer: David Fearon   Date: August 1994

DF: Our book is *Managing in Organizations That Learn*. You are a leader in management education and organizational development, fields that span this title and its implicit question, "Does the learning organization require a different way of managing?"

PV: I'm pretty sure that my own mainstream interests are not quite what people are today calling a "learning organization," as I understand it. But, I'm certainly not working against the concept, nor in contradiction to the concept. I'm not quite sure where I am on it.

There is no such thing as an organization that doesn't learn, anymore than there's such a thing as a human being who doesn't learn. That would be one of my main quarrels with the organizational learning movement. We're talking as though there are organizations that learn and there are organizations that don't.

What I would say is that the original theory of machine bureaucracy does include an unstated postulate of learning. "Learning" is that the organization notices when people inside the system are not behaving as they are supposed to; or when roles are not being played as they are supposed to; or when results are not occurring as they're supposed to. It then includes control mechanisms for bringing the actual behavior of the people in the organization back into conformance with what is intended by the normative design. So, you might call it a "normative equilibrium process," where the designers of the organization, typically top management, have decided this is the way it's suppose to run. Consequently, they have "noticing" or learning systems for detecting when it isn't. They use authority, usually coercive, to bring it back into the state that it's supposed to be in. That also qualifies, in my opinion, as organizational learning.

DF: Yes it is. It's not the kind of learning we're writing the book about!

PV: It's not very happy learning. It creates an environment of fear, evasion, low morale and high turnover. But, if we call it nonlearning, I think we're creating a pretty serious confusion. So the question to me is not the question between organizations that learn and organizations that don't; it is whether the organization has learning structures and a learning culture that enable it to learn the things that it needs to learn to remain viable in the environment, present and future.

That's where bureaucracy falls on its face. It is blind to so many external trends in the environment. Or it presumes that those trends will cancel out; or will be such slowly evolving things that no dramatic action will be needed by the members of the organization. This set-up is in every management textbook, yet bureaucratic structures are not fit for turbulent environments.

However, just because management realizes they're in a turbulent environment, it still doesn't mean they know what they need to learn to survive and prosper in that turbulent environment. But at least they may wake up to the fact that some kind of learning is going to have to go on, if they're going to keep from becoming extinct.

"Extinct." That's the familiar language that you get that shows there is a whole new ball game, not business as unusual, heard in statements that executives are making these days. One of the quotes that I like is by David Hurst.[1] It goes something like this, "The chief problem of managers in North America is finding tomorrow's business." What he means is, as an executive, you cannot know today, in a highly dynamic, turbulent environment, what business you're going to be in five years from now. So your problem is to do the environmental scanning and the positioning and the learning and all the preparatory work so that you will maximize your chances of discovering businesses that you can transition into without tearing yourself apart.

This is what drives all of us crazy at universities. That tomorrow's higher education must be very different is readily apparent to anyone who looks; but we see so few universities doing what they need to be doing to make the transition. They just keep blithely going on with the same grading systems and degree structure, the same classroom design, the same promotion criteria that they had in the 1950s. It is as though they were going to be able to have 100 students per section of "Psych 101" for a face-to-face lecture at 9:00 am on Monday, Wednesday, and Friday, just as they've always had. There are plenty of commercial businesses that have the same problem; they can't face the learning they have to do.

DF: Is that kind of learning that hard to face?

PV: I think it can be very scary, yes. Because, in a way, a big piece of it is **unlearning**; a big piece of it is letting go of patterns and traditions and structures and habits. It means casting oneself adrift on a sea of possibilities.

For people whose careers are riding on short-term decisions, whose numbers are looking good today, to cast oneself adrift on a sea of possibilities is a pretty heroic act!

DF: Yet a necessary one.

PV: Another piece of the problem here is that I'm not sure exactly what "unlearning" means. I mean it may just be a cliché. Unlearning may be biologically impossible for an individual organism. I don't know if you really can change the "software" in the brain the way you can change the software in the computer. I kind of doubt it.

DF: One would just tell one's brain, "Delete files."

PV: That's one of my favorite definitions of culture. "Culture is software." Culture is the software, but the problem is there is no "reveal codes" key! So, you can't know what's programmed in there very easily. The learning, then, is very stressful and very scary. You can't know whether you're doing it right. You can't know what to benchmark.

To me, by the way, all this talk about benchmarking is laughable. When everybody is learning, what is the point of benchmarking? If the truth be told, those companies that look like they might be candidates for benchmarking may not agree with their fame. If you go inside and actually ask them intensely or insistently whether they know what they're doing, they'll tell you, "No, we don't know what we're doing, we're just experimenting; we're just trying these things on for size." Then, you say, "Well do you realize that you're being held up as a paragon; you're being benchmarked all over the world?" At that point, many executives will say, "Well, I sure as hell wouldn't benchmark us! Anything we're achieving is just very temporary and very accidental. Check with us next week, we may have changed it."

DF: But, at least they're still viable!

PV: This is a quote about learning that will probably get into my forthcoming Jossey-Bass book, *Learning as a Way of Being*, in one form or another.

> As this book goes to press, the world of education and training for managerial leadership is heavily occupied with ideas about learning, under the separate but related rubrics of "organizational learning" and "the learning organization" (then I cite some literature for those things). For our purposes, organizational learning means *learning that goes on inside an organization*. Usually we would be talking about the learning of an individual; but it could be of pairs or teams of people also.
>
> The organizational learning movement is thus occupied with questions on the nature of learning in organizational environments and with what managerial leaders can do to enhance learning processes within organizations. The great contribution here is to see the managerial leader role as impacting the kind

of learning that goes on in an organization and to define that role to include responsibilities for enhancing the learning of others.

It's only regrettable that the insight of the "manager as teacher/mentor/coach" and as a leader/facilitator of learning has not been a dominant part of the definition of the managerial role from the dawn of management theory. Why has it taken us until 1990 to figure this out?

The learning organization is certainly a place where high quality human learning goes on; but something more is being said here by the switch of the noun and the adjective. The "learning organization" is a different kind of social system than what has been the dominant concept of organization theory, with a few landmark exceptions such as Argyris and Schon, Weick, and maybe some others.

The learning organization is not grudgingly and creakily lurching from one stable state to the next, as the world around it changes. As an organization which is constantly learning, it is *permanently beyond the stable state.*[2]

The learning organization, in contemporary vision, has achieved a new kind of internal structure and process, marked by imaginative flexibility of style in its leadership and empowered contribution by its membership. It is constituted to learn and grow and change; as opposed to the traditional bureaucratic models which are constituted to be stable and predictable in their operations – to hold the line and not to change.

One obvious thing about the notion of the learning organization, of course, is that it takes human beings to refashion organizational structures and processes to achieve these learning organizations. These human beings themselves have learning to do, if they're to lead or participate in this refashioning.

The dynamics of learning organizations depend on new behavior by their members and their constituents. We come back, therefore, to the relative health of individuals' learning abilities and to their understanding of the kinds and degrees of learning that are involved in leading the evolution toward learning organizations.

In the context of my book, that quote is simply a nod to the organizational learning and learning organization movement. What I want to talk about is this very last clause: *"the relative health of individuals' learning abilities and their understanding of the kinds and degrees of learning that are involved in leading the evolution toward learning organizations."* My book is, in a way, about executive learning. Whether you're trying to become a learning organization or not, I'm more interested in the fundamental issue of executive learning.

Now, with my somewhat conservative or skeptical hat on, I'm not sure we're going to make it to what Senge and others are calling "learning organizations." I don't know how dependent your book and your thinking is on some of that work.

DF: We are covering that field.

PV: Fundamentally, in my terms, **a learning organization is an organization that is organized beyond a stable state**. It has achieved that position, not just at the level of conceptualization and not just at the level of its formal ways of talking about itself, but at the level of its daily behavior among people. This means it has radically changed its culture.

Margaret Mead once went on a hunt for any human cultures whose fundamental organizing principle was change.

DF: And found none, right?

PV: She found one. In her book, *New Lives for Old*, she identifies them. It's a South Seas island culture called the Manus. My recollection of what she says about them is that they are a culture that had been invaded constantly by Polynesians, Japanese, Malaysians, Americans, British, French. Their island had just been continuously occupied by one sea power or another for hundreds of years. What they had become was a kind of chameleon. They could just blow with the wind and take some pleasure in experimenting with new patterns of culture, as they experienced one new tidal wave after another of change.

She's got a discussion that goes on two or three pages about these Manus. I haven't read it for a while, it's buried somewhere in my files. Leave it that there's not a lot of precedence in human history at the organizational level to have achieved a culture that continuously reinvents itself in any very significant ways, at least within the space of a human lifetime.

So, I guess, in my heart, I would be on the side of those who were a bit skeptical about the learning organization, as to whether or not it can actually be realized. It is a charming concept, a very attractive concept, in that sense. It's like a lot of things that have been written in the organizational development field over the last 30 years. You envision a pattern of relationships, whether you call it a total Theory Y organization or have an organization that is like a "Jack Gibb" organization, full of trust and open communication.

In a certain sense, the learning organization is the latest idealization of a form of organization that would be better given the environments we're operating in than what we have. But whether we're going to get there on any significant scale or not is unclear to me. The jury is still definitely out on that question.

Frankly, I'm not even impressed by the number of case studies that are coming out of organizations that have seemed to have moved rather dramatically in the directions of learning organizations. We need at least ten or maybe more, maybe 20 to 25 years, before we can say that a particular organization has really made this breakthrough. This would be when it has permanently or at least quasi-permanently, for all practical purposes, gotten itself out to a basis of conscious, continuous learning in the sense that we mean learning. Unless we're just going to let the phrase "learning" become a relatively empty label; if, that is, the word learning is going to retain meaning at all, the behavior can be learning only if the entity that is doing it is engaging in pretty substantial change, continuously.

I don't think I'm on the "learning organization" band wagon, at least as I understand it. The chances are certain that the people up at MIT and others who have looked into this have looked into all these objections or concerns long since. But their response might also be that if organizations can't get on that continuous change basis, they're going to be overwhelmed.

DF: Are organizations becoming overwhelmed?

PV: I think it is already happening, yes. I think it's happening in the public school system. I think it's happening in the court system, in the health system; it's certainly happening in the universities; it's happening in the military. It's happening all throughout society. Interestingly enough, there is a relatively little known theorist, Geoffrey Vickers, who forecast all of this as long ago as the early 1960s.[3]

Vickers had a very dark vision. It was that the rate of change in the environment is faster than the rate of change that organizations can absorb; therefore, organizations are going to grow progressively out of synch with the environmental needs. Ultimately, they're either going to become black holes of just little empty rituals, which is what has happened in a lot of universities and in a lot of churches. They are still surviving, but the performance of their mission is practically a joke, relative to the role they used to play. Or they're going to tear themselves apart and fragment into a lot of pieces. Or they're going to be torn up with internal conflict and their missions are going to transform into a lot of just-to-make-it survival strategies.

There's an interesting subfield of sociology or organizational behavior which you could call the field of "organizational breakup." Maybe all this stuff about downsizing that we are seeing is kind of an early manifestation of a broader field, where the organization simply cannot sustain itself any longer in the environment and it just goes belly up.

DF: You mentioned the executive as the focus of your current work. Our book is not so much about the learning organization *per se*, as it is about systems and processes for which managers have traditionally been responsible. Our question is how those systems and processes facilitate, cause, block, perhaps accelerate or decelerate the learning process? Or does management have nothing at all to do with learning?

I'm listening to you talk about the dilemmas of being out-raced by change facing institution after institution. Is the guilty party the executive, and managers who work in some hierarchical support of the executive? Should they be led out with cuffs on their wrists. I mean metaphorically, who's guilty; who can we blame?

PV: I think we're probably pretty much on the same wavelength there. But, I'm not big on the heroes and villains game in any type of problem discussion. If there is a villain to be implicated in my book, it is the "philosophy of institutional learning." This has unintentionally and systematically disqualified all these men and women managers whom we're talking about from engaging in the kind of learning they need to engage in in order to do this change work we're talking about.

My book is full of a lot of fairly pointed criticisms about the idea that learning is supposed to go on with an expert in a classroom, in a curriculum, be graded, be conducted individualistically – all those familiar things that some of us management educators have been complaining about.

Our Organizational Behavior Teaching Society has been one of the leaders in trying to modify institutionalized learning. But, you know, as a fellow member, that what we've achieved is just a drop in the bucket. Many in the Society, just judging from what I can see on our list in the Internet computer network, are prisoners of the institutional learning system. They don't have any idea how else managerial education can go on in the typical classroom environment.

DF: As a member of the OBTS, I agree.

PV: We've got this huge educational system, underpinned and undergirded with a very elaborate philosophy that is profoundly engraved on all our consciousnesses. It operates as a brake on any kind of innovation where we try to think about how a particular executive group might be shaken loose to look at the world afresh.

DF: To let go.

PV: Yes. You know I've got this concept that you and I were talking about a few days ago of the "reflective beginner." That's a very exciting idea to me and I'm going to give it plenty of play in my book. But, like the learning organization concept, it could just be a romantic ideal. Our culture is set up to so thoroughly and profoundly and completely *punish* learners, it distracts learners from doing the psychological and spiritual work they need to do in order to be healthy beginners.

There are so many traditions and practices that embarrass the learner, humble the learner, distract the learner, punish the learner, inappropriately reward the learner, render the learner dependent and addicted; I mean, just completely render the learner dysfunctional! With that as a background, what sense does it make to talk about executive leaders becoming effective learners?

That's where I'm throwing down the gauntlet. It is that we've got to go back to this and rethink this educational or learning philosophy that we're bringing to these problems.

DF: Not just to the MBAs and so forth. It seems to me that almost every professional group, legal, medical, tend to be locked in the same old paradigm. Do you know of executives who are freer of that institutionalized learning orbit? Are there some doing things that seem to make their organizations more able to "work without a safety net," if you will?

PV: Yes, there are, at the organizational level. The ones that are "working without a net" are not framing what they are doing as learning, however; they're framing it as "crisis management," or "problem-solving," or "winging it." They are not connecting what they are doing with what they understand learning to be.

At a more individual level, a lot of us have actually engaged in quite creative learning with respect to what we call hobbies, in which we've pretty much had to steer our own ship and feel our own way. This is a noninstitutionalized kind of learning at our own pace. It doesn't mean we haven't taken courses and we haven't read books, but we've done it in a different frame of mind than when we're in formal schooling. And I really think a lot of that informal learning is already there. A hopeful characteristic of all this is that **the human being is a natural learner.**

So, the problem is to get the "garbage" out of the way, so that human beings can approach learning tasks more naturally, more innocently, more freely. Those conditions are more likely to exist when we're operating in a "hobby mode," so to speak. We might call it puttering around; we might call it experimenting, or "mucking around" in something. The words we would use would have that kind of off-hand, informal quality to them.

A lot of us have learned word-processing or computer network skills, just kind of inductively, by making mistakes. It would be an interesting little research project to find out how many members of the Organization Behavior Teaching Society List have ever read a user manual, studied a user manual.

DF: I didn't. I set a coffee cup on mine.

PV: I've only known two or three people who specifically studied user manuals. There is an administrative assistant in our building, not a faculty member, who, when he gets a new computer, opens the box, puts the equipment on his desk, then he sits down and he reads the user manual. Unbelievable! I mean he doesn't even turn the thing on before he reads the user manual. The other way is the mode of learning that I'll bet you and most of us practice. It is a much more informal, almost random form of learning.

DF: It seems like, in those "informal" situations, we enjoy running up against the blockages; we try something, carom off, then try another way, until we get beyond the block.

PV: I'm very conscious about the learning strategy that I practice with my word-processing software. Every time I want to do something that I used to be able to do on a typewriter or always wished I could do, I try. That's when I will open the user manual and find out how to do that; but, I don't open the manual until I have come up against something that I don't know how to do.

Over a period of three to four years, I will probably learn half of what the software would allow me to do. There are still a lot of bells and whistles which I don't even know exist in it. But, I've become very confident. It has an *organic* developmental process, rather than sitting in a classroom and listen to somebody talk to me about WordPerfect or watching a video on WordPerfect. My learning has been in relation to self-needs, not externally exposed objectives.

DF: Have we jumped to the conclusion that there is a natural energy for learning in the individual? That manager/leaders would serve this natural process by removing learning blocks that are apparent? And are managers to be there to anticipate and help remove the blocks that aren't apparent, but pop up like icebergs in the North Sea?

PV: Well yes, it's analogous to what we all used to say about Herzberg's notions of job enrichment. Herzberg, I think, first started this whole point of view that there is natural motivation to work; that the thing to do is to get the garbage out of the way.

DF: The dissatisfiers.

PV: It is to *stop* doing things, rather than to necessarily start doing things. I think there are a lot of disincentives in the typical organizations to the kind of learning we want people to engage in.

DF: So we're saying, "Stop doing all that hardball 'managing'. Do the managing that supports learning, or do a lot less of the other."

PV: Yes, maybe it's an application of this notion of **empowerment** that everybody is excited about. What we really want to do is empower learning. The way you empower people is by taking restrictions off them.

Maybe a practical question that could be asked of a manager in the present environment, whether his or her organization was moving smartly toward becoming a learning organization or not, is, "What are you doing that is tending to discourage learning in your people." Then, give that manager some help identifying those things. It would be an interesting list.

DF: They could first ask themselves, "What are others doing to discourage my learning?" This would build some empathy. Almost everyone is managed by someone else. Once we've done the introspection, then we can ask it of our co-workers. It could produce very revealing lists!

PV: It would make a nice little exercise to ask a group of managers what the disincentives to learning are in their own jobs. In what ways does the climate of the organization tend to discourage learning? Then hit them with the booming question, *"Now, what are you doing to perpetuate these practices?"*

DF: Right. I don't think I want to ask myself this in regard to my own management classrooms!

PV: Unfortunately as "keepers of the flame," we management professors are at the top of the heap in this institutional learning philosophy. We benefit, or we think we benefit, from the 12 or 16 or more years of indoctrination in learning processes that our students have had.

No wonder the first day of class in college and in graduate school is so ritualistic. Everybody knows what the first day of class is supposed to be like. Occasionally one of us organizational behavior professors will come in wearing a clown suit or will come in on a pair of in-line skates or fax in an announcement that I'm somewhere on campus and the class's first assignment is to find me or whatever. Occasionally, one of us will pull something like that and it will be the talk of the school for a few days. Then everyone will go on about their business as usual. That same bold person, I now say with a 30-year perspective on this whole process, who was doing that in their late twenties and early thirties, is no longer doing that in their late forties and fifties.

DF: Right again. We've been beaten down. My "Nobo the Clown" suit is in deep storage. Peter, we're talking about moving towards a self-examination of what managing means to learning in organizations. We seek to reveal managerial practices and patterns of thought arising while a person is doing the work of managing. I've noticed literally hundreds of books swamping managers with "new" paradigms to be embraced – "or else." Now, we have the learning organization that could look to them like one more management fad.

What advice have you for the person who is opening our book, perhaps a bit shell-shocked by the onslaught, about handling, perhaps even integrating, all these ideas about changing management?

PV: I'm reminded of a quotation from Joseph Conrad, I believe it was in *Lord Jim*. I agree that we are bombarded with all these new ideas, these injunctions to do better to improve ourselves, onward and upward and so forth. As you say, American managers are probably bombarded with more advice then probably any other occupational group in human history; unless it is parents.

So, this Conrad quote doesn't solve the problem, but it certainly nails an alternative point of view: "Hang ideas, they are tramps, vagabonds, knocking at the backdoor of your mind, each taking away a little of your substance, each carrying away some crumb of that belief. In a few simple notions you must cling to if you want to live decently and you want to die easily." Well, you and I and all of our colleagues are living contradiction to that principle. I don't think that's exactly right, but it has a certain appeal.

I am not sure that I would pick Peter Senge's particular five disciplines (as developed in his book, *The Fifth Discipline*). But, his cognitive strategy of trying to identify some qualities of character and mentality which are needed to navigate through all the turbulence would be, in my best judgment, the right one.

We educators let our curriculum get so fragmented, so hyped up with . . . I was going to say irrelevancies and trivia, but I don't mean that. It's so hyped up with details and side trips and sub-points and elaboration and amplifications and complications, that the poor learner has lost sight of those four or five disciplines.

In ancient times, there was the Trivium and the Quadrivium, the three core subjects and the four core subjects. We have let that all dissipate or fragment into a million little pieces. Today's graduating MBA, except in a very few institutions, does not walk out knowing anything that even remotely graphs on what managerial leadership is.

I did an article in *Management Inquiry* here a couple of years ago called "Running an organization." It was an attempt to formulate this notion of running an organization as the fundamental reason for having an MBA program. My argument was that if a student walks out the door not knowing anything about running an organization, as most of them do, then we've lost our reason for existence. I think I flatly said we ought to give students their money back.

Amid the ideas and techniques and research findings and colorful concepts and increasingly seductive graphics and all that stuff, video tapes, virtual reality – this unbelievable explosion of available information for thinking and talking about management in organization – amid all that, I think it's still possible to articulate "what the keel and what the rudder" need to be. This is in the sense that Peter Senge and Steven Covey are trying to articulate basic principles; that's the right direction to go.

DF: These new principles become managers' "head protectors," if you will, from the swarms of new ideas. The paradox there is they need also to remain open to ideas, choosing what seems most important to sustaining their organizations, yet not really being sure they have chosen well.

PV: My own impression is that, historically, the way we have helped the human beings cope with incredible variety and change in the environment is by supplying them with *dogma*. That is to say, statements about what is the truth that you cling to. That's kind of what the Joseph Conrad quote says, the few simple notions one must cling to if one would like to live decently and die easy.

The problem is, though, that dogma has been itself rendered obsolete by social and technological change. The strategy of teaching people "subjects of substance," which they are to regard as truth, has been overwhelmed. It actually began to be overwhelmed in the 19th century, in which Nietzsche and Kierkegaard were among the first to know this well; that you were not any longer doing a person a service by teaching them doctrine and dogma. Despite all they were committing to mind, they were just going to get pummeled by life. You can still see remnants of that with the fundamentalist religions that cling to very black and white ways of talking.

Senge's strategy is a different one. There is no content to the five disciplines. There's no one right form or content of mental mastery or mental modeling or personal mastery. Even the systems idea is content free. He's talking about ways to *use* the mind-body-spirit entity, rather than teaching content on mind, body, and spirit that people are going to cling to if they want to "live decently and die easily."

We can debate whether Senge's five are the right five or whether it's three or seven or whatever it is; but, the main point is that there are some ways of developing oneself in mind, body, and spirit which are good preparation for the world we're living in and increasingly moving into. That idea I think is sound. This, Senge has developed beautifully, in that it constitutes an answer to the question "what is to be learned?" It sets the learning agenda. If you combine the learning agenda that Senge has said with the concerns that Vaill and perhaps others have for new ideas about learning itself, you might begin to have the ingredients for a way of talking about management/executive development that would be quite interesting and quite appropriate for the organizational world of the future.

DF: You say there is an emerging agenda on learning that would help executives and other managers focus on things that they need to think and do to bring about vitalizing learning in and of their organizations. What needs developing from this point on?

PV: There is the whole area of intercultural learning. You may have heard me say over the last decade or so, that one of the astonishing things to me in my cross-cultural management class with MBAs is their beliefs, which I guess they get from the broader society as well as perhaps from their own professors in International Business.

They come into my Cross-cultural Management class assuming that what the class is going to be about is a recitation of facts about other cultures that they're going to; that their head is going to be filled up with just data about cultural patterns of other cultures. That's what they expect, and they have a very hard time letting go of that expectation. This is even though I have a couple things that I do at the beginning of the semester that demonstrates pretty dramatically that there's no way in 15 weeks that you can begin to teach 30 MBAs very much about other cultures.

My course focuses on the process of getting outside one's own culture and opening oneself to the characteristics of other cultures and focuses on the process of doing that; rather than on the content of what you're going to discover when you go to Bangkok, or when you go to Lapland, or wherever.

I have forgotten right now whether Senge or others have put intercultural learning on the agenda of indispensable awareness. I would certainly put it there as a core process with which managers need to be comfortably adept.

DF: What does it do for people when they learn to open themselves up to the characteristics of other cultures? How does this modify their minds, their outlooks?

PV: What they're able then to do is see the *intrinsic* validity of another culture's way of doing things. They no longer feel that there is some kind of competition between their way of doing things and the other cultures, as if somebody's right and somebody's wrong. That's the big problem with intercultural relations. You are so unaware of yourself as a cultural expression that you think that everybody else in the world, in one way or another, is just a sort of variation on you. If they don't do things the way you do things, they must be wrong. That's called **ethnocentricity**.

The value of being aware of the process of opening is that you're in a posture of inquiry and of curiosity, having suspended for the moment your commitment to doing things your way. My argument is that that's the posture to be in, if you're trying to manage in an intercultural environment. So the trick is to get into that frame of mind.

The great Edward Hall's phrase for it is, "getting beyond your own culture." Some talk about transcending culture, some about bracketing your own culture, while you're investigating the nature of another one. But, you've got to somehow learn how to lift yourself out of the everyday consciousness of your own culture. If you don't, you will simply look at everything through the lenses of your own culture. Because your own culture has been familiar to you, you know how to make its principles and its values work. It's quite unlikely that you're going to find, looking at other cultures through the lenses of your own culture, that which, in other cultures, is superior.

DF: The progression of that seems to be discovering better ways of doing things across all sorts of lines. It is done in acts of genuinely opening to the other culture. This brings into your mind their way of doing something to mix with your way; so the amalgam of that is an altogether new way of doing things.

PV: The term that is used for that amalgam is the phrase **cultural synergy**. Unfortunately, cultural synergy tends to be a rhetorical expression that people just toss around. If we're serious about it, the learning problem is, "What frame of mind does one need to be in, in order to honestly be able to explore the ways to integrate one's own culture with another culture?" Synergy is not just going to be a piece of rhetoric, it is honestly going to be a new condition, a kind of new temporary culture, as it were.

The frame of mind one is in, as one seeks to do this amalgamating process, is crucial. It is not just tacking on. It's not as if we're going to eat soul food for lunch and Mexican for dinner and have an all-American desert and call that a synergetic diet. It is true at the biological level the body will make synergy out of all those foods; but we're not talking biology, we're talking psychology here. Just eating three different cuisines is not synergistic.

One set of organizations in the world that have probably discovered more about synergy than many multicultural organizations are sports teams. This is where you are finding synergies between white and Afro-American culture and, increasingly, European culture. You can't play the game if you're going to just play out of one culture or another.

DF: Yes, teams are moving from region to region, the fans from each region have their own particular "casts" on the game and way of relating to the players. I imagine the players do sense a tremendous amount of diversity in their experiences.

PV: That's right, it can tear a team apart.

DF: And yet, players have to remain focused, in order to win.

PV: The performing arts organizations also have faced up to some problems of synergy. You may have many different cultures involved in the performing troupe or in the orchestra. What they do is find a way to relate their own native cultures to the **culture of the performance**.

The culture of the performance is a kind of temporary culture, as it were. They each find a way to hook on via their own native culture. The performing arts spend a lot of time evolving and nurturing and growing and developing that temporary culture that surrounds the theater troupe or surrounds the orchestra. They know how to go into that gear, when they're working together in the performing mode.

DF: So it takes a lot of preparation in order to have spontaneous synergy.

PV: That's right. There is a very powerful tradition that sustains the idea of a culture operating while the symphony is being played or the play is being performed. I think it's doable. People have learned how to do this in organizations that would learn to thrive globally. But it has not been learned in the managerial world; particularly Americans, for we are just on the bare front edge of realizing what's involved here.

I've a doctoral student who's doing research on trust formation in strategic alliances. She has done some preliminary interviewing and literature search. What she's finding, as you would expect, is a lot of American managers who are quite insensitive to how the trust formation process becomes more difficult, more fragile, more problematic as the cultural differences that the parties are bringing to the table become greater. She's kind of astonished, herself coming from one of the East Asian countries, at the American managers to whom she's talking. Their attitude is that, "We just introduce ourselves; we make sure the other side knows that we're basically good people; and then we sit down and we start negotiating."

She wonders why these managers don't realize that their Japanese or Chinese counterparts, for example, are going to want to drink tea and go tour temples for the first two days of the visit, before they utter or say one word about business. And don't they understand the kind of gift giving that's going to go back and forth between the Chinese delegation and the Americans? And I say, I don't think so.

DF: I'm just getting this overwhelming feeling of a parallel to the interculturalism of the external relationships that you're discussing to a kind of interculturalism of the firm. Each functional unit seems to have a self-contained culture. Then there are managers and "nonmanagers." There is a subculture of "being a manager," with its own codes of dress and decorum, trappings and myths. The "workforce" has its own culture. I get the sense of the same problem cited by your graduate student, that American managers see themselves as apart, in their own management culture. We are asking them to open themselves to the "other" cultures. I imagine the first response of the American manager would be, "Well yes, we support training. We 'walk the talk' out on the shop floor." Yet, do they have a glimmer of an idea what it means to create these synergies, to really appreciate and merge ideas with those on the "other side"?

PV: I mean that's why I have reached the conclusion, at least in this book I'm working on, I just have to spend a lot of time talking about our prevailing assumptions about learning *per se* and that is kind of prior in my opinion to saying very much about exciting new approaches to bringing a learning climate into the organization.

I absolutely agree that the organization has to have a more stimulating learning climate than it has had up until now. I have no problem with that insight. It is embraced in that quotation from my book that I read you. My only regret is that its taken 50 years of management theorizing to stumble into it! I support what you said, and think the idea of your book is right on target, in that respect. But I think anybody who is writing about learning has to see that gap between managers and employees. I mean this, not just in America, but really in the developed world, because we've exploited this American management model and its culture all over the world. We all have to see that millions of quite intelligent people are already unconsciously programmed with ideas about what learning is. Those ideas have to go back onto the table for examination, if we are going to talk about transforming the learning climate of the organization.

Let me give you a really powerful example of this. Most of us, certainly most of the readers of your book at one time or another in their lives will have sat in a really first rate, Harvard Business School-type case discussion. This would be either at one of the leading business schools or perhaps later in some management development experience they had. So I think we can assume that most professional managers these days, certainly people in the training/development field, know a first rate Harvard Business School case discussion when they see one.

Isn't it interesting to witness all the powerful thinking that goes on in those discussions, with all the insight people have, jumping out of their seats with excitement as they see implications and aspects that they hadn't seen before? Lines of thinking emerge and the discussion takes unexpected turns when somebody puts a new interpretation on a piece of data that everybody thought they understood and so forth. The atmosphere can get very electric and extremely involving.

In the best case, a really very powerful consensus can emerge about what's the problem in the case and what some of the major lines of action ought to be to deal with the problem. It doesn't always happen with that level of intensity and with that degree of consensus, but it certainly can. The fact that it can is what keeps the idea going as a teaching method.

All that is preparatory to the point I want to make which is: "Isn't it interesting that in all the 70 or 80 years or more that those kind of discussions have been going on in management topics, isn't it interesting that as far as I know, I've never heard of a corporation trying to do its main business through a case methodology."

From a logical point of view, there is absolutely no reason why a strategic management discussion of the next five years of this company's life couldn't be done in a Harvard Business School case method discussion mode. Logically, there's no reason why it couldn't be done. Psychologically, there are all kinds of reasons why it couldn't be done and the reason companies don't use the methodology for real.

They might use it in an off-line, safe mode; but they wouldn't use it for real, because it blows the control of top management. The danger is that people will start coming to conclusions around the room that are not the party line. So no management in its right mind would bring in a top quality case leader, a Michael Porter or somebody. For all I know, it does go on and I just don't hear about it; but I don't think most management would bring a Michael Porter in and sort of toss the company's strategic future up in the air for discussion in a case method format with several levels of management participating.

What it says to me is, to the extent that I'm right about this, about the fact that it's not happening, it dramatizes how far the typical corporation is from real commitment to a real learning environment. It indicates how much they are concerned with keeping control of the kind and rate of learning and the people who get to engage in it.

If the learning organization idea and the organizational learning notion are going to have any impact at all, people have to be willing to allow *all* kinds of learning experiences in the organization that, up to now, they've been prevented from having. Why? Because we just don't want to open that "can of worms."

DF: That's our management culture talking: "Pandora's box," "cans of worms," "don't rock the boat," "don't upset the big guy." You made a wonderful list in your talk to the Eastern Academy of Management of the signs of pathologies of organizations that can't cope with running in the "white water." We can make a similar list of all the reasons why one ought not to open up learning as you have stated this. All of it has to do with avoiding recriminations from those who are "above" them.

PV: One of the sayings that I've always loved is, "Once you open a can of worms, it always takes a bigger can to get them all back in." Many companies simply do not want to mess around with the bigger can. The bigger can involves transformations of the hierarchy; it involves increases in the trust level; it involves empowerment down the line; it involves everyone taking a longer view of the organization's position in its environment; it involves transforming the relationship of the organization to its customers. It involves integrating qualitative factors with the financial factors, so that you're not just obsessed with some narrow definition of the bottom line.

A lot of companies are hearing those speeches from people like you and me; and they're reading about these notions in the popular management literature. But it's a long step from reading about how you've got to think differently and how you have break the old paradigm, to actually committing yourself to doing it.

DF: You told me that your newest book is focusing on the executive. What are you going to tell the executive about the "bigger can"? Is there some way you can tease them out of this outworn command and control mindset?

PV: Well, I don't know. There are four things that I'm going to talk about in terms of learning. One is that I'm going to check in with my own thinking about **systems thinking**. I agree with Peter Senge's writings about the value and virtue of systems thinking. What I'm going to focus on is how systems thinking is learned. A second one is culture; again, talking about learning **processes for culture**. A third one is **leadership**. One of the real anomalies is how many people are talking about all the exciting new things that leaders are suppose to be able to do; but nobody's talking about how they are going to *learn* those things.

The fourth one is **spirituality** and learning processes. It is one of the great tragedies of our culture, beyond business, to our society in general, that millions of us have not had it pointed out to us that **spirituality is a learning process**. Instead, the impression one gets from the way our culture handles religion is, "learn the basics, the catechism, the language, before about the age of 16 or 17, then just believe all that for the rest of your life." I can't think of one signal or one scene in our culture that suggests to people, particularly young people, that if spirituality means anything, it means a lifelong process of progressive deepening and enrichment of one's spiritual consciousness. That idea is just not out there in the air.

We treat spirituality like we treat algebra, as something you've learned; then, when you've learned it, you pass that milestone, and you're done with it. Every serious religious tradition, of course, makes it very clear that it means nothing if you don't treat it as a daily process, a lifelong path. But religious leaders have not succeeded in implanting that idea very deeply in people's awareness. So the result is that people don't really expect to have a continuous process of spiritual enlightenment. It's really too bad. Unfortunately, the irony is that unlike any other subject, spiritual enlightenment has no upper limit; there's no way you can say "well I've now done it all."

DF: We're just "spiritual enough" to stay in business through 1995, some might say.

PV: It's really almost that way. If weren't so tragic, it would be amazing that we low-ball spirituality, just like we low-ball every other subject. With spirituality, however, there is an infinite range of ideas, applications, and inner experiences. You are "messing with the divine." That means it's *unbounded*.

DF: There is an infinite supply of potential insights that you can create in exploring spirituality which can be part of that amalgam of the learning we need to be effective in action.

PV: Yes. I said this in the essay I wrote for Suresh Srivastua's book.[4] Intercultural relationships and intercultural learning is eased enormously if you are able to perceive the spiritual nature of the members of the other culture. In fact, one reason why culture is such a tough boundary is because it's hard to perceive the spiritual nature across the boundary. We use the word "compassion"; well, compassion is a spiritual quality. Still, we maintain the walls between "unlike" groups by not perceiving each of the others' spiritual natures.

DF: Spirituality seems like the "ground water" flowing under the surface of all the learning that we have been talking about. Are we really asking the reader to go through a major overhaul of his or herself to tap into this hidden well-spring for moving learning? Or are there more gentle transitions in store for us?

PV: In the Recovery Movement, the "Twelve Step" people are the ones that put the concept of denial into everyday conversation. It's quite possible that all the work that's going on about the subject of learning these days will trigger some feelings of denial in some people: "It can't be that bad. After all we do know how to do that; we did solve that problem."

There is a lot more learning going on, functional, effective learning in organizations, than perhaps we are giving them credit for. Organizations are not absolutely antithetical places to learning. We are saying, however, that they need to become freer, more innovative, more flexible places. There are kinds of learning that they need to do, particularly reading and understanding their environments, present and future.

Organizations are not well set up to do this. I remember back when I was doing a lot on the subject of strategic management, one of my realizations was that the structure you have determines what you can see out in the environment. Your structure gives you a bunch of telescopes out into the environment. There still may be things going on in the environment that you don't have any telescopes for. You only know about these things vaguely from the Sunday supplement or the evening news. You don't know what the immediate implications for you are. You've got to develop some "eyes and ears" for that particular set of trends.

One general answer, so the reader doesn't feel too down and out, is that a lot of good learning has gone on already in organizations. My candidate for the sphere in which organizations have been the most creative in a learning sense is

R & D. Here, they try to come up with new products or interesting new versions of old products; to create new manufacturing and engineering processes for making those products. The impact of engineering on organizations is enormous. Whenever I get into a discussion where people are criticizing engineers, I like to say, "Look around you. Every single artifact in the entire world is engineered." They had to figure out what it was supposed to do, how to produce it, and then "debug" the process, until it turned the idea into reality.

Developed cultures have demonstrated unbelievable capacity to engage in creative learning on the technical material dimensions. Now what we're facing are a bunch of problems that aren't solvable by technical material solutions, purely. We're suddenly over into learning what needs to go on so that people grow more closely together; so that they understand each other better; so that they understand themselves better; so that they see further into the future than scientific logic will take them and use their intuition more creatively. There are bunches of learning tasks for which the standard engineering learning mode is not adequate. The challenge is to invent and learn, over the next few decades, intrapersonal, interpersonal and organizational methods and modes of learning, rather than purely technological and material modes.

That would be one thing I would say to somebody who was really feeling overwhelmed with all this – that we already know, intuitively, a lot more about learning than perhaps we think we do.

DF: Realizing our survival now depends on also developing as learners of the "soft side" of the enterprise – relationships, values, spirit – will we invent better ways to learn, as we once did with our technical materials? Perhaps this calls for a new type of engineering with a small "e."

PV: I would like to check in with a strong, strong warning not to use "engineering" for the kind of learning that goes on in the social world. The metaphor I like the best is one that has occurred to other people. The first place I ran into it was in Bennis and Slater's book *The Temporary Society*.[5] It is an agricultural metaphor. You are a gardener: you're stroking things into being; you're nurturing them into being. They have an intrinsic developmental processes of their own. You are trying to work with those intrinsic developmental processes to simply make sure that the potential, as best as possible, is realized.

That is a much better metaphor than the metaphor of an engineer, of designing and constructing something. Actually this links over into a field of studying the development of systems. Systems have an internal growth potential that is in a state of continuous actualization. The best survey of all of this that I know of is Mitchell Waldrop's *Complexity*. That is one line of answers I would indicate to leaders who are restlessly looking for ways to understand this "other" learning.

A second thing I think I would want to remind such a person is that learning, under the right conditions, can be a matter of joy and delight. This may seem startling, in that our Western intellectual, control-oriented approach to education has learning framed in terms of something that's painful, that is a struggle, something that one only does when one has to, something that one usually just doesn't feel good about as it's going on. As long as we hold that set of assumptions unconsciously about learning, of course we're going to be nervous when somebody comes along and says we're going to have to engage in all this superhuman learning for the rest of our lives.

If you think about a set of jazz musicians, mutually exploring the possibilities of a new work's structure and having fun playing off each other, they are taking some delight in that. Or, if you think of a group of close friends in a strange city, out on some kind of adventure together, there are plenty of examples of how human beings can have the time of their lives, as learners. That would be a major challenge for managerial leaders; to try to achieve qualities of **lightness** and **adventure** in the learning that their companies and other organizations are going to have to be doing.

DF: If the learning is going to go on in a mode of running scared and of terror, then who wouldn't want to get out into an environment like that? I sure wouldn't want to be in an environment where I was running scared for the rest of my life.

PV: We know joyful learning is possible. It is not a pie-in-the-sky, idealistic statement. There are lots of situations that most of us have probably experienced at one time or another where human beings can just have a wonderful time together, while they are on an adventure; where they don't know what's going to happen next and they really are in an exploratory mode, including some pains and frustrations and some "scary parts." Yet, somehow those pains and scary parts are in the broader context.

There are games of "Dungeons and Dragons," where going on adventures together, exploring things together, is very much alive in our culture today among young people. That is a positive thought, for it could mean that tomorrow's managerial leaders are going to keep the spirit of Dungeons and Dragons going in their workforce, so to speak.

DF: Let's hope we don't stifle that emerging sense of adventure. My gut tells me that is our main hope.

PV: We can avoid stifling adventuresomeness if we take it seriously, and take it for what it is which is – human learning, happening in group situations, under the right kind of supportive conditions. I can certainly see how the reader would feel like this is a titanic problem; but it's only a titanic problem if you treat learning as an add-on to everything else that we're all trying to do these days. If you treat it as an add-on, then what it looks like is, "these guys with their organizational learning books are basically saying I have to spend another 20 hours a week making myself current. I don't know when the hell I'm going to have time to do that!"

DF: We saw that happen when quality was introduced as a highly valued outcome. It meant moving the customer's needs to the center of all business propositions. It seemed, in many applications of TQM that I have read about, that the whole notion of managing for quality was kept at arm's length by the regular management cadre, kept as an add-on. Quality improvement activities are an extra burden that you do in addition to your regular work. There are some organizations still stuck in that dualism. There are others that have discovered the wonderful interplay between so-called regular work and the work it takes to continuously improve quality. They have developed the seamlessness of those two dynamics. I hope our books on organizational learning do not cause managers to treat learning as a separate system, with its own bureaucracy with a "Vice President of Learning."

PV: I'm sure we will live to see it. It's already happening. Look at all these companies that are setting up learning academies and institutes. A lot of companies have put millions of dollars into building their own little mini-universities; all coming out of learning as an add-on model. They are scratching their heads about whether or not they're getting as much bang for the buck as they'd like.

DF: Are there other ideas that you would like to share?

PV: I have made up the expression: a **process frontier**. It is reached when an organization is faced with having to do something that it has never had to do before – make a whole new mode of product, deal with a brand new kind of customer, respond to a new government mandate, meet the novel actions of a competitor. They have got to transform themselves in one way or another, but they have no idea how.

DF: That "never before moment."

PV: Yes, so they're in the position of having to make up an organizational process. Total Quality Management put everybody on a process frontier, but they didn't know they were on a process frontier. They thought that Deming knew how to do it, so they hired Deming to come in and tell them how to implement Total Quality Management. But, Deming didn't have a clue as to how to implement it. He knew what it would look like when it was up and going, but he didn't know how you get from here to there. And nobody else really did either, and probably most still don't.

Interestingly enough, our field of organization development is a set of ideas and practices for inventing organizational processes. Or, as I like to say, **OD is a process for improving processes**. The trouble is that OD people have never understood it that way, so OD has never had a theory of itself, at least a public theory, that could be passed on and developed to guide helping organizations invent processes for things they didn't have any processes for. And so, the result of this is that OD has drifted over into being a set of content ideas.

I think there is a whole mentality that goes with being on a process frontier, where you sort of realize you're trying to do something that you've never done before. You are in a completely different frame of mind. As I like to say, you're in a "beginner mode."

The problem is how to be a creative, effective beginner, with other people, right there in front of other people. Our culture doesn't support people very much in being confused and puzzled and mystified. To me, that's another kind of challenge, if we're going to engage in learning in a very dynamic and turbulent world. It means we are continually on these things I call process frontiers. It means we're going to be continually mystified and puzzled.

Quite by accident, in the newspaper here in Washington a few weeks ago, a sportswriter, of all things, made a reference to something John Keats, the poet, once said. The sportswriter, in his column, says, "the poet, John Keats, once asked what quality was essential to a person of achievement. Keats decided that something he called 'negative capability' was vital. By negative capability Keats wrote, 'that is, when a man is capable of being in uncertainties, mysteries, doubts, without any irritable reaching after fact and reason'."

That was said nearly 200 years ago by a poet; but the ability to just dwell in mystery and doubt, without demanding necessarily that somebody come up with the right answer – that there be a piece of software that will solve all your problems or some consultant would come in and solve all your problems – is still a rare quality. Yet, I think it's a form of learning that is absolutely essential to the world we are in now and moving into.

You asked, David, how much the academic and continuing educators of managers must change, in order that managing builds a capacity for valuable organizational learning. I see that as *our* process frontier; yet, the only honest answer to that one is that I haven't the slightest idea! But, let's get going on it. In fact, there are plenty of men and women, particularly in corporate training and development groups, who are getting going. They've already intuited that they've got to transform their approach to executive training and development.

I don't see much real work going on in the universities, however, to transform the institution. I see a lot of us talking about it and writing about it while hoping that other organizations will do it. I don't see very much happening in universities that you would call a transformation of the academic education of managers. I see mainly just tinkering around the edges. I guess if I had to say one sensitive thing about what we need to do in undergraduate and graduate universities, it is to start conducting ourselves as though our main mission was to prepare the student for lifelong learning. It becomes instead of learning economics, how to learn economics; instead of learning computers, it becomes how to stay in touch with the technological rampage of computers; instead of learning facts about human behavior, it is how to engage in continuous inquiry into the meaning of human behavior.

In other words, all these subjects that we are throwing at our students can be transformed into vehicles for the lifelong learning process. We will then have substantially reduced our obsession with filling up the student's head with what we arrogantly call knowledge.

DF: This way, students can make their own ways and change their own knowledge, for they will know that it came from their own creativity and learning acumen, not just from ours.

PV: We are, by filling the student's head up with facts about these various subjects, not preparing them for the world of the future. I don't want to be so black and white as to say that there are no facts that we should bother trying to impart. I do think, however, that our main focus ought to be not on fact transmission, but on the transmission of a *mentality*.

It is to help the student acquire a mentality, so that they will be able to generate their own facts in the future. It's the old aphorism, "I give you a fish today and you eat today. I teach you how to fish and you eat for life." We are not teaching our students how to fish, we just aren't, and that's the "dirty little secret."

I want to be very sure that a reader of what I'm saying reflects on the following. What I'm saying is about preparing the student to engage in his or her own lifelong process of inquiry and fact generation and deepening understanding of the world around him or her. This is not new and I know it's not new. The literature on education and the development of young people for the future needs of society is "called to arms" on this very point. What *has not* happened is my main point. We have not managed to create the academic organizations that deliver that value system.

The academic organizations that we have created deliver mountains of facts. The student is a "dumpster" and each one of us is a huge truck; we back up to the classroom each day and turn on the hydraulics and we let them fly. The students all walk out bulging, but within a few hours they have passed it all and it's back to the soil where it started.

The work for us as educators is not so much coming up with sexy new facts to teach. It is coming up with new ways to conduct ourselves, so that we consistently impart the spirit of learning and development of mind, body, and spirit to the student.

That is why, by the way, all of our vaunted emphasis on research is misplaced, because of the way we are emphasizing research. We do our research off line, out of sight of students. Then we come back to them with new fistsful of facts which we hand them. The student never gets to see our process of inquiry, not the passion with which we're chasing our questions. They never get to see the dilemmas we face along the way and all the tough judgment calls we make as we try to figure out what we've got and what we're doing. They don't get any real exposure to that, even doctoral students. They certainly don't get it as a college sophomore. The result is that students are screened from the very thing

I'm talking about. Even for professors who are the superb creative inquirers, the current system hides those qualities from the student.

DF: . . . students who, ironically, are paying for us with tuition, so we can do all that other work that seems to be more in line with our promotions and tenure.

PV: The majority of professors are not now, and perhaps never were, in much of an inquiring frame of mind to begin with. They, basically, are high level information storage and retrieval machines. And what they're just real good at doing is transmitting a text book to the student.

DF: Well, we management educators surely have some work to do, but you and I are still young enough to do it, aren't we? Aren't we?

Thank you, Peter, for this searching conversation.

Notes

1 David Hurst, "Why is strategic management bankrupt?" *Organizational Dynamics*, Autumn 1986.
2 Donald A. Schon, *Beyond the Steady State* (New York: Norton, 1971).
3 See, e.g. Geoffrey Vickers, *Value Systems and Social Process* (New York: Basic Books), 1968.
4 Peter Vaill, "Executive development as spiritual development", in S. Srivastua (ed.) *Appreciative Management and Learning* (San Francisco: Jossey-Bass, 1990).
5 Warren Bennis and Philip Slater, *The Temporary Society* (New York: Harper and Row, 1968).
6 Mitchell Waldrop, *Complexity* (New York: Simon and Schuster, 1992).

Relational Management

Nicholas J. Zangari and Steven A. Cavaleri

Introduction

During the past two decades there has been a shift in business practice that represents no less than a watershed transformation in the way organizations are managed. This change has been precipitated by concomitant changes in the natural sciences. The changes that we speak of spring from diverse sources of wisdom and cannot be fairly attributed to any particular school of thought. Wheatley[1] has described the emergence of a "new science" that is changing the way managers think about the way we organize work, people, and life. While it is not clear how the new discoveries in the physical sciences, such as quantum physics and theories of dissipative structures, will affect management practice in the long term, it is clear that three major discoveries are beginning to profoundly affect our beliefs about the nature of organizations. The first is the finding, from quantum physics, that the mere presence of an experimenter, or observer, may influence the outcome of an experiment. This finding raises questions about the role of managers as independent agents of change who seek to exert their will on a system. This leads us to consider redefining the role of the manager as a biased participant-observer, who is part of the system, not an objective outsider. The second lesson comes from systems science and suggests that parts of a system often, unexpectedly, form linkages to each other in ways that run counter to reason and create outcomes that defy traditional explanation. Finally, from the physical and systems sciences comes the notion that the resilience that an organization shows in withstanding stress may depend on the hidden patterns of information, known as feedback loops, that define the relationships between various parts of an organization. In our view, these changes are causing us to reexamine the notion of what it means to manage.

Our preliminary observations suggest that this new era will usher in a deeper appreciation of the origins of many patterns of organizational dynamics, and lead to a new model of managing that emphasizes the importance of learning as a catalyst to performance in organizations. The purpose of this chapter is to outline a framework for an emerging approach to managing that reflects many of these changes, and we believe that it incorporates a synthesis of several newly emerging understandings about the nature of organizations and the management process. A strong case could be made that the connotations of what it means "to manage" have changed so much in recent years that it may not even be appropriate to refer to this process as "management" any longer. Surely, the view that managing is a process of controlling resources is an anachronism and, as many people have come to realize, the notions of controlling and organizational learning are often incompatible.

One way to add clarity to our understanding of what it means to manage is to create another word that more accurately describes the aspects of management that are not oriented toward control. Another approach, one that we have chosen, is to describe a vision of another view of managing that is based on a different set of assumptions other than the "control model" of management. In this chapter we will offer a conceptual sketch of an alternative to "control-outcome management." We call this new approach **relational management**.

Relational management is based on the premise that people and organizations have some natural self-organizing capacities that are usually ignored or diminished by managers. We view the essence of relational management as a process of self-development for managers spurred by creating ever-deeper personal understandings of how patterns of relationship affect performance in organizations. By the word "relationship" we mean the reciprocal patterns of influence that emerge over time in organizations. Such reciprocal patterns often are exacerbated by the responses of managers to perceived situations, and over time are likely to generate recurring patterns of: (1) fixed and expected perceptions, (2) programmed responsive actions, (3) selective attention to expected effects of their actions, and (4) creating degraded explanations of the meaning and relationship between their actions and the effects which they are creating. In our view, managers are continuously trying to create a meaningful, albeit tentative, explanation of how their actions yield certain effects. In one sense, we could say that managers are continuously trying to create their own theories for how things work, at work. Chris Argyris calls these tentative explanations **theories of action**. He proposes "In order for theories of action to be tested in everyday life, it must be possible to derive from them the actual behavior for effectiveness. In other words, theories of action must produce actionable knowledge."[2] We concur with Argyris and add that, for managers, useful knowledge must include a way of understanding the patterns of relationship that influence organizational performance.

In our view, relationships most often form among four key elements in organizations that we call the "four P's of relational management." The four P's are **people, performance, processes**, and **patterns**. For example, a manager may develop a pattern of responding to the news that profits are declining by trying to increase the efficiency of production processes in order to cut costs. Once cost cuts are made managers wait attentively to see if the next period's financial reports indicate the effects of their cost-cutting efforts were successful.

If the profits continue to decline, then subsequent rounds of cost cutting are likely to take place. These efforts may go beyond actions to improve efficiency, and often include layoffs of personnel, and renegotiating contracts with supply vendors. If this cycle of cost cutting continues over time, not only do the managers need to be aware of their original reasons for cutting costs, but now they have also formed a pattern of cost cutting. In forming such a pattern they have also subtly created a self-reinforcing cycle of events which will cause their attention to be diverted away from alternative actions and policies. This managerial effort is intended to close the circle of the perceived need to act, to respond, to pay attention to the effects of the response, and to take further action or informed nonaction. Here you see a relationship, or recurring reciprocal influence, that emerges between people, performance, processes, and patterns.

By developing a useful knowledge of how relationships affect performance in organizations, managers no longer have an external reason to unnecessarily rely upon control as the basis for their managing. Surely, there are many managers who prefer to use control-based assumptions to guide their practice of managing, but we propose that those reasons are largely based in either personal need or cultural norms and traditions. By contrast, the relational manager is free to use this deeper understanding of relationships as a basis for helping to support the natural self-organizing processes within organizations. Yet many managers must wonder whether such notions as self-organization have any place in organizations. We suggest that the self-organizing perspective is just part of a broader shift in thinking that is taking place in response to a number of new insights developed through inquiry in the various fields of science.

A New Way of Seeing

The idea that changes in scientific thinking could lead to changes in other parts of society, such as politics and business, are not new. For example, in Europe, during the 18th century, the new science of rationalism produced a dramatic effect on people and science. The era became known as "The Age of Reason" and people learned the value of using logic and the scientific method for solving problems. The dominant world view shared by people at that time supported the use of such methods. Leading thinkers of the time assumed that the mysteries of the world could be unraveled by objectively seeking the truth, measuring, and quantifying all unknown factors in a situation, and by reducing complex problems to their simplest elements.[3] This view of reason suggested that people need only to take a mental step back to see the problems of the world more clearly, and then use logic as the scalpel to dissect the complexities of the universe. To some extent it worked. Many scientific revelations have been made using this approach. Unfortunately, these early scientific approaches only told part of the story. Use your imagination for a minute to mentally trace how such forms of thought have been applied wholesale to the social sciences and management. Most likely, you will have no difficulty in imagining thousands of ways these ideas have been incorporated into our world. Or perhaps you have, like many people, come to assume that these aspects of life are the way that things are supposed to be and just accept their place in the world as "a given."

From F. W. Taylor and his scientific management approach, through to Michael Porter and his models for strategic analysis of competition, the Age of Reason lives on in the form of management theories. Unfortunately, the scientific ideas that formed the fundamental philosophical roots of these management approaches are now considered, at best, to be half-truths. If this is the case, what does it suggest in terms of the validity of current, popular management theories? While the views of scientists may be changing rapidly, the assimilation of these views in the form of a transformed practice of management has been slow, and sometimes arduous. Yet a number of new approaches to managing, that reflect these new perspectives, are being called for by leading theorists, such as Europeans Peter Checkland, Charles Handy, Ronnie Lessem, Reg Revans, Fritz Schumacher, and Werner Ulrich. American authors including Chris Argyris, Peter Senge, John Sterman, Peter Vaill, and Meg Wheatley are all leading the charge to fundamentally change the way organizations are managed to reflect the dynamic, complex nature of these systems and their environments. The theme that is heard to echo throughout the messages of these visionaries is that it is no longer sufficient to manage organizations by simplifying them into mechanical bits and pieces that can be quickly fixed.

Certainly, there will always be plenty of well-defined problems with simple solutions in organizations, but these will not be characteristic of the vexing, chronic conditions that so often defy simple solutions and bring organizations to the brink of failure. In these, the slimy underworlds of organizational morass, this is where the complex entanglements of the problems and solutions of the past, present, and future meet to yield conditions that frustrate the efforts of even the best managers. It is the place where problems are like thickets of underbrush: it is impossible to define where one ends and another begins. Such problems defy simple description and definition. Therefore, we must shift our attention to developing tools and languages that offer ways to deeply understand and act upon such systems. Here, in the traffic jams of the organizational world, learning is the process that will help managers develop a richer understanding of the relationships that will lead to balancing the competing forces in organizations: an ultimately better economic performance. Individual, team, and organizational learning is all part of the paradoxical notion that a chaotic process may yield stability. It is the goal of this developing work, that we call relational management, to outline how people may manage such organizations that learn.

Relational Management

There are several reasons why we have chosen the name relational management. The most important reason, we believe, is that organizational life can be understood more deeply when viewed in terms of patterns of relationships, over extended periods of time, rather than when seen in terms of linear chains of strategies and outcomes. Many popular management approaches, such as business process re-engineering, are based on designing and implementing processes that facilitate the accomplishment of goals by focusing the attention of managers on outcomes, not relationships. Relational management is a process that continually identifies ways to reinforce beneficial relationships and balance ones that are not mutually beneficial. The manager who practices relational management sees all problems in a context where they are joined with other issues, rather than seen in isolation. Here, managers improve the functioning of the whole by finding innovative ways to better articulate the relations among the parts of the whole.

Relational management is **appreciative** in that it is based on the recognition that beliefs precede action and "facts" are only seen as hard data if they are preceded by a manager's predisposition to value and focus upon certain sets of facts, rather than others.[4] Finally, relational management regards situations as being defined based on the interpretations of managers. Simply, any situation may contain many potential meanings. Traditionally, when a situation is well-known and stable most managers seek to turn the situations to the organization's economic benefit, in other words, they focus on optimizing efficiency. However, when a situation is not well-known and is dynamic, a manager may offer a greater service to the organization by charting the uncharted waters of complexity and helping others to become proficient at charting these murky waters too. In other words, we see the key role of the manager as not being one of optimizing the relations between organizational inputs and outputs, but rather to increase their own learning and the learning capacities of others in the organization.[5] Some managers will argue that some waters which others describe as being murky, or not well understood, are really simple and well understood. Here, relational managers must learn to recognize that complexity often exists in the eye of the beholder. In either case, whether complexity is an objective characteristic of a situation or just a way of looking at the world, perception and learning can play an important role in the work of managers.

The role of learning and inquiry is central to the appreciative qualities of relational management. In this view, a manager is seen as a participatory observer who works in the midst of dynamic situations, which usually offer few simple solutions. Here, the most effective strategy for managers is to focus upon increasing their own and others' capacities for learning. Doing so is not always easy, fun, or risk-free. Learning in organizations begins with a commitment to one's personal development and culminates in the development of shared meanings among the members of an organization. Along the way, they must continually examine the validity of their own beliefs and those of others without being paralyzed by self-doubt. Both the importance of action and reflection need to be in balance. As Peter Checkland has noted, the manager's work is to bring theory and practice together. Therefore, in order to learn from experience, managers' actions must inform their thinking and vice versa. Their ideas must continually be grounded in reality, yet it is a reality which is often being redefined. By striving to engage in the paradoxical process of being both active and reflective, managers may begin to see relationships more clearly.

Practicing Relational Management

Relational managers are participant/observers who are actively engaged in a continuous process of fitting together their own style of managing, their personal beliefs, and the needs of the people and organization which they serve. There are many types of personal beliefs which are relevant to management, such as beliefs about one's self (identity and sense of self-worth) and about others such as whether others have good intentions and are trustworthy. However, another belief system may prove to be of even greater value to relational managers. Relational managers seek to discover their own fundamental beliefs about the laws, principles, or mechanisms by which causes produce effects. In other words, they seek to discover, reconsider, and validate their basis for judging how things happen in organizations. On the surface, it would appear to be unnecessary to pursue such a path of self-discovery as a prelude to any management process. After all, don't most managers already know what they believe? This issue is not as simple as it would at first seem.

Persuasive arguments have been offered by writers such as Argyris and Senge that at least a portion of the beliefs held by most managers offer incomplete, and often non-systemic explanations of cause and effect in organizations.[6] These and other writers have proposed that managers perceive and act in ways that are shaped by such belief systems. More importantly, most managers seem to make decisions on the basis of hidden beliefs which offer partial explanations of cause and effect, but often lead managers into thinking they are comprehensive explanations. It is extremely difficult to understand the value of relational management if one holds hidden beliefs that suggest that outcomes, rather than relationships, should be the focus of the attention of managers. Since relational management is primarily concerned with defining and understanding relationships, managers who wish to be relational managers can take the first step in this direction by becoming aware of limitations in their own belief systems. By thinking in terms of relationships one can help facilitate beneficial ones and compensate for ones that limit an organization's ability to meet its potential. A number of the important differences in the beliefs that would be held by a relational management in contrast with those that are the basis for traditional management approaches are summarized below.

Traditional	*Relational*
Focus on parts	Focus on whole
Static	Dynamic

Traditional cont'	Relational cont'
Hard systems	Soft and hard systems
Production output	Quality and value
Planning	Capacity to react
Training	Action
Hierarchy	Horizontal
Objective reality	Subjective reality
Hard information	Hard and soft information
Behaviors	Beliefs and value
Outcomes	Relationships

Geoffrey Vickers suggests that managers are often likely to remain unaware of the belief systems that drive their behavior. Such hidden beliefs are likely to predispose managers to valuing, recognizing, and favoring certain choices over others without even being aware they are doing this.

Manager's self-inquiry

It's relatively simple to determine what others believe by observing their actions. It's more challenging for managers to discover their own beliefs. One simple, yet often effective, place to start is by inquiring what it is that you believe about the importance of people in organizations. Do you view people as assets? Do you regard them as physical assets, intellectual/knowledge capital, or sources of energy? Once you've spent some time considering this question, then try to envision how your beliefs will influence your stance on personal and organizational learning. See the Hanover Insurance example later in this chapter to learn how one company dealt with these basic assumptions.

Clearly, it is unrealistic for managers to strive for complete objectivity in the way they view things. On the other hand, if they can see more clearly how they may act to remove impediments to the natural flow of organizational processes they can help foster a dynamic balance within a system. This notion of fostering dynamic balance is contrary to the traditional idea that managers should control the mechanical processes that yield outcomes. The relational manager believes in the natural rhythm and flow of organizational relationships, and seeks to manage by helping these relationships return to a state of balance, not to control them. If they can see more clearly how they may take actions that will remove impediments to the natural flow of organizational relations and dynamics they are acting in a way that "honors the system." Most management approaches do not honor the system, that is, the inherent wisdom of the people and processes in the organization to self-organize in ways that are beneficial are often overlooked. Hence, the notion of the manager as "balancer" or "magician" runs contrary to the traditional idea that effective managers should exert control over organizational processes that generate important outcomes. The relational manager, on the other hand, believes in the innate wisdom of people and processes to ultimately establish a natural rhythm and flow of organizational relationships. They seek to manage organizations by helping these relationships return to a state of balance where things flow more naturally, not to control them. One author has described the essence of 'flow' as "being so involved in an activity that nothing else seems to matter."[7] When a natural flow is present in relationships work seems effortless.

For example, when a good basketball team is in a state of "flow" where the natural synergies of the players are yielding the desired outcome, there is no need for the coach to take action. Yet many an inexperienced coach is inclined to meddle with the flow, rather than to stand back and admire the marvelous chemistry among the players. The tendency is to overcoach, overcontrol, and not honor the inherent natural abilities found in human systems. Especially when managers live in fear that they must demonstrate tangible efforts to manage, they are likely to overcompensate in this direction. Furthermore, if a chronic pattern of frequent overcontrolling behavior develops it is likely to introduce "blockages" to the natural processes of self-organization that exist within human systems.

Scientists Humberto Maturana and Francisco Varela have described a natural self-organizing process within all natural systems, called **autopoiesis**. They propose that all natural systems have the ability to define themselves in ways that will produce autonomy and organize themselves for this purpose. This is not to say that a process of chaos ensues, but rather a system must be allowed to experiment with various ways of being in order to reach the best way at a given time. Eventually, as these natural forces that support growth and stability become established there will be a coalescing of forces into a recurring pattern of relations that will generate order amidst the chaos. This process is known as **structural coupling**. According to Maturana and Varela, "We speak of structural coupling whenever there is a history of recurrent interactions leading to the structural congruence between two (or more) systems."[8]

From our view, relational managers are able to think and act in ways that are distinctly different from traditional management practitioners. They have deeper understanding of themselves, and a broader understanding of organizations. They subscribe to the following precepts for managing:

1 See and understand key relations between yourself, and the many systems of the organization.
2 Avoid taking unnecessary actions to control other people or systems.
3 Be conscious of your own potential to create blockages in the flow of human and other systems.
4 Intervene in systems to facilitate the rebalancing of the flow when necessary.

In many respects, the way of the relational manager will seem paradoxical and unnatural to the mechanical control-oriented manager. Traditional management is based on action, commanding, and controlling. Relational management is predicated on helping, modeling the dynamic tension between action and nonaction, and allowing self-organization and flow to develop. Relational managers are able to use the tension in the manager's role as the guy wire that keeps them aware of the natural state of balance in themselves and the organization. The relational manager does not shy away from action, she or he just appreciates the value of well-timed action or non-action in getting results. "Silence is the warrior's art – and meditation is his sword."[9]

In the relational management process there are four key ways that managers may help to create a relational management system. They can:

- Help others to increase their capacity to discover the basis for their own mental models;
- Help others to think in terms of both relationships and outcomes;
- Help others to develop the skills to build relationships with other stakeholders, such as customers, suppliers;
- Help others to understand the natural wisdom of nonaction by modeling it in their relationships with them.

Clearly, relational management is based on some beliefs which are different than many of those which are the foundation of traditional management. More clearly, some managers are very comfortable with the more traditional approach, while others seek something new. After reading over the comparison of some of the key assumptions for the two approaches it may be that one or the other resonates with you and feels more natural.

The Relational Management Process

As with any management system, an idealized mental image of what is desired is the beginning for the relational management process. This process starts with the executives or leaders developing a rich picture in their minds of the configuration of relationships that they wish to maintain or develop. This enables the manager to define the context of what is important or valued for other organization members. Max DePree has said that "The first responsibility of a leader is to define reality."[10] To relational managers this infers a process in which they engage in a dialogue with other team members to outline the relational context of their work. Specifically, this means defining and outlining the many connections that compose each relationship and the broader patterns of those relationships.

The role of figure and background are very important in the process of perceiving relationships. One can easily see the differences in how various painters have experienced and portrayed these figure–ground relationships. For example, the French impressionist painters, such as Monet and Manet, expressed figure and ground relationships in a way where the contrasts between the two are often quite subtle. The artist Escher has played with figure–ground relations where either figure or ground may be mistaken for the other. Consequently, a sense of illusion is often created: a psychological "sleight of hand," so to speak. The process of helping others form their own mental picture of a situation must exist before they can recognize it in reality. Yet leading another through such a process of realization is anything but methodical. As noted Gestalt psychologist, Fritz Perls, once observed, "Experience is largely reported in metaphorical terms, and its sharing with others has traditionally been the province of the poet and novelist."[11]

There are many tools available, such as systems modeling, that can facilitate this process but, despite them, the process of conveying the meaning of relationships to others remains largely an art. The specific approach chosen will depend on the needs and expertise levels of the managers.[12] Regardless of the method chosen, the mere process of conceptually outlining the mechanisms that serve as the foundation for these relationships will provide a vehicle for helping managers to develop a deeper appreciation for the nature of the relationships that surround their work. In the context of the relational management process, learning is viewed as being a product of managers' heightened capacity to contact those assumptions and beliefs that drive their actions. When managers are able to expand their ability to see whole webs of relationships, the organization of which they are part will begin to reflect similar abilities. Said another way, managers committed to their own learning and growth in these areas will tend to pull the organization along with them. This cannot be forced through an organization.

It is our belief that all organizations exhibit a type of learning that is the product of collective human experience. What is learned in organizations is influenced by the underlying assumptions held by the members of that organization. Therefore, it is important that managers remain aware that even when it isn't obvious, organizations are always learning. What they are learning is another matter entirely. Much of this learning takes the form of theories of action about relationships. Simply, most managers are continually seeking to discover what they can do to improve performance. All managers selectively choose to focus on certain relationships as potential sources of insight about performance and they ignore others. When you choose to interpret the meaning of relationships in a certain way, you actually leave out other interpretations. Why is this important? It illustrates the significance of assumptions in decision-making because those assumptions influence our perceptions and choices of what we will give our attention. Over time, we begin to see a pattern or network of relationships that has a seeming degree of permanence. This soon becomes the framework or structure through which we interpret the meaning of our experience and the happenings within an organization. Robert Fritz in *The Path of Least*

Resistance defines structure in this way: "The structure of anything refers to its fundamental parts and how those individual elements function in relation to each other and in relation to the whole".[13]

For the relational manager the key parts of this definition are how the fundamental parts of an organization function in relation to one another and how they relate to the whole. Another difference between traditional managers and relational managers lies in the perception of their relationship to the system. Traditionally, managers have assumed that they are "outsiders" in relation to core processes, such as manufacturing or product development, and often regard their role as being similar to enzymes in a chemical reaction. That is to say, they see their role narrowly as "catalysts" to the ultimate chemical reaction without binding to those chemicals themselves. By adopting the perspective of the outsider, managers have often viewed their prime mission as problem-solving. The logic of the catalytic manager was: (1) jump into the system, (2) use my expertise to solve the problem, and (3) jump out of the system. Most often the "fix" offered by catalytic managers means developing solutions to well-understood, relatively routine problems, such as minimizing costs, raising productivity, and increasing efficiency as way to optimize short-term economic performance. Often, the hidden belief of catalytic managers is that in order to optimize economic performance they must ignore conflicts between economic performance and other influences, such as human factors, by avoiding the noneconomic factors. For instance, long-term solutions will be sacrificed if they require short-term increases in expenses, loss of productivity, or uncertainty regarding profitability. Another example would include cutting research and development funds due to expense problems caused by decreasing market share. While this is a viable short-term solution, it often creates even larger problems in the long run. Similar decisions to reduce staff or eliminate training and development budgets may appear to generate the desired results in the near term, but can generate larger, even more damaging problems down the road. From the perspective of the catalytic manager people tend to be viewed in utilitarian terms that focus on economic performance. Catalytic managers view themselves as being expert problem solvers who, like a mechanic, fixes the automobile and gets it back on the road without concern for who is driving it or where it is going.

This approach exists in dramatic contrast to relational management. The relational manager's learning results from a much different view of the manager's role and relation to the system. Relational management is a response for dealing with what E. F. Schumacher has described as "divergent problems" – problems "which cannot be solved by logical reasoning."[14] From a systems perspective, divergent problems exist when two problems are tightly coupled and efforts to improve one problem cause worsening of the other. For example, high-speed assembly lines are usually quite efficient, but normally result in high levels of worker alienation and boredom. Similarly, many of the methods used to improve problems of worker alienation and boredom usually lower efficiency.

The "sociotechnical" systems movement pioneered by companies such as Volvo and Saab have tried to reconcile this divergence by optimizing both human and techno/economic factors. As Reflexite Corporation CEO, Cecil Ursprung, observed in the interview recorded later in this book, Henry Ford responded appropriately to the conditions of his time and set up compatible management systems and work processes that were incredibly successful. However, times have changed, people are better educated and motivated to participate in discussions.

Peter Senge argues that such problems are often dealt with by employing a "shifting the burden" strategy in which fundamental solutions to problems are avoided in favor of more expedient short-term fixes. For example, Senge notes that companies are often prone to attempt to grow by trying to sell more to existing customers rather than by broadening their markets. Some other typical examples of this pattern of behavior are shown below.

Fix	*Trade-off*
Short-term profits	Long-term profits
Action	Reflection
Overwork	Health
Deferred maintenance	Preventative maintenance
Downsizing	Product development

Divergent problems are increasingly common as systems (business, government, education, learning) evolve into more complex forms. Within complex systems managers usually experience more barriers to understanding the relationship between cause and effect that influence performance. Many non-systemic efforts initiated by managers have been known to produce unanticipated side-effects that run counter to what their intuition would lead them to expect. As a result divergent problems are not easily resolved by the use of quick fixes. Rather, problems are more effectively dealt with by gradually developing an understanding of each problem as a part of the larger systems that provide its context. Many total quality management programs have demonstrated that continuous improvement processes are often quite useful in resolving ill-defined problems.

The emphasis on creating fundamental solutions to problems over time allows the relational manager to develop a deeper appreciation of the systemic relations that create and sustain problems. But what differentiates relational managers from all others is that they also use the continuous improvement process as the basis for their own continuous learning about how they interact with the situation. There is a growing body of evidence that reflective observation alone is simply insufficient to enable managers of complex organizations to readily solve problems. As John Sterman of MIT has noted, there are many scholars who have called for managers to become more adept at systems thinking and action-based learning. Yet Sterman comments, "The barriers to learning include the dynamic complexity of the systems themselves; inadequate and ambiguous outcome feedback; systematic misperception of feedback; inability to simulate mentally the dynamics of our cognitive maps; poor interpersonal and organizational inquiry skills; and poor scientific reasoning skills. To be successful, methods to enhance learning about complex systems must address all these impediments."[15]

Although all managers must be concerned with a more systemic view of problems, focusing on relationships often leads to an inward focus in an organization. The redirection of a manager's focus from external issues to more inwardly focused concerns often arises from the realization that organizational performance can be the product of the dynamic interaction of complex internal relations, as well as external forces such as competition. For example, internal decisions pertaining to capacity planning, over the long run, have the potential to affect order backlogs, delivery times, sales, and profits. Unless a company holds the sterling reputation of a Harley-Davidson, their inadequate production capacity usually translates into longer delivery times, lost orders and sales, as well as declining profits.

There are two aspects of this inward focus on relationships. One has been created by the trend toward decentralized processes for decision-making driven by beliefs in empowerment and localness. The other provides the necessary context for those decision-making processes to work effectively.

A key concept behind decentralizing decision making is Schumacher's "principle of subsidiarity" which, in essence, holds that higher authority levels within an organization should not make decisions which can be made effectively at the lower authority level. The consequences of violating this principle are a reduced sense of ownership and control of functions essential to the lower level's and overall organization's success.

The falling bank card: a case of confused identity

One example of the principle of subsidiarity is a customer who received an unexpected phone call from his credit card bank. The customer had been actively searching for a credit card from a different bank since his current card carried a high interest rate. A few days before the customer was ready to make the switch a customer service representative from the current credit card bank called the customer to assess his level of satisfaction with the card and the bank's service. The representative asked a series of, apparently programmed, questions regarding the quality of the bank's service. The customer expressed generally high levels of satisfaction with the quality of the bank's service over the nearly six year period. Near the end of the conversation the representative asked the customer if there was

Continued on p. 338

anything else she could do. The customer paused, and quickly wondered whether he should tell the person of his dissatisfaction with the credit card rate. After all, the customer thought, "What can a customer service representative do about the credit card rate – that must be an upper management decision?" The customer took the chance to vent his unhappiness with the bank and said, "By the way, I think your interest rates are too high." Expecting to hear that she was sorry, but that was a matter of bank policy, the customer was not nearly prepared for what he would hear next. The service representative replied, "Would you feel better if I lowered your rate by 5 percent for the next six months?" The shocked customer stuttered something in the affirmative and the caller ended by saying, "Okay, it's done . . . will there be anything else today?" Trying to recover from the experience the customer said goodbye and paused to think about what had just happened. Here was a customer service representative from a very large bank who had just lowered the interest rate on a credit card over the phone to satisfy a customer.

How could this happen? Obviously, someone in the bank honored the principle of subsidiarity. If the customer service person had to field the customer's anger without the power to do anything about it, both they and the customer would hang up the phone feeling "disconnected" in their relationship.

Managers need to concern themselves with the structural relationships between the central core/power base of the organization and its decentralized operations to be certain that the power to act and the responsibility for actions are in the same place. This is a constant process of aligning the power and functional relationships to the corporate vision. Relational managers need constant and effective feedback to work with this process effectively. The other aspect of focusing inwardly in the organization involves providing context for the decision-making process. To be effective in this capacity, managers need to concern themselves with the human relationships which are established with superiors, peers, and subordinates as well as relationships these people have with one another within the organizational structure.

The Human Side of Relational Management

Relational managers are inclined to focus their attention on networks of relations that compose whole systems, rather than on individual parts. Similarly, they understand that people who work in organizations bring their whole self to work each day, not just their work self. The notion that bringing one's "whole self" to work, and not just the work self, is regarded as natural and important in relational management. Much in the way that cultural diversity within organizations helps to offer different perspectives on problems, the presence of the whole self at work offers similar benefits. The whole self includes body, mind, spirit, consciousness, emotion, and connections to family, friends, hobbies, and other outside activities. Although, in some cultures, learning via intellectual development is highly valued, on a more global scale it is clear that there are many means by which people may learn to be productive at work. Some people might arrive at an insight into how to better serve customers through pure reason, while others may empathetically relate to the needs of customers they have met in a focus group. Simply, the more channels one has available to see the nature of "relationships that matter" to the organization, the better.

Viewing people as whole or full members of an organization is a critical step in providing context and meaning to work in the relational organization. As criminals are less prone to steal from someone they know, managers are more likely to recognize each person's capacity for contributing to the relational organization if they view them as whole persons, rather than in utilitarian terms. On a broader scale, the effect of adopting this view throughout an organization is that patterns of decision-making also change. Here, the role of power within the organization becomes implicit, rather than explicit. By interacting multi-dimensionally with their respected colleagues, managers are able to nurture a critical relationship that becomes the basis for both input into decisions and feedback regarding the effects of decisions. Our experience has led us to believe that people are more willing to tell you what they really think when the basis of a dialogue is human being to human being, and is based on trust and respect, rather than in the context of a formal reporting relationship. The stereotype of the manager who is surrounded by "yes-people" who obediently nod with approval to all suggestions made by the "boss" is all too common for comfort in Western cultures. As Laura Freebairn-Smith has noted, managers often become insulated from what is actually happening around them because of various social and informational barriers that prevent accurate information from getting through to them. In our view, this is also the result of receiving information outside of the context of a holistic relationship. Engaging in meaningful conversation with colleagues is particularly important in sensing the level of ownership, understanding, and commitment to the core values and beliefs of the organization. This feedback provides a barometer of the state of learning within the organization.

When managers interact with others on the basis of their position in the organization's power structure, they will get feedback based on the dynamics of power-oriented, superior–subordinate relationships. Our experience suggests that this type of a dynamic produces barriers that act as a powerful filter in the feedback process and often masks a manager's weak interpersonal skills by compensating for them through the use of power. Ackoff distinguishes "power over" someone versus "power to." Power over is exerted to get people to do what they would not ordinarily do voluntarily. Power to helps gets people to do voluntarily what is desired.[16] The theme of empowerment is not new, nor sufficient to support relational management. As Sterman and Senge have observed, empowerment without a broader understanding of each individual's relationship to the whole is a recipe for disaster.[17] The relational manager empowers others, not just for personal development or performance, but to engage them as team members in a dialogue that offers insight into the relational possibilities of work. Such possibilities include redesigning work to be more whole, envisioning ideal futures, and imagining the type of relationships that will be necessary to support the attainment of those futures.

In organizations where authority to act and responsibility for those actions are aligned at the lowest or most "local" level, managers who can provide context and obtain unfiltered feedback can more accurately assess what is being learned and what is being accomplished.

Creating a Relational Organization

Relational management is evolving from numerous and diverse influences. The practical implications of this approach may be inferred from the work of people such as Russ Ackoff, Chris Argyris, Kermit Campbell, Peter Checkland, Robert Greenleaf, Bill O'Brien, Peter Senge, E. F. Schumacher, and Abraham Zaleznick. Relational management is a process based on the eclectic belief that various tools, theories, and insights developed by these people can be integrated in a practical way that can expand an organization's capacity for learning. The theme of relational management is that the leverage created by learning, amidst conditions of complexity and divergent problems, enables economic and financial performance to be achieved. There are six major areas in which relational managers play an instrumental role in transforming these concepts into the reality of the relational organization. These six areas in clude designing systems which increase the capacity of other organization members to:

(1)   Identify and communicate those key structures which assist or hinder efforts to achieve the organization's vision.

(2)   Disseminate and receive information to and from other members and parts of the organization in such a way as to provide context – a sense of perspective and connectedness. Here, managers become storytellers who can paint the relation between foreground and background with their stories.

(3)   Serve as a prism whose function is to generate important questions (rather than answers) about key structural and human relationships which affect the achievement of the organization's vision.

(4)   Serve as an institutional memory for all that is learned. As keepers of "the flame" of the organization they essentially act as living embodiment of its shared vision, values, and beliefs. This requires a systemic view and one which understands the structural relationships that are part of that system.

(5)   Lead learning and build community. In this context, leadership is the
      power of achievement harnessed through commitment. Leaders in a learn-
      ing organization have the ability to draw out of others that which can be
      freely given, but not coerced. Learning in organizations is far from being
      a risk-free pursuit. However, by building a community with commitment
      to learning and to valuing diversity a supportive ecology for knowledge
      may flourish.

         Learning leaders are committed to their own personal development
      first; this goes beyond managerial development. The power in this com-
      mitment is the simultaneous choice to follow other learning leaders along
      the learning path, and also to choose one's own development as the per-
      sonal vision on that horizon. Contrary to the beliefs of the utilitarian
      manager, the relational manager views such personal development as the
      gateway to economic achievement. Relational managers must provide a
      laboratory environment which allows organizational and personal develop-
      ment through experimentation.

(6)   Act as capacity builders. Relational managers endeavor to enhance those
      parts of a system that can potentially yield what Peter Senge calls "high
      leverage changes."[18] That is, by making judicious choices concerning in-
      vestment in future capacity, managers may make subtle decisions that
      produce profound results. For example, by recognizing that the capacity to
      create knowledge is an organization's most critical competitive force, then
      it becomes possible to support the development of this force by investing
      in organizational learning. This approach exists in stark contrast to the
      traditional managerial approaches which are based on problem-solving.
      Problem-solving focuses on minimizing the negative forces in an organiza-
      tion, while relational management emphasizes expanding the positives to
      crowd out the negatives.

   Clearly, the relational organization is one that relies upon the shared involvement of all its members. In order for a relational organization to become a
reality managers must be conversant in the language and concepts of relational
management.

The Skills of the Relational Manager

Relational managers possess skill in understanding and using a wide variety
of management tools. There is little doubt that well-defined problems will still
continue to exist and require the attention of relational managers. Relational
managers do not practice their art in place of more traditional management
approaches. Rather, all approaches are regarded as having value under a
given set of circumstances. The relational manager places her or his emphasis
on building the organization's capacity for learning in the context of
relationships. However this is done in a way that complements, rather

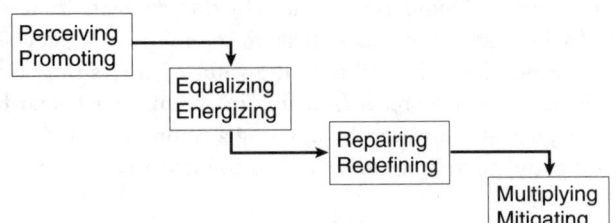

Figure 11.1   PERM – the essential skills of the relational manager.

than replaces other established managerial tools. The essential skills of the relational manager are included in the acronym, PERM, illustrated in figure 11.1.

Briefly, the elements of the relational manager's toolbox contain the following skills:

P

Perceiving with the realization that one's perceptions are the product of one's beliefs. No one sees reality directly without filters.
Promoting learning opportunities for others.

E

Equalizing relationships by balancing negative and positive forces.
Energizing learning by supporting the free flow of information and unblocking the places where people want to let their performance flow.

R

Repairing relationships by serving as a model and resource to those partners who want to strengthen areas of weakness and soreness.
Redefining the meaning of relationships *vis-à-vis* performance.

M

Mitigating the natural effects of entropy, destruction, and fear.
Multiplying one's efforts by creating high-leverage systemic changes built on an understanding of the dynamics of relationships.

By engaging in these actions, by reflecting upon their impact, by communicating the insights gained, the relational manager provides "context," a critical element in learning. Context is the description of various relationship structures and the ways in which they are connected. This context is given meaning in relationship to the organization's vision of its purpose, values, and goals. The vision defines what relationships are important and provides focus on the ways they are connected.

Managing from a relational frame of reference requires that attention be paid to continually being aware of new, emerging, or developing patterns of causality. For example, a company that is experiencing dramatic growth may supplement its workforce capacity by subcontracting to outside vendors. However, as time goes on this may obscure the need for beginning planning for new plant construction or expansion. Ultimately, the lack of core internal capacity may introduce much higher levels of complexity associated with the management of large numbers of vendors in diverse areas of the business. In the language of systems thinking, a shifting-the-burden archetype gave way to an emerging limits-to-growth pattern.[19] Peter Senge's description of feedback loops is important here. His mapping of cause and effect provides a new tool to understand the structure of the interaction between cause and effect. The concepts of "time delays" are important because these interruptions in the receipt of feedback tend to distort or obscure or simply postpone the manifestation of the cause/effect structure. In the prior example, the time delays are inherent in recurring patterns where limitations on capacity also serve to restrict future growth and tends to encourage managers to do a better job of managing vendor relations, rather than planning for the construction of a new plant. In the late 1980s, Miller Brewing built a new brewery in New Jersey to accommodate growing demand. By the time the plant was complete, demand had slackened and the plant never opened. It was sold to a firm outside the industry for an entirely different purpose.

This idea of taking action to shorten feedback loops is important to relational management. First, it keeps managers focused on structures (relationships between parts and wholes, cause and effect). Why is this significant? Systems thinking has as a fundamental belief that structure influences behavior over time. If managers have a hope of changing the business behaviors required to earn a profit and create learning organizations, then the focus must be on understanding and influencing those structures rather than leaving the structures implicit and unchanged. Trying to change behavior is not the strategy.

Second, by keeping feedback loops (the relationship between cause and effect) short, Schumacher's Principle of Subsidiarity can be applied to the decision-making process required in business. For example, by delegating authority and accountability to front-line service people, the relationship of the cause and effect between business decisions and customer satisfaction is clearer. The service person knows quickly if the customer is satisfied because that feedback is not distorted by time or information delays inherent in a decision-making structure which requires corporate office approval.

Simply said, the shorter the feedback loops, the fewer delays and distortions between cause and effect. The less distorted the picture of reality is, the more focused the decisions can be on business choices at hand. The short feedback loop concept can also be applied to the human relationship aspect of relational management and learning/leadership. As manager, the shorter your feedback loops are with the people you interact with, the better context and information you will receive. As a relational manager you need to get close to people to understand them and their feedback, and for them to understand you. This is done through your peer-to-peer, human-to-human relationship with them. The shorter the "distance" between your influence on people and their influence on you, the greater the sense of connectedness and context. This is fertile ground for leadership.

A key approach for keeping feedback loops short between managers and colleagues is through a mentoring, coaching, storytelling relationship with subordinates. Often managers confuse delegation of tasks or decision-making based on authority, with delegation of their human relationships with others. In fact, delegation of the decision-making process makes sense – both from a reductionistic management approach and the Schumacher concept of subsidiarity. Decisions made at the lowest or most "local" level tend to be based on a more accurate sense of the business reality and higher levels of ownership when authority is aligned with responsibility.

However, managers should understand that by coaching at that level rather than making those decisions, they have an opportunity to observe the operating structures in place at that decision point. They can ask key questions to draw out and reveal the operating relationships.

In a sense, mentoring is a way of keeping *indirect* control because of the feedback it provides to the coach about the decision-making structure. The storytelling aspect of coaching is providing the context for the connection between the "local" task or decision and the overall vision of the corporation. This helps add meaning for subordinates as they perform the tasks. It provides a sense of worth and helps raise self-esteem. This sense of connectedness is important in generating quality and productivity improvements. So far, relational management has been described as having these attributes:

- An understanding that a focus on system structures reveals insights into system behavior (a key tenet of systems thinking);
- An approach which focuses on keeping the relationships between cause and effect (the feedback loops) as short as possible, not only in terms of focusing business decision-making as close to the customer as possible, but also in terms of shortening the feedback structure between manager and subordinates at the human relationship level;
- The existence of mentoring relationships as the structural mechanism to provide context to workers;
- A focus on people and their wholeness as well as business process.

How can these attributes be connected in a model which expresses the relationships and structural connections?

Schumacher describes a basic tension between an organization's need for order and its need for creativity – what he calls the "antimony of freedom and chaos." Understanding that there is dynamic tension in organizations between their need for order and their need for entrepreneurial creativity and risk-taking, a key relational question arises: What structures exist that connect order and creativity in a given organization? Further, which structures tend to unbalance this relationship? What structures can be built to capture and channel the dynamic tension between order and creativity into movement toward the corporate vision?

The relational management "model" can be expressed in terms of four key structural components and their relationship to one another. They are:

1 The corporate vision of goals and possibilities. This, in effect, defines the boundaries of company decision-making.
2 The corporate core. This includes its values about people, the economic goals, the company belief system about the way economic and human decisions are made and from which emanate the power to make decisions necessary to conduct business.
3 The entrepreneurial or experimentation process (what Schumacher calls "chaos"). This is the leading edge of the company as it expands and migrates toward the vision.
4 The structural relationships which connect the vision, core, and entrepreneurial elements. These include person-to-person, person-to-system(s) and systems-to-systems relationships.

The graphic expression of this model is illustrated in figure 11.2.

Each of the structural relationships between the core and entrepreneurial process can be viewed as a feedback loop. One element of the feedback loop which moves toward the entrepreneurial component is the flow of power and values from the core. What flows back to the core reciprocally is the learning generated at the creative edge by the utilization of that power in the context of the corporate values.

This learning has the dimension of increased problem-solving ability which, if effectively applied to the economic and human decisions the corporation must make, can strengthen the power of both core and entrepreneurial processes. This learning also provides feedback to the core about how experiments have affected values and beliefs. This feedback becomes the basis for reinforcing and/or modifying those beliefs.

Regardless of mental model, the manager has a responsibility to connect it with economic performance. The method the relational manager uses to make this connection is practiced with a focus on structures. Relational managers have a challenge to understand the corporate vision of which they are a part. They need to understand the various models that have an evolving influence on their craft. Finally, they must be able to apply these theories in a way that generates desired economic performance and human commitment to the vision.

In the context, the role of the relational manager is largely one of:

1 Deciding which questions need to be asked about economic performance, people, and process in the quest for the corporate vision.
2 Exploring the ideas triggered by those questions.
3 Acting on those ideas through testing and experimentation.

The questions to be concerned with fall into three broad structural areas. First, managers will question the relationship between the power to act and

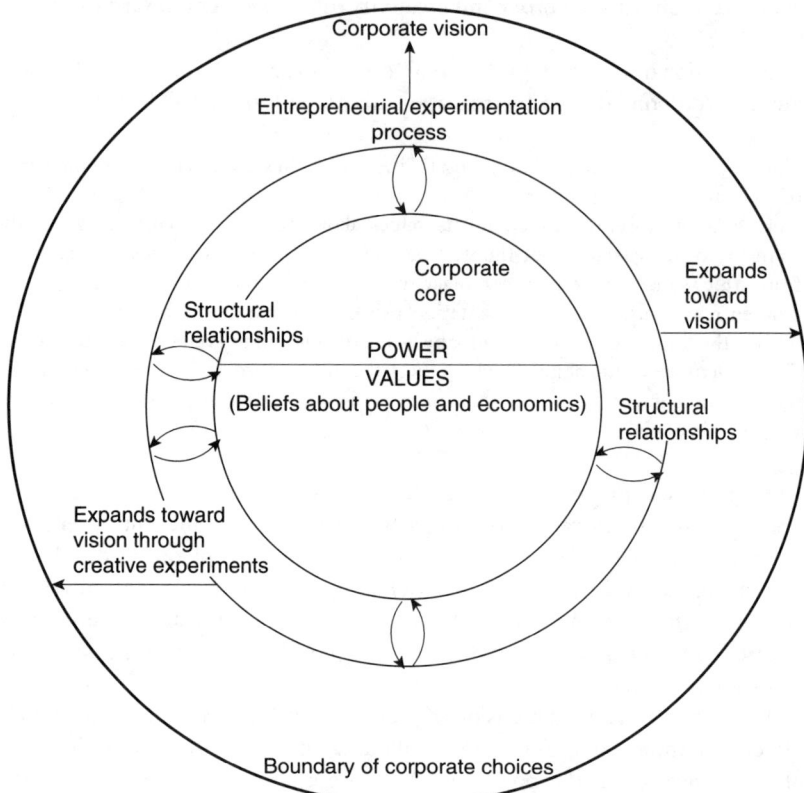

Figure 11.2   The relational management system.

degree of direct accountability for the exercise of that power. For example, are authority and accountability at the maximum leverage point for generating the desired economic performance and sense of employee well-being or are they structured in such a way as to strengthen and maintain order and control at the expense of experimentation (risk-taking) and learning?

Second, what is the relationship between the corporate core values/culture and economic performance? Do the corporate values contribute to the achievement of economic goals or are values maintained at the expense of long-term economic performance?

Third, what is the relationship of employee well-being (in a holistic sense) to economic performance? What is the relationship of context and a sense of connectedness to economic performance? What is the relationship of an employee's sense of congruency with core values and vision and its bias toward risk-taking?

Where these questions lead the relational manager depends on the answers and the additional questions these inquiries generate.

Exploring and Acting on the Ideas: A Hanover Insurance Story

As a local operating arm of the Hanover Insurance Company under Bill O'Brien, retired CEO, the Connecticut branch was a testing ground for many of these theories. The insights which resulted from the bias of experimentation and the practice of the core values provide an illustration of how relational insights can help achieve the dual goals of achieving desired economic results and ongoing development of people.

Connecticut consistently ranked among Hanover's top branches for growth, profit, and expense efficiency. They embraced the opportunities to learn from the ideas of Peter Senge, John Beckett, Chris Argyris and many others. They were also committed to learning from each other as part of the organization's long-term development plan. The local organization was able to build a local vision which supported the corporate vision of being a vision-driven, value-guided company. The local vision articulated a desire to be a leading-edge field office with a high reliance on relationship strength, people development, technical competency, and a bias toward experimentation. Superior economic performance was an integrated component of the local vision.

The field office developed a series of insights about the structural relationships between certain forces at work in their environment and their ability to progress toward their vision. Some of the key structural relationships were:

1 The relationship between their ability to view the long-term consequences of decisions and the number of crises generated or avoided.
2 The relationship of employee turnover to quality, productivity, expense efficiency, customer retention, and profitability.
3 The relationship of employee selection, and subsequent employee development, to turnover.
4 The relationship of employee well-being to productivity and a sense of "owning the job."
5 The importance of good personal relationships with the distributors of the product and its impact on growth and profit.
6 The relationship between risk-taking through controlled experiments and long-term expense efficiencies and growth.
7 The relationship between the management team's ability to provide employees with context and a sense of connectedness and their ability to sustain superior economic performance.

The articulation, questioning, and analysis of these relationships over time provided a rich context against which to make the daily business decisions about adding to staff, budgeting for a project, or finding ways to improve service to customers.

Employees often commented about the absence of crisis management and their own commitment to achievement. They were a constant source of feedback about the marketplace and excellent ambassadors for their company.

In both the Claim and Policy Processing departments, management focus on the structural relationship between employee turnover and performance on key profit and service issues led to significant changes generated by the management team. These included improved employee selection for open positions with a better match of job skills and mind-sets to the job demands and a formal ongoing training and development program in each department. Service performance, quality ratios, and employee productivity improved.

The management team also conducted a number of small-scale experiments designed to better understand (and shorten the feedback loop to/from) the customer. Service satisfaction postcards were sent out with every transaction. Every negative response was personally answered by a member of the management team. Department and job structures were modified to test for increased effectiveness in serving customers and sustaining economic performance. The principle was: "Don't be afraid to try it; don't be afraid to make a mistake." By remaining focused on the key structural relationship, the possibilities of a big mistake were minimized. By keeping decision-making authority as close to the customer as possible, the field office was able to keep customers happy that they would have otherwise lost.

The insights developed from a focus on systems, structures, and people helped sustain long-term performance. However, it is a slow process – one which requires persistency and faith that the techniques which develop out of the insights will eventually work. By keeping feedback loops from customers to the branch and from employees to the management team as short as possible, the ability to maintain focus while adjusting to the environment was developed. All of this helped in the evolution toward the corporate and local office visions.

The Challenges Facing the Relational Manager

The foremost challenge for any manager who wants to contribute to organizational learning is a personal one. The manager who desires organizational growth and learning must first be committed to his or her own growth and learning.

Given the commitment to personal growth, managers then face the challenge of:

- Developing a vision of where they want to be – personally and in the context of the organization.

- Integrating the human values within the business by focusing on wholes, connections, and the dynamic relationships which exist between people and systems.
- Recognizing that viewing management through the prism of structures and relationships is a specific mental model in itself. This means keeping sight of the point that relational management cannot be done from a perspective outside the relationships. When done from a perspective outside those relationships, this can become relationship manipulation.
- Questioning how the manager can influence the business system, of which they are a part, at key leverage points in that system.
- Developing a feedback mechanism which provides the context of where they and their subordinates are in the operating system, how the relationships in that operating system are interacting and where they want those relationships to go.
- Providing an environment which balances the need for experimentation with the need for control.

Conclusion

Relational management is evolving as a practical articulation of theories and insights of people like Senge, Argyris, Fritz, Greenleaf, Oncken, Zaleznick, Schumacher, Beckett, O'Brien and others. At this point in its evolution relational management is as much a vision as a reality.

For managerial practice, the basic skills of relational management are:

1 View problems in terms of structures; ask relational questions to stimulate thinking.
2 Make a personal commitment to learning, especially absorbing the thinking of those listed above.
3 Delegate decision-making to the lowest or most local level that is competent to handle in the long term (Schumacher).
4 Do not delegate interpersonal relationship cultivation. Address relationships on human-to-human level regardless of hierarchy. "Coach" as a way to get information and get your story across – as a way to provide context.
5 Keep your feedback loops short to minimize the distortion of information. Get decisions through the chain of command; get context from direct interaction on the human relationship level.

The basic premise of this approach, namely the ability of managers to be able to recognize and respond to the imbalances among relationships, is neither new nor visionary. From social relationships in such arrangements as marriages, sports teams, and communities the importance of relationship between people has always been known. However, the notion that the class of phenomena we label as relationships may be expanded to include other nonhuman constituents, such as the relationship between sales and profit or among worker satisfaction and the design of an assembly line, is slightly more novel. However obvious these ideas may be, the core notion of relational management remains that organizations are composed of a web of relationships and, when these relationships are "out of balance," then the many systems within an organization will not respond as expected or desired by managers. The unintended side effect and enigmatic consequences of managerial decisions are often attributed to chance or evil competitors, rather than to blockages and imbalances within the organization. Consequently, by ignoring this interpretation of management it is possible that the underlying causes of these blockages become further ignored and more problematic.

The first step toward dealing with such circumstances is to accept the possibility that such organizational elements as relations, flows, and blockages even exist, and they have a potentially important influence on performance. Transforming one's thinking and recognizing how one systemically has ignored the possibility of such interpretations, may alert some managers to the realization that both relationships and outcomes are important in organizations. Further, it may eventually become clear, as the field of relational management evolves, that both relationships and outcomes are interdependent. In some organizations they will mingle together to form a seamless web in a knowledge ecology.

Notes

1 M. J. Wheatley, *Leadership and the New Science* (San Francisco, Berrett-Koehler, 1992).

2 Chris Argyris, *Knowledge for Action* (San Francisco, Jossey Bass, 1993), p. 250.

3 Willis Harman, "Shifting context for executive behavior: signs of change and revaluation", in *Appreciative Management and Leadership*, Srivasta, Cooperider, and Associates (eds) (San Francisco, Jossey-Bass, 1990), pp. 37–54.

4 The notion of appreciation originated in the work of British theorist Geoffrey Vickers. He has written a number of books including *Freedom in a Rocking Boat* and *Human Systems are Different*.

5 Peter Checkland, "From optimizing to learning: A development of systems thinking for the 1990s", *Journal of Operational Research*, 1985, vol. 36, no. 9, pp. 757–67.

6 Peter Senge, *The Fifth Discipline* (New York, Doubleday, 1990) and Argyris, *Knowledge for Action*.

7 Mihaly Csikszentmihalyi, *Flow: The Psychology of Optimal Experience* (New York: Harper and Row, 1991), p. 4.

8 Humberto Maturana and Francisco Varela, *The Tree of Knowledge* (Boston: Shambala, 1987), p. 75.

9 D. Millman, *The Way of the Peaceful Warrior* (Tiburon, CA: H. J. Kramer, 1980), p. 82.

10 M. DePree, *Leadership is an Art* (New York: Dell Publishing, 1989), p. 11.

11 F. Perls, R. Hefferline and P. Goodman, *Gestalt Therapy* (New York: Bantam, 1977), p. 28.

12 For further reading see Senge, *The Fifth Discipline* and P. Checkland and J. Scholes, *Soft Systems Methodology in Action* (Wiley: Chichester, 1990).

13 Robert Fritz, *The Path of Least Resistance* (New York: Fawcett, 1989), p. 6.

14 E. F. Schumacher, *Small is Beautiful* (New York: Harper and Row, 1975), p. 97.

15 John Sterman, "Learning in and about complex systems", *System Dynamics Review*, 1994, vol. 10, no. 2–3, pp. 291–330.
16 Russell Ackoff, *The Democratic Organization* (New York: Oxford University Press, 1994).
17 John Sterman and Peter Senge, "Systems thinking and organization learning: acting locally and thinking globally in the organization of the future", in *Transforming Organizations*, T. Kochan and M. Useem (eds) (New York: Oxford University Press, 1990).
18 Senge, *The Fifth Discipline*, p. 64.
19 Senge, *The Fifth Discipline*.

12

Learning from the Core:
The Heroic Leader and
Conscious Organization

Sharon Seivert, Alexander N. Pattakos,
Frederick Reed, and Steven A. Cavaleri

Introduction

The thesis we will examine in this chapter is that learning is a natural process not only for human beings, but also for the human systems within which they work. Learning is a primary survival tool, "as strong as the sex drive,"[1] and instinctive to all living organisms. Therefore, in the same way that all life has some level of intelligence and all human beings have the ability to learn, all human organizations have the potential to become "learning organizations." The realization that learning potential, however, requires **heroism** of leaders, for they must launch the effort with their *own* process of learning. In this way, they can bring themselves and their organizations into increased **consciousness** – a deliberately developed awareness of themselves and their own learning processes. Learning, then, is here defined as an ongoing process of discovery about oneself and one's world. It is the bringing of the unknown and the unconscious into one's conscious awareness.

Heroism and the Adventure of Learning

Learning is, first and foremost, an adventure of self-discovery. It requires both leaders and organizations to tackle the fears, confusion, unconscious pulls, and lethargy which often thwarts learning, change, or improvement efforts. Consequently, the leadership needed to develop learning organizations requires a different form of risk-taking than has been encouraged in the past. Instead of tough-minded executives who focus externally on wiping out the competition or internally on directing activity and maintaining control, we will need individuals who have the courage to face and deal with their own issues, including their and others' fears about a tumultuous present and an uncertain future.

Such learning leadership, as we define it here, is a "selfishly altruistic" act. Biologists Humberto Maturana and Francisco Varela, in their ground-breaking *The Tree of Knowledge* describe how species survival is often dependent on members of the group taking risks that appear altruistic – for example, a worker ant who gets food for the whole colony. Maturana and Varela contend that such acts are actually "altruistically selfish" and "selfishly altruistic," – as it clearly benefits the individual that the group survives.[2] The risks that accompany a leader's modeling such learning in an organization may include: having to challenge the unconscious assumptions which are buried in the organization's culture (for example, what it takes to be "real executive material"), putting oneself at risk of ridicule, investing time and effort with no guarantee of results, or possibly even suffering reprisal from those who do not want anyone around them to rock the boat by embarking on a course of self-discovery. The good news in human systems, however, is that the individual is likely to benefit from the process of learning, even if the group does not. We contend then that learning organizations require, as a first step, that their leaders act "heroically" by taking their own journeys of self-discovery, thereby modeling and leading the way for co-workers. But exactly how does one do this?

The supposedly unknown territory of self-discovery has maps galore for us: there are stories common to all cultures about regular people who transformed themselves into heroic leaders. The following metaphor, borrowed from Seivert and Pearson's *Heroes at Work*, is a not atypical cross-cultural map for heroic leadership:

> In ancient days, knights (*middle management*) could not become rulers (*top executives*) of the kingdoms (*workplaces*) until they had:
> journeyed into the woods (*the dark, entangled maze of their inner selves*);
> slain the dragon (*faced and learned from their own inner monsters*);
> claimed the treasure or found the Holy Grail (*rediscovered their souls*);
> rescued the princess (*integrated their opposite female or male side, i.e. grown up and become a real person*); and
> brought their new-found heroism, treasure, and princess (*what they learned*) back to rejuvenate the Wasteland Kingdom (*the lifeless organization*).[3]

But what does this myth-encoded message mean for today? To begin the heroic journey, leaders do not have to take up residence on an analyst's couch or go to retreats where they bare their souls, hold hands, or walk barefoot over blazing coals. The good news is that all the ingredients for an adventure of self-discovery await leaders behind their own office doors: there are, after all, plenty of complicated maze-like riddles to figure out, an occasional fire-breathing dragon in the way, and hopefully, buried treasure which will reward all the effort! To embark on a learning journey, leaders merely need to embrace the mind-set that work is an indispensable part of their lifelong learning adventure, and that their workplace is as good a place as any for self-discovery to occur. The adventure of learning can begin in the midst of daily action and in dialogue with other members of the organization. It's primarily a matter of becoming *conscious*.

Learning as a Process of Becoming Increasingly Conscious

The famous psychiatrist Carl Gustav Jung wrote prolifically about the human psyche. According to Jung, each individual psyche was composed of conscious and unconscious aspects (see Jung's model of the human psyche in figure 12.1).

In *The Structure and Dynamics of the Psyche*, Jung described the human psyche as including the following three levels: **consciousness**, the **personal unconscious**, and the **collective unconscious**.

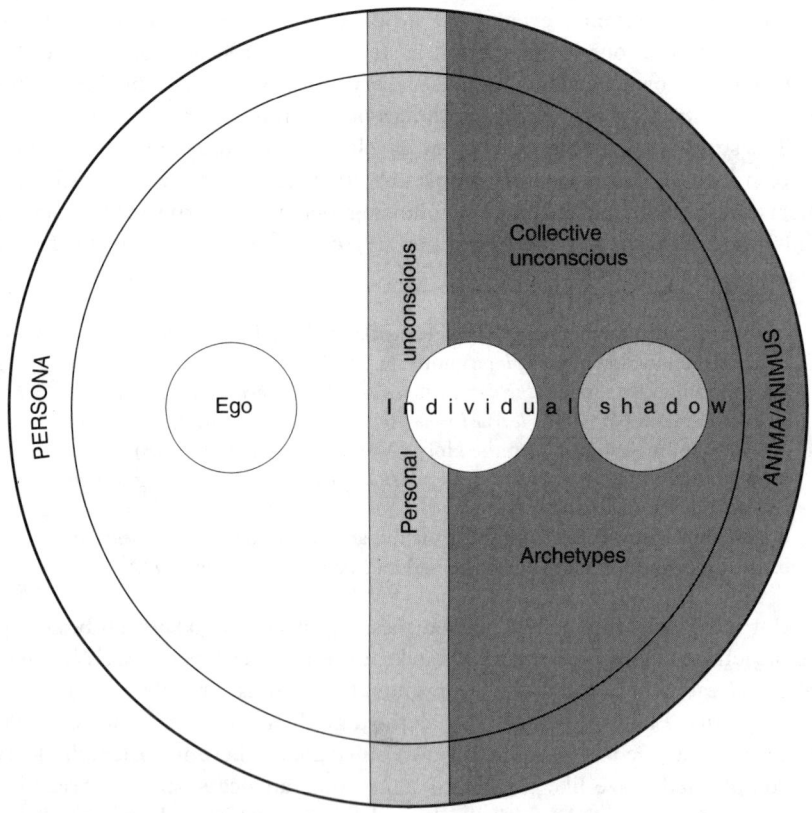

Figure 12.1   Jung's model of the human psyche.

According to Jung, consciousness included the following: perception (via the five senses – seeing, hearing, etc.); the process of recognizing and evaluating those perceptions; intuition ("the perception of the possibilities inherent in a situation"); volitional processes (directed, "free will" impulses); instincts (for body survival and/or instincts which bubble up from the unconscious); the act of paying attention (a directed, "rational" apperceptive process); and undirected apperceptive processes such as fantasizing and dreaming ("irrational" processes which he described as the "results of unconscious psychic processes obtruding themselves upon consciousness.")[4]

Particularly relevant to our discussion of learning is Jung's work on the unconscious (which includes both a personal and collective unconscious.) The personal unconscious includes parts of our lives that we have forgotten (or never paid a lot of attention to, or actively repressed), yet which are still stored away in our minds, like the contents of dusty boxes stored in the attic. The collective unconscious consists of species memory (similar to animal instincts): mythological motifs (such as the classic story of the heroic journey we described above), primordial images, archetypes, cross-cultural stories and richly meaningful symbols, all of which appear in both the collective myth and the individual dream. Jung described the collective unconscious as follows: "the totality of all archetypes . . . the deposit of all human experience right back to its remotest beginnings . . . a living system of reactions and aptitudes that determine the individual's life in invisible ways . . . a living fountain of instinct [from which] flows everything that is creative."[5]

The concepts of the personal and collective unconscious have profound implications for individual and organizational learning – making the process of learning more one of remembering, of **calling up learning from inside** rather than one of taking in ideas and information from the outside. Viewed this way, learning is actually an easier process: instead of expending considerable time, effort, and money to stuff yet more data into our brains, we learn by bringing that which is currently unconscious into our consciousness. For the rest of this chapter we will examine the scientific arguments for this thesis and its implications for both individual and organizational learning. Because the learning we describe herein involves every part of us, including our deepest selves, we refer to it as **learning from the core**.

Learning from the core requires effort of a different kind: it requires us to slow down, listen to ourselves and pay attention to what comes up, to trust and follow our instincts. It demands of us the daily effort and courage to see life though our own eyes, to experience it with an inquiring mind and a strong, open heart. For many of us, that prospect is scary: frankly, we would prefer to keep busy rather than face this kind of raw, undiluted learning. Yet it is indispensable to becoming the kind of leader who can take the first critical steps to shaping a learning organization. This path is not easy, but the alternative is worse. As best-selling author, Marianne Williamson, said: "It takes *courage* – this is often called the path of the *spiritual warrior* – to endure the sharp pain of self-discovery rather than choose to take the dull pain of unconsciousness that would last the rest of our lives."[6] And, we would add, it is that "dull pain of unconsciousness" which can drain our own energy and our organization's vitality, leading to the sort of workplace Wasteland Kingdoms we see all around us.

Obstacles to Heroic Leadership and Change Efforts

The path to leading a learning organization is strewn with many obstacles, not limited to, but certainly including, the following:

- It requires a significant initial effort to change; therefore it *appears* easier to remain unconscious;
- The "adventure" of becoming conscious causes discomfort, even pain, before it produces tangible results or causes pleasure and joy;
- Unconsciousness is reinforced in most organizations whereas pushing for consciousness is punished;
- Not only workers, but also many leaders feel drained of their vitality, powerless to affect real change in their organizations;
- Many workplaces have "tyrant kings" or petty despots firmly in control who feel threatened by change of any kind;
- By and large, people tend to be afraid of the unknown.

Obviously, any one of the above could suffice as a learning/risk-taking disincentive. Many people do not expend the effort to learn because of a low-grade, chronic anxiety which Edgar Schein has labeled "'Anxiety 1,' the anxiety that is associated with inability or unwillingness to learn something new because it appears too difficult or disruptive."[7] We see this a great deal in monolithic governmental bureaucracies or impersonal corporate structures where talented individuals have given up trying to buck the system. Discouraged, they merely put in their time. Those who have not been completely beaten down turn their creativity elsewhere – to their families, community, second jobs, or avocations. Thwarted from learning in that workplace, they are determined to learn and grow elsewhere.

To counteract the deleterious effects of workplace anxiety, W. Edwards Deming argued that fear must be driven out of our organizations.[8] Why? Fear is the first obstacle to the adventure of learning, keeping the individual from even stepping onto the path. And there's more. Fear is toxic: it can pollute an entire system, adversely affecting everyone. Interestingly, when we ask workers the characteristics of their worst and best bosses, the one issue that surfaces every time is fear. The worst bosses are described as inspiring fear or being afraid – sometimes both! They are controlling, micro-managing, not trusting of their workers: they try to keep people down and are quick to blame and find fault; they are often out of control emotionally (either volatile and unpredictable, or cold and noncommunicative); and alternately, sometimes they are timid, hesitant, and afraid of making necessary decisions. On the other hand, the best bosses are described as being unafraid: they take risks, encourage their employees to grow, are supportive, communicate easily and frequently, have multiple sources of power (informal/formal), and they are decent to the people around them. In short, they have taken some version of the individual heroic journey described above and have taken responsibility for their own actions.

The issue of fear is directly related to another task for heroic leadership, that is, to recognize and bring out the learning potential in one's workers. This ability distinguishes the good leader from the great. Leaders can release the learning potential in other members of their organizations by: (1) consistently modeling their own heroism so that others can feel that it's safe to experiment and learn; (2) letting people know what boundaries/parameters/authority issues exist so they don't blindly slam into an invisible wall; (3) determining a baseline of what is known and unknown, conscious and unconscious within the organization; (4) establishing systems within the organization to foster and support the learning that takes place; and finally (5) understanding just how it is that individual and organizational learning occur – a task this book is designed to assist. This then is what we mean by "heroism" in leadership. It can set off a wildly virtuous cycle of self-discovery and learning within an organization. The possibilities – after such an organization-wide learning cycle has begun – are endless, exciting, completely out of control, and therefore a bit scary. No wonder Peter Vaill said, in his interview with David Fearon, that to cast oneself adrift on a sea of possibilities is a heroic act.

How Learning Happens: Autognomics and Joy

Learning is a natural process; as such, current methodologies of teaching actually inhibit learning by force-feeding us "information" from external sources which we must be "motivated" to ingest and digest. (See Peter Vaill's "dump truck/teacher" analogy in the interview at the start of this section.) An alternative definition of learning is presented by **autognomics**, which means "self-knowing." Autognomics is an evolving science which describes the learning characteristics of autonomous systems (such as individual humans and organizations). Autognomics, which is described extensively in the following chapter, combines the biological concepts of **autopoiesis** (described by Maturana and Varela), the pragmatic philosophy and **semiotics** of Charles Sanders Pierce, and the mathematics of **axiology** (a scientific theory of value designed by Robert S. Hartman). According to autognomics, learning is not what results when we are spoon-fed our school lessons by our teachers; rather *learning is knowledge the system gains about itself via sensations that arise from its interaction with its environment.* Autognomics, then, reframes our understanding of learning, from an outward directed view of the world to an inward view of one's self. It differs from the traditional definition of learning: we do not perceive what is out there, but rather we meet what is outside us with who we are (our current ideas and values and interests), thereby choosing and filtering our perceptions.

Autognomics contends that perception is not a "rational" process where we take in what is objectively out there, but rather a mix of the following three dimensions by which autonomous systems (for example, you or I) interact with and make judgments about their environments: these are **intrinsic**, **extrinsic**, and **systemic** "valuing" of our selves and our world. Unfortunately, most traditional teaching proceeds backwards from (or remains fixed at) the third or systemic level. In contrast, all autonomous systems learn best when they follow this natural learning process:

1 Start with intrinsic valuing (the experience of the individual, what is of value to that person);
2 Then move to extrinsic valuing (events repeat so that something is noticed, judged by the individual for its qualities, e.g., as being good or bad);
3 Then form a "system" or law of thought, a generalization or extrapolation, which allows that individual to predict what ought to happen under a similar set of circumstances.

Autognomics argues that a mix of these valuings is necessary for optimum learning and that, based on pragmatic usefulness, a mix of these three valuings could constantly shift. If we stay at the first (intrinsic) level, no knowledge is ever accumulated that would allow us to benefit from our experience. However at the third level, our knowledge becomes static, fixed in a certain mental model, quickly obsolete in a rapidly changing world. Hartman's work argues that the priority of valuation must be intrinsic first, extrinsic second, and systemic third, particularly when dealing with living things – and that only then can they evolve into their full potential. Moreover, autognomics theory and the heroic model would agree that such valuing of the self is an excellent strategy for individual and organizational success; that is, when individuals start their learning process from the intrinsic dimension, they are likely to be more completely and fully "themselves," they bring all their talents and abilities to the table. Morever, the leaders who allow and encourage such learning are likely to witness an increase in workplace creativity, autonomy, diversity, tolerance, and harmony.

It is important to note that as the world changes faster, concepts (extrinsic) and laws (systemic) become obsolete faster. Indeed, autognomics challenges any form of organizational "systems thinking" to make certain no theory and accompanying intervention is applied before discovering that organization's values; a process which requires becoming increasingly conscious of hidden aspects of the organization (such as organizational culture) which need to be involved in the learning process.

Intrinsic valuing, then, is the "core" from which all learning must proceed. Accordingly, the learning leader(s) and organization(s) will increasingly need to shift their value mix so that they first attend to the often-ignored intrinsic dimension. Leaders need to continually ask questions of themselves and others: "What do *I* believe about this matter?" "What do *I* really want?" "What is important to *me* in this matter?" "What is *my* personal experience?" At first glance it may appear that autognomics could foster a self-centered attitude and promote a selfish way of being. However, we would argue that by asking such questions, leaders are actually engaging in "selfishly altruistic" behavior – helping the group survive by making certain they and their organizations bring into consciousness what is true and real and important to them personally. They are being "grown-ups" who assume full responsibility for their actions. This vigilant self-awareness will also keep leaders from making the occasionally fatal mistake of acting against what their "gut" tells them and instead accepting what some well-credentialed "expert" (in a particular school of systemic thought) says is true.

Starting the learning process with intrinsic valuing translates behaviorally to leaders operating from the immediacy of their own experience, moving into and through the world based on what they personally *feel* to be true, what they want to learn, what they themselves see, hear, and touch rather than settling for the opinions of external sources. In organizations it would mean that people would be empowered so they could develop pride in their work via intrinsically motivated activity rather than be pressured to "fit in" to prescribed definitions of what is a "good employee" or a "good job." According to Skye Hirst, cofounder of the Autognomics Institute, the problem with learning any other way is that we get "hog-tied" with the "*H*ave to, *O*ught to, and *G*ot to" prescriptions that are external to us. Over time we lose our internal compass, the source of our power and energy; we forget our dreams and who we are. If we continue on that course we will become partial beings: automatons who work nine-to-five, who do what we're told, but who have no sense of what's real for us, no love of learning. No adventure. No joy.

> On the vigil of Pentecost, the knights and ladies of Camelot were gathered together when they suddenly heard a loud thunderclap and were visited by a blindly bright light and presence of the Holy Spirit. As they sat there – dumbstruck – the Holy Grail appeared in their midst.
>
> When the Grail finally disappeared, all the knights agreed to take a vow to seek the Grail and bring it back to Camelot. However, because the knights believed that it would be a disgrace to go forth in a group, each knight determined to enter the forest at a point that he, himself, had chosen, where it was dark and there was no path.[9]

The lesson from this most famous of Western myths is the same lesson of the modern science of autognomics: to find your best self, you must choose your own path of learning. *Indeed, autognomics encourages us to dig up what society, including our learning institutions, has encouraged us to bury – our unique identity, and with it our unique learning potential.* In *Heroes at Work*, Seivert and Pearson argue that whereas in the past our cross-cultural stories allowed only for the most brave and lucky to become heroes (the one lone gunman riding into town who saves the day for all the helpless, but grateful townsfolk), now our problems are so complex that it is time for *all* of us to discover and contribute our special gifts to our desperately in-need organizations and societies.[10] In a way, our organizational and social problems are like big puzzles, with all of us holding a small, but unique – and perhaps critical – piece of that puzzle. To the degree that we take charge of our own lives and learning, our organizations too will be infused with new life and learning. Autognomics, then, this esoteric blend of several new sciences, recalls an ancient map which leads to learning that matters, to learning that sticks, and to learning that brings with it a personal sense of aliveness, joy in our work, and strong vital leadership for coherent, well-integrated organizational action.

We will now examine a model of human systems learning which describes multiple "levels" of potential learning. These levels start at the most conscious and move into increasingly unconscious levels. It is our contention that accessing these deeper levels, bringing them into consciousness, is necessary for lasting learning.

Levels of Learning: The Conscious and Unconscious in Individuals and Organizations

There are many levels at which a "human system" (an individual, a department, an organization, a community group or society) can learn. The following conceptual framework can help a leader not only understand human systems development but also clarify the "levels" of learning that are required for personal, professional, or organizational changes to occur and *be sustained*. Unfortunately, too many personal change efforts or organizational interventions are more disruptive than effective – the learning doesn't take, it doesn't last, the old behaviors and problems soon recur. Why? We would argue that the learning did not take place at the deeper, less visible levels of the entity.

I (Sharon Seivert) remember very clearly one fine summer morning when my father asked me to dig up a dandelion in our front lawn. If we mowed over the dandelion, he said, we would simply cut it off at the top – then it would not only grow again from the root, but we would have unwittingly spread its many seeds elsewhere. If we jerked the root up suddenly, we would get only part of it and it would sprout again sometime later. For lasting change, if we wanted to be rid of the dandelion for once and for all, we would need to remove its entire root. Intrigued, I began to dig a small circle in the soil around the plant. I dug and dug for the root, impressed and discouraged by its depth. Finally my search was rewarded, and I pulled the dandelion, with the last of its long, persistent root, completely out of the ground.

We see too many leaders today "mowing over" organizational problems that have deep roots, problems which sometimes penetrate all the organizational levels we are about to discuss. Many leaders become frustrated with improvement efforts because they sense they are throwing good money after bad, wasting their own and everyone else's time. And indeed, they often are. We hope the multidimensional framework for human systems development (figure 12.2) which we present here can be of help. This framework, from a model by Alex Pattakos, integrates six key levels of human systems: environment, behaviors, capacities, values/beliefs, identity, and spirit. It is our thesis then, that for lasting learning to take place, it must somehow reach to, then emanate from, the (often unconscious) levels of the human system.

Environment refers to those aspects or elements of a human system that are external to, and provide the operational context for, the entity. Leaders and organizations are usually quite aware of their environments, which is probably why change efforts tend to be first directed here. Such efforts could include "restructuring" the organization – moving around people, furniture, offices. Often, however, such activity gives the appearance of change more than the substance. Improvement efforts directed at the environment tend to be short-lived. These are often quick-fix interventions – cases which prove the adage "things change in order to stay the same." Since this is the level of the entity where change is most readily accepted and easy to do, human systems unfortunately are predisposed to seek modifications in their operating environments without probing more deeply into themselves – much as we individuals first try to hide those few extra pounds under loose-fitting clothes rather than modifying

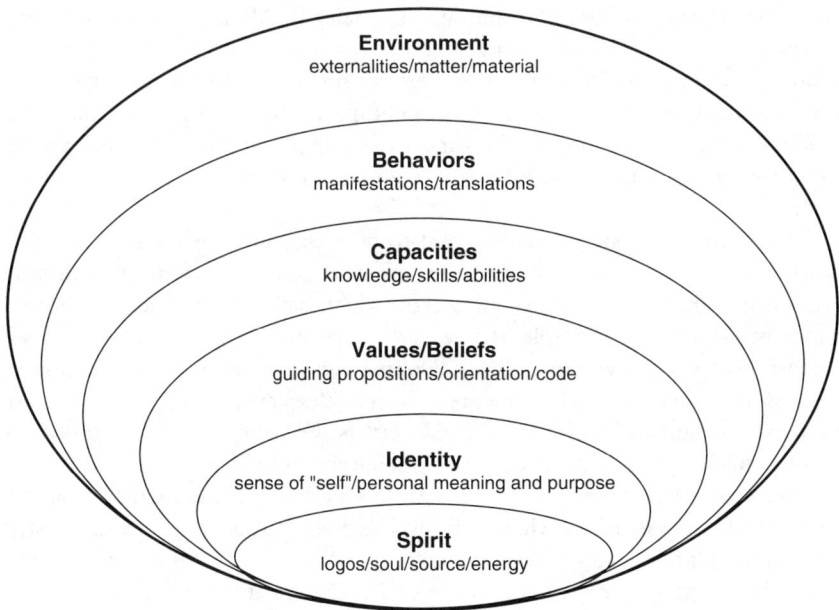

Figure 12.2 A framework for human systems development.

the health habits which caused – and will continue to exacerbate – the root problem.

Behaviors are another level of the organization which is quite visible: for example, it includes how members of the organization treat each other and their customers, what they say on or off the record about the company and its product(s), in short their actions, interactions, communication patterns, inactions, and interpretations of established rules of conduct. Real learning at this level would result in enduring behavior modification, which is why so many change efforts are directed at this level of the organization, for example, instituting incentive or reward systems, or moving to pay-for-performance. And, such carrot-and-stick approaches definitely can change things – at least for a while. However, behavior modification strategies typically still leave intact operating conditions and other causal factors for the original behavior. In organizations under significant stress, leaders sometimes motivate, reward, or threaten their employees into behaviors that increase productivity temporarily. However, if new behaviors do not arise from deeper learning, they will soon dissipate into dysfunctional "accommodations" (for example, finding short cuts), or the old behaviors will simply return once the heat is off.

Capacities are the knowledge, skills, abilities, and aptitudes associated with performance. This too is a visible, easily accessible level for organizational change efforts and learning. Organizations tend to focus their training and development or continuous improvement efforts at this level, in order to build their performance capacity in some way: for example, training a new work team in Statistical Process Control techniques. Capacity-building, in this sense, refers to an entity's *ability* to act, to manage its resources so it attains its goals, to monitor and evaluate its performance against predetermined measures of success. Besides the ability to act, the notion of capacity also involves the *willingness* to act. Whether or not an individual or organizational entity is willing to learn or do something is determined by the next dimension in the framework: values/ beliefs.

Our **beliefs** are the things we hold to be true, our convictions about the world and how it operates. Our **values** are a set of beliefs about what things, what behaviors are of more or less worth, which have a higher versus a lower inherent value.[11] For example, if I *believe* that people should always put in an honest day's work, I will most likely live that *value* and appreciate it in others. Therefore, although not the same, beliefs and values are intertwined in human systems learning and will be discussed here as the next level. Clarification of values and beliefs is not an easy task for either individuals or collectivities. Indeed, it is much easier for an entity to focus attention and resources on the previous three dimensions which this level directly (but usually unconsciously) influences. Unfortunately, lasting change is unlikely unless an entity's beliefs and values support, rather than sabotage, that change at that time.

The importance of values to organizational development and the craft of leadership has been the subject of much recent management literature (for example, Stephen R. Covey's best-selling *Principle-Centered Leadership*). After examining value systems from a broad, cross-cultural perspective, S. K. Chakraborty of the Indian Institute of Management in Calcutta concluded that ". . . ethics and values, therefore, must remain at the centre of our concern for human response development."[12] Noting that emotion is the motive power behind intellect, he quotes Albert Einstein who once declared that "the intellect has a sharp eye for methods and tools [capacities], but is *blind to ends and values*."[13] It is no wonder then that raw intellect and knowledge by themselves prove so inadequate to affect significant personal or organizational change. For example, although I may know I need to exercise more, and although I have the capacity (proper motor skills and maybe even a brand new home Nautilus), I just won't be able to make it happen until I summon up, from deeper inside me, the emotional charge for motivation.

The relationship between the level of values/beliefs and the next level of an entity – its **identity** – is strong and direct. When we examine our values and beliefs, we are following Socrates' advice to "know thyself," and we can begin to get some sense, an outline, of who we are. Identity is the "essential character" of an entity. It is what makes one person or organization inherently different from another. In much the same way that each of us has a sense of "who I am" and how we are different from and similar to each other, we can also discover the identity or character of an organization – the "who we are" together.

Indeed, an entity's sense of self largely determines how the above dimensions in our human systems framework manifest themselves. The more secure an entity is with its identity, the more likely it will be able to accept the challenges of growth and change with confidence and be successful. Unfortunately, "identity crises" are common to both people and organizations – largely because we do not have a strong sense of our selves, of who we are. An organization's identity, for example, may be defined or perceived differently by its various managers, workers, and customers. Integrating these differing perspectives into a coherent, high-functioning *whole* becomes a learning challenge for everyone involved. Often this task is made all the more difficult due to the complexity, fragmentation, and fluidity of our work and personal lives. Hence Professor Stanley Deetz's statement that "identity production may well be the most important product of most companies."[14]

S. K. Chakraborty identifies two layers of the human personality that, according to Indian psychology, comprise the essence of identity or "self": the empirical, surface self, or *vyavaharika vyaktitwa*; and the transempirical, deeper self, or *parmarthika vyaktitwa*.[15] The former is the same as the secular or material self (the personality which distinguishes us from others) and the latter is the same as the spiritual self.

Learning from the Core

A spiritual self? The hotly debated concept of spirit enters our discussion now because each individual identity must be realized in the context of a larger, connected whole. We do not live our lives or do our work in isolation. **Spirit** or **soul**, then, is that common essence which connects us all. Learning from the core, as we define it here, requires that we also learn at the spirit or soul level. Soul is defined in *Webster's Collegiate Dictionary* as the animating principle or cause of life, the immaterial essence, and also as spiritual and moral force. Spirit is defined as the animating life principle, the soul, as well as courage and the ability to withstand threat. For the purposes of this chapter, we will use the two terms interchangeably.

Many leaders would argue that there is no such thing as spirit or soul, or that the topic is not relevant to organizational learning. Indeed, learning from the identity level would make a vast improvement in the organizational learning efforts we have seen, and any leaders who choose to end their learning quest here would still be well rewarded for their efforts. However, other learning theorists – and sages throughout the millennia – hold that deeper learning is possible. Indeed, although the heroic quest for self-discovery is often sparked initially by search for one's unique identity, continuing that journey inevitably results in learning about spirit, soul, our essence – the ways we are profoundly *connected*. We urge leaders to consider this one more step in the learning process because we believe that it is this most fundamental level that is the *source* of all learning: Spirit is the "witness" who is actually doing the valuing, examining the beliefs, acquiring new skills, and delineating an identity – in short, the core of us which is actually doing the learning.

Spirit or soul, by definition, is that which cannot be touched by the physical senses. This makes the topic incredibly difficult to deal with "rationally." Despite its inherently elusive and unprovable quality, the discussion of spirit in the workplace has grown dramatically in recent years. Why? We believe it is because so many people are experiencing their workplaces as increasingly stressful and lifeless. In response to this widespread dispiriting phenomenon, a flood of recent management books have appeared suggesting that we can bring vitality, life, and order to such "wastelands" with a new management paradigm – one filled with *heart* and *soul*. (See for example: Tom Chappell's *The Soul of a Business*, Matthew Fox's *The Reinvention of Work*, J. Hawley's *Reawakening the Spirit at Work* and Pearson/Seivert's *Magic at Work: Camelot, Creative Leadership, and Everyday Miracles*.)

Michael Ray of the Stanford Business school writes of this emerging management paradigm: "The gateway from the old paradigm to the new is the individual, and changes in the individual come from the inside, from inner consciousness or spirit," adding that spirituality in this context does not refer to religion but rather to the "power of inner wisdom and authority and the connection and wholeness in humanity."[16] And Lawrence Miller states that we are "lucky to be living in an age" when management is rediscovering its soul: which he defines as "a 'good,' higher in scope and priority than any short-term decision or action, which exerts overriding influence on all actions . . ."[17]

Learning on a spiritual level has important implications for organizational learning. We find that people on quality work teams we've trained describe the experience as being one of the best of their work lives: they accomplished so much, they broke down personal and departmental barriers, and they thoroughly enjoyed the process of working together, of getting to know and trust their teammates. They sometimes describe the work team experience as feeling that they had became a part of something that was significantly greater than themselves. Peter Senge uses the Greek word *metonoia* ("shift of mind") to describe the essence of this "great team" experience which he felt was critical to forming learning organizations.

> For the Greeks, it meant a fundamental shift or change, or more literally transcendence ("meta" – above or beyond, as in "metaphysics") of mind ("noia," from the root "nous," of mind). In the early (Gnostic) Christian tradition, it took on a special meaning of awakening shared intuition and direct knowing of the highest, of God. . . . To grasp the meaning of "metanoia" is to grasp the deeper meaning of "learning" for learning also involves a fundamental shift of movement of mind. . . . Real learning gets to the heart of what it means to be human. Through learning we re-create ourselves. . . . Through learning we extend our capacity to create, to be part of the generative process of life. . . . This then, is the basic meaning of a "learning organization" – an organization that is continually expanding its capacity to create its future.[18]

Senge also defines another word which is critical to collective learning: **dialogue**. Senge distinguishes dialogue from discussion, suggesting that the former is a necessary condition for team learning to take place. Senge notes that the word "dialogue" comes from the Greek *dialogos*, which is made up of the root words *dia* ("through") and *logos* (roughly translated as "the meaning"). In dialogue, he says, a group accesses a "larger pool of common meaning," which cannot be accessed individually.[19]

However, it is interesting to note that the root *logos* is also commonly used in the original Greek to mean *spirit* – which significantly alters the above translation of dialogue and comes closer to what we believe is the truth of people's deepest learning experiences – that they need to "pass through spirit." The Jewish philosopher Philo of Alexandria suggested that logos is the "highest idea of God that human beings can attain . . . higher than a way of thinking, more precious than anything that is merely thought."[20] For Philo, the logos was divine; it was the source of energy from which the human soul became manifest. Karen Armstrong notes that St John had made it clear that Jesus was the Logos and, moreover, that the Logos was God.[21]

Interpreting logos as a manifestation of spirit or soul carries with it significant implications, both conceptual and practical, for organizational learning. Clearly, it suggests that dialogue is much more than "collective thinking" – often an all-too-cerebral process which stops short of fully engaging the participants. The process of dialogue enables individuals to experience that they are connected – either through common meaning or common spirit, or both; that each of us is part of a great whole. Becoming more conscious of the spirit of a human system will foster dialogue which, in turn, will result in learning from the core. In this way, learning can be organic, congruent, and thoroughly integrated system-wide, rippling naturally from this deep and central place into and throughout every level of the entity. Moreover, learning from the soul level can significantly reduce the debilitating stress, alienation, fragmentation, and malaise currently associated with work today. To personally experience that we are connected in profound ways to each other and the world around us is most comforting and liberating. Moreover, this realization tends to spontaneously give rise to heroic leadership, because all the little fears and anxieties that otherwise bedevil us seem small in comparison to the hugeness of spirit.

The Case for Organizational Consciousness

We have just defined human systems (individual and organizational) as consisting of multiple levels, some of which we tend to be more aware of than others. In this section we will present arguments that effective organizational learning will occur to the degree that an organization is conscious of itself, the degree to which its normally submerged levels are examined, understood, and known to itself. We begin this part of our discussion then by asking: Do organizations have a consciousness which is separate from their members? And, from a slightly different perspective: How can organizations learn if they do *not* have a consciousness?

As esoteric as the topic of "organizational consciousness" appears at first blush, it has some real-life, practical applications for effective organizational learning and change efforts. In *The Age of Unreason*, Charles Handy argues that the rate of change is speeding up so much it has now become "discontinuous."[22] As such unpredictable external forces act on organizations, their long-term viability will increasingly be dependent upon an internally generated stability which can only come from a core consciousness of itself. In this section we will borrow upon the wisdom of great minds who have tackled the definition of the individual and collective consciousness and unconsciousness.

The case for organizational consciousness has been made by biologists Maturana and Varela. In *The Tree of Knowledge* they describe human social systems, such as our workplaces, as **metasystems**. In other biological organisms, such as animals or plants, the components of that organism have maximum dependence on it (my finger does not have a life apart from me). Human social systems, however, are "metasystems of components with maximum autonomy, i.e. components with many dimensions of independent existence."[23] I definitely "have a life" apart from work; moreover I can move from one metasystem to another. These human metasystems – our organizations, our societies – clearly also "have a life" apart from me. And, according to Maturana and Varela, it is a life which is capable of generating a new phenomenon: its own mind and consciousness.[24] We argue here that metasystems such as organizations can grow into an awareness of their separate consciousness, much as we individuals do as we grow up. At a certain age, small children who look in a mirror will think they see another child. Later, however, those children realize that the mirror is not someone else, and not themselves, but rather a reflection of them. This is an evolved form of "self-consciousness." Similarly an organization can clearly differentiate itself from another and it can articulate those differences. For example, when engaged by good leadership it can clearly describe its environment, behaviors, capacities, values and beliefs, cultural identity – and, in some cases, it can eloquently describe its soul. Upon examining itself and looking at other organizations, it can determine in what ways it prefers the way it is and in which ways it might like to be more similar to the others. It knows its boundaries, who is within and outside it, and who is fully or only partially functioning within it. These are all manifestations of organizational consciousness.

Looking back at Jung's definition of the human psyche, we will now put forth the argument that organizations have many, if not all, of the above aspects of the individual human psyche. The organizational metasystem appears to have the above described aspects of consciousness: for example, its components act collectively in both rational/directed and irrational/instinctive ways. It thinks objectively, and it has feelings as a system (any leader who does not believe this probably is not paying sufficient attention to "employee morale"). And interestingly, an organization can even fantasize and figuratively "dream" about its future and about solutions to current problems (via techniques such as organizational brainstorming, visioning, future search activities, and dialogue).

We believe that organizations have both a personal and collective unconscious. The organization's personal unconscious can be accessed by paying attention to organizational memory. Indeed, in the crush of doing daily business, organizations all too readily forget even recent history and repeat the same – often very costly – mistakes. The organizational learning provided by deliberately accessing the organization's "personal unconscious" would have significant and immediate pay-off.

The collective unconscious of an organizational psyche has potentially extraordinary implications for organizational learning. Obviously, the great advantage to accessing what we already collectively know is that it is a very fast, efficient way to learn. However, we have to be quiet long enough to call up treasures from the deep parts of us, to dialogue internally with ourselves or externally with others, thereby accessing this deep pool of common meaning/spirit. Accessing the metasystem's and individuals' collective unconscious is potentially a breakthrough process for organizational learning. Indeed, it may explain why the process of dialogue is so exciting. The question then presents itself: Is the key to organizational learning that we bring the collective *unconscious* increasingly into our collective *consciousness*? We believe that the answer is "yes" – and that the implications for leaders are staggering. However, before we discuss tools for leaders who wish to bring the collective unconscious into their organizational consciousness, we will first add the perspectives of other sciences to the argument for organizational and collective consciousness.

Learning, the Collective Unconsciousness, and the Hologram

Jung's work on the collective unconscious is echoed in modern science's model of the hologram. A hologram is an image, a three-dimensional picture made with the aid of a laser, an illusion that looks absolutely like reality. The hologram has been used as a powerful metaphor by such great modern thinkers as neurophysiologist Karl Pribram and physicist David Bohm to explain previously inexplicable phenomena in their respective fields. Pribram used the hologram to answer the question of how specific memories could be stored throughout our whole brains. Pribram found that, much as the entire holographic image remains whole no matter how many times it is divided, human memory was similarly whole, and that surgically removing even large portions of a brain did not erase an individual's memory.

David Bohm began his landmark work by observing that individual electrons, once they were in plasma, "stopped behaving like individuals and started behaving as if they were part of a larger and interconnected whole."[25] (Certainly this is an organizational ideal for which many leaders strive!) Bohm's research drew the attention and support of Einstein; both believed that quantum physics theory was incomplete. Later Bohm came upon the metaphor of the hologram, which he used as a tool for explaining both the explicit and implicit order which exists in the Universe. In his master work *Wholeness and the Implicate Order*,[26] Bohm asserted that there is a constant, flowing, dynamic exchange ("holomovement") between the tangible reality of our daily lives (the explicit, unfolded order) and a deeper, unseen level of reality (the implicate, "enfolded" order). Bohm argued that *everything* is connected into a seamless holographic fabric – no matter how separate and distinct things or people appear.

Fortunately, holographic theory allows that we as individuals are not indistinguishable parts of an undifferentiated universal soup – obviously we still have our own unique identities and other qualities. However, as Michael Talbot claims in *The Holographic Universe*, we get into trouble when we ignore "the dynamic interconnectedness of all things"; that is, our fragmentation and insistence on separateness is responsible for our inability to solve systemic, organizational, and societal problems. According to Bohm, consciousness and matter are not really separate; consciousness is present to some degree in all matter, and therefore ". . . just as every portion of a hologram contains the image of the whole, every portion of the universe enfolds the whole."[27]

Holographic theory, then, would argue that all individuals in an organization carry and reflect every aspect of it, much as every cell in the human body contains the same DNA code for that whole body, and much as we each have access to a wealth of understanding in the collective unconscious. Hence many organizational leaders and consultants now argue that random interviews throughout an organization (for example, of a receptionist at the front desk or an RN in the cardiac unit), give at least as accurate an image or picture of the organization as would interviewing a vice president. In most organizations the top executives write up vision, values, and mission statements and then pass them down through the organization. However, to quote Duke Ellington, "It don't mean a thing if it ain't got that swing." Unless members at all levels of the organization can easily paraphrase the meaning of these statements, they are not part of the organization's consciousness – and nobody is going to be dancing to that tune.

Bohm's work on the interconnectedness of all things provides an explanation for how individuals within an organization can be interconnected and how we can be connected to our organization. The hologram therefore provides a modern scientific theory for the linkages that occur between and within individuals in human systems. As Bohm stated: "Deep down the consciousness of mankind is one."[28]

The Many in One: Tools for Making Leaders and Organizations More Conscious

We believe that the primary task of heroic leaders is to make themselves, those they supervise, and their organizations, more conscious. What individuals in organizations and work teams may first become aware of, as they evolve consciously, are the ways they are very different from each other. Autognomics theorists argue that in a creative universe, diversity is the only reliable strategy; that if the intrinsic dimension takes precedence in learning, then people come to value their own uniqueness. Fortunately, a part of this same process is that they also learn to value others. In this way a respectful diversity is possible: I can value you as a person (your intrinsic self) while still not valuing any of your particular beliefs (which are extrinsic or systemic-based). Unfortunately, in any relationship or organization where the intrinsic learning dimension is devalued, extrinsic or systemic-based differences among people are emphasized, leading to less interesting individuals and more serious division among them.

All the theories we've been discussing in this chapter converge to agree that the organization will prosper from this form of individual learning; that is, that it leads to an increasing *organizational* "value," where the organization itself becomes worth more due to the increased diversity, harmony, and autonomy of its members.

We will now examine some tools by which leaders can move themselves and their organization into increasing consciousness. First we will focus on organizational culture, as much of what we have previously discussed as being invisible and unconscious in an organization is encoded in its culture. These would

include its values/beliefs, and its identity. As we define it here, other aspects of
an organization – such as the more readily observable environment, behaviors,
and capacities – are organic outcomes, surface reflections of its culture. (Organizational culture in turn is a reflection of the deeper level of its core spirit or soul.)
Edgar Schein defines organizational culture as:

> A pattern of basic assumptions – invented, discovered, or developed by a given
> group as it learns to cope with its problems of external adaptation and internal
> integration – that has worked well enough to be considered valid and, therefore, to
> be taught to new members as the correct way to perceive, think, and feel in relation
> to those problems.[29]

Similarly, Maturana and Varela define human system culture as behavioral
patterns which have been stable through generations. Although similar to other
learned behavior, they say that "it is peculiar in that it arises as a consequence of
social living over many generations while its members are continuously
replaced."[30]

When societal or organizational culture is unconscious, people inside those
systems believe that this is the way the world is – therefore there is neither
reason for, nor hope for, change. This is ethnocentricity, a virulent type of
learning disability. This is why, when asked about a "learning agenda" for
executives, Peter Vaill puts intercultural learning at the *top* of his list. He says in
his interview with David Fearon that in opening up to other cultures people
become able to see intrinsic validity in the way they do things, not someone
being right or wrong. People are so unaware of themselves as a cultural expression, they think that everyone is a variation of them. Managers need to learn how
to lift themselves out of everyday consciousness of their own culture, and
discover ways of doing things differently. This results in what Vaill calls "cultural synergy."

There are many approaches to making organizations conscious of their cultures, a few of which are listed here. For example, the *Hartman Value Profile*,
developed by Robert S. Hartman, can help leaders examine their own and their
organizations' intrinsic, extrinsic and systemic values. The *Organization Beliefs
Indicator Process* (by Beliefs Partners) surfaces unconscious organizational beliefs, and then helps the organization determine and address areas of blockage.
The Organizational Culture Index (Seivert) defines ten different kinds of organizational cultures which are based on ancient archetypal, cross-cultural human
patterns. Such easily recognizable patterns draw on the collective unconscious
and provide a nonjudgmental language for real dialogue, for learning about
ourselves and the cultures within which we live and work. All the above instruments are helpful as tools which gives leaders and members of an organization
insights into their own organization's culture while inviting them, as Peter Vaill
suggests, to examine other cultural possibilities and break out of their ethnocen-

tricity. For example, people are often surprised to see how very differently various cultures might respond to the same set of circumstances. In the example given below, ten organizations are all threatened with significant market share loss by a strong new competitor whose impact on them was not anticipated. Interestingly, each culture is likely to react quite differently to this same stimulus. The cultural archetypes here are based upon ten "pure" types from the *Organizational Culture Index*.

Organizational cultural archetype	What organizations with different cultures are likely to "learn" from the same situation. Their beliefs/values which are reinforced and resulting behaviors
Innocent	Primary belief is that the world is a safe place, therefore any major disruption leads to puzzlement and shock. How could this happen to us? Reaction is to personally approach customers who have left/could leave and play on their loyalty, circle the wagons as much as possible. Learning is that things which they thought were perfect, are not; or deny that things are as bad as some say, play down or ignore the problem.
Orphan	Belief that it's a dog-eat-dog world is reinforced. Strategy is likely to be to attack in kind on any possible front. Immediacy is strongly felt, as organizational survival is believed to be at stake. Behavior tends to be to respond quickly one way; then, if that doesn't work, try another; and if that doesn't produce quick results, flail. All this activity could be accompanied by an attitude of "woe is me."
Seeker	Belief is that serious questions need to be asked; you may not be on right track, may need to set out in a different direction. Learning includes curiosity about how you and competitor are distinct. What exactly makes them a force? Learning is around clarification of your uniqueness. Behavior is to advertise that uniqueness or maverick quality, and play upon potential customer's seeking for something better.
Jester	Belief is that competition is a game, this is a new challenge, and it's fun to try to outwit opponents. Learning comes while trying to change the game itself or beat them at their own game. Behavior is to respond with a barrage of inventiveness and even more innovation (the better,

faster, cheaper mousetrap approach), or sometimes trickery (humorous tactics or making fun of opponents) in order to recapture market.

Caregiver   Belief is that clients must be served, they need *your* help, *you* care the most about them and their welfare. Organization evidences sincere concern about how loss of market will affect current clients (the competitor will just take their money and run), and also for staff members who are laboring under increasingly difficult circumstances. Learning is that even more sacrifices may have to be made.

Warrior   Belief is that the marketplace is a battleground, where you are engaged in warfare and only the strongest survive. The barbarians are at the gate. Questions asked will be: why didn't we know about this attack sooner? Who fell asleep at the watch? Learning is that we need to work harder, faster, and better; we must rise to this challenge. Behavior is likely to be a strategically timed attack at heart of the enemy.

Magician   Belief is that learning is the reason for life and that such problems are opportunities to improve organization, to grow and develop in new ways. "Welcome" situation as a mirror for the organization, a way to learn how to improve product/service. Behavior would include benchmarking with competition and others, dialoguing with internal and external individuals, doing an environmental scan, clarifying values, vision, and mission.

Ruler   Belief is that you are at top of industry and competitors are upstarts, interlopers who need to be put in their place. Behavior is to find out who in the organization needs to know what in order to not unduly alarm others while responding appropriately (not over or underrespond) to threat. Learning is to shore up territory you already have, and play on reputation and prestige to bring back wayward customers.

Lover   Belief is that your product or service and company are the best ever; that all you need to do is reach people with that message and they will be convinced because the product will speak for itself. Learning is to get the word out to more people about the meaning and real value of your product (in which you believe absolutely), and perhaps recontact current or wayward customers to remind or persuade them of the same.

Sage   Belief is that there is a logical answer to loss of market share and that studying the problem, analyzing the data, and making a new plan will remedy the situation. Learning is the need to get data, analyze it, make a plan and then act. Try to look at the issue from a detached perspective – perhaps receive feedback from customers who have left. Research overall picture of what is happening in industry/world markets.

All of the above-listed tools would assist leaders in their own and their organization's learning process by asking the questions necessary to bring the invisible aspects of an organization's culture to light so that change efforts will be tailored respectfully for that organization. Moreover, awareness of other cultures, including a variety of possible responses to the same situations (as demonstrated in the example above) allows the organization's leaders to start becoming more conscious of alternate ways of doing business.

All of the instruments listed above can also give individual leaders helpful insights in their own process of self-discovery. With the *Hartman Value Profile* and *Organizational Beliefs Indicator Process*, for example, leaders would have their own individual profiles of beliefs and values to examine. The *Organizational Culture Index* has a counterpart for the individual: the *Heroic Myth Index*, where individuals determine which archetypal heroic story dominates their lives now. The *Myers-Briggs Type Indicator* is the most widely used personality inventory in the world; it can give individuals great insights into their individual personalities, working, leading, and learning styles.[31] Because the MBTI so respectfully describes the different gifts of individuals, it is often used to improve working relationships in organizations. Indeed all of these instruments, and many others, can be used by leaders to promote dialogue and camaraderie in work teams.

In addition to the above tools, individual leaders have an infinite number of tools at their disposal to help them with their journey of self-discovery. Choose wherever you wish to enter "the woods." Some people start by getting reacquainted with the parts of themselves they've been too busy to acknowledge by taking a few moments of quiet time behind a closed door to listen to themselves, and watch the mind ramble. Write down whatever bubbles up. Try writing a journal every morning and/or writing down your dreams. Go to a bookstore, walk around, and see what catches your eye. Seek out a friend or colleague who seems to have some emotional or spiritual depth and have a quiet supper together. Take classes that intrigue you. Do something that is pure fun – just for the joy of it.

Leaders who find the above not to their tastes can use the help of more scientific techniques which are designed to help us reconnect with our deeper selves. For example, some companies have used a cybernetic bio-acoustic entrainment system known as GENESIS to help managers to break through old patterns of thought and behavior.[32] Leaders can also use applied kinesiology, a new science which calls up body wisdom which is often censored by the mind. It is amazingly simple to use (see exercise).[33]

Applied kinesiology's truth and lie detector test[34]

Touch your thumb to your first finger on your stronger hand, forming a small circle. Now place the thumb and first finger from your other hand inside that circle, so that they can act as a lever to push the other two fingers apart.

You can set up a very simple "yes/no" test in this way. For a yes answer, instruct the body to give muscle resistance so that the joined circle, thumb to finger, stays strong and does not come apart despite the pressure you put on it to push it open. For a "no" answer, instruct the body to weaken, relax and have the fingers come apart easily.

Now try your first quiz. "Give me a yes." Try to push the loop apart; it should stay strong. Then, "Give me a no." Again try to push your fingers loose; they should part easily. Try this a few times to make sure you have the hang of it. Then try your name. "My name is . . ." The response should be clear. Then you can move on to increasingly difficult questions – no essays here, always phrase your questions so that a simple yes/no answer from your "gut" is possible.

This is an easy truth or lie detector test, and a simple way to get to your intrinsic valuing of something. It is especially handy if it's been a long time since you've listened to your deeper self.

Summary and Conclusion

In this chapter we have woven together diverse theories – autognomics, heroic mythology, a model of human systems development, and modern science – to argue for "learning to the core," a process by which individual leaders and their organizations become increasingly conscious of normally unconscious aspects of themselves.

In this way, heroic leaders – like the noble knights of Camelot – can choose to take their own unique paths to find the very best of themselves and bring back the wealth of what they've learned from all their journeying, so that they and their workplaces can thrive. And to all you good readers who have come with us to this point: please take our best wishes with you as you continue your adventure of self-discovery. Here's wishing you grace and Godspeed.

Notes

1 Peter Senge in lecture at MIT, Cambridge, MA, January 1991.

2 Humberto Maturana and Francisco Varela, *The Tree of Knowledge, The Biological Roots of Human Understanding* (Boston: Shambala, 1987), p. 197.

3 Sharon Seivert and Carol S. Pearson, *Heroes at Work: Understanding and Transforming your Relationships, Work, and Self* (College Park, MD: Meristem Publishers, 1988).

4 Joseph Campbell (ed.), "The structure of the psyche" *The Portable Jung* (Reprint of Carl Gustav Jung's *The Structure and Dynamics of the Psyche. Collected Works*, vol. 8, 1930) (New York: Viking Press, 1971), pp. 25–27.

5 Campbell, *Portable Jung*, p. 44.

6 Marianne Williamson, *A Return to Love: Reflections on the Principles of A Course in Miracles* (New York: HarperCollins, 1992), p. 116.

7 Edgar H. Schein, *How Can Organizations Learn Faster?: The Problem of Entering the Green Room* (Cambridge, MA: MIT Sloan School of Management, 1992).

8 W. Edwards Deming's 14 points, "Obligations of Management," from M. Walton, *The Deming Management Method* (New York: Putnam, 1986), pp. 34–36.

9 Carol S. Pearson and Sharon Seivert, *Magic at Work: Camelot, Creative Leadership, and Everyday Miracles* (New York: Doubleday/Currency, 1995), from chapter 3: "The Call of the Grail".

10 Seivert and Pearson, *Heroes at Work*.

11 The common definition of "value" is used here rather than its autognomics definition as one of three ways autonomous systems interact with and make judgments about their environments.

12 S. K. Chakraborty, *Management by Values: Towards Cultural Congruence* (Oxford: Oxford University Press, 1991), p. 58.

13 Ibid., p. 47.

14 Stanley Deetz, *Transforming Communication: Transforming Business* (Cresskill, NJ: Hampton Press, 1995), p. 63.

15 Chakraborty, *Management by Values*, p. 65.

16 Michael L. Ray, "The emerging new paradigm in business", in J. Renesch (ed.), *New Traditions in Business: Spirit and Leadership in the 21st Century* (San Francisco: Berrett Koehler, 1992), pp. 29, 36.

17 Lawrence M. Miller, *American Spirit: Visions of a new Corporate Culture*, (New York: William Morrow & Company, 1984), p. 184.

18 Senge, *The Fifth Discipline*, pp. 13–14.

19 Ibid., pp. 240–1.

20 Karen Armstrong, *A History of God* (New York: Ballantine, 1993), p. 70.

21 Ibid., p. 109.

22 Charles Handy, *The Age of Unreason* (Boston: Harvard Business School Press, 1990).

23 Maturana and Varela. The Tree of Knowledge, p. 198.

24 Ibid., p. 223.

25 Michael Talbot, *The Holographic Universe* (New York: HarperPerennial, 1992), p. 38.

26 David Bohm, *Wholeness and the Implicate Order* (London: Routledge and Kegan Paul, 1980).

27 Talbot, *The Holographic Universe*, pp. 48–50.

28 Renee Weber, "The enfolding-unfolding universe: a conversation with David Bohm", in Ken Wilber (ed.), *The Holographic Paradigm* (Boulder, CO: New Science Library, 1982), p. 72.

29 Edgar H. Schein, *Organizational Culture and Leadership* (San Francisco: Jossey-Bass, 1985), p. 9.

30 Maturana and Varela, *The Tree of Knowledge*, p. 201.

31 For more information on the *Hartman Value Profile*, contact the Autognomics Institute, 32 Williams Avenue, Mystic, CT 06355.

   For more information on the *Organization Beliefs Indicator Process*, contact Beliefs Partners, c/o Dan Karney, 21 Robins Lane, Berwin, PA 19312.

   For more information on the *Organizational Culture Index*, contact GREAT WORK, 10 Magazine Street, #1004, Cambridge, MA 02139.

32 For more information on the *Heroic Myth Index*, contact GREAT WORK, 10 Magazine Street, #1004, Cambridge, MA 02139.

   For more information on the *Myers-Briggs Type Indicator*, contact Consulting Psychologists Press, 3803 E. Bayshore, Palo Alto, CA 94303.

33 GENESIS® is manufactured by Bio-Innergy Systems, Delaware, Ohio.

34 This applied kinesiology technique for self-discovery, and many others, are taught by Judith A. Swack and Associates, 400 Hillside Avenue, Needham, MA 02194; 617-444-6940. See also Judith Swack, "The basic structure of loss and violence trauma imprints," *Anchor Point Magazine*, March 1994.

13

The Implications of Autonomy for Learning in Organizations

Frederick Reed and Sharon Seivert

The cycle of the machine is now coming to an end. Man has learned much in the hard discipline and the shrewd, unflinching grasp of practical possibilities that the machine has provided in the last three centuries: but we can no more continue to live in the world of the machine than we could live successfully on the barren surface of the moon.

Lewis Mumford, The Culture of Cities

Introduction

Throughout this chapter we will argue that the modern cultural affection for machines does not provide a useful starting point for effective learning at the individual or organizational level. The resulting obsession with objective facts and what *ought to be* are actually roadblocks to learning since they stifle the diversity, creativity, and the freedom to explore alternate points of view that are essential to real development. We believe that only through a fundamental change of personal and cultural philosophy can the ideals associated with the notion of a "learning organization" be attained.

We will suggest that a more appropriate philosophy can be based on the essential features of autonomy, such as the theory of **autognomics** we will outline here. Only by emphasizing the essential features of autonomy, including intrinsic identity, the primacy of action, and the critical role of values, can we regain our full potential for learning and development. And, as part of the bargain, we may also regain some of the humanity that we lost in the era of the machine.

Say goodbye to the world-as-machine

Over the past several centuries, wondrous things have been achieved through the paradigm of the machine. In that time, humankind has created great machines: not only technological wonders such as the electron microscope and the space shuttle, but in organizations as well. Two hundred years ago, the idea that the activities of hundreds of thousands of individuals could be closely coordinated toward a single purpose would have seemed as fantastic as any modern technological marvel. Yet many current organizations, from multinational corporations to governmental agencies, do just that by using tenets of the machine paradigm, such as functional specialization and hierarchical control.

We have, in fact, learned and achieved much from the "practical possibilities" of the machine. Yet, there is also an increasing feeling that we have given up something important. Much has been made of the effect on the human spirit that our emphasis on the machine has had. We have given up much of our humanity to the cause of building bigger and more efficient organizational machines. No one is spared this toll. From top executives to manual laborers, everyone seems to be required to act less human, to be less fully themselves, to suit the needs of the organizational machine.

Organizations have also paid the price, inheriting both the strengths and weaknesses of the machine model. The one critical weakness we will discuss at length here is the *machine's inability to learn and change.* Just as one does not expect a printing press or steam turbine to modify itself to meet evolving conditions, one should also not expect an organization that emphasizes its machine-like character and efficiency to do so either. Moreover, the real world in which organizations and individuals must survive has stubbornly refused to act very machine-like, regardless of how much we force our paradigm on it. The very unmachine-like chaos of Nature, the unpredictability, complexity, uncontrollability, just plain *messiness* of the real world, has proven to be quite harsh on machines of all forms. As a result, one of the greatest threats to both modern organizations and individuals is obsolescence: failing to keep up with rapid changes in the world around them.

Due in large part to the success of our machine technology, the world in general is changing at an ever-increasing rate, aggravating our inability to learn and adapt. For individuals, the result is often unemployment and alienation that leads to calls for more and better job training and placement. For organizations, the resulting business failures and stagnation lead to calls for better use of information system technologies, more effective management controls, and other improvements. But in either case, these responses often originate in the same machine paradigm that contributed to the problem in the first place. And, as Albert Einstein said, "Problems cannot be solved by the same consciousness that created them." Machines, by their very nature, are not self-adapting or *autonomous.* Improving learning by building better machines is a futile strategy. It is only the deep-seated cultural affection for the machine model that keeps us unaware of this futility. We believe, however, that it is an awareness that is vitally important for our future survival.

Daedalus, of ancient Athens, was a great inventor and architect. King Minos of Crete commissioned him to construct the best maze the world had ever seen to house the horrific Minotaur, a monster with a bull's head and a man's body. Daedalus, a great intellect, was up to the challenge; he made a maze so complicated that no one could possibly find the way out. To appease the Minotaur the king fed him every year 14 young Athenians, seven men and seven women. These poor souls were thrown into the maze and left there to wander without hope until each was found and devoured by the monster.

At the urging of Minos's daughter Ariadne, Daedalus aided one of the youths, Prince Theseus, in killing the bull and escaping from the labyrinth. Furious, the king threw Daedalus with his son, Icarus, into the maze.

But Daedalus used his inventiveness to make wings for himself and his son. Together they flew from the labyrinth. Unfortunately, much to the grief of Daedalus, Icarus did not survive the journey – he flew too near the sun, then fell into the sea and drowned.

The myth of Daedalus illustrates a serious question for us today: We are a world of great inventors, but our inventions have a dual potential – for great benefit or great disaster. In truth, we, like Daedalus, have created the maze into which we have been thrown. We might survive what we have created – but will our children? And, what are we going to do? How are we going to use our great ability to learn and adapt in a way that improves their chances for survival?

Overview

We claim that the quality of learning we strive for cannot be achieved at the individual or organizational level without changes in philosophy. We need to become aware of the implications of our fundamental assumptions about people, organizations, and the world around us, so that we can act intelligently to better our future.

In order to elaborate on this assertion, we will require some new intellectual "tools" to help stake out a new perspective on learning and organizations. The primary tool we have in mind is a theory of autonomous systems called autognomics. Much of the chapter will be spent acquainting the reader with the basic principles of autognomics and the perspective it brings to understanding natural systems, including people and organizations.

We will then examine some consequences for learning to get a feel for the practical import of this new conceptual tool, and what it translates to for organizations, their members, and their leaders. In the process we hope to expose the crumbling foundation of rationalism that simply cannot support the weight of a true learning organization.

The Problem With the Machine Model

Of frogs and blocks and tables

By now, anyone with even the smallest interest in science and philosophy has been bombarded with claims of the coming of a "new science." The counter-intuitive findings of modern physics, such as the inherent uncertainty and observer-dependence of quantum mechanics, and the breakdown of "normal" space and time in the theory of relativity are probably the most well-known harbingers of this new science. Somewhat less well known is an ongoing revolution in the science of what might best be termed "living" systems. This revolution is currently being fought on the battlefields of epistemology (the philosophy of knowledge), cognitive science, psychology, and theoretical biology, among others. Its impact is being felt in a wide variety of applied domains such as computer science and its subfield artificial intelligence, medicine, social policy, and even in organizational management.

A key issue in this revolution is how we, or intelligent systems in general, come to know things. At present, nearly all of what is considered mainstream science and technology conforms to a single broad tradition that we will call **rationalism**. According to this tradition, information is about persistent *things* in an objective world. In this scheme, assertions such as "the block is on the table, I am in the doorway, frogs are green," and "you are reading this book" are, if true, information about the state of this objective world. Determining the truth of such assertions is a matter of comparing the assertion, say "the block is on the table," with some objective determination of whether the "real" block is on the "real" table. It is important to note that, according to this rationalist perspective, the truth of these assertions is completely independent of who is doing the determination and for what purpose. In other words, the *subject* (the system doing the observing) has been completely removed from the picture.

And so it should be, the rationalists claim. After all, if you are going to be rational, you can't allow your actions to be persuaded by subjective opinions that have no basis in objective truth. Consequently, in rationalism, intelligent systems such as humans and organizations are thought of as complex input–output mechanisms (in other words, *machines*) that take in information about the world through their senses (albeit, perhaps incompletely or inaccurately), compute appropriate responses based on this information, and then act accordingly. Acting on beliefs that are not grounded in objective information would be, well, irrational!

For example, assume that my purpose in life is to collect blocks. With my rationalist eyes, I take in visual inputs of information with which I construct an internal representation of the world that includes assertions such as "the block is on the table" and "I am in the doorway." From the information contained in this model, I am then able to calculate a path from my current position to the table. Finally, I walk along the calculated path and collect the block. For argument's sake, it is also possible that when I get there I might need information about frogs to distinguish the block I seek from any stray frogs that also might be on the table (perhaps I am collecting blocks at the zoo).

The downside of rationalism

On closer examination, however, such rational explanations of behavior lead to many philosophical as well as practical difficulties. These difficulties are perhaps most apparent in the field of artificial intelligence (AI), which attempts to convert general theories of knowledge, learning, and intelligence into explicit instructions to a computer system. For the most part, the AI community has relied on theories and technology born in the rationalist tradition to build systems that process information inputs and compute "intelligent" outputs. Clearly, if this scheme were even mildly successful, it would offer valuable insights into how to better organize "intelligent" organizations as well. Unfortunately, this has not been the case. AI, and in less obvious ways all forms of science and technology including management and organizational science, are beset by a number of intractable issues that arise from the fundamental beliefs of the rationalist tradition. These problems include the following:

- **Of the overwhelming possible information within the scope of perception, how does the system choose which information to attend to within the limits of processing power and time?** In the last example, did I add information about the color of the table, the kind of wood it was made from, the position of windows in the room, and so forth to my world model before I acted? Probably not, or else I might have been there all day getting my information. But how did I know what was an important input before I put it to use?
- **How do new objects and concepts arise in knowledge?** The assertion that "frogs are green" certainly seems like a fact whose truth is independent of the observer and time. But surely one can imagine that there must have been a time before frogs were "frogs," included in some more general grouping of "things-that-live-in-ponds." But if our senses are simply providing us information about things in the world, why would they not have immediately informed these ancient observers of frog-things and their green color? If the answer to this question has anything to do with some observer in the distant past "inventing" a frog-thing to be distinguished from the rest of the pond-dwellers, then a rather large crack has suddenly appeared in the foundation of rationalism: the *subject* has returned.
- **What guides the learning process?** Suppose I arrive at the table, only to find the block I sought, with no frogs to complicate the problem. After a few such occurrences, you might say I would "learn" that frogs do not often sit on tables with blocks. But, of course, I did not find any tigers, school buses, wheelbarrows, or an infinity of other things on these tables as well. Did I learn all this too? Not all of this information is useless to me. It is comforting to know that I can (usually) approach the table without taking precautions to prevent being mauled by wild animals or run over by large vehicles. But the rationalist idea that I learn by adding information to a mental model representation of some objectively defined world would seem to

require that I have to learn, thing by thing, what I can expect to *not* find on tables with blocks.

- **If the truth of knowledge is defined as its correspondence to the "real" state of the world, what objective means are available for determining such truth?** What do my eyes really tell me about the block on the table, and how do they enable me to ascertain the truth of the assertion that "the block is on the table"? If the truth of this assertion is solely determined by comparing it to the "real" situation, how do my eyes perform this comparison? Physiologically, my eyes simply convert photons into electrochemical nerve pulses. They have no way to "reach" beyond me and directly determine the "real" truth. If so, does this mean I have no reliable way of determining truth at all?

While rationalism offers no satisfactory resolution of the above issues, adherents to this tradition argue, as reported by Winograd and Flores, "that the only conceivable alternative is some kind of mysticism, religion, or fuzzy thinking that is a throwback to earlier stages of civilization."[1]

Au contraire! The rationalist tradition is actually the throwback to earlier stages of civilization. Its primary supposition, the existence of an independent objective world that causes our perceptions of it, is one that has been effectively criticized for over a century. Rationalism actually follows closely an ancient tendency to assume that other external agents (in the old days, demons and spirits) are behind what we personally experience. Relativity and quantum mechanics have conclusively shown that the notion of an objective world does not apply to the very small and very large aspects of our reality. In the middle ground of our everyday experience, where our common objects reside, the rational view of the world has until now remained entrenched. However, because of its emphasis on persistence, certainty, and objectivity, rationalism does not provide an effective foundation for learning and dealing with a complex and rapidly changing world. We have reached a point in human development where abandonment of the rationalist tradition is necessary if intelligent systems, from ourselves to our societies, are to survive and prosper.

In this chapter, we will consider an alternative learning model that may at first jar the reader's sensibilities, but will allow us to gain new insights on learning and organizational change. We should note, however, that no theory or framework for describing organizational learning can be absolutely and for all purposes the "right" one. Theories always are about something in *some* respect, and but not in *all* respects. Any theory will emphasize certain dimensions of reality and neglect others. For example, a traditional accounting model of an organization can usefully explain the current financial health of a company, but says nothing about the "intellectual capital" from which new products and services will arise to provide long-term viability. We are arguing here that rationalism is not unconditionally wrong, but rather that it has proven to be less than satisfactory as a basis for understanding the processes of learning and change.

A New Perspective on Learning: Autognomics

The alternative framework, or paradigm, that we will use in this chapter is called **autognomics**, which means "self-knowing." Autognomics is a synthesis of several threads of intellectual history and theories that have been overshadowed to date by the manifestations of rationalism. While unfamiliar to most people, these threads are not new or revolutionary. They and autognomics have been quietly developing and evolving over many years, hidden in the shadow of the more sensational discoveries and inventions of modern rationalist sciences and technology.

The essence of autonomy: autopoiesis

A good place to start in describing autognomics is with the essential differences between machines and **autonomous systems**. The theory of **autopoiesis**, most closely associated with Humberto Maturana and Francisco Varela, provides much of the insight for making these distinctions.[2]

Consider the act of design as it relates to a machine (a nonautonomous system.) When a person designs a machine, she or he decides how that system should respond to an environment as defined by the designer. The designer assumes that the machine will not respond to inputs that have not been provided for, and that the machine's responses will be guided by "laws" provided by the designer.

But what if there is no designer? Who decides what an *autonomous* system will respond to? How does an autonomous system know what external effects its actions will have? If a system is autonomous, it cannot inherently rely on outside sources for information. It must be capable on its own of determining its relationship to the surrounding environment – of creating its own information. And, if the environment changes, the autonomous system must be able to modify this relationship in a timely and effective manner, again, on its own.

These requirements for autonomy should not be underestimated. Their implications for fundamental concepts such as information, meaning, and learning are quite profound. Let's step for a moment completely out of our daily reality and the machine-paradigm that normally colors our understanding of it. Let's say that tomorrow, on your way to work – just hypothetically now – you are abducted by aliens and taken to live with them on their planet. However, because their environment is hostile to human life forms, your abductors put you in a windowless box that you cannot leave. All you have access to are some "meaningless" gadgets: lights, buttons, and levers that you can only assume are means of sensing and acting on the environment outside the box. You are an autonomous system in a strange new world. Assuming the aliens do not intervene, you will have to survive on your own, using only these gadgets. Clearly, any "meaning" you assign to the gadgets cannot be based on their correspondence to "things" outside your box, since there is no way for you to know what "things" are outside except through the gadgets themselves. The only reliable meaning you will be able to give to certain lights or buttons will be in terms of other lights and buttons. You might invent strange new forces and beasts to explain and organize the relationships between your sensations and actions, but these "things" are clearly of your own doing, they are not imposed on you from the outside as "information."

In principle, these are the same kind of challenges facing every real autonomous system, such as you and me, right here on planet Earth. And in a way our task is more difficult because we do not have any predefined set of status lights (sensations) or levers and buttons (ways to act on the world) provided for us. Clearly, the concepts appropriate to a designed machine (e.g., "inputs" and "information" about external "things") will not suffice as an explanation of how an autonomous system actually operates. In other words, an operational theory of autonomous systems cannot rely on designers and other omniscient helpers. Autopoiesis addresses these concerns by posing a radically different way of looking at such systems. One of its principal creators, Francisco Varela, acknowledged the disbelief that would greet his proposal:

> . . . almost every researcher in neuro-science will take as dogma that (1) the nervous system acts by picking up information from the environment and "processing" it, and that (2) this processing is adequate because there is a "representation" of the outside world in the animals (or human being's) mind. The brain is a machine to produce an accurate picture of the world, . . . the brain as computer is by now a common sense notion.
>
> Vis-à-vis this predominant opinion, it might seem arrogant to propose a viewpoint that is exactly the opposite, namely, that the nervous system operates as a closed network with no inputs or outputs, that its cognitive operation reflects only its organization, and that information is imposed on the environment, not picked up from it![3]

The main points of autopoiesis include the following assertions.

(1) **The identity of an autonomous system is a closed network of relations defining the *organization* of the system. These relations are manifest as physical processes, or *structure*, maintaining the relations called for in the organizational identity.**

An identity is what makes something distinct from all others and the surrounding environment. Clearly, you are you and I am me, and fortunately our identities keep us from getting confused on that point. But we must be careful in how we define identity for autonomous systems. In particular, we must be careful not to rely on an observer or reference to the environment, else we lose the essence of autonomy.

As a result, autopoiesis defines identity as a **closed network of relations** within the autonomous system. This network is closed in the sense that it has no defining relationships with anything outside of it. Thus, identity is defined independent of its surroundings and can be referenced completely from *within* the system. Consider the alternative. If one's identity were even partly defined in reference to some external condition, changes in this external condition would automatically alter one's identity: something completely unacceptable for an autonomous system.

The second element in our definition of identity employs the term **relations** to emphasize the non-*thingness* of identity. Identity is not determined by the structural components that might constitute the system at any particular time; rather, it is defined by the relations among these physical processes, their organization. Since the autonomous system must be able to change structurally as it grows and evolves, its identity cannot be based on its structure, or else its identity would be in a constant state of flux.

For example, a tree is the same tree whether it is a seedling or 100 feet tall. Its identity as that same tree is defined by the specific relationships between various metabolic and other processes that provide for food production, tissue growth, reproduction, and so on. And, most importantly, these relationships will differ from tree to tree, even within the same species. In other words, two trees that appear identical to outside observers will not grow exactly the same under the same conditions.

(2) **Autonomous systems adapt to maintain this network of relations (its identity) in the context of its enclosing environment.**

In other words, the system changes its structure to maintain and express its identity so as to continue its distinction from the background. Let's take the example of a tree in your front yard. If you decide to install a driveway, that tree will adapt when you pave the ground next to it by proportionately reducing the amount of roots and foliage on the affected side. What remains the same are those key relationships in its organization that ultimately define this particular tree in contrast to other trees or the environment itself.

(3) **Interactions with the environment are not inputs of information, but rather are potential disturbances, or perturbations, of the network of organizational processes.**

If a physical interaction has no effect on these essential processes, then it is of no consequence to the system. If the interaction does perturb the processes making up the organizational network, the system will respond according to a function of its own unique organization, not according to any objective "informational" content of the perturbation. If such perturbations are regular or persistent, the autonomous system will infer that there is something in its environment causing them. The world the system creates from organizing these distinctive perturbations is the system's **cognitive domain**. If, for example, the ambient temperature around our hypothetical tree were to change, and this change had no effect on the physical processes reflecting the key relationships in the tree's organization, then this change would not be a perturbation (i.e., it would not be "information"). On the other hand, if this change in temperature were to perturb the organizational processes, the tree would respond, if possible, by settling into a new state (for example by dropping leaves or inhibiting sap flow) that mitigated the effects of the perturbation while maintaining constant the key organizational relations. There is, of course, always the possibility that the system cannot adequately respond while maintaining the key organizational relations – for example, if you decided to cut down and dig out the tree in order to install a wider driveway, the tree's identity is lost.

(4)   **Learning, then, can be viewed as changes to the structure of the living system that allow it to continue to respond to environmental perturbations in such a way, if possible, as to successfully maintain its identity.**

Finally, we have a glimpse at a new perspective on learning. By altering its structure, and therefore the nature of environmental perturbations, the system can "learn" to more reliably maintain the critical relations in its organization which define its identity. In autopoietic terms, the system becomes **structurally coupled** to its environment in a way that maintains its identity. The system discovers a way to successfully relate to and exist within its environment. Suppose that a particularly "smart" tree in your yard detects new patterns in environmental perturbations (say the fall days get cooler much faster than they used to). More fantastically, it could then alter part of its structure into what we, as observers, would call a thermometer, particularly sensitive to kinds of environmental changes we as observers would call temperature changes. This new structural element could be further connected to other processes within the tree and possibly even a "memory" device for recording fluctuations (to be used, for example, in determining the rate of average temperature drop over the past month). As a result of this new structural coupling between the tree and its environment, it would be able to respond to changes in outside temperature in a more timely and effective manner for maintaining the key organizational relations, such as by preparing for winter more reliably than before.

Of course, we do not observe or speak of trees as "learning" this way, but rather through a process of natural selection over many generations of trees. "Intelligent" entities such as humans, on the other hand, have a nervous system whose structure is more rapidly alterable to support complex structural coupling changes based on personal experience.

Regardless, however, of how we might describe the behavior of the tree, there is no reason to believe that this hypothetical "intelligent" tree actually has any knowledge of a "thing" called temperature or a thermometer. Therefore, even though we might use the term "temperature information" to explain the tree's behavior in *our* cognitive domain, it is not appropriate to infer that the tree has as an "input" of information about temperature in *its* actual operation.

The value of autopoiesis for us is that it provides a sound starting point, as opposed to rationalism, for constructing more practical explanations of how complex autonomous systems learn and adapt. As shocking as it may sound, we are abandoning the notion of information as corresponding to the state of things in an objective world. With our new perspective, we redefine "information" as: "knowledge of the system about itself, its actions and the internal regularities that arise from its interaction with its environment." In short, we have turned information from an *outward* directed view of the world to an *inward* view of one's self.

Learning and autonomy: semiotics

While the theory of autopoiesis is able to provide fresh and important insights into individual and organizational learning, it was intended only to offer the minimum conditions under which true autonomy is possible. We will now build on this foundation what might be called a *symbolic* description of the processes by which an autonomous system actually couples with its environment, learning to act more effectively in maintaining and expressing its identity. In short the problem we will next address is how the system structurally changes to more successfully express its identity. For this, autognomics relies on the theory of semiotics proposed by Charles Sanders Peirce (pronounced "purse"), the American logician/scientist/philosopher, around the turn of the 20th century. For our purposes, the semiotics of autonomous systems is a science of sorting out reliable acts (those that regularly produce expected results), from unreliable acts (those that result in unexpected or random results). Clearly, the best you could hope for would be for all your actions to always produce the result you expected. Peircian semiotics offers a normative (i.e., what ought to be) symbolic theory of how real autonomous systems actually learn to act effectively.

Semiotics is a science of sign processes, or **semiosis**. In the case of autonomous systems, all of the system's sensations and acts, both mental and physical, are named by internal signs. Going back to a previous example in this chapter, if you were locked by aliens in that windowless box on some strange planet, probably your first inclination would be to name (i.e., associate a sign with) each of the simple lights and levers immediately available to you. Technically, these things are all acts: the lights represent actual and potential acts of sensation, and the levers represent potential and actual outward acts. Starting out with only these primitive acts, semiosis constructs composite acts of ever greater complexity, diversity, and trustworthiness.

So, say one of your sensors seems to correlate with elevated temperatures within the box, and thus presumably outside the box as well, so you name it the "thermometer" sensor. Assuming these elevated temperatures were threatening to you, one of your goals would be to learn how to maintain this "thermometer" sensor in a limited range of values. Remember, your only means for accomplishing this are the primitive outward acts (e.g., the levers) available to you. You would begin by learning that operating certain levers produces repeatable results in terms of the primitive sensory acts available to you. One of your most critical tasks will be to distinguish such reliable acts from those whose results are unpredictable, since acts whose results are unpredictable are essentially useless to you. As you continued to act, you would eventually learn that certain combinations of named outward acts produced repeatable results made up of combinations of already named sensations. These combinations you would also name as reliable acts, and they too could eventually become components of even more complex acts. Ultimately, by learning such reliable acts, you would be able to effectively act so as to maintain that certain "thermometer" sensor within acceptable limits, and, more generally, mitigate any other threats to you, in your role as surrogate identity in this autonomous box thought-experiment.

According to semiotics, for every act there would be a **case**, describing the situation prior to commencing an act, a **rule** describing the performance of the act, and the anticipated **result** of the act. In essence, all of your knowledge would be in the form of a repertoire of such named three-part acts. At no time would you be constructing or processing an internal representation or model of the external world based on the rationalist notion of information. Instead, you are in a constant process of evaluating the results of acts, choosing appropriate ends to be achieved, creating and refining means to these ends. This difference between *information processing* and *act processing* is crucial to real autonomous systems.

From the perspective of information processing, the system must respond appropriately to all of the potential inputs that the world might produce. In other words, information processing offers no inherent limitations on the variety of information inputs the system must process. This presents a significant problem for autonomous systems in a real environment that is infinitely more complex by comparison. In practice, such as in the field of artificial intelligence, a designer or a subtle "hidden hand" is required to assist the system in distinguishing what is important and what is not.

Semiosis, in processing acts rather than information, makes the subtle but crucial change (from rationalism) of placing action before sensation. As a result, the variety of sensations is inherently limited by the repertoire of acts the system is capable of performing. While this by no means guarantees that the system will be a viable one (e.g., its repertoire of acts may or may not be sufficient for survival), it does guarantee that the processing of sensations will always be within the capacity of the system, no matter how simple the system is. Thus, semiosis and act processing provides a much more reasonable explanation of how real, autonomous systems actually do cope with the complex world around them, regardless of their own complexity or lack of it.

As a more practical example of semiosis at work, consider that your business is entering a brand new market with an innovative new product. Traditional wisdom would say to gather information about this new market, develop an appropriate marketing plan of action, then execute it. But what is this "information" that you are collecting based on? Are the market segments you are quantifying something "real," or are they simply artificial constructs or groupings that were useful for marketing your last product? Are the rules that you go by now in developing your market plan similarly based on the past? If so, how do you expect them to work if your new product and market are really new? In actuality, you are more than a little like the poor soul locked in the box on that strange planet. You have no direct way of knowing your environment any more than the person in the box: you must learn by acting and noting the results.

So, you begin with primitive acts: a trial release here, a simple announcement there. Then you observe the results: how many units are shipped, how many phone calls did you get? Sooner or later, you will observe regularities in these results and give them a name (maybe a new conceptual market segment). Ultimately, just like the person in the windowless box, you will have learned which acts are reliable ones that you will be able to use in achieving your objective, which is (no, not profit!) maintaining your identity (of course!)

Another important part of the theory of semiosis is the tension between pure chance and pure generality. Pure chance is the uncertainty associated with surprise. That is, no matter what regularities of sensations have occurred in the past, there is always the chance that something completely surprising may occur. At the other end of the spectrum, there is pure generality or predictability. Through the process of semiosis, the system continually strives to eliminate surprise, or in other words, attempts to act with perfectly predictable results. In an artificial world that was of limited complexity and did not change, the semiotic system would actually converge on a state where all thought would be in the form of prediction (e.g., if I do *this*, I will get *that* result). In such a world, the system could eventually eliminate all surprise. At the other extreme, if reality provided no regularities at all, there could be no generalization, no prediction. And so, all thought would be limited to what could *possibly be* (e.g., I wonder what would happen if I did this). Obviously, our reality is somewhere between these two extremes. But the actual point is a matter of judgment, not established fact. The semiotic system is therefore constantly reassessing its beliefs about what acts will be most effective, and indirectly about how surprising the world really is. A large part of the process of semiosis is in adjusting these beliefs based on the success of past judgments. The acts that make and refine these and other important judgments are referred to as **valuative acts**.

Judgment and values: axiology

Valuative acts are also an essential aspect of autonomy. Systems that exist in a real and complex environment must act in a timely manner and under conditions of considerable uncertainty. Judgments must be made that close the loop of action/sensation even when the options are many or ill-defined. And, for the autonomous system, these choices must be completely self-determined. Machines, on the other hand, do not make judgments in this sense. They may make selections based on their inputs, but these are ultimately guided by the implicit judgments of the designer encoded into the design of the system itself.

A primary assertion of autognomics is that these valuative acts substantially determine the differences between individuals in their behaviors. Even under similar circumstances, two semiotic systems will learn and adapt in quite different ways if their values differ. In order to better understand values and their role in learning and behavior, autognomics integrates a scientific theory of value (**axiology**) largely attributed to Robert S. Hartman, a modern American philosopher. Through empirical study as well as logic, Hartman arrived at three fundamental categories of value that mesh well with the valuative judgments involved in semiosis. These three categories in order are:

1   **Systemic value** – judging according to a finite number of attributes, each of which may be one of only a finite number of options. This is the valuing according to law. That is, I have a system of generalities (laws) that allow me to make predictions. Such a system, however, requires that I be able to judge the acceptability of something: whether or not it fits the rules of this system, whether it's ruled in or out, or whether it makes the cut. For example, I believe I can predict that a worker will perform successfully in a job if he or she is judged acceptable, according to certain attributes that my system defines (e.g., education level, experience in certain tasks, etc.) and acceptance criteria for each attribute (e.g., Master's Degree, three years of programming experience, etc.). If I were interviewing candidates for a job on this basis, I would be valuing them systemically. Simply put, no one gets interviewed unless at a minimum they meet these systemic criteria. In this case, the emphasis is on what *ought to be*.

2   **Extrinsic value** – judging according to a finite number of attributes, each of which may have essentially infinite number of options. This is valuing according to concept. I have an ideal in my mind and I rank everything against that ideal concept. For example, I want to buy a chair; that process requires that I evaluate a finite number of chair-attributes (e.g. I want it to support my lower back, be comfortable and adjustable). But for each of these attributes, I will accept an infinite number of options (i.e., I am open to surprises on how a certain chair might fulfill these chair attributes). According to how a certain instance (e.g., a specific chair) fulfills these finite attributes, I am able to judge goodness/badness of every chair I look at (e.g., a chair without a comfortable seat would be a bad chair). Similarly, I might interview job candidates and pay special attention to prior job references, the schools they attended, what I can discern from their interview answers about

how good their judgment, team work, and responsibility might be. I would then select the final candidate by ranking all of them against each other (good, bad, better, worse) and my concept of the ideal candidate. The emphasis here is on what *is*.

3 **Intrinsic value** – judging according to an infinite number of attributes, each of which may have an infinite number of options. Thus, no preconceived restrictions are placed on the judgment, allowing for a valuing of true uniqueness, allowing for the entrance of surprise. Valuing someone you have just met as a unique person would be intrinsic valuing. Because there is no describable set of attributes against which we intrinsically value something or someone, such judgments cannot be fully put into words. Instead they are generally "felt" as immediate physical reactions. Thus, for example, "true love" is often surprising, unmistakable, and cannot adequately be put into words, despite all the noble attempts by poets and songwriters. In another example, intrinsic valuing of job candidates is often not a component of the formal interview process, but may play a considerable role nonetheless. For example, if someone is hired because an interviewer "just had a good feeling" about this person, or my "gut" told me that everyone would like to work with her, or I realized during the interview that he could make a unique contribution to the organization, then intrinsic value is at work. Especially when valuing living things, intrinsic valuing emphasizes what *could be*.

In summary then, if I go to an art museum for the first time and say "I don't know anything about art, but I know what I like – and I like that," then I am doing intrinsic valuing. Later, if I develop an eye for what constitutes "good art," for example it has realistic perspective and uses color well, then I am extrinsically valuing the works of art. As an art "expert", I might state that I hate cubism, then I have partitioned those art works off; all cubist works are out, pretty much everything else makes the cut and will be considered. In this case I have done systemic valuing. The relationship of these value dimensions to the problem of successful adaptation to a changing reality should be clear. There is a natural order of valuing as more is learned. Each value dimension provides a different view of the world on which judgments may be based. Intrinsic valuing emphasizes the immediate, the creativity and change in reality, where each new moment is unlike any other. Extrinsic valuing categorizes these actual experiences based on a measures of similarity found useful in practice. Systemic value emphasizes the stability and order that has gone before through the creation of theories or laws.

Autognomics: an integration of three theories

Thus, for our purposes, autognomics can be seen as three independent theories integrated into one. Autopoiesis provides the fundamental requirements for autonomous systems and gets us off on the right track concerning the notion of information and learning in such systems. Of critical importance is the role of identity in determining the effect of environmental perturbations, and thus the entire basis for learning and adaptation. Peirces's theory of semiotics offers a symbolic explanation of how autonomous systems actually do go about learning and refining the acts necessary to preserve and express this identity. Semiosis, in stating that living systems process acts rather than information, challenges rationalism by saying that action precedes sensation. Finally, the axiology of Hartman provides a solid basis for understanding how value judgments play a role in determining the actual path of learning and behavior in unique individuals.

We are now finally ready to begin examining, in the context of the autognomics framework, assertions concerning how individuals and organizations learn. These assertions are examined in the next section.

New Perspectives on Learning

What one sees is largely determined by what one expects to see. However, the rationalist tradition has tuned our perceptions to emphasize the persistent, stable features of reality, and neglect the processes of change. With our new perspective, however, we are prepared to look at the same reality and see new things, seemingly contradictory to what rationalism led us to believe. In this section, we will examine three implications of autonomy and autognomics with respect to learning and compare them with traditional wisdom. They are:

- Learning is a natural process, a most vital instinct since it deals with immediate survival;
- The driving force for learning is maintenance and expression of identity; and,
- Organizational learning shares the same processes of learning as individuals, with language providing the critical connectivity.

Learning is a natural process

Nowhere in our discussion of the process of learning and adaptation has the need arisen for teachers, workbooks, or classrooms. Clearly, autonomous systems would not be very autonomous if they required external assistance in a process that is central to their existence. But according to traditional wisdom, do learners themselves contribute everything to the process of learning?

Our most telling clue is found in the prominent and important role given to educational institutions. Modern culture places little value on learning done outside the confines of educational institutions. When one looks at the primary activities of such schools, one generally finds time is spent *motivating* students to learn, *providing* them information, *monitoring/ranking* their progress, and *ensuring* meaningful academic standards are met. Considering the extraordinary cost of such educational institutions to our society, one can only conclude that these activities are believed to be necessary for effective learning to occur. In other words, traditional wisdom does not hold that learning is a natural, organic process, but that the learner must be compelled to learn.

Our culture actually believes that "motivators" such as gold stars, competitions, and enticing multimedia instructional technology are essential for students who will otherwise not be motivated to learn. Traditionally, we also believe that the transfer of preprocessed information to the student is the basic process of learning (especially considering the money spent on textbooks and other "information sources"). And surely we must believe that if left unmonitored and unmotivated, the learner would soon settle back into some nonlearning state more "natural" to humanity.

But our new perspective leads us to question this traditional wisdom. If information is not a representation of some objective external world, how can it be directly transferred from one to another? If my judgments about what is important to learn are made according to my unique value perspective, how can there be learning standards? If my need to learn is driven by my desire to maintain and express my identity, then why must I be provided with external motivation?

If learners are machines, then "obviously" we must use external force or direction (i.e., motivations), programming (i.e., processed information), and control feedback (i.e., testing, monitoring) to achieve our (not the machine's) goals. On the other hand, if learners are autonomous systems, whose autonomy is respected and valued, then just as "obviously" they must decide what is important and how it should be learned. If ultimately the final reason for being is to express a unique identity, how does the concept of motivation even come up? This last question is so important, it is addressed by itself in the next section.

Learning's driving force: identity

Asserting that learning was a natural, organic process almost seemed like a corollary to our perspective of humans and organizations as autonomous systems. The hard part was showing that our cultural predisposition is contradictory. And so it is with explaining the **motivation** of learning. Who decides what is important enough to be learned and causes it to be learned? Based on the fundamental requirements for autonomy, it is clear that the system by and for itself determines what effort is to be put into learning and where, all for the sole purpose of maintaining its defining organization, its identity. From this perspective, there is no more need for motivation to learn than there should be to breathe or sleep. The more interesting question is how this compares with what our culturally accepted machine-model of learning tells us.

It seems clear that we as a culture take it as our right to determine what ought to be taught in schools, and thus take responsibility for motivating the learner to learn what is taught. Consider for example, the current emphasis on education that provides the student the capability to "compete in the global marketplace." In the United States, this has almost become a mantra of politicians, school boards, and administrators. They "know" what it takes to compete in the global marketplace because they have looked at what has worked in the past and have projected educational requirements into the future. Thus, in axiological (i.e., value-theory) terms, they are systemically valuing the content of education. They are applying a law or theory based on past experience that allows them (they think) to predict what will happen if a student receives what they have defined as an "acceptable" education. Consequently, a broad range of motivators are used to encourage compliance, including fear of the consequences of noncompliance. In other words, students and schools who do not meet these acceptability criteria are punished severely. Schools face loss of funding and accreditation. For students, the educational system labels their educational experience, and indirectly the student, a "failure" (as in "you failed algebra").

Pervasive as systemic value is in the educational systems, it is not surprising that it also permeates organizational culture as well. In many businesses, one's position and job title exactly specifies what *ought to be* either known or learned. In fact, the very notion of job requirements/descriptions is a tool for ensuring that learning be guided into productive channels by job seekers. In other cases, organizational training plans are devised based on what ought to be learned to prepare the organization for future endeavors.

The point, we think, should be clear. In a rational culture, it is easy and natural to expect that learning would be guided in a rational way. One difficulty with this approach is the ill-considered basis for such rationality. In a world that is changing ever faster, predictions of future usefulness tend themselves to be less useful. This observation is one reason for the increasing importance of diversity. If the single rational approach turns out to be wrong, we are completely out of luck. We have done precisely what the old adage told us not to do, that is, put all our eggs in one basket. We have no alternatives. But if a diversity of approaches are taken, there is a much greater chance that one or more of them will turn out to be viable. Unfortunately, systemic valuing of learning does not allow for diversity. It insists on a clear demarcation: consequently, there are only acceptable versus not acceptable educations.

Another difficulty with this rational approach to education and learning becomes clear when we distinguish between what is taught to us (and expected to be learned), and what we actually learn. The basic requirements of autonomy cannot be discarded when the enclosing environment believes otherwise. That is, *what is learned is still determined solely by the identity of the learner*. In the case of school children, they learn that the world values learning systemically, and so should they if they want to get along. This lesson is learned so well in fact that when these school children grow up and become part of the workforce, they value themselves almost exclusively by what "the system" says they ought to be, to the exclusion of all other considerations.

This externally derived identity has an unintended, but nonetheless tragic result: it essentially disconnects the learner from the most important guide to learning, the intrinsic self. Without our internal compass, this constant internal reference point for valuative judgments, our natural coherence of action and learning, is lost. It is only feebly replaced by externally induced motivations and standards of accomplishment. A main point of this chapter is that ineffective learning, in both individuals and organizations, is largely due to this serious disconnect. It is a culturally induced and approved learning disability, and it costs each of us dearly. Fortunately, through a process of self-discovery, we can bring back an awareness of an internally derived identity, an intrinsic valuing of one's most inner self, which some refer to as our spirit or soul (see discussion in chapter 12).

We should point out, however, that this process of "reconnecting" to the intrinsic self is not necessarily a simple one. If external motivations are suddenly removed after a lifetime of emphasis, a real learning system (individual or organization) will not revert to intrinsic motivation quickly or easily. For example, in the past several decades, many schools in the United States and elsewhere have engaged in limited experiments that allow senior high school students to select all or some of their courses from a wider offering of electives. These experiments have often been described as failures because the students still underachieve in the courses they select, and their selections are based strongly on which courses offer the least challenge (e.g., everyone decides to take basket weaving together for a lark.) While some may take this as evidence for the need for strong external motivation, we believe it is more a matter of timing. In general, the longer one has spent in an educational system suppressing individual interests, the more difficult it will be to remember and reconnect to these interests when called upon. As for these experiments, a more proper test might have been to allow grade school children the opportunity to choose their curriculum. If such changes are to be instituted for older students, and even more importantly, for adult learners, they must be made gradually and in concert with a process of self-discovery.

We, of course, have overgeneralized to make our point. All schools and organizations are not uniformly systemic in their outlook. For example, one can find schools (albeit not very many) at the other end of the spectrum. We have one such school in mind: it is the Sudbury Valley School in Framingham, Massachusetts (and a small number of other schools using Sudbury as a model). In this school, there are no courses, no teachers (although they do have an adult "staff"), no attendance requirements, and only one graduation requirement: that the students defend before a public meeting that they are ready to become responsible members of society. What this school offers is a place and time for students to learn on their own and in groups. From an autognomic perspective, this organization places complete reliance on the natural learning process and intrinsic valuation on the learner, recognizing that any interference, even well-intentioned, will inhibit it. According to some of the founders of the school:

> The process of self-direction, or blazing your own way, indeed living your life rather than passing time, is natural but not self-evident to children growing up in our civilization. . . . [and, we would add, most adults too].
>
> Sudbury Valley School was established not as yet another institution to enshrine courses, but as its antithesis, a place where internal growth and the path of each student is sacrosanct. The processes that have value at Sudbury are the private ones that take place within the minds and souls of each student. . . .
>
> To participate in an activity where the clash of unequal bodies is transformed through teamwork, the pursuit of personal excellence, responsibility and restraint into a common union of equal souls in the pursuit of meaningful experience has been one of the most profound experiences of my life.[4]

We believe there could hardly be a better description of an ideal learning organization!

Thus, a key to effective learning, at both the individual and organizational level, is awareness of self, of one's unique identity, as well as one's connectedness to a greater whole, or spirit. This awareness provides two essential boosts to learning: it taps into a motivational source of unlimited power, and it provides a "rudder" to ensure that learning and action are always focused and coherent.

However, the applicability of these assertions to human organizations should be made clear. Up until this point in the chapter we have included both individuals and organizations under the category of autonomous systems without much explanation. In the next section, we will attempt such an explanation using the perspective of autognomics.

Individuals and organizations as learners

With all the emphasis on autonomy, one might get the impression that we have de-emphasized group or social interaction. This impression would be wrong. The structural coupling that is the heart of learning and survival applies not only to the inanimate surroundings of the autonomous system, but to other autonomous systems in the environment as well. Thus, autonomous systems couple with other autonomous systems to form higher level systems that increase the survivability of all involved. This process can occur over and over, providing many levels of what are called **autonomous meta-systems**. Our own bodies can be considered a higher level meta-system of the individual cells that make it up. Similarly, we as individuals can structurally couple to other individuals to form families, teams, and all other sorts of organizations, including societies and even an entire human population we on very optimistic days refer to as the world community. Modern ecology even has a term for the autonomous system that includes the entire earth: the Gaia.

Clearly, if we are to survive and prosper, we must do all we can to encourage effective learning at all these levels of autonomous systems. And if our new perspective is to be of value, it should apply to all these learning systems. Yet many people will resist the idea that any theory or paradigm that applies to individuals such as you and me could also apply to organizations and whole societies.

Probably the most difficult problem people have with attributing the same fundamental characteristics to such higher-order organizations as are attributed to biological entities is the form of structural coupling they undergo. Human beings, for example, are held together by skin, bones, and whatnot into a physically linked set of local components. From the rational perspective, this is much easier to understand; here is a material cohesiveness that provides an observable mechanism – the body – for the local cause and effect necessary for a machine-model system.

However, in order to appreciate the similarity of individuals and organizations as autonomous systems, one must recognize *language* as an equally capable medium for structural coupling; in organizations language acts as do chemical compounds and blood in our bodies. However, this view of language is unfamiliar within the rationalist tradition: rationalism takes language to be a matter-of-fact transmission of information between a source and destination. Words, phrases, sentences, and so on are thought to be statements about the world, that is, information. Autognomics, on the other hand, recognizes language as just another form of semiotic act, performed with the expectation of a particular result on the hearer. Words and sentences have no inherent meaning as information.

"Wait!" you say. "This has gone too far. Everyone knows that words mean things. What kind of twisted mind would think otherwise. For example, take 'The sky is blue.' What could this possibly mean except that there is a thing called 'sky' and its color is 'blue?' Really!"

Well . . . let's look at this example. Had we inserted this sentence apparently *without reason* several paragraphs before, one could only expect that all our readers would have, without fail, thought to themselves, "what do they mean, 'the sky is blue'?" And they would do so not because the words *sky*, *is*, and *blue* are unfamiliar to them, but because the phrase would strike them as an unreasonable linguistic act in the context of that paragraph at that time (for example, if we had inserted "the sky is blue" in the middle of the Sudbury school description). Apparently, if language is used without reason, it has no meaning. The only way the linguistic act "the sky is blue" has meaning is if it is used in context to produce a response in the intended listener. For example, if I were coloring with my three-year-old son and said "the sky is blue," I would expect this to produce a response something like increasing the likelihood that he would choose the blue crayon rather than the red one for coloring in the sky of his picture. I am certainly not just trying to convey an objective "fact," independent of any context. (Actually, the sky is often not blue.)

In practice, of course, we dispense with all this conscious wondering over how our language couples our actions with others, and use the gross approximation that it does just convey information in most cases. However, that we are consciously aware of only the informational character of our language does not deny the actual reason we use language to produce anticipated responses in others. For example, if I say "This report needs a lot more work," I expect that language to produce a certain range of responses.

And so, in principle, the internal process of semiosis by which the individual learns to effectively act can be directly extended to include others so as to form an organizational process of semiosis with the same features as the internal one. According to this perspective, words, phrases, and so on are signs whose meaning is mutually negotiated for use in coordinating the activity and associated semiosis of the engaged languagers. What this means is that language, our communication in our organizations, is as vital to organizational life as the blood pulsing in our veins is to ours. According to biologists Maturana and Varela, ". . . the network of conversations which language generates . . . constitutes the unity of a particular human society." And they add, "The unique features of human social life and its intense linguistic coupling are manifest in that this life is capable of generating a new phenomenon . . . *our mind, our consciousness.*"[5]

Applications of Autognomics to the Learning Organization

Consistent with what we have said so far, we do not expect you to take this chapter as "information" and put it directly to practical use. Instead, we can only hope that you will incorporate the arguments we have made into your ongoing personal process of inquiry and discovery. In all likelihood, you would not have read this far if you were not questioning the traditional view of learning and organizational development. Being generally of a philosophic nature, the principles discussed in this chapter can only provide a new foundation for further inquiry – hopefully leading ultimately to learning in, and through, action.

We can, however, offer an example of how one might use the conceptual lens of autognomics to gain new insights into organizational learning and management. Consider, for example, one of the most salient trends in modern management theory and practice: Total Quality Management (TQM, also known as Continuous Quality Management, Process Management, etc.). TQM has been analyzed, interpreted, adopted, thrown out, praised, and criticized probably more than any "theory" of management in history. Yet, considering the tremendous range of variants of, and opinions about, TQM, we can only conclude that it remains largely misunderstood. How can this be?

From an autognomics perspective, TQM is fundamentally about a shift in values. Consider what often exists in organizations without TQM, what we might call the *classic* form of organization (although certainly many organizations still fit this description). The predominant basis for judgments, or value, in such organizations is the **bottom line**. Management is a matter of managing costs: material costs, labor costs, overhead costs, and so, within the context of an all-encompassing accounting system. According to this system, any change can be characterized as a cost change and the net impact on the bottom line calculated accordingly. Employees at most of the levels of such an organization are generally considered one-for-one replaceable, their key attribute being their cost. As long as employees behave acceptably and perform their job according to the job description, they are doing all the company expects of them.

Clearly, such an organization is steeped in **systemic value**. Things are judged according to a finite set of attributes, in this case primarily cost, which can only have a certain range of measure (i.e., dollar amount). The cost accounting system of rules and laws generalizes over all situations, allowing one to predict the result of any change within the system at any time or place. Behaviors and actions are judged according to formal and unstated rules as being acceptable or not acceptable.

The primary weakness of such an organization, which is a direct result of its overemphasis on systemic value, is that it cannot change when current reality undermines the systems of rules and laws that are based on the past. Thus, everyone knows of at least a few classic organizations that managed themselves right into obsolescence, all the while clinging to the same rules and systems, exclaiming "This should not be happening."

Enter Deming, Juran, Crosby (and others) who looked at the classic organization and said: Do not manage to improve the bottom line – manage instead to produce a quality product and the bottom line will take care of itself. In practice, this means constantly improving things, making things better. With TQM, managers are advised to collect data on everything; do not rely on what *should* be happening, find out what *is* happening. Document your *real* processes. See your employees as more than a cost; take advantage of their expertise, their skills, the important role can they play in the process of continuous improvement.

This is clearly a shift to **extrinsic value**. Products, behaviors, and processes are no longer acceptable or not acceptable, they are judged on a continuum of goodness, always with room for making things better. In systemic value, there is no way to distinguish between levels of acceptability; thus there is no incentive to improve! However, in extrinsic valuing organizations, even employees can be made "better" through an emphasis on training and continuous learning.

The problem that commonly arises, however, is that most managers, having been indoctrinated into the classic model of organization, are simply not prepared for a shift in fundamental values. Most managers sincerely want to change. Managers may participate in executive TQM overviews and seminars, establish work teams, draw up a new training plan – but still only see what their systemic perceptual filters allow them to see. "This is how we *ought* to do process action teams." "Sure, training sounds like a great thing to do, but what is it going to *cost* me?" "What do we *have* to do to win the Baldrige Award?"

Of course, there are plenty of management consultants and theorists that also did not see the depth of change required for TQM, and were all too happy to translate TQM into a more palatable form for "practical" (i.e., systemic) managers. Unfortunately, the result has been the diffusion and dilution of TQM principles that one sees today – and the resulting disillusionment often voiced as "Hey, this TQM isn't all it's cracked up to be" or "We tried TQM and it just doesn't work."

The primary advantage of TQM's emphasis on extrinsic value is that it opened the door for reality to intrude on the operations of the organization. If things *really* are not going well, your data collection will tell you. These facts (extrinsic value) take precedence over any idea of what the process *ought* to be (systemic value). And so, as reality intrudes, the organization naturally and continuously adapts its systems, processes, and rules in response.

So, if the classic organization is overly systemic, and TQM asserts the proper role of extrinsic value relative to systemic value, where does **intrinsic value** fit in? Emerging management literature touts concepts such as "management by intuition," self-directed work teams, dialogue, personal mastery, managing "from the heart," and so on. These notions all point towards a new recognition of intrinsic value in organizations. A "pure" intrinsic-value organization would be one that had no rules, no procedures, no job titles, no planning. In short, it would choose to continuously respond to immediate reality in all its complex and unpredictable glory.

Buddha and the balanced, or, tie goes to the runner

In our mind, the "ultimate" form of organization would be one that adheres to the principles of scientific inquiry laid out by Peirce. In autognomic terms, such an organization would put intrinsic value first, extrinsic second, and systemic third, yet all in a particular balance determined by the identity of the organization. This is not to say that intrinsic valuing completely displaces extrinsic or systemic valuing. Balance is the key.

While we have emphasized intrinsic valuing throughout much of this chapter, we have done so because it is so repressed in our society and organizations. We need to clearly state, however, that in practice all three value dimensions are important. To achieve a workable balance requires an attitude one might call the "middle way," as described in the following story:

> Early one morning the young prince Siddhartha, in search of enlightenment, stole out of his father's palace and forever left behind his life of luxury. For many years thereafter, he practiced severe austerities, wandering in poverty and fasting in the

unforgiving heat and sun. Then one day, as he was lost deep in meditation, a musician and student happened to pass by. Siddhartha overheard the elder musician state that if an instrument was strung too loose, it would not sound, yet if it was wound too tight, the strings would break. Neither extreme would produce the beauty of music. Siddhartha was hit with a sudden jolt of understanding. At that moment he left his life of austerity as suddenly as he had left his life of indulgence – forever after adhering to the path which he, as the Buddha, called The Middle Way.

Another way of looking at value balance is through the baseball rule "Tie goes to the runner." If the ball and the base runner arrive at the base at what can only be judged to be the same instant, the benefit of the doubt goes to the runner who is called "safe." In other words, the rule is to choose *life*, to keep alive the possibility of a future run scored or a play at home plate, for the game to continue on. An "out" would dash these possibilities, bringing the game one step closer to its end.

Similarly, when values dimensions are balanced, there will be circumstances when each one of them will become appropriately emphasized. On the other hand, there will be times when the judgment will not be so clear-cut. In these cases, autognomics suggests that the "tie" go to the higher value dimension: intrinsic followed by extrinsic, then systemic. In other words, the rule is to choose what might be, potentiality, over what is or should be. Only in this way can the system effectively change with the world, and become tomorrow more than it is today – to learn.

Of course, managers who are still reeling over the shift from systemic to extrinsic value are not likely to enthusiastically embrace this even more dramatic value shift. The inclination to return to the comfortable stability of systemic value is still quite strong. This conservatism evidences itself today in the popularity of systemic quality standards such as ISO 9000, and management practices based on computer software engineering (for example, business "re-engineering"). These trends clearly indicate that the world-as-machine paradigm will not give up its sovereignty easily or in the near future.

Conclusion

Our goal in this chapter has been to urge you to begin a process of personal inquiry questioning the prevalent assumptions and beliefs that underlie most modern theory and practice of individual and organizational learning. We have formulated the question as a matter of choosing between a system-as-machine paradigm and an autonomous system paradigm.

Yet, regardless of how the question is framed, we are not alone in strongly believing that there must be a radical and fundamental shift in our cultural inclinations if we are to more reliably attain the ends we seek. Thoreau wrote in *Walden*: "I see young men, my townsmen, whose misfortune it is to have inherited farms, houses, barns, cattle, and farming tools; for these are more easily acquired than got rid of. Better if they had been born in the open pasture and suckled by a wolf, that they might have seen with clearer eyes what field they were called to labor in."[6] Similarly, we have inherited from our ancestors a way of thinking, a philosophy, that is more easily acquired than got rid of. Eugene Pendergraft, a founder of autognomics, wrote as did Thoreau, "men labor under a mistake," in this case, "under the inherited idea that they receive rather than create information."[7] The fallout from this mistake is staggering: individuals, organizations, and societies are led to oppressive and sterile notions of learning, development, and action.

At stake is not simply a matter of reducing education and training costs or raising corporate profitability. Effective learning is not just desirable, it is the key to our survival! Francisco Varela conveyed the importance of freeing ourselves from this mistake when he wrote: "To me, the chance of surviving with dignity on this planet hinges on the acquisition of a new mind. This new mind must be wrought, among other things, from a radically different epistemology which will inform relevant actions."[8]

It is our fervent hope that this chapter, and others within this volume, contribute to such a change of mind.

Notes

We would like to thank the scholars and associates of the Autognomics Institute, in particular Norman and Skye Hirst, and Eugene Pendergraft, for their assistance in exploring the meaning and implication of autonomy.

1 Terry Winograd and Fernando Flores, *Understanding Computers and Cognition: A New Foundation for Design* (Norwood, NJ: Ablex, 1986), p. 16.

2 Humberto Maturana and Francisco Varela, *The Tree of Knowledge: A New Look at the Biological Roots of Human Understanding* (Boston: Shambala, 1987).

3 Francisco Varela, *Principles of Biological Autonomy* (New York: North Holland, 1979), p. 238.

4 From Daniel J. Greenberg, *The Sudbury Valley School Experience* (Framingham, MA: The Sudbury School Press, 1987); first quote by Hanna Greenberg, p. 66; second by Daniel Greenberg, p. 70; third by Michael Greenberg, p. 120.

5 Maturana and Varela, *The Tree of Knowledge*, p. 223.

6 Henry David Thoreau, *Walden; or, Life in the Woods* (Boston: The Library of America, 1985), p. 326.

7 Eugene Pendergraft, "The future's voice: organizing principles for the information age" (Unpublished manuscript, 1993).

8 Francisco Varela, "Laying down a path in walking: A biologist's look at a new biology and its ethics", *Cybernetic* 1986, vol. 2, no. 1, p. 6.

PART V

Transforming Organizations for
Learning and Performance

Interviews

Interview with Cecil Ursprung
Chief Executive Officer, Reflexite Corporation
and
David Edgar
Vice President of Human Resources

Interviewer: David Fearon   Date: September 1994

DF: Our book is *Managing in Organizations That Learn*. When the entire Reflexite employee-owner group was named Entrepreneur of the Year by *INC.* magazine in 1992, it surely caught our attention that your company is not only pioneering in the uses of light-reflecting materials, but in different ways of managing. You are the lead person in this regard, Cecil. How *do* you manage here?

CU: Thinking about managing this way goes against the great majority of themes and rules by which institutions have been governed these many years. Authoritarian ways of doing things came from the experience of the military and the church. During the early part of the twentieth century, when Henry Ford was building production lines and people were coming off farms and from foreign countries to go to work in those automobile plants, people had very little relevant knowledge, unless they were craftsmen. Otherwise, most were uneducated or undereducated, including language capabilities. Many who were immigrants didn't speak English back then.

Henry Ford, whose way is kind of a catch-all image for managers of that era, responded appropriately to these labor conditions. He set up compatible management systems and work processes that were incredibly successful. Frederick Taylor was a hero in those days for very good reason. Turnover in 1917 at the Ford plant in Dearborn was 170 percent. So for all those reasons it was necessary to have interchangeable people. The evidence of the wisdom of that approach is in the results that the US obtained using it to gain economic dominance in the world – 40 percent of the world's GDP after World War II.

We had tremendous success, until the times changed. Now people are much better educated and motivated to participate in decisions effecting their work. They want to have more control over their lives including their workplace situation. The historic models are now increasingly suboptimal after a good 75 year run.

This is strikingly evident in some of the newer industries, computer software, for example. The people doing the work in those organizations are just as well-educated, just as intelligent as the people who are leading the organization. They just have different functions. These employees have different needs and desires and different satisfaction quotients, different sources of motivation than existed 50, 70, 30 years ago.

Bright managers, I believe, will recognize that what they learned in an MBA program in, say, 1966 about management as planning, directing, controlling, can forget as much of this as one can. It is time to break some new ground that is relevant to people in workplaces today. Many of the people that I talk to who are in a similar situation as us at Reflexite aren't visionaries or social experimenters. We consider ourselves to be very pragmatic managers looking for what works.

DF: Results still matter.

CU: Oh, yes.

DF: The old system produced results, until results fell off. You still need similar results to satisfy customers and stakeholders. You're looking for better ways to create those results within the new workforce. Would you say the key then *is* the workforce? It is the realization that an employee has a full mind at work here at Reflexite and the confidence to use it in securing the company's future?

CU: Yes, but then I'd add the word "potential," because people won't automatically use their minds. Everybody brings along a lot of baggage, so people do not automatically do that expansive kind of thinking on the job. The managers in an organization have to create an environment where people feel comfortable, where they can take risks to try something new. If that works, they are willing to do more. Yes, change in the composition of workforce is a big, big driver.

The other significant driver is the globalization of business. In the fifties and sixties, it didn't matter really that GM and Ford and Chrysler did things the same way. It didn't matter that there were all these patterned settlements with the UAW that were very, very generous, because the automobile business was a very profitable business, even if all three raised their prices in concert.

DF: We customers went along with it back then.

CU: The workforces in those organizations all came from the same environment. The management in those organizations all came from the same environment, all went to the same schools, or at least schools that were teaching the same management principles, and that's fine as long as that's the edge of the circle. The problem came when someone from a different circle, namely the Japanese, came into the market and began to compete with a very different workforce. They managed with different technological paradigms and management principles. For a period of time they "cleaned our clock."

DF: They also honed in on customer requirements here and around the world. They knew us better than we knew us. So we have the change-drivers of the high, untapped potential of the workforce. Secondly the globalization of competition. Are there any other factors you think are causing us to rethink management?

CU: Those are enough. There are other things that are going on. Improvements in logistics and transportation, communication. Things that gave societies advantages in the past, natural resources for example, low labor costs, are nearly nonexistent today. *This leaves us with people.* If you can gain an advantage by educating, training, and developing the people in a society, then that is a sustainable advantage.

A strong example in the last 20 years is Singapore and what they have done. Now, they have a kind of government that can get things done, so to speak. I realize they didn't have to worry about a lot of democratic principles. But, if you look at the results, Singapore got started with a rather unskilled, low-cost labor force. Over the past years, they have developed a highly skilled, educated, trained, and highly motivated workforce. This is the major competitive battlefield, this new global era.

DF: Reflexite is becoming a worldwide, networked company, with associated businesses in several countries. You have patented technologies which, some 20 years ago, gave the founders, the Rowland brothers, an edge over the far bigger companies in your industry. I'm sure you're still advancing on the technological side to be competitive. Would you say, however, that your emphasis to developing Reflexite people is the good news for those stakeholders who would tie their future well-being to your firm?

CU: The technology that we have resides in the minds of people. Reflexite has made, successfully I believe, two very difficult business transitions in the last ten years. The most difficult any organization makes is the transition from the entrepreneurs to the next generation of management. That's a kind of an "adoption" process that takes place. It takes place only once in an organization's life, when the entrepreneurs hand it over to the next group. It's a very difficult one. Many organizations don't survive it.

Just below that in difficulty, particularly for a technology-driven company like Reflexite, is the *transfer* of knowledge from the inventors and the founders to that next generation of technically oriented people. Can those new people be inspired to use all of the hard work as a foundation and then build on it?

Technology is applied knowledge, particularly for a young company with an emerging technology like ours. There is on any given day equal parts art and science that go into this technology. It is not codified; there is no "bible of microprisms" to be handed down. There is a tremendous portion of this technology that resides in the minds of the people who work here. So to answer your point, technology and people are really one and the same.

DF: In other words, if you did some things, unwittingly, to diminish the reasons that people would want to work for your place, you would be sending a good portion of your technology out the door?

CU: They are inseparable. Maybe someday, when our microprism technology is mature and people have taken the time to write it down, it might be different. Now, I do know that in our organization they're inseparable.

DF: What have you folks evolved and designed here that you think makes the employee not only a valuable resource, but an active contributor to the learning of this company? Is being an employee-owned company a mainstay?

CU: Ownership certainly gives people a financial stake in the company, which for most of us is important. I think for many people ownership goes beyond having a financial stake, of coldly calculating the stock value once a year. I think it gives our people an emotional commitment to Reflexite and our mission. There is a broader concept of ownership that can occur. It does not necessarily occur, but can occur in an organization, if you nurture and encourage that sort of emotional attachment. I think this deeper commitment is one of the reasons this organization has such low voluntary turnover.

Ownership is a key ingredient to the learning that goes on here. A lot of the learning that goes on and gets applied at Reflexite goes on when people get outside the building. Reflexite employee-owners are free, of course, to choose how they spend their free time. It's thrilling to come in here on a Monday morning and talk, in random conversations, about work-related things they were thinking about or getting done over the weekend. They take pleasure in thinking about the company!

DF: That's the acid test.

CU: How do people spend their own free time? I have found that a number of people here spend that time thinking about work, thinking about how to make things better. So ownership I think is a large factor in the equation. I wouldn't necessarily call it essential, but certainly highly desirable. It gives people something greater that comes of their work than a pay check. We feel the "pull" of the mission, to be chosen by our customers for having the best products and services. If you have stock ownership, but you don't have an appropriate work environment, a supportive work environment; if you have an old management model and just an ESOP program, you're just not going to get anywhere.

DF: There are many such innovations growing from the experience of companies like Reflexite. They seem to get lost in the translation within companies that lack the fundamental spirit that leaders have carefully cultivated here at Reflexite, over the years.

CU: It has been my observation here that the limitations on what can be accomplished in the organization are not set by the people doing the work; I think those limitations are set by us, the managers. Some of us don't want to take the risk and share the power necessary to create the environment where people can contribute. Secondly, there are some of us who have crossed that hurdle and we want to do the right thing, but we don't know what the hell to do!

DF: That is why we are producing this book, to speak to people who are out there trying to manage so organizations are enriched by their collective learning. We're out there groping around for new directions, as well. We know what the wrong things to do are like, but the new ways to manage are just taking shape.

CU: I did not learn what I am talking about in school. I have gained, through experience, a wonderful business education that wasn't there in the 1960s. Some books are starting to emerge now, but it was some five years ago that most of the ideas that we got that had some validity either came from articles or from seminars. It's that new.

DF: Would you say now that a lot of the ideas that are working are coming from within Reflexite's walls?

CU: I think there are two discoveries that we have made that are relevant. We've tried a lot of ad hoc stuff. It works for a while but you've got to have somebody sustain it all, so you've got to institutionalize. The thing that we've found in that area that works best for us is the quality improvement process. Everybody can be involved. There can be a common language. There is a very strong connection between efforts and results.

Secondly, I think that how you structure an organization – the roles and responsibilities you assign within that structure – can either be a mild plus, it's not going to be a huge plus, or a big negative.

DF: What would be some of the "plus" arrangements that you have created so far in your structuring that are keeping you from going to the negative side?

CU: You train the people. Encourage the people. Make learning easily available. Then begin to transfer those management functions that used to be centralized. It seems to work well in New Britain to transfer those functions to work groups and help them figure out within the team how to get the functions done. Now, when you do this it is absolutely essential that you make information readily available throughout the organization. You can't hold it close.

DF: But that's your "power"! Holding onto company knowledge means power in the old management system. It was predicated on the notion that I know more than you do, therefore I am more important than you are. You are saying that for your new work centers to flourish, those employees need information that is traditionally "owned" by managers?

CU: If people are better educated, better motivated, have information to make decisions, then tell me what you need managers for?

DF: Well, managers are needed for stitching things together, so that the work of individual units is connected to a well-functioning whole. Perhaps managers are those who are not designated for mainly operational work, but concentrate on organizational work?

CU: It's a different job to manage in the way you have indicated, but it's very high-level work.

DF: It's very cerebral, isn't it? Managers are not working with a safety net or a "how to manage manual" any longer. I look at Matt Guyer, your Reflexite of North America Director of Operations, as a prototype of the manager who flourishes with decentralization. Wouldn't you agree?

CU: Yes, he is.

DF: What is it about Matt that makes you confident that you're on the right track? How does he work differently than you would expect a typical plant supervisor to carry out the work?

CU: People like Matt as a person. And, he's not the only one coming up in the industry. I meet a lot of these young people at the Leaders for Manufacturing Program at MIT, where I go from time to time. They don't have any baggage. They don't have 20 years of experience that they've relied on that they're having to throw away. They're starting in the new world, so to speak. So, they certainly are motivated to figure out what works. Because they certainly want to be successful, they don't feel bound to repeat failed history. Some people that have been around 20–30 years are also very adaptable. You can't make a blanket statement. They are embracing new ideas and methodologies and throwing off some of the baggage that they bring with them. Still, I am optimistic about young people like Matt out there making a difference in organization through-out the country.

DF: Is "being liked by people" the difference?

CU: I would use the word "respect" rather than like. There are times when the people in leadership positions have to make decisions that they believe are correct but not necessarily popular. If, however, those decisions are made with a backdrop of caring for the people in the organization – with that important kind of credibility – people will say, "I don't necessarily like this, but I respect the person making the decision, so I'll abide by the decision."

DF: It seems that they also have a clear context for those tough decisions because employees have been helped to gain full company knowledge.

CU: Yes. In Matt Guyer's case, his positive personality and being liked has been a big plus. What is making him successful, though, is that he is very inquisitive. He always asks "why?" He's always saying, "Why have we done it this way?" He's is in his third basically different job in this company in just a few years and growing quite nicely. He's successfully demonstrated, time and time again, that he is a change agent. Matt goes out and gets new ideas and brings them in. Because of his ability to build rapport, he is able to bring other people with him, and they can bring him along, too. Some employees have really good ideas that they find difficult to communicate. Matt makes sure they are heard. He's done it in our shipping and materials area. He's done it in quality; and, now he's doing it in operations as a whole. That willingness to extend his learning to wholly new responsibilities is really the key to his success, and I've told him that.

DF: How does this open sharing of authority relate to your role? How do you have to be as Chief Executive of this company? I agree that I think that is what would work very well at the level that Matt is performing – the shop floor. Almost everyone is looking to the top of an organization for that symbolic leadership.

CU: It has changed for me, as the company has grown. Not long ago, it was essential that I lead by demonstrating, by involving myself directly with the people who were involved with me in this chain. I think the big part of the change happened two years ago when we split the US organization into two parts and I became disconnected physically. Now, we have 85 employees out of 326 here in our new Technology Center. I have daily contact with a distinct minority of people in the company. I'm having to figure out new strategies for creating and maintaining the kind of environment I feel we need in the company.

One element that used to be important but is now essential is the people we pick to lead our profit centers. Do they buy into, live, and promulgate the values that I think are critical to Reflexite's future? There are leaders in businesses across this country who know how to keep values intact while the company grows. I am just learning how to do this.

DF: How do you keep working on the values yourself? What kind of inspiration do you work with, what kind of folks do you interact with to keep you fresh in all of this?

CU: I don't think it's a matter of fresh in terms of values and principles, I think those are pretty stable. I think that the freshness comes in the different ways to communicate the values, to express, to actualize, so that the values themselves stay visible in the minds of our people and are factors in how we all behave. That's what you really want.

DF: How do you measure those factors that are most important to attaining high levels of what your stakeholders value?

CU: In business organizations, an essential part of our being is to obtain results, objective quantifiable results. It's been demonstrated time and time again that in American society, measuring things is a good way to draw people's attention. They get people to rally around, to set targets, to have new breakthroughs, to try things and then measure again and see if you get an intended result. So measuring, whether it's financial statements or quality improvements or widgets produced, is a good thing to do.

Measuring is a good management tool that need not be limited to managers. It can be practiced throughout the organization, with people having requisite basic skills, access to information and computers, and so on. We can all measure and monitor, intervene and change something, monitor again and improve things. It works and we do it.

There are more qualitative ingredients to the success of a company in this kind of environment that we live in today that are incredibly difficult to measure. I've talked with Dave Edgar and our management team about the fact that we have reasonably sophisticated ways to measure the results obtained in the nine or ten profit centers that we have scattered around the world. We don't have the same sophisticated pulse-taking and measuring techniques for the more qualitative things we want to be as people no matter where Reflexite is in the world.

Dave and I have talked just recently about trying to equalize that; to get across to the managing directors of profit centers that some of these less objective things such as training and development of people are as important as "Did you meet your profit plan?".

DF: How do each of you in the management team stay in tune with all these data?

CU: We do it by osmosis and we talk about it at meetings with managing directors. We try to make a good example as we bring them in here. This month, we are conducting the first ever employee survey in the company and it's being done right by [a leading personnel consulting firm]. And they are learning that we are quite a unique organization.

DF: They probably don't have words for some of the things you folks do as employee-owners. It will be a good learning engagement for them, too.

CU: It is. They're having fun. It's going to work out. One of the things I am hopeful that we will get out of this is some measurement of peoples' feelings and perceptions on these more qualitative issues. I will be able to go back to a managing director and say, "Ownership doesn't mean enough in your organization. It's important in this total company, so we're going to measure this again in two years. We expect to see improvement here. What are you going to do over the next two years to create this kind of situation in your organization?"

Now, we begin to get some yardsticks on the more qualitative aspects of work life in a highly decentralized organization. I have hope; I do not yet have any evidence.

DF: It just occurred to me as I was listening, that is one of the real flip-flops for the managers of today versus yesterday. The managers of yesterday could be quite confident that if those quantified measures worked, their careers were in good shape. So they worked really hard to work out their quantitative, analytical skills. In fact, our business schools base most of our training on skills for analysis and quantification. The message is that it is hard numbers that truly matter. Yet, the flip-over is that for companies that are becoming like Reflexite, managers are more accountable for the "soft side" of people's value systems where judgment resides. This has more to do with qualitative factors that are measured intuitively or subjectively.

CU: The picture you painted first is still true, it is still quite pervasive in this country in particular and particularly in the short run. One of the things that bothers me the most about the prospect of Reflexite ever becoming a publicly owned company is the "quarterly mentality" that pervades the companies traded on the stock exchange. While we are not, it is still in the air. The owners of those companies are measuring the management and the people in that company every 62 or 63 work days, it's absolutely ridiculous.

DF: That's pressure! And they're measuring the wrong things in some ways too. They're measuring them but they're using those measures to indicate the wrong things. The health and the worth of the company.

CU: That needs to change; it really needs to change. People need to be held accountable by the owners and the board of directors, of course. But time frames must be opened up to allow us to open and thoughtfully grow the potential of the company. It is my own accountability that Reflexite ought to grow its profits by 20 percent per year measured over any five year period. There have been, however, quarters in years where that has not been the case. There have been times when I know that my behavior would have been different had I been subject to a different yardstick. I think it's a big problem.

DF: Most companies I visit have posters prominently displaying their customer-focused vision and mission statements in most public areas, as does Reflexite. Again, to values. How do you and your management team act so that these noble words are real thoughts, underpinning daily practice at Reflexite?

CU: Two thoughts. It has been demonstrated to me time and time again that a team, when people really operate as a team, will make better decisions than any individual member of the team can make. The work done at the Yale school of Organization and Management offers good decision models when an authoritative decision needs to be made, and an advisory or collaborative decision needs to be made. I agree with those contingencies. There are circumstances that require one to make different styles of decision. Decisions about principles should not be consensus decisions. Those are black and white. You stand for something, or you don't; but in cases where advisory or collaborative decisions are appropriate, I think that better decisions come from teams. Whether it's top management, in a work center or in product development, teams work best here at Reflexite.

I find that sometimes, however, even with my own senior experienced, mature, able people, that I can't get a team decision with the participation that I need. I have a very definite feeling people are waiting for me to make a decision or people feel that I have an agenda and something's going to happen and they are not going to get in the way of it.

DF: . . . and that you're just going to wait until they say what's on your mind?

CU: This tells me I have more work to do on team-building. I remember how frustrated I got at my house, not long ago. Our management team was having a planning retreat. I was looking for creative ideas and wasn't getting anything but silence. I think it is because everybody thought that I had something on my mind, so I was going to go through the motions. Then, I was going to say, "Okay, here is what is going to happen." To break the ice, I cited an example of a time when someone came forward to affect my thinking.

DF: You were reminding them that they can actually change your mind?

CU: That's right. Now, I'll tell you something else. I do not know another way to get people to believe their ideas matter in this company, than to model this as CEO with my management team. As we were about to start this interview, you talked about how people bring "baggage" from their past, when entering an innovative corporation. This makes them either unwilling or unable to change, for they have no model, other than their past, to go by.

DF: Yes.

CU: This is a very personal example. I do not know any other way to run this company than with extensive team involvement at every level. I find reinforcement from the examples of other successful companies, from the other CEOs with whom I talk, and certainly, from the Board of Directors of this corporation who are tremendously talented, experienced executives.

Well, we talk about "teams" around here. Thank goodness that Dave Edgar and I got rid of "family." We used to talk about the "Reflexite family." Wrong, really wrong. I am glad we truncated that early. Teams go about doing the company's business. Families are another aspect of our lives altogether.

Within the senior management team, the five of us, I am told how much they like the openness of our approach. Going to Maslow's hierarchy of needs, they are saying that there is real self-actualization going on. There is power sharing that none of them had experienced in their past organizations. They had been in middle-management. Now they come into our team environment and they're able to participate. They have direct impact on the future of a company.

DF: This must put a great deal of energy into the company's leadership.

DE: Yes, the feeling of power also comes from the fact that you can get a group of people to share ideas and influence each other. The good thing is that what you decide together happens very fast afterward, because all the principals are involved. To me this is a real "turn-on." This is an effective group with whom I can sit down and do lobbying. This lets me actually have an impact on the direction of the company. Maybe the idea I come in with is not the idea that we go out with; but, it's that *forum* to exchange ideas and then do something on those ideas that matters.

In other networks outside Reflexite, with other HR folks, for example, we exchange ideas. I come back, but maybe nothing really happened. Here you can network with the people that have the power and ability to move the business rather rapidly. That's lot of fun!

CU: It's important that our management team be willingly proactive about sharing the responsibility and power we have from the organization throughout the organization. I think we do a reasonably good job at that. An employee survey that we have being done by that consulting firm will tell us how well we are doing or not doing in this sharing. It may tell us that we have a lot further to go. Perhaps there is some saving grace in saying, "Well if teams are a good way to get things done at Reflexite, what's the matter with a top management team?" Our team has to work the same as the other teams in the organization upon which we now depend for producing a high quality product using the full talents of everyone involved.

DF: A lot of things that are done in "new ways" still look like the old. You still have a shop floor and you still have people making the product. Surely their relationships have changed, as your work centers are formed; but they still have to move material into finished form and do all those practical things. In a sense, it is "putting new wine in old bottles." Perhaps transformational change does not always require wholly new organizational forms to be constructed. Would it mean, however, that ways people act with each other in these structures have to be fundamentally different? Specifically, you still have an executive committee, of sorts, yet you count on members not using their power to politic for their self-interest.

CU: When I came to Reflexite, I was struck by the low level of political activity that existed in this company. I was very interested in trying to figure out why. What I figured out is that there was no real payoff for negative politicking. The two founding brothers of this organization, two engineers, were very interested in the technology and moving their patented technology forward. They showed no interest in internally competitive politics. Instead, they fostered a spirit of mutually beneficial ownership that goes on today. Rather than take it for granted that this will go on unattended, I work to see that it is institutionalized in every possible way.

DF: I imagine it would be a great relief for someone to come to work here, after being battered by corporate politics in more traditionally hierarchical companies.

CU: Yes. There are some subjective things you can do and there are some objective things you can do. For example, we dont have any discretionary bonuses here, because in my experience this led to lots of politics. We don't have any perks here either. Those special advantages for managers, parking spaces, fancy offices, club memberships, do not add value; instead, they bring negative value to whatever an organization is trying to do.

When we do find people in the organization engaging in some political activity, we try to make sure there is no big payoff for it. You "call it out" and get to root causes. People do bring political habits from other places they have worked that used to pay off for them. It is vital that they learn such attitudes and actions are not tolerated here, for they work against all our company values. Accordingly, we are very careful about who we bring into the company, what kind of personality they project, background experience from which they came. This is terribly difficult to figure out in an interview situation, but we have to be attuned to signs that a person might not come to respect our open culture. I hope that new people will feel about it as I did, when I came aboard, "Wow, this openness is really great!". We can learn to ascribe different values in a situation, that we don't have to fear making mistakes or need to set up others to avoid blame.

DF: Reflexite has a product line, the prismatic, light-reflecting sheet material that would seem to me has infinite possible applications. Furthermore, the team atmosphere that you have been discussing opens the creative potential of employees to explore and try these new applications. This is a powerfully fortuitous condition for a global company to be in. Would you agree that frontier is set by the extent to which Reflexite people "manage to learn"? I hope so, for this is the gist of our book!

CU: I have no expectation to come back in to work Monday, Dave, and say, "Eureka!". We are searching out the ways.

DF: Maybe the people that succeed you 50 years from now will appreciate what you are going through, but my gut tells me that you and a lot of other leaders of organizations of all types are really involved in starting over. The marketplace and technologies are just that new. Peter Vaill, a professor from the George Washington University whose interview also appears in this book, calls becoming a beginner, a "reflective beginner." In this regard, Cecil, I don't see you at all as a nonexpert, but I do appreciate the look in your eyes which our readers will not see. There is an eagerness to learn in them that I am fortunate to see in my college students. When they have a new idea, they light up with a wonderful kind of hopefulness.

DE: I think Cecil stated it well a couple of nights ago talking to that group of superintendents of schools whom we hosted for the Connecticut Business and Industry Association's Total Quality Education Institute. They were asking Cecil how he felt about Reflexite's remarkable progress through the many new things we are doing. He said that he is actually in a mild state of dissatisfaction. It is analogous to always being kind of halfway to our goal. We *are* a much different company than we were seven years ago, when I joined the company as VP for Human Resources.

We do have lots of Reflexite people realizing their potential; but we don't measure ourselves by where we were five-six years ago. We measure ourselves by where we are today versus where we think we can be. With that kind of attitude you can celebrate your successes, then you go back to being "mildly dissatisfied." We know we are not where we can be. I think that's healthy. It is a driving force.

CU: Three years ago, we were halfway into where we wanted Reflexite to be. Now, we are halfway in to where we want to be, yet far ahead of where we were then!

DF: The ballet is a metaphor that may capture what you are saying about remaining mildly dissatisfied. I have heard its dances described as being in a fluid state of constant falling. To dance, one has to risk putting oneself off balance in public! Then, they must stay just a tad off balance for most of their performance. It takes a lot of practice to "fall ahead" as planned. So must it be for you at Reflexite.

DE: In our early Crosby Quality Training sessions, they used the comparison between a hockey game where all hell breaks loose and a ballet. Most companies are too much like a hockey game. We are trying to become more like a ballet. We can predict our movements with some level of success.

DF: Reflexite's performance deserves a "standing O."

Interview with Matthew Guyer
Director of Operations
Reflexite of North America
New Britain, Connecticut

Interviewer: David Fearon

DF: We hope to characterize management in our book as a positive presence in that it allows organizations to respond very quickly to external changes; accordingly, to make internal corrections, adjustments, and improvements on a very timely basis. How does this resonate with you?

MG: It makes complete sense. It is in keeping with the culture that Cecil Ursprung has developed and the emphasis he puts on different kinds of things. I realized early on that the only way we were going to get an awful lot done was to share the responsibilities among all employee-owners. There were so many things going, running their courses so fast, that a few managers could not possibly cover them. Customer demand was growing, but we had one or two people who were sort of directing the actions of 78 people. Each of these did specific tasks, only when they were told to do so. When those tasks were completed, they would come back and stand in a line in front of the manager waiting to be given another specific discrete task to go do.

DF: They would actually do that?

MG: Oh yes, absolutely. I remember these lines among my most striking memories when I first started working here just a few years ago. I am sure it must be worse other places. Reflexite is fairly progressive, or we think we are, in a lot of ways. Yet, not so long ago, there were 30 or 40 people on each shift, all adults coming from all different kinds of backgrounds, lined up in a single file outside the foreman's office at the beginning of the shift. It took a good 20 minutes, until every person had gone through to be handed a small piece of paper. That was a "job card" prepared through a series of clerical steps to tell them how many pieces to make. They go out to the machine listed on the card, make the specified pieces, then come back to stand in line to be reassigned to another machine to make other pieces.

DF: It sounds like programming a machine. This little card represents their "cog-in-the-wheel" duties for the work day.

MG: Right. They didn't necessarily set the machine up when they got to it. It was usually set up for them. If they ran into a problem, they'd just stop and wait to tell their supervisor when the supervisor came around. That supervisor would then go find the maintenance person. Meanwhile, the machine would be down and the person would just be sitting there, or would go off to the break room. While the employees were making the piece, if they had a problem or question about the quality of the material or something related, they again would stop and refer this to the supervisor. The supervisor would then take the matter to the Quality Department. They would make a ruling from a database of information the department had. When they were done, they would give the card back. Again, there would be a series of clerical functions that would result in that information getting entered into the computer. The excess material laying on a work table would be picked up, taken away, and packaged by somebody else in another department. Eventually, orders were processed.

DF: It is obvious, in hindsight, that you could not keep that functional system going and meet demands for high quantities of high quality goods. Yet, looking over the plant floor from your office window, I see nothing that resembles lines of people waiting for their next job card.

MG: What we have evolved into now, and keep trying to continually evolve, is teamwork. People now have all the the critical information about the complete customer orders that they are going to generate in their work centers. Now, when they come in at the start of their shifts, they go right to their work centers. Second shift arrivals meet with their first shift counterparts in an overlapping period to learn what is going on and transfer the customer orders still needing attention.

Today, as new orders come into the company, they print them up at the appropriate work center. We used to print them way up stream so it took five days for orders to make their way to the shop floor. Now, team leaders in the work centers to which orders are directed by customer service, coordinate them with the team running the five or six machines in their centers. These folks have a much better hand on the pulse of what is going on in their work center. They can rotate among the operations, yet each runs the same equipment with some degree of regularity, so they become familiar with the machines as they are run. This attunes them to when something's wrong. If a person is on a machine for a few hours, as in the old days, making a set thing and then not coming back to that machine for weeks, sensing that something is going wrong is unlikely.

We've assigned specific maintenance people to specific work centers. They go there whether something's wrong or not, which is a revolutionary thing for us. As I mentioned, they used to wait. A complaint would go from an operator to a supervisor, maybe from the supervisor to the plant manager, maybe next to the maintenance manager, and then down to a maintenance person who would schedule that repair. Finally, it got done.

Now we have the maintenance people out there every day, so that they know the teams. They become part of the team, sharing a sense of pride in the team's results. These technical people now train the operators and educate them in how to take care of a lot of the equipment themselves. That then frees them up to actually start making improvements to the equipment. Now, we have the team members communicating to the maintenance people, ". . . if we could put another roll here then we could wind up this material while the machine is still running. And, if we could put slitting blades here we could slit it while it winds up instead of having to do a second stage. It would save time." They talk about a whole lot of different things, now, from safety issues to improvements in throughput and quality.

DF: Gee, what does this leave for you and the other managers to talk about?

MG: That's a whole new frontier for us too. I think for me one of the biggest things has been that now we now know each of our five work centers on each shift is expert at knowing what they make, for whom, and why it is important. Each is like a microcosm of the whole Reflexite Company.

Teams have a business going on within our entire business. They now order their own raw materials into their work center from an internal supplier, another department. They schedule the jobs. They rotate the people, because there's a real drive and peer pressure to rotate people. They ensure that everyone is cross-trained within their work center so that they are able to rotate. And they receive and analyze computerized performance reports. Teams ascertain the open orders and backlog that they have, the percentage of the backlog that's overdue, anything like that. We put in telephones, desks, and computers, file cabinets, everything they need to manage the business from the work center.

This also allows our customer service representatives, and everyone else, to call, communicate through voice mail or make personal visits. Whatever works with those work centers, as opposed to again going up and down through all these different ladders in the organization. Communication is now direct and swift. It's allowed us to go from five days to get an order to the floor to a maximum of 15 minutes to get an order to the floor. This is an amazing cycle time improvement. From a management point of view it has many implications to our customers for quality and service.

DF: Remarkable. What made it all happen?

MG: Imagine me trying, all by myself, to schedule the two-thousand plus potential different products that we make here; doing so across more than 60 people working over 17 hours a day minimum! I would probably try to keep a handle on all of that myself, or do it through a production manager or some staff arrangement. It would be impossible for me to communicate with the people to educate and do everything; impossible and it is a fairly small company. It certainly wasn't a strategy to grow with.

This work center approach is the best thing I could come up with. I am sure that it is not going to be the final version. We change it as we go along. Yet, the main difference for me, in meeting my overall responsibilities for the plant, is that I now know that everyone knows what we are doing here!

By having five work centers I know there are five manageable units out there that are so much more competent at running their small portion of the company than I could ever be at trying to look at the whole overview of it. So, I can communicate with five team leaders and hopefully get a message across to 40 people on that shift and those five team leaders during the course of their week. They sit down with me at the end of the week to communicate the issues and needs of the 40 people on that shift back to me; without my sitting down with all of those 40 people which would just be unreal to try to do. I do the same with our support teams – materials management, human resources, engineering. If I were to try to centralize material planning, there's no way I could keep a grip on ordering materials in the right amounts with all of the nuances of doing that. These people do know them and can do it themselves.

DF: You brought about these changes in less than two years! Why do you think, Matt, that there are still perhaps thousands of men and women in this country who manage with responsibilities like yours, yet who want to keep that centralized grip on their operations; who need that grip and cannot conceive of letting go? Why do you think that force is so strong? I assume at one point, when you were becoming more involved in the managing of the plant, that you felt that you needed to get a grip on it and to have that grip and felt that force in you.

MG: I sure did. I think that's a huge issue these days. I am sure it always has been so in manufacturing and probably works the same way in service companies. *The change is in people more than technology.* As an example, we have team leaders now, drawn from the groups. We used to have a supervisor and an assistant supervisor on each of our three shifts. Those six people were all indirect labor. They spent most of their time in the production office. Each had a locked toolbox that contained tools that were to be used by their shift when someone from that shift wanted or required the use of a tool. They saw every order to be manufactured, sorted them, ripped them into discrete orders, decided how to disseminate them on the shop floor.

When we started the process of making things the way they are. I spent a lot of time talking to those six people about how their jobs would change. I presented the value of taking a lot of the portions of what they do and pushing them down to the people who could do them closer to where the real work is getting done who would have a better grip on them. That would then free up the supervisors to get involved in a whole lot of new things that they had never done before in terms of actually improving the process.

DF: How did that come across initially?

MG: It didn't come across well at all. I knew we managers needed to get outside the work processes, so that we could tweak them for improvements and clear the road for progress. Yet, they saw themselves as so much a part of the process, it was, at first, unimaginable that this workforce could get along without their direct control.

DF: Did they eventually go along?

MG: Out of the six people, three or four "bought in," two not at all. There was absolutely no progress there. The way it's shaking out now, with some transfers to our technology center and a couple of retirements, we just have one person left really out of that six that is still an indirect labor contributor. He finally did come around to it. I remember I jotted it down in my notebook the day it happened. He came in my office and said. "I need something to do. I sat in my office for two hours this morning and straightened up my whole desk. I have sharpened all of my pencils, did everything I could, then sat and looked out my window." His office is next to mine. He's got a window right there that looks out on the shop floor. He said, "I saw people walking back and forth talking to maintenance people, talking to engineers. I saw product flowing around. I saw what might have been conflicts or questions or different issues arise. I saw customer service people walking in front of my office, but nobody needed me!". He told me it was really scary at first. Then, he said, "All of a sudden, I knew you were right. I do have something to do, but it is not fire fighting."

This made my week. We found a slew of things for him to do: set up productions and improvements, cataloguing peoples' skills, planning for future skill development and future classes helping work centers produce annual reports. We had a whole list of problems that we had never gotten to for corrective action and improvement. These were things and ideas he could never get to because he was always caught up in the day-to-day clicking of the gears with never a chance to step out of it and not be drawn into it. Now he's doing all kinds of things we need. He just came back yesterday from spending three days out in the field in the Chicago and Wisconsin areas with one of the customer service people and the regional territory manager who lives out in Chicago. They called on 15 customers from all different bases of our business. You never could have done that a few years ago. The management at that time could never have imagined that we could let him out of the building. What would have happened if he wasn't here?

DF: Everything would have fallen apart. That's an excellent anecdote. My impression there is that all the time that person was feeling needed, because he was so directly engaged in the process, he was getting better and better at doing just precisely what he was expected to do. In other words, he was learning. I sense that he had learned so well that he almost didn't have to think about it anymore. He was a very competent person. The environment shifted under the six you decentralized and it brought him to the outer edge of his familiar competencies. He "let go" and trusted you.

This case is analogous to everyone we're talking about who is holding on so tight to their supervisorships, managerships, even their functional VPships and their CEOships. They're saying, "I know how to do this well. It's made my company somewhat successful. I've gotten my degrees. I've posted my certificates on the wall. You're asking me now to almost start over again, very publicly in front of people I used to look after!" They, you, your associates, even I as a management professor, have little choice but to count on our learning abilities, and wade into the ambiguity.

MG: You probably handle it differently depending on who you work for or what kind of support you have. I think some of the fear comes from people that say, "If they can all do it so I can leave for a week or two am I still needed at all?" Yes, we can be, if we have the support from the top and the realization that there is an awful lot of development you can do in the business.

Where do you start? What do you do? It does require totally different skills.

I think the way that we have tried to address it is by prioritizing what it is *organizationally* that we are trying to get done, what are the top things to work on? The former supervisors' goal is help the teams succeed. Secondly, they can make sure that we are maximizing the use of raw materials. A couple of our raw materials are extremely expensive. They can work with the teams to come up with creative ways of making sure none is wasted, tracking and measuring this with them as they learn what works best.

Of course, we need skill building to learn new ways of managing. One of the first things for this manager was to help him develop a new system of time management. Where once his day was blocked out in routines, so that his time was managed for him, now he had to manage his time. Because his role became more to bring people together to learn and solve problems, he was trained in managing a meeting, in creative brainstorming, in listening and other leadership skills.

This need for skill development extends to every team leader. We brought all the team leaders to a Joel Barker program the other day on paradigms and hunting for paradigms. None of them even knew what a paradigm was. We have since been doing a lot of talking about their new responsibility as leaders to be open and aware of the ideas of their associates; about how to hunt for new opportunities and work through what keeps you and others from being receptive to them. This is something that would not have been considered a few years ago, nor needed, for they wouldn't have had occasion to use it. If we had sent people off to a lot of these things a few years ago they would have come back and gotten very frustrated.

DF: Matt, it would seem that every person in your plant is in some stage of moving away from the comfort zones of the old jobs with their cards and simple routines. This means taking risks. The higher they are in the company, the longer the fall. Does it look to you and them that there is no safety net? Or have Cecil and his team made it possible for people to deal with those fears of change? How do they communicate this so that it reaches the shop floor?

MG: Credibility. It starts with Cecil and works through me as plant manager. Without trust, most of what I have told you we are doing would be a hard sell at best. To the extent that we are believable, that when we say something is going to happen it is not just "hype," they will accept empowerment. The practical fear is that management will trick them into empowering other people, so they can cut you. If you can get over this potentially big stumbling block, then I think the challenge is to start preparing people to deal with taking on these new responsibilities.

I was surprised, going into this, by the new challenge of getting people to take themselves seriously. It was a transformation of self-image to think, "I am not just someone who makes X product"; or "I am not just someone who churns out these reports." Instead, we worked for each of us to be able to say, "I am someone who can actually be creative; I am someone who can learn these different things; I am someone who can do these things and more. I'm a business person."

The growth comes when we believe there is value in not just producing a given product or report yourself that you can tap down on the table and put a staple in it and put your name on; but that you realize you're making progress through helping other people be successful too.

DF: What are you doing to foster this new self-image among your employees?

MG: What we're doing right now I think is pretty fascinating to watch. We've taken about 65 people and over the years we have done English as a Second Language programs. We've gone into communication programs for the graduates of that. This is to take ourselves to the next plateau of work center performance. An experiment that seems to be working in this regard is that instead of using the textbooks that the community college teachers usually bring, I am using articles that I rip out of business magazines, *Businessweek*, *Industry Week*, *Harvard Business Review*, whatever, *INC.* magazine. We're talking over articles about the business environment, work teams, quality. They pick an article, read it, and then present it to the class and lead a discussion. We're finding that almost no one in the class has ever heard of, let alone read, an article in a business magazine.

DF: That's incredible. Yet, they have been employed for a long while as adults.

MG: And they don't think of themselves as being business people. Why would I need to read an article in *Businessweek*? One of the articles that we did, they invited me to see presentations on Wednesday, a couple of days ago, one of the articles that I had ripped out and that I had sent to Cecil and his team was an article from *Businessweek* about 3M, our biggest competitor, something about "3M's labs are back." It was circulated. When I went to class, a native Polish-speaking member brought in a new, bacteria resistant 3M sponge referred to in the article. She had made a graph of their revenue stream going up over the years. She's in there talking about how 3M is our competitor, that their technology is coming back. This shows, she pointed out, the importance of Reflexite's new product development. I'm thinking, "This is amazing!" Here are people that may have never thought before about our best response to our competition. Job security is an issue with them, of course. As a result of her leadership with this article, I sensed they were beginning to think more like business people.

DF: That's a fine story. The workforce that started when this company was born, some 20 years ago, is by and large still here. Now you are leading them into investigating and trying "modern concepts" about reorganizing so that they can participate in managing Reflexite. I know it may sound crass to say so, but you could have left these employees out in the cold, hiring instead more technically educated workers who abound in this state. You would not have had to include

English lessons and other remedial training in your cost structure. Yet what you are doing is taking these very same folks and creating some kind of magic which I wish we could bottle and share everywhere. You kept them, kept the faith, and Reflexite is flourishing. What's the magic?

MG: I guess there are a couple of things coming together. Some of this spirit came from the founders of the company and got passed along. They once had an option to cash out of the business to an outside buyer, but chose not to because they could not get guarantees that the jobs would stay in Connecticut with the workforce. That sacrifice helped to show that such commitment is in our culture. Cecil reinforces this at every juncture. We are aware of the incredible damage it does to lay people off, unless we are close to having to close our doors. We would do all kinds of things that a traditional company would not do before we would do a layoff, before we would replace people, or upgrade. This goes both ways. These people have stuck with us through some hard times and growing pains. We are as good as we are today, because of them.

DF: What about you? When it came to choosing the top leader for this North American operation, they could have gone out and recruited a "hot shot," big-school trained manufacturing engineer. Weren't you also somewhat of an underdog?

MG: I am not sure that underdog is the right word at Reflexite. Many of us do not necessarily come from the traditional backgrounds that you would use to stack the deck in a traditional way. You could hand pick people who look that good on paper, or you could trust the business to those of us who have grown with the company. We have invaluable knowledge gained from constant contact about our products with customers, suppliers. We know the "ins and outs" of this business that could be learned nowhere else.

It definitely happened with me and I definitely do feel the same responsibility. When I started, I didn't ever intend to end up in manufacturing. After I got out of school, I was done with college, I really wasn't sure what I was going to do or where I would end up. I started working part-time in the Reflexite shipping department, almost on a lark. Six dollars an hour was better than no dollars an hour and after traveling across the country I had pretty much expended my resources and needed to generate some more so I could buy myself some time to figure out what the next step was.

In the process of being here and watching the company grow there were a whole lot of different things I thought could be improved and I would jot them down on napkins and pieces of paper, thinking I would pass these insights along when I moved on. I would say, "Here are a bunch of things I noticed. You ought to put these shelves here and line this thing up over here." Most of it was knowledge I had from living the process and using common sense. I didn't know anything about shipping or factory layout or anything; but I was a victim of it or a participant in it. Some things just made sense. As I left, I typed my list, gave it to them, and said, "Thanks, it's been great."

I got a call a couple months later saying, "We've still got the list on the desk and we haven't done a single thing on your list. Would you want to come back as a consultant for a couple months and try to help us execute a few of these things?" I said, "Wow, a couple thousand dollars and I will be a consultant; isn't this amazing!" So I came back and started doing that. Then they said "There is so much going on and we see positive change, do you want a job?"

DF: What did they figure out to call you then?

MG: They called me a management trainee. I was the first ever and I think maybe the last as I know it. I spent time in shipping, managing that. Then, the quality control manager went on maternity leave and decided not to come back, so I fell into doing that for a little while. That was in a sequence of events when Cecil started looking at continuous improvement processes to do company-wide. I accepted that implementation project and began to learn all I could about TQM. It was very new to us, new to a lot of small companies. It still is maybe. I could become the Reflexite expert on it, but there was so much that we could work on that I could stay just ahead of where the company's actual progress was. In the process of laying down some fundamentals, I started visiting other companies. There I saw work cells and process teams. I came back and said, "Wow, we've just got to do some of this stuff." One thing led to another.

When we split the company up to create the Technology Center and Reflexite North America, the new president coming in from our Canadian business was one of the most receptive to the idea of work centers and teams. He offered me a job to stay here, rather than go on being a corporate quality person. It would be to "move everything around." He was again kind of an underdog himself, if you want to call it that, having more knowledge of marketing than manufacturing. We are both younger than your typical model of president/ operating officer. So we said, "Let's just do it!". I showed him a book called *The New Manufacturing Challenge*, read it, had dinner a couple of times and got real excited about our emerging vision of how we could change things here. We just started doing it, while developing the vision with people everywhere. Our intent became noticeable when we started cleaning things up on the shop floor that had been ignored for years.

DF: You are tailoring this outside management learning to your own unique business situations.

MG: Yes, it's constantly changing and moving as we're challenged by new things we read and see. People in the work centers have taken hold, putting up a convincing argument against our best laid plans for combining two work centers into one. How often do the employees on the shop floor in a traditional company solicit the plant manager and say, "Your layout is wrong. We ought to be one work center"? I had to gauge my response, then say. "Hey, they probably know better what's going on. Get out there, Matt, and feel it, look closely." They sold me. Centers four and five are now Work Center Forty-five! It's working great, a lot better than it did before.

I think there is something about our culture that we all carry with us at Reflexite. What is valued are the contributions that you make and how you get things done. It is evidence of real performance that matters, not what was on your résumé when you showed up at the door.

DF: Would this openness stand up when the chips are down and you all feel pressured to drive the business or else?

MG: The pressure has been on, since I took on these new responsibilities about a year ago. I had thought I would have a production manager reporting to me, when I accepted the offer, someone to be an intermediary and help with the communications. It worked out that I was asked to go ahead without one. I assume at first we would bring in a production manager or engineer in a team-based company to import some new ideas and implement them. To make a long story short, I was soon faced with the challenge of pulling off doing my job with no traditional intermediary to the work center teams. They were so new, that we had not even developed team leaders *per se*. Abandoning any thought of a traditional plant structure, we went to having five people on each shift, five new team leaders, work with me directly on every aspect of operation. In keeping with the vision of this company, I soon had these groups of five being innovators and implementers in the business. They lead, whether I'm there or not.

I run the business with them, now, but it was not so long ago that this role would not have dawned on any of the ten. Most had never been in formal leadership positions before, a lot had never read a business management article, like we talked about before. Most are not native English speakers. So the first few months were pretty tricky. What we have been doing is an endless amount of talking. I "download" into these ten people everything I possibly know and what I think is important for them to develop as skills. This is how I leverage myself throughout the business.

About six months into it, what I was describing before with the remaining supervisor no longer having people knock on his door and come in, was happening to me! All of a sudden, I started to get a full sense of calm. It was just amazing. I relaxed and looked out this window to the shop floor. There weren't people coming to me saying "When's this order going to be done?" or "What does this customer want?" Or, "We just ran out of X size boxes, and can you believe what they shipped us this time". I can look out now and see things taking place smoothly, see people growing as conflicts are resolved. I see product flying out to our customers! I can watch the overall numbers of the business. Now my work is to invest in those people out there, so they go on learning how to do everything better. This is instead of trying to drive a 30 million dollar company myself.

DF: I am looking out there now. No one is looking back to see if "the boss" is watching. Pretty refreshing!

MG: Two years ago we had 82 people doing about 12 million dollars in business. Now, we're down to 64 people in direct labor and we're hoping we're going to do 34 or 35 million in business. There is still tons of capacity out there. It is not that we have made huge technological breakthroughs. We've made some smart moves and changed some machines around and taken some steps out of the process that were redundant. The bigger thing, however, is that out there people are so much more involved and are driving things. They are not waiting for commands; a far cry from those lines waiting for job cards.

DF: To sum it all up, you presented the image at first of the people literally coming here to serve the machines. Now, several years later, particularly since you became plant manager, machines are working for the people.

MG: Sure. I remember listening to a Philip Crosby tape in which he said that a key part of our business is that we give people lives. We give our employees lives. It's true. And now we give Reflexite life. You wake up thinking about new ideas for the company, driving to work, and everything is Reflexite. You've got to shut off once in a while! It's not because you're scared of a deadline, it's not because things are bad, it's just because you're so engaged in what you're doing.

DF: The company is in your heads. You are engaging what I call in a chapter for this book, everyone's "managerial minds." That it gives you all a livelihood is particularly noticeable in an employee-owned company. Sharing the management of this plant among fellow employee-owners must bring enormous satisfaction, when revenues grow so nicely.

MG: Absolutely. I'm having a ball. The results have to be there if those more skeptical don't buy in on faith to what we're doing. Even if the results weren't as strong as they are for me, based on the kind of response that we are getting from people and the kinds of things we are doing I am delighted.

Two weeks ago we did a leadership retreat with those ten team leaders. Now there is nothing great about us for doing it, but I don't think there are an awful lot of other people doing leadership retreats with direct labor employees. Not that that makes us progressive, but I think that we're starting to realize that and what we were trying to do that day was to make those ten team leaders realize that as individuals, whether it is in their communities, at work in their work centers, or their families, that they are leaders. Like you said, everybody has a "managerial mind." Everybody has a leadership responsibility too. These ten people happened to be selected to be team leaders and even though they had never been leaders before, they have whole new responsibilities now.

We did exercises about what are the characteristics of leaders that we have respected in our pasts. Here are some of the global characteristics that people have come to associate with good leaders. You mentioned something earlier about traditional educational background not being an impediment to their involvement. They had listed good listening skills, a decent sense of humor, honesty and trust, and good communication, things that people with wide varieties of educational backgrounds, wide varieties of cultural backgrounds can have in abundance. No one was going to have to go off to MIT to learn to become a Reflexite leader. They all could work on what they had gained inherently from their home and community roles.

We ended that retreat talking about the day when none in the plant would just say, "I work on a machine at Reflexite. I make stickers. I make truck tape." Instead, we strive for this identity: "I'm a business person. I'm a leader. I've got these responsibilities that go above and beyond being there by seven-thirty, punching out by four, and keeping my scrap to a minimum. There's a whole lot more that I've got going on." That just does enrich someone's life and can't help but improve our results.

DF: Thank you, Matt, for "reflecting" so well on your fellow employee-owners.

Case: Learning and Growth at Reflexite Corporation

David Edgar
Vice President of Human Resources
Reflexite Corporation

A couple of weeks ago I bumped into Dave K. in the cafeteria and he told me how happy he was to be working at Reflexite. He thanked me for hiring him a few years ago. There was a smile on his face and a bounce in his step. I told him I felt the same way – that I too am happy to be working at Reflexite. We laughed and shook hands. And as I walked back to my office there was a little more bounce in my step as well.

We have many people like Dave K. in our company and it is that fact which gives me the most satisfaction. Dave is a Team Leader – material flow at our Avon, Connecticut plant, Reflexite Technology Center. He joined us as a machine operator about five years ago after working for a few years in the construction trade. He took a big cut in his hourly wage, but he wanted some job security and a company that would give him a chance to be somebody, to get ahead. After a short time, he transferred from manufacturing to shipping, then was promoted twice. Two years ago, Dave became a team leader at the newly formed Technology Center.

After just a few years with the company, Dave has more than $50,000 worth of Reflexite stock in his Employee Stock Option Plan (ESOP) account, but his happiness goes far beyond money. He loves his job and he's involved with Reflexite. He has passion for his work. His job goes well beyond shipping out rolls of plastic reflective material to our member companies. His "work" includes doing whatever he can to make Reflexite become a better company. He's a member of our ESOP Education Committee. He has spoken before hundreds of people at an ESOP Association convention in Washington DC about what being an employee-owner at Reflexite means to him. He has traveled with me (and another employee-owner) to Philadelphia recently to participate in a Department of Labor sponsored forum to discuss alternatives to corporate downsizing. He is a member of our new Employee Opinion Survey Committee and he's always an active participant in our employee meetings. Dave is *involved* with Reflexite.

In his Team Leader position, Dave supervises only one person. Like all our Team Leader positions, his is a very hands-on position requiring a combination of physical labor and leadership. He seems to thrive in our very flat organizational structure. He has a taste for learning. With no formal education past high school, he is now taking a college course at night. He eagerly participates in company training programs. Dave, I think, is a very good example of what we're trying to accomplish at our company.

There is a keen understanding at Reflexite that people are our limits. We are not limited by market size: we are a $50 million company in a world market of reflective products that exceeds one billion dollars. Nor are we limited by cash flow. We generate enough profits to invest in our growth which has averaged 30 percent per year for the last ten years. We are limited by the quality and capacity of our people. We are limited by the vast difference between average performance and superior performance.

The most important thing I do for the company, therefore, is to recruit and help grow superior performers. How do we grow people like Dave at Reflexite? I have summarized below some of the features at our company that promote learning and growth. Not all of them will apply to other organizations, but I'm sure many of them do. I know they work for us. The first three have to do with sharing.

Sharing Information

People in our organization – and in all organizations – have a thirst for knowledge. The more they know, the more they want to know. The fact that the majority of our stock is owned by the employees intensifies that need to know. We have a fundamentally sound communications program at Reflexite, but we realize companies can never do enough in this area.

Our communications program consists of quarterly plant meetings for all employees, monthly team meetings for employees involved in manufacturing, a brief monthly newsletter published by our Quality Improvement Team, a large "active" bulletin board, monthly "Owner's Reports" detailing how the company is doing financially, and Quarterly Reports that include financial and other important company topics. This sounds like fundamental blocking and tackling, but I am continually amazed at how many companies don't invest time in these type of activities.

Sharing Rewards

A company with a fair and respected reward-sharing system has a much better chance of getting employees to "buy in" and become involved. Our compensation philosophy at Reflexite is simple, well-communicated, and has stood the test of time. It covers four areas of compensation: base pay, benefits, perks, and incentive pay.

Base pay throughout Reflexite Corporation is modest – competitive, but not better than average. This helps keep our fixed costs under control which, in turn, helps keep our products competitive in the marketplace. Benefits are above average. Since our employees own most of the company and tend to stay with the company for a long time, we feel benefits should be above average. Perks are nonexistent. We don't feel people should get special benefits or be treated differently because of their job title.

Our incentive pay programs are designed to be outstanding. They are a very significant part of our total compensation program. Short-term incentive pay is cash. Almost all of our employees are on a monthly formula-based profit-sharing program called the Owner's Bonus. Long-term incentive pay is stock – our Employee Stock Ownership Plan (ESOP). The Owner's Bonus and ESOP create a win/win situation between employees and all shareholders. Employees can only benefit under these plans when all shareholders benefit.

Our reward-sharing system at Reflexite does not flow from the fact that we are successful. On the contrary, much of our success, I think, is a result of our reward sharing. When people know they will receive a fair slice of the pie, they will put all their effort into increasing the size of the pie. Many companies have no profit-sharing system. Others have a year-end Christmas type of bonus that arises out of a paternalistic culture. At Reflexite we want our employees to share profits on a monthly basis even if there are no profits (losses must be made up in subsequent months). This helps to keep them very engaged with the business on a continual basis.

Sharing Power

Sharing power is probably tougher for most of us than sharing information and rewards. It is even more important. We continue to stumble around a bit in our efforts to promote employee participation but we have some nice success stories as well. At our Reflexite North America plant in New Britain, Connecticut, ten working Team Leaders report to our Director of Operations. They no longer report to shift supervisors who reported to a production manager who reported to the Director of Operations. A new flat organization combined with a transformation from a traditional job rotation system to dedicated work teams has opened up tremendous opportunities for learning and employee involvement. None of this would have been possible without an enlightened manager and a completely new work structure.

These team leaders (like Dave K.) are "turned on" most of all by the power they can now exert in their jobs. They are making decisions that used to be made for them. Because they have the best information to make these decisions, the quality of decision-making and the speed of decision-making is now much better. It turns out that sharing power increases your own power and increases the power of the organization.

Many of us have a tough time letting go of the power to make decisions. But when we do, we are amazed at the results. People have considerably more capacity to make decisions than we give them credit for. Most of the time they will rise to our level of expectation (or beyond it). It is a lesson that we continue to learn at Reflexite.

Raising the Bar

Over the past three years, we have put a great deal of emphasis on raising standards throughout the organization. To join our company now, you have to be able to leap over hurdles that were not there in the past. These have been incorporated into our recruiting process. Likewise, the standard for success on the job has been rising and will continue to rise.

Our Performance Management System has been revised to focus more on training and development needs. People are measured on job knowledge and skills, as well as participation. Employees complete a self-evaluation form which asks them, among other things, what skills they acquired or developed during the year and how they put these skills to work to increase their value to the company. They are asked what they did to help their fellow employee-owners succeed. Those that supervise are asked specifically what they did to develop their people and increase their value.

A Reflexite Learning Center has been established and courses are taught in a new training room. Many of our instructors are employees who have never taught before or even made group presentations. They probably benefit more than the students. A resource library has various books, tapes, videos, and so forth that employees are encouraged to use to help develop their own careers.

We have an active wellness program that encourages employees to work out regularly in our fitness room. Quarterly wellness seminars are held on company time. Employees go through an annual wellness screening and receive a variety of 100 percent medical plan coverage as a reward for their participation. Fitness contests are sponsored to promote use of our fitness room.

By raising the standards and expectations in the areas of recruiting, performance, skill development and health, a certain climate develops over time whereby people take their careers very seriously. The number of people that are "coasting" goes down dramatically. We think that's happening at Reflexite and that bodes well for learning and growth – for our employees and for our company as a whole.

Quality Improvement Process

Every company needs certain vehicles that allow employees to participate in decision-making. At Reflexite, being an employee-owner just was not enough. Our Quality Improvement Process, however, has been successful in getting a critical mass of employees involved with continuous improvement. Our Quality Improvement Team is a cross-functional group of mostly nonmanagement employees. Charged with implementing the various steps of our quality process (supported by top management) they have assumed leadership roles in the organization. A variety of employees have served on Corrective Action Teams that are formed to attack serious issues, and probably over half our employees have been involved with our Employee Assistance Request System (EARS) which empowers employees to tap into our quality improvement process by pointing out circumstances that prevent them from doing the job right the first time.

We have learned, through our quality improvement process, the power of measurement. Measurement leads to a focus on improvement which leads to results. Our quality process, along with technology and ownership, has become one of three fundamental building blocks for Reflexite. The attitude of continuous improvement has extended well beyond the products and services we deliver to our customers – it has been taken to heart by the vast majority of our employee-owners.

Corporate Goals

We have the same five corporate goals today that we had ten years ago. They are qualitative, not quantitative. We feel that if we do these things well, the numbers will naturally follow. One goal concerns keeping our technology at the state-of-the-art, one concerns new product development, and another concerns quality. Two of our five goals concern people: to provide professional and personal growth opportunities for our employees, and provide mechanisms for all employees to share in the rewards of our future success and to participate in decisions that effect their work.

It's a bit of a cliché to say that building an organization committed to learning and growth starts at the top. But it's clearly a big help to define these types of people related goals from the very start, and continually measure ourselves against them. In the long run, it certainly helps grow people like Dave K. who, in turn, grows Reflexite.

14

Integrating Learning and Organizations

John M. Montgomery and Frank Scalia

The Present State of Learning in Organizations

Organizations, like people, learn – or do they? To paraphrase a statement attributed to B. F. Skinner that "Rats learn . . . people don't!", maybe organizations do not either – or at least not very well. In reality, both individuals and organizations are capable of learning. The capability to learn is particularly well developed in human beings. Through the centuries, the development of individual learning, its nurture, refinement, expansion, and almost universal application, has resulted in what we see as truly phenomenal progress.

However, our organizations' learning capability has not progressed at the same pace. We would argue that there is a reason why organizations, historically and today, have not recognized the importance of their capability to learn. Thus, they have not focused on the enhancers or inhibitors of this learning. In fact, some of modern organizations' most common and sometimes desired characteristics may be antithetical to an organization fully exploiting its learning capability. In particular, conventional management theory and style actually inhibit the integration of effective learning in organizations. It is our premise, consistent with the thoughts of our fellow contributors, that the true "learning organization" is a thing of the future – but an idea whose time has come.

Learning organizations need more than individual learning

The integration of learning in organizations requires more than simple attention to individual learning. While the learning effectiveness of individuals within organizations is a necessary condition to effective organizational learning, it is hardly sufficient. While we would agree with Argyris's[1] observation that individuals are the agents of both organizational action and learning, there is clearly more to the story.

Characteristics that determine effective organizational learning

Effective learning in organizations, then, could be expected to be dependent upon both individual action and established characteristics of organizational performance. As discussed later, it is dependent on a very different kind of leadership and management.

One can expect that the things that determine the effectiveness of organizational learning are:

- Associated with the purpose, vision, and values of an organization;
- Affected by the organization's structural/design attributes; and
- Related to the way the organization performs.

Responses from today's organization leaders

If we were to ask the leaders of today's organizations what are the characteristics of an effective learning organization, we would expect to get a broad range of answers, including "I'm not sure what you are talking about." If we were to attempt to identify organizations that at least seem relatively effective learners, we would expect little consensus, and even if there were, five years from now we would expect the conclusions to change. We also would expect to find that effective learning seems to occur randomly, and may be associated with differing, sometimes contradictory organizational characteristics.

This kind of variability is expected, as the idea of effective organizational learning is in a primitive state. While a mounting body of evidence is being collected, and interest is directed to the issue, we are not yet at a point where we can systematically identify the key ingredients to integrating effective learning into organizations.

However, there is no reason to believe that we cannot create a more highly evolved learning concept and, as a result, a radically different organization – one that is truly an effective learning organization. To accomplish this objective requires much more than establishing a reasonable and accurate conceptual base, it will require the use of a vision and system of management strategies that fully support effective learning. We view today's organizations operating at the lowest level of a Maslow-like hierarchy of needs, that is, at a survival level, particularly in the for-profit sector, where attention to both survival and security is critical.

How Organizational and Individual Learning Differ

Shared consciousness in organizational learning

The single most important difference between individual and organizational learning is the **shared consciousness** that underlies and creates effective organizational learning. That shared consciousness is maximized and made most effective by properly managing the group processes that are the basic engines of modern organizations.

Gordon Lippit's "Multocular Process"

In the early 1980s, the late Gordon Lippitt conducted an experimental doctoral course called "The Multocular Process."[2] The term **multocular** referred to the use of multiple ways of viewing and thinking about a problem. While Lippitt's interest was in the improvement of group (organizational) decision-making, he was nevertheless also dealing with the question of organizational learning. He was attempting to push the boundary of effective learning by using a highly directed, structured, and organized group process. Lippitt's recognition of the ability of organization to step beyond individual effort, and his belief that existing models of organized action could be improved, have a great deal in common with Senge's arguments in *The Fifth Discipline*.[3] Only the labels are different.

Essence of organizational learning

The idea of multiple views, of alternate ways of seeing, of viewing, and then shaping reality from many different perspectives, is central to effective organizational learning, along with the continual testing of ideas and ultimate comparison to performance. The difference between individual and organizational learning reflects the idea that the whole is greater than the sum of its parts – the parts here being learning individuals. The level of connection and organized patterning of organizational learning are also of a different kind and are themselves characteristics of shared consciousness.

In fact, individual and organizational learning may not even be the same logical type. The expanded capacity of organizational learning to significantly improve organizational performance and to overcome the limitations, failures, or loss of specific individuals also makes it different from individual learning. While the learning of individuals relies on acquisition of facts and experiences, the retention of such things, and the subsequent selection from memory for application to new situations, the learning of organizations goes beyond these processes. In fact, they may be taking them for granted while the learning organization focuses on the group processes that expand and empower shared consciousness. Effective organizational learning relies on the traditional processes of individual training and education, but it attends to improving group performance, expanding communication, focusing on creating learning values and motivation, and creating a culture of continual improvement. To improve these processes also requires considerable attention to the use of new technological innovations, such as information technology, and a systems approach to problem-solving.

Organizational Need for More Effective Learning

Stability a vanishing attribute

It is now a fact that accelerating change makes organizational stability a vanishing attribute. Organizations that ignore change in their environment, increased competition, changed interests and values in their employees, increasing demands by their customers, or changed social tolerance for their impact on the environment are in jeopardy. Some fail, others simply perform poorly. A recent example is the US Congress that continued to grow and spend without significantly improving the quality of its product or the image of its service to the American people.

Rapid advances in technology

Another significant aspect of the rapid rate of change is the continuing evolution of technology. Innovations occur so frequently now, that in many industries – computer software, for example – the cycle time for developing, marketing, and selling a product before it becomes obsolete is only a couple of years. The ability to gear up, perform effectively in a rapid burst, and then quickly change to a different process and product is crucial.

Rapid change's impact on organization

Looking within the organization, this rate of change also has a significant impact. Since information important to the well-being of the organization can come from almost any source, it becomes extremely important to open up communication and decision-making possibilities both vertically and horizontally. The practices of using quality circles, multidisciplinary task forces, management retreats, and group strategic planning sessions, are all rudimentary attempts to accomplish the process of changing and adapting (implicitly anchored in learning). Our experience with these existing modes of group interactions is consistent with Senge's view – that too many of these efforts result in an outcome below the capability of the least talented member. However, we have also experienced such efforts which resulted in outcomes that went beyond what conventional wisdom thought possible. The success of Chapparel Steel is an example where sharing of most tasks and decisions is expected of all employees. The difference may sometimes be in the composition of the group, that is, the extent to which the diversity of the expertise and perspective contributes to the synergy. In other cases, the failure may be traced not to group composition but to a failure to use effective group processes such as those discussed earlier in noting Lippitt's Multocular Process.

Rate of learning needs to surpass rate of change

Learning and the rate of change are inextricably mixed. Revans has stated that learning must surpass the rate of change if an organization is to survive over the long term.[4] If the rate of change continues to increase, then the effectiveness of organizational learning must also. However, it will require active vision, leadership, and tenacity to overcome the many hurdles to creating effective organizational learning.

Assessment of organization and its environment

An organization which effectively assesses those aspects of itself and its environment that bear on its survival and performance will naturally live longer and perform better than its competitors. Effective organizational learning bears on:

- The essential principles and meaning of the organization (its vision);
- The processes that introduce and reinforce the essential culture and values of the organization;
- The quality and effort of organizational members;
- Structures and processes that create effective action;
- The assessment of action as it occurs and the prompt feedback and correction of its quality;
- Environmental scanning and control;
- Attention to stakeholders and maintenance of constructive relationships;
- Creation and nurturing of patterns of reflection, development and renewal; and
- An attitude of openness and bias toward change.

Clearly, organization learning is tied to all the characteristics that bear on organizational performance and ultimate success. As organizations have become more sophisticated and other modes of improvement no longer result in significant change, learning may be the last significant mechanism for substantive positive change. "The rate at which organizations learn may become the only sustainable source of competitive advantage, especially in knowledge-intensive business."[5]

Why integration of learning into organizations is difficult

There are a number of reasons why the integration of learning into modern organizations will prove difficult, and why examples of learning organizations are few and far between. While some may claim we are in a post-bureaucratic era, there are still many healthy, thriving bureaucracies in all sectors of society. We also find an increasing dependency on highly specialized job functions, which makes holistic thinking difficult and tends to increase the levels of complexity found in any organization. Authoritarian leadership still exists in many organizations – another barrier to acquisition of necessary information and collaborative decision-making. This discussion focuses on the characteristics of modern organizations which constrain the integration of effective learning.

Three essential attributes

Learning organizations not only have skilled people and "skilled" processes, but also have acquired (learned) experience, which increases adaptability and probability of success, particularly in turbulent and uncertain conditions. In examining these three characteristics – **skilled people, skilled processes**, and **acquired experience** – skilled processes is probably the one that could benefit most from attention to effective learning strategies. The processes of organization that dictate the level of learning and effective adaptability have been described extensively using cybernetics by Stafford Beer,[6] but not widely integrated into modern organizations. A notable exception is the use of systems dynamics modeling, as developed by Jay Forrester[7] at MIT and recently popularized by Senge.[8] The systems or organizational perspective contributes a high potential improvement to effective learning by systematically explaining and considering complexity, rates of change, connections, effective organizational control points, and the characteristics which improve adaptability.

For organizations to become more effective learners, they will need to address and better integrate these three attributes: (1) people skills, (2) process skills, and (3) acquired experience. To accomplish this will require recognition of the need to more completely integrate the lessons of the human potentiality movement with those of systems engineering and organizational cybernetics. Both the improvement of the "soft-people-skills" and the harder technological skills, for example, information selection, acquisition, analysis, and prediction will be required to approach the concept of an effective learning organization.

Prepared to survive the unexpected

An effective learning organization is clearly better prepared to survive unanticipated environmental events, whether the collapse of primary markets, unexpected competition, or loss of a major constituency. It is also clear that an effective learning organization is more likely to perform toward its optimum, providing maximum performance in times that are good for business. Such organizations can also be expected to actively "create" their own futures in a more rapidly changing world, rather than simply reacting to change – even if such reaction is adaptive and results in survival. Last, there is a powerful focus in the effective learning organization on understanding how organizational actions will affect the broader community at large and a strong principle working toward societal synergy and compatibility. Even so, the path to creating effective learning organizations will be difficult.

Organizational Constraints on Learning

Four essential elements of the true learning organization are (1) vision, (2) culture, (3) principled value system, and (4) leadership support.[9] Whether that leadership is in the form of a CEO of a manufacturing firm or the administrative board of a church, it serves as the primary source of meaning, shared values, and resultant culture that underlies the direction of members' behavior – and therefore organizational action. In modern democratic societies, that leadership is collaborative, and it fails when it ignores or misreads the values, interests, and views of those who comprise the organization and those who are important external stakeholders.

Bureaucratic strategies that limit effective learning

Equally constraining on effective learning are traditional bureaucratic strategies, mainly in the areas of centralization and highly developed, rigid control strategies. Also important as a learning constraint is the tendency toward increased and more formalized specialization.

Centralization places decision-making as far removed from actual events and effective local experience as possible. Such organizations always develop a model of action that relies on field or local functions for implementation and a specialized centralized "staff" for operational and policy evaluation and strategic decision-making. As American business has come to realize over the past few years, this model is slow to acquire, acknowledge, and act upon key changes "in the field" important to success. Frequently this is because those who first discover them are not considered legitimate sources of evaluation information, or because their views must filter up a rigid chain of communication and be approved by the centralized professional staff. Centralization also tends to limit the flexibility of local decision-makers to act quickly without the approval of centralized authority. This, of course, limits the implementation of any learning in a timely manner and erodes needed commitment.

Communications are frequently distorted, filtered, or ignored. Discourse is infrequent and difficult. "Lessons learned" are of a narrow perspective and frequently exacerbate problems rather than correcting them. Competition between bureaucratic units becomes dysfunctional and is difficult to control.

Rigid control strategies

There are important characteristics of bureaucratic control that affect learning separate and apart from their centralized aspect. The basic purpose of rigid, overdeveloped control strategies is to eliminate the variability introduced by the human element. Bureaucracy excels at providing a highly reliable standardized set of actions to accomplish a specific purpose – a purpose which has been consciously planned and considered. The control which discourages free-form or novel organizational response as a protection against ineffective planned action is the same control which discourages "good" novel behavior in the learning context. Fundamentally, the whole concept of rigid control is antithetical to the practice of organizational learning. By its nature it discourages free thinking, spontaneous action, individual reflection, and developing local or unitized repositories of learning behavior and experience. Bureaucratic control has not yet "learned" to differentiate between "good" and "bad" exploratory behavior, therefore making the same mistake that society has made in similarly failing to differentiate such differences in an ecological sense, contributing to our environmental difficulties.

Model-in-use

Another constraint characteristic of existing organizations is the actual management model-in-use and the cause of its obsolescence. Those of us who have spent considerable time in a variety of work organizations recognize that it takes many years of hard work and limited responsibility before one is even considered for a senior position of authority (the one compelling exception is the short-lived trend of the seventies to hire young MBAs for such roles). If one finally reaches that elevated position, one normally relies on an education 20 or 30 years out of date, particularly in the management/leadership arena. A career of hit-and-miss experience has directed survival and maintenance of the status quo rather than systematic understanding of modern change strategies, recognition of human potentiality, or the confidence or tools to face head-on the expanding challenge of shifting social and technological bases.

Short-term goals

A further constraint on improved learning, at least on the American scene, is the continued focus on relatively short-term goals. One should expect to see a direct correlation between the willingness and ability of an organization to integrate effective learning strategies and its long-term goal orientation. Learning strategies take time, energy, and are sometimes long-range investments, for example, in expanding developmental activities of individuals or organizational units early in their careers or implementation. Its focus is on preparing people rather than repairing them. Significant evidence of return on investment may take many years, much as the belated American emphasis on quality, but will be equally as important.

Theory X management

Another significant constraint on learning is what we term a "dark side" mentality regarding organizational members – a form of mental model as described by

Senge.[10] The phenomenon was described many years ago by McGregor and termed Theory X management.[11] Despite much attention to the subject by students of management, and much evidence supporting the dysfunctional character of this style of management in most organizational settings, many organizations still practice this style based on a deep and sincere conviction that most employees are fundamentally inept and cannot be trusted. A leadership mentality which cannot accept the possibility of significant improvement in human potential, or has a basic distrust of the work force, will not be able to support effective learning in organizations.

The cost of fully integrating learning into organizations

Maybe the most important set of constraints, from some points of view, is the real and perceived costs of fully integrating learning into modern organizations. Whatever specific learning behaviors are eventually developed and perfected for use, they will clearly have profound effects on today's dominant ways of doing business. Recognition of the enhanced need for application of a broader and more comprehensive set of considerations, additional attention to indirect and subtle issues, and more conscious active decision-making, will force leaders and managers to spend more time on reflective thinking behaviors. They will need to demand the same from other organizational players. The time, and therefore the expense, associated with planning and decision-making will necessarily increase. Increased inclusion of a broader base of organization members in these activities will also have an added expense. The addition of consistent, systematic evaluation of operational and ongoing experience will also add costs. "Skunkworks" activities, more formal "intelligence" operations, operations research, and new forms of simulation, prediction, and forecasting, will also add additional burdens to most organizations.

Whether adoption of these activities results in new structures and subunits or simply utilizes existing organizational members and functions in new and challenging ways, such as in "virtual" subunits, the result will be an added initial set of costs. In times of increased competitive pressure, turbulent markets, or inconsistent or changing customer demands, justifying this expense in many organizations will be extremely difficult. We predict this will be as difficult in government and other nonprofit settings, where cost containment is becoming as important as in the competitive business environments. However, successful companies, such as the leading performers in the nuclear power industry, have used these challenges as the justification for transitioning to learning effectively.

Reward systems

We view today's dominant organizational reward systems as another significant constraint on effective organizational learning. There are two reasons for this.

First, these systems strongly reward individual effort at the expense of group or collaborative effort. This discourages collaborative effort and strong motivation for truly effective teamwork. It also discourages teaching and other support behaviors, which are necessarily indirect organizational functions that seldom receive strong visibility. The second reason relates to the fact that the present reward systems (promotional opportunities and bonuses, awards, and other forms of recognition) are poor reflections of cause and effect, actual contribution, and those who are effective organizationally. They remain flawed by favoritism, personality cultism, inaccurate information or evaluation, and ineffective timing.

Learning Disabled Organizations

Some might claim that an evaluation of modern organizations' learning disabilities is retrospective and therefore not instructive. The whole issue of organizational ethics plays an important role in such an evaluation. Those organizations that pay little attention to the learning fundamental of the principled value system mentioned earlier, or view their ethical responsibilities very narrowly, can be predicted to get into trouble. Recent troubles at a major US bioengineering company may be attributable to a marketing strategy which appears to operate right at the legal limit. When that happens, the consequence to the organization's effectiveness is often all out of proportion to the actual initiating act. It is a hard and fast rule that once an organization is seen to lie, cheat, steal, or worse yet, cover up significant errors, overall trust and forbearance for that organization's future actions is severely eroded. One-time errors that are exceptions and not indicative of normal organizational behavior are treated as if they are everyday occurrences. Both the public and institutions with significant power over organizations, such as financiers, government regulators, or the media can be counted on to overreact and modify their behavior toward the organization in a negative manner.

A recent case in point is the allegation of exaggerated billing at a major US defense contractor, a situation divulged by a high-level financial executive. Whatever additional profit that could have been expected from such cheating will be more than erased after settlement with the whistle-blower executive and a final accounting with the federal government. Equally important, but more difficult to assess, is the long-term damage to this company's reputation and relationship with a key customer, Uncle Sam.

Turbulent, or consistently evolving environments, will tend to show us our most visible and vulnerable poor learners. Stability may not require the level of directed learning that we envision necessary for organizations coping with rapid and continuous change. In so far as there remain pockets of stability for some industries, or nonprofit and public institutions, organizations in such an environment may not find the transformation to a learning organization as pressing or as justifiable.

Organizational Characteristics Supporting Learning

Principled leadership

As with any other significant aspect of directed organizational behavior, only top-level attention and vision can overcome the resistance to change and inertia that makes choosing new ways of doing things so difficult. Since effective learning will probably require broad fundamental change in most organizations, the leadership will have to initiate a major culture shift with all of the effort that entails. In order for this to happen, most leaders themselves will have to undergo a major value shift consistent with the model presented earlier. The challenge placed on leaders should not be underestimated. Extremely strongly held views and gut-level values antithetical to integrating learning will have to be modified and replaced with a vision, attendant principled leadership, and a supporting value system much different from that most of us know.

Fortunately, there are guideposts to show us the way. Covey's[12] concept of **principled leadership**, what we and others know as "stewardship," provides a starting point. Top-level leaders who behave and lead as if they are stewards are well equipped to respect and behave according to sound ecological principles from both a business and societal perspective. They will tend to take the long view, balance the direct and indirect, understand that investment is sometimes most necessary when it seems the most difficult and least affordable. Learning leaders will focus on clearly differentiating between legitimate cost saving improvements and cutting into organizational muscle much better than is presently done.

Developing a learning culture

A leadership integrating learning will develop a culture and policies that continually support learning behaviors, particularly when times are tough. We would expect this to be an evolutionary process, passing through the stages shown in figure 14.1.

For such a culture to take root and bloom, three essential characteristics will have to be developed and reinforced. They are (1) controlled competition, with encouragement for collaboration; (2) openness – in terms of sharing the fuel of effective learning, information, feelings, intuitions, weaknesses, mistakes, creativity, and so forth; and (3) trust – in leadership, members' competence, trust that mistakes will not result in punishment, and developed trust in the capability of a learning environment to result in individual and organizational success.

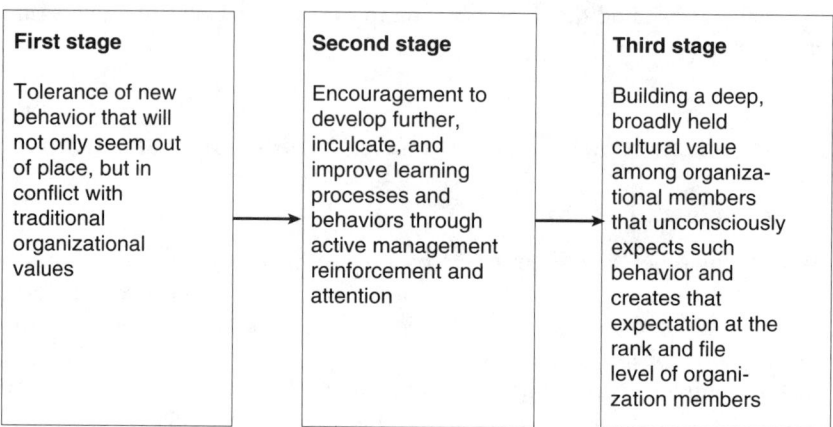

First stage	Second stage	Third stage
Tolerance of new behavior that will not only seem out of place, but in conflict with traditional organizational values	Encouragement to develop further, inculcate, and improve learning processes and behaviors through active management reinforcement and attention	Building a deep, broadly held cultural value among organizational members that unconsciously expects such behavior and creates that expectation at the rank and file level of organization members

Figure 14.1   Three essential characteristics needed for organizations to grow.

Time expenditure

The whole issue of appropriate time expenditure may require radical change. For a learning posture to be effective, time must be spent on behaviors that are not necessarily perceived as, or directed at, producing a product or delivering a service. The whole concept of using play as a productive organizational tool seems a likely characteristic of an effective learning organization. Not only do we know that play is an essential component of individual learning (and therefore is assumed to be so in the organizational setting), but we also know that play is probably the most powerful motivation in most adults. Workers who experience no or little play at work channel their energies to play activities away from work and direct their best energies toward that play. Employees who regard their work as fun or play are generally (if not universally) the most highly motivated and the most successful of organizational members. An effective learning organization will find the means to overcome a widely held view in most work organizations that work should not be fun, and if it looks like it is, someone needs to be punished.

Mistakes viewed as learning opportunities

Processes that aim to learn from and take advantage of mistakes will become a much more widely used tool to improve performance. Error and mistakes will be widely viewed as nothing more than opportunities to learn, and will not result in negative reinforcement unless found to be willful or negligent. Processes to practice new behaviors or skills will be more extensively utilized, with an end of learning from errors and correcting them before the real thing happens. While such techniques are widely used in complex building and engineering projects, they could be expected to become much more utilized in all manners of organizational activity.

Management generalists and thinking individuals

Activities which focus on the improvement of human relations, communications, group and team processes, performance evaluation and improvement, process experimentation, and above all, goal and activity integration, will take on new meaning, new emphasis and begin to dominate management's efforts. Since such activities are already acknowledged to be long-term efforts, their increased emphasis may aid the transformation to a broad acceptance of leading and managing toward long-term viability and success. For any of this to happen, organizational members will be more and more required to think as "technical generalists." Significant effort toward educating members to understand the broad implications of their actions and responsibilities and reinforcing behaviors and processes that encourage thinking and performance with broad interests in mind will be necessary. Leaders will have a much greater responsibility to use their acquired abilities in this area to encourage such thinking throughout their organization.

The learning organization must be composed of thinking individuals. In far too many organizations, an individual taking the time to think – or to learn – without any immediate application is viewed as a nonproductive daydreamer. A businessman turned professor told his former corporate colleagues that he had done more thinking in his first three months in the academic world than he had done in his last three years in business. The reason he presented was that he now had license to think and reflect where before it was coupled with guilt for not doing something "more productive."

Use of information technology

Equally important is a strong, aggressive use of modern information technology (IT). Local area networks (LAN), e-mail, access to the Internet, computer-aided design (CAD) systems, on-line libraries, and information repositories are tools which exponentially increase the capability to communicate horizontally and vertically within the organization. These provide prompt, inexpensive access to important external information. Through the directed use of such systems and their associated equipment, important cultural change can be more easily adapted to and accepted. Resistance to opening up communication channels and sharing much more information with organization members is more easily overcome when such fundamental behavioral change is linked to the transition to a "high tech" environment. Another important advantage of the aggressive use of IT is the expanded capability it gives the organization to develop and maintain a much improved structured corporate memory. At the present such attempts are limited by the time and expense of maintaining vast paper files and the cost and time associated with the human retrieval and interpretation necessary for use.

Principle of continuous improvement

Last, but not least, is the adoption of the principle of continuous improvement. This principle is central to the total quality management movement (TQM) and also critical to integrating effective learning in organizations. From a learning perspective, it serves the same function as in TQM – that is, to serve as a fundamental goal and motivator to avoid complacency and self-satisfaction. It serves as a positive irritant that keeps the collective mind active and continuously searching for better ways to see or do things. As a mental frame or mind set, it aids in maintaining an overall awareness or acuity of the entire surrounding environment, such that changes which can be exploited or protected against can be anticipated or at worst promptly responded to after they occur. Such an active and intense mental frame becomes more and more necessary as the rate of change in markets, people's values, government intervention, and technological innovation continues to increase.

How Does a Learning Organization Look and Behave

Today's learning organizations may actually appear different from the norm, but are more likely to be nondescript from a structural perspective. Since the concept of effective structure for learning is still in its infancy, it should be expected that present characteristics have not been changed or are in a state of transition. The first signs of an organization's moving toward a more effective learning posture are probably more process-based than structural anyway. Flatter organization structures and decentralized decision-making are now accepted organizational characteristics which are acknowledged to be necessary for modern organizational success and also are supportive of effective learning.

Example of commercial nuclear power companies

In the best of commercial nuclear power producers, we have found organizations that focus on and improve their performance by dealing with key behaviors that generate effective learning. The organizational characteristics we describe are real. They can be found in the best nuclear performers to one extent or another. While our example represents a composite, it typifies a number of specific organizations.

The electric utility industry has been undergoing a profound set of changes, driven by new laws opening them up to intense competition and increased consumer pressure for reasonable rates. The nuclear segment of the industry has even greater pressures driving its viability because of the strong continued emphasis on improving safety – an emphasis that is seldom cheap.

As a result, nuclear operations have become more focused on what makes safe, effective, and efficient power production. Their characteristics which are consistent with our conception of effective learning organizations are:

- The nature of their leadership;
- An informal process of directing learning, creating an open and supportive environment for critical thought, continuing evaluation of decision-making and implementation, and strong support for suggested improvement from all employees;
- Acknowledging and supporting the costs of learning – treating them as a good investment;
- Demanding top level performance at all levels, never being satisfied with the status quo, always searching for ways to do better;
- Supporting a sophisticated system of practice and performance feedback, which together provide tangible improvement in a number of key performance areas.

Leadership totally committed   The leaders of these operations live their vision and their high performance standards. They not only "talk the talk" but walk the walk. They have instilled a culture where a strong learning–execution cycle not only exists but flourishes. They can be characterized as heavy on communication. There is a great deal of interaction on issues between relevant parties. Failure to communicate concerns or views is viewed negatively, teamwork is strongly encouraged, and opportunities to practice upcoming evolutions occur regularly. An extremely strong training and education environment exists and employees are encouraged to sharpen their skills throughout their careers. These activities are heavily financed by the company and receive active attention by senior management. Career assignments are viewed as having both an immediate execution purpose but also a developmental aspect. Large numbers of employees at all levels are placed in "developmental" assignments. Here they get a feel for the issues and concerns of most if not all of the critical functions that must work well in an integrated fashion for overall success. In fact, activities which support overall integration of goals, attitudes, philosophy, planning, assessing, and executing are the bread and butter of these operations and in our view the most critical of those characteristics that make for effective organizational learning.

Management's expectations and treatment of mistakes   Another key part of the learning environment at these operations involves the management expectations placed on employees. There is a sense of high expectations and exceptional demands on all organizational members. They are considered professionals and they are expected to perform exceptionally. There is a strong collective focus on pursuing challenging goals, and a sense of accomplishment when things are done well. Rewards and recognition are shared at all levels of the organization. When things go poorly, blame is also shared. If a failure occurs, management accepts failure on its part to prepare people adequately. The situation is analyzed and widely communicated so that as many people as possible understand the lessons to be learned. Even though the performance demands are extremely high, management recognizes that people make honest mistakes. Therefore, while the broad communication of mistakes may lead to embarrassment, it is a collective embarrassment, which is quickly replaced by the focus on preventing its occurrence again.

Specialized responsibilities The level of functional teamwork is also very high. While these nuclear operations have managed to improve without undue resentment between functional departments, it requires a special recognition of the value of specialized responsibilities, rather than specialized functions, a recognition that we consider an emerging characteristic of the learning organization.

Companies integrating learning into organization These operational companies are an example of organizations that are high on the learning curve of integrating learning into their organization. They have focused their attention on that which matters. Significant resources and time are spent on cognitive activities. Human process activities are directed and structured to attend to learning and execution. Relevant business methods which work are kept, those that don't aren't.

Two examples to serve as models and challenge thinking

Other interesting examples may serve as models or otherwise challenge our thinking. First is the symphony orchestra, an example used by Peter Vaill, Professor of Human Systems at The George Washington University (who was interviewed in Part IV of this book) to demonstrate the characteristics of a high performing system.[13] The symphony orchestra has as a primary purpose the interpretation of the world's great orchestral music, a purpose which it fulfills by studying and performing such work. Secondarily, it has a steward function of maintaining and continuing this tradition in society plus providing a livelihood for competent musicians. These purposes are clearly not separable, but are reinforcing and integrated.

The work product is, in this case, very clearly defined. The component parts are largely predetermined, such as the notes, the assignment of parts to various instruments, the timing and pace of delivery, how and when various musical voices interact with each other, and what volumes are expected from various instruments at various times. All these things were predetermined by the composer. Within this relatively constrained framework, however, the conductor, soloists, and other musicians solely determine the quality and spirit of the performance within some interpretative freedom.

For the symphony orchestra to be a "high performance" system, it must perform at the very top of its performance range. Everything must fit together correctly and at the right time. Individual errors must be eliminated or be of a nature that go unnoticed. To remain viable, most symphony orchestras do perform at this rarefied level, although knowledgeable observers will identify various levels of performance within a range of high performance which distinguish the best from the second best, and routine performances from the rarely occurring exceptional.

A second example is the professional sports team. Its purpose is to play particular sports games as performances, and to win more of those games than its opponents. Like the symphony orchestra, players each have a role. As play occurs, they are each to fulfill a function, and for the action to be successful, those roles must be executed at the proper place, times, and intensity. The game is sometimes sloppy, but can be intricate. Motivation is a key factor in who wins the game, and is frequently the key to an underdog winning.

Effective learning integrated into both example organizations

Effective learning has been integrated into these two types of organizations. On the organization level one can observe the natural cycle of activity and rest. The time of performances is always a small percentage of the overall time available, at least for those examples that are accepted as the best in their field. Practice and study fills a substantial part of the organization's time, and within that time is intense attention to improvement, objective assessment of performance, and experimentation into new or different approaches. Individuals are competent, the best of the best, who in these cases have devoted most of their lives to perfecting their skills and abilities. They are all expected to fulfill their roles to the best of their ability. Individuals who do not meet the strictest standards of motivation, skills, behavior, or performance are quickly separated from the organization. They may remain in the field, as in the case where a baseball player is sent to the minors, but are removed at least until they show some positive change in their ability to contribute.

These examples may be viewed skeptically as not particularly representative of the conditions most organizations find themselves in. While that may be true, they still represent living examples of the effective integration of learning into organizations. In particular, they can serve as learning laboratories to study and better understand what conditions account for the rare exceptional performance that almost becomes spiritual in nature. This evidence of an infrequent higher plane performance that individuals, teams, and other groups seldom experience, at least suggests that there is an inherent quality within the organization to move beyond our current understanding of human capability – particularly group or organizational capability. This phenomenon may be what Senge refers to as a possible sixth discipline.

Managing the Learning Organization:
Executive Perspective

Managing an effective learning organization is different. It begins with a new form of strategic thinking that can view learning and its organizational application in the following way. Integrating learning into the fabric of the organization requires a conceptual shift away from traditional "theories of the firm." The learning concept can replace traditional theory as the cornerstone of organizational purpose, culture, and action. It pervades all other characteristics, structure, and activities and through its cognitive, integrative power provides a potential higher level of organizational existence, maturation, and performance. It can be viewed as a creature on a higher evolutionary plane.

The kind of strategic thinking that can create such a "new" organization is first and foremost focused on intellect and reflection. The importance of objective, critical thought becomes central to the culture and its actions. By necessity, the philosophy and process of learning become highly directed, a phenomenon that distinguishes a true learning organization from all others.

Understanding concept of systems thinking

This strategic thinking is grounded in **systems thinking**, whether it is called that or not; for balance, integration, and the understanding of subtle and complex relationships are essential and best understood from a systems perspective. The concept of human systems, still rudimentary as an area of study, will be drawn upon to understand the characteristics of high-performing human systems better, what feeds and nurtures them and what is harmful to their health. Human performance will be one of the first areas in which a learning organization can be expected to find significant improvement, both in terms of finding stronger motivators and improving the skills and process of human endeavor.

The direction required reflects the recognition that learning processes and activities are only effective when they support and are focused on those issues which matter, that is, they are critical to the organization's effective functioning and long-term viability. Thus, the strategic thinking of a learning organization acknowledges good and bad learning, and is selective and directive in its encouragement of specific principle and application. One can expect in a world and society which is increasing the power of connections, communications, restriction on activity, and public influence, that a "correct" set of principles directs the effective learning organization. This set of principles is integrative, ecological, stewardly, spiritual, and humanistic. In their book, *The Good Society*, Bellah et al. describe the "democratic learning community." We believe, by definition, the effective learning organization is a democratic learning community.[14] It reflects the highest potential of human activity and avoids the mean-spirited and destructive as both wrong and ineffective.

It deals in futures and is extravagant in its possibilities and fantasies. It is active in its belief that an alternative future can be created which improves human potential and creates additional abundance. It is more protective of human resources and may find itself using Covey's basic principle that the principled organization has as its primary goal "to improve the economic well-being and quality of life of all stake-holders."[15] Therefore, a much stronger focus will be placed on all aspects of the human equation. People will be expected to be more competent, they will be given much stronger support to assure that competence is both created and maintained. While lifelong employment may not result, longer relationships (and better ones) can be expected between the learning organization and its competent members. The psychological contract between employee and organization will be revisited, with added benefits to both.

Transitional leaders needed

A new kind of executive will be needed. Many of the old strengths and skills may be immaterial, if not counter-productive. Those whose strengths are quick decisiveness, impatience with discussion or reflection, closed or emotional decision-making, will not be able to lead in this environment. Those who cannot teach and mentor will also be at a disadvantage. The transitional leader will have a major task of changing many of the fundamental "rules of the game" that successful organization members have spent a lifetime learning and coming to rely on.

Paradoxically, transitional leaders may need to behave as beneficent authoritarians, demanding change and culling out those who cannot adapt to the need. While this approach may be vital to the transition, leaders must change approaches once the transition is made to sustain progress or, quite possibly, must be replaced themselves. We may need a cadre of temporary leaders with the unique skills to bring about the necessary changes, "turnaround experts" for learning organizations.

We believe the process of succession will also require revisiting. At the present, there is a distinction between successful and effective people.[16] We believe this reflects significant weaknesses in traditional selection techniques. Those who focus on promotion appear to do better and go farther than those who focus on doing their jobs well. Such a process is counter-productive to maximizing competence and results in producing leaders whose skills may further their personal careers, but may not provide the necessary talent or interest to maximize the organization's performance.

Human and systems skills needed

The resistance to changed values and new focuses will be high. The kind of expertise needed in various parts of the organization will require reexamination. The present parochial process which decides which expert will lead must change. No longer will it be adequate to place a technical expert in charge.

Engineering organizations will need leaders who are more than competent engineers. Other firms will need leaders who are more than financial wizards or marketing pros. The new leader will require a general background in important technical areas but will most need additional broad understanding of human and systems skills.

Most importantly, presuming a broad-based education and experience base, the transitional learning leader must have been proselytized. He or she must have the faith, be a true believer in the power of effective learning, and have the intellect, interpersonal skills, and wisdom to create a very substantial change process. Such leaders can be created by modifying our educational and experiential objectives. In the educational arena, barriers between traditional fields of expert study need to be removed and professional schools need to focus predominantly on integrative studies.

Traditional concepts of cost-effectiveness will be challenged

Organizations will need to focus on the nature of their financial planning, policy, and control functions. Organizations which allow the strict, traditional financial function to dominate decision-making will find it difficult to make the transition to the effective learning mode. The learning organization must be willing to challenge and change the traditional concepts of cost effectiveness. It must question differently what is necessary versus nice to have as expenditures and investments. It must also reconsider the traditional power and authority of financial controllers who have such a great influence on budget and expenditure decisions. In acknowledging that the transition to a learning organization will have potentially significant startup costs, it will prove necessary to reevaluate the existing cost structure and fundamental organization assumptions from a financial perspective. This can initially increase costs, but can be justified if taken as an investment effort with a long-term payoff.

From a human and process productivity perspective, the best justification for investing in learning is the almost universally accepted recognition that present organizations are moderately to excessively wasteful. Most manufacturing processes have room for additional improvement. Most services can become more productive, and most individuals can improve their productivity. The 80/20 rule still applies (20% of the people do 80% of the work) indicating that great strides in individual productivity and effectiveness are possible and necessary. TQM, as the first major learning movement, bases its justification on many of these facts.

Strategic thinking and decision-making methods change with organizational complexity

The effective implementation of learning processes and behaviors, such as additional time for reflection, team and group discourse, practice, and creative analysis, requires that these activities be free to be creative within broadly defined goals and direction. Thus, the directedness of effective learning provides the structure and method of measurement to assure that there is a positive outcome, that is, tangible products that will serve to justify the activity. With time, the accumulation of learning products and processes will provide the evidence of learning's utility, cost-effectiveness, and adaptive value.

For example, some organizations are learning the value of improving people processes as a direct and measurable improvement activity. Bose Corporation, maker of high fidelity audio systems, introduced the idea of "JIT-2," a modified just-in-time inventory scheme. To reduce the hostility and distrust between vendor and manufacturer created by short deadline pressure, Bose let the vendor representatives work next to their factory floor almost like their own employees. The vendor representatives were allowed to (1) determine what orders were needed and (2) do the ordering. This innovation then spread to IBM, Ingersoll Rand, and others.[17] At Planning Research Corporation (PRC), a federal contractor in McLean, Virginia, shrinking market and changing products require ultimate cooperation and teamwork between divisions to ensure survival. The past practice of individual independence, going different ways, and minimizing internal communications became too costly.[18]

The necessity of the learning organization is based on the challenge of increasing complexity. Our traditional processes for dealing with complexity are to simplify, generalize, and then hope that we guessed in the right direction. Complexity is handled in technical organizations by much more formalized and complex analytical tools. For example, the building of modern jet liners is designed and "mocked up" on large networked computer systems, so that the extensive detail and complex set of relationships can be both conceptually and spatially tested before the first prototype is begun. As organizational complexity increases, and strategic thinking and decisions must deal with this complexity, new ways of handling human and decision-making complexity must be developed. An important area for additional integrative research is in the arena of group decision-making, particularly in dealing with difficult areas involving disparate values, human satisfaction, and scarcity of resources. Further work along the lines of Lippitt's attempt at developing a "multocular process," which brings together and balances group decision-making needs to be done. It should include consideration of objective, dispassionate analysis with value judgments, and expand upon systems modeling and nonlinear, intuitive decision-making. These have promise for providing more effective solutions to some of organizations' more intransigent problems.

Management's new appearance and role

The management of the effective learning organization may not seem a management at all, at least, not in the traditional way it has been defined. The traditional functions, as described by Fayol,[19] of planning, organizing, commanding, coordinating, and controlling, are already of questionable viability and effectiveness in many organizations. In organizations which create human competency and depend on it, they may actually be counter-productive. The functions which appear to be most central to tomorrow's effectiveness differ. They are vision, integration, teaching, analyzing, and coordinating. Where managers commanded, and then led, they will now be expected to govern in a collaborative fashion. Other important functions will be coaching and advising. Leading by example will remain an important management tool. The learning manager/leader will be a critical thinker, dedicated to creative thinking, intellectual exploration, continuous searching for new and different ways to be better, constantly attentive to the signals of a changing environment. All of this may be too much to ask of much of today's management.

As the old control mentality changes, fewer "managers" as such are necessary. The learning organization will probably decrease the overall numbers of managers in recognition that it is better not to have a manager than to have one who is actively opposed to, or poorly skilled in, the learning functions. A new class of manager might better be thought of as shepherd, drover, or steward. The style and type of personality of the new manager may be very different and selection and development of such people will require new directions and more leadership attention.

While we have discussed important competencies for the learning manager, there seem also to be important characteristics that should be screened out. These are the "reptilian-brain" manager characteristics, after the Robert Bly description of the oldest part of the human brain's control of the baser human instincts.[20] Unfortunately, much organizational behavior remains imbedded in the unconscious, and much unconscious behavior remains directed at satisfying the instinctual needs of power, dominance, fight or flight, territory, and predatory activity. Those individuals who reach management positions because of strong unconscious drives for power, domination, and gamesmanship, and who unthinkingly behave toward others in response to these needs will not make effective learning managers. We believe there is clearly a self-selection process that occurs in organizations which makes these types successful. Nevertheless, informed, conscious succession, which identifies and screens out such individuals, is both possible and necessary if a learning environment is to be established. The behavior patterns of the learning manager will necessarily shift away from the traditional activities to the new ones. We believe that Mintzberg would find very different results if he were to view what managers do in a learning organization.[21]

Signs of a different form of management

At the heart of a learning organization, we would expect to find signs of a very different form of management. While we have described the directions that we believe will be associated with such organizations, those directions will be successful only if they are realistically and effectively implemented in the day-to-day activities of the organization. Our experience with most change projects in organizations indicates that inadequate concern for, and attention to the details of, implementation are the major causes of disappointing results. The enthusiasm that accompanies setting directions, making critical decisions, and communicating the new vision to those who are expected to live it, is seldom carried over to the development, implementation, and reinforcement of the more mundane policies, procedures, and logistics that are equally essential to an effective outcome. Contributing to this problem is the traditional tactic of dividing the effort so that the most senior and knowledgeable people "think the great thoughts" and "set the broad policy," while the job of translation and connection to the everyday and fuller detailed activity is delegated to a lower level – usually with a minimum of communication and explanation and with an accompanying loss of commitment.

Observing and understanding how such divisions of labor actually occur and how communications between and among them play out is an essential first step in beginning the process of integrating learning into the organization. In those organizations which fail to understand the lost opportunity in motivation, understanding, increased individual potential and resultant competency, increased effectiveness cannot result. The organization must "learn" what its people believe is expected of them and modify that belief as may be necessary.

Clear organizational policy on expectations of members

A clear policy on what the organization expects of people will be necessary but difficult. A learning organization requires above all competency, of a high intellectual character. This does not mean every member requires a Ph.D. It does mean that within the "functional space" of each member there is (1) a strong knowledge and performance base, (2) a level and integrity of intellect poised to question what is going on, and (3) a genuine interest in pursuing self-interest through the success of the whole.

Such a policy must first determine what is necessary of members and may require changing hiring standards. It may also require substantial initial retraining and redirected acculturation of existing organization members. Management must face the issue of **empowerment** and the anxiety that most managers feel when that word is mentioned in polite conversation. Empowerment is a key to an effective learning organization and can only be effective when pursued in a disciplined and thoughtful way. Successful empowerment begins with competent individuals. It results in effective learning and resultant improved performance when it is directed toward what is important to organizational performance. It serves as its own fuel for success as its victories increase the confidence of management, and the experience level and resultant contributions of the empowered. The key role for management policy in this area is continually to reinforce the goal of improving organizational performance; letting the empowered function effectively with minimum interference; and providing the course correction, coordination, advice, and logistics necessary to produce high quality decisions and activities that enhance both performance and the organization's future ability to perform even better.

Policy for handling complexity and rigidity

Another major policy area involves the learning organization's handling of complexity and rigidity. As organizations grow and technology evolves, both the business of the organization and how the organization does its business increase in complexity. The operating environment tends to become more rigid as problem-solving accumulates more and more standard solutions to day-to-day issues. Years of well-intentioned management activity provides more and more constraints on functioning until effective performance is actually limited by the policies, procedures, pronouncements, rules, structures, processes, and activities which have as their ostensible purpose the enhancement of effective performance. An excellent example is the proliferation of operating and regulatory procedures in the commercial nuclear power industry.

We see excessive complexity and rigidity as phenomena that can be severely dysfunctional to operations and also to the effective integration of learning. While there is clearly a functional need for some minimum level of complexity for effective functioning, there is also a whole separate class of complexity that does not further the actual things that matter. The learning management will search out and remove such complexity as a matter of policy, and also assure that a higher level "policy of policies" encourages flexibility and discourages unnecessary complexity and rigidity. Such a direction might be called a policy of simplicity.

In furtherance of such a direction, flexibility in treatment of employee activities, time, family and community life, and work options all further the need for competency and an environment that supports consciousness, creativity and critical thinking. Flexibility in terms of who does what also furthers the goals of expanding experience of members, increasing sensitivity to the role of other's functions, and bringing fresh thinking to how things are done and to problem-solving. Implementing such flexibility is difficult for managements that have poor performance assessment and measurement capabilities, as they rely on indirect, and sometimes meaningless measures of performance, such as presence at a specific location and the appearance of frenetic activity. A learning management will rely on competent judgment to serve as a performance measure, aided by objective measure when appropriate, and provide policies that protect the flexibility of competent members.

Communication in a learning organization

One of the truisms of organizational life is that the formally stated goals, beliefs, and policies of an organization frequently differ from the actual action, activities, and understandings of organizational members in general. It is always illuminating, sometimes devastating, to have a candid discussion with a working organizational member and find that some clever policy, developed at the executive level, has been somehow turned inside out, upside down, and not only bears no resemblance to the original intent, but is being robustly implemented contrary to it. Such stories are legendary and reflect poor vertical communication and feedback.

Communications in a learning organization will be structured to assure accuracy and openness to critical information. Since effective learning requires both enhanced intellect and comprehensive and accurate information (i.e. empirical evidence), communication processes, sources, channels, and feedback loops will require serious attention. The integrity of information sources is critical, as is the fidelity and richness of information processed. In an engineering, linear logic sense, improvement in classic information theory aspects, such as redundancy, feedback loops, and verification, will help assure that learning is effective.

Maybe more importantly, attention to the human aspects of effective communication is necessary for effective organizational learning. The management of a learning organization will have strong policies and practices of broadly shared communications, both vertically and horizontally. Moreover, communications outside the organization will also be open and extensive, as in the earlier example of Bose Corporation and JIT-2. Listening will be recognized and emphasized as the single most important element of a learning organization's communications. Communications will be continual, conversational on a real-time basis, exemplifying what Senge refers to as "discourse". The communication of sincere belief in the activities supporting learning will also be heavily emphasized by leadership, since this is the only effective method of convincing members of the reality of a changed organization. Much more management time, particularly senior management time, will be spent "living its learning" with all levels of members throughout the organization.

Managing internal relationships, recognition, and rewards

A learning organization will improve the ability to manage its internal relationships, particularly with labor, on a different plane. A learning environment, to be effective, will have to depend on trust, which is essential to openness, which is key to learning. Relationships must be based on mutual respect, a conviction in others' competence and desire to do the right thing, and faith that the organization will protect and reward individuals and groups who pursue the organization's interests. Since human nature dictates that some percentage of members will try to take advantage of such an environment, management must be prepared to take prompt and public action to communicate to others that such behavior is not tolerated. Some situations may require prompt separation from the organization since subversive, destructive activity in any organization is easy to engage in and has negative effects out of all proportion to the activity.

Trustful, open environments are critical to effective learning and they are extremely difficult to create and maintain.

Recognition and reward may become modified in such an environment. Encouragement of key behaviors through recognition is an effective management tool which would require only different direction. For example, to elicit open communication and accurate information from subordinates, a manager could encourage questioning and criticism from subordinates on management actions and additionally strengthen the belief that the leadership not only wants to hear bad news, but is willing to respond positively to it. A positive response to team building and openness behaviors, and a negative response to turf building, infighting, personality cultism, predatory behavior, and other classic "reptilian brain" behaviors will strengthen and expand the willingness of members to consistently engage in those key behaviors essential to effective learning.

The Learning Organization – The Challenge of Getting There

Prognosis for general evolution to learning organizations

Our prognosis for a general evolution to effective learning organizations in the short term is not good, particularly in the United States. The two elements we consider most critical to integrating effective learning in organizations – a strong emphasis on intellect in general, and a broad, integrative mode of thinking (what Senge calls "systems thinking") – are inconsistent with modern American culture and organizational directions in general. We believe the trend in America has been away from critical thinking, toward segmented easy-way-out strategies, partially driven by increasingly turbulent business conditions, but equally caused by a shortsighted, quick-fix reactive mentality and deteriorating standards of educational performance and self-reliance. In addition, we believe a very strong environmental disincentive is acting against the adoption of an effective learning orientation, at least in the for-profit sector. That disincentive results from strong competitive pressures and the turbulence associated with the modern business environment. These conditions, many beyond the single organization's control, may play against the ability to establish and move toward the learning environment.

On a broad scale, it is difficult to conceive of an environment driver powerful enough to shift the collective mind-set toward the principles, values, and interests that support a general understanding and implementation of those factors that would create learning organizations. However, as we see some small nucleus of such organizations beginning a transformation toward that end, always driven by necessity, one can speculate that such organizations will sporadically appear. This will be particularly true in situations where environmental conditions force it, or where naturally occurring learning-directed leaders randomly appear.

Successful examples will eventually become standard

If the concept of an effective learning organization truly has merit, particularly as a broad application, time will help build the successful examples which always eventually become the standards that others follow. If the concept finds enough favor with the academic community, it will find its way into curricula and eventually become part of the bag of tools of the next generation of organizational leaders. Such changes take time and sometimes lead actual implementation in organizations, while at other times lagging it. Management innovation has no single institutional source. While the idea of learning organizations is specifically intellectually oriented, it seems to us that its most effective proponents will come from the ranks of challenged organizations who find it their best hope for viability and success.

As organizations like the nuclear power industry have already "learned" the value of transforming toward the effective learning organization, and now have the conscious processes and culture in place to continue that evolution, others will see the outcome – performance improvement – and at least attempt to copy the process. However, unless those who attempt the effort make the mind shift that requires fundamentally addressing the basic existential issues at the heart of a learning organization, their efforts will be misspent. Just as it has taken years for companies to evolve to true quality-driven organizations, the shift to becoming learning-oriented will take time.

A work environment conducive to learning

The process of learning, as we envision it, is not necessarily conducive to achieving strong support in the American work environment. Americans are known for constantly being in a rush. We tend to equate continuous activity with hard work, and in most working environments, we view the passivity of reflection with suspicion. We may be tolerant of small periods of the stuff, but we would consider an individual a shirker who spent too much time at it. During lean times the proposed adoption of significant learning activities would face considerable resistance for this reason alone. Moreover, since many of the behaviors associated with learning, would, at least in the short term, be difficult to justify from a narrow cost-effectiveness perspective, attempts to transform to a learning organization would be difficult.

As we have emphasized repeatedly in this chapter, organizational learning will come about when management provides a supportive, nurturing environment conducive to learning. As we have attempted to argue, many if not most, of those critical management actions, attitudes, and policies, that support learning are familiar and have been advocated for other reasons previously. The idea that learning can only work under supportive conditions should be obvious.

Outcome for government sector

In the government sector, the same questions can be raised, but different factors affect the outcome. Cost considerations are just as relevant, and two major additional factors come into play. First is the difficulty for many agencies to develop a vision, focus their attention on what matters, and provide the strong leadership necessary to transform the organization. Congress ultimately controls such things, and in the political environment, there is a tendency to make everything important. Second, complexity and rigidity are mainstays of government, deeply imbedded in the conditions of bureaucracy, legalism, and detailed policy and procedure.

Interestingly, the Clinton administration has targeted these conditions for attention as part of the National Performance Review[22] initiative sponsored by Vice President Gore. Among the many parts of this initiative are included strong empowerment pronouncements and more flexible (and sensible) cost control mechanisms, contracting procedures, and workplace rules, with the goal of providing more efficient and effective delivery of government services. Whether these initiatives take hold, and provide a more supportive environment for integrating learning into government organizations, remains to be seen.

Visioning and Communicating Learning Directions and Goals

"Paradigm shift" in philosophy and purpose

Conceptualizing organizations from a learning perspective provides, in our view, the potential for a fundamental "paradigm shift" in the philosophy and purpose leaders and managers bring to their roles in organizations. In directing an organization toward effective learning, a leader provides a direction that by its nature is embedded in a principled, humanistic, and hard-nosed performance-oriented philosophy. The tough mindedness so often associated with leaders, who sacrifice unprofitable ventures, preside over significant layoffs, fire existing management en masse, cut legal and ethical corners to gain prompt financial goals, still resides in the learning-oriented leader. The difference is that his or her tough mindedness is tempered by a broader, long-term, more integrated understanding that recognizes that the organization's assets wear shoes. While some of the above outcomes may be required, the odds are that they will only be implemented if absolutely necessary and, in the case of crossing legal/ethical lines, will not be viable options.

Leadership focuses on "visioning"

The learning integrated into the organization is itself tough minded. It has direction, always with direct or indirect connection to the performance and/or improvement of the organization. The learning leader, more than anything else, embodies a constant searching for doing better on what matters, and builds relationships and processes which exhort everyone to be on the same lookout. The leadership focuses on defining what matters and communicating concrete goals that define improvement, what is now called **visioning**. Using Covey's metaphors, it provides the compass and encourages the organization to create the map and build the roads.

It shifts from the traditional expectation and practice of demanding hard work to the more difficult and challenging task of demanding smart work. More radical, the new "work" may not look anything like traditionally defined work. As part of a complex of learning activities, "work" may appear to be play, fun, reverie, or even rest. The old adage that many of us grew up with, that success is 99 percent perspiration and 1 percent inspiration, is no longer operable in an effective learning organization. The discipline that will be required to manage a ménage of learning activities and cycles may at first appear to have no discipline or structure at all.

The leadership of such an organization, to effectively integrate learning as a firm and established cultural phenomenon, will recognize the difficulty in communicating with employees that such new and potentially frightening values, attitudes, behaviors, responsibilities, and opportunities, are for real. For most organizations, these characteristics will not only be foreign, they will have been strongly discouraged during most if not all of employees' work careers. Overcoming the vast amount of "unlearning" that must proceed any broad-scale employee buy-in to the new direction will be difficult. However, the tools to effectively deal with such major change issues involving basic gut-level processes are relatively well understood and applicable.

Prediction of expected payoff

An important part of communicating and promoting the concept of the learning organization is to provide some credible prediction, or estimate, of what potential payoff can be expected in the normal work organization. How much more can we squeeze from organizational performance by applying effective learning techniques? If we accept that there must be some limit to effective output, just as there is with engines, nuclear power reactors, and cows (they can only produce calves once per year), we can ask how far learning can take us toward that limit. One qualitative answer to that question comes from the earlier comment made on how much effort and resources go wasted in today's organizations. We believe there is a tremendous amount of raw human potential, in the form of motivation, energy, willingness to be responsible, and basic competency, lying fallow in organizations. Second, the efficiency and cost-effectiveness of separate industrial and organizational processes have also not been fully tapped. Therefore, we conclude there is a tremendous potential for improvement, which can only be tapped and its limits explored if we learn how to do it.

Factors determining successful integration of effective learning

In summary, the success of efforts to integrate effective learning strategies into modern organizations will depend on many things, not the least of which is the establishment of a learning leadership. The recognition that organizational improvement in the real world is immensely challenging, and can only come from coordinated, integrated intelligence, is surprisingly simple, and as surprisingly, goes largely unrecognized. Consciousness, as the mental quality which first binds thought, reflection, and learning, is largely absent in our everyday lives. Much of our time is spent operating unconsciously or semiconsciously, even by those of us who would claim to be reflective and thoughtful by nature.

Organizational activities become executed by habit. Where consciousness occurs it may be misdirected. Developing high quality, sustained, focused activity on an organizational issue is not that common. Time constraints, work overload, or lack of focus on what matters, may discourage the practice of directed consciousness. We believe that many organizational activities occur by rote. Senge claims the key to creating learning organizations is the transition to systems thinking. This may be the key to creating a learning leadership, for we would agree that systems thinking necessarily underlies the discovery of the conditions that will maintain viability and effectiveness in a rapidly changing world.

However, we believe the establishment and encouragement of directed consciousness at all organizational levels is at least as important to the implementation of an effective learning organization as the adoption of systems thinking. Implementation issues remain the Achilles heel of organizational change. There is no reason to believe they will not be so for the challenging task of integrating learning into modern organizations. The exploitation of intelligence, as mind, is one characteristic that probably separates humans from the other animals. The active use of mind, on a broad scale, at all levels, is to us the glue of a learning organization. If learning leaders understand this fact, and find effective ways to establish this as a much more frequent and robust activity – as an inherent part of the culture – then the idea of effective learning may prove itself a first principle of effective and improved organizational life. Time will tell.

Notes

1 Chris Argyris and D. A. Schon, *Organizational Learning: A Theory of Action Perspective* (New York: Addison-Wesley, 1978), pp. 8–29.

2 The "Multocular Process" was an experimental course taught by Gordon Lippitt in the early 1980s at George Washington University. It was attempted twice and abandoned.

3 Peter Senge, *The Fifth Discipline: The Art and Practice of the Learning Organization* (New York: Doubleday/Currency, 1990).

4 R. Revans, *Developing Effective Managers*, quoted in Ronnie Lessem, *Developmental Management: Principles of Holistic Business* (Oxford: Blackwell, 1990), p. 32.

5 Senge, *The Fifth Discipline*, p. 349.

6 See, for example, Stafford Beer, *Platform for Change* (New York: Wiley, Corrected reprint 1978), Stafford Beer, *Decision and Control* (New York: Wiley, 1966), Stafford Beer, *The Heart of Enterprise* (New York: Wiley, 1979), and Stafford Beer, *Brain of the Firm* (New York: Herder and Herder, 1972).

7 Jay Forrester, *Principles of Systems* (Cambridge, MA: MIT Press, 1980).

8 Senge, *The Fifth Discipline*.

9 Stephen R. Covey, *Principle-Centered Leadership, A Fireside Book* (New York: Simon & Schuster, 1992), p. 296.

10 Senge, *The Fifth Discipline*, p. 8.

11 Douglas McGregor, *The Human Side of Enterprise* (New York: McGraw-Hill, 1960).

12 Covey, *Principle-Centered Leadership*, p. 296.

13 Peter Vaill, 'The purposing of high performing systems," *Organizational Dynamics*, Autumn 1982, pp. 23–39.

14 Robert N. Bellah et al., *The Good Society* (New York: Alfred A. Knopf, 1991), p. 16.

15 Covey, *Principle-Centered Leadership*, p. 296.

16 Fred Luthans, "Successful vs. effective real managers", *The Academy of Management Executive*, May 1988, pp. 127–32.

17 *Wall Street Journal*, January 13, 1995, Sec. A, p. 1.

18 *Washington Post*, December 19, 1994, Sec. Washington Business, p. 1.

19 Henri Fayol, *General and Industrial Management*, translated by C. Stoers (London: Pitman, 1949).

20 Robert Bly, *American Poetry: Wildness and Domesticity* (New York: HarperCollins, 1991), pp. 52–63.

21 Henry Mintzberg, *The Nature of Managerial Work* (Englewood Cliffs, NJ: Prentice-Hall, 1973).

22 Vice President Al Gore, *Creating a Government that Works Better and Costs Less* (Report of the National Performance Review) (Washington, DC: US Government Printing Office, September 7, 1993).

15

Strategic Planning as a Tool for Building Learning Capacity

James Thompson and Joan Weiner

The world we have created today has problems which cannot be solved by thinking the way we thought when we created them.

Albert Einstein

Introduction

In the following pages, we consider strategic planning as a forum for learning and discuss how managers can boost organizational learning by taking the long view. We introduce tools that help provide a system-wide sightline across traditional functions and disciplines.

As an academic subject, strategic planning has been around for over 50 years. In stages of popularity, planning comprised strengths-and-weaknesses inventories, business case studies, "five forces," discounted cash flow (DCF), economic valuation analysis, core competencies, strategic intent, and so on. Each methodology generated fresh insight from the history of the organization and provided some time for managers to reflect on important questions:

- Where are we going?
- What are our resources?
- What if we tried something new?
- Who are the customers?
- How do we add to shareholder value?
- What do we do better than – or not as well as – the competition?

Spreadsheet financial forecasts usually accompanied the responses. With VisiCalc, 1-2-3, and Excel, personal computer-based spreadsheets proliferated and, in the case of DCF, dominated thinking and planning. The computer-aided spreadsheet prompted "what if?" questions that led to "so what" and "what now?" inquiries. This effect generated a next step, exploring creative alternatives. By examining possible financial outcomes, managers attempted to look at the whole of their organization, supply chain, competition, customers, and environment. The emphasis shifted from qualitative to quantitative analysis; planning took on its own structure and lost its principal purpose – to stimulate the manager's imagination and help the organization to learn.

While the value of strategic planning has been questioned,[1] it can play an important role in developing a learning organization. Concerns about strategic planning question whether the techniques used are capable of dealing with rapidly changing global market conditions that face an organization. Doubters also question whether the techniques themselves have become so ossified, both in structure and application, that they do not promote organizational change in response to changing needs. If that is so, it probably mirrors conditions throughout the firm.

Planning and Learning

For the learning organization, planning should provide techniques for checking how well the organization is doing in meeting its goals. The method should lead managers to reflect on that organization's core mission.[2] A subtler question is whether "doing well" is truly part of the mission. This is an example of what Chris Argyris calls "double loop learning": one loop provides feedback on maintaining defined activities, and a second loop changes the way in which the firm meets objectives or changes the objectives themselves.[3]

Over the past ten years, we have seen a tighter coupling of firms and markets. The line tying suppliers and the consumer has little slack. Information moves more quickly today and will be more quickly exchanged tomorrow. The slack is disappearing, the time delays shortening. Rather than existing as a separate entity, the organization is part of a system in which the parts and their traditional roles are blurred by rapid market transformation. As time delays compress, manager decisions are judged less by their effect on the organization and more by their effect in the system.

Strategic planning is the organizational forum for expanding the knowledge base and management's thinking skills. If the forum is closed to the introduction of new disciplines, the organization's capacity to learn is limited to the accumulation of experience. The lessons from the experience are repeated, and over time, nothing new is learned. If the forum is open to learning methodologies, the range of possible learning is expanding and dynamic. Simply taking a new view of old experience creates a new experience.

Within the study of systems and organizations, there is ongoing debate about the appropriate approach to planning. Even the co-authors of this chapter have far different approaches for working with organizations. For this chapter our goal is to explore how planning contributes to developing the learning organization, and we offer one approach to increasing learning capacity.

Some Necessary Definitions

We use the term **learning** in the sense described by Herbert Simon as "any change in a system that produces a more or less permanent change in its capacity for adapting to its environment . . . we can distinguish between acquiring information (stored data structures) and acquiring skills (stored procedures)."[4]

Organization is the term we use for a firm, government entity, company, school, and the like. Organization expresses the notion of people working together for a common purpose.

Planning refers to strategy formation for an organization. In its simplest sense, planning is thinking ahead.

Policy is the heuristic or rule that governs a stream of actions. It is not limited to the "policy" written in organization manuals. Policy is as concrete as the decision rules for ordering inventory, and as abstract as a rule-of-thumb employed by consumers when choosing to purchase a product.

A **system** may be described as an entity or "whole" generating behavior and comprising two or more interacting parts.[5] As used in this chapter, however, system should convey some generality of purview, some complexity in the issues, and a wholeness of perspective.[6]

System dynamics is a conceptual framework for understanding how and why systems perform as they do. The issues or problems involve quantities that change over time and the notion of feedback (figure 15.1).

Feedback is the transmission and return of information. When information sent by one part of a system is acted upon by another part in the system, it produces a response. (This use of the word "feedback" is different from its common use.) If we follow the path of information and action, it forms a **loop** of cause and effect in which results from the past affect future actions.[7] To help visualize one type of feedback, you may think of interest accruing on a bank balance. As the balance increases, interest income increases, further increasing the balance and so on (see figure 15.2).

Skill is acquired by remembering and using the answer to previously solved problems and remembering and avoiding previous traps. Evidence of a skill is found when one performs the steps necessary to perform requisite actions. Skill level is judged on a scale of effort required to remember and perform the necessary steps. That is, when the steps are conscious and explicit, skill is relatively low and, when steps are recalled effortlessly, skill is relatively high. A skill once learned is not easily alterable, especially when the steps are generalized and stored.[8]

To better see what we mean by skill, you may wish to try an experiment. Most people sign their name without thinking of the process, that is, with great

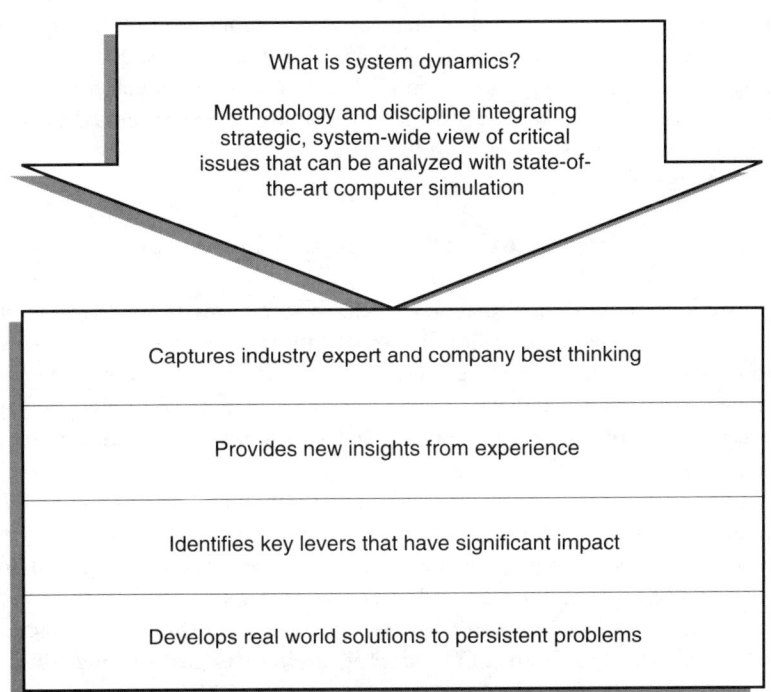

Figure 15.1   What is system dynamics?

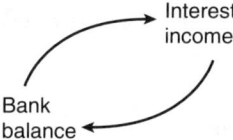

Figure 15.2   Interest accruing on a bank balance.

skill. Try thinking of how you form each letter of your name as you sign it. You will likely note that the letters appear different, almost contrived, compared to the highly skilled signature. Further, try to change the way that you form one letter in your signature – to make it clearer to read. Compare that signature to your automatic signature in a week or so; you will find that changing something that is automatic, and deeply known, is difficult. So our personal skill at anything, including learning, becomes automatic, effortless, and quite rigid as we perfect the skill. And so it is for organizations. The deeply embedded skill for producing a perceived result or consequence of action is automatic; with practice our routine for solving problems becomes quite rigid. In organizations we can find evidence for this in policy manuals on inventory procedures, on how to build a product, and on strategic planning. That is, someone at some time learned the necessary steps to accomplish a chore. Those steps produced an apparent success, and someone recorded those steps – to save others the expense of making a similar discovery.

Organization Design and Defenses

Organizations are designed to achieve goals in some time frame (fiscal month, quarter, year, or planning cycle). The goals are translated into policies, with perceived performance measured against the goals. Any difference between perceived performance and the goal is a mismatch or gap. An intolerable gap is an accumulation of exceptions which provokes an action. This is **management by exception** . . . and it is the nub of strategy.[9]

Virtually every organization sets on a course with an intention to pursue that course until information indicates that they are off the mark. Then the system attempts to correct – to get back on course. This behavior is a powerful goal-seeking feedback loop, one that underlies how businesses conduct themselves. So the underlying *strategy* is to keep on doing the same thing until a signal is received to correct the course. Forrester[10] illustrates this goal-seeking system as shown in figure 15.3.[11]

Most managers have been trained to look for signals of differences and make small course corrections. In effect, they behave like a furnace's thermostat. This poses a major problem when their house is on fire. Worse, when policies are not structured to produce the desired goal, the goal remains unattained and the gap between expectations and performance continues to widen.

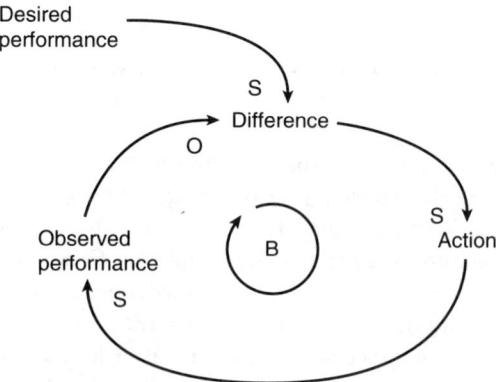

Figure 15.3 Goal-seeking feedback loop. Note: From Jay W. Forrester, "Structure of any policy," *Collected Papers*, 1975, p. 173.

Argyris[12] indicates that the difference between the desired goal and the goal that the organization is structured to accomplish is protected by defensive routines. These routines are themselves part of the skills of the organization – a part of the structure of the system. When the goals and practices of the system are not aligned, no amount of effort will bring about the desired results. This is not surprising when stated this way. But as Argyris indicates, when the difference is not discussible, the lack of communication seals off the organization from change. On the other hand, when cause and effect are illuminated, it is possible to improve the organization.

This is the heart of our proposition: The strategic thinking process is fundamental to the learning organization, and in order to increase learning capacity, the organization must first see a need to improve. Goals and the policies to achieve those goals must be examined and aligned. And since there is no perfect set of goals and no perfect set of policies to achieve those goals, the learning organization must have an automatic process for critical thinking and learning. This automatic process is strategic planning.

Testing outcomes in a simulation model

A manufacturing company in its formative stage was struggling with an ownership question. The shareholders included key employees and three large corporate investors. The corporate investors each had a different motivation for their investment: capital appreciation, strategic technical alliance, and allied market development. Early on, the investor with the allied market development interest asked to "cash out".

The client was planning to seek a suitable replacement, from a small pool of companies in a similar industry to the withdrawing investor. The managers wanted an investor group that would permit investment in new capacity. They were at odds over what type of new investor would be best. Their arguments reflected their respective backgrounds: technology development, manufacturing operations, and market development.

To break the deadlock, we developed a system dynamics model of market and company growth with a sector for the influence of the Board of Directors. In this exercise management described a profile of potential investors who they believed would share their goals and whose votes would contribute to stability in the investor base. The team tested alternative voting decision-rules and outcomes. The result was a crisp description of potential investors and a short search for the appropriate new investor.

Before our involvement, the managers assumed that an additional strategic technology partner would yield the best result. Our synthesis

Continued on p. 472

described a type of venture capitalist known for a medium-term view and desire for cash dividends.

The process illuminated important issues with a new light. The managers' willingness to try a different approach opened the way to fresh analysis, consensus, and increased organizational learning.

The Planning Process

Strategic planners often express frustration generated by the expectations their colleagues hold that planning will provide a correct view of future activity, a proper forecast, and an organization designed to maximize rewards from investment.[13] However, the *process of planning* contributes to the illumination of issues and can lower defensive routines. Managers need time out from day-to-day affairs to think about the longer term and to contemplate issues with a broader horizon viewed from higher ground. The process of planning can be case study, business case, assessment of core competency, systems thinking inquiry, or another form. The question is which available methodology produces the most desirable result for the smallest investment. Forrester provides some insight into the process and its potential outcomes:

> To understand planning, and to understand its failures, we must see the planning process as part of the total structure of [an organization]. Long-range forecasting and planning methods are in no sense different from any other policy that controls action within a system. Methods and policies are based on *current* information which converts that information into a *present* course of action. There is no information available to us out of the future. There are no actions which can take place in the past or the future. We act only in the present. *Long-range planning is simply another of our many processes for converting history into current activity.*[14]

"Systems thinking" provides a starting point for experimentation. Viewing the organization as part of a system puts the strategic thinker in the role of organization architect. However, if the formation of strategy ends with an exhaustive description of conditions that are likely to be encountered, description of competing structures, and a set of designs, the builders are left to construct without design testing and analysis. It is cost-effective to first build a model for testing how a design will fare under a variety of conditions and allow for criticism of functional, ergonomic, and aesthetic design characteristics. The same holds true for organization strategy. The exploration and analysis of model outcomes enriches insight.

Modeling for insight

The Industrial Products Group of a manufacturing client noted that its on-time order fulfillment to distributors slipped from near 100 percent to below 50 percent over a ten-year period. Group general managers adopted policies to expedite overdue orders that accumulated in backlogs. Periodically, manufacturing capacities were increased and average utilization was about 80 percent, but the delivery problem worsened with each year. Over the past three years, sales personnel reported that distributors were stocking more and more substitute products from competitors. IPG witnessed a gradual decrease in total market served even though end-user surveys indicated that demand was rising.

Management believed that its manufacturing processes could be reengineered to provide a 10 percent increase in throughput. After the tweaking, management wanted the sales force to be armed with the best selling techniques to carry the message to distributors. IPG called on its consultants to examine its manufacturing methods and the effectiveness of its sales force.

The consultants examined the supply chain processes and distribution channel strategies of IPG. As an experimental part of the engagement, the consultants built a high level simulation model of the entire value chain. They noticed that IPG's capacity planning and allocation were based on orders received from distributors who made their orders on recent average sales of IPG products.

By exploring feedback links in the model, the team noticed that a tighter coupling of actual end-user demand with IPG's capacity planning functions increased overall system effectiveness. The distributors did not capture orders for IPG products that were fulfilled with competitor's products when IPG products were unavailable. As part of the "sales effectiveness" program the consultants suggested that sales calls include a request for this data. With the help of the simulation model and improved end-user demand data, they estimated that capacity utilization would rise about 20 percentage points (to full utilization) and that distributor stock outs would decrease approximately 30 percentage points. (See the stock and flow diagrams in figure 15.4.)

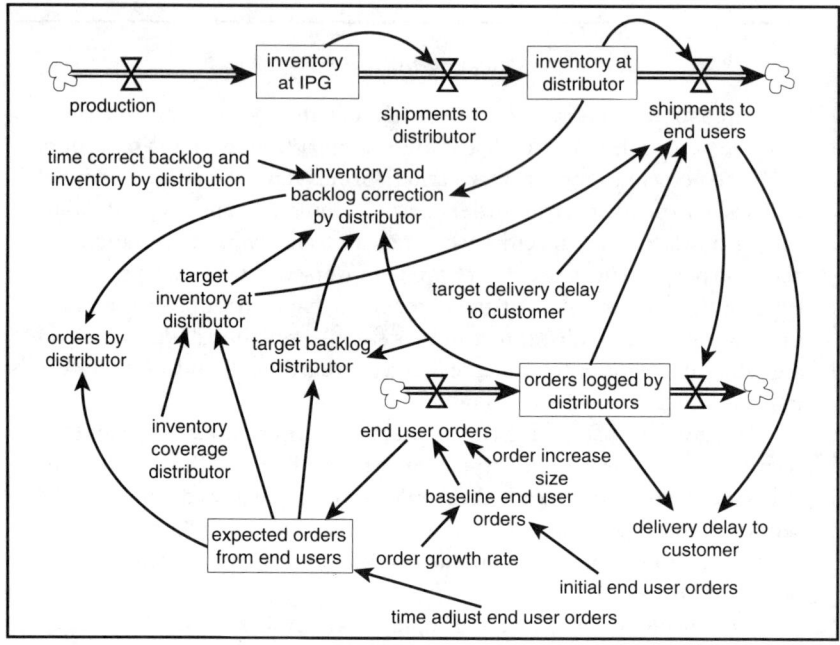

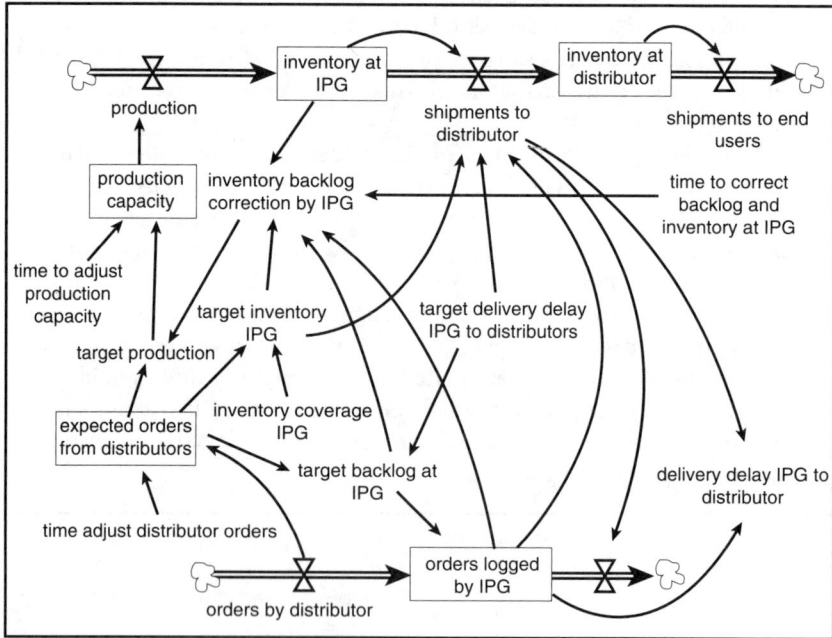

Figure 15.4   The value chain analysis from the IPG case. Top: structure for distributors' ordering decisions. Bottom: structure of IPG's capacity planning system.

System Dynamics in the Planning Process

Strategic planning groups are often expected to make accurate predictions of events in the distant future, an impossible chore. However, when managers expect planning to help improve the organization's adaptability – that is, to increase the learning capacity of the organization – it is possible to meet the expectation and make something worthwhile.[15]

Production and Distribution

Distribution centers put us at a competitive disadvantage because they cost too much ... but our customers (and their customers) want us to maintain delivery service times

Production   Dealers   End-Users

Distribution   Geographics   Products

System Dynamics Approach

1. Recognizes that distribution centers do not act in isolation; rather, they are part of a larger system...
2. Allows us to answer questions that lead to benefits for the entire system:
   - What happens if we close a center?
   - Which distribution structure will help sales double over the next five years?
   - If we want to change our product mix, do we need a different distribution structure?
   - Is our problem better solved by closing distribution centers or changing production schedules?

Senge points to the importance of creating a common, shared understanding for the value of design and its strategic role in an organization.[16] When incorporated in strategy formation, system dynamics can provide powerful insights into how and why structure determines behavior. Randers describes how system dynamics captures the essential process.[17]

System Dynamics Modeling Process

Identifying Cause and Effect

Familiarization with the general issue

Definition of the questions to be addressed –
   What caused performance?
   What are the likely effects of a given policy?

Description of the feedback loops that are assumed to cause the interesting behavior, making mental models explicit

Model Building

The process of formulating a dynamic model

Testing and Analysis

Analyzing model behavior and response to different policies
   Do the basic mechanisms cause the interesting behavior?
   Does the model include the important variables?
   Are the relationships reasonable?
   Are the inputs plausible?

Implementation

Making results accessible to all
Aligning vision, policy, and action

Practical experience indicates that these steps hardly ever proceed in the neat sequence implied by the table.[18] The process from conceptualization through implementation involves revisiting steps to refine ideas.

In the first stage of the process, Identifying Cause and Effect, the group's mental models come to the surface.[19] As team members describe an issue of interest and the cause of performance, their intuition is challenged. The process involves gathering data – usually in graphs – that illustrate significant symptoms or trends that concern managers. The graphs are used as a reference for the question of what causes that performance. The group is asked to form an opinion to be challenged, a hypothesis of cause and effect.

In the next stage, Model Building, one or a few members of the team will transfer the issues to a computer model to simulate the performance of the "system." As the model comes together, its structure and the outcomes from simulations are reviewed by the team. An explanation may be refined or even discarded if the model fails to simulate expected results. The model helps to show that ideas were incomplete or assumptions were inaccurate. This is not a loss; it is part of the learning.

Testing alternative strategies in a model provides the group with a common framework for proposed changes to the organization. The model captures and simulates organizational behavior and serves as a learning laboratory for testing potential improvements. So, when proposed changes produce an unintended consequence, the team can trace the cause of the side-effect to see *why* it occurs. In spreadsheet models, attention focuses on *what if*. Learning *why* the model – and the real world – behaves in a certain way is at a much deeper level than asking *what if* in a spreadsheet.

Finally, implementation takes managers beyond the modeling process. It is a challenge to communicate learning across functions and disciplines. The model is useful for setting goals and performance standards used to measure achievement. It may be used to create a microworld, a computer-based learning laboratory that helps others in the organization learn both how and *why* changes are necessary. But Implementation is more; it comprises the mobilization of an entire organization and alignment with the new vision. It is the action step that completes one learning cycle and generates the next.[20]

Microworlds and Alignment

Senge's *ATP* case illustrates a pleasing use of strategy formation with a simulation model.[21] The client was an operating division of a large public company. The division managers had a disturbing conflict regarding a correct marketing strategy for an advanced technology product.

The management team constructed a computer simulation model with a formulation for the relative attractiveness of products available in the marketplace. They tested alternative strategies for increasing the use of the company's product (see figure 15.5). When an appropriate strategy was settled on, a microworld was constructed from the simulation model. All division employees were encouraged to play the role of managers in the microworld. Their objective was to increase the customer base, increase sales, and maintain an acceptable level of profitability. The employees tried various tactics to improve performance in the simulated market.

When they concluded their experience, they were invited to a seminar that explained the causal relationships in the model and analysis of the aggregate results of their tactics. The process satisfied employees that the proposed company strategy produced a desirable result and achieved a significant alignment of goals in the face of conflict.

Competitive Strategy

Organizations rely on the recollections of experienced managers – seasoned participants in the system. The ability to recognize patterns of performance, relate observed patterns to current situations, and take decisive actions, is a large part of the job description for managers. Their ability to recognize patterns is part of the knowledge base of the organization. However, that learning capacity relies on a model of the real world in the manager's mind. This mental model is based

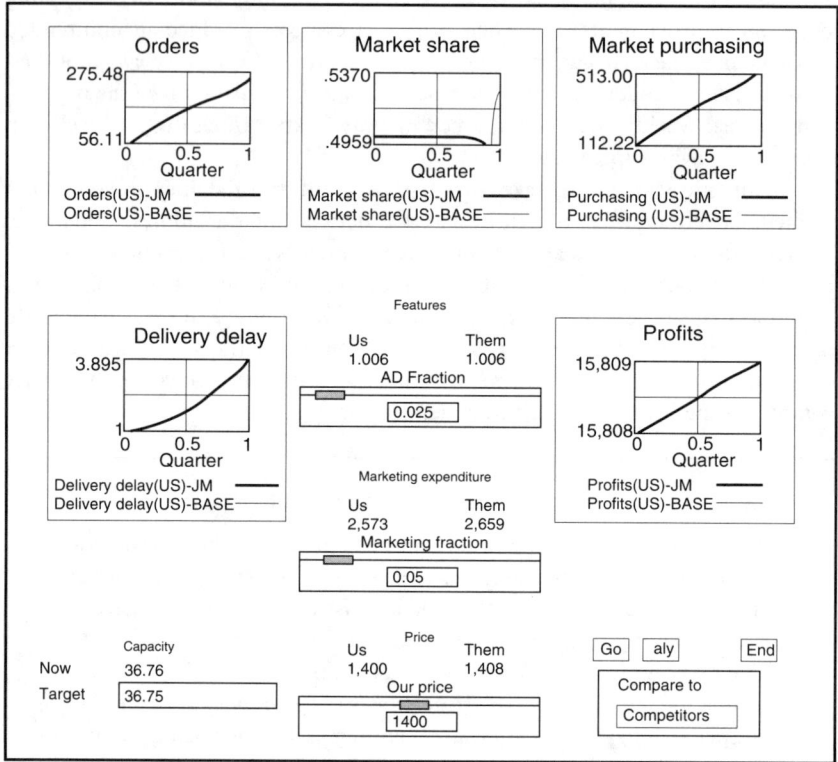

Figure 15.5 "Flight deck" of a management flight simulator (**Aaron** – Software from LeapTec).

in a natural language such as English, Japanese, or French. A simulation model enriches the manager's informal models and more subtle insight is available.

The marketplace is a complex network of relationships and competitive dynamics. The cause and effect of actions taken by competitors is central to the planning process. Are *they* doing it in response to something that *we* are doing? As experience accumulates, responses become reliable and, in a sense, predictable for employees, customers, suppliers, and competitors. This feedback idea is central to system dynamics methodology. But it is unlikely that a firm's competitors will participate in formulating a model; so how are *they* represented?

Through observation we may "reverse engineer" a set of tendencies of another firm and the market. Simulation modeling allows the organization to test its assumptions about competitors. The model will simulate performance that is recognizable to other system participants, in this case, the planning team. Combined with a searching inventory of a firm's best skills, a model helps illuminate where and why an advantage can be obtained. By exploring the model, it is possible to gain insight into the competitive consequences of a strategy.

"Hidden loops"

Bookings and sales of a high technology product grew in a stair step pattern from quarter to quarter. A team, made up of system dynamics consultants and managers from the company, focused on the problem. After extensive interviews and brainstorming with marketing and operations personnel, the team concluded that delays in increasing production capacity were at the root. The customer ordering pattern reflected the customers' concern with delivery schedules. The proposed solution was to increase production capacity at a constant rate based on expectations for market growth rather than waiting until firm orders justified increasing capacity.

As the competition adopted advanced product design and production techniques, its product delivery scheduled gradually shortened. Our product caused our customers to handle it in production in a special (costly) way. As the conventional product delivery schedule approached our delivery schedule, our product was less attractive and customer demand weakened accordingly.

So while the capacity limitation problem clearly existed, it was overwhelmed by a more critical loop: customer satisfaction with the price and relative utility of the product.

Demand was sensitive to customer satisfaction, and the addition of production capacity during periods of weak customer demand alleviated a problem. The undesirable consequence from adding capacity was due to a hidden loop – one that tied the competition's response to the client's design advantage.

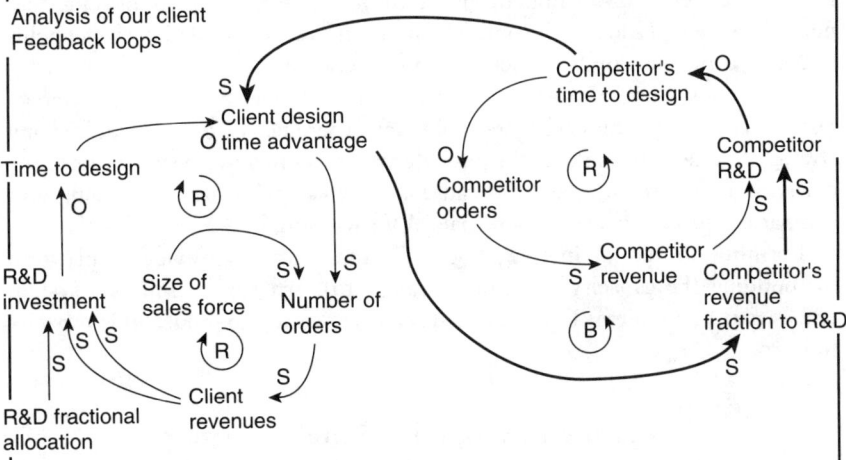

Figure 15.6 Causal loop analysis with hidden loop.

Figure 15.6 is part of a causal loop analysis of the case. The larger arrows highlight the crucial links in the "hidden loop."

System Dynamics as a Tool for Learning

Strategic planning allows time for managers to think about the competitive practices of their organization and competitors – a time to think about the results of decisions in the marketplace. In informal strategy sessions, participants are left to guess the outcome of a change in strategy. Their learning is limited to thinking about different things instead of thinking about things differently. **Systems thinking** emphasizes the importance of looking beyond the events and actors – how performance is dictated by the structure of the whole, the system.[22] It is the structure of the system that automatically generates the pattern of performance. Systems thinking stresses capturing structure in causal loop diagrams. However helpful, a blueprint of the system structure does not show how that system behaves. Such a diagram can only hint at the outcomes that will be produced by the dynamic interaction of the feedback loops within this structure. The prime value of computer simulations is that they enable managers to visualize the connection between this dynamic structure and the performance that it creates over time.

A system described in a causal loop diagram often generates surprising outcomes in a simulation model. It is difficult to accurately guess from looking at a "blueprint" the conditions when one feedback loop will dominate system performance. A reinforcing loop will generate growth or decay without limitation when operating in isolation, and a balancing loop seeks a goal. Although a particular loop exists in a system, there is a question of whether that loop may affect behavior under *any* conditions. The causal loop diagram does not indicate when a loop will come into play – if ever. A simulation model helps to define conditions under which a loop is operative.

A planning team is integral to the process of model building and strategy testing. Learning comes from the full team experience of forming and testing strategy.[23] The team explores the possible structures to describe what causes the behavior of interest. When the cause and effect are tested in a computer simulation, team expectations are crucial for learning.[24]

Forming strategy – in the present for the future – provides a platform for building the capacity of an organization to learn about itself as a system and as part of a system. Exploring cause and effect in the model adds capacity to learn.

Investing in Organizational Learning

Building a first strategy simulation model within an organization has a cost. The strategy team must first agree that there is room for improvement and that they are willing to try a novel methodology to develop a model. As the team increases its collective understanding of feedback and dynamics, learning and experimentation also increases.[25]

The initial investment in learning how to construct and employ a system dynamics model can be relatively small. Several organizations are creating stocks of models that may be incorporated in a larger model structure. These may be found in the System Dynamics National Model of the Sloan School at MIT; the *System Dynamics Review*; journals of operations research; MIT Library working papers, masters and doctoral theses; the generic structures of Senge's *The Fifth Discipline*; the model libraries included with iThink® and Vensim® software; and competitive dynamics models such as Aaron™.[26]

Information technology is leading toward widely distributed use of models throughout organizations. The model becomes a collective laboratory for experimenting: the manager sets up new assumptions or a change in structure to one in the corporate library, runs an experiment, and analyzes outcomes. When

Sample Issues	
Global	• How could the consolidation of North/South Korea impact imports to Europe? • How would the end of Castro's rule impact Florida?
National	• How will federal financial guarantee legislation affect the commercial banking industry? • How will environmental concerns continue to influence America's relative cost to produce?
Industry	• What are the key countries for a trade bank to focus on ? • What drives price fluctuations in the oil market?
Corporate	• What set of policies will produce a "healthy company" in five years? • When does a company's core competence work against it?

Division	• Where is the competitive leverage in our client's direct sales force? • What should the distribution network look like?
Product Group	• Which product mix can generate the most revenue from unrelated investment? • Is it better to license a product or develop a product in-house
Department	• Which employee behaviors should be rewarded to increase productivity? • How does our policy to expedite late orders lower customer satisfaction?
Function	• Will a new call-directing technology help the client respond to customer questions more quickly? • How does product quality impact employee morale and lost time?

the model is linked to historical data files and commonly shared models, the stage is set for continuous learning and thoughtful experimentation.

Practicing learning to learn

In a workshop designed to introduce managers to system dynamics modeling and systems thinking, we move quickly to producing small, interesting, simulation models. The participants usually have no previous experience with system dynamics modeling. One team focused on the growth of the marketplace for financial derivative products. They wished to find causes for the explosive growth of the market. Their goal was to develop a model to test alternative points for stimulation of demand.

Continued on p. 483

The team first developed a causal loop diagram which they believed adequately described the market growth. The causal loop diagram included about five or six loops comprising 20 or so highly abstract concepts. When they tested their thoughts in a model, they were initially frustrated that they could not finish a model in minutes. They instructors visited with the team for several minutes each half hour. We challenged them to describe one or two loops that were central to their theory. The team produced a two–loop diagram that they presented to one instructor. Their conclusion was tinged with skepticism – "This is ridiculously simple. It will produce nothing interesting."

The modeling went quickly and resulted in a simulation run within a half hour or so. Just prior to running the simulation, the team was asked to express their expectation for the outcome of the simulation, the pattern of the output. The simulation result was far different from their expectations. The team assumed that they had done something wrong and needed to start all over. The instructor encouraged them to analyze the behavior of their model by tracing around each loop to see what they could learn. The questions asked: Is the model an accurate representation of their notions and were their notions about the way the real world worked accurate and complete?

After tracing causality around the model loops, they determined that the model accurately represented their notions. This was a breakthrough. They went on to consider a new question. Were they satisfied that they knew the causes of market growth in the real world?

The team satisfied themselves that the model was insufficient to explain the real world system as they saw it. However, the model could help them learn about the dynamic implications of their own notions. In the team's exercise they had broken through a defensive routine: "I have to fix this model and make it work," changed to "I can learn from this." They laid a cornerstone for building a capacity to learn.

Each workshop team achieved similar results. The insights from modeling are often subtle but rarely unimportant. Increasing the capacity to learn required melting barriers to learning, increasing confidence in newly developed skills, and reflecting on the results of the process.

Summary

In the organization, routine decision-making is based on its values and recent feedback. The process of forming strategy provides a time to think about those values, performance, and structure. Learning why and how an organization generates its performance adds depth to experience. The process sharpens thinking and provides the focus for examining important issues. Planning with system dynamics deepens understanding of *why* things work, creating a survey of possibilities. This learning increases organizational robustness – a feedback notion itself.

Appendix: Conceptualization with Causal Loops

Causal loop drawing is a skill in itself; it requires talent and practice to develop competency. Interpreting a diagram requires talent and practice, too. A poor or inappropriate diagram may divert attention from the important issue and, worse, may obscure subtle issues. As an alternative, stock and flow diagrams can lead to an understanding of the systemic causes. Stock and flow diagrams may yield the best results in cases in which the team identifies where the issue arises but the causes are less apparent.[27]

An example of double-loop learning

Argyris[28] describes defensive routines that organizations adopt to protect themselves from threat or embarrassment from personal and organizational failure to meet governing variables. He describes how the design of management information systems can be part of the defensive routine of firms. Ackoff[29] illustrates how the mismatch between actual results, information feedback, and governing variables causes organizations to untrack. Organizations and individuals invoke powerful defenses, such as denial or obfuscation, because they refuse to examine whether their goals and milestones are appropriate.[30]

Argyris[31] describes organizational learning as single- and double-loop learning. The principle is that an organization learns in two ways: a short-term reinforcement loop (the single-loop) and an adjustment of underlying values (the double-loop), illustrated in figure 15.7.[32]

In the single-loop, actions are repeated when they do not produce the intended consequences. In the double-loop, the lesson learned from a mismatch of intentions, actions, and consequences leads to an adjustment of the system's goals, standards, or governing variables.

We offer an interpretation of the "single-loop" in causal loop format in figure 15.8.

The diagram may be interpreted as a system in which certain actions cause desired consequences and the actions are repeated *automatically* until the consequence of the action meets the governing variable or goal. An interpretation of the "double-loop" is presented in causal loop format in figure 15.9.

The outer circle, or double-loop, provides for an adjustment of the governing variables. When desirable results are attained as a consequence of certain actions, the system responds by increasing its goals. On the other hand, the governing variable decreases if consequences do not match.[33] The *automatic match* of actions and consequences deeply ingrains the governing variables.

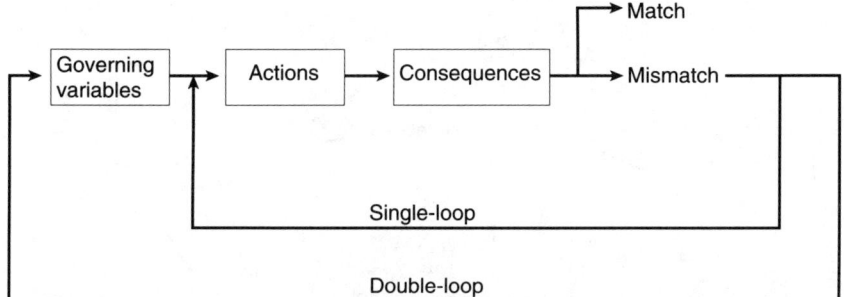

Figure 15.7 Single-loop and double-loop learning.

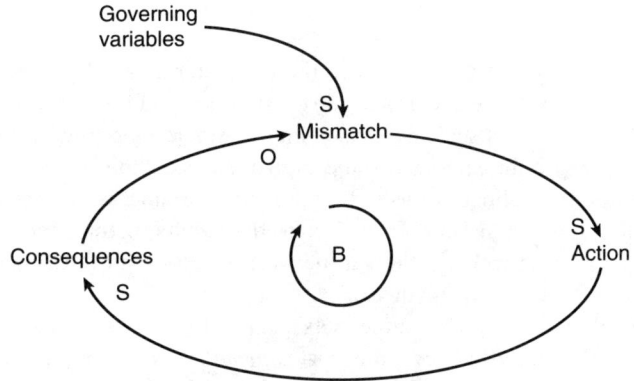

Figure 15.8 Single-loop learning.

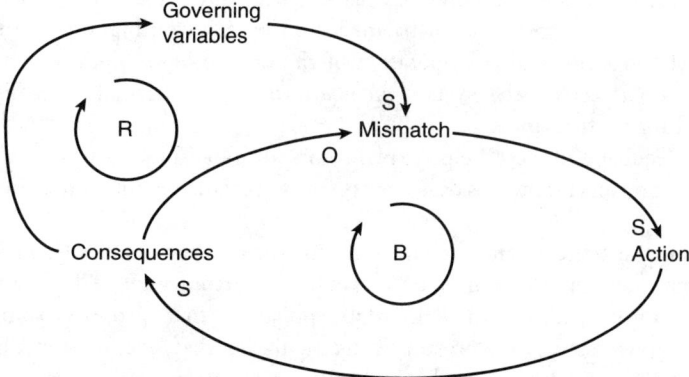

Figure 15.9 Double-loop learning.

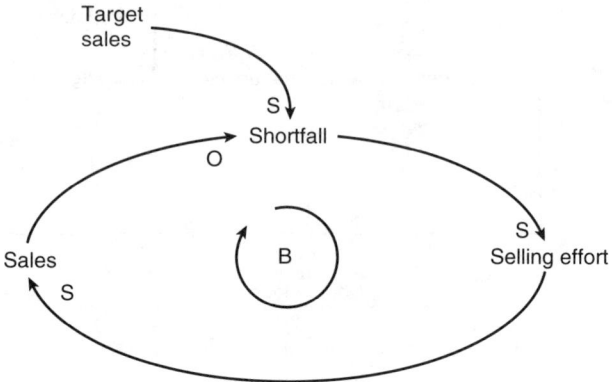

Figure 15.10   Structure of a sales department.

To illustrate, say that a sprinter runs the 100 meter dash. The sprinter's goal is to achieve a record time in competition of six seconds. The governing variable is a finishing time of six seconds. Following the single-loop, the runner would continue to prepare for each race – and measure success in each competition – by that standard. Failing to meet the governing variable of six seconds, the runner will always try harder. If we isolate the results of this loop alone, the runner is attempting to close the gap between results achieved and achieve a very high standard of performance.

With the double-loop, the runner sets a standard of six seconds for the 100 meter dash. Failing to achieve the goal *automatically* causes the governing variable to change, and depending on the time delay for making the adjustment, the governing variable may be changed a little or a lot at any one competition.

With each successive experience, the governing variable is adjusted up or down based on the accumulated experience until the results and the governing variable come into a balance. Setting a governing variable that is achievable does not end the operation of the double-loop. That is, when the double-loop is active, the system *automatically* is encouraged to change the standard for performance.

This feedback process helps explain how an individual or an organization moves to improvement. A sales department's structure is illustrated in figure 15.10.

Where the policies and practices of an organization do not produce the goal, significant problems may be created. The organization will continue to employ, automatically and with skill, practices that produce something other than the goal. The result is likely to be that everyone within the organization works harder, and the absolute goal remains unattained, with an ever-widening gap between expectations and perceived performance. Consider

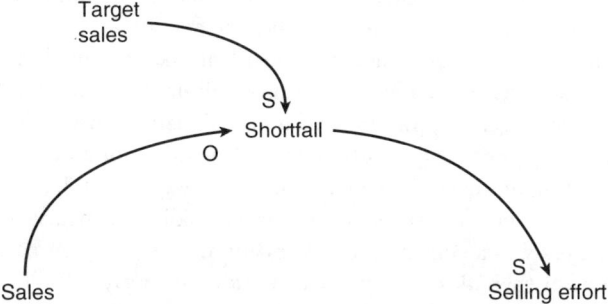

Figure 15.11 Selling effort not linked to sales.

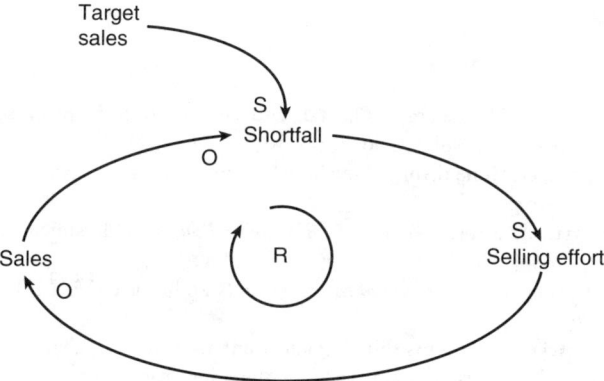

Figure 15.12 Selling effort decreases sales.

a sales department in which the selling effort is not linked to sales, illustrated in figure 15.11. In this system a shortfall triggers increased selling effort, but no increase in sales. Now, consider an organization in which selling effort *decreases* sales (figure 15.12). Here, as the shortfall increases, selling effort increases, sales decrease and the shortfall increases. Although the case is extreme, it illustrates a vicious cycle or *reinforcing* feedback loop.

Effect of information delays

Information is delayed in the performance monitoring systems so that the actual shortfall or gap is unknown. It is implicit in management by exception systems that managers need information about performance only when the historical performance deviates from the system's tolerance for errors. And since managers have a finite capacity for information processing, most of the information they receive on performance gaps is aggregated – an accumulation of errors and time delays before corrective actions can be implemented.

The manager draws on a mental model[34] of the system or performance patterns to reason that systemic performance will be thus-and-so in the future based on the manager's application of a stored pattern from the past. The maturity of management is proportional to its tolerance for ambiguity in measuring and reacting to the performance gap. Managers with a tolerance for errors and who "still deliver the results" are rewarded. Skilled managers – those who operate effortlessly in a collection of errors and delays – rely on pattern recognition to control their desire to react to performance gaps. Skilled managers draw on their experience within the system and recognize a pattern of behavior of the system. The recognition of the pattern allows them to anticipate a change in the system performance.[35]

Notes

1   See, e.g., Henry Mintzberg, "The fall and rise of strategic planning", *Harvard Business Review*, 1994, vol. 72, no. 1, pp. 107–14.
2   Peter F. Drucker, "The theory of business", *Harvard Business Review*, 1994, vol. 72, no. 5, pp. 95–104.
3   Chris Argyris, *Strategy, Change, and Defensive Routines* (Marshfield, MA: Pitman Publishing, 1985).
4   Herbert A. Simon, *The Sciences of the Artificial* (Cambridge, MA: MIT Press, 1969), pp. 118–19.
5   Russell L. Ackoff, "Systems thinking and thinking systems", *System Dynamics Review*, 1994, vol. 10, nos. 2–3, pp. 175–88, quotation from p. 175.
6   George P. Richardson and Alexander L. Pugh III, *Introduction to System Dynamics Modeling with DYNAMO* (Cambridge, MA: MIT Press, 1981), p. 1.
7   Ibid., pp. 1–3.
8   Argyris, *Strategy, Change, and Defensive Routines*, p. 84.
9   Ibid., p. 86.
10 Jay W. Forrester, *The Collected Papers of Jay W. Forrester* (Cambridge, MA: Wright-Allen Press, 1975), p. 173.
11 A causal loop diagram may be interpreted as follows: The variable at the tail of an arrow *causes* or *influences* the variable at the head of the arrow. There is no implication that the causes shown in the diagram are the only causes or influences – there may be others not shown on the diagram. "S" at the arrow head indicates that the caused-variable changes in the same direction as its cause (i.e., the partial derivative of the variable with respect to the cause is positive).
    A loop can be assigned an overall polarity – either reinforcing and positive or balancing and negative. A negative polarity – indicated by "B" enclosed by a looping arrow – means that a change in any variable in the loop will tend to be negated as its influence flows around the loop. As a consequence, balancing loops are spoken of as being goal-seeking or controlling.
    A positive polarity – indicated by "R" enclosed by a looping arrow – indicates that a change in any variable will be reinforced as its influence flows around the loop.

Consequently, positive loops are often considered to be self-reinforcing. J. Hines and J. Thompson, "Designing new federal financial guarantee programs", Working Paper #WP 3678 (Cambridge MA: Sloan School of Management, 1994).

More detailed explanations of causal loop diagrams and influence diagrams may be found in Richardson and Pugh, *Introduction*, pp. 25 ff. and E. B. Roberts, *Managerial Applications of Systems Dynamics* (Cambridge, MA: MIT Press, 1978), ch. 1. Peter Senge, in *The Fifth Discipline* (New York: Doubleday, 1990), pp. 73 ff. offers an explanation in a more managerial context, and in *Feedback Thought in Social Science and Systems Theory* (Philadelphia: University of Pennsylvania Press, 1991), George P. Richardson offers an explanation in tracing the historical development of the notion of feedback in the social sciences.

12 Argyris, *Strategy, Change, and Defensive Routines*. Also *On Organizational Learning* (Cambridge, MA: Blackwell, 1992) and *Knowledge for Action* (San Francisco: Jossey-Bass, 1993).

13 Mintzberg, "The fall and rise of strategic planning".

14 Forrester, *Collected Papers*, p. 167 (emphasis added).

15 Simon, in *The Sciences of the Artificial*, describes the emerging science of design and an increasing appreciation for the fact that organization policy structure determines outcomes. He focuses on the value added by a thorough exploration through simulation models – a survey of the possibilities. Simon emphasizes the importance of applying a rigorous methodology in arriving at cause and effect, including feedback in the methodology, and avoiding the seduction of prediction (pp. 129, 170–2).

16 Senge, *The Fifth Discipline*, p. 206.

17 List adapted from Jørgen Randers, "Guidelines for model conceptualization" in Jørgen Randers (ed.) *Elements of the System Dynamics Method* (Portland, OR: Productivity Press, 1981), p. 119.

18 James H. Hines and Dewey W. Johnson, "Launching system dynamics", *Proceedings of the 1994 International System Dynamics Conference*. Stirling, Scotland.

19 J. A. M. Vennix, D. F. Andersen, G. P. Richardson and J. Rohrbaugh, "Model building for group decision support," in John D. W. Morecroft and John D. Sterman (eds.), *Modeling for Learning Organizations* (Portland, OR: Productivity Press, 1994).

20 See, e.g. Kolb's cycle of experiential learning: David A. Kolb, Irwin M. Rubin and James M. McIntyre. *Organizational Psychology: An Experiential Approach to Organizational Behavior* (Englewood Cliffs, NJ: Prentice Hall, 1994).

21 Senge, *The Fifth Discipline*, pp. 251–7.

22 Jay W. Forrester, "System dynamics, systems thinking, and soft OR", *System Dynamics Review*, 1994, vol. 10, nos. 2–3, p. 248.

23 Alan K. Graham, John D. W. Morecroft, Peter M. Senge and John D. Sterman, "Model supported case studies for management education", in Morecroft and Sterman, *Modeling for Learning Organizations*, p. 238.

24 Argyris, *Strategy, Change, and Defensive Routines*, p. 81.

25 Hines and Johnson, "Launching system dynamics", p. 2 and Forrester, *Collected Papers*, p. 164.

26 iThink® and Vensim® are system dynamics application environments – modeling tools in computer software that allow for the construction, testing, and analysis of system dynamics models. Aaron™ is a configurable market growth and product diffusion system dynamics model based in Vensim. iThink is available from High Performance Systems, Inc., 45 Lyme Road, Hanover, NH 03755. Vensim is available

from Ventana Systems, Inc., 149 Waverly Street, Belmont, MA 02178. Aaron is published by LeapTec, PO Box 8460, Warwick, RI 02888.

27 For a description of causal loop diagrams, see note 11 above.

28 Argyris, *Knowledge for Action, On Organizational Learning*, and *Strategy, Change, and Defensive Routines*.

29 Russell L. Ackoff, "Management misinformation systems", *Management Science*, 1967, vol. 14, no. 4, pp. B147–56.

30 In moving from the views of Argyris to the methodology of system dynamics, there is potential for distorting or losing an important notion. The causal loop diagrams are offered more as a bridge to Argyris's work rather than as a supplement. That is, Argyris's double-loop work stands on its own.

31 Argyris, *On Organizational Learning*, pp. 8 ff. and *Knowledge for Action*, p. 50.

32 Figure 15.7 from Argyris, *On Organizational Learning*, p. 8.

33 Argyris, *On Organizational Learning*, p. 9.

34 Jay W. Forrester, *Industrial Dynamics* (Cambridge, MA: Productivity Press, 1961).

35 Argyris, *Strategy, Change, and Defensive Routines*, pp. 86–90 and *Knowledge for Action*, p. 55.

16

Managing in a Culture That Values Learning

Craig C. Lundberg

Introduction

Two general questions focus the discussion of this chapter. The first question is: How does organizational culture influence learning in and by organizations? The second is: What does this impact of culture on learning in and by organizations imply for managing? To respond to these questions I shall be discussing four related topics: the nature and form of organizations (the learning organization), the process of change that changes organizations (organizational learning), the nature and function of the shared meanings that support learning in and by organizations (organizational culture), and those persons, and their activities, responsible for creating, maintaining, and developing organizations (management).

Why are the two focusing questions and this chapter worthy of our attention? From the outset of this book you have read repeatedly both about the need for more and better learning in and by organizations and about the array of forces and circumstances within organizations that make managing so that organizations learn so challenging. We only need to be reminded that a capacity for learning and thus changing for continual improvement is seen as a crucial feature for both organizational and managerial survival and success in what we know to be an increasingly competitive, complex, and changeful world.[1] The more fully managers understand their organizational circumstances, the more likely they are to act appropriately and effectively in them. The more fully managers understand the effects, both intended and unintended, of the way they manage, the more likely they are to enhance learning in and by their organizations. Since cultures in organizations explain so much about behavior, it follows that an appreciation, and an informed understanding, of organizational cultures is not only useful but perhaps is a prerequisite for organization management now as well as in the future.

The discussion that follows will be organized in four sections. The first section will provide a way of understanding what organizational culture is and what it does for organizations and their members. The second section will review how individuals and organizations learn and how the learning by each is transferred to the other. The third section describes the form and functions of a learning organization and the part that culture plays. Finally, I will discuss how managers lead learning organizations and influence individual and organizational learning.

Toward Understanding Cultures In Organizations

For a little over a decade, organizational cultures have increasingly attracted attention and study by managers, consultants, and theorists. Long the idea central to the discipline of anthropology, culture is one of the most familiar aspects of everyone's experience. We all grow up in a culture, work and live in cultures; we intuitively know about culture and use it every day. For example how we read this book is learned, widely understood, yet typically out of our awareness. Noting it is in English, we read it front to back, read the pages top to bottom, and each line left to right. Excessive familiarity makes culture difficult to understand, much less think about crisply. Because organizational culture is so familiar, and because it is both a relatively new and rapidly growing field, the idea of culture in organizations has come to have a diversity of meanings.

While definitions of organizational culture abound, it is possible to distill what is common across them.[2] Doing so, it can be seen as generally agreed that organizational culture:

- Is a shared common frame of reference, that is, it is shared by some significant portion of organization members, and is largely taken for granted by them;
- Is socially acquired and transmitted by organization members, that is, it is learned;
- Can be found in all fairly stable social units, of any size, that have a reasonable history, that is, it endures over time;
- Provides organizational members with guides for their behavior, that is, it governs;
- Provides a common psychology, that is, it denotes what is unique and contributes a shared identity;
- Is symbolic, that is, it is manifested in observables such as language, things, and patterned behavior to which are attributed meanings;
- Is, at its core, typically both invisible and determinate, that is, it is ultimately composed of a configuration of values and assumptions;
- Is modifiable, but not easily so.

Culture, as these definitional themes show, is both the source and vehicle of organizational meanings. Culture is the phenomenon of organizations by which reality is constructed: it allows members to see and understand particular events, actions, objects, utterances, and whole situations, including one's own behavior, in an acceptable way that is sensible and meaningful. Two organizations performing the same task do not necessarily perform it identically, for example, the Celtics do not play basketball in the same way as the 76ers. Organizational culture in one sense is the reservoir of solutions to an organization's ongoing and anticipated tasks as well as occasional crises – from managing internal affairs to surviving in the external environment, from maintaining morale to dealing with growth or decline, from measuring performance to reviewing product-service offerings. What has been found to work consistently over time is symbolically expressed and maintained through patterns of thought and behavior and other devices as guides to future actions, for example, "how we do things around here." Organizational culture, thus, is what is taught and reinforced to members as the proper way to perceive, to think, to feel, to act. Cook and Yanow,[3] for example, note that over two decades the Juilliard String Quartet has replaced all but one of its original members yet retains its distinctive style – learned by each new member through the playing of music in rehearsal and performance but never through explicit conversation.

The general idea of organizational culture reminds us, correctly, of the enormous extent to which reality is both socially constructed and symbolically mediated. The idea of culture suggests that (1) what is most important about organizational events and processes is not what happened but the meaning of what happened; (2) the meaning of events and processes is determined not simply by what happened but by the way that members interpret what happened; (3) for many of the most significant events and processes in organizations it is often difficult or impossible to know what happened, why it happened, or what will happen; (4) this pervasive uncertainty and ambiguity about organizational events and processes undermines simple, rational, linear managerial approaches; and, (5) under such conditions while organizational events and processes may often be illogical, random, fluid, silly, disconnected, and essentially meaningless, managers and members alike create symbols and impose meanings to reduce ambiguity, resolve confusion, increase predictability, and provide direction.[4]

Through its meaning-infused symbols and patterned activities, organizational culture provides much that is invaluable to organizations and their members. As noted, culture specifies what is unique to those who share it, thus it gives an identity to organizations and parts of organizations as well as enabling members to create part of their own identities. Also as previously noted, culture is the basis for direction as well as order and coherence – the meanings of where the collective "we" are going and how we are related. Cultures provide the rationale and supportive reasoning for an organization's vision, strategy, and all required activities and responsibilities – saying in effect what we are jointly about and why we bother doing it. Cultural meanings serve to mobilize, guide and control member energy – what emotions and behaviors are desired, appropriate, and taboo. Organizational culture meanings fill the void of uncertainty too; it is therefore a primary source of anxiety reduction for all members. For these and similar reasons, we begin to understand that culture is strongly functional for both organizations and their members in that it provides meaningful responses to the sorts of questions, typically unvoiced, that pervade human existence: Who are we? What are we about? How should we behave? The challenge to managers is how to comprehend organizational culture, manage within it, and how to influence it.

Popular writing about organizational culture typically emphasizes uncommon but easily noticed features such as heroes, exotic ceremonies, dramatic stories, strange labels, and so on and relies on colorful anecdotes to convey their significance, for example, the pink cadillacs of Mary Kay Cosmetics, R&D skunkworks, a security guard prohibiting a CEO from entrance without approved ID, managers rolling up their sleeves to "pitch-in" to meet shipment deadlines, musicians playing "gigs," and the like. While these features easily capture our attention it is similarly easy to miss their essence, namely that they are symbolic and their meaning is found in how these particulars reflect a larger, more invisible set of more or less deeply shared understandings. Serious investigators of organizational culture, in contrast to casual observers, now portray culture as a layered phenomenon composed of three interrelated levels of meanings – from relatively easily observable to mostly invisible.[5] Figure 16.1 summa-

---

The Manifest Level

    Symbolic artifacts

    Unique language (jargon, slang, sayings, slogans)

    Organization stories (sagas, myths)

    Ritualistic activities (rituals, ceremonies)

    Patterned conduct (norms, customs)

The Middle Level

    Strategic beliefs

The Core Level

    Values

    Assumptions

Figure 16.1   The "levels of meaning" framework.

rizes the component ideas and the hierarchy of levels which outline a "levels of meaning" conceptual framework for comprehending organizational culture. Before describing this framework, however, it is important to emphasize that culture in organizations is usually plural. There often is an "umbrella" culture for the organization as a whole. Within this umbrella culture, each subsystem (e.g. regions, divisions, departments, occupations, other groupings) may have its own culture, more or less consistent with the umbrella culture on the one hand and the cultures of other subunits on the other hand.

The most easily observed and understood features of culture are at the manifest level. These are relatively visible in that careful, systematic listening and observing will reveal them. They are relatively easy to understand simply because most members who have been around awhile can articulate their meaning. There are five manifest features. First, there are organization-specific symbolic artifacts, that is, objects that possess some meaning beyond what they are, for example company logos, photographs of founders, furniture style, and so forth. Second, there are unique language elements: an organization-specific vocabulary (jargon), slang (argot), and sayings and slogans as well as their nonverbal counterparts. Third, there are organizational stories about significant persons and events, some essentially accurate such as stories of organizational heroes (sagas) and some elaborated beyond the facts (myths). Fourth, there are ritualistic activities of two types: regular events that reaffirm and signify what is important (rituals), and important but less regular events that signify transitions or enable something deemed important to happen more easily (ceremonies). Fifth is patterned conduct, those behaviors that reflect unwritten rules that inform members what is and is not appropriate behavior and what is the preferred style of relating (group norms and organizational customs). Individually and collectively these five manifest features function to predispose members to experience organizational events, activities, and things in certain ways, to define problems in acceptable ways, to perform within acceptable limits, and to strive toward common ends. Experiencing these manifest features of the organizational culture over time, members acquire and come to share a unique common psychology familiarly understood as organizational "know-how."

At the middle level of meaning are a set of strategic beliefs. These beliefs are not the long-range plans, strategies or policies pronounced by organizational spokespersons. Rather, strategic beliefs are the fundamental if general shared convictions about the organization's (or subcultural unit's) major survival tasks. There are four basic types: those of strategic vision – what the organization can become and do and what it will not attempt; those about capital market expectations – what is believed necessary to keep lenders and investors satisfied; those about product-market competition – how and why the organization can succeed in its industry and in its set of suppliers and consumers; and those about internal managing – what operating practices support the other beliefs. These strategic beliefs are usually "in the mind" of the organization's influential leaders, shared and understood but not often consciously so, and their meaning is often at least partially appreciated by other members. Some strategic beliefs may be articulated but typically they must be inferred from the stream of decisions made over time. They actively shape the manifest cultural features discussed above, and reflect the cultural core we turn to next.

The deepest level of cultural meanings, the core level of the framework, is a set of organization-specific values and assumptions. The configuration of this set of values and assumptions constitutes the basic character of the organization. This core serves as the set of premises and aspirations that impacts on the vast majority of organizational thought and actions, both formal and informal. Values are the collective sense of what should be striven for or avoided. Values then are the real ideals, basic aspirations, and sins of the organization. Assumptions are the shared premises with which the organization's leaders view or imagine the reality they exist in. Assumptions therefore refer to basics: the nature of time, truth, human activity, fate and chance, human relationships, and which classes of people should get preferential treatment. A central value and assumption has to do with change – whether change is really possible, whether it is desirable, how it should be initiated and by whom, and how managed. Experienced managers will appreciate that change-related values and assumptions vary enormously across organizations and subunits, and may or may not be reflected in faddish rhetoric. Cultural cores may be characterized as falling along a strong–weak continuum, where strong means the core is both intensely held and widely shared, that is, the more members who accept the core values and assumptions and the greater their commitment to them, the stronger the culture. The core level of meanings is essentially "taken for granted" and thus invisible. To know the core requires making general inferences based upon an enormous, factual amount of information about organizational practices – usefully facilitated by an outsider since understanding ones' own culture will be biased by being captive of it.

With an appreciation of what cultures in organizations are and do and a framework for understanding them, we can begin to see how culture may impact learning in and by organizations as well as foreshadow how culture either constrains or promotes managerial actions *vis à vis* learning. Does the culture assume that learning by members and the organization is possible and feasible? Does the culture value such learning? Do the strategic beliefs necessitate the changes that learning provides? Do the manifest features, the norms, rituals, stories, language, and so forth, encourage learning processes and structures? And does the culture tend to liberate or tie the hands of managers who wish to create and develop learning in and by their organizations? Before exploring these questions, however, we need to clarify what learning in organizations is.

On Learning in and by Organizations

In this section I wish to clarify two things – how individuals and organizations perform and learn, and how learning by individuals and by organizations may become the learning of the other. The discussion will proceed by first outlining a relatively simple descriptive model that accounts for all organizational behavior including learning. After clarifying what "learning how to learn" is, the discussion will turn to the processes by which individual learning becomes organizational knowledge – diffusion, and the process by which organizational knowledge is learned by individual members – socialization.[6] Finally, what all of this means culturally will be examined.

At the outset it is important to point out that the two units of analysis discussed, individual organizational members and the human systems in which individuals have membership, that is, organizations and their subunits, are open systems. They are open systems in that they receive and give energy and information to their environments. Since the environment is never static, never stable, open systems that persist are continually adapting themselves to their environment. Hence, by definition, open systems naturally learn. Learning, therefore, is not something special that people and organizations do once in a while, rather it is naturally continuous. Learning for individuals and for human systems of all sizes and degrees of formalization is a matter of about what, when, how much and how well, and under what conditions. Learning, in essence, becomes understood as the natural, ongoing, outcome of organizational behavior. But, we ask, how might organizational behavior be described so that we might enhance learning?

Ongoing organizational performance and learning occurs through a sequential cycle of four subprocesses or stages: observation, assessment, formulation, and implementation. This experiential cycle has been identified over and over as fundamental in organizational psychology, organizational development, total quality improvement, management development, and so forth.[7] To **observe** is to notice or attend to the components, actions, and events of experience that the mental categories of a human system (again, individuals or larger systems, e.g. teams, departments, organizations) predispose or permit being perceived, that is, that which is culturally relevant. To **assess** is to reflect on that which has been observed, that is, to note how well actions meet relevant standards or goals, and to interpret or explain why this has occurred. Again this is culturally anchored. To **formulate** is either to decide to continue the behavior that resulted in what was observed or to design some hopefully more appropriate behavior – usually within cultural bounds. To **implement** is to initiate, within cultural limits, either the prior or the new behavior, thereby providing a test of the formulation and the new experience which can then be observed, commencing another cycle. Each of these processes, of course, can occur either in or out of the conscious awareness of the individual or persons who make up the membership of some human system. To summarize these points made or implied so far: this inquiry cycle describes both ordinary and unusual organizational behavior as well as learning, it applies to both individuals and to all sizes and types of human systems, and it is culturally guided.

Each of the processes that constitute the four stages of the performance–

learning cycle just outlined interestingly functions in accordance with its own rules almost always unknown or only partially known by the person or system – and typically strongly influenced by culture. The process of observation will be guided by cognitive rules about accessing memory, that is, what part of that already known is deemed relevant and important, and rules of attention, that is, what is worth noticing in what circumstances. The process of assessment will be guided by rules that specify relevant aspirational levels of performance or behavior modification, and rules of interpretation, that is, what sorts of explanation are permitted so as to make sense out of what has been observed. The process of formulation is likewise guided by two kinds of rules, rules for information search, that is, about the allowable cost of resources and time and the scope of information search, and rules for designing activities, that is, about the specificity, formality, and areas of applicability of activities. The process of implementation is guided by rules about the time frame needed to implement an activity and the time allowed for an activity to produce a noticeable level of desired output, and rules about what are acceptable levels of resource cost to implement or refine an activity. It should be emphasized that these rules are seldom known to members or to organizations but if known open up alternative choices. Figure 16.2[8] summarizes the basic performance–learning cycle and the types of rules governing its four subprocesses.

In order to show how the cycle works, one begins with a very basic but seldom considered question – how does organizational performance occur? To

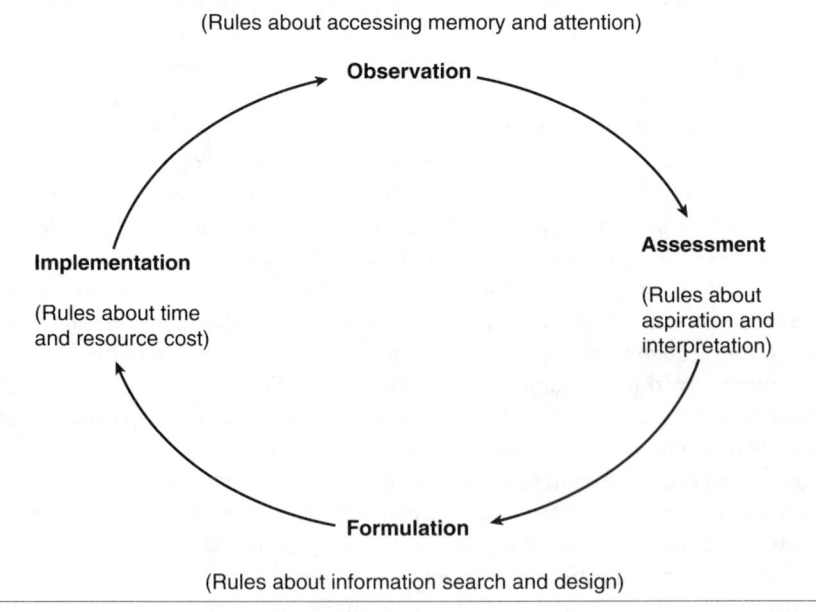

Figure 16.2 The basic performance learning cycle.

answer this question, we begin by reminding ourselves that organizations and their subunits are purposive, that purpose is defined in terms of specific outcomes, and that outcomes are the product of members believing and performing a set of actions that supposedly lead to outcomes. Performance in any organizational circumstance may now be described as follows: members observe what they have learned to pay attention to, that is, the things, actions, and events that supposedly contribute to outcomes (this is a comparison of outcomes against intended goals and standards); when no appreciable difference is noticed, the type and amount of behavior observed is continued. However when a performance gap is noticed (a difference between goals or standards and observed performances) it is labeled a problem and action is initiated to alter either the goals or standards that apply or the amount or type of outcome-relevant behavior. Actions taken are those previously learned when the problem is a familiar one. When successful, these actions taken are reinforced. When not successful or when the observed performance gap is novel, new actions not already learned are required. In these cases, search is undertaken, new tactical actions selected, and experimental action initiated. Those actions that appear to be successful are then retained, that is, added to the set of learned responses, and we can say learning has occurred in that these actions will in the future influence what is observed, assessed as either a familiar or a novel problem, and so forth. For both individuals and for organizations then, the difference between performance and learning turns on whether performance gaps are perceived as being familiar or novel, which in turn is a function of what is observed, how it is assessed, the formulation of actions, and the criteria utilized to judge implementation success.

In the workings of the basic performance–learning cycle two types of changes can be seen: (1) those changes that get both individuals and organizations back on track, where the "learning" is basically a reaffirmation of what works; and (2) changes where the "learning" is the acquisition of a new way of working and what was perceived as a novel problem will henceforth be seen as a familiar one. Both familiar and novel problems, however, will reflect what organizational members have learned to pay attention to, or to observe, and how what is noticed is assessed, or interpreted. Cultures in organizations are significant here; culture says in effect what will be surfaced and how it will be examined – and surfacing and examining may vary widely among different cultures. In one organization, for example, it may be legitimate to only occasionally observe a limited range of things and only very large performance gaps are thought to be real problems – familiarly, "If it ain't broke, don't fix it." In contrast, another organization might legitimate observing just about everything, with even small or incipient gaps perceived as real or potential problems, for example managers of TGI Fridays restaurants regularly sit in every seat in the establishment to experience it as their guests do.

Up to this point, learning has been characterized as the consequence of surfacing, that is, bringing to awareness and expressing this awareness, and examining it, judging whether something already known or done continues to be acceptable or not. It should be emphasized that these processes are defined in large part by culture.[9] What if an organizational culture valued learning? It seems likely that the organization's cultural assumptions about change would tend to see change as inevitable, perhaps necessary, natural, and feasible. Its values would have change as desirable. Its strategic beliefs would encourage the surfacing and examination of the future, organization–environment relations, stakeholder interests, and all aspects of internal managing. Its manifest components, that is, its stories, norms, rituals, and so forth, would reflect and support continuous surfacing and examining. A culture that valued learning would have learned how to learn, that is, the organization and its members would have learned that surfacing and examining leads to learning.

When we say that an organization values learning and more or less routinely surfaces and examines the appropriateness of its goals and the adequacy of its goal-seeking activities and all that which supports them, this means that it is the organization's members who are actually doing it. Socialization is the process by which members learn organizational cultures. Socialization can be formal, for example through selection, orientation, training, performance appraisal, and reward practices, and so forth, or informal, for example, as members experience customs and rituals, hear stories, acquire jargon, and learn the meaning of artifacts, and so forth. While critical for new recruits, socialization continues, though maybe not as explicitly, throughout every member's organizational career. The more socialization a member experiences, the more he or she will share the meanings of the organization, and become committed to and identified with it. Being socialized into a learning organization means that members have learned how to surface and examine activities and beliefs, and the importance of doing so, and more or less routinely do it.

When an individual learns something of value for his or her job, subunit, or organization, it may not automatically become general knowledge. Individual learning must be communicated and shared throughout to have strategic impact. Diffusion is this process. The diffusion of individual learning will be a function of the symbolic importance of that member's roles or position, the size, extent, and degree of coupling of organization networks, the existence of a substantive organizational language, as well as the degree to which the message is couched positively. One executive's direct report, for example, when given a directive sometimes asked, "Why is that necessary?" While initially discomforted, upon reflection the executive realized that this questioning tended to stop him from giving poorly thought out directions. He then began to publicly ask for the reasons behind the ideas, suggestions, and orders he heard. This practice is now a widespread norm throughout the organization, increasing both understanding and thus compliance and eliminating most unwarranted changes. Both socialization and diffusion processes are of course culturally defined and legitimated – it is the culture which says what is real, what is worthy, and to what extent and how it should be shared.

Recapitulation

In the first section of this chapter organizational cultures were described as a three-layered system of meanings that all organizations develop over time: a system of meanings that says in effect what the organization is, what it can become, and how it will function. This section then introduced a cycle of fundamental activities that demonstrated how both individuals and organizations perform and learn. Organizational learning was characterized as the general process which occurs when surfacing and examining activities occur. It was shown that organizational culture greatly influenced whether an organization will promote and reinforce organizational learning as well as the processes of socialization and diffusion that support it. When the culture values learning, the organization may be termed a learning organization. The clarification of what the form and components of a learning organization look like is taken up in the next section.

On the Learning Organization

To understand what learning organizations are and how they function it is necessary first to explore the idea of an organization as a meaning–action system, second, to carefully explicate what this means for all organizations, and, third, to examine how this characterization allows us to say what are the defining attributes of learning organizations.

The basic building block for thinking about all behavior and organizations is knowledge, defined here as a probability that some action will result in some outcome. As children for example, most of us quickly learned that slowly touching a flame will burn our fingers. Some people believe that living in sin means they won't go to heaven. Many retailers think that store location is the key to sales volume. Some executives assume that managing participatively increases employee satisfaction and that satisfied employees will be more productive. From these few examples we note that knowledge can vary from being about specifics to about the very general, from having a high probability (almost certain) to one quite low (only sometimes), and from being based on first hand factual experience and thus easily verifiable to being guessed at or simply imagined. Also knowledge ranges from that which is personally unique to that which is shared widely. Regardless of its type, knowledge is always learned. Regardless of its type, knowledge purports to explain how things work, that is, it gives meaning. People use knowledge therefore to understand, to justify, and to predict, that is, knowledge is about the meaning of actions.

Organizations exist to accomplish something that individuals can't do alone. Members therefore have to coordinate some of their behavior with each other. To behave in a coordinated fashion requires members to share certain kinds of knowledge. Sometimes this shared knowledge is jointly developed, that is, learned, and sometimes it is communicated from others and accepted (socialization, diffusion). Shared knowledge that is organizationally important and functional is about that which earlier was noted as what culture does for us: it informs members who we are, what we are about, why we bother doing it, and how we should do it – both generally and specifically. Organizations then, give meaning to activities.

With an appreciation of what organizations as meaning–action systems generally are, they can be described more fully. For all organizations, regardless of their size, type, or degree of formalization, three levels of meaning (philosophical, governance, and operational) and two levels of action (strategic recipes and activity routines) may be discerned. Each of these meaning and activity levels can be viewed as a component of organizations. When we specify how they relate to one another (in general, meaning components influence action components, and, more encompassing levels influence less encompassing ones), the outline of a model of organizations emerges. Figure 16.3 diagrams this model. At the core of meaning, at the deepest and most general level, is a configuration of values and assumptions. This component is labeled **philosophical** because these values and assumptions refer to what some sets of people jointly understand to be real and true. As already noted in describing organizational culture, this philosophical core conditions a set of **governance beliefs** (shared general knowledge that guides strategic relationships and internal managing) which in turn influences a body of specific, **operational expectations** (how-to-do-it knowledge). Actions in organizations occurs at two levels of generality. The more general are **strategic recipes**, action guides which specify when, where, and how particular activities should be enacted. Strategic recipes can take many forms. Intentional recipes are contained in mission statements, formal structures,

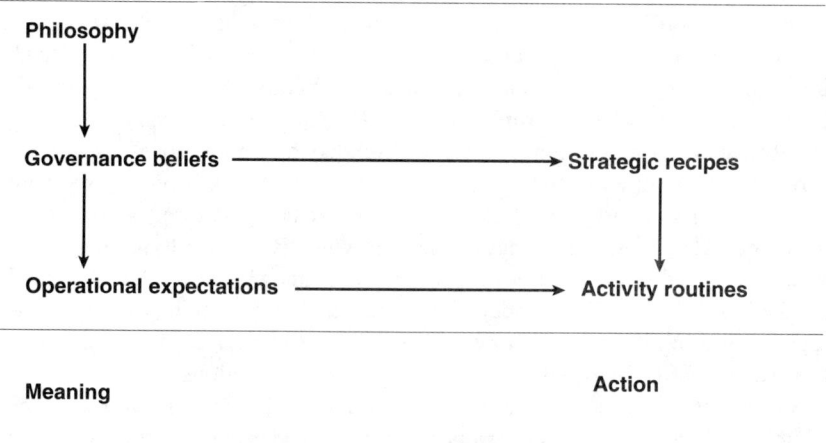

Figure 16.3 Organizations as meaning–action systems.

technologies, professional codes, strategy pronouncements, policies, and managerial systems. Informal recipes may be found in customs, ceremonies, sagas, and myths, and in the meanings attributed to major symbolic objects. Actions at the operational level are defined by routines which describe how to specifically accomplish activities. Again these activity routines may take several forms and may be both formal, for example, job specifications, rules, and regulations, and informal, for example, norms, rituals, and stories. The outcomes of particular activities constitute what can be called **individual performance**; the outcomes of assemblies of activities can be called **organizational productivity**.

The five components just outlined delineate in a general way the content of learning in organizations. Individuals can and do learn (socialization, diffusion) about organizational routines and recipes, about operational expectations, governance beliefs, and the organization's philosophy. When these types of content are widely shared and accepted the organization can be said to have learned. An organization's memory therefore consists of its recipes and routines.[10]

Utilizing this conception of organizations as meaning–action systems, we now turn to what differentiates a learning organization from a performing organization. Recall that the essence of learning in organizations was described as the process of surfacing and examining – now understood to be the surfacing and examination of the five meaning and action components. A learning organization exists when there are: (1) values and assumptions that say in effect that continuous learning is desirable and necessary, (2) governance beliefs that justify and explain the surfacing and examination process, and (3) strategic recipes that provide guidance in terms of how and when the surfacing and examining of each of the five components and their interrelationships should happen. Without these features, individual learning of course may occur, and, if diffused and accepted, will become part of the organization's memory as well as part of the socialization of members, but the organization has not learned how to learn. Learning in organizations can and does occur in all organizations. What distinguishes learning organizations from others is that a learning organization has learned how to learn in an ongoing way – the periodic surfacing and examination of why and how work is accomplished is built in both formally and culturally.

As has now been emphasized, learning organizations are distinguished by having strategic recipes that give form to the surfacing and examining of all that is organizational. These recipes outline a cycle of learning which consists of five kinds of activities, each performed by an associated role. Roles need not be tied to either positions or persons in a one-to-one way: a person may enact one, several, or all. The first learning recipe activity is to monitor the outcomes of routines, singularly and in combination, as well as other strategic recipes and related beliefs and expectancies, noticing any performance gaps and incongruities among them, and give them expression. The role associated with **monitoring** is that of "surfacer." The second activity is to alert and convince relevant and influential organizational members about surfaced concerns of importance

so they will be examined. The role associated with **alerting** is that of "advocate." The third learning recipe activity is to examine observed gaps and incongruities to see if they impede organizational functioning and outcome
achievement. The role associated with **examining** is that of "analyst." When
existing routines, recipes, and their guiding expectations and beliefs are judged
as dysfunctional or inadequate, a fourth activity is triggered, namely the design
of more appropriate routines, and so forth. The role associated with **designing**
is that of "designer." Finally, newly designed routines and/or recipes, beliefs
and/or expectations, are authorized and then communicated to appropriate
organizational members. The role associated with **diffusion** is that of "authorizer." This sequence of five learning recipe activities (and roles) – monitoring
(surfacer), alerting (advocate), examining (analyst), designing (designer), and
diffusing (authorizer) – describes the cycle through which organizational learning occurs.

Recapitulation

A learning organization can now be said to exist: (1) when five learning activities
are initiated and performed by their associated roles, (2) when these activities
function to surface and examine the meaning and action components that define
organizations and their subunits, (3) when these activities are regularized and
legitimated by a special type of strategic recipe, and (4) when all of the above
reflect values about learning in and by organizations to meet changing external
and internal circumstances.

On Managing Learning Organizations

In external circumstances of rapid change and increased environmental complexity, organizations not only lose stability but more and more have to live with
uncertainty.[11] Distinctive competence under these conditions will accrue to
"clever" organizations of "clever" people which can effectively adapt to external
circumstances and anticipate probable futures.[12] In addition to effectiveness,
therefore, the primary organizational criterion will be learning. Whereas high
formalization of organizational structures and systems provides for control,
coordination, and predictability under conditions of stability, bureaucratic-like
structures are flawed as learning systems in at least three ways: "First, choices
about the values and purposes . . . are separated from the performance of those
activities. Second, the learning of organizational members is focused on narrow,
specific tasks with routine procedures. Third, feedback about results is so frag-
mental that individuals do not really learn how their performance affects the
overall task."[13] Conditions of complexity and rapid change require more organic, loosely coupled or scattered organizational forms. Organizations that
favor learning have similar profiles in action:[14] they present real-time opportu-

nities to learn from experience dealing with a flow of work, feature cultures that emphasize feedback and disclosure, encourage and reward risk-taking and experimentation that contribute to overall performance, variously seek to empower employees, and often make use of boundary-spanning devices such as cross-functional teams. Federalist, Shamrock, and Network forms are exemplars – in each the central core of these forms provides guidance from a low profile with the real initiative and energy of the organization coming from its differentiated, semiautonomous parts. When organizations are differentiated and have relatively low levels of formalization, control, and direction, their internal integration and governance more and more comes from the organizational culture. It follows that organizational success and survival will depend increasingly on cultures that promote and sustain learning. It also follows that managing in learning organizations will require new mind-sets and new competencies, for example, seeing managing less as control and more as leadership.

The leadership of learning organizations appears somewhat paradoxical. On the one hand, leaders have to facilitate the improvement of tactics and strategies for achieving existing goals, that is, they have to manage. On the other hand, leaders have to see to it that members surface, examine and choose among competing assumptions, values, goals, structures, systems, and so forth, so that their organizations continuously learn, that is, they have to liberate and empower. Among the useful questions managers might ask themselves in this regard are: Do I tend to think that questioning how and why things work is solely management's job? Do I believe that rules are needed because without them people won't do the right things? How open am I to having others question my reasoning for things? When I insist on something, is it because it fits the past or the future? How well does this particular exemplify our general purposes and direction? Do I actively model the behaviors I want from others? How well do my associates learn and what am I doing about it? Leaders, of course, can no more command learning than they can command spontaneity. Leadership in a learning organization is ultimately a matter of shaping and sustaining a culture that values learning.

In a learning organization, leadership roles will exist beyond those familiar ones necessary for organizational achievement and maintenance. Learning organizations require three unique, critical leadership roles – those of champion, educator, and steward – all of which have antecedents in the ways leaders have contributed to organizations in the past.

The learning organization **champion** initiates and maintains the need for learning as a valued organizational purpose. The function of a champion is to focus member attention on learning as a prerequisite for strategic and tactical success. Sometimes the champion does this explicitly as when learning in and by the organization gets articulation in the organization's vision statement, is incorporated into the mission statement, and/or expressed as an organizational objective or in a dominant metaphor. Attention is also directed to the value of learning by a champion through his or her everyday behavior, for example, showing interest in it through questions and suggestions, "attaboys," and other behaviors. The champion, one way or another, says to the organization in effect, "learning here, by us, is necessary and not just nice; learning is part of who we are, what we do."

The learning organization **educator** promotes learning in and by his or her organization in several ways. The educator fosters organizational learning by actively modeling the surfacing and examination of governance beliefs and strategic recipes, encourages and teaches the use of learning process activities and roles, and is vigilant about keeping the organizational rhetoric about learning close to reality. In addition the educator sees to it that history is reinterpreted to emphasize learning, that myths and stories that extol learning get reinforced, that individual's learning is appropriately diffused, and that members are appropriately socialized. Educators also intervene to see that learnings become part of the organization's memory by being encoded onto management policies, systems, structures, and other recipes and into job designs, work rules, rituals, and other routines – especially those that institutionalize learning how to learn.

The learning organization **steward** supports all other learning roles, that is, the other leadership roles of champion and educator, and the learning process activity roles of surfacer, advocate, analyst, designer, and authorizer. The steward sees to it that resources of time, money, ideas, and competencies get to learning-related role incumbents. Stewards actively intervene to see that management systems are designed so that they are supportive of learning, for example, that reward systems reinforce learning as well as performance, human resource systems attract, retain and develop members who are open to learning, that communication systems encourage diffusion and socialization, and so on. The steward also actively prevents the diminution of the effort and discipline that sustained learning in and by organizations requires, for example, he or she aids in defusing defensiveness, buffers pressures for just performance outcomes, thwarts exaggerated self-interest by members, and so on.

Leadership which brings attention to, promotes, and supports learning in and by organizations is both symbolic and real, impacts both meaning and action. The three leadership roles for learning may, and usefully are, enacted by more than one person – for the organization as a whole (usually but not just top management) and for each organizational subunit. The caveat for enacting all learning roles is the same as in everyday management – first believe, then behave enthusiastically, consistently, and redundantly with as much cultural sensitivity as possible.[15]

Concluding Commentary

Learning in and by organizations reflects the cultures of an organization – from the philosophic cultural core which values learning and assumes it is a necessity in a changeful world, to the governing beliefs that shape the strategic recipes that call for the periodic surfacing and examination of all that's organizational, to the operational expectations manifested in the activity routines by which work is done. As organizational culture becomes increasingly understood as not only the vehicle of organizational meaning and sense-marking but also as a major guidance system, managers and other members of learning organizations quite naturally become more attentive to the symbolic side of their organizations for promoting and protecting learning processes. A set of leadership roles is emerging which collectively facilitates the cycle of inquiry and renewal which is organizational learning. Through leadership roles of champion, educator, and steward, managers serve their learning organizations by modeling learning promoting beliefs and expectations and designing – in recipes for learning, diffusion, and socialization. Organizational culture both fuels and fosters learning in organizations, as well as learning by organizations. Managing for learning by members and by the organization is managing with and through culture. The possibilities are exciting for personal and professional development and for organizational transformation.

Notes

1 See A. G. Bedian, "Contemporary challenges in the study of organizations." *Journal of Management*, 1986, vol. 12, pp. 185–201, and P. M. Senge, *The Fifth Discipline: The Art and Practice of the Learning Organization* (New York: Doubleday, 1990).

2 C. C. Lundberg, "Surfacing organizational culture", *Journal of Managerial Psychology*, 1990, vol. 5, pp. 19–26.

3 S. D. N. Cook and D. Yanow, "Culture and organizational learning," *Journal of Management Inquiry*, 1993, vol. 2, pp. 373–90.

4 L. G. Bolman and T. E. Deal, *Reframing Organizations: Artistry, Choice, and Leadership* (San Francisco: Jossey-Bass, 1991).

5 See, e.g., W. R. Dyer Jr, *Culture Change in Family Firms* (San Francisco: Jossey-Bass, 1986), C. C. Lundberg, "Working with culture", *Journal of Organizational Change Management*, 1986, vol. 1, pp. 38–47, and E. H. Schein, *Organizational Culture and Leadership* (San Francisco: Jossey-Bass, 1985).

6 M. A. Glynn, T. K. Lant and F. J. Milliken, "Mapping learning processes in organizations". In C. Stubbart, J. Meind and J. Porac (eds.) *Advances in Managerial Cognition and Organizational Information Processing* (Greenwich, CT: JAI Press, 1994).

7 See, e.g., C. Argyris and D. Schon, *Organizational Learning* (Reading, MA: Addison-Wesley, 1978), W. E. Deming, *Quality, Productivity, and Competitive Position* (Detroit: Ford Quality Education and Training Center, 1992), D. A. Kolb, *Experiential Learning: Experience as the Source of Learning and Development* (Englewood Cliffs, NJ: Prentice Hall, 1984), and E. H. Schein, *Process Consultation*, vol. 2 (Reading, MA: Addison-Wesley, 1987).

8 Figure 16.2 is adapted from C. C. Lundberg, "Expanding OD theory and practice: an organizational learning perspective." In F. Mesaraic (ed.), *Advances in Organization Development*, vol. 4 (Norwood, NJ: Ablex, 1996).

9 C. C. Lundberg, "On organizational learning: Implications and opportunities for expanding organizational development." In R. Woodman and W. Passmore (eds) *Research in Organizational Development and Change*, vol. 3. (Greenwich, CT: JAI Press, 1989), and C. Hampton-Turner, *Creating Corporate Culture* (Reading, MA: Addison-Wesley, 1992).

10 J. R. Walsh and G. R. Ungson, "Organizational memory." *Academy of Management Review*, 1991, vol. 16, pp. 57–91.

11 P. F. Drucker, *The New Realities: In Government and Politics, in Economics and Business, in Society and World View* (New York: Harper and Row, 1989).

12 C. Handy, *The Age of Unreason* (Boston: Harvard Business School Press, 1989).

13 K. E. Watkins and V. A. Marsick, *Sculpting the Learning Organization* (San Francisco: Jossey-Bass, 1993), p. 19.

14 See L. Honold, "The power of learning at Johnsonville Foods." *Training*, 1991, vol. 28, pp. 55–58, M. E. McGill and J. W. Slocum, "Unlearning the organization", *Organizational Dynamics*, 1993, vol. 22, pp. 67–79, and Watkins and Marsick, *Sculpting the Learning Organization*.

15 C. Siehl and J. Martin, "The management of culture: The need for consistency and redundancy among cultural components." Presented at the annual meeting of the Academy of Management, Boston.

17

Creating a World-Class Total Learning Organization

James A. F. Stoner

Introduction

A friend of mine was a student 25 years ago in Cambridge, Massachusetts, a city where students in her field frequently cross-registered for courses in two excellent universities. She recounts, with considerable relish, an observation one of her fellow students – a teaching assistant – made. It went roughly as follows: "I've noted that in the courses at your school, the prof starts by telling us what isn't known in the field, and then builds the course around it. In my school, we would never teach anything unless we were absolutely sure it was true."[1]

As I read the rich collection of chapters in the preceding pages, that university story kept recurring to me. A quarter century ago, my friend recognized that there was something very special about her school. Part of that specialness I think resembles what we now call the nature of learning organizations. The specialness that she and the authors of the chapters in this volume describe seems very precious and very important. The question we have now is how can we nurture it? And we ask that question even as we continue to grope with what "it" *really* is.

This chapter discusses three topics: (1) a potentially useful way of looking at managing for organizational learning, (2) what top managers can do to promote more effective learning, and (3) what the rest of us in those organizations can do.

The discussion of the first topic suggests that it may be useful to look at world-class learning organizations as the next step in the evolution of effective management systems. The second topic builds on this evolutionary perspective, suggesting three things top level managers can do to contribute to moving their organizations toward world-class learning. In the discussion of the third topic, three things other organizational members can do are suggested. For top managers and for the rest of us, the three items will relate to personal learning, control, and change.

At the end of the chapter a few afterthoughts deal with humility in the midst of paradigm change and the possibility of transforming the nature or organizational leadership. An addendum essay on learning from the quality revolution is also attached.

Samurai pathfinders

As one of the editors observed as this chapter evolved: "My view is that managers face a learning challenge much like the leadership challenge discussed by Kouzas and Posner.[2] Are managers forever condemned to undercut mindlessly their own future success by sticking with the ways they have viewed the world and managed in the past rather than to change themselves in any meaningful way?"

One warning about the actions suggested here for top managers and for others: rather than suggesting relatively minor incremental changes, more fundamental shifts are sought in thinking and acting that could make a lasting difference to the organization. These actions will also change the managers themselves and such actions that help us to change ourselves are among the boldest actions any of us can take.

The actions will require considerable courage. We will ask individuals to plunge whole-heartedly into nontraditional roles, new activities, and new ventures – setting examples for others to follow. Combining the stereotype of Samurai warriors as individuals fully and boldly committed to a course of action with Hal Leavitt's concept of corporate pathfinding – finding the right questions to ask and finding the right directions in which to lead – ways will be suggested in which individuals can be "Samurai pathfinders."[3] Although the risk to the organization of each of these actions may be trivial, the risk to some individuals' self-images may be great.

Leading and contributing to the emerging learning revolution will require considerable *unlearning* of some previously useful skills and perspectives. The need for unlearning may be much more unsettling than the widely recognized needs for new learning. Being skillful at learning doesn't necessarily mean that one possesses the same level of acumen in replacing worn ideas with more appropriate ones.

Is this "*déjà vu* all over again?"

The *déjà vu* quotation is, of course, from Yogi Berra, baseball hall-of-famer, pundit, and innovative linguist of considerable repute. The question is, however, very serious, and it is likely to be asked repeatedly: "Is our current interest in learning organizations still one more management fad or is it pointing toward something more enduring?"

Rather than being merely a fad, the pursuit of world-class organizational learning capabilities may well be one more step in an evolutionary process of increasing organizational competence and awareness. If that is so, achieving this world-class learning status may well be the most important goal, or strategic priority, of all organizations. Contributing to that goal may, likewise, be the single most important priority for all organizational members.

World-Class Learning as the Next Step in Organizational Effectiveness

Perhaps the most widely quoted short prognosis on the importance of becoming a learning organization comes from Arie de Geus of Shell Oil; it now appears in various forms in textbooks, as well as in two chapters of this volume: "The ability to learn faster than your competitors may be the only sustainable competitive advantage."[4]

The popularity of the quotation suggests that it conveys something more than catchiness. It captures an opportunity and a warning: the exhilarating opportunity for any organization to become and to continue to be a leader in its field, and the dark warning that failure to achieve revolutionary rates of learning will doom even the currently most successful organizations.

The chapters of this book suggest that becoming a truly effective ("world-class") learning organization requires a major management paradigm shift from the traditional Tayloristic command-and-control management systems that are still the most frequent form of managing in most industries around the world. The chapters also suggest close linkages between the organizational changes that are visible as the global quality revolution has unfolded and changes that are starting to become visible as a global learning revolution begins to become apparent. Becoming a world-class learning organization (wclo) may be a continuation and extension of a progressively better understood path toward increasing organizational effectiveness.

From traditional management to dynamic world-class learning organizations

Becoming a world-class learning organization represents both a paradigm shift from the command-and-control management paradigm and a continuation of a continually evolving quality management paradigm ("dynamic tqm"). This possibility is illustrated in figure 17.1.[5]

From TM to pqm In figure 17.1, the triangle on its base is labeled TM for the "traditional management" paradigm. The triangle represents the well-established pyramidal shaped command-and-control management system consistent in large part with the writings of Henri Fayol, Frederick W. Taylor, Max Weber, and many others. We are all familiar with such organizations because we have worked in some form of them for virtually our entire working lives.

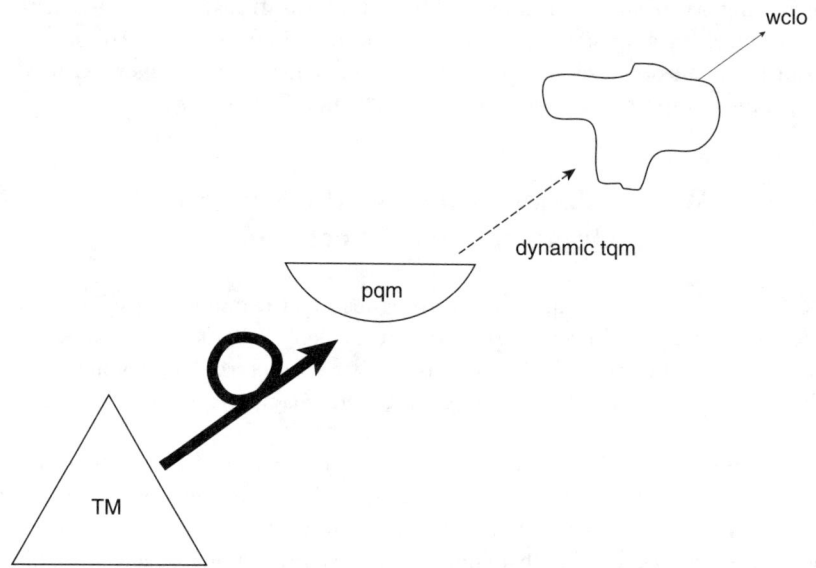

Figure 17.1   From Tayloristic command-and-control to dynamic TQM to world-class
learning organization.

The next two shapes to the right, that look like a looping arrow leading to an
inverted Frisbee, represent the early stages of the evolving quality management
paradigm. The "pqm" label on the inverted Frisbee suggests a static snapshot
of the dynamic tqm management technology as it exists at a given moment in
time. We use the term pqm (partial quality management) in place of the widely
used term TQM (Total Quality Management) for two reasons. One is to
emphasize that virtually no organization has fully absorbed all the capabilities
for excellence contained in the evolving dynamic tqm management technology
– no one is doing *total* quality management; they are, at best, doing *partial*
quality management. The other is to avoid the controversy and confusion
that have arisen about the "T phrase." TQM has so many widely varying
definitions that use of the term has become a barrier to effective communication.

The shape of the Frisbee suggests an inverting and flattening of the traditional management pyramid. The inverting of the pyramid in the figure suggests
two of the many tqm changes: rethinking the nature of the organization to put
the customer (rather than top management) on top and rethinking the nature of
managing so that managers are on the bottom of the organization, "supporting"
the workers above who, in turn, serve the customers on top. The flattening of
the pyramid represents the de-layering of the organization, reducing levels of
managers in the chain of command and empowering individuals to take more
initiative.

The looping arrow represents both the turning of the organization upside down to put customers on the top and the transformation of a great many other things within the organization. (Readers who are fans of the artist E. C. Escher might like to replace the looping black arrow, in their minds, with a thicker coiling cylinder containing Escher-type white fishes swimming to the right blending into black birds flying to the left. Such a version would represent transformation more graphically than the black arrow does.)

Dynamic tqm Further to the right, the first dash-lined arrow suggests continuing evolution and the ameba shape represents the quality management paradigm as it continues to evolve. Together the dashed-line arrow and the ameba represent the continuing evolution of tqm – "dynamic tqm." The ameba shape is used to suggest an organization that has reduced the boundaries that separate it from the outside environment, re-integrating itself with customers, suppliers, other stakeholders, and the communities in which it operates.[6]

From dynamic tqm to dynamic wclo Finally, the last dashed-line arrow heading off to the upper right represents the continued evolution of management technology toward a world-class learning organization.

Defining a world-class learning organization

In an article entitled "Building a learning organization," David Garvin has offered a definition of a learning organization which is modified here to define a world-class learning organization.[7] The modified definition is:

> *A world class learning organization is an organization that achieves revolutionary rates of learning and performance improvement by becoming exceptionally skilled at creating, acquiring, and transferring knowledge, and at modifying its behavior to reflect new knowledge and insights.*

The world-class learning organization may turn out to be best interpreted as the natural continuation of the evolution of the dynamic tqm management technology or it may more usefully be interpreted as a new paradigm. Either way, it will certainly represent a major change from the traditional management paradigm as we have come to know that paradigm in the last 100 years.

The number one corporate and individual priority

If becoming a world-class learning organization is a viable goal, then it becomes the most important strategic task facing virtually all organizations. The chapters in this volume support the view that progress is being made in learning how to become a more effective learning organization, that it is starting to become possible to identify candidates for the world-class learning organization designation, and that it may be possible to start talking about defining the technology of world-class learning.[8]

The previous chapters also support the view that, for most organizations, becoming a world-class learning organization will involve, at the very least, a complete shift of the dominant management paradigms of the people managing those organizations. A shift in management paradigm is the most fundamental shift any manager or organization can experience – it is far more impactful than changes in market-focus, turnover of top management, financial stringency, or even change in dominant production technologies. It is likely to involve heart-wrenching changes or heart-mending ones – or both.

If becoming a world-class learning organization is the organization's first priority, it must also be the first priority of top management and of all organizational members. The change is so great, the methods to get there are so little understood, and the avenues currently apparent rely so heavily on exploration, inquiry, risk-taking, innovation, multiple initiatives, and acceptance of errors, that pursuit of revolutionary rates of learning will require the commitment and involvement of all organizational members, not just a few top-level leaders.[9] Leadership will need to come from the top and also from everywhere in the organization.

Leading From the Top

Having observed a great many companies in action, I am unable to point to a single instance in which stunning results were achieved without the active and personal leadership of upper managers.[10]

This quotation is from Joseph M. Juran, recognized as one of the two major American quality leaders of the 20th century. The stunning results he is referring to are order of magnitude improvements in defects, cycle-time, and cost combined with parallel increases in customer satisfaction, sales revenues, and profitability. Of all the lessons learned from the global quality revolution, probably the one most universally agreed upon is the importance of top-level leadership.

If there is to be a learning revolution yielding revolutionary rates of learning parallel to the rates of quality improvement that are coming from the quality revolution, similar types of top management leadership will almost certainly be necessary. (I will return to the word "almost" under the heading: "An Afterthought on Leadership").

To become quality leaders of the type Juran acknowledges, managers with a history of success in the traditional management paradigm had to make dramatic changes in the ways they viewed the world and how they managed. They had not only to learn many new things, they also had to unlearn some of the most critical perspectives and skills that had gotten them to "the top."

Three key areas of change for top-level managers that will be important for the learning revolution relate to top managers' personal learning, their relationship to power and control, and their relationship to organizational change. Managers who will enable their organizations to achieve revolutionary rates of learning will need to achieve significant personal growth in each of these areas. In each case, the habits and perspectives that yielded success in traditional management systems are likely to be at least partially a barrier to providing leadership for world-class learning.

Becoming a student again: learning the lessons of the quality revolution

The traditional management paradigm has long assumed that at each successively higher level of the organizational hierarchy knowledge and wisdom increases. This stereotype clearly contains important elements of truth. When promotions are well handled, especially capable and wise individuals move toward the top. The top offers a breadth of vision and a confluence of information streams that allow upper managers to see and assess relationships and connections that individuals buried more deeply in the bowels of the organization may not perceive. And the greater years of experience represented in upper management may lead to more wisdom and better perspectives.

However, the exalted status of upper managers has always led to dangers that they will think they know more than they do and that people around them (with the possible exception of their spouses) will support them in such beliefs. In the transition between paradigms, when we come to believe that much of what we used to "know" is no longer true, the accumulated knowledge and wisdom may be more of a barrier to success than an advantage. Rather than utilizing their knowledge, skills, and wisdom to be teachers, supervisors, coaches, and mentors, top managers may need to adopt the mindset of being "students" once again. Bob Galvin, retired Chairman and CEO of Motorola, provided an excellent example how this could be done in the late 1970s and 1980s as Motorola was embarking on its quality journey.

> To set the example, he began to admit openly "he did not know what he did not know," and began asking "what do you think other people know that I don't know?" . . . Active questioning led Motorola executives to the concepts of humility and listening – humility in the sense that they were willing to admit that they did not know or have all the answers, listening in the sense that they were willing to hear how others did similar tasks in the search for the most efficient and effective way.[11]

Managers who choose to become students once again, as Bob Galvin did, can combine their traditional leadership role with the nontraditional learning role by becoming co-inquirers with all other organizational members. Galvin became a key learning leader in an inquiry that started with the question "How can we become more competitive?" In many respects that question has not changed at Motorola, and the inquiry has continued to reveal a steady progression of powerful and sophisticated approaches to achieving organizational excellence.

In the article noted earlier, David Garvin has demonstrated how effectively lessons learned from the quality revolution can be applied to the pursuit of world-class learning by describing five building blocks of effective learning organizations. He describes the five building blocks as systematic problem solving, experimenting with new approaches (which is motivated more by opportunities and expanding horizons versus the current difficulties that stimulate problem-solving activities), "learning from their own experience and past history, learning from the experiences and best practices of others, and transferring knowledge quickly and efficiently throughout the organization."[12] He illustrates each building block with numerous examples from companies that are recognized quality leaders.

The addendum at the end of this chapter summarizing some of these lessons serves as a guide for top managers who are ready to become students once again and want to start with a continuing inquiry into the lessons learned from the quality revolution.

Two processes of change

As valuable as it may be to find and apply the lessons learned from the quality revolution to guide the learning revolution, there may be an even more useful way to take advantage of the experiences arising from the quality revolution. That would be to explore the similarities and differences between the continuing quality revolution and the emerging learning revolution – in essence, an inquiry into the two processes of change. From this perspective, managers would be continually looking at how learning organizations are evolving and comparing the phenomena they observe against the way quality driven organizations have evolved in the past and continue to evolve. In addition to conducting the inquiry at the level of organizational comparisons, it may also be useful to explore the value of looking at world-class learning as a technology of managing. In this perspective, the inquiry would examine the ways in which the learning technology of the learning organization is evolving. The notion of pairing total quality and organizational learning is not new. Following on the path trod by masters such as Robert Pirsig, author of *Zen and the Art of Motorcycle Maintenance*, Ronnie Lessem has introduced the concept of **Total Quality Learning**. According to Lessem, the Japanese have been successful in creating their own version of learning organizations by drawing on their cultural, spiritual, and philosophical traditions. He notes:

By contrast, we in the West, drawing upon our Judeo-Christian and Greek traditions need to create learning organizations in which *self-knowledge, self-realization*, and the progressive *individuation* of our institutions become our own hallmark. In such learning organizations, we shall ultimately find, quality will be born out of nothing less than a holographic form of integration between the different "learning fields" in which we work, between total learning and quality management.[13]

Freeing people to rediscover themselves and quality in their work is not always a simple matter in organizations where the unspoken messages about power and control linger in the air, despite whatever rhetoric may be offered up by top management.

Rethinking control: empowering the board to monitor top management

Power and control are key issues for effective performance in the traditional management paradigm. Successful managers have frequently been masters at building power, maintaining tight control, and playing organizational politics. The fear of losing traditional forms of power and of losing control have been two of the greatest barriers to achieving effective transitions from traditional management practices to quality-based ones. They are certain to represent continuing barriers in subsequent steps toward world-class learning organizations.

Empowering organizational members has been one of the keys to success in the quality revolution. It may not have come easily for top managers to "give up control" but many have done so. And in doing so they have often discovered new ways to look at control and some have come to believe they have far greater control in the tqm paradigm than they ever did in the traditional management one.

Top managers can contribute toward more effective organizational learning by continuing along this path of empowering organizational members below them in the traditional hierarchy, but Samurai pathfinding will require greater boldness. That boldness could take the form of empowering the board of directors to provide leadership in the learning revolution. One way to do so would be to re-negotiate the contract between the board and top management in a form that makes top management responsible for achieving organizational learning and the board responsible for monitoring top management's performance in doing so.

A tradition of lack of leadership by corporate boards   Joseph Juran refers to top-level leadership as a critical element for achieving revolutionary rates of quality improvement. However, this does not actually refer to the very top of the organizational pyramid – the board of directors. It refers to the level just below the board – the CEO and other top managers. Boards have virtually all been "no-shows" at the most important organizational event of the century – the adoption of the quality management technology necessary for corporate survival. Without Samurai pathfinders in this realm, boards of directors are almost certain to repeat that performance for the learning revolution.

Top-level managers have long been adept at selecting, co-opting, and controlling boards of directors to a point where boards virtually never dominate the top-level managers in a manner similar to the way every other hierarchical level dominates the level below. Such domination would probably be undesirable, but the disempowerment of boards by top-level managers goes so far that most boards rarely influence top management strongly. The major exceptions tend to occur when prolonged management failure has become so damaging and visible that even the most obtuse boards are forced to act – out of public embarrassment and fear of legal liability. In the US, the recent case of Morrison & Knudsen Corporation's CEO William Agee and its board of directors is a prime example of top management's ability to manipulate boards.

Murray Weidenbaum has summarized three major criticisms of the performances of corporate boards of directors: (1) boards routinely provide "ceremonial rubber-stamping of the views of management," (2) "the board's deliberations are dominated by the CEO, who typically also serves as chairman," and (3) boards "are plagued with conflicts of interest."[14]

Although the "root cause" of the ineffectiveness of most boards is surely the success of CEOs in controlling selection, reward, and retention of board members, a contributing factor – not emphasized by Weidenbaum – is the lack of clear, limited, and achievable priorities for the board. As just one example: there is wide disagreement about the basic constituency of boards of directors. Does the board owe its allegiance exclusively to the shareholders, as Weidenbaum and many others seem to believe? Or, is the board responsible to a much broader constituency of stakeholders (as both Lee Preston[15] and Robert Golembiewski[16] argue)?

In a time of rapid global competitive changes, the very survival of even the most historically successful organizations is now a matter of critical concern for boards of directors and the top managers the boards theoretically "oversee." W. Edwards Deming, Joseph Juran, and many others have argued that the type of shift of the dominant management paradigm discussed earlier is a key driving force in this global quality revolution. Their intuition seems to be correct, and it offers a compelling argument for using this new understanding of learning organizations to create a framework to guide the survival for virtually all organizations. With organizational survival at stake, we can now suggest a set of standards against which corporate board performance can and should be judged. Ironically, it is the board's "subordinates" (top management) that hold the key to teaching the board what its core obligations are and for re-negotiating the board's contract to make it responsible for meeting those obligations. And ironically, doing so will require top management to give up the power over the board it has worked so hard to gain.

The board of directors' key obligations   The three most important obligations of boards of directors for at least the beginning of the 21st century should be:

1 to ensure that the organization adopts the world-class quality management technology required to achieve and sustain global competitiveness,
2 to ensure that the company's chief executive officer and chief operating officer possess the management skills and styles to make that management technology work, and
3 to ensure that the organization begins and pursues the inquiry into the nature of world-class learning organizations and the skills and styles of managing appropriate for leading and sustaining them,

As progress on the third obligation is achieved, the fourth obligation should emerge naturally:

4 to ensure the adoption of the learning organization philosophy as a whole, of learning organization elements as they become understood, and of the top-level management skills and styles required to support effective organizational learning.

To set the groundwork for the fourth obligation, each of the first three obligations requires considerable learning by the board, but the board's performance in pursuing and achieving them can be assessed. For example, on obligation 1, models of world-class organizational systems and processes, like the Baldrige Award criteria, are becoming widely recognized as providing useful templates for excellence, and are being used to monitor improvement. A recent survey reported by Karen Bemowski and Brad Stratton describes ways in which improvement efforts in thousands of companies are being guided by close to a million copies of the Baldrige application that have been distributed to companies since the founding of the award.[17]

On obligation 2, the skills, knowledge, and wisdom that support revolutionary rates of quality improvement have been modeled by many managers in a wide variety of industries and countries. Besides Robert Galvin of Motorola, the blending of styles of managing for quality and learning is evident in the work of Winston Chen and Ko Nishimura of Solectron in the electronics industry, Don Petersen of Ford in the automobile industry, and David Lawrence of Kaiser Permanente in health care. In Japan there are many examples of such leadership including Konosuke Matsushita of Matsushita Electric Company in electronics. European examples include Jan Carlzon of SAS in transportation services.

The chapters in this volume contain many ideas for guiding boards in developing criteria appropriate for monitoring the performance of top management on obligations 3 and 4. However, once again, the greatest payoff will very likely come from asking the questions rather than finding the answers. The board can play its greatest monitoring role by becoming co-inquirers with top management, rather than in becoming top-level cops.

Kicking the quick fix habit: learning to dance with implementation and inquiry

When the CEO of Alcoa was asked at the Juran Impro Conference, in 1990, what was the hardest part of the quality transformation for himself and the other top managers in his company, he replied without hesitation that it was to stop doing what they had done so successfully in the past – that is, that which had enabled them to reach the top of the organization. He and his colleagues had to learn to take the time to understand the organization's problems, to gather appropriate data, and to get to root causes, so that solutions would actually have a chance of yielding sustained improvement and not merely cure symptoms for a short time. They had to abandon skills honed over decades that enabled them to size up complex problems quickly and then to take bold, decisive actions. They had to abandon that apparent boldness and decisiveness that got them to the top and for which they were handsomely paid.

The traditional management paradigm has long exalted exactly the type of leadership that the CEO of Alcoa, and many others, have concluded contributes more to the problems of declining competitiveness than it offers as part of a solution. Abandoning this traditional managerial style and reframing top managers' contribution to emphasize building organizational transformation on organizational learning, rather than on quick fixes, will require much bolder, decisive leadership in a new realm – the realm of learning to do the dance between inquiry and implementation.

Dancing with inquiry and implementation   The well-established management practice of "solving problems" with "programs" that are "implemented" has made it easy to forget that learning is a continuing dance with inquiry and implementation. Because of the natural tendency to develop programs to capture what has been learned, and the demand for programs both from buyers and sellers, it is likely that the search for the secrets of effective learning organizations will yield many total learning organization programs. As top managers find themselves implementing total learning organization programs, rather than engaging in a continuing process of inquiry, they will need to keep returning to the dance between inquiry and implementation.

Leading from Everywhere

Just as war is too important to leave to the generals, organizational learning is too important to leave to the top managers.

Each of the three Samurai pathfinding steps that top leaders can initiate are also available, to some extent or in some form, to the rest of an organization's members. Other organizational members can and should also become students once again: learning the lessons of the quality revolution, with appropriate adaptations, to achieve revolutionary rates of organizational learning. They should rethink control and support the empowering of the board to monitor top management's performance in pursuing these revolutionary rates of quality improvement, and of organizational learning. They should also kick the quick fix habit, and doing so will probably be easier for them than it will be for top managers.

Supporting and contributing to top management's Samurai goals will not be as bold for people below the top as leading the pursuit will be for those at the top. If that is the case, what would be comparable Samurai pathfinder goals for the rest of us? Three possibilities in the same areas of personal learning, control, and change are:

1 Creating responsibility for finding and capitalizing on opportunities: developing the skill of appreciation,
2 Creating responsibility for leading upwards: "just starting," and
3 Creating responsibility for leading change: pioneering co-creation.

The term "creating responsibility for" is used in each of the three Samurai goals to provide a salient, and perhaps painful, reminder of just how big a change in thought and action is being suggested. One of the major lessons the traditional management paradigm has taught over and over again, with enormous success, is that almost everyone in organizations is powerless. For many years, people have been expected not to know more than their bosses, not to teach their leaders, and not to take initiative on their own, and so bosses frequently encounter "resistance" when they change the rules and expect "subordinates" to become empowered when they tell them to be.

Creating responsibly for finding and capitalizing on opportunities: developing the skill of appreciation

One of the striking changes in the shift from the traditional command-and-control paradigm to the modern quality management one has been a shift in tone. The problem-oriented, right/wrong and somewhat negative tone of traditional approaches, like management by exception, is being replaced. In its place a more opportunity-oriented, "nothing-is-right-or-wrong: there-are-just-results-to-be-learned-from," positive tone appears in the language and actions of dynamic tqm. This shift in tone is likely to be as useful and valuable in the pursuit of world-class learning as it has been in the pursuit of world-class quality. While the skills and attitudes of criticism are appropriate for the tone of traditional management practices, the skills and attitudes of appreciation are likely to be more appropriate for world-class learning. Many of the tools and much of the philosophy of quality management are positive, optimistic, and opportunity-finding in tone, and are thus well-suited for supporting organizational learning.

A particularly promising approach to integrate positive inquiry with organizational learning is known as "appreciative inquiry." As David L. Cooperrider and Suresh Srivastva write: "The appreciative mode awakens the desire to create and discover new social possibilities that can enrich our existence and give it meaning. In this sense appreciative inquiry seeks an imaginative and fresh perception of organizations as 'ordinary magic,' as if seen for the first time – or perhaps for the last time."[18]

Taking leadership in finding new, positively based methods of individual and organizational learning contains an element of boldness and offers a chance to make a difference in how organizations learn.

Creating responsibility for leading upwards: "just starting"

Leading upwards – "just starting" to make changes to improve quality and organizational learning in the absence of top-level commitment and leadership – may require more boldness for other members of the organization than empowering the board will require for top management. Although leading upwards may not fit the stereotype of how traditional organizations are managed, the quality revolution would probably not yet have started if many individuals who are well below the top had not done just what Dr Deming recommended – they "just started" . . . long before top management got the idea. The proposal that people should start the learning revolution within the company, whether or not top management is ready, by leading top management to discover its obligations in this realm, is intended to parallel the suggestion about empowering boards of directors. Although it is similar to the suggestion to empower the board, it is probably more bold than that suggestion.

The opposite may at first seem to be true. When top managers have worked so long and hard to disempower boards of directors, intentionally empowering those same boards may seem like a wildly bold suggestion, or even an insane one. The argument that empowering the board may be less outrageous than leading the quality and learning revolutions from within the company stems from an understanding of time horizons. If CEOs actually choose to rewrite their contracts with their board in terms that commit them to deliver first-class performance as quality and learning leaders, the concept will be very innovative, but the implementation will be very safe for most CEOs. With the tenure of most CEOs running in the range of from three to six years, most Samurai-pathfinder CEOs will probably be retired by the time the board has really learned to do its new job, and has learned how to do an effective job of judging the CEO's performance. It is the successor CEOs who will have to dance to the tune of this new piper who plays the tune of the learning organization.

Creating responsibility for leading change: pioneering co-creation

It is very early in the learning revolution to guess how we will actually move toward becoming world-class learning organizations. What will be the steps in the inquiry-implementation dance? What music will we dance to? Pragmatically, the answers will most certainly emerge from discoveries made throughout organizations, rather than by top management fiat. Over time, we will learn how to become better learning organizations by improving our learning rather than by making the "right" initial decisions, developing the "right" sets of programs, and implementing them successfully.

One of the ways of exploring how to learn that can be pioneered by people not at the top of the organization can be called "cocreation": the shared exploration and creation of new organizational possibilities. The appreciative inquiry approach described in the addendum is one type of co-creation. Another has been described by George Land and Beth Jarman.[19] Noting that: "The way every growing organism makes broader, deeper, and more inter-penetrating connections has been shown to be nature's most powerful method of moving beyond a Breakpoint," they describe a set of seven principles that fits well with the positive tone of appreciative inquiry. Their seven principles are:

- See the potentials and possibilities in everyone
- Offer mutual support
- Extend equality to all people
- Bring about the circumstances in which everyone can win
- Recognize that whatever you focus on expands
- Eliminate judgments
- Trust and love one another

Exploring approaches like these are far from traditional in our present organizations. The words and phrases have a "touchy-feely" tone that is potentially threatening in most organizations – very different from "the way we do things here." Exploring these and other nontraditional approaches to change and transformation requires much more courage than purchasing a well-packaged program for promoting organizational change that is built upon a collection of familiar tried-and-true techniques, and is phrased in a familiar and comfortable vocabulary.

An Afterthought on Leadership

Although at present there is little reason to doubt that top-level leadership will be as necessary for achieving world-class learning as it has been for achieving world-class quality, one caution may be in order. That caution relates to the changes in organizational processes that the quality revolution is creating and that the learning revolution will very likely extend. If we are in the midst of one or even two paradigm shifts, we simply do not know what leadership, organizational structure, and organizational power will look like when the quality and learning revolutions have run their courses. Although it is not yet clear, it is entirely possible that the natural evolution of self-organizing learning processes will significantly modify the dominance of the top over the rest of the organization. The internal organizational changes that are both contributing to – and being stimulated by – the quality revolution may be assuming a life of their own. They may eventually lead to a quantum leap in the natural process of evolution toward world-class learning capabilities with or without top-level leadership and commitment. Like the leader of the Paris mob during the French Revolution, someday top management may need to run ahead to get in front of the mob as it moves in the direction it has already chosen or be left behind as the crowd moves forward on its own.

Addendum: Learning from the Global Quality Revolution

The quality revolution has generated sufficient evidence of the causes of quality to enable some enlightened speculation about which managerial practices work and which do not. These "lessons learned" from the quality revolution may serve as useful guideposts for the heroic leaders who are "out front" in the emerging learning revolution. A few of these possible lessons are suggested below – in terms of positive actions to take and in terms of errors to avoid.

In the 1991 article cited earlier, Joseph Juran discussed how the early winners of the Baldrige Award for quality achieved their successes and drew eight lessons from them "and from the experiences of 20 or 30 other companies that have achieved similar results but did not receive the award." The lessons were:

- Stretch goals: Stretch goals needed to be set and achieved, such as order of magnitude reductions in defects and of cycle time.
- Big Q: The concept of Big Q had to be adopted – with "product" meaning services as well as goods, "processes" meaning business processes as well as production processes, and "customer" meaning "all who are affected, internally and externally."
- Process ownership: "Clear ownership of multifunctional process must be assigned."
- Infrastructure for improvement: "An infrastructure for improvement must be created."
- Dedicated work: "A lot of work is required."
- Top management leadership: "Upper managers must personally lead the effort."
- New management system: "The Taylor system must be replaced."
- Integrating quality and business planning: "Quality goals must be incorporated into the business plan."[20]

Juran also noted that successful companies used competitive benchmarking effectively, "implemented improvement processes at a revolutionary pace," "provided extensive training," "used employee involvement to an unprecedented degree," publicly acknowledged contributions of individuals and teams, and made quality improvement a regular part of everyone's job.

In an article a year later, Blanton Godfrey (a close associate of Juran's), Don Berwick, and Jane Roessner summarized ten lessons from the emerging quality revolution in the health care field. Nine of the lessons they listed seem to apply equally well to achieving revolutionary rates of quality improvement in all industries.[21] These are summarized below. (The tenth is unique to health care: "The involvement of physicians is extremely important.")

1 Committed leadership investment is the *sine qua non* of effective TQM: 'Almost all leading experts agree that effective quality management 'begins at the top' (or, at the very least, is 'owned by the top' soon after it begins.)"
2 Several bottlenecks hamper TQM: Insufficient facilitation, insufficient board involvement, rapid turnover of staff and executives, mergers and restructuring, excessive word-crafting of statements of mission or guiding principles.
3 It's easier to begin than to keep going: A common trajectory is: the CEO gets interested, decides to commit resources, including financial, to the effort; appoints a manager in charge of quality – and promptly becomes distracted by the myriad pressing issues of personnel, the annual business cycle, budget shortfalls, and the like.
4 Structure is critical if TQM is going to work: Elements common across successful organizations include quality councils; a quality director; a strategic quality planning process; trained facilitators; a process of nominating, selecting, and supporting quality projects; and an information and analysis system that contains customer satisfaction information, and internal quality and efficiency measurements.
5 Quality management is much more than quality improvement projects: Total quality management "involves a fundamental change in business strategy and management culture – one, and only one, element of which is quality improvement projects."
6 Training alone is not enough: "Training – like quality improvement projects, and like benchmarking – is a critical element of total quality management; but the part should not be mistaken for the whole."
7 Measurement drives TQM progress: "Often just the very act of measuring something causes blinding flashes of the obvious and almost instant improvements."
8 (Health care) projects save money: "Repeatedly, we hear of financial returns of 5:1 or more for specific improvement projects." "We have seen improvement projects that removed anywhere from ten to eighty percent of the work in a process."
9 Customer focus is the real bottom line: "The bottom line in any quality focused organization is not financial – it is the customer."

A number of lessons learned from the quality revolution seem likely to be quite applicable to the emerging learning revolution. Each reader will see possibly applicable lessons in the lists above. Just three that stick out for this observer are:

1 The value of competitive benchmarking. In the quality revolution, the use of competitive benchmarking has become an extremely valuable tool for breaking down resistance to improvement (defeating the deadly NIH – or, not invented here – syndrome), empowering individuals throughout organizations to set and achieve improvement goals far higher than managers could force upon them, and finding or inventing new ways for the organization to achieve those goals. Competitive benchmarking may yield very similar results in the pursuit of revolutionary rates of organizational learning.

2 The value of explicit models of world-class organizational performance. For Japan initially, and for the United States later, the development of the explicit models of organizational excellence that underlay the Deming Prize and the Malcolm Baldrige National Quality Award have focused energies on key areas of improvement and fostered continuous learning about the nature of organizational excellence. The search for and testing of such models may be one of the exciting parts of the learning organization adventure.

3 The need for organizational transformation at a very deep level. The prevalent quick fix mentality of many American managers that has frequently been a barrier to quality improvement will very likely also be a major barrier to effective organizational learning. Deming's 14 points' message and Juran's call for replacement of the Taylor system of management focus attention on this need for transformation. The dramatic levels of organizational transformation being achieved by leading quality companies may reduce the tendency to deny that profound change is achievable in a business society hooked on only short-term solutions to long-lasting problems.

Four errors not to repeat

The experiences of the global quality revolution also suggest at least four errors to be avoided in the pursuit of world-class learning and in attempts to apply the lessons learned from that effort. They are: (1) denying, (2) static labeling, (3) forgetting to dance with inquiry and implementation, and (4) waiting for the top to act. The essence of each block to creating learning organizations is suggested below:

Lesson 1: Denying: "It won't work in my company (country, industry, function) because . . ."   Although the first clear payoffs from adopting early quality management practices were starting to emerge by the mid- to late 1950s and although two of the key leaders in the global quality revolution were Americans, three to four decades were to pass before significant numbers of American companies recognized that a new management technology was available for adoption.

The process of denying the usefulness of the new management approaches followed a painfully familiar path. First the new management was labeled "Japanese management," therefore, many American managers (and academics) claimed the techniques could not be adopted by non-Japanese organizations.

When Japanese companies took their manufacturing techniques abroad and achieved revolutionary rates of quality improvement in plants outside Japan, the interpretation of managers in service firms was that the tqm technology was purely a manufacturing technology and that it would never work in service industries.

When service companies achieved similar results, such as the achievements of Federal Express that enabled it to win the Baldrige Award and Florida Power and Light's successes that led to the Deming Prize, many functional managers argued that the approaches could not be used in finance, marketing, human resources, and legal services. In due course, similar successes were achieved in each of these areas. Along the way, the usefulness of the quality management technology was also denied by many in the governmental, educational, and not-for-profit sectors.

We can anticipate that many managers will believe that their industry, sector, organization, or function cannot achieve revolutionary rates of learning even after they have seen others do so. And, they will also turn out to be wrong – probably at little or no cost to themselves and enormous cost to their organizations.

The moral is that no matter how successful others may be as a result of a management approach, some people will say, "It won't work here!" And the lesson to be learned is: Expect that if some organizations and functions can achieve revolutionary rates of learning, all can do so. Devoting resources to proving that revolutionary rates of learning can occur where they have not yet occurred will pay far higher dividends than efforts devoted to proving that "it can't be done here."

Lesson 2: Applying static labels: "Once you label me, you negate me" Søren Kierkegaard   The adoption of systematic, company-wide, quality management in the United States has been severely hampered by a deep misunderstanding of what it means to manage for quality. Managers thought they "knew" that quality management referred only to a limited inspection function in the production department. They reasoned that it was not a major factor in company success. In the mid-1980s quality was a passé term to many. In 1986, the faculty of the first business school in the United States to throw out its required core management course and its upper level offerings and build its program around a dynamic interpretation of the new quality management technology intentionally avoided the label "quality management" because so many managers "knew" what quality was and that it was not very important. By the late 1980s and early 1990s, the word "quality" was "in," and, for many, the label TQM stuck. For some authors TQM, or some other label, meant a broad all-encompassing and dynamically evolving management system. Deming and Juran have always been clear about the pervasiveness and evolving nature of dynamic "tqm" (although TQM was a term that particularly galled Deming). Most leading quality champions have long used an expansive versus a restricted interpretation.

By the early 1990s, quality management was again being interpreted by many who did not recognize the global nature of the quality revolution in a very restricted way and was "out" once again. It was frequently treated as merely the "quality circle" technique, or as team-based small-scale improvement projects statistical quality control, or as misapplied quality programs. Again, people tried to define the new TQM in terms of the old, command and control system. One of the more popular of these "narrow" interpretations of quality is the one used by Michael Hammer and James Champy in their enormously successful best seller *Reengineering the Corporation*. They interpreted TQM (and all other "manifestations of the contemporary quality movement") as a "program" restricted to small-scale incremental improvement of existing processes with the aim of doing better what is already being done."[22] They rediscovered and successfully "repackaged" a technique that many quality experts considered one of the well-established quality management techniques. Large-scale business process improvement became "corporate reengineering" and the profits rolled in.[23]

The moral is that people will define the new approaches in terms of their past understandings of old approaches. "Square pegs will be forced into round holes." And the lesson to be learned is: expect that the inquiry into the nature of world-class learning organizations will lead to a number of static and narrow definitions of what a world-class learning organization *really* is. Some of these definitions will lead us to waste energies, at least for a while.

Lesson 3: Forgetting to dance: "TQM and TLO are programs to be implemented." The well-established management practice of "solving problems" with "programs" that are "implemented" has made it easy to confuse dynamic tqm with a static "thing" and not to see it as a continuing process of inquiry. The same danger will face the learning organization inquiry.

When TQM has been seen by managers as a program to be implemented, it has often been treated as a set of procedures, rules, and activities, rather than as an evolving process focused on learning what the customer wants or will want (and what other stakeholders want or need). Learning successively better ways to exceed those wants can also be forgotten: implementation can replace inquiry.

In an insightful, but unfortunately titled article "The ten reasons why TQM doesn't work", Oren Harari[24] describes a series of errors that are frequently made when the quality management inquiry is incorrectly translated into a TQM program, and when TQM is defined very narrowly in such a program. (A more descriptive, and much less catchy title might have been, "Ten errors frequently made in translating quality management approaches into TQM programs.") The 10 errors Harari discusses are:

- focusing people's attention on internal processes rather than on external results;
- focusing on minimum standards;
- developing a cumbersome quality bureaucracy;
- delegating quality to "quality czars" and "experts" rather than to "real" people;
- not demanding radical organizational reform;

- not demanding changes in management compensation;
- not demanding entirely new relationships with outside partners;
- appealing to faddism, egotism, and quick-fixism;
- draining entrepreneurship and innovation from corporate culture;
- having no place for love.

Even in summary form, virtually all of these points speak clearly of the dangers of converting an inherently company-wide, dynamic transformational process into static and narrowly focused programs. Harari's comments on the last two points make it clear that they also deal directly with this issue. In discussing the draining of entrepreneurship and innovation, Harari notes that "obsessing internally until one achieves zero–defects, 'do-it-right-the first-time' routine is a dangerous luxury that often slows down new breakthrough development in products and services. It is the latter that are the cornerstone of business success."[25] In discussing love, he observes: ". . . when all is said and done, TQM attempts to make quality happen via an analytically detached, sterile mechanical path. What is missing, frankly, is emotion and soul."[26] When the excitement and thrill of inquiry is replaced by the routine of implementation, the quality and learning journeys lose their juices and electricity.

Because of the natural tendency to develop programs to capture and test what has been learned, and because of the demand for programs both from buyers and sellers, it is likely that the search for the secrets of effective learning organizations will lead to the creation of many TLO programs and position titles. And the frequency of errors like these listed by Harari suggest that the translation of a dynamic learning process into a set of programs is fraught with considerable risk.

The moral is that if any management philosophy can be turned into a simple technique or precise program it will be done. And the lesson to be learned is: expect efforts to understand the nature of effective learning organizations to lead to learning organization programs that stress implementation at the sacrifice of inquiry. As we find ourselves "implementing a TLO program," rather than engaging in a continuing inquiry, we will need to keep returning to the dance of balance between inquiry and implementation.

Lesson 4: Waiting for the top: "We can't get started until top management leads the way."   Waiting for top management to take the lead in learning about and then adopting quality management approaches has been a major barrier to rapid improvement in many companies. "Quality begins at the top" means that committed leadership by the top is needed to achieve revolutionary rates of quality improvement. It does not mean the CEO was always the first quality champion and that every corporate quality revolution was initiated, *de novo*, by the CEO.

When organization members have failed to take the initiative in championing and experimenting with new quality ideas and approaches, they have deprived top management of one of their major sources of learning about quality – the successes achieved in their own companies by independent initiatives. As wonderful as it might be if top managers were uniformly more intelligent, insightful, wise, and better informed than all other organizational members, it is very unlikely that many companies fit that description and even fewer violate the tqm slogan that "none of us alone is smarter than all of us together."

The moral is that people who wait for top management to lead the way may think they are playing it safe by not acting boldly to do what they know is right out of their own accord. But how safe is it to be in a company that is being surpassed by its competitors who are truly learning? That is not job security. The lesson to be learned is that: Organizational members will frequently look to top management for clear and unequivocal commitment to becoming a world-class learning organization. When such commitment is not visible they should start or continue on their own – leading top management to lead.

Notes

1 The friend is Professor Ellen Greenberg, currently a Fullbright Scholar at the University of National and World Economics in Sofia, Bulgaria.

2 James M. Kouzas and Barry Z. Posner, *The Leadership Challenge: How to Get Extraordinary Things Done in Organizations* (San Francisco: Jossey-Bass, 1995).

3 Harold J. Leavitt, *Corporate Pathfinders* (Homewood, Illinois: Dow Jones-Irwin, 1986). The use of the Samurai leader metaphor first came to my attention in personal growth seminars offered by Landmark Education. Of course, the stereotype of Samurai warriors also includes a deep reverence for tradition and a lack of innovation, so the term Samurai pathfinder may sound to many like an oxymoron.

4 Arie P. de Geus, "Planning as learning", *Harvard Business Review*, March–April, 1988, pp. 70–74.

5 Figure 17.1 is adapted from James A. F. Stoner and Frank M. Werner, *Managing Finance for Quality: Bottom-line Results form Top-level Commitment* (Milwaukee: ASQC Quality Press and Morristown, NJ: Financial Executives Research Foundation, 1994). Used by permission.

6 Richard L. Daft, *Organization Theory and Design* (St. Paul: West Publishing, 1995), p. 490.

7 Garvin's original definition is "A learning organization is an organization skilled in creating, acquiring, and transferring knowledge, and at modifying behavior to reflect new knowledge and insights". David A. Garvin, "Building a learning organization," *Harvard Business Review*, vol. 71, no. 4, p. 80.

8 A number of Japanese wclo candidates are discussed in a recent book by Ikujiro Nonaka and Hirotaka Takeuchi, *The Knowledge-Creating Company: How Japanese Companies Create the Dynamics of Innovation* (New York: Oxford University Press, 1995).

9 Milan Zeleny, Robert Cornet and James A. F. Stoner, "Moving from the age of specialization to the era of integration", *Human Systems Management*, 1990, vol. 9, no. 3, pp. 153–72.

10 J. M. Juran, "Strategies for world-class quality", *Quality Progress*, March, 1991, pp. 81–85, quotation from p. 84.

11 Stoner and Warner, *Managing Finance for Quality*, p. 151.

12 Garvin, "Building a learning organization", p. 81.

13 Ronnie Lessem, *Total Quality Learning: Building a Learning Organization* (Oxford, UK: Blackwell Business, 1991), p. 15.

14 Murray Weidenbaum, "The evolving corporate board," *Society*, March/April, 1994, pp. 9–16, quotations from pp. 9–10.

15 Lee A. Preston, "Corporate boards and corporate governance", *Society*, March/April, 1995, pp. 17–20.

16 Robert T. Golembiewski, "By whose warrant? Multiple contexts for ownership and control," *Society*, March/April, 1995, pp. 21–26.

17 Karen Bemowski and Brad Stratton, "How do people use the Baldrige Award criteria?" *Quality Progress*, May 1995, vol. 28, no. 5, pp. 43–7.

18 David L. Cooperrider and Suresh Srivastva, "Appreciative inquiry in organizational life," in Richard W. Woodsman and William A. Pasmore (eds), *Research in Organizational Change and Development*, vol. 1 (Greenwich, CT: JAI Press, 1987), pp. 129–69, quotation p. 164. See also Suresh Srivastva, David Cooperrider, and associates, *Appreciative Management and Leadership: The Power of Positive Thought and Action in Organizations* (San Francisco: Jossey-Bass, 1990).

19 George Land and Beth Jarman, *Breakpoint and Beyond: Mastering the Future Today*. (New York: HarperBusiness, 1992), pp. 189–90.

20 Juran, "Strategies for world-class quality", pp. 83–4.

21 A. Blanton Godfrey, Donald M. Berwick, and Jane Roessner, "Ten lessons learned: how quality management really works in health care", manuscript, 1992. Available from the Juran Institute, 11 River Road, Wilton, CT 06880. An earlier version appears in Donald M. Berwick, A. Blanton Godfrey, and Jane Roessner, *Curing Health Care: New Strategies for Quality Improvement* (San Francisco: Jossey-Bass, 1990), pp. 144–58.

22 Michael Hammer and James Champy, *Reengineering the Corporation: A Manifesto for Business Revolution* (New York: HarperBusiness, 1993), p. 49.

23 Robert Cole has provided a clear and useful critique and appreciation of Hammer and Champy's contributions in "Reengineering the corporation: a review essay", *Quality Management Journal*, July 1994, pp. 77–85.

24 Oren Harari, "Ten reasons why TQM doesn't work", *Management Review*, January 1993, pp. 33–8.

25 Ibid, p. 37.

26 Ibid, p. 37.

Epiloque

Interview with William J. O'Brien
former Chief Executive Officer
Hanover Insurance Company
and
member of the board of governors
MIT Center for Organizational Learning

Interviewers: Nicholas Zangari, Steven Cavaleri, and David Fearon

Date: September 1994

Q: Bill, you have often said, "Planning should be an exercise in learning; not an annual ritual of predicting the future based on extrapolating from current results." Can you share with us your perceptions of the value of traditional planning approaches?

WO: Planning, as it is conducted in many corporations, can often be destructive to the process of learning. *Planning should be a way of enhancing people's capacity for learning.* Many conventional approaches to planning dull the minds of managers, rather than enrich their mental models. Because such types of planning don't really engage the creative minds of managers, they frequently are not able to probe the deeper issues facing an organization. For many organizations, planning has become nothing more than an administrative ritual, which is used by top management to "hold people's feet to the fire." The results of such planning processes are misleading – ultimately, they provide management with a neat, linear map of a territory that is essentially organic and constantly changing. So the map, while appearing user-friendly, often misleads the users about the direction in which they are heading.

Q: What are some of the deeper issues that you think planning should address?

WO: By reframing planning as learning we are able get at some of these deeper issues. For instance, one issue that is often avoided is the commitment to developing the capacities of individual workers at all levels of an organization.

Organizations are the beneficiaries when employees are able to make wise judgments in the face of complex situations. When organization members learn to nurture relationships with their colleagues, both inside and outside of an organization, everyone wins. Planning can facilitate this type of learning in organizations. These capacities are the preconditions for modern corporations handling the rapid changes in competitive environments that we see so often today. But these conditions won't occur if "the plan" is developed in a way where the people who implement it never have the opportunity to discuss its underlying assumptions. If they don't understand the broader context from which the map was drawn you end up with people complying with the plan, rather than activating it.

Ultimately, the game of business is not won by companies devising the best plan. It is won by your employees learning more deeply than competitors' employees. In essence, the key is to have more people in your organization who are able to "out-think" your competition.

Q: How does a company move from those planning methods which are centered on control to ones which stimulate learning for a dynamic environment?

WO: I don't have a formula for planning that fosters learning, nor have I ever seen one. The Royal Dutch Shell's "scenario planning" process is enormously impressive, but I don't know of a perfect role model for anyone to follow. Royal Shell's planning process works by laying out a series of alternate paths to the future, as opposed to predicting the "correct" future.

Regardless of the planning method which is used, I believe that all of them should be able to promote the development of five core competencies. They are:

1 **Conversation:** Despite sophisticated technology, conversation will remain our most important instrument for learning. I find many Westerners inept at serious conversation around contentious issues, that is, subjects around which our deepest assumptions are different. To learn, we must be able and willing to make these fundamental, and often implicit, assumptions explicit and subject to testing.
2 **Systems thinking:** It is essential that we learn the language and theory of systems thinking to augment the traditional reductionistic understanding of issues.
3 **Scenario planning:** I recommend reading *The Art of the Long View* by Peter Schwartz.[1]
4 **A contrarian approach:** This enables you to contrast your assumptions and mental models. A higher, sharper focus comes from taking the other side and looking back at your ideas.
5 **Proreflection:** Companies need to create an environment where reflection is valued and encouraged.

Q: Why would companies want to "let go" of control over their employees in the name of learning, when they still view themselves as succeeding in the first wave, by saying, "Just give us one more year with the heavy-handed economic tools and we'll fix this business"?

WO: Today's circumstances favor learning-centered organizations, yet it may take another generation for CEOs to catch on to this. Undoubtedly, there are some CEOs who are leading impressive changes today, but very few people are comfortable with, and successful at, making dramatic interior changes. Of course there will always be pseudochange in organizations. It will be recognized as such by people in those organizations who will, accordingly, withhold their voluntary followership. There are enormous numbers of people in the "baby boomer" age who will really move things along in the direction that we have been discussing over the next decades.

Q: What is drawing people to the vision of organizations that compete by learning?

WO: The human species is evolving intellectually and emotionally, as well as physically. I suspect that we are at a point in history where we are going to see a unifying of the spirit and the material realms that have been kept separate for the past five centuries. Organizations, the ones that are teleologically attuned, will be the ones that are going to create this unifying effect – by converging reflection and action into a true learning cycle. Many people in business are still very uncomfortable with notions pertaining to the concept of spirit. Yet with this unification, I believe, we will be pulled toward much higher levels of organizational learning.

Q: How does one go about leading this liberation of the spirit of which you speak?

WO: Let me bring it down to basics. Once children grow to somewhere between 12 and 21 years of age I believe there is little additional teaching which can be done to affect their fundamental character. When you are president of a company or a manager, what you really need to do is put business in a perspective so it connects what is already etched into people's minds about core values with their vocational tasks. As a manager who leads learning you help to crystallize and illuminate it for them. On the other hand, if you think I could go into a company and infuse ideas into their heads that will stick, you are mistaken! Leaders, in this emerging future, will act to create organizations that can provide a context of meaning for what people already know. They will then proceed from this shared understanding to act and learn together.

I get to talk to a lot of people in middle management through my consulting and affiliations. They often say, "Hey Bill! I believe this stuff about learning, but I'm only in the middle and this is risky." My answer is: "It's risky, but less so than to stay in a place where obsolescence is coming fast."

Q: The ways in which people have managed in the past often keep people from learning how to add value to their organizations. Is there a need to fundamentally reshape the process of managing?

WO: Managing, as it is traditionally understood, is based on scientific principles that are generally logical and sound. Managing evolved relying on science as its backbone in those times when there was tremendous pressure to produce material goods. My grandparents worked seven days a week on farms or elsewhere for room and board, and had no discretionary income. As a result of those bureaucratic management systems, which we now tend to criticize, many people were relieved from the oppressiveness of physical labor. It also has produced a phenomenal standard of living here in the United States. Not everyone agrees with the pattern of how wealth is distributed; but it is quite apparent to me that the prevailing management system still "kicks out" enough goods, so that the standard of living can be relatively high throughout much of the world. Despite these accomplishments, this system has limitations.

The needs of many people today, in organizations, are very different than during my grandparents' era. People's needs and consciousness have risen since then, and they are continually ascending. Our job, as leaders of learning, is to get people and systems in organizations ready to move to the next plateau. This requires managers to begin turning their attention toward integrating much of what we have learned in the past century about the human nature into organizations. We managers are very smug about our knowledge of economics and finance; but what do we learn in our business schools about promoting human potential in organizations?

Q: What would you advise that managers do to manage in support of organizational learning?

WO: Change themselves!

Q: Are you saying that by engaging in activities which raise our self-awareness this will open us to new ideas for managing for learning?

WO: Simply, people are human beings first and instruments of production second. When managers are able to harness the power of learning in organizations, we'll all be far more productive. At Hanover, all we did was the "blocking and the tackling" of the insurance game better than our competitors. For 20 years, we hardly ever had a new idea! Our learning meant that we became better at doing the basics of insurance. Finally, we discovered that these "new" basics that we discovered had more to do with the creative efforts of all our employees than it did with "managing the business." Managing, the old way, means to control employees to the point of suppressing their self-reliance and creating a codependent relationship with managers.

I cannot conceive of a stockholder organization being operated other than from the flow of power from the stockholders to board of directors, to the CEO, to direct reports and on through the organization. However, the difference comes in how managers choose to use this system. Will they use it for people's learning or against it? We need to learn how to use this power with a profound respect for human beings and their development. The major challenge to managers of the future will be to construct a high moral climate in the pursuit of truth among a diversity of relationships. That is what it means to be an "empowering environment." I do not think the actual downward flow of power in institutions is going to change. The change will be in enabling the horizontal flows of power to develop freely.

Q: How did you go about changing the environment at Hanover?

WO: We pursued "scholarship" – that is, thinking more deeply and reflecting more. As we reached out around us, within as well as outside of the company, we got more "hooks" in our heads. The more hooks, the more ideas there are to hook onto.

All of sudden, back in the early 1980s, this idea of the learning organization took off in the business world. Back then, there was Chris Argyris's Model II, and double loop learning. That was followed by the work of several people on mental models and paradigms. Peter Senge and Daniel Kim became involved as consultants to Hanover, and built further on this theme of the learning organization. Work on dialogue, the value of conversation, was explored, as was the idea of "community building." While all of this work added value at Hanover, I must caution managers against raising false expectations about what can be done. Each organization is unique, and it doesn't apply equally well to all. The other field that had an impact at Hanover was systems thinking. Conversation and systems thinking are the principle disciplines within this enormous umbrella we call "organizational learning." One of the exciting things we are doing at MIT right now is putting learning historians on all of our projects. The way something is perceived by historians will largely influence what is learned by succeeding generations. The Boston Tea Party, for example, could be seen as a heroic, symbolic event in the name of freedom. It could also be viewed as a bunch of rowdies breaking the law. It is all in the way the scribes passed this history on down to us. We lose a lot of truth about what really happened as events go on. Learning historians are going to mark what and how things happened by scribing their view of events.

Q: Will the ideas of organizational learning lose some of the shimmer once they are tried by managers?

WO: Yes. Like most new ideas, they could be oversold. Fortunately, many of these basic ideas are fundamentally quite sound. They will survive the turbulence and go on to have a positive impact on organizations. Still, it's usually the case that such innovative ideas tend to merge slowly into the consciousness of corporations. Sometimes they are slowed because people near the "firing lines" may not seem to be ready for such things as systems thinking or mapping organization culture. As a result, there is an opportunity for colleges to prepare and send out graduates who can apply these newest theories in organizations.

Q: How is the employee of the future, say in the year 2012, going to be performing differently than he or she might today?

WO: I envision six characteristics that will differentiate them from their predecessors. They are:

1 *Organization members are going to focus down at the work and out to the customer.* Right now, most people focus upward. The rule of thumb for surviving is: "Tell me what you want, boss, and I'll do it. What's going on? What vice-president is in and what vice-president is out?" Instead tomorrow's employees will be focusing on how we can all get our work done better.
2 *There will be a much, much deeper understanding of connectedness with other activities; even activities outside the company.*
3 *They will understand context.* We were talking about the role of the manager before. One of the most fundamental roles of a manager is not to tell people what to do, it is to provide the context so they can figure out what to do better. One of my hardest jobs at Hanover was to get *context* into the company education program.
4 *There will be a propensity and time for tomorrow's employees to reflect on their work.* This may not necessarily be done in long periods of time, but every so often, to stop and consider the unfolding story of the company.
5 *Much learning will be hidden from easy view.* A person could walk into the plant or the office in the year 2012, and not discern any of the differences that I'm talking about here. The interior or personal differences within people will, however, be enormous.
6 *Product and service quality will achieve such high levels that a quality distinction will be rather minimal between products.* Successful marketing will be *relationship* marketing.

Q: One of this book's chapters is on "relational management." It is about understanding relationships. We believe that it's critical to this whole new form of learning in organizations. Do you agree?

WO: There is movement from a political-bureaucratic decision-making basis to making things work on the merit of ideas. This is matched by an opening of the flow of information from its once manipulated and tightly controlled state, to a state of *openness*. There is also a larger dimension of localness emerging from these other conditions, localness in how people at different levels of a company relate to one another. It is based on a principle of "subsidiarity" – the idea that it is an abuse of power for someone at a higher level in an organization to intervene, if the one at the lower level is competent to fix the problem him or herself. By honoring localness it builds self-reliance in the worker, relieving dependency on an external manager.

These are the kind of values required to expel many of the political behaviors that are capable of polluting an organization's ecology. The values of openness and localness have already helped in companies like Federal Express, which has a phenomenal culture. There are not many Federal Expresses around. The older a company gets the more difficult it is to sustain. That is, the more you have successive generations away from entrepreneurial management, the more "infections" that occur in its organizational ecology. The temptation is to adopt some values that the CEO and friends think are appropriate without ever going through the process of mapping and curing the organizational "diseases." This gives the needed context to mobilize the people to adopt the newly espoused values. The map of an organization's culture guides selections of the "antibiotics," which are values to counter them.

DF: Thank you, Bill.

Note

1 Peter Schwartz, *The Art of the Long View: Planning for the Future in an Uncertain World* (New York: Doubleday-Currency, 1991).

Index